A Tour of the Darkling Plain

J-31 Dunster House - Harvard University - Cambridge 38, Massachusetts

Dec 7. 1950.

Dear Miss Glasheen:

Yes, I tried the very thing you suggest.

But I found that *F—s Wake* addicts are a curious band of cats: they think everybody else is a benighted flounderer and that they — each one — hold *the* answer. They didn't want to pool their insight; they didn't want to contribute to a Master-Copy. I came away from the meeting very angry — but with just enough evidence from the crumbs they let fall, to feel assured that their superior "initiated" hauteur

---

"I sent the list to several Joyceans, hoping they could add to it. Thornton Wilder . . . responded generously with additions and encouragement." Adaline Glasheen

The first page of Thornton Wilder's letter of 7 December 1950
Courtesy, Beinecke Rare Book and Manuscript Library, Yale University

A Tour of the Darkling Plain

The Finnegans Wake *Letters of Thornton Wilder and Adaline Glasheen*

EDITED BY
Edward M. Burns
with
Joshua A. Gaylord

University College Dublin Press
Preas Choláiste Ollscoile Bhaile Átha Cliath

First published 2001 by University College Dublin Press,
Newman House, St Stephen's Green, Dublin 2, Ireland

© The Estate of Adaline Glasheen, 2001

© The Wilder Family LLC, 2001

Introduction and notes © Edward M. Burns and Joshua A. Gaylord, 2001

ISBN 1 900621 54 1 (hardcover)
1 900621 55 X (softcover)

All rights reserved. No part of this publication may be reproduced, stored in a retrieval system, or transmitted in any form or by any means, electronic, photocopying, recording or otherwise without the prior permission of the publisher.

Cataloguing in Publication data available from the British Library

Typeset in Ireland by Elaine Shiels, Bantry, Co. Cork
Printed in Ireland by ColourBooks, Dublin

Contents

List of Illustrations	vii
Acknowledgements	ix
Introduction by Adaline Glasheen	xiii
Editor's Introduction	xxi
Editorial Statement	xxvii
Short Titles	xxix

The *Finnegans Wake* Letters of Thornton Wilder and Adaline Glasheen, 1950–1975   1

APPENDICES

   I   Of the Four Old Men in *Finnegans Wake*   589
         Thornton Wilder

   II   Memorandum: rê Frank Budgen's "Joyce's Chapters of Going Forth By Day"   592
         Thornton Wilder

   III   "*Finnegans Wake*: The Polyglot Everyman" [Draft A]   595
         Thornton Wilder

   IV   "*Finnegans Wake*: The Polyglot Everyman" [Draft B]   607
         Thornton Wilder

   V   Letters to Dounia Bunis Christiani, Scarsdale, New York   612
         Thornton Wilder

VI	A Puzzle Thornton Wilder	620
VII	Twins Thornton Wilder	623
VIII	"The Strange Cold Fowl in *Finnegans Wake*" Adaline Glasheen	626
IX	Helen Joyce 1962 Adaline Glasheen	650
X	Helen Joyce 1963 Adaline Glasheen	652
XI	Another Painful Case Adaline Glasheen	662
XII	City Adaline Glasheen	666
XIII	Historical and Literary Figures in Joyce's Work Adaline Glasheen	671
XIV	George Reavey to Thornton Wilder	673

BIBLIOGRAPHIES

General Bibliography	676
Bibliography of the Published Works of Thornton Wilder on James Joyce	679
Bibliography of the Unpublished Works of Thornton Wilder on James Joyce	679
Bibliography of the Published Works of Adaline Glasheen on James Joyce	680
Bibliography of the Unpublished Works of Adaline Glasheen on James Joyce	684

INDICES

Name Index	685
Finnegans Wake Page/Line Index	705

List of Illustrations

The first page of Thornton Wilder's letter
   of 7 December 1950   Frontispiece
Courtesy, Beinecke Rare Book and Manuscript Library,
   Yale University

Adaline Glasheen in Paris for the Fifth International
   James Joyce Symposium, June 1975   xii
Photograph by Fritz Senn

A page from Adaline Glasheen's letter of 8 January 1954   xx
Courtesy, Beinecke Rare Book and Manuscript Library,
   Yale University

A page from Thornton Wilder's letter of
   16 October 1960   xxx
Courtesy, Beinecke Rare Book and Manuscript Library,
   Yale University

James Joyce in Paris, 1934   2
Photograph by Roger-Viollet, Copyright: Lipnitzki-Viollet

Thornton Wilder and Isabel Wilder on board the SS *Olympic*,
   July 1954. En route to London for rehearsals of
   Wilder's play *The Matchmaker*   66
Photographer unknown, Private collection

A page of Thornton Wilder's working notes for *Finnegans Wake*   124
Courtesy, Beinecke Rare Book and Manuscript Library,
   Yale University

A page from Adaline Glasheen's letter of 30 March 1960   249
*Courtesy, Beinecke Rare Book and Manuscript Library,
   Yale University*

Adaline Glasheen at the Fifth International James Joyce
   Symposium, Paris, June 1975   556
Photograph by Fritz Senn

Thornton Wilder and Isabel Wilder at the Lawn Club,
   New Haven, 1972   566
Photographer unknown, Private collection

Acknowledgements

It was Isabel Wilder, Thornton's sister, who first suggested to me her brother's letters to Adaline Glasheen as a possible project after the publication of the Gertrude Stein–Thornton Wilder letters. Her conversations helped paint a vivid picture of what Wilder and Glasheen were like as fellow Joyceans, thus encouraging me toward this project. The support of Ulla Dydo and William Rice, with whom I edited the Stein–Wilder letters, was crucial for me in undertaking this project. They are my silent co-workers on this book. I am grateful to the late Donald Gallup for his friendship. Charlotte Hegyi, the archivist at the Warren Hunting Smith Library of Hobart and William Smith Colleges, Geneva, New York, which houses Glasheen's papers, made each visit one to be fondly remembered. She thoughtfully made work spaces available to me and helped me make the most efficient use of my time. The staff at the Warren Hunting Smith Library made my work a pleasure. Patricia Willis and Vincent Giroud, curators at the Beinecke Rare Book and Manuscript Library at Yale University, and Ralph W. Franklin, its director, have, over many years, given me much support. The award of a Beinecke Library Fellowship made possible a rich and exciting period of research at the Library, and I remain grateful to the staff, particularly Stephen Jones and Tim Young, for their assistance.

Ken Anderson, who was helping me with computer problems, suggested that a fellow student in the Doctoral English Program at New York University might be interested in helping me on this project. Thanks to him I made the acquaintance of Joshua Gaylord who quickly proved his value as a colleague on this project. What had begun as a job to check my transcriptions of the letters soon evolved into an editorial partnership. Joshua has, from the outset, worked on every facet of this edition: helping to check references and sources, working to keep in focus the delicate balance of what and what not to annotate, and controlling my urge toward encyclopedic footnotes. His knowledge of Joyce's texts was invaluable.

In her Preface to *Census I*, Glasheen writes of Wilder, James. S. Atherton, Matthew J. C. Hodgart, Hugh Kenner, and Richard Ellmann, all of whom had helped her with identifications: "None of these five people were known to me. They had nothing in common but an interest in Joyce and a desire that *Finnegans Wake* should become more available to the common reader. Their generosity to the census was disinterested and abstract and speaks very well for the intellectual climate of our time." I can but only echo her thoughts when I think of the assistance given to me by a vast number of Joyceans who were unknown to me. Ruth Bauerle read through the entire manuscript and offered trenchant comments on how it might be improved. Her eye for detail was truly extraordinary. Joshua and I are deeply in her debt. Fritz Senn, a friend of both Wilder and Glasheen, answered many queries about them and about *Finnegans Wake*. Sam Slote gave generously of his time.

In the notes to these letters are present innumerable writers, friends, colleagues, archivists near and far who gave generous help and interest. We are grateful to: Michael Begnal; Morris Beja; William S. Brockman; Ross Chambers; Henry Chen; Vincent J. Cheng; Eric Concklin; Luca Crispi; Vincent Deane; Gregory Downing; Bernard Duyfhuizen; Sydney Feshbach; Richard J. Finneran; Paul Franklin; F. Gayle-Twombly; Sean Golden; Willard Goodwin; Jon Grennan; Michael Groden; Ian Gunn; Clive Hart; Mathilda Hills; John Kidd; Erwin Levold, Archivist, the Rockefeller Archive Center; Alex Lines; Patrick MacCarthy; Anna A. Malicka, The Lewis Walpole Library, Farmington, CT; Russell Maylone, Curator, McCormick Library of Special Collections, Northwestern University Library; J. Mitchell Morse; Vara Neverow; the staff of the Newberry Library, Chicago; Merry Pawlowski; Ronald Prowse; Patrick M. Quinn, University Archivist, Northwestern University Library; Mark Rose; Peter L. Shillingsburg; Bonnie Kime Scott; John Train; Bjorn Tysdahl; Dirk Van Hulle; David A. Ware, Archival Assistant for Reference, Harvard University Archives; and Marta L. Werner. The members of the James Joyce listserv and the *Finnegans Wake* listserv were often silent educators and helpers.

I am grateful to my colleagues at William Paterson University for the support they have given me and for their kindness in answering many questions. Catarina Edinger, Brad Gooch, John Mason, and Martin Weinstein were particularly supportive. I have received released time to aid my research, and I wish to thank the various faculty committees who supported my requests. Provost and Executive Vice President Chernoy M. Sesay, Associate Provost Stephen Hahn, and Nina Jemmott, Associate Vice President and Dean of Graduate Studies and Research, and the staff of the Sarah Byrd Askew Library cooperated in supporting my research. A sabbatical leave allowed me the opportunity for uninterrupted research time. My friends Joan and Antoine Chapman, John Leeper, Joseph Margolis, Guy Poitry, and Abdellah Taïa, know my debt to them.

Hugh Kenner kindly gave permission to reprint his letter of 9 February 1973 to Ralph Carlson. John M. Ridland, Professor of English at the University of California, Santa Barbara, granted permission to reprint Glasheen's article from *Spectrum*. The family of Thornton Wilder, particularly Tappan Wilder, have been supportive of this project, and I am grateful for their permission to print these letters and the unpublished Wilder materials included in this book as well as Isabel Wilder's letters to Adaline Glasheen. Francis Glasheen has kindly given his permission to print his wife's letters and her unpublished essays. Barbara Hogenson, representing the Wilder Estate, has been cooperative on all matters large and small.

Joshua and I wish to thank Megan Abbott for her support of this project. Working with Barbara Mennell of the UCD Press has been a rare privilege, and we also extend our appreciation to Elaine Shiels for her excellent job of typesetting this very difficult manuscript. Support for the publication of this book has also come from the Estate of Paul Thek and my close, and deeply missed friends Louise and Michel Leiris.

Edward M. Burns
New York
October 2000

Adaline Glasheen in Paris for the Fifth International James Joyce Symposium, June 1975
Photograph by Fritz Senn

Introduction

Letters About James Joyce's Finnegans Wake
*Written 1950–1975 by Thornton Wilder
to Adaline Glasheen*[1]

ADALINE GLASHEEN

In the late 1940s some friends and I took to playing around with *Finnegans Wake*, enjoying ourselves and doing our best to unriddle bits of that difficult and entertaining book. In 1950 I made an alphabetical list of such proper names as we had found at given lines and pages. I sent the list to several Joyceans, hoping they could add to it. One of these was the late Thornton Wilder who responded generously with additions and encouragement. For a quarter of a century, he went on to write these valuable letters. We met sometimes, we talked about *Finnegans Wake* for hours on the telephone. I am more grateful than I can say for his wit and openhanded kindness, and for the friendship and the work we shared.

As Thornton Wilder knew, I saved his letters. I did not reread them, but recollected them as a rich vein, exhausted when I made three censuses of *Finnegans Wake*, 1952, 1962, 1977.[2]

I was wrong to think the letters exhausted of interest, for when I reread them in February, 1977, they seemed to me to be full of matter which—out of ignorance or in a hurry—I had used inadequately or improperly. I now think the letters contain insights, clues, peripluses which are well worth the attention of the adventurer setting forth into the wild blue *dédale* yonder.

The letters are also an abiding record of a particular past—the amateur's age of unriddling. It was a time when *Finnegans Wake* was yet outside literature, criticism, scholarship, when it had no price on the literary exchange, when it seemed capable of solution or dissolution at any moment. The amateur age had its faults—work was done wastefully and in isolation from Joyce's other works; the age had its virtues—work was imaginative, unstructured, freely shared, and great delight was taken in our unexampled chance to explore a charming and enigmatic landscape.

The age of the amateur unriddler is gone by. It is commonly said and not quite truly said that because *Finnegans Wake* was so hard to read and so uncertain of permanent literary value that only the amateur could afford to unriddle it, spend time as if it were dirt, read for three years, read for twenty out of twenty-four hours, and then sit down and write long letters to another fancier of *Finnegans Wake*. It sounds improbable as I tell it, but it went on something like that.

The amateur age was over when Mr Hart published his *Concordance to Finnegans Wake* in 1963, and when Mr Hart and Mr Senn founded *A Wake Newslitter* which has been published since 1964.[3] The *Concordance* makes possible production of useful scholarly work—e.g., studies of verbal motif, foreign word lists—by those who have not read *Finnegans Wake*. Scholar's time will be cut even shorter when, as is highly desirable, we get the sixty-three thousand [unique] words of *Finnegans Wake* onto computer cards. Amateur unriddlers still flourish, mostly underground. No amateur unriddler of Thornton Wilder's quality and endurance has surfaced of late, but there is sure to be one.

Thornton Wilder's best letters are working-papers which have a technical elegance which will be lost on those who do not know *Finnegans Wake*. Indeed these pages and pages of bare exegesis may look menacing in their potentiality, like a thousand and one pages of quadratic equations cast before the non-mathematical. Though often playful, these letters are rarely personal or autobiographical, but they will remain of high interest to historians of *Finnegans Wake*, to historians of literature, and, of course, to the Artist.

I think we do not talk about the Artist today, but Joyce did, and the word will get fashionable again. Henry James also talked about the Artist and James built a procrustean paradigm into which persons who work at unriddling *Finnegans Wake* must inevitably fit. I refer to James's teasing fable, "The Figure in the Carpet" which goes like this:

Vereker, an admired novelist says (it may be a lie) that his art is governed by a secret quality which his readers have not noticed; it is "the string the pearls were strung on, the buried treasure, the figure in the carpet"; trying to find out the unknown quality becomes an obsession with certain of Vereker's readers, eats them up alive as those who hunt cryptograms in *Hamlet* are eaten up alive; on the last pages of "The Figure" the novelist is dead, along with his secret or no secret; one of the obsessed survives him and infects a new victim who, we guess, will infect another who will infect another and so on to the end of the world.

"The Figure in the Carpet" is the Artist's retort, his neatly turned revenge on his natural enemies; for Vereker's obsessed readers are "subtle devils of critics." James sends them to a well-made hell where their life and judgment of literature are alike destroyed by alternations of hope of finding out and despair at not discovering.

Like Henry James, Joyce used his own writings to bait traps for his critics. One bait was *Ulysses*; it was published in 1922, and for a decade was celebrated or savaged as a supreme rendering of modern chaos. Then in 1934, Joyce published a Scheme of *Ulysses*[4] which demonstrates (it may be a lie) that his critics were ignoramuses because *Ulysses* is no chaos, but comically overstructured as a means of burlesquing the epic conventions of the *Odyssey*, which is the string Joyce's pearls are strung on.

I am happy to read *Ulysses* under a Homeric or any other dispensation, for it is an endlessly funny and sustaining book. But publication of the Scheme did Joyce's reputation no good, led critics to say that *Ulysses* explained was *Ulysses* stripped of its interest.

Perhaps so as to catch these carpers, Joyce left no Scheme to explain *Finnegans Wake*, or, at any rate no Scheme has been found. The obsessed—some of them—dig for the Scheme under Irish cromlechs and Roman oaks; and it is quite in the cards that a Scheme will be forged as Piltdown Man or the Jensen Report or the portrait of Mr. W. H. were forged by men too truly in love with a theory.

Joyce left no statement, saying: "I have buried an explanatory treasure of heart and mind under an Irish dunghill or in *Finnegans Wake*." What he did was more horrendous and amusing—he left behind him *Finnegans Wake* which is a dream of incessant treasure hunts, the treasure being of all sorts—female chastity, the lost word of the Freemasons, the source of the Nile, the means of justifying God's ways to man, Schliemann's Hissarlik, Tutankhamun's tomb, Neanderthal Man, the wheel, the arch, the alphabet, how to square the circle, how to reach dramatic climax, how to end the world.

In *Finnegans Wake*, the treasure is not found because the treasure-hunters are of an appalling inefficiency—they lose or misread the treasure map, question the wrong witness, accept a lying guide; they quarrel with each other, their intelligence gaps, attention lapses, will weakens, and they start new, more elaborate treasure hunt[s]. Dogged they are, but dogged doesn't do it. I suppose the treasure hunt to be a variant on the common dream of trying and trying and always failing to catch a train.

The reader of *Finnegans Wake* cannot help being caught up in the process of exasperation in which hope springs eternal and is cast down. If the hunters do not find the buried treasure, they never abandon the hunt; a wealth of hints, signals, downright statements assure hunter and reader that if they will but push one more stone up three hills they will find the purloined letter at exactly 11:32 this very morning.

Raised hope, dashed hope puts even the hardheaded reader into a state of altered consciousness, common sense surrenders to the lure of drugged and soliciting language, language artfully arranged to say several things and their opposites at the same time.

A book so long (628 pages), so dense, so hypnotic will always be a hunting ground, more or less happy, for minds that have lost their balance and perhaps found something better. Indeed, it may be boasted that it is to lunatic fringes, lovers and poets that *Finnegans Wake* most naturally and directly speaks. The danger used to be that *Finnegans Wake* would speak to no one else[,] would remain an intensely private, arcane, uncultivated tract, lying outside the classroom and the library where harmless drudges sort and preserve artifacts and hand them on to posterity. If an artifact looks aberrant and moon-struck, the more it needs help, needs domicile in an institution—Gertrude Stein was wise to leave to the Metropolitan Museum the portrait Picasso painted of her.

Finnegans Wake would have gotten into classrooms and libraries sooner or later, for it is a work irresistibly rich, entertaining and pedantic, but it might have taken a long time to get in, such a long time that it would have been stripped bare of immediacy and have accreted no critical or emotional tradition.

As things fall out, the consummation devoutly wished for came rather quickly: in less than half a century *Finnegans Wake* lies down with academic lambs. One of the reasons it is safely domiciled is that Thornton Wilder, who was a detached, intelligent man, bore steady witness to the power of *Finnegans Wake* to fascinate and compel. Note that in these letters Thornton Wilder speaks more than once of being obsessed with and laboriously disengaging himself from *Finnegans Wake*.

It must be said that, used in its purely Joycean sense, the word "obsession" does not indicate extremity of situation, but merely that the reader is playing the game of *Finnegans Wake* by its own rules. Like all writers and actors, Thornton Wilder had a lively, accurate eye for what game or paradigm he played in; he knew he sometimes played in a variation on "The Figure in the Carpet" which went like this: Joyce is the novelist Vereker, dead with his secret; I am the obsessed, the entrapped; I am not an entrapped critic, but a novelist, entrapped by another novelist; this last fact is a wicked turn of the screw which Henry James would finely have appreciated.

It is a grim, interesting, instructive part to play, but Thornton Wilder was not eaten up by *Finnegans Wake*, he always disengaged himself and went about his own writing.

Note about *The Skin of Our Teeth* and *Finnegans Wake*

It cannot always have been easy for Thornton Wilder to bear witness to the literary excellence of *Finnegans Wake*, for long before our correspondence began, he had had to face the unmeaning charge that his play, *The Skin of Our Teeth* takes more than should be taken, without acknowledgment, from *Finnegans Wake*.[5]

I have not read the charge, nor answers to the charge; but I have often read *The Skin of Our Teeth* and *Finnegans Wake* and marveled that anyone could postulate guilty connection between them. Yet in one of these letters Thornton Wilder says—without elaborating—that *The Skin of Our Teeth* "leans on" *Finnegans Wake*.[6] It seems worthwhile, therefore, to say why I think it does not lean.

One thing is plain, both writers pillage with both hands from some of the best known stories in the Bible and produce, as Byron and Milton did, their own portraits of Adam and Eve, Cain and Abel, Noah and his family. Both Joyce and Wilder are aware that they have been preceded at Bible-pillaging by anonymous medieval authors of *Adam and Eve*, *Cain and Abel*, *Noah*, plays that belong to one or more of the Mystery cycles. Joyce and Wilder are both aware that they have been preceded by the author of the medieval Morality play, *Everyman*, which was revived with great success in England and America in the first decade of this century.

Here ends important resemblance between *The Skin of Our Teeth* and *Finnegans Wake*.

However frivolous and unmeaning the charge, it would have been an exasperating charge to answer because in the 1940s few knew what is in *Finnegans Wake*; and, at the same time, "everything" (or the cunning pretense of everything) is in *Finnegans Wake*. Everything includes all the great exemplary fictions—e.g., fictions out of Greek tragedy, Homer, Shakespeare and the Bible. In *Finnegans Wake*, they are arranged as if they were contemporaries, fellow citizens of one town; and they are visited as such exemplary fictions are visited in the *Divine Comedy*. (Dante scholars have made out the path of visitation: Joyce scholars have not.)

Considered as a sort of encyclopedia, *Finnegans Wake* contains exemplary fictions and also contains examples of every literary form, including drama, the imitation of significant action. (See "Buckley and the Russian General," *Finnegans Wake*, 337–355.)

But, for rather profound and pervasive reasons, no action in *Finnegans Wake* is efficiently performed, but always botched like the hunt for treasure; therefore, no artifact is satisfactory, complete or functional. Again and again the attempt is made to build a wall or fashion a dramatic narrative, but the attempt is vain as hell—the wall is aborted before it can keep out cold, the drama is inhibited before it attains dramatic climax.

I cannot say whether imitation of botched or frustrate[d] action is suitable to the theatre: it certainly cannot purge us of pity and terror; it ought not make us laugh. But I do know that it is Samuel Beckett, not Thornton Wilder, who brings on stage imitations of the action of inhibition, explores the dramatic possibilities of clonic quietism.

With blighted form and inhibition of dramatic climax, Thornton Wilder's plays have nothing on earth to do. *The Skin of Our Teeth* is a well-made play with a clear, affirming message: History repeats itself and, by faith and works, Man survives in the teeth of natural disaster and war. Survival is celebrated as an uncomplicated good.

If there is no likeness of temper or intention between *Finnegans Wake* and *The Skin of Our Teeth*, there is every possible likeness between *The Skin of Our Teeth* and the plays of the Mystery cycle; every dramatic device or piece of stage business in *The Skin of Our Teeth* has its equivalent in devices of the Mystery plays or in the conditions of their performance.

The Skin of Our Teeth and the Mysteries both retell stories from Biblical history and stories from no other source; both repeat the story as soon as it has been played; both are works in which the man in the street acts high and sacred roles; both modernize their ancient source; both adapt ancient history to their local habitation—Wakefield, Excelsior, N. J.; both add to Hebrew history the comedy and highjinks of Durham or Excelsior (the highjinks include stage disasters and interplay between actors and audience, an interplay which may be inferred from the craftsmen who present "Pyramus and Thisbe"); both the Mystery cycles and *The Skin of Our Teeth* teach lessons of good conduct.

These resemblances seem to me so exact, entire and obvious that I daresay they have been pointed out twenty times by critics of Thornton Wilder's works. The force of the resemblance particularly struck me when last Christmas time, I saw a remarkably fine BBC production of the Old Testament part of the Chester cycle. To see it played is to know the sole ancestor of *The Skin of Our Teeth*. To see it played is also to know that *The Skin of Our Teeth* is excellent when perceived as a 20th century variation on the Mysteries and not as some yards of plain cloth, spun off from the elaborate, layered web of *Finnegans Wake*.

The charge that *The Skin of Our Teeth* plagiarizes *Finnegans Wake* is a footling charge, which damaged critical perception of Thornton Wilder's achievement by putting it into unmeaning configuration with James Joyce's achievement. As well pair off Samuel Beckett and George Eliot. The talents of Wilder and Joyce are incongruous; the bodies of their writings have no members in common; comparison between them has the value and character of nothing.

Note

The Cabala, *The Ides of March*, *Theophilus North*, *The Woman of Andros* all suggest that Thornton Wilder had an abiding impulse to educate women (God knows they need it) by showering them with cultural information, like Henry Higgins to Eliza Doolittle in *Pygmalion*. This pattern seems to repeat itself in these letters that Thornton Wilder wrote me about *Finnegans Wake*.

The appearance is misleading because Thornton Wilder's letters are here isolated from the letters I wrote him (I believe they are in the Yale Library). They shower him with information of my own and information that I received from others with whom I corresponded. Some little account of the composite nature of *Finnegans Wake* unriddling will be found in my Census, "Acknowledgments."

1. Glasheen read photocopies of Wilder's letters when she reviewed the "Preliminary Calendar" of Wilder's correspondence prepared by Carolyn France for the Warren Hunting Smith Library at Hobart and William Smith Colleges. This statement, written in February–March 1977, was meant to accompany the letters. The manuscript is on eleven typewritten pages with additions and corrections in Glasheen's hand. There are two pages of handwritten notes which she marked "Keep WHS Library." Typing errors have been silently corrected. In the title, Glasheen typed "1951," this has been changed to conform to the first letter—1950.

2. See Glasheen bibliography for publication details.

3. The first issue of *A Wake Newslitter* appeared in March 1962. Eighteen numbers were published irregularly, in mimeograph format, until December 1963. The new series began publication in February 1964 and continued until December 1980. Under the title *A Wake Newslitter: Occasional Paper* four issues were published between August 1982 and September 1984. The entire run of *A Wake Newslitter*, the "Occasional papers," and *A Wake Digest* is available on CD-ROM, *A Wake Newslitter*, published by Split Pea Press, Edinburgh, Scotland, www.harent.demon.co.uk/splitpea.

4. A schema (Glasheen writes scheme) of *Ulysses* was first published in Stuart Gilbert's *James Joyce's 'Ulysses': A Study* (London: Faber & Faber 1930, numerous reprints), in the chapter, "The Rhythm of *Ulysses*." Joyce had circulated information about the structure of *Ulysses* in letters (see particularly Joyce to John Quinn, 3 September 1920, in *Letters I*, 145–146). The most complete published schema is in chapter 14, "The Plan of *Ulysses*," in Hugh Kenner's *Dublin's Joyce*, 226–227.

5. In two numbers of the *Saturday Review of Literature* (19 December 1942, 3–4; 13 February 1943, 16, 18–19) Joseph Campbell and Henry Morton Robinson charged that Wilder's *The Skin of Our Teeth* was not an original work but rather a thinly disguised Americanization of *Finnegans Wake*. See TW to AG, 18 July 1952, n. 4.

6. TW to AG, 18 July 1952.

January 8, 1954

Dear Mr W.,

Do you know I don't even know when Joyce's birthday is. Tell me that, tell me what you say to the Joyceans, tell me what a gathering of Joyceans is like. I have always been surprised by the relative luridity of the proceedings at the Dr Johnson celebrations, but I imagine a Joyce festival will be more subdued. You probably attach yourself to Dr. Johnson out of a fear that you are basically a faun or a maenad, to Joyce because you know you pass the plate in church, and know it all too well. In any case, please tell me fully about the party.

I feel as though a great deal of FW must have happened since I wrote you and I will presently go through my notes and see what small things have. No, I really do think Hodgart's Shakespeare is definitive in that I believe he has collected every demned WS echo in FW. What he does with them is not, but neither is it offensive as the frameworks of so many J. articles are. I have written another article which one journal has turned down and the other is having the opportunity of doing. Oddly enough, it is on <u>Ulysses</u>, not FW and, perhaps just because I am out of my real field, I consider it a most superior production. Doubtless I will feel that I have to tell you all about it one day, if it shouldn't be accepted anywhere. I will only say that, whether my article is itself good or bad, I can prove that there is an undiscovered myth elaborately worked out in <u>Ulysses</u> and it explains why the Scylla and Charibdis Scene has to take place in the public library. Jim Atherton is sending us a 36x36 ox 17th century oil portrait of a Hapsburg Infanta. Why did I never think of sending you anything like that? He hasn't told me why he is sending it, so I can't tell you. Now it is presumably on the way after a long wrangle with the British customs. When Atherton wanted to sell the picture, he could get nothing; when he wanted to export it they accused him of sending a national treasure out of England. Well, this is one fruit of an FW correspondence. Atherton and Hodgart met each other for the first time at Christmas at the British Museum where they were to look at the FW ms there, only it turned out they weren't ready. H. is going to fix up and have mimeographed his list of songs, of all kinds, in FW and I will bespeak one for you if you like. I saw it in rough form and am going to see it again before mimeographing, but it was quite fx vast and had lots in it I didn't know. He and I are determined not to make any more lists of anything but actually try to work out what each section says--ha--don't say it. I had a perfectly awful time with the Joycean writer, Hugh Kenner, who sent me a book that he has written on Joyce. Parts of it were brilliant, I thought--he's quite hot on FW and the liturgy for instance--but Kenner's is what I imagine the RC party line is going to be on Joyce and I find it ebominable. All hail to technique, xxxxxxixxkkx damn Joyce's people. Stephen gave up God the Father so as his just desserts he gets Bloom the father--grrrr. I wrote, though politely, what I did think (I had to tear up three letters, as my husband says, you can't accuse somebody you've never met of spiritual pride) but he has not replied. This paragraph, not the most exciting of paragraphs will show you how one little Joyce clique is making out.

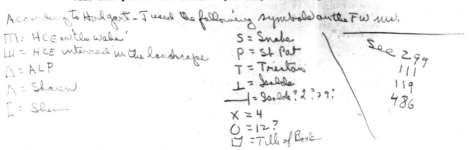

A page from Adaline Glasheen's letter of 8 January 1954
Courtesy, Beinecke Rare Book and Manuscript Library, Yale University

Introduction

EDWARD M. BURNS

When Thornton Wilder was playing the role of the Stage Manager in *Our Town*, in August of 1939, he wrote to Gertrude Stein and Alice Toklas of *Finnegans Wake*: "One of my absorptions and consolations during these occupied and hot six weeks has been James Joyce's new novel, digging out its buried keys and resolving that unbroken chain of erudite puzzles and finally coming on lots of wit, and lots of beautiful things has been my midnight recuperation. A lot of thanks to him." For the remainder of his life Wilder read and reread Joyce's novel seeking new insights that might help him unlock its underlying patterns. For twenty-five years his passionate companion on that journey was Adaline Glasheen.

In the Fall of 1950, at the suggestion of Charles Bennett, a friend at the Yale Library with whom she was reading the *Wake*, Glasheen sent Wilder a preliminary list of characters in the novel. "When my list was in an inchoate state," she wrote in her Preface to *A Census of "Finnegans Wake"*, "and contained no identifications, I had it mimeographed and sent it to a few Joyceans. One of these was Mr. Thornton Wilder who treated it with heavenly kindness and generosity. He gave me a number of valuable identifications and wrote me at length about *Finnegans Wake*. He has a writer's creative understanding of the book that no harmless drudge can hope to duplicate."

At the time that he and Glasheen met, Wilder was a distinguished man of letters. Born in Madison, Wisconsin, on 17 April 1897, educated in China and in California, Wilder attended Oberlin College for two years and then transferred to Yale College where he received his Bachelor's degree in 1920. His first novel, *The Cabala*, was published in 1926 and his play, *The Trumpet Shall Sound*, was directed by Richard Boleslavsky at the American Laboratory Theatre in New York the same year. In 1928 he received the Pulitzer Prize for his novel *The Bridge of San Luis Rey* (1927). He was widely sought after as a lecturer, and in 1930 he accepted the invitation of his old college friend Robert Maynard Hutchins to teach writing and classics in translation at the University of Chicago. Other novels and plays continued to be published in the next two decades: *The Woman of Andros* (1930), *The Long Christmas Dinner and Other Plays* (1931), *Heaven's My Destination* (1935), *Our Town* (1938) and the screenplay for Alfred Hitchcock's film *Shadow of a Doubt* (1942). In 1943 he won his second Pulitzer Prize for his play *The Skin of Our Teeth*. During World War II, he was commissioned and served in the Army Air Corps Intelligence service in North Africa and Italy. His novel in letters, *The Ides of March*, was published in 1948. At the time the *Wake* letters begin he was the Charles Eliot Norton Professor at Harvard University.

Wilder's interest in Joyce began in his college years. As a well-known novelist, he was an active supporter of Joyce, and in 1927 was one of the 167 writers and artists who signed a statement protesting the unauthorized publication of episodes of *Ulysses* by Samuel Roth. When Padraic and Mary Colum told Wilder in the Fall of 1940 of Joyce's situation in France, he began a campaign to petition the Nobel Prize Committee to award Joyce the prize in literature, thereby providing him with desperately needed funds. Wilder wrote to Padraic Colum on 8 October 1940 that if enough writers, artists, and intellectuals would sign a letter it "might help in removing the one doubt remaining in their mind about J. J.—that he was obscene (there our college president's signatures would help, tho' I have not yet approached Pres. Conant [of Harvard University]) and that he was an obscure rarified clique writer." Wilder proposed that the letter be for "the committee alone, not to be published over here, and that it would contain a dignified statement . . . of J. J.'s distinction and influence, but without 'vast superlative claims.'" He reported to Colum that "Van Wyk Brooks, Eugene O'Neill and Aldous Huxley have answered cordially," and he told him of his conversations with Sinclair Lewis and Dorothy Thompson about trying to bring pressure on the Nobel Committee. In a post script to his letter Wilder wrote that "O'Neill and Lewis expressly said that should this venture fail they would like to contribute to any fund collected for J. J." Wilder also solicited Robert Maynard Hutchins and Archibald MacLeish among others to sign a letter to the Nobel Committee. From the material in Wilder's archive it is unclear whether such a letter was ever sent or whether Wilder accepted Sinclair Lewis's opinion that the Committee would be "annoyed and antagonized by recommendations."

In November 1940 arrangements were made for Joyce and his family to leave Vichy, France, for Zurich. Maria Jolas and Padraic and Mary

Colum asked Wilder to help organize a committee to raise the 30,000 Swiss Francs (about $7,000) demanded by the Swiss authorities to guarantee that Joyce and his family would not be a charge to them. With about half of the money deposited in the Bank of Manhattan Company, the Joyces were permitted to enter Switzerland on 14 December. A month later, on 13 January 1941, Joyce died. The committee which had been formed in October reconstituted itself and, on 15 February 1941, as the Joyce Memorial Committee, launched an appeal for funds for Joyce's family. Wilder along with Maria Jolas and others signed a letter explaining that "these several friends feel it would be breaking faith with him if they didn't endeavour to help those who were dependent on him and whose situation, now that he is gone, is, on the financial side, even more distressing than before." Wilder would later contribute to the fund to place a statue of Joyce by Milton Hebald in the Fluntern Cemetery in Zurich.

Wilder met Joyce in 1921 on his way back to the United States to take a job at the Lawrenceville School for boys in New Jersey; he saw him at Shakespeare and Company, Sylvia Beach's Paris bookshop.[1] Two years later he recommended the bookshop to a friend traveling in Europe, suggesting that he give "my best regards to Miss Sylvia Beach, the publisher of *Ulysses* whose author I met in her shop." Wilder would never mythologize his brief encounter with Joyce the way he would his meetings with Freud and his relationship with Gertrude Stein. But he paid Joyce the compliment of alluding to his work in his own writings. The description of the downpour in the last paragraph of *The Woman of Andros* echoes the closing paragraph of Joyce's "The Dead." On the title page of *Heaven's My Destination* Wilder identifies the lines "*George Brush* is my name;/America's my nation;/ *Ludington's* my dwelling-place/And Heaven's my destination" as the "Doggerel verse which children of the Middle West were accustomed to write in their schoolbooks." While this may be true, it is remarkably similar to what is written in Dedalus's geography book in *A Portrait of the Artist as a Young Man*: "Stephen Dedalus is my name,/Ireland is my nation./Clongowes is my dwellingplace/And heaven my expectation." At the end of Act One of *Our Town* the cozy world of Grover's Corners is contrasted throughout with the immense universe—most notably when George Gibbs's sister Rebecca recalls the address a minister scrawled on an envelope which moves in stages from the nearest, "June Crofut, the Crofut Farm, Grover's Corners, Sultan County, New Hampshire," to the ultimate, "the Universe; the Mind of God." The progression is remarkably like Stephen Dedalus's inscription on the flyleaf of his geography book: "Stephen Dedalus/Class of Elements/Clongowes Wood College/Sallins/County Kildare/Ireland/Europe/The World/The Universe."

The Skin of Our Teeth came under intense scrutiny by Joseph Campbell and Henry Morton Robinson shortly after it opened in October 1942, and Wilder was accused of having plagiarized his play[2] from *Finnegans Wake*. At the time, Wilder did not defend himself or his play. Edmund Wilson, an early and enthusiastic reader of *Finnegans Wake*, did, however, in an essay, "The Antrobuses and the Earwickers," published on 30 January 1943. Wilson and Wilder had had long talks and had exchanged letters about Joyce. In a note to a reprint of his seminal essay, "The Dream of H. C. Earwicker," Wilson writes about Wilder: "I have also had the advantage of discussions with Mr. Thornton Wilder, who has explored the book more thoroughly than anyone else I have heard of. It is to be hoped that Mr. Wilder will some day publish something about *Finnegans Wake*." Wilder never directly answered Campbell's and Robinson's charges, but in a Preface he wrote in 1957 for an edition of three of his plays he wrote of *The Skin of Our Teeth*: "The play is deeply indebted to James Joyce's *Finnegans Wake*. I should be very happy if, in the future, some author should feel similarly indebted to any work of mine. Literature has always more resembled a torch race than a furious dispute among heirs."

x x

Adaline Erlbacher was born in Evansville, Indiana, on 16 January 1920. She attended Central High School there and later the University of Indiana. She transferred to the University of Mississippi, and in 1939 earned her Bachelor's degree. It was as a student there that she met and married her husband Francis Glasheen. In 1940 she completed her Master's degree at Washington University in St. Louis. Her essay, "Shelley's 'The Wandering Jew,'" a systematic reading of the poem's complex history and allusions, follows a methodology similar to the one she used for *Finnegans Wake*. She taught at Wheaton College in Norton, Massachusetts, from 1943 to 1946, and during the summers she worked on government projects. After the birth of her daughter Allison in 1946, she occasionally worked in the Farmington Village Library.

Adaline Glasheen's involvement with Joyce began in 1950. As she wrote in her Preface to *A Census of 'Finnegans Wake'*: "I started, hit or miss, to draw up an alphabetical list of such proper names as I could discern in *Finnegans Wake*. I did it for the diversion of the thing and because I could never find given passages or people. I had also a vague idea that listing all the people in *Finnegans Wake* would solve the riddle of the book." In the Preface she acknowledges the limitations of her *Census*. She also tells of the remarkable group of people she had turned to for help in her identifications: James S. Atherton, Matthew J. C. Hodgart, Hugh Kenner, and Richard Ellmann. Of these men and Wilder she writes:

"None of these five people were known to me. They had nothing in common but an interest in Joyce and a desire that *Finnegans Wake* should become available to the common reader. Their generosity to the census was disinterested and abstract and speaks very well for the intellectual climate of our time."

The publication of *A Census* brought her into contact with other Joyce scholars. A unique feature of her appendage to *A Census*, "Out of My Census," published in *The Analyst* in 1959, is her identification of her "donors," who in addition to the names mentioned in her Preface now included Fritz Senn, Gerard O'Flaherty, George Painter, J. Mitchell Morse, Mabel Worthington, Ruth von Phul, and Father William T. Noon, S. J. Her archive, in the Warren Hunting Smith Library of Hobart and William Smith Colleges, is a feast for those wanting to understand the development of *Finnegans Wake* studies.

Asked in a "Promotion Questionnaire" for *Census II* about any "Special study undertaken and qualifications for writing this work" she replied simply, "I just kept reading *Finnegans Wake*." Glasheen describes herself in *A Census* as a "harmless drudge." She was anything but, as an examination of her massive notes on the *Wake* and the flow of incoming correspondence with Joyce scholars around the world reveals. In the 1950s and early 1960s she never attended meetings or conferences about Joyce. Even when Wilder spoke before the James Joyce Society of New York, she found reasons to decline the invitation to be his guest. This shyness changed with the publication of *Census II* in 1963. The tenacious scholar, whom many Joyce scholars knew only from her lengthy typed or handwritten letters, found pleasure in teaching at the University of Buffalo summer seminar, and in giving papers at national and international conferences. In the early 1980s she was diagnosed with Huntington's Chorea, a disease which made her unsteady and produced rigidity in walking. Her slurred speech, another manifestation of the disease, embarrassed and frustrated Glasheen, who took great pleasure in the excitement of communication. She died in 1993.

x x

These letters begin formally, "Dear Mr. Wilder," "Dear Mrs. Glasheen." It is not until 1954 that the relationship they had forged through Joyce begins to take on a sense of intimacy, and they refer to each other by first names. Both Wilder and Glasheen had curious and seeking minds and they found, in their effort to unlock the mysteries of *Finnegans Wake*, a spark that ignited their imaginations. These impassioned letters, often written with great urgency immediately after a discovery, celebrate Joyce's novel and help explain why it continues to fascinate readers.

Richard Ellmann in his Foreword to *A Census* comments on the single minded sense of purpose that Glasheen brought to her work on *Finnegans Wake* and of her "inspired power of detection." Of her indispensable book, he writes: "We may now understand a little better what so far we have perhaps only admired." In her Preface Glasheen writes of the reader of *Finnegans Wake* who finds himself "on the well-trodden darkling plain swept with confused alarms of struggle and flight. He and Joyce set out to explore the plain, to find who is fighting and why. All night they walk in Viconian circles about the plain and come back with nothing to report save that the struggle goes on. If the reader had walked with Kafka, say, or Arnold himself, morning would see him near dead with discouragement; but Joyce is an athletic and exhilarating guide. He tells jokes all night; he is brave without calling attention to his bravery; he finds struggles, however ignorant, a sign of vitality; he has no grievance, no notion that it is all a dirty trick. 'It was,' Joyce says, 'allso agreeable . . . touring the no placelike no timelike absolent . . .'" These letters and essays of Thornton Wilder and Adaline Glasheen are maps of Joyce's almost boundless range of references, symbols, and allusions. They are published to encourage others to tour the plain of *Finnegans Wake*.

1. See TW to AG, 18 July 1952.
2. A letter Wilder wrote on 17 December 1942 to the editor of *The Saturday Review of Literature* answering Campbell's and Robinson's charges was, after it was reviewed by his family and his attorney, never sent. See "A Footnote to *The Skin of Our Teeth*," in *The Yale Review*, 87, 4 (October 1999), 66–76.

Editorial Statement

This edition collects and prints completely the extant letters exchanged by Thornton Wilder and Adaline Glasheen from 1950 to 1975. For the sake of continuity and completeness, Glasheen's letters to Wilder's sister Isabel are also included—thus making available a total of 255 letters that speak, almost exclusively, to their shared passion for Joyce's *Finnegans Wake*.

In preparing this edition, we recognize that no edition of letters, not even a facsimile edition, can be a substitute for examining the holograph original. This edition organizes aspects of the letters in a uniform manner while keeping idiosyncrasies in the body of the letter as close as possible to the original to give a sense of how they were written. The heading of each letter indicates the recipient, where it was sent, the type of original, and its current location (see Short Titles listing for abbreviations). Postcards and their images have been identified, telegrams reproduced in their unique forms. We have standardized the dates on the left, adopted the form of day/month/year, and silently opened up abbreviations for the month. Dates determined from postmarks or internal evidence are given in square brackets. We have standardized the return address to the right. Interpolated information is enclosed in square brackets. Salutations, closing signatures, and postscripts have been standardized.

In the body of the letter we have tried to give some sense of what the original was like. For example, Glasheen generally did not indent—we have maintained this formatting. Wilder peppers his letters with lines and an "x" or a "—" to indicate a section break; he also frequently uses the paragraph sign ¶. We have maintained these indications. Unless specifically referred to in the letter, we have not indicated the color of the penciled lines. To avoid confusion with editorial insertions, which throughout appear in square brackets, we have changed Wilder's and Glasheen's brackets to braces { }.

These letters were often written in great haste; a letter received in the morning was sometimes answered by the afternoon. Both Wilder and

Glasheen looked upon the letters as part of their on-going conversation about *Finnegans Wake*. We have, therefore, maintained their punctuation. Where the lack of punctuation might lead to confusion, we have used square brackets to indicate that we have supplied it. We have, however, maintained each writers' style in using Mr. or Mrs.—with or without the period—since this seems to be a vestige of education and not an error. Because so much of this material deals with permutations of words used by Joyce, we have tried to make a distinction between spelling errors and intentional word play. Obvious errors have been silently corrected. More questionable errors have been indicated by "i.e." Wilder, although a fluent reader and speaker of several languages, often left out accent marks—we have not supplied them. Occasionally, each made marginal notes on the letters of the other. These have been included in square brackets and introduced with either "TW" or "AG" to indicate who has made the notation.

All references to *Finnegans Wake* have been checked, and where either writer was faulty in their line count we have corrected them using "i.e." All page and line references are to the 1959 Viking Press edition. Where a page begins a section both Wilder and Glasheen sometimes counted from the bottom. Using "i.e." we have indicated the now standard practice of counting from the first line of the page.

Annotations to these letters were discussed at great length. To comment on each and every name, or to cite the prodigious scholarship of the last fifty years, would overwhelm these letters and diminish the excitement both Wilder and Glasheen felt as they tried out ideas on each other. Some of these ideas found their way into the various editions of the *Census*—others did not. It is assumed that the reader of these letters will have access to the standard works of Joyce scholarship—including Glasheen's *Census*. When a reference needed clarification, we have supplied it and cited texts available to Wilder and Glasheen: James S. Atherton's *The Books at the Wake: A Study of Literary Allusions in James Joyce's 'Finnegans Wake'* (1959) and Matthew J. Hodgart's and Mabel P. Worthington's *Song in the Works of James Joyce* (1959) being two examples. References to books and articles are fully cited in the bibliography and are given abbreviated titles in the notes.

Short Titles

AWN   *A Wake Newslitter.*
FW   James Joyce, *Finnegans Wake.*

Letters

AL	Autograph letter unsigned.
ALS	Autograph letter signed.
APC	Autograph post card unsigned.
APCS	Autograph post card signed.
TL	Typed letter. Handwritten additions and corrections are silently incorporated.
TLS	Typed letter signed. Handwritten additions and corrections are silently incorporated.

Manuscript Locations

Berg	The Henry W. and Albert A. Berg Collection, The New York Public Library. Specific collections are noted, e.g., Berg-Gotham for the Gotham Book Mart Collection.
HWS	The Adaline Glasheen Archive in The Warren Hunting Smith Library of Hobart and William Smith Colleges, Geneva, New York.
Northwestern	University Archives, Northwestern University Library, Evanston, Ilinois.
Texas	The Harry Ransom Humanities Research Center of the University of Texas at Austin.
Yale	The Beinecke Rare Book and Manuscript Library, Yale University, New Haven, Connecticut.
YCAL	The Thornton Wilder Collection in The Yale Collection of American Literature, The Beinecke Rare Book and Manuscript Library, Yale University, New Haven, Connecticut.

"Thornton Wilder's best letters are working-papers which have a technical elegance..." Adaline Glasheen

A page from Thornton Wilder's letter of 16 October 1960
Courtesy, Beinecke Rare Book and Manuscript Library, Yale University

A Tour of the Darkling Plain

The Finnegans Wake *Letters*
of Thornton Wilder
and Adaline Glasheen

James Joyce in Paris, 1934
Photograph by Roger-Viollet, Copyright: Lipnitzki-Viollet

1950

To Adaline Glasheen, Forestville, Connecticut

[MS. ALS—HWS]

7 December 1950

J–31 Dunster House
Harvard University
Cambridge 38, Massachusetts[1]

Dear Miss Glasheen:

    Yes, I tried the very thing you suggest.
    But I found that F———s Wake addicts are a curious brand of cats: they think everybody else is a benighted flounderer and that they—each one—hold *the* answer. They didn't want to pool their insights; they didn't want to contribute to a Master-Copy. I came away from the meeting very angry—but with just enough evidence from the crumbs they let fall, to feel assured that their Superior "Initiated" hauteur contained just as great an ignorance as my Loquacity.[2]
    Every now and then I plunge for a year at a time into the book. Shorter intervals are no fun. Now I'm deeply immersed in other things.[3] When can I accord myself another "year"? I don't know.
    I thank you for Cherry Jinnies. [9.13]
    Out of so many hundreds I send you for fun and for beauty:
p. 244 next to last line Hsiang is Chinese for elephant.
    245 line 6 Mei—Chinese for girl.[4]
      "   " 8 The German engineers Siemens built the Arklow lighthouse
p 542 eighth and ninth from the bottom [i.e., 542.28–.29]:
    Dr Bethel Solomon[s] (a friend of mine) was long President of Dublin's Rotund[a] Maternity Hospital[5]

The Lock is Dublin waterfront slang for the Hospital of St Margaret of Cortona—for "fallen women"[6]

I'm specially working on The FOUR OLD MEN—throughout; the Nocturne p. 244; and the Radio Speech from middle of p. 539 to 554. If you find any real rare 'uns (naturally I have hundreds of the more immediately-found—share 'em with me![7]

All best wishes
Sincerely yours
Thornton Wilder

1. Wilder arrived in Cambridge, Massachusetts, on 30 October 1950 to take up his residence as Charles Eliot Norton Professor of Poetry at Harvard University for 1950–51. His general subject was announced as "The American Characteristics of Classical American Literature" (*New York Times*, 8 November 1950, 27).

2. Wilder may be referring to a meeting on 4 December 1949 where he discussed how an analysis of *Finnegans Wake* might be undertaken. The meeting at the Grolier Club was arranged by John J. Slocum, a founding member with Frances Stelloff and Leon Edel of the James Joyce Society of New York in February 1947. In a letter to Richard M. Kain, Slocum wrote of the evening, "The Seminar was a most incredible flop with Nathan Halper, Jim Gilvarry and Hugh Kenner [who were then graduate students] refusing to open up on anything they knew. It resulted in a duel between John Kelleher and Thornton Wilder, with both emerging the loser" (carbon, Slocum to Kain, 14 December 1949, Yale). In addition to Kelleher, who taught at Harvard University, others present were Cleanth Brooks of Yale, William York Tindall of Columbia, Herbert J. Cahoon of the New York Public Library at 42nd Street and compiler with Slocum of a bibliography of Joyce, and the publisher James Laughlin (see Slocum to Harriet Shaw Weaver, carbon 3 December 1949 and to Richard M. Kain, carbon 3 December 1949, Yale). In the fall of 1961 Glasheen wrote to John Kelleher about Shakespeare and *Finnegans Wake*. She may have mentioned Wilder's reactions to her research, and this prompted Kelleher to remember the 1949 meeting: "I always have difficulties with Thornton Wilder's readings, due I think to a fundamental difference of approach between us. I remember attending for my sins a meeting (I think it was the only one) of a high-power Joycean group at the Grolier Book Club of New York when Wilder was in the chair. He was proposing that we approach this great book, the greatest of our age, with full intent to master it, and advocating a 'line by line, word by word, if necessary syllable by syllable' analysis. I argued, I imagine hotly and incoherently (for I stammered like hell at that time) that such an approach was pointless, that the book must be taken entire, its outer form realized, its ground rules learned, its humor understood, before any interpretation could be of much value. It is just as easy to do, or approximate, Joyce's associational stunts on your own; and unless you know what the ground rules are—*his* ground rules—you have no way of knowing whether your guess is good or not. Wilder listened and restated his proposal. I sputtered some more. I don't remember any result" (20 October 1961, HWS).

3. During the Fall semester, Wilder delivered five lectures: the opening lecture on 8 November 1950, which included a discussion of passages from Melville; on

15 November he lectured on Thoreau, on 29 November on Dickinson, and on 6 December on Whitman. On 20 February 1951 he lectured on Poe. A sixth lecture was planned but never delivered—Wilder debated in his journals whether it should be on Hawthorne or on Melville. During the Spring semester he taught a humanities course that included Cervantes' *Don Quixote*, Stendhal's *The Red and the Black*, Melville's *Moby-Dick*, and Tolstoy's *War and Peace*. Three of Wilder's Norton Lectures were published in *The Atlantic Monthly*: "Toward an American Language" CXC, 1 (July 1952), 29–37; "The American Loneliness" [Thoreau], CXC, 2 (August 1952), 65–69; "Emily Dickinson," CXC, 5 (November 1952), 43–48. These essays are revised and printed in Wilder's *American Characteristics*. See also Wilder's *Journals*.

Wilder maintained Cambridge as his base until mid-August 1951, when he returned to his home in Hamden, Connecticut. On 14 September he sailed on the SS *Veendam* for Europe. Entries in his journal after this date show him still working on ideas related to the Norton Lectures.

4. This information comes from a letter to Wilder from Achilles Fang, 10 November 1950. See TW to AG, 30 August 1951, n. 7.

5. In an unpublished journal entry for 24 September 1948 (#411, YCAL), Wilder writes, "Yesterday Isabel and I house hunting [in Dublin] had tea with Dr. Bethel Soloman [sic], President of the College of Surgeons, eminent gynecologist, and former chief of the Rotunda Maternity Hospital. And sure enough he's in Finnegans Wake in H. C. E.'s great broadcast = ' . . . in my bethel of Solyman's I accouched their rotundaties. . . .' [542.27–.28]." Glasheen's entry in *Census I* is based on Wilder's information. In his autobiography, *One Doctor in His Time* (London: Christopher Johnson, 1956), Dr. Solomons (1885–1957) writes of his meeting with Wilder: "When Thornton Wilder came to Dublin, he decided to rent our mews in Fitzwilliam Square, but he was unfortunately called to a first production of one of his plays in Paris, and so we missed the pleasure of having him near us. I had just finished reading his latest work on the letters of Caesar [Wilder's epistolary novel *The Ides of March*] and he kindly corrected several misprints in my copy for me. He was then working on a glossary for that remarkable book, James Joyce's *Finnegan's Wake* [sic], and he was able to assist me to make something of the import of this amusing work" (189). According to his autobiography, Solomons was only the third Jew to receive a medical degree at Trinity College, Dublin, and was the first Jewish specialist in the city where there was then only one Jewish general practitioner (218). Wilder and Dr. Solomons, who probably met through Lady Longford of the Dublin Gate Theatre, saw each other on at least three occasions. Despite what Dr. Solomons writes, Wilder left for the continent to see friends and to fulfill lecture engagements in Germany.

6. This information may have come from telephone conversations Wilder had with John Francis Byrne about Joyce on 30 September and 7 October 1948. Byrne was a fellow student with Joyce both at Belvedere College and University College Dublin. In an unpublished journal entry (#416, YCAL), Wilder writes: "The call from Mr. Byrne. He didn't know much about it, but we looked over a few sentences and he gave me here and there a clue: 'Lutetias in the lock' [542.29]; 'Forum Foster' [542.18]." This will be great fun, to publish an elucidation of portions of the Great Broadcast. To agitate the matter and then withdraw, leaving it to other hands. Everywhere the embarrassment of well-read Dubliners about this book: partly because of its half-glimpsed obscenity and blasphemy, partly because no one has time or perseverance (the liberation from England has upset them as much as the struggle did) and partly

the same kind of discomfort that cultivated Mississippians must feel in the presence of Faulkner's novels." See also Byrne *Silent Years*.

7. The "Nocturne" was a favorite section of Wilder's in the *Wake*. He first elucidated it on Friday, 12 January 1940 along with the opening three paragraphs and the close from 626 at the New York apartment of Mabel Dodge Luhan. He returned to it again and again in his impromptu talks about the *Wake*. For a detailed description of the talk and reaction to it, see Wilder to Stein, 28 January 1940 in Burns and Dydo, Stein/Wilder letters. Wilder returns to the Nocturne passage in other letters. See TW to AG, 21 December 1951.

1951

To Thornton Wilder, Hamden, Connecticut

[MS. TLS—YCAL]

6 June [1951][1] [83 Red Stone Street
 Forestville, Connecticut]

Dear Mr. Wilder,

Back in winter you wrote me a very kind and charming letter about *Finnegans Wake*. Now I am sending you a list I made of some of the people who turn up in *Finnegans Wake*. I made the list last winter when my child had swollen glands, and as lists go I don't think it too awful. But I have very little respect for lists or list-making. Shaw was wrong—those who can't don't teach, they make lists.[2]

At any rate, here the thing is. Sometimes it does help me find people. Actually, it was spending four days hunting through *Finnegans Wake* for Gipsy Devereux that impelled me to begin listing.[3]

Have you ever read a detailed account of the Commission that inquired into Parnell's authorship of the letters that it turned out [Richard] Pigott forged?[4] It does much to illuminate the fourth section of *Finnegans Wake*, at least, I think it's the fourth section—the one that begins "As the lion" etc.[5]

I know you must be a very busy man. Please don't feel obliged to acknowledge the list. Or to look at it for that matter.

 Yours sincerely,
 Adaline E. Glasheen

1. Written in response to Wilder's letter of 7 December 1950.

2. The "list" is a mimeographed early version of what would become Glasheen's *Census*. At the suggestion of either Warren Hunting Smith or Charles Bennett she sent it to Wilder and Malcolm Cowley, an editor at The Viking Press, among others. Cowley replied to Glasheen on 21 August 1951: "It is certainly an amusing idea to list the proper names in *Finnegans Wake* and, with annotations and cross references, the list would indeed be useful to readers of the novel—but we can't see any prospect of a popular demand that would be large enough to justify publication in these days when book manufacturing has become extremely expensive" (HWS).

3. Gipsy Devereux, hero of the Joseph Sheridan Le Fanu (1814–1873) novel *The House by the Churchyard* (1863). See Atherton, *The Books at the Wake*.

4. See MacDonald, *Diary of the Parnell Commission*. Glasheen wrote about Parnell in her 1959 article, "Joyce and the Three Ages of Charles Stewart Parnell," in Magalaner, *A James Joyce Miscellany, Second Series*. MacDonald gives a day by day account of the Commission which sat for 128 days beginning on 22 October 1888 and ending on 31 October 1889. The Parnell Commission, as it came to be called, was constituted by the House of Commons to make a general inquiry into the "Parnell Movement." Following the first reading of the Bill of Coercion in February 1887, which would have granted England special rights to coerce members of the Land League whom they judged to be "cowardly miscreants" (vii), *The Times* published a series of articles under the general title "Parnellism and Crime" designed to destroy the credibility of Parnell and his supporters. "It was on 18 April that *The Times* produced its trump card, supplied by Pigott: the facsimile of a letter written in long hand on one side of a folded sheet of paper and on the other side signed at the top 'Yours very truly Chas. S. Parnell'" (Kee 526). The letter is dated "15/5/82," nine days after the Phoenix Park murders of Thomas Henry Burke, Permanent Undersecretary in the Irish Office, and Lord Frederick Cavendish, Chief Secretary for Ireland. In a different hand, the text ran: "I am not surprised at your friend's anger but he and you should know that to denounce the murders was the only course open to us. To do that promptly was plainly our best policy. But you can tell him and all others concerned that though I regret the accident of Lord F. Cavendish's death I cannot refuse to admit that Burke got no more than his deserts. You are at liberty to show him this, and others whom you can trust also, but let not my address be known. He can write to [sic] House of Commons" (Kee 526, MacDonald iv). Following a demonstration at Hyde Park against the Bill of Coercion in April 1887, *The Times* published additional articles designed to discredit Parnell's National League. The "facsimile" letter appeared to confirm that the members of the Land League which Parnell, Michael Davitt, and Andrew Kettle founded in October 1879 and Parnell dissolved in October 1882 when he formed the National League, were part of a conspiracy of "dynamiters and assassins." Other letters by Parnell appeared in *The Times* articles. Parnell formally denied the authenticity of the letters on the floor of the House on 6 July and demanded a select committee of the House to investigate the letters. By an Act of Parliament, a Commission of Judges was appointed to investigate the serious charges brought up in *The Times* articles in addition to the authenticity of the Parnell letters. On 22 February 1889, Richard Pigott, a journalist and newspaper owner, admitted that he had been bribed to write the letters against the interests of Ireland. MacDonald writes, "The notion of Piggot's appearing in the character of injured innocence set the audience off, once

more, into a fit of laughter" (161). When the Commission resumed testimony of Monday, 26 February, it was announced that Pigott had escaped London and gone to the continent. A warrant for his arrest was then issued charging him with forgery and perjury. News of his suicide in Madrid, Spain, reached London on 2 March. In desperate need of money, Pigott had sold his declining newspapers, the old-fashioned Fenian and anti-Land League *Irishman* and *Flag of Ireland* to Parnell for £3000—Parnell closed them and started his own paper, *United Ireland*. Pigott used letters written at this time to trace Parnell's signature. See also Corfe, *The Phoenix Park Murders*.

5. *Finnegans Wake*, I. iv, pages 75–103.

☐

To Adaline Glasheen, Forestville, Connecticut

[MS. ALS—HWS]

12 June [1951]   Dunster House
                                                 Harvard University
                                                 Cambridge 38, Massachusetts

Dear Mrs Glasheen:
   That silence was only me in the hospital enjoying a sacro-iliac dislocation.[1]

x

Can I have this list all for mine? for keeps?

x

Prof's [Harry] Levin and [John] Kelleher would give their eye-teeth for copies.
   Can I serve as intermediary (oh! only briefly—they'll be in ocean-deep correspondence with you soon)[2]

x

Sure, you've got yourself now into unending work.
But I don't say this deploring it but felicitating you.
It's a virus—but not a depressant.

x

I'm deep in tasks: readying my Norton lectures for the printer; always margin-work on Lope de Vega; a little project in Palestrina—sounds like it could call in your aid on "liturgical echoes"—[3]

So I send you not the result of deep exploration, but a few straws caught in passing and always with the reservation that I may be stoutly wrong.

Page 211 [.2]: Will of the Wisp and Barny the Bark are Yeats and Shaw who get a Nobel Prize for their devoted mother.[4]

Victor Hugonot was Atkinson's factor for selling poplin ties on the quais. [.18]

Conditor Sawyer was Peter Sawyer, the founder of Dublin, Georgia, USA [.28]

Honor Bright was a prostitute found murdered in the Dublin Mts [.33]

You can give Gough his title of General [.25]

Tib is an old nickname for Isabel(la).
    Hence too Bold Bet backwords TEB 624 [.18] Is it.
The cat is also Boald Tib on p. 28 [.5]—or is that our little Miss Issy?
Is that the family dog Percy—or is their dog Olaf =
    All this to be dug out: 235, 568, 569, 594, 613, 454

So you don't include characters from books?
    So you can remove
        Dimitrius O'Flagonan who belongs to the Ezekial-Irons-Hyacinthus O'Flaherty (Posidonius O'Fluctuary 80)— Stark crowd in "The House by the Churchyard" 27 [.25], 80 [.28–.29], 87 [i.e., 27.23], 363 [i.e., 362.5]

You can remove the asterisk from before Oglethorpe:[5] He left funds in Dublin to release prisoners from debtors' prison.

Won't you give remove the question-mark after Madame Gristle {Steevens} seeing she's in the list of hospital benefactors on p. 20? [i.e., 40.34]

    x

Derzheer-Dair's Herr 289 [.8], 69 [.8] is just a German Der Erz-Herr = The Mighty Lord (combining with the old song "There's hair like wire,["] etc) and with Erz = brass

    x

Heavens, is 342 [.11], the only de Valera?

    x

Dew vale, Clod = Claude Duval, the famous highwayman; on p. 457 [.11] he may also be the Emperor Claudius of 121 [.1].

    x

Can you put in an entry for James Harmensen—who founded the anti-Calvinist sect called the Arminians whom he brought to Ireland—he [is] buried half-way down p. 466 [.25]—"harmanize" and in mind uncle Hare probably?

x

Barnado = Orphanage in England [253.31]

x

p. 184 [.35]   Padre Aguilar—(is he there?) the 4th Evangelist with his aguilar = eagle and Layteacher Baudwin is John's everpresent ass—why Baldwin? Ah ho is his bray—usually accompanies him too {eg. 533 [.21–.22]}

p. 69 [.32]   Herr Betreffender: Germ. merely means "when it concerns, before-mentioned.["]

Beurla p. 132 [.27] Irish for the English language.

p. 157 [.34]   Mrs Cornwallis-West = Mrs Patrick Campbell (not his first wife— Winston Churchill's, step-mother, because she had a title.)

p. 62 [.34]   An asterisk for Lotta Crabtree?—our great American soubrette of the 70s and 80s?

pp 31 [.17–.19] & 29 Can we believe that MM Manning was mayor of Waterford and Luke Elcock mayor of Drogheda? or bishops?

p. 13 [.13, .9] Fiery Farrelly and Miry Mitchell I've always taken for (pardon it) the Archangels Raphael and Michael—but they are also (we are afraid they are listening) the twin boys in their cribs.

p. 299 [.22]   Simperspreach Hammeltones = "Single speech Hamilton."

p. 140 [.1]   Benjamin Lea for Bill Guin[n]ess {here as tho' the name of a Pub.[}]

p. 573 [.26]   I suppose Wadding is Luke Wadding who founded the Irish College in Rome in 1625 = He is in the center of page 24 [.20] under Waddlings Raid where his first name gives us the Old-Man and Evangelist in its proper order.

p. 386 [.18]   Merquus of Pawerschoof. Mark-Munster we have been told lives (373 [.1]) at the Fourcourts (S. in Dublin, Naturally). This become[s] Porecourts [5.36]—German for Court is Hof. So ennobled he is Marquis = and under the guise of a horse—he is the above, pawing, with allusion also to Lord Powercourt?

p. 254 [.2]   Rurie, Thoath—these are deformations of the Three wants—WAVES of Ireland (here I can't read my own notes RUR?, Tooha and CLEENA see also bottom of p. 23[)]

p. 536 [.32–.33]   Those four judges: Lord Tone, John O'Feely or
                   John Whalley, Benjamin Code and (Judge?) Wright.
p. 542 [.23]   Aren't those two separate reformers Elizabeth Fletcher
                   and Elizabeth Flem[m]ing—ElizaBOTH? and you see,
                   both quakers?
p. 543   line 2—there's de Valera
                   line 18—I always took William Inglis for William III.
545   5th line from the bottom [i.e., .32]: that Gomez is also
                   [in] Ulysses 740:28
                   For magmonimoss [545.32], give us a well known doctor
                   in Dublin Dr Mosse
548   Do you want to put in the firms (lower third of the page)
                        Prim Bros—drapers Grt George's St [.26]
                        Slyne and Co ladies' tailors 71 Grafton St [.26]
                        Sparrows' (can't read my notes = ?Dalton St?) [.26]
549 (top) [.2]   J. Leonard Co Chemists 19 N. Earl St
                   John Dunphy chemist and hairdresser, Crosshaven [.2]
552 [.26]   Tellforth's glory = Telford was the organ-builder
552 [.29]   forty-bonnets = Joyce has been reported to have been so
                   amazed on hearing that Rebecca West had forty hats that
                   he strewed it all over the book see 283 note 1; 333 [.25],
                   243 [.4][6]
553 [.13–.14]   Jean de Porteleau = John Waterman = these are the
                   statues as you go down O'Connell St.
                        Sir John Gray, Father Theobald Matthew,
                   Admiral Nelson—then I get lost.
                   {Lordy, this is the longest letter I ever wrote.}
                   Ma'am, you've started a real indispensable monument.
                   Your pastime has become an obligation.
   Do plan about 3 years from now to do it again—after having
gleaned recommendations from far more reliable and diligent
enthusiasts than I am.
   And in the next version, please plan to put a brief "aid" with each
name:
         E. G.
              D'Esterre (killed by O'Connell in a duel) 52 [.29–.30]
                             x
              Philpot, Sara (see Curran, Sarah) [210.30]
              Curran, Sarah, d. of Philpot Curran; she was Robert
                   Emmet's *fiancée*.
         And so on:
         And cross-references for the deformations:

Dunders de Dunness 213 [.34–.35], see Dunn
Dunn, Irish hat-makers 213 etc.
x
And in a future edition won't you need a subdividing guide to the line on the page. The Seminars in Columbia and Harvard apparently have a celluloid frame—marked for lines—so they can place it on each page:
[Wilder draws a sheet with lines numbering 5 then 10]
And so you could give
D'Esterre (killed by O'C, etc) 52.29
Oh, madam, it's not *me* urging work on you it's the force within *you* that incited all this.

Cordially
Thornton Wilder

1. On the morning of 1 March Wilder awoke with severe pains in his back, his legs, and his thighs. He taught his morning class on Stendhal's *The Red and the Black*, but in the afternoon the pain was so severe that he was taken to the Stillman Infirmary in Cambridge. Later he was transferred to Phillips House at Massachusetts General Hospital where he remained until 30 March.

2. Levin, Professor of English and Comparative Literature at Harvard University, was the author of *James Joyce, A Critical Introduction* (1941) and editor of *The Portable James Joyce* (1947). Kelleher was a Professor of Irish History and Literature. Beginning in the 1948–1949 academic year they jointly taught a seminar on *Finnegans Wake*. Glasheen sent her list to Levin in July. See AG to TW, 5 July 1951.

3. In October 1950 Wilder finished an article, "New Aids Toward Dating the Early Plays of Lope de Vega," published in *Varia Variorum Festgabe für Karl Reinhardt dargebracht von Freuden und Schülern* (Münster Koln: Böhlau-Verlag, 1952, 194–200). A second essay on Lope de Vega's plays, "Lope, Pinedo, Some Child-Actors, and a Lion," was published in *Romance Philology*, VII (August 1953), 19–25. Both are reprinted in *American Characteristics*. Wilder discusses his "Plan of Work" for Lope and Palestrina in *Journals*, entry 491, 30 December 1950. In the work of Palestrina, which he had first encountered while a student at Oberlin College, he wanted to find "themes which Palestrina associated with the Virgin Mary (not merely formally but intimately) and which he introduced into the Masses (even those not acknowledgedly based upon her motifs) precisely because she is only once alluded to in the Mass" (88–89).

4. Yeats won the Nobel Prize for Literature in 1923; Shaw won the prize in 1925.

5. In *Census I* Glasheen writes: "An asterisk means I don't know who somebody is. A dagger means a name is made up of two or more people. If part of a name is italicized (*Finn* MacCool or Tim *Finnegan*) it means that the person is listed under that name and spelling in the *Census*" (1).

6. West's essay, "The Strange Necessity" (1928), opens as she is leaving Sylvia Beach's book shop, Shakespeare and Company, having purchased Joyce's *Pomes Penyeach*

(1927). She meditates on the poem "Alone," and why she considers it to be bad. In imitation of *Ulysses*, West wanders about Paris making observations about Joyce's work, observing people in the streets, and visiting her dressmaker. She then visits a milliner's shop "which the head *vendeuse* of a famous house had just started as her own venture and had ordered three hats, and had sat playing with the models, two on my lap, one on my head, changing them about, little dove-like things that laid wings of dark felt softly against the face; I was amused by their contrast with their maker, who leaned over me, trying to sell me more . . ." (44–45). Joyce, perhaps having heard about West's love of hats, and retaliating against her imitation of *Ulysses*, included allusions to her hats in *Finnegans Wake*. In his notes on the *Wake*, Wilder listed additional references to "forty bonnets": 20.27, 379.23, and 519.7 (#315, YCAL). In "A Point for American Criticism," William Carlos Williams responds to West's essay: "In summary: Rebecca West makes (is made by) a mold; English criticism, a product of English literature. She states her case for art. It is an excellent digest but for a world panorama inadequate. She fails to fit Joyce to it. She calls him, therefore, 'strange,' not realizing his compulsions which are outside of her sphere. In support of this, she builds a case against him, using Freudian and other nonliterary weapons. She is clever, universal in her informational resorts. What is now left over—Joyce's true significance—his pure literary virtue—is for her 'nonesense.' Of literature and its modus showing that she knows nothing. America, offering an undeveloped but wider criticism, will take this opportunity to place an appreciation of Joyce on its proper basis" (185). West responded to Williams's essay in her "Letter from Europe," *Bookman* (New York) LXX (September 1929), 664–668. Beckett's essay "Dante . . . Bruno. Vico . . . Joyce" in *Our Exagmination* also briefly responds to West's criticism of Joyce. See Briggs, "Rebecca West vs. James Joyce"; see Scott, *Joyce and Feminism*.

☐

To Adaline Glasheen, Forestville, Connecticut

[MS. ALS—YCAL]

[postmark: 2 July 1951]   Dunster House
Sunday morning   Harvard University
                                Cambridge 38, Massachusetts

Dear Mrs. Glasheen:

    Some stray notes to keep you eager.

x

Please send a copy of the census to Mr. John TRAIN 370 Park Ave NY.[1]

He will send you (when he finishes it late next fall) the *catalogue raisonnée* of all quotations in latin in FW. (He has not yet located "Quâ rê. . . . unde gestium? festinas" 202 and passim.[)]

I haven't located Harry Levin's summer address yet. If you send his copy to me, I'll forward it.

x

Healy, Tim (former Gov. Irish Free State) in "Healiopolis" 24 [.18]
Lalor, Fintan (political writer) 25 [.9–.10]
Pankhurst, Gloria (suffragette) 388 [.28]
White, Pearl (actress in silent movies—"The Perils of Pauline") bottom p. 394 [.35–.36]
?Ars, Curé of ("Curer of Wars") 440 [.10]
Gill, ? (publisher on O'Connell St) 440 [.14–.15]
Ratti (family name of present Pope?) 458 [.6][2]
"Tich, Little" (London Music hall star) 465 [.29]
Krishnamurti (Hindu philosopher) 472 [.15]
Hamazum, Mrs 494 [.35] (the Amazon River, associated with her sister the Nile, here and on p. 627 [.28–.29])
Coleraine, Kitty (ballad; she dropped a pitcher of milk) 210 [.33–.34]
Melmoth, Sebastian (*alias* of Oscar Wilde) under subustioned mullmud 228 [.33]

x x x

You'll ease your road and illuminate us if you disentangle lots of the allusions to the Four Old Men: try from p. 476

Matthew Gregory (Walker?)   Ulster (Amagh) MAN; HEIGHT
                                                FIRE
Mark Lyons   Munster (Cork etc) LION, LENGTH
                                                and Breath; AIR;
LUKE MeTCALFe Tarpey, Leinster (also a Welshman) OX
    SOLIDS & BOUNDS. EARTH
John Walker (are they perhaps all Walkers) McDougal
    [(]connaught) EAGLE. Point; WATER
Luke is perhaps Tarpey because Gaelic Tarbe = bull = OX, his Evangelist's "beast."
All this with many a vexation is distributed through 57, 94, 367, 476, 368, 514, 223, 536

Their residences in Dublin + are	372
Their animals.	367
Their faces	368
Animals again	332, 573

Direction of compass	534
As playing cards	286, 202
As Cardinal Numbers	282

And their great Book, of course, begins on p. 383. The wonderful twilight of senile decay at Mrs M[a]cCawley's Poor House—maybe ALP's Marg. Earwicker's maiden name was M[a]cCawley anyway.

x

You will get often disheartened.

The chief occupation of FW-specialists is the Concealing From Others How Little They Know.

Don't let's you and I be among them: let us proclaim loudly that we know nothing about the book.

In the long run we must and can expose them: not by superior knowledge, but by superior candor

(Provincetown June 30,—returning to Cambridge Monday)[3]
Oh, dear, here it is still unfinished. I'd better send it off.
I repeat: to keep you eager.

faithfully—urque ad aras
Thornton Wilder

---

1. Wilder met Train, a student at Harvard (B.A., 1950; M.A., 1951), during his Norton Professorship. Train was the head of the Signet Club and inducted Wilder as an honorary member. Train took a Master's in Comparative Literature, and under John V. Kelleher he prepared a "Latin Glossary of *Finnegans Wake*" which was never published. Train was a founder and managing editor of *The Paris Review* (1952–1954) and later became a successful investment counselor, writer, and government official.

2. "Present Pope" is misleading. The reference would be to Ambrogio Damiano Achille Ratti (1857–1939), Pope Pius XI (1922–1939).

3. Wilder arrived in Provincetown, Massachusetts, on 27 June and returned on 2 July. This letter is postmarked Brockton, Massachusetts.

To *Thornton Wilder, Hamden, Connecticut*
[MS. TLS—YCAL]

5 July [1951]　　　　　　　　　　　　[83 Red Stone Street
　　　　　　　　　　　　　　　　　　Forestville, Connecticut]

Dear Mr. Wilder,

Nothing is easier than for me to stay eager about Finnegans Wake and nothing is easier than for me to confess my ignorance about it. I don't know why the Letter comes from Boston, Mass. I don't know why Kate (who I suppose is Kathleen ni Houlihan) is in charge of the museum. I don't know why the Prankquean looks like a poss of porter pease. I don't know why the Norwegian Captain wants a suit or sowterkins. I don't know what the cad with the pipe said to HCE in the park. I *think* he said (35 [.15–.16]) "Give us the loot in you my dear old friend," but this is open to various objections. Oh I could go on indefinitely but these are enough to expose my blank ignorance. You, however, must not admit ignorance. A friend of mine who heard your Norton lectures has written me that you are a Great Mind. Great Minds never admit ignorance, and what is more important, never admit that there is a process in greatness.

I have a new copy of *Finnegans Wake*.[1] It is a revelation. Hence some additions to my census.
　　Adonis (a Jonas), 434 [.27]
　　Sara Allgood, 21 [.30] ?
　　Aquinas, 240 [.8]
　　Belshazzar, 146 [.13]
　　Dion Cassius, 391 [.23]
　　Disraeli, 27 [.1]
　　Luke Elcock (another) 447 [.12, .14]
　　Guinevere, 28 [.1]
　　Harry Lorrequer (a Lever hero), 228 [.21]
　　Victor Hugonot, 133 [.21]
　　John F. Larchet (orchestra leader at the Abbey) 222 [.2]
　　Joseph Maas, 165 [.2] (singer)
　　Mullocky (151 [.24]) is Malachy and his circle of gold

p. 13 [.9, .13]—if Miry Mitchel is St. Michael, which I do think, why isn't Fiery Farrelly Lucifer and not Raphael?
Von Moltke, 333 [.13]
Ney, 10 [.15]
A Becket and O'Toole also 59 [.6–.7]
Soult, 10 [.14]
Sturluson [i.e., Sturlason], Snorri, 551 [.4]
Synge, 549 [.3] (where is the sedulous singe?)
Vousden, Veneralble [FW: Venerable] Val—439 [.17–.18], 50 [.15] wa[s] a Dublin music hall entertainer, but that is the kind of thing you know
Wadding 573 [.26]—was Luke an historian? All the others in the passage are, aren't they? Gilbert, Warre, D'Alton.

Another thing I saw with the new copy was p. 534 [.21–.22] "the best begrudged man in Belgradia who doth no[t] beleaseto our pavio[u]r . . .["] (and down the page) behavio[u]r [.31]. Is this not the lim[e]rick about the old man of Moldavia who couldn't believe in our Savior, so he started instead with himself as the head, the cult of decorous behavior?

My husband thinks that "Foun[d]litter. Shown geshotten" at the bottom of 420 [.35] is a play with the Elizabethan word "shotten" meaning to have littered, as in "shotten herring."

I read in a book that "Auden" (279 [note 1]) is from Odin. Also that Asa is a name of Odin and that he was the first to teach runes to men. This makes more sense than Peer Gynt's mother, don't you think? Also (154 [.23]) "orlog" was in the Norse religion the primaeval law which carries "Let thor be orlog" back to Genesis.

None of these are very world shaking, but little by little and so and so. I will try to work on the old men. I will start right away, but I can't get on so fast in summer as I can in winter because we have a farm that weighs on my mind in summer.

I have sent copies of the census (I adopt your term and from now shall pretend it was my own) to Mr. Train and one to Mr. Levin just care of the Harvard English department. I thought that would be easier than troubling you.

As well I have said everything, for I have to shell peas for supper. If I were a Virginia Woolf sort of feminist, I would feel that this excused my inferiority as a Joyce worker. But really it doesn't. I have brilliant ideas over the wash tub, and it was peeling shrimp that I realized that Hircus Civis Eblanensis was the name of a person and place and a thing.

Thank you so much. You are all that is kind and encouraging. I just thought of an odd thing. I have read only one book of yours—The Ides of March—but I have read it eight times.

               Sincerely,
               Adaline Glasheen

1. There are six copies of *Finnegans Wake* in the Glasheen archive: The Viking Press edition of 1939, two copies of the 1947 edition, and the editions of 1964, 1966, and 1976. The revelation may have been that of seeing the text without all of her previous annotations.

To Adaline Glasheen, Forestville, Connecticut

[MS. ALS—HWS]

30 August 1951   50 Deepwood Drive
                                                                Hamden 14, Connecticut

Dear Mrs Glasheen:
    Saddest story in the world: I had to put all Finnegans Wake reading aside for some other things I have to do. {But not before I'd worked two days on the avatars of the Four Old Men—and now I've mislaid those notes; if they turn up I'll forward them to you.}
    I sail for 6 weeks in Europe, leaving Sept 14.[1] Then I come back to work in the vicinity of the Princeton Library (on my Thoreau, Poe, Melville matters—very fascinating, too. Between you and me, don't reading FW habituate us to reading *anything* with quadrupled attention?)[.] Then I shall have time to reopen FW again.
    From your last letter I've copied your readings into my text.
    Don't be so modest—most of them had completely escaped me.
    105 [.19] older nor the Rogues. . . . after Walter Pater in The Renaissance.

111 [.32]. Boucher. May be you[r] archeologist.² But probably mostly an allusion to the burning rubbish heap on which the hen found the letter. French: BÛCHER, a pile of wood. Jeanne D'arc was burned at the bûcher.

About the metals:

I have a totally unproved theory that the (atomic) elements in various sequences march through the whole book . . . . . . as do the colors of the rainbow (all contained in the black of night) . . . as does the world of sound (vîa Guido d'Arezzo's scale).³ In other words the whole physical universe is woven into the web of HCE's thoughts.

But you are certainly right that Gold x Silver x Brass-Bronze x Lead-Tin come to the surface in relation to the Viconian cycle at pp 140 and 398–9.⁴

So far I've shied away from the complexities of the Ondt and Grasshopper and the Mookse and the Gripes. I leave those to my sixties.

154 [.23] thanks for orlog. = keep it related to Horloge = French, clock and (p 77 [.13]) Africans oorlog = war.

Oh, I've found some notes on the Four Old Men.⁵ Remember first they are four sycamore trees outside the window (Grogram's pasture) with a donkey tied to the fourth (i.e. St. John's ass and the ass is of course a Christofer.)

And probably secondarily as the bedposts (whence the Evangelist's via the old goodnight prayer) on the fourth of which hangs. . . . ? . . . Mr. Earwicker's collar? To your forty-two avatars could you add them as musicians (twice on p. 533).

You ask me about Salt etc relative to the Trinity. Deponent answers not, not knowing. Also rê p. 367 [.8] "Mask One" as "Mark One"—Huckleberry Finn: I doubt that he had that in mind. S. L. Clemens took his penname from the plumb-line call of the river-pilots. I think here the allusion is to the actors in the old commedia d'arte— usually ridiculous old doctors, clowns, etc, who were technically called *maschere*.

I have the feeling that, this time, I've practically failed you.

That's because I've been so beset and betorn by so many far less interesting matters.

x
x

One last word:
You're doing a splendid and a "classical" task.
But don't feel that you have to hurry.
Patience for thoroughness.

And—for the present—work at it *at that level*: the Proper Names: men, women (and animals?) referred to in FW.

You'll only become insecure and distressed and discouraged, if you start to haul into your net a lot of the other intentions and symbols etc in the book. {Naturally, you can *see* them, for your own interest; what I mean is, for the purpose of this census.}

If you do wish to extend your labors you might be assembling a second census called, say, Refrains, slogans, and Recurrent Phrases in FW.

x

If you have time, do write me once more before I sail (Sept 14) about your plans, hopes, fears, problems.

x

Have you all the Oriental resurrection divinities and solar heroes collected for the last book [IV, 593–628]? Catch all those Parsi, Hindu, Norse, Egyptian Gods in some Encyclopedia of Religion.

x

Nothing makes me happier than to hear you say that you need boosting and encouragement,—not at all. Of course not—this is the Grand Old Book of the first half of the 20th Century.

"Where once we led so many car couples have follied since" . . . . . p. 623 [.21–.22].

x

Kate, who shows tourists around the house, may be Kathleen Na H—n, but she is also Widow Kate Strong, the maid of all work in the Earwicker Home.

x

And never lose the FUN of it.

Cordially
Thornton Wilder

pp 398–399

Yes, apparently the Four Old Men are each serenading her in person {Each is a musical instrument—drum, reed, fife and brass! which is new}

And as you say: There she is in the four Viconian parallels: MOTHER . . . . . Bride . . . . Widow . . . . and (?) Rediviva.

And speaking are Ulster-Matthew
        Dingle Boy—Kerry—Munster—Mark
        —Luke, but place not given
        —John, and (where is the Cross of Cong?) [399.25][6]

And there is Sunday
   Monday
   —midweek
   Friday–Sat.
—And gold, silver, copper, iron.

x   x

   Now apparently she is now the wife of John—of Bohermore = Moherbore to the Washte (p 373 [.5]) in Connaught. Mark on p 399 [.9–.10] regrets that she bides with King Cedric—Sitrig—Sigrig Silkybeard (as Sig Sloomysides—from sloom, sleep out of the Anglo-Saxon). Which gives you another Sitric. {In your census I'd put it Sitric Silkybeard, Danish Conqueror of Dublin, and put Cedric Sigric etc as cross references. Note that as so often John (here Sig) is accompanied by that grogram grey donkey—why he is here a "barnacle goose" [FW: gander] I do not know.

   The song is a play on the then popular Lambeth Walk—elsewhere referred to in the book. And Lambeg Island is off Howth Head—by [i.e., but] why all those Lomboog Lunbag Limibeg—I don't know.
   There's no end to it

TW.

   A Chinese scholar named Achilles Fang would have delighted Joyce.[7]
   This letter and my conversation with him was a sample of one of the several maladies which beset FW-maniacs. He has Monoculitis = for him a Chinese reading outweighs all others.
      p. 244 [.13]. Tinct-tint—maybe Chinese listen. But Lordy it's the bough brushing against the window all night—and here it is: listen to the sound; and observe the shade of color.
      He wants Mei so much to read solely a young girl that he doesn't see
      Christmas remembers May
      You'll remember Me (in the song)
      Sir Henry Yule remembers the Chinese Girl he left behind him.
I'm through with this.

1. Wilder arrived at Le Havre on 24 September and traveled in France and Italy before returning to New York on 5 November.

2. Glasheen drops her identification of "Boucher" as Jacques Boucher de Crèvecoeur de Perthes (1788–1868) from *Census I*. Boucher was an archaeologist and a writer of tragedies and fiction.

3. Guido d'Arezzo (*c*. 990–1050), the Benedictine monk who devised the four-line musical staff and developed solmization in music which employs a series of syllables used in vocalization and for practice in sight singing.

4. In *Census I* Glasheen writes of Giovanni Battista Vico (1668–1744): "Italian jurist and philosopher. From his great work *Scienza Nuova*, Joyce took a great deal for FW, particularly a way of looking at human history." See Beckett; see Atherton *The Books at the Wake*.

5. Wilder may be referring to notes he made in his journal on 23 February 1940 ("The Four Old Men In Finnegans Wake" and "The Four Evangelists," note 13, YCAL). See Appendix I.

6. The Cross of Cong was, at one time, in the Augustinian Abbey of Cong in County Mayo. The famous gold cross, which is believed to have once contained a relic of the True Cross of Christ, is now in the National Museum of Ireland in Dublin.

7. This sentence, and the remainder of the letter, is written on the verso of a letter from Achilles Fang to Wilder on 10 November 1950, the day after Wilder had given a talk on "Obscenity in Modern Literature," at the Dunster House Forum. Fang writes: "With regard to your explication of the 'oriental foliation' in FW 244–245 last night, I venture to remark that it was 'merciless as wonderful' (FW 252.6). In 'It darkles, (tinct, tint) all this our funnaminal world,' the words in parentheses can certainlly mean 'listen, listen'; for 'ting' (pronounced *t'ing* [ideogram]) is a Chinese word meaning 'to listen'—in fact, the word occurs quadrupled in 294.23–.24. (By the way, 'funnaminal' is printed 'funnominal' in the Mime of Mick Nick and the Maggies [219–259]. I wonder if that is not better reading, for 'a selfmade world' of 252.26 seems to be anticipated by 'nominal world.') The third word in 'Elefant has siang his triump' is a Chinese word (standard transcription: *hsiang* [ideogram]) meaning 'elephant.' Finally, it would be better to read 'Mei' in '. . . Yul remembers Mei. Her hung maid mohns are bluming' as a Chinese word [ideogram] meaning 'plum flower'; as 'hung' [ideogram] . . .I[t] means 'red' (vide 'mohns'), 'hung maid' can be read as 'hung mei' (red plum-flower), a usual name for girls (like 'Rose' in English). Übrigens, please accept my thanks for your spirited defense of modern writers. P. S. 'Mei' [ideogram] also means 'sister' or 'girl' (vide 'maid')." Fang's doctoral dissertation was "Materials for the Study of Pound's *Cantos*" (Harvard 1958). See also TW to AG, 7 December 1950.

Written in an unidentified handwriting at the bottom of Fang's letter is "Science & Society Vol. III or IV Margaret Schlauch." This is a reference to Margaret Schlauch's article "The Language of James Joyce" in *Science & Society: A Marxian Quarterly*, III, 4 (Fall 1939), 482–497.

To Thornton Wilder, Hamden, Connecticut
[MS. TLS—YCAL]

1 September [1951] [83 Red Stone Street
Forestville, Connecticut]

Dear Mr. Wilder,

As always, so nice to hear from you, and so solidly helpful too. I have not worked on FW of late owing to home decoration, and now I have a houseguest and another coming tomorrow who will want to talk about Faulkner. But and however[.]

I am fascinated with your idea of the elements marching through the book. I had thought about the relations of the spectrum and the musical scale. Was it not Newton who tried to work out a correspondence between the spectrum and the scale? 7 notes, 7 primary colors? Something like that. I've always thought this was mixed up on 492 and 494, but I don't know much about music.

But there *is* a place in Luke's speech (p. 399). Balbriggan is in Lenister [.14]. And Cong is in Ulster though the cross I believe is in Dublin now.[1] Is the barnacle gander [399.10] a possible domestic joke? Do you not think "she was always mad gone on me" [399.22] brings in another of history's fadeless wonder women?

Our correspondence having progressed this far I will reveal a Horrid Thing. I do not really think that FW is a dream. Or rather, I think Joyce uses the dream as it is used in "The Pearl" or "The Thistle and the Rose" or "Pilgrim's Progress," as a device for the suspension of reality. And I further think that the Freudian approach is the most barren. I know that this conviction strikes everyone as being not heretical but inane. Nevertheless it is mine and I thought I should mention it.[2]

197 [.36]–198 [.1] "Tune your pipes and fall ahumming" is a direct quotation from an anon. ballad "Doran's Ass."

88—7 from bottom [i.e., .30]—"there—is—a—pain" etc. is "There is a Green Island in lone Gougaune Barra / Where allu of songs rushes forth like an arrow" which is also the source of "from lone Coogan Barry his arrow of song" on p. 93 (last paragraph) [.28–.29]. A poem by J. J. Callanan.³

p. 95 What is the tie up of the 4 with the Cunningham family? Here it is Minxy and in their section it is with Martin?

96 [.33]—I think I know why Joyce is so fond of "Securus indicat orbis terrarum." It is the phrase that drove Newman out of the Anglican church though not into the Roman.⁴

356 [.14] "whereom is man, that old offender, nother man, wheile he is asame." Human nature being what it is, "same" is practically the only word I remembered from a German course. I guess it explains this version of the riddle, but do the other riddles have similar points?

316—(line 1) "Pukkelsen." Pukkel (I am told) is Norwegian for hunchback.

318 (3 from bottom) [i.e., .34–.35] "plight. . . snorth" the 7 deadly sins, here combined with the spectrum

332 (line 1) "Snip snap snoody" is snipp snapp snute the conventional ending to Norwegian fairy tales.

348 [.26–.27] "For lispias harth a burm in eye but whem it bames for norone screeneth" is Moore's "Nora Creina," "Lesbia hath a beaming eye" etc. See Lesbia Looshe on 93 [.27–.28]⁵

413 The paragraph beginning "To the Very Honorable" is a parody (that isn't the word—I never know what to call what Joyce does) of Swift's "On the Death of Mrs. Johnson." The phrase "only too fat" occurs in Swift.⁶

420–421—You may know that many of these addresses are the addresses of the various residences of the Joyce family in Joyce's childhood and youth.

378 (just under middle) [.20–.21] "Tiemore moretis tisturb Badday! The playgue will be soon over, rats[!]" Is this not a combining of the refrain from Dunbar's "Lament for the Makaris" "Timor mortis conturbat me" and Nash's Brightness falls poem? Nash has "And full

swift the plague runs by." I always associate the two poems in my mind. Maybe Joyce did too.[7]

These are very minor thoughts of mine. But to tell the truth I think everybody should work at minor points of FW. So little is known about them that people are bound to make bad or silly mistakes about the big ones. They start with the symbolism because Freud has made symbolism sound so easy to us all, and then break down on foolish details that a child of the Dublin streets could correct them on. Besides Joyce was getting at something that may include but isn't Freud and Jung, something less fussy but a good deal more important I should say.

I hope you have a lovely time in Europe, and at Princeton when you come back.[8] Yes, reading FW does alter one's reading habits. Sometimes with good literature you wonder if other writers weren't unconsciously working along Joyce's lines and he perhaps unconsciously rooting up the essence of literary creation. Not a very clear speculation but I know what I mean. And how thin so much writing is after FW! Me, I have no plans. I mean to work on FW and hope to go to the Yale library soon. I would like to write an article on Trollope who—after Joyce—is really really *the* most fascinating problem I can think of.

When you come back from Europe may I write you if I think up anything clever about FW?

    Faithfully,
    Adaline Glasheen

What connection has the 4 with the variations of stop, please stop, etc? [124.4–.5, *passim*]

1. See TW to AG, 30 August 1951, n. 6.
2. Possibly a reference to Edmund Wilson's two part article on *Finnegans Wake* which first appeared in *The New Republic* in 1939 and was later collected, with a note written in 1964, in *The Wound and the Bow*. Wilson advanced the idea that the novel was in fact the record of Earwicker's dreams: "Earwicker has been drinking off and on all day and has perhaps gone to bed a little drunk. At any rate, his night is troubled. At first he dreams about the day before, with a bad conscience and a sense of humiliation: then, as the night darkens and he sinks more deeply into sleep, he has to labor through a nightmare oppression" (199).
3. Slightly misquoted from "Gougana Barra," a poem by Jeremiah Joseph Callanan (1795–1829): "There is a green island in lone Gougana Barra,/Where Allua of songs

rushes forth as an arrow" (*The Poems of J. J. Callanan*, Cork: Daniel Mulcahy, sold by James Duffy; Dublin and London, 1861, 65–67).

4. John Henry Newman, as a leader of the Oxford Movement founded in 1833, argued that to revitalize the Anglican Church there should be a return to the beliefs and practices of the early Christians. Newman's translation of the phrase is "The universal Church is in its judgments secure of truth." In *Apologia por Vita Sua*, he writes: "What a light was hereby thrown upon every controversy in the Church! not that, for the moment, the multitude may not falter in their judgment,—not that, in the Arian hurricane, Sees more than can be numbered did not bend before its fury, and fall off from St. Athanasius,—not that the crowd of Oriental Bishops did not need to be sustained during the contest by the voice and the eye of St. Leo; but that the deliberate judgment, in which the whole Church at length rests and acquiesces, is an infallible prescription and a final sentence against such portions of it as protest and secede" (110). Newman left the Anglican Church in 1843 and was received into the Roman Catholic Church in 1845.

5. In "Lesbia Hath a Beaming Eye" in Thomas Moore's *Irish Melodies* (numerous editions beginning in 1808) the eyes, robes, and wit of Lesbia and the poet's love Nora Creina are compared—with the "simple, graceful" Nora winning the poet's admiration.

6. Jonathan Swift writes of Esther Johnson, the Stella of his *Journal to Stella*, just after the news of her death: "She was sickly from her childhood until about the age of fifteen: But then grew into perfect health, and was looked upon as one of the most beautiful, graceful, and agreeable young women in London, only a little too fat" (391).

7. William Dunbar (1460?–1520?) the Scottish poet. The poem is an elegy to Dunbar's predecessors beginning with Chaucer and his contemporaries ("Makaris" meaning makers or poets). The Latin phrase Dunbar uses means "The fear of death confounds me," and is a refrain from the Anglican Office of the Dead. In Thomas Nash's (or Nashe, 1567–1601) only surviving play, *Summer's Last Will and Testament* (1600), Summer, the season, asks Will Summers, the jester, to "Sing me some doleful ditty to the lute,/That may complain my near-approaching death." The song that Will Summers sings, "Adieu, farewell earth's bliss," is a dirge for humanity. Glasheen here cites the second stanza: "Rich men, trust not in wealth,/Gold cannot buy you health;/Physick himself must fade./All things to end are made,/The plague full Swift goes by;/I am sick, I must die:/Lord, have mercy on us" (Nashe 195).

8. When Wilder returned on 5 November, he spent several days in New York and at his home in Hamden, Connecticut, before leaving for Princeton University on 18 November. He remained at Princeton, seeing friends and working in the library until he returned to New York on 24 November.

To Adaline Glasheen, Forestville, Connecticut

[MS. ALS—HWS]

[postmark: 4 September 1951] 50 Deepwood Drive
Hamden 14, Connecticut

Dear Mrs Glasheen:

JOTTINGS:

¶ Rushed to copy in your nuggets.

¶ Yes, Joyce precisely shows what happens when you've known the psychoanalytic lore and have "forgotten it" i.e. passed beyond it. G[ertrude]. Stein said: "Granted all Freud is true—what of it?" It's description—like all science—like the parts of the eye.[1]

¶ Of "tune your pipes"—every bit helps. No one has yet found the basic plan for the movement of Anna Livia Plurabelle.

¶ The Cunninghams may receive some light from their appearance in Ulysses;[2] have you the Word List for that drawn up at the U. of Wisconsin on WPA funds?[3]

¶ Oh, yes, Trollope is the Great One. Because he just looked and told. Didn't push and alter to satisfy stresses within himself.

¶ Yes,—I'll announce my return to you and greedily await some more of these beauties.

¶ Now Why are the Four Old Men out of their proper order, middle of p. 378 [.15–.17]?

Moto-metus-solum-Methuselah and Matthew but I don't know why.
Bulley—Ox of St. Luke and perhaps Napolean.
Cowlie—That could give us a feminine for bull, all right, but Mark gets the syllables also on p. 367 [.28] "where coold by cawld." Of course, often we find a word reversed = maybe it implies that we're under the influence of Cancer the Crab who goes backward = which gives us . .L. . . u. . . . s.

{In the second paragraph of the book [3.11]—but maybe I talked to you about this before—"not yet though all's fair" we're under GEMINI the twins and CANCER. Nathanjoe was Swift's own reversal of his name [3.12]}

Diggerydiggerydock = (John McDougal and perhaps Richard III?[)] and the

Bazeness = the Donkey via a French vulgarity [378.16].
Oh, dear! stumped again.

If you're doing animals—try:
    p. 177 [.22] Bethgellert—by Snowden, Wales. Prince Llewelyn's deer hound Gellert, unjustly slain, symbol of faithful guardianship of a baby.

I guess Barefoot Burn p. 204 l. 6 = is only half Bobby Burns; Pheagh MacHugh O'Byrne—famous brigand who in Elizabeth's time kept a chieftan's court at Ballinacor House on S. E. slope toward Rathdrum. Joyce first printed Wary Wade, then changed to Wallowme (Wallowa r. in Oregon) and to get the splash in.

I guess you've got the GONNING sisters (coalesced with Maude Gonne again p. 508, 9th line from the bottom [i.e., .28].
    I'm so unsystematic that I'm now probably submitting info to you which you first fowarded to me.
                  x   x
    I suppose you saw that the Library of the University of Buffalo bought great crates of Joyce papers. Harry Levin[4] went to see them: tells me there are work-sheets for Ulysses and FW.[5]
    He sort of shut up like a clam when I asked him {all FW workers shut up like clams except you and me} if there was a Schematic Diagram for the "intentions" behind FW.

            Gotta hurry to the Dentist
            Sincerely
            T. Wilder

---

1. Wilder met Freud on three occasions, on 13 and 25 October 1935 at Freud's home in Grinzing, a wine village in the countryside north of Vienna, and in London in June 1939. For an account of his meetings with Freud, see Wilder to Stein, 14 October 1935 and 24 June 1939 in Burns and Dydo, Stein/Wilder Letters.

2. Martin Cunningham, based on Matthew F. Kane, chief clerk in the Crown Solicitor's Office in Dublin Castle, appears as a character or is mentioned in *Dubliners* ("Grace") and *Ulysses*. See Benstock; see Appendix II in Joyce, *Dubliners*, ed. Terence Brown.

3. Miles L. Hanley (1893–1954), assisted by Martin Joos, Theresa Fein, and others, *Word Index to James Joyce's 'Ulysses'* (Madison: University of Wisconsin Press, 1937; rpt. 1944, 1951, 1953, 1962, 1965). Hanley indexed the Random House (1934) text of *Ulysses*. Joyce was so amazed and pleased with the compilation that he saluted Hanley, "the madison man," in *Finnegans Wake* (25.4). Glasheen's copy of the 1937 edition is in HWS.

4. See TW to AG, 12 June 1951, n. 2.

5. In the summer of 1950, through funds given by Margaretta F. Wickser in memory of her husband, Philip J. Wickser, the University of Buffalo acquired from Librairie La Hune, acting on behalf of the Joyce family, a collection of manuscripts, including notebooks used in the composition of *Ulysses* and *Finnegans Wake*, letters, books, and family portraits belonging to Joyce. The works were exhibited in Paris at La Hune, 170 Boulevard Saint-Germain, from 8 October to 12 November 1949. Most of the material belonging to Joyce had been saved by Paul Léon and his brother-in-law Alexander Ponikowski in 1941 prior to a public sale at the Hotel Drouot in Paris to satisfy the claims of Joyce's landlord. During the sale, most dealers withdrew from the bidding when they realized that Léon was buying the material back for the Joyce family. The collection of the University of Buffalo's Poetry/Rare Books Collection was enhanced by the purchase of Joyce materials from the collection of Sylvia Beach. See Gheerbrant, Connolly, and Spielberg.

☐

To Thornton Wilder, Hamden, Connecticut

[MS. TL—YCAL]

[5 September 1951]   [83 Red Stone Street
Wednesday   Forestville, Connecticut]

Dear Mr. Wilder,

I hope the dentist was not too horrid. I suppose he was. I would as soon go to a Beauty Shoppe as a dentist and the other way around. I went to the dentist fifteen times last winter because I hadn't gone in ten years because I prefer suffering in a lump.

I trouble you with another letter before your flitting because I think that while you are in Europe, bodily separate from the earth that nourished your current enthusiasms, while you are in Europe you ought to think about writing a book about *Finnegans Wake*. You know all the reasons for writing it so I'll leave them out. You must know that the dark tower of FW needs you as the white clapboard school does not. I admit to prejudice. I don't like all those 19th century American men. They—Thoreau, Emerson, Melville whoever—were what Emily Dickinson calls "enabled" men.[1] Please think on it.

Mr. [Harry] Levin clammed on me. He said my census was "valuable" and could he put it with some thematic indices the Joyce seminar had? I said yes and did the thematic indices include one on the Prankquean and the Norwegian Captain? And if it did could I please have a copy? And he said if I came to Cambridge I could see the index. Here our relationship may stand until it rots.[2] I also sent a copy to Mr. Edmund Wilson who was really nice but, between you and me, doesn't know boo about FW. He said I should revise the list and get it published, a little trick (published I mean) that I should think was about as easy as splitting an atom on the kitchen table.[3] All of which leads me back to the point that if *you* wrote a book about FW people would read it because you are Thornton Wilder and you could persuade them to read FW and that would—oh heavens the limitless vistas!

This is what I make of Motometusolum. . . Bulley. . . Cowlie. . . Diggery etc on p. 378 [.15–.18]. I don't think much of what I make, too elaborate for one thing. I think they are the 4 Vico ages maybe, not the 4 old men exactly. I am badly educated and never took Latin because my mother was progressive but out of the Latin dictionary I get: *Moto* is to move, stir, agitate: *Metus* is fear of the God of; *Solum* is lowest part, foundation, earth. All of which could add up to the thunderclap— "Moving of earth brings harms and fears / Men question what it did or meant."[4] The bull is a sexual animal. Cowlie—well it does include "lie" as in death. (This sounds feebler and feebler.) But rather convincingly Diggerydiggerydock suggests a clock, hence time which is right for 4 or Johnny and the mouse ran up (so rises from death) and then down to business or baseness as usual, beginning the fall from grace all over again. On the other hand Methuselah is indicated. Oh dear.

Barefoot Burn is the same I guess as 126 [.13] "went nudiboots with trouters into a liffeyette." I had kind of guessed it was something like the real name of a stream that flows into the young Liffey. There's an awful lot of Burns in FW, isn't there?

I will not jot. This letter is a Serious Call. Do you want it on your conscience that you left Finnegans Wake to the Levins who (in the words of a boy I once knew) "has it in the head but don't give out none"? Do you want to dine at journey's end with Bronson Alcott[5] or with James Joyce?

Good Europe to you.

                       Sincerely,
                       [unsigned]

1. The phrase is in poem 1207 in *The Complete Poems of Emily Dickinson*, edited by Thomas H. Johnson (Boston: Little, Brown & Co., 1960). First published in 1891, where it was titled "The Preacher," the second stanza reads: "Simplicity fled from his counterfeit presence/As Gold the Pyrites would shun –/What confusion would cover the innocent Jesus/To meet so enabled a Man!"

2. See Levin to Glasheen, 9 July 1951 (HWS). Glasheen's correspondence to Levin has not been located. The "thematic indices" were explained to Glasheen in a letter of 20 July 1961 from John Kelleher: "The first couple of times Harry Levin and I gave a seminar on FW we set the students to making a theme index of the book, each student being assigned a couple of major and four or five minor topics to follow through" (HWS).

3. Wilson's letter is not in the Glasheen archive at HWS, and her correspondence with Wilson has not been located. Glasheen does not mention to Wilder Malcolm Cowley's letter of 21 August 1951 (HWS), from the Viking Press, in which he turns down the idea of publishing her list. See also TW to AG, 12 June 1951, n. 2.

4. This may be Glasheen's interpretation of the Latin words.

5. Bronson Alcott (1799–1888) was a member of the American Transcendentalist movement.

☐

To Adaline Glasheen, Forestville, Connecticut

[MS. ALS—HWS]

[postmark: 9 September 1951]   50 Deepwood Drive
                                 Hamden 14, Connecticut

Dear Mrs Glasheen:
    Note:
    How many ways has Joyce of telling us what time it is?
p. 213 [.14]   Fieluhr {"Wie viel uhr ist es["]?} . . What age is at?
    Then three back / back / bach and PING PONG PANG.
            Quarter of. . . . of what?
    {N. B. He added the Pingpong! There's the Belle for Sexaloitez etc since its first printings in 1925, and 1927—"Transition."[}]
p. 244 [.25]   What era's o'ering? Lang gong late—Then three phrases about the moon. And Ark? (Will there be another stroke?). No!
            Quarter of . . . . of what?

NINETEEN FIFTY-ONE

Now returning to the PING PONG PANG phrase (variants on there's the bell for sächseleute—a Swiss festival for the "Winter Man"![1]
    p. 58 [.24] Two* (Peingpeong)
    p. 32 [?35.23] Two*
    p 213 [.18–.19] Three* [2]
    p 268 [.2] Three (ringrang)
    327 [.23–.24] Two
    379 [[?.30 FW: BENK BANK BONK] Two (but look at the Dang. Ding Dong. Dung. Dinnin on the bottom of
        p. 377 [.35–.36]
    528 [.18, .26]   Three—the Dang is nine lines below the Ding Dong.
    536 [.11, .9]   One? Sacks eleathury. . . BAM—but there is a (bonze!) three lines above. But not capitalized.
    {for some reason all these variants on Ring the bell for Sächseleute seem to recur with mighty "mixed sex" overtones.}
    And if he is giving us the "quarters strick off" how does he convey the full hour?
    When we're in a second quarter do we get more dual or binary phrases? Yet that two pints on p. 58 is amid a flock of triple-phrases.

Note: The three passages marked with a red dot were all added after his first (periodical) printing—*He added them late*!
    That on p. 327 *was* in his first printing (maybe it was then he got the idea. . . . if it is an idea.)
    For the other appearances I've not been able to make a verification of the earliest text.

    Could that be a 3-bells opening on p. 593 [.1]?
    Look at all the FOURS on pp 554 and 555.
    And after having counted BACKWARD is that MIDNIGHT on p. 403?
    Well, if 403 is midnight
    There's a fine Three-bells for quarter of 12 on p. 383 (heading a chapter whose whole business is to work in fours.)

    Now maybe the stop, please stop, stop become also another device for striking the quarter hours [124.3–.5]. Heh?

    How can you tell me it's my duty to write about FW when all I do is to make it clear how far I am from a glimmer.

No, the shoe's on the other foot. I'm having a feeling of wonderful relief: *I don't have to sit up until 3 in the morning any more because Mrs Glasheen is working out* FW *for us.*

For many chapters I've surrounded with red brackets all the material that he added after the first printing.

It's amazing how seldom he changed a phrase or eliminated a phrase; always he merely added more. The few times he did change a phrase it was ever so slightly and the early form is always much simpler. For instance: begin bottom of p. 209 [.34]: Vivi vienne etc was formerly: Long live little Anne, old Anna, high life chipping her and raising a bit of jeer or a cheer every time she'd neb in her culdee sack of rubbish she robbed.... ¶ See how he wove in five rivers long after the first printing?

Goodbye. I'm running away from all this. No, I'm not taking the volume abroad with me. It's a leech. It would devour all the time.... the time that Lope and Palestrina and those American classics that you hoot at, don't take. But MAYBE I'll be back at the conundrums when I get back. By the way, the Nancy Hands is a pub near the Phoenix Park. Isn't that upsetting?

    Sincerely
    TW, the renegade

Very amused by the acct of Levin's and Wilson's reception. Don't give it a thought. They have to maintain the pretense of acknowledging it's a masterpiece—but what good is the assertion of being a believer unless he'll also concede it the 1000 hours a year and they won't do that—and they know they spend their 1000 hours on books that can't hold a candle to it. But still they hold their pretense: your census caught them out.

---

1. "Zurich's most important contribution to *Finnegans Wake* is its annual spring festival, called the *Sechseläuten* or *Sächsilüte* in Swiss German. . . .We have Mrs. Giedion-Welcker's testimony that Joyce made a point of attending this festival when in Zurich and watched the ceremony with all its details very closely. . . . Sechseläuten takes place on the third Sunday and Monday of April. Sunday is the children's day. Children dressed up in old-fashioned period-costumes form a procession and take with them a stuffed effigy on a cart, a snowman made of cotton named the *Bögg*, who represents Winter. The next day, always a half-holiday in Zurich, the members of the craft-guilds, most of them in their traditional costumes, parade the principal streets with marching bands and carts decorated with flowers, or representing

scenes from the city's history. Towards six o'clock the procession moves to the Bellevue Square or Sechseläutenplatz, where a wooden pyre has been erected, and the Bögg put on a pole. Promptly as six o'clock all the city's bells begin to ring out, fire is set to the pyre, and the winter demon is ceremoniously burnt at the stake. Guildsmen on horseback gallop round the bonfire while bands play the tune of the Sechseläuten-Marsch. A huge crowd cheers when the flames reach the Bögg, who is filled with explosives, and when one of his limbs or the head comes off with a bang. After the ceremony the guilds separate to have their meals and then spend the night visiting one another, carousing, singing, and speech-making. The Sechseläuten, while resembling other spring festivals, is peculiar to Zurich . . ." (see Senn, "Some Zurich Allusions in *Finnegans Wake*," 2–3, the essay has not been reprinted).

2. These three passages, marked with a red dot, are referred to later in this letter.

To Adaline Glasheen, Forestville, Connecticut

[MS. ALS—HWS]

[postmark: 6 November 1951]
N[ew] Y[ork] Nov. 6. Just in.[1]

Dear Mrs Glasheen:
   This is not a letter.
   Just a palliative to your phrase "a state of desperation."
   Besides how could I comment on your items without my precious book before me.
   But 244 is first: How Night falls over the Zoo in Phoenix Park— hence all the animals.
   Nancy Hands [244.20] may be both a ship and a racehorse but here she is a variant of Anna all right.
   Alvemarrea [244.14–.15]: the bell: a sea weed: and the tide. Avond [244.31] = Dutch for evening. Yes, dog and wolf are out. Gill [244.23] = Gall of the Gap = a proverbial brigand: and also the man who threw all those stones at Earwicker's pub door; now he is among the constellations and the stones he left behind him have become the milky way. Laohen [244.30] is Liar via the Chinese. There's lots of Chinese and Japanese in there—when I get my book I'll give you the notes.

Since we're at Chapelizod where [i.e., we] are at the very house by the churchyard on which the novel was written by {forget his name now but *you know*}² and churchyard gives us (for fun) Kierkegaard—as a merely passing allusion to a tormented religious thinker (but *how* great).

Mr. Kelleher like all Irish thinks the novel can be unlocked by a knowledge of Gaelic and Dublin talk—*so* tiresome of them. That is but one shade in the vast spectrum.³

37 [.13]: I met with you too late etc. Also: Joyce's famous arrogant remark to Yeats.⁴

35 [.15]: Guinness thaw tool in[.] If Mr. Kelleher didn't give us the English of this recurrent phrase I suspect it was because it was highly indelicate.⁵

Doesn't Glugg have a tooth age [i.e., ache] because he is little Jerry in his crib and we visit his infant wailing in the Movie-scenario scene?

I may find some not-too-assured answers for some of the rest later.

In the meantime deeply grateful for the resources you are marshaling. When I've settled down, you'll get reams.

Enjoy yourself. Don't get nerves. Accept the fact that it's slow, slow.

Sin————ly
Thornton Wilder

---

1. Wilder arrived in New York early in the morning on 5 November. This letter would appear to be a response to a missing Glasheen letter of 1 November referred to by Wilder in his letter of 21 December.

2. Joseph Sheridan Le Fanu's novel *The House by the Churchyard* (1863).

3. In the absence of Glasheen's letter, Wilder's comments on John Kelleher remain unclear. Wilder met him at a meeting of the James Joyce Society in New York on 4 December 1949, and he saw him again when he was Norton Professor of Poetry at Harvard University, 1950–1951. Wilder may have attended the seminar on Joyce Kelleher taught with Harry Levin (see TW to AG, 7 December 1950, n. 2; AG to TW, 5 September 1951, n. 2). Wilder may be drawing on these experiences. The extant correspondence from Kelleher to Glasheen begins in 1961; there are no extant letters from Kelleher to Wilder. Some of Kelleher's work on Joyce appeared in *Accent V*, "Joyce Digested," (Spring 1945), 181–186, and in *The Analyst*: "Notes on *Finnegans Wake* and *Ulysses*," No. X, March 1956, [1]–9; "Notes on *Finnegans Wake*, No. XII, April 1957, 9–15; "Notes on *Finnegans Wake*," No. XV, March 1958, 9–13.

4. Ellmann quotes Yeats: "Presently he [Joyce] got up to go, and as he was going out, he said, 'I am twenty. How old are you?' I told him, but I am afraid I said I was a year younger than I am. He with a sigh, 'I thought as much. I have met you too late. You are too old'" (1982, 103).

5. The Irish "Conas tá tú indiu mo dhuine uasal fionn?" is translated by O Hehir as "How are you today my fair gentleman?"

To Adaline Glasheen, Forestville, Connecticut
[MS. Telegram—HWS]

5 December 1951   Washington, D.C.

LETTER FOLLOWS CORRECTING MISTAKE CORDIALLY[1]

THORNTON WILDER

1. The mistake is explained in the next letter.

To Adaline Glasheen, Forestville, Connecticut
[MS. ALS—HWS]

[postmark: 5 December 1951]   The Hotel Raleigh
                                Pennsylvania Avenue at 12th St.
                                Washington 4, D.C.

Dear Mrs Glasheen:
   Now for a while I'm going to fail you—but I know that you're now strong in the faith and will continue so.
   I'm en route South—to find a lonely bungalow to work on some tasks.[1]
   But I've found a substitute. Her husband, too, is a teacher. She has four (wonderful) children, but Joyce's two last novels are the burning center of her interest. Please send her the census:
       Mrs. Rudd Fleming
       211 Elm Street
       Chevy Chase 15, Maryland[2]
   And look, simply look at my enclosure. I wrote the parents of my joy: A. L. P. is indeed, the richest warmest most varicolored picture of feminine {female: notice how ugly and ungracious our English language

is in relation to the matter!} nature in all modern literature,—since Tolstoi's Natasha.

Without waiting to ask your permission I'm also going to lend Polly Fleming a letter or two which you wrote me, so that she can see the kinds of interest you bring to the great book.[3]

Don't be mad at me. I'll return to the circle when I've finished the other tasks.

                    Sincerely yours
                    Thornton Wilder

Dear Mrs Glasheen—[4]

I did that old mistake—sign of distraction and worse—I put the wrong letters in the right envelopes. Here's yours. Be an angel and forward yours either to Mrs Rudd Fleming 211 Elm Street Chevy Chase 15 Maryland (including please yours to me!); or else to me which will reach me circuitously as I am driving today to Florida. Me at

         care Wiggin and Dana
         205 Church St
         New Haven
         Connecticut

                    Sincerely yours
                    Thornton

1. On 5 December Wilder began a leisurely drive south to Florida where he remained until 6 March 1952.

2. Rudd Fleming was a professor at the University of Maryland, College Park, and also taught at the Institute of Contemporary Arts in Washignton, D.C., where he helped organize a series of guest lecturers; Mrs. Fleming ("My given name: Mary Duke Wight. I changed it to Polly when I was 15, at camp.") taught at various colleges and at the Institute. They first met when Wilder visited Ezra Pound at St. Elizabeths Hospital in Washington D. C., on 16 March 1949. In a letter, Mrs. Fleming wrote of the meetings with Pound: "Rudd and I were both teaching at the Institute of Contemporary Arts in Washington when we met Mrs. Pound at a reception for T. S. Eliot. Maida Richmond, wife of the director, asked us to sit on a sofa with her and keep her *down*. (She kept jumping up to see if Eliot had arrived yet.) At that time Pound was the only one who had translated any of Laforgue's poems. (Except V— a woman who had translated the *Moralités légendaires*—prose poems in the form of tales.) . . . I was translating poems, and had been told to see Pound who was at St. Elizabeths. Rudd was working on Greek plays, and we told Mrs. Pound about that. She said Pound would be interested, and gave us a date to come to St. Elizabeths. I went first, but spent all the time telling Pound about Rudd,

and brought him the next week. They immediately started work on Greek, and I didn't show Pound my Laforgue translations until the next July! (That was from early Jan. 1949.)" (letter received, 31 August 1995). In 1951 Pound and Rudd Fleming completed *Sophokles/Elektra* (Cary Perloff's introduction gives details on how Pound and Fleming worked). The Flemings were admirers of Joyce: "I had a Joyce group who met weekly at our house—we read Ulysses and then Finnegans Wake aloud" (letter received, 31 August 1995). Rudd Fleming's article, "*Quidditas* in the Tragic-comedy of Joyce," had already been published when he met Wilder (*University of Kansas City Review*, XV, Summer 1949, 288–296). A second article "Dramatic Involution: Tate, Husserl, and Joyce" was published in the *Sewanee Review*, LX (Summer 1952), 445–464.

3. According to Mrs. Fleming, Wilder did not send her letters from Glasheen—only a copy of the *Census*. "He put me in touch with Mrs. Glasheen, but also with Patricia Hutchins who had done a photographic book on Joyce's Dublin and wanted to do one on Pound" (letter received, 31 August 1995).

4. This additional note is written on a torn telegraph form. Glasheen forwarded Mrs. Fleming's letter to her. Wilder retrieved this letter from Mrs. Fleming and sent it Special Delivery to Glasheen.

☐

To Adaline Glasheen, Forestville, Connecticut

[MS. ALS—HWS]

21 December [1951] 1440 North Atlantic Ave
  Daytona Beach Fl[orid]a.

Dear Mrs Glasheen:
  My work's going so badly and I've left so many things undone (Christmas cards etc) that what can I do better than fling myself into dissipation and reopen FW.[1]
  You notice I didn't answer any of your questions in the letter of Nov. 1. Chiefly because I didn't know the answers.[2]
  But you asked some about the Nocturne on p. 244.[3]
  Night falls on the Zoo in Phoenix Park. It's during a truce in the children's games and fights and will soon be interrupted by Thunder.
  It darkles [.13]. {perhaps memory of Dargle Bay S. of Dublin.[}] (tinct, tint) added by Joyce since the passage was first printed in Transition Feb 1932 [i.e., 1933][4]

you notice this "tilt tinkt" on p. 560 line 14 is definitely related however to the front door—tho' why there it should be to awaken the Master of the Threshold (Linen) and God himself (Bog is Russian for God.)[5]

Isn't this again the bough brushing the window outside their bedroom?

Here it means SOUND and COLOR darken

funnaminal world [.13]. {in 1933 he wrote funnominal} wonderful!

Marshpond [.14]—if it's the pool the Liffey makes by the pub in Chapelizod I've seen it. I didn't know the tide water could get there.

But are we sure of the real scene of this house?

by ruodmark verge [.14] {added since 1933} Gaelic Ruadh = red, pronounced Rua: + roadmark and perhaps a road or cross.

Alvemarea [.14–.15] + Vesper prayer + marea tides + alva marina dried sea kale. You call attention to 198 line 8 Havemmarea where maybe the Hebrew Eve and a river have inflected it.

obscuritads [.15]: Spanish to get in the children and the young frogs?

belves [.15]: Joyce originally wrote beastes. Latin belna + bells?

frieren [.16]: it seems to trouble you that they are cold?

—to be not doing [.16]—sleepy rhythm gives us nodding or just for rugs [.16–.17] . . . probably some Dutch hidden here. Ferox could give us our Zoo.

Zoo Roud [.17]. Dutch: KOUD = cold.

(Drr. . . . . Ha) [.17–.18] added by Joyce since 1933. Yes. Deucalion and Pyrrha but the fire is also the Paschalis fire of St. Patrick and final supreme beauty we have the Greek word for goodnight Kaliperas.

I don't know what this Ha is except to prepare the next Haha [.19] and to introduce an ironical tone.

This is a foliation of homes and homelife and the next phrase is the Japanese formal address of inquiry [.18–.19]. As the foolish one [.19]—may be also the oriental deprecation.

{I'm always liking to turn words around and fooli' almost gives us Liffey.}

Haha [.19] is Japanese for Father. It is also that civilized ditch in a garden which the French call "saut de loup."

Huzoor [.19]: don't know. It's OE cough and it's a disease of sheep.

At house [.20] = ?Attis

Tospitty [.20] = near to Greek "at home."

Nancy Hands [.20] = whether tavern or racehorse or ship it's here Anna all right and the next word

Tsheetshee [.20] = Japanese for mother

{Tsheetshee—Ark [.26]!? No!} added by Joyce after 1933.

The wolf dog [.21] I don't know—I suspect an Astronomical datum.

Gill of the Gap [.23]—HCE's assaulter, who left the rest of his stones behind after pegging some at his door p. 37 line 8 and p. 73 last paragraph is now in the sky: we cannot yet see the Milky Way

What time is it?

The three repeated phrases about the position of the moon suggest Three bells = ? quarter of nine? [.25–.26] see also p. 469 line 21 . . . stay still in reedery . . . [244.28] {maddening: sure there must be some concealed church latin here.}

Tranquilla [.28] was an estate, now a Convent S. of Dublin

For some reason he has changed Phoenix Park's Deergarten to Deerhaven [.29]. I'm now stumped: up to Nuathan [.31], except that ii [.30] is Norwegian for some small birds. And can't you hear some latin like this . . . tu malis tuque silentii?

Was *avond* [.31] Dutch for evening. Avon is Irish for riverwater.

Now Jolas (Transition Feb 33) told us long ago he got from Joyce the Flections of the five Roman watches of the night [6]

    vespers = AVOND
    conticinium[.31] = early part of the night
    concubium   lying together [.32]
    intempestas noctis   wildering of the night [.33]
    gallicinium   cockeedoodle [.33]
    aura ante lucano aubens} [.33]

Panther monster [.34] = Pater Noster. Yes, little Shem dreads a panther. Don't know why.

[margin: {Panther Monster to . . . .so Beast: added later by Joyce}]

{Oh, I forgot Lord the Laohun: A Chinese scholar[7] at Harvard told me Laohun makes Tiger and Sheutseuyes makes LION! [.31–.32]}

Now: send tomorrow barrel loads[.34] of Benjamin *Lea* Guinness's stout.

    liebe German love could make a macaronic liebero = I shall love and amaró could make an Italian: I shall love. But maybe I'm crazy.

While loevdom shleeps [.34–.35] = Old Melodrama While London Sleeps; plus the (German) Lionworld sleeps plus?

El enfant [.35] = the baby elephant.

Hsiang [.35] = Chinese for elephant. Siang is Burmese!

{Does the ear hear FANT-A-SI?}

Eliphas good Greek; but Job's Eliphas says we're all sinners [.35]
Kneeprayer [.36] = doesn't the ear hear the British nipper?
Tusker [245.1] = means (1) to beat the bush for game but (2) the lightboat at the S. E. coast of Ireland will which set off in HCE's mind the roll call of the lighthouses of Ireland.
Salamsalaim [.1] = Arab and Persian for Peace.
Then a moment's smuttering from the monkeys = Rhino may not be a big pig but he's a big sausage [.1–.2].
Joyce found frantling [.3] in Urquhart's translation of Rabelais.
Bring on the lights [.4] = both the Jewish Feast of Lights and the old song: "With the help of Hannigan's Aunt" [.5] and little Shaun's (Johnathan + Jokanaan) flashlight. [margin: Channukah's tomorrow]
Now intermixed foliation of Lighthouses and Chinese allusions.
When otter leaps in outer parts [.5–.6] = song from the Bohemian Girl (Balfe b. in Dublin) = When other lips and other hearts (their tales of love shall tell).
(Otters leaping on the coasts where the lighthouses are)
Then You'll remember Me [.6].
Sir Henry Yule (explorer in China will remember the Chinese girl he left behind him.[)]
December-Xmas will remember May.
Mei [.6] = Chinese: sister or maid.
The lighthouses are like Chinese lanterns and like flowers hung = red Hung mei [.6] = red plum flower.
Mohn-blume [.7] = German poppy.
look, to greet those loes. . . . amethyst [.7] = have ransacked all Shelley for this. Is it in Thomas Moore?[8]
Arcglow [.8]- - -
The lighthouse at Arklow like a sapphire seafire [.8] built by the Engineers Siemen is a lure to sailors. {Joyce liked this so much he repeated it on p. 549 line 18.[}]
And the lighthouse at Wexford [.8] warns (like Capt John Warneford Armstrong, the informer, in the pay of Lord Castlereagh) the smugglers who might try to steal in between the peninsular known as the Hook and the Crook (from which the proverbial expression came)

And I can believe that that's only scratching the surface.
And even if we got all at *this* level we still wouldn't have anything essential.
I feel sure that all sorts of other schematizations are "controlling" this passage.
Astronomical and calendar.

Musical key or mode (tinct tint may be also Ti Ti B♮)
Colors of the Spectrum.
And so on.

There's one of your items I'll venture to approach.
"277 (line 2) Ochonal is O'Connell and the note must refer to the toga-like drapery of his statue. Perhaps someone vandalized the statue?"
Is the statue equestrian? I think it is. Otherwise read no farther.
The statue is mentioned p. 553 [.14] Conall Gretecloke.
p. 214 line 11 "Is that the great Finnleader himself in his joakimono on his statue riding the high horse." etc
Now back to p. 277
his famous cloak—his sevencoloured soot—Alas—(Ochone!) has got dirty; it's sooty, it's ebon colored; is lamp black [.1–.3].
And in the note [n. 2] = rappe is German for a black horse (p. 190 line 196 [i.e., 196.11] "he's an awful old reppe"—where a color scheme seems to be working from black to red—last line "roughty old rappe." [.24])
Why should he associate the Rape of "Lucrease" [n. 2] with O'Connell unless it's coalesced with HCE?

Anyway, I've enjoyed it
                    x
No, I've never had a secretary. What would she think of our correspondence? Resign in exasperation at all the things I ought to be doing for the edification and laetification and indoctrination of Others.
¶ Have you jockeyed about with anagrams of Proteus (the original name for this book?[)] The Earwickers are PORTERS on p. 560 [.22–.35].
¶ Does it mean on p. 405 lines 4–6 that the Donkey is the writer of that or those chapters? and on p. 478 line 8 that he as Hanner Esellus or Hanno the Esel is the interpreter for the quartet?
Nobody knows a thing about this book!

                    Cordially
                    Thornton Wilder
                    (now Dec 26)

---

1. Wilder was revising his Norton Lectures for publication.

2. A letter from Glasheen presumably lost. See TW to AG, 6 November 1951, n. 1.

3. A favorite passage of Wilder's. This letter is a line by line reading of the Nocturne passage. All line numbers here refer first to page 244 and subsequently to page 245. See TW to AG, 7 December 1950, and 6 November 1951.

4. "Continuation of a Work in Progress by James Joyce," in *transition*, No. 22, February 1933, [50]–76. The "It darkles" passage begins on page 66. Between April 1927, the first issue of *transition*, and April–May 1938 fragments of "Work in Progress," *Finnegans Wake*, appeared in seventeen installments in the literary magazine founded by Eugene Jolas and Elliot Paul.

5. These lines (from "you notice") are written in the margin, circled, and an arrow drawn to "(tinct, tint)."

6. Eugene Jolas, "Marginalia to James Joyce's Work in Progress," in *transition*, No. 22, February 1933, [101]–105; see particularly section XI, p. 104.

7. Achilles Fang, see TW to AG, 30 August 1951, n. 7.

8. "The Young May Moon," in Moore's *Irish Melodies*.

☐

To Thornton Wilder, Hamden, Connecticut

[MS. TL—YCAL]

28 December [1951]   [83 Red Stone Street
Forestville, Connecticut]

Dear Mr. Wilder,
I am sorry your work is going badly, and hope that by the time you get this it will be going so well that you will look blankly at this letter as though at a strange woman who has assailed you at a cocktail party. For my own part, I was enchanted to have so much information and it so delightful about 244–5. I had found out almost nothing more about the passage for myself. "lolave branches" (line 4, 244) must be lulave— a palm branch dressed with myrtle or willow, carried at Succoth rites.

277 [.2]—about O'Connell and his statue. I saw a picture of it in a book on Dublin. Not equestrian. The effect is of a Roman senator, draped in a cloak that is half or more than half toga. This at least suggests a common nationality with Lucrece. I am half of a mind that

O'Connell is the Mann in the Cloak to whom ALP gives a collera morbous on 211 [.1]. What did he die of in Italy?

Speaking of ALP's children—there are certain people whom I feel must be hidden in the list. For instance, Wilde. For instance, Wellington. I want to make blind and gouty Gough (211 [.25]) Wilde on account of Speranza[1] and account of the Symposium [211.24].

I am fascinated with the idea of Porter being Proteus since I have given much thought to Porter and its possible significance. Speaking of anagrams I spotted three last night. On p. 223 (2nd half) [.28] "Oh theoperil! Ethiaop lore, the poor lie" are all anagrams of Heliotrope!

405 [.4–.6]—yes, I had always taken it that this section and the one following were told by the ass and all very reminiscent of medieval dream poems and Pilgrim's Progress.

the 4. p. 78—here they are the four of them as the Viconian ages again Birth at the end of the first paragraph, marriage, death and "as it was let it be, says he" and then they become the 4 elements. I don't know about the four gods named here as corresponding, but Agni is the God of fire which is right for Matthew Gregory. Then 95 I hadn't noticed that they have exactly the same speeches that they have 398–99, even to the same phrases.

137 (2nd half) [.22–.23] "by stealth of a kersse her aulburntress abaft his nape she hung"—again a play on "The ancient Mariner" as on 512 [.4, .22].

You will have to bear with me now. I have read Vico and I have been bursting, teeming with Vico and will perish if I do not discuss it with someone.

I was very surprised by Vico because having read articles on Joyce and Vico I expected something other or at least different from what I found. I don't know how to say it all.[2] First, I was far more *struck* by Viconian counterparts in *Ulysses* than FW. Molly as the plebeian Venus, the whole extra dimension that knowing Vico gives to the Cyc[l]ops episode—these things are more immediately striking whereas in FW Vico is organic and, as it were digested and transformed. Oh Lord, I'll Never discuss this properly so you won't think I'm a fool.

To take the small and obvious things. Vico cleared up the second
section of FW for me since once you know who Hosty is the section—
in general—clicks into place and of course clears up the companion
parts of the tavern scene.³ I think too, don't you, that the opening of the
second section must be imitated from Scott's historical novels? I've just
been reading Quentin Durward.⁴ Vico's struggles of plebe and patrician
obviously add another dimension to Buckley and the Russian General.⁵

Vico too explains all sorts of small things, like the use of fables, the
meaning of lots of words—*pura et pia bella*, viricorda—all sorts of
scattered little things. I even wonder if Vico's passages on *indigetes*
or *inde genti* doesn't in some way explain Undy gentian festyknees on
23 [.20] etc. I should like sometime to ask you about all these things
for you must have been thinking about them much longer than I have
and probably noticed a great deal more.

I had got the idea from articles and the Skeleton Key that Vico said
that birth, marriage, death were respectively associated with the first,
second, third Viconian age.⁶ I couldn't find a word of this in Vico.
He merely says they were civilizing steps and in paragraph 11 he says
marriage was the first of the human things. (I took 20 pages of single-
spaced notes on Vico, hence my facility at tossing him around.) Then
of course, there are really three Viconian ages and two states of nature
which are not really one. So on these two scores, as I hesitantly see it,
Joyce is employing his own scheme of things or using someone elses.
(Please believe I am very hesitant.)

Now another thing—and please do not despair of my intelligence—
I can't see that Joyce uses the Viconian ages at all in the general
machinery of Book I. There are millions of Viconian details, especially
in Sections I and II.⁷ I think he starts up the Viconian machinery in
"The Mime" just as he starts up his Christian machinery there. For
instance much of "The Mime" deals with people imitating things or
acting them out as one does in a Mime but as one does, according to
Vico, in the first or divine age when one acts out one's meanings by
gestures and imitation. The ending of "The Mime" 258–259 is pure
Vico with the thunder and the people going into habitations and so on.⁸
(by the by, 258 1st paragraph [.13] "I hear, O Ismael, how they laud is
only as my loud is one" plays on the Shema "Hear O Israel, the Lord
our God, the Lord is one") I don't know about the textbook section but
the tavern section and the honeymoon are certainly heroic and then
Shaun's two books of preaching are human, very.

Oh dear, oh dear, I have the feeling that I'm not getting all this just right, and I can't of course go into it all at once. If you have time be an angel and write me a letter and tell me what I should have got out of Vico. I guess I had better buy the book because I had only six days to read and take notes on it. Charles Bennett is very particular about my not keeping Yale books any time.[9]

Another thing. I know I must often sound far more upset about FW than I am. I am, indeed, easily upset but always about peripheral things. I have been honestly and deeply upset by inheriting two Victorian sofas, but the graver issues of existence—love and death and Finnegans Wake find me ever calm and detached. I say I am nervous, I am desperate and it is only a manner of speaking. FW is for me just a thing it is more fun to think about than most other things. The energy that many a woman lavishes upon white dotted swiss curtains or the league of women voters I lavish on FW. And what a wise wise female that makes me.

Oh oh, I just remembered another 4 passage. On p. 160, 2nd half [.27–.28]. Here are the four—billfaust—Belfast—cork—philip deblinite and Mr. Wist or West who is rightly Johnny. I don't really understand this

[unsigned—or part of letter missing]

---

1. The nom de plume of Lady Wilde, Jane Francesca Wilde, *née* Elgee (1826–1896), Oscar Wilde's mother. She maintained a salon at her home in Dublin, and after her husband's death, in London where she had moved.
2. See Beckett in *Our Exagmination*. It is not certain what articles Glasheen read. In her archive there are several pages of notes on Vico and Joyce.
3. *Finnegans Wake* I, ii (30–47). Glasheen writes in *Census I*: "When one has read Vico on the class struggle, this section presents few difficulties" (xix).
4. Scott's novel, published in 1823, is set in 15th century France. Quentin Durward is a member of the Scottish Archers, guards to Louis XI of France. He is sent to bring the young Countess Isabelle de Croye to the protection of the bishop of Liége. They fall in love during the journey.
5. *Finnegans Wake* II, iii (309–382). Glasheen writes in *Census I*: "'How Buckley Shot the Russian General' describes the death of the father at his son's (Shem's) hands" (xxi). In her entry Glasheen writes: "Hosty is the personification of Vico's plebe, eternally in revolt against the patrician." Her entry is expanded in each subsequent edition of the *Census*. See also Nathan Halper, "James Joyce and the Russian General," *Partisan Review*, XVIII, 4 (July–August 1951), [424]–431. In a letter to Wilder of 26 August 1953, George Reavey, scholar and translator of Russian literature, responds to a Wilder letter: "[O]n the same *page* [5.5–.6] opens a theme I have been studying myself: *Wassaily Booslaeugh*. I have identified W. B. as *Vassily*

Buslayev (this is *entre nous* for the time being), the hero of two very good Novgorod sagas—apart of course from the other associations and *RAM*—ifications (namely Buckley etc.). There are certain elements in the saga in the character of the hero which explain why Joyce would have used him—as one of the main characters it seems to me. . . ."

6. Joseph Campbell and Henry Morton Robinson, *A Skeleton Key to 'Finnegans Wake'* (1944).

7. *Finnegans Wake* I, i (3–29); I, ii (30–47).

8. "The Mime of Mick, Nick, and the Maggies," II, i (219–259).

9. Charles Bennett, a research associate at the Yale University Library working on the Boswell papers, borrowed books from the Library for Glasheen. In her "Preface" to *Census I* Glasheen thanks Bennett "who gave me my first copy of *Finnegans Wake*" (xvii).

1952

To *Adaline Glasheen, Forestville, Connecticut*

[MS. APCS—HWS]

[postmark: 22 January 1952]   1440 N. Atlantic Ave
Daytona Beach Fl[orid]a
Until Feb 8[1]

Dear Mrs Glasheen:
    It's simply splendid that Captain Cenler has rec'd from the King of Denmark the order of the Danabrog; but we mustn't forget that Anna Livia Plurabelle got it first on the top of p. 549 [.1].[2]
                              x
    Your new light on the Four Old Men is brilliant.
                              x
    But I'm under geasa[3] not to open that glorious book for four months. Then I'll read it all through again—as a reward for good behavior.

                Cordially
                Thornton Wilder

---

1. Wilder left Daytona Beach on 8 February and traveled in Florida to Winter Park, Sarasota, and Sanibel Island before starting his return trip north on 6 March.
2. The Order of the Dannebrog was founded by Valdemar II Sejr and revived by King Christian V of Denmark in 1671. Originally limited to fifty nobleman, in 1808 the order was enlarged and opened to all Danish subjects irrespective of class and rank. Captain Cenler has not been identified (letter received, Royal Danish Embassy, 3 March 1998).
3. Word invented by Wilder.

To Adaline Glasheen, Forestville, Connecticut

[MS. ALS—HWS]

24 May 1952 Newport R[hode] I[sland]

Dear Mrs Glasheen—
    Fa—sin—a—ting letter.[1]
                            x
    First your questions. For the first time in years I am in one of my working hideaways without a copy of FW with me. Sign—not of flagging interest, but of harder work at other things.[2]
    Atkinson [43.10]. Did I seem once to know something about an Atkinson? All I can think of now is that he is the Englishman ("Tommy Atkins") of those three guards
HCE met in the Park.
    Where did I get the info about Peter Sawyer founding Dublin, Ga.[3] Am not sure, but I think it first showed up in some notes on FW written by the Librarian of the National Library Dublin, which I read in the Ms room at the New York Public Library.[4] Someone had mentioned they were there at our meeting of the J. J. society one evening at the Grolier Club—you should have been there. Couldn't Joyce have found it in the Encyclopedia Britannica?
    "Honor Bright (Meretrix)" [211.13] was told me—again I grope—by Padraic Colum.[5]
    Gough's Statue.[6] Decapitated by rioters, etc. where did I find that. In a guidebook to Dublin I think, in the Yale Lib. I roamed up and down the shelf devoted to the city and country.
                            x
    So you see I've relapsed into being useless to you.
                            x
    What a beauty—that discovery of Stanihurst.[7]
                            x
    And Kate Strong [79.27]. That's it. And always assoc. with that cleansing powder or fluid whose name I have forgotten.
    Yes, I tried to identify the speakers in the Pure Jaun section [474.1]—but I only got a short ways.
                            x
    I'm eager to get back home and write in all these new findings.
                            x

The Lewis Carroll paper is fine. How moving it is to hear that it will first appear in Amsterdam!⁸

                      x

Now as to the census.

It seems to me that you will have to cruelly limit yourself—define your task and stick within your boundaries. You can't propose a 900-page book which it could easily be.

                      x

For instance: "A CENSUS OF PROPER NAMES in FW."

This means that you can't have an entry on, and called, DOGS. You can only include dogs which have specific names.

At most you can enter

Dogs: see Ralph the Ganger, Fido, (etc[)]

You could not have MUSIC—Lord! where would you end up?

It will not be a subject-index.

This self-restriction will cost you pain—but it will save you seven years' work.

                      x

As to the usefulness of such a census—oh, just trust. It will not be the guide to FW or a Chart of it—we can now see that that will not be done for many many years (unless J. J.'s secret charts turn up somewhere . . . oh, yes, he had them, and took good care to destroy them probably.) but your census will be a completely justifiable and indispensable piece of apparatus for those who come after.

                      x

Pedestrian?

You are needlessly voicing some imaginary person's description of it.

My Sherlock-Holmes work of dating the early plays of Lope de Vega is grubbily terre-à-terre. It is not criticism or insight or aesthetic. It is pedestrian: but its results will enlarge our knowledge of his life, methods of work, everything.⁹

                      x

G[ertrude]. Stein said that the *only* interest in the world is the interest in how creativity works in anybody,—anybody. Your census is the preparation for an inquiry about a very extraordinary operation of creativity.

                      x

Now I'm going to end with my usual cry—

We still know very little about FW.

This collection of the million-and-one hidden allusions is perfectly all right in its way; it is not pedestrian and it is not inessential—but it must not be mistaken for a throwing-light on the Book as a whole.

The real clock-work springs of the book have not yet been uncovered.

I'm sure there is always a hidden reason why he suddenly goes into an "oriental foliation" why ALP's gifts to her children are in precisely that order and no other. And so on.

x

Your grandchildren will know.

In the meantime it is fun to be among those pushing further and further toward the major schematic scaffoldings.

x

The man servant. I thought it was Joe—in the section devoted to him in the questionnaire. But he may be Tom-Tim. In other words, I don't know.

x

No, I haven't seen the Rowntree passage in the London Times Supplement. I will find it at my N. Y. club next week.[10] Very interested—because I'd love to know what ties together all those heartbreaking and very funny things in the "respectable" section.

x

Faint not. Flag not. Why not send me a sample biography and other type of entry in the Census, *pro formâ*?

> Sincerely ever
> Thornton Wilder

---

1. Wilder is referring to a lost letter. Wilder arrived in Newport on 19 May and remained until the 28th.

2. Wilder was working on revisions to his Norton Lectures, his article on Alexander Woollcott, remarks about Sidney Kingsley to be given on the occasion of his being given the Award of Merit Medal for Drama by the American Academy of Arts and Letters, and a project to write a film script with Vittorio De Sica, "Rain in Chicago," based on Ben Hecht's 1934 novel *Miracle in the Rain*. The project, for Warner Brothers, which would have been De Sica's first American film, was abandoned.

3. See Glasheen's article, "Laurens County," in *A Wake Newslitter*, N.S., X, 5 (October 1973), 77–78, which expands the Peter Sawyer entry in *Census III*.

4. Glasheen trying to follow up on these "notes" asked a friend living in New York to go the New York Public Library. She wrote to Glasheen on 14 July 1952: "When I asked him [Herbert Cahoon of the New York Public Library] about the ms. notes he said that the only ones he ever heard of were an informal letter written by James Hayes, head of the National Library of Ireland in Dublin, to I have forgotten whom but which are now at Yale" (signed ? Jarmela, HWS). The "notes" were a letter sent by Richard J. Hayes, Director of the National Library of Ireland, Dublin, to John J. Slocum in October 1949. In a letter to Hayes Slocum wrote that he was planning

"to bring them up at the first meeting of the Joyce Society this Fall for the delectation of the members" (20 October 1949, Yale). The "notes" by Hayes are not in the Slocum papers, and it would appear that Slocum returned them to him. The letter from Hayes was probably read at the meeting of the James Joyce Society of New York held at the Grolier Club on 4 December 1949 (before Wilder knew Glasheen). See TW to AG, 7 December 1950, n. 2.

5. The playwright and novelist (1881–1972). He was for many years president of the James Joyce Society of New York. With her husband, Mary Colum (1887–1957), a journalist and critic, wrote, *Our Friend James Joyce* (Garden City, NY: Doubleday, 1958).

6. An equestrian statue that stood in Phoenix Park, Dublin. Sir Hugh Gough (1779–1869) was a British military commander, who fought under Wellington at Talavera where his horse was shot under him. The Gough Statue was erected in 1880 and was cast from canons taken by troops under his command. The statue was beheaded at Christmas 1944. It was restored, but completely destroyed by an explosion on 23 July 1957.

7. David Alfred Chart uses a passage from the Irish historian and classicist Richard Stanyhurst (or Stanihurst, 1547–1618) as an epigraph to his *The Story of Dublin* (1907: rev. ed., London: J. M. Dent & Co., 1932). Joyce, without mentioning Stanyhurst's name, uses, with some modifications, the passage from Stanyhurst's *A Treatise containing a plane and perfect Description of Ireland* in the *Wake*, 540.5–.8. Glasheen also found that Joyce had probably gotten the information on Kate Strong, "The most odious of Dublin tax gatherers" from Chart (231). See Atherton, *The Books at the Wake*, 91.

8. James S. Atherton, "Lewis Carroll and *Finnegans Wake*," in *English Studies: A Journal of English Letters and Philology*, XXXIII, 1 (February 1952), 1–15. The journal, the subtitle varies, was published in Amsterdam by Swets & Zeitlinger. The revised and expanded essay is chapter 6 in his *The Books at the Wake* (124–136).

9. See Wilder's "New Aids Toward Dating the Early Plays of Lope de Vega" (1952) in his *American Characteristics*, 257–266. His research notes are in his archive at YCAL.

10. In a letter to the London *Times Literary Supplement*, 23 November 1951 (749), James S. Atherton wrote of the use Joyce made in *Finnegans Wake* of Benjamin Seebohm Rowntree's *Poverty: A Study of Town Life* (London: Macmillan & Co., 1901; new edition, 1922; rpt. 1910 printing, New York: Garland Pub., 1980). The material is revised and expanded in *The Books at the Wake* (75–79).

To Adaline Glasheen, Forestville, Connecticut
[MS. ALS—HWS]

[postmark: 2 June 1952]   50 Deepwood Drive
   Hamden 14, Connecticut

Dear Mrs Glasheen—
   Some more ramblings.
   Thanks a million for Mr. Atherton's paper.[1]
   And for the Rowntree. I don't get much out of the Ibsen-tea, but will try again[2]

   Cordially T. W.

624.
   Your note rê Tib, Tabitha, Tybalt. Yes, Shakespeare plays on Tybalt—tom cat in Romeo (and Orson Welles played him so!)[3]
   "Who taught you those trides?" asks ALP. Bold Bet Backwords TEB [624.17–.18].
   Now turn to 28.5. TIB is a woman's name from ISABEL. (Common in English home-life, I'm told.)
   THEOBALD = THIBAUT = TYBALT.
   BOALD TIB = THEOBALD = TYBALT = male cat.
   TIB is also pejorative = hussy.
   So Mother ALP is mentioning that she has noticed an incestuous color in HCE's devotion to daughter Lillypet Isabel (as on the top of p. 627.)
   So what is your CENSUS to do? Is the family cat TIBBY—with a psychological momentary identification of the cat with the daughter?

439.17
   All right; many thanks for "Valentine Vox. Ventriloquist."
   Its foliations are difficult.
   Where did I get that there was also a popular musical hall artist called Venerable Val Vousden (perhaps some one like Padraic Colum who never remembers anything quite right or quite thoroughly). This may be Valentine Vox in a Joycean disguise.
   Double V and W. are one of ALP's signatures, aren't they? Isn't she the little jockey Winny Widger 39.11 and doesn't the double V get its start from Veni, vidi, vici?

Anyway: we met the voliantine-valentine eyes on p. 20 [.34–.35] where it is identified with a WINNIE. Then on p. 50.15 we get a "volunteer Vousden" who is hardly ALP but who coalesces Valentine Vox with a Venerable Vousden (if such existed.) Then on your reference p. 439.17 we do seem to get the two together again[.]

245.8
You say this is the smallest point you ever made; I can make it smaller: Hook and Crook are the two points that enclose the bay. Smugglers came (and so did we) through by hook and crook. Capt. John Warneford Armstrong was an informer in Lord Castlereagh's pay.
262. Note 2 [i.e., 3]   Tynwald is also the Manx Parliament
288 note 4 Ally Sloper—character invented by British humorist W. G. Baxter—also on pp. 248 [.10], 319 [.18] and watch out for coalesance with Alsop's ale.
368.32 [i.e., .29] You can have the song Willy the Weeper—but note that this is also the Donkey following the Four.[4]

The Rowntree is fascinating.[5]

If you do Proper Names—must you get *all* the Rivers? oo! All the Cities and parts of cities?

You've got me all upset by asking who the Handyman in the house and pub is. There's his section on p. 141 [.8–.26]—Question 5 on the Questionnaire. [H]e empties "old mans" [.9] (slang for what's left in a glass) sells newspaper, tobacco and sweets: after buggelawrs [.14] Joyce had originally written innhome daymon, outhouse dinell— and then it goes into a want ad.
Is his name Behan? 27.31 which brings us to Maurice Behan "boots about the Swan" 63.35
Or is the Tom Bowe Glassarse (plus: don't throw things at people in glass-house; plus) and Timmy the Tosser 27.1
Which gives us another Tom-Tim doublet on p. 342.3 Tomtinker Tim . . . his unremitting retainer . . . ; and brings Tom and BEHAN together on 412.18. . . . "For the teom bihan. ."
Anyway I don't think it's the Joe of the ostensible answer on p. 141.
You notice the inverted TAK for Kate at the end of Question 6, top of 142. {and 245.34[}] [arrow to margin: And what do we make of Watsy Lyke (JJ originally wrote Like) on p. 245.33]

For the Census
  Nash 75.20 is from Hebrew NAHASH a serpent
  Bog 76.31 Russian: God
  robur curling 112.35 Halley suggested a constellation Robur Caroli—Charles's oak.
  [C]occolanius or Gallotaurus 118.13 Rooster-sheep or Rooster-bull—probably hides Coquelin, the actor who created Chanteclair,—no, Sarah Bernhardt did.[6] Well, I'll drop this.
  131.35 Taishan, sacred mt. in Shantung (This I get from Ezra Pound's Cantos, another whopping puzzle-book.[)]
  132.35 Yes, Gorky wrote The Mother
  133.19 Foliation of operas. If I'm not mistaken Eleazer is a character in Halévy's La Juive; and Raoul is in Meyerbeer's Les Hugenots.
  146.34 Grimm's law: read B = V; G for K; R for L. bigtree are all against gravestone and you (also) get Victoria against Gladstone.
  158.7 The reeds are whispering King Midas has asses' ears. [margin: Midas p. 481.33 p. 482.4]
  168.5/6 In the earlier printing Joyce wrote Jaffe for Mac Jeffet. Anyway it is Japheth son of Noah—like Jophet p. 189 [.31].

  Shem's ancestors on p. 169. In some way these indicate that he was descended from the Gods:
  Ragonar [.4] = O. Norse REGIN, RÖGN = the Gods
  Hairwire [.4] = see that old musical hall song "hair like wire coming out of the Empire" d—n it, now I can't find it something about Erzheer like wire = German Highest Lord + copper and gives the notion of God in Lightning [margin: Found it!!! 289.9]
  and then Blogg probably has our Russian Bog = God [169.5]

  Somewhere I am told Joyce has buried deep a side-swipe at his patroness Mrs. Edith Rockefeller McCormick who gave him a pension in Zürich but stopped it abruptly when someone told her that Ulysses was indecent.[7]

  240.27 Anaks [A]ndrum—here the old man himself—but the Dioscuri were called the *Anaces* from Gr[eek] Anax lord and andros, man.

251.17 You got Imogen for Cymbeline—representing birthmarks

441.11/12 You got Yeats' Countess Cathleen and selling her soul to Mephistopheles.

458.6 You got the last pope's family name RATTI.[8]

Have you found all the allusions to his children? Georgio in the first paragraph—and somewhere there's a lucydlac [203.26]? and all the Nora and Barnacle and Stanislas?

1. Atherton's "Lewis Carroll and *Finnegans Wake*." See TW to AG, 24 May 1952, n. 10.
2. See TW to AG, 24 May 1952, n. 14. The phrase "Ibsen-tea" is not used by Atherton. In comparing passages from pages 543–545 in *Finnegans Wake* to passages in *Poverty*, he makes reference to Joyce's "teawidow pension" (545.4) which can be explained by reading Rowntree. "A tea company started a scheme under which a regular purchaser of a quarter pound of their tea per week on being left a widow is entitled to a pension of 5s. per week during her widowhood—the only apparent condition for the continuation of this pension being that she continues to buy the regular quantity of tea each week" (London *Times Literary Supplement*, 23 November 1951, 749; see Atherton, *The Books at the Wake*, 78.)
3. Orson Welles (1915–1985) was a member of a company organized by Katherine Cornell and Guthrie McClintic that in 1934 took three plays on a cross country tour: Shakespeare's *Romeo and Juliet*, George Bernard Shaw's *Candida*, and Rudolf Besier's *The Barretts of Wimpole Street*. During the tour, Welles played Mercutio, but before *Romeo and Juliet* opened at the Martin Beck Theatre in New York on 20 December, Brian Aherne joined the company and was given the role of Mercutio. Welles played Tybalt and the minor role of the Chorus. Wilder, with the actress Ruth Gordon, saw the production on 29 December. Wilder had met Welles in Chicago in the summer of 1934, shortly after Welles returned to the United States after almost two years in Europe, acting, painting and writing. In Ireland, the eighteen-year-old Welles joined the Gate Theatre of Dublin, directed by Hilton Edwards and Micheál Mac Liammóir, and scored a huge success in the role of Karl Alexander, the Duke, in Lionel Feuchtwanger's *Jew Süss*. An article about the production, and the success of the young American, appeared in the *New York Times* on 8 November 1931 (VIII, 4). Wilder, who was passionately interested in the theater, and kept lists of European productions in his notebooks, remembered the article when he met Welles in Chicago in June 1934. In August, with letters of introduction from Wilder to Arthur Hopkins, the producer, and Alexander Woollcott, the journalist and radio personality, Welles went to New York. It was Woollcott who introduced him to Cornell and McClintic.
4. Hodgart and Worthington in *Song* cite the song as "Willie the Weeper (Minnie the Moocher)" See 340.31 and 368.29.
5. See TW to AG, 24 May 1952, n. 14.
6. Benoit Constant Coquelin (1841–1909), the French actor-manager who, in 1897, created the role of Cyrano in Edmond Rostand's *Cyrano de Bergerac*. He died while studying the title role in Rostand's *Chantecler*. When the play opened in 1910, Sarah Bernhardt (1844–1923) played the title role.
7. Joyce's relationship to Mrs. McCormick, and her decision to cut off the stipend is discussed in Gorman, 262–265.
8. See TW to AG, 2 July 1951, n. 2.

To Adaline Glasheen, Forestville, Connecticut

[MS. ALS—HWS]

18 July [1952]
                                                    50 Deepwood Drive
                                                    Hamden 14, Connecticut

Dear Mrs Glasheen:
    Joyce's books.
    I don't know.
    Can I guess? That Joyce never had the money nor the assurances that he would reside long in one place—sufficient to buy the library his vast reading implies. He used every possible lending library in Paris—popular and technical.[1] The only time I ever saw him was in Sylvia Beach's "Shakespeare and Co."—rue de l'Odeon with his finger in the backs of books in the shelves.[2] I'll bet you about all he owned was dictionaries. But there was certainly a battery of volumes in Irish history and Egyptian religion—and those titles are worth knowing.
    The fact that you are in correspondence with this remarkable Mr. Atherton consoles me.[3] For there's no doubt about it: I've failed you. And up to the elbows in chores and projects I must continue to fail you for some time. I only open my FW when a letter from you comes—then I greedily write in the notations you furnish me (which too often I return to you, mistakenly, as findings of my own.)
    As soon as I can find (a) paper (b) string (c) gumption (d) a post office, I'm going to send you a present. For your collection. From Aug. 1 to Sept 15 I shall be at the MacDowell Colony Peterborough New Hampshire, writing a play which *leans* on Kafka's The Castle just as my last play leaned on FW.[4]

                Vale!
                Selah!
                Mizpath!
                Thornton Wilder

    Any light on the New York street allusions in FW. West 23rd St 549.15 or 32 W. 11th St (yes, that damned 1132 again)?

1. For a listing of books Joyce had in his library at the time he left Paris in December 1939, which are now in the collection of the University of Buffalo, see: Gheerbrant; Connolly, *The Personal Library of James Joyce* (1955) and *James Joyce's Books* (1957). For the books Joyce left in Trieste when he moved to Paris in 1920, see Gillespie.

2. Wilder's only meeting with Joyce was in Paris in August 1921 at Sylvia Beach's Shakespeare and Company, a bookshop-lending library, at 12 Rue de l'Odeon. Beach, who had founded her shop in 1919 in the Rue Duputyren, had recently moved to the Rue de l'Odeon, across the street from her friend Adrienne Monnier's bookstore La Maison des Amis des Livres. Beach was the publisher of *Ulysses* (1922), *Pomes Penyeach* (1927), and *Our Exagmination Round his Factification for Incamination of Work in Progress* (1929). Wilder, in Paris after finishing a year's work in archaeological studies at the American Academy in Rome, was returning to the United States to teach French at the Lawrenceville School near Princeton, New Jersey.

3. The correspondence between Glasheen and Atherton (1910–1986) began in the spring of 1952. Atherton's letters to her are in her archive at HWS.

4. Wilder arrived at the colony, where he had first gone in 1924, on 1 August and remained until 4 September. The colony, a retreat for musicians, artists, and writers, was founded in 1908 by Marian Nevins MacDowell in memory of her husband, the composer Edward MacDowell. Wilder was a colonist for many years and actively supported the colony. The uncompleted "The Emporium" is Wilder's "play which *leans* on Kafka." See the two scenes he completed and his working notes for the play in his *Journals*. The play, "influenced by both Kierkegaard and Gertrude Stein," combines "the atmosphere of Kafka's *The Castle* with a Horatio-Alger theme" (Gallup in *Journals*, 295). Wilder worked on the play in 1948–1949 and returned to it in 1953–1954 when he eventually abandoned it. The play which "leans" on *Finnegans Wake* is his *The Skin of Our Teeth*, which opened in New York on 18 November 1942, and won for Wilder a Pulitzer Prize for Drama. A controversy over Wilder's use of the *Wake* was initiated by Joseph Campbell and Henry Morton Robinson in two issues of the *Saturday Review of Literature*, 19 December 1952, 3–4 and 13 February 1943, 16, 18–19. See Appendix VIII, "Thornton Wilder: January 1942 to May 1943," in Burns and Dydo, the Stein/Wilder Letters for information on the writing of the play, its first production, and the Campbell–Robinson–Wilder controversy.

To Thornton Wilder, Hamden, Connecticut

[MS. TLS—YCAL]

30 July 1952 [83 Red Stone Street
Forestville, Connecticut]

Good God, my dear Mr Wilder, how am I to thank you for this munificence? And I must in spite of saying I wouldn't! You said a present. I pictured *a* volume, something on Joyce of course. Not all this. How does one express a state of panting, of being overwhelmed of— of more than I ever can say?

How I have wanted transition with the Joyce things.[1] How I have wanted . . . But no, it is at times like these that your trade of communication by the written word breaks down. In Heavens name accept and believe in my heartfelt thanks not only for the books in themselves but also for your goodness in sending them to me. It was a thing so out of the ordinary nice for you to do.

I do not want to weary you with thanks. The thanks are there—solid and not to be altered—a fact of the universe like your goodness.

                Yours
                Adaline Glasheen

1. The copies of *transition* with "Work in Progress" which Wilder sent Glasheen are not in HWS.

To Adaline Glasheen, Forestville, Connecticut

[MS. ALS—HWS]

16 August [1952]   until Sept 15 =
                                                 The MacDowell Colony
                                                 Peterborough New Hampshire

Dear Mrs Glasheen:
    I resolutely did not bring my FW up here. FW is the best underminer of good resolutions that I know,—next to Lope de Vega.
    It's a great shock to [me] that a Jonathan Sawyer and not a Peter Sawyer founded Dublin Ga.[1] It just goes to show. The other day I drove into Dublin N. H.—eight miles away—murmuring: "there were 24 mes" {no I've forgotten the phrase now; burgeoning in the United States of Amiracle while the Yanks were Heckling the Empire: something like that.}
    Yes, yes, indeed, I shall rejoice to read your book. {Sorry, I spielt "rejoice" wrong.}[2]
    I don't know any *writers'* colony. This is a composers—painters—sculptors—writers colony. Each lives in a studio deep in a wood. Lunch is brought by a truck. From 9 to 5 you sharpen pencils or read George Simenon[3] or write letters or watch for passing deer or torment ants or listen to the rain or gaze at Mount Monadnock until gradually gradually you go to your desk and do some work. Supper is at six; as the majority of your fellow-penshioners are young dissonant composers the table-talk is music-shop. You can't return to your forest-buried studio in the evening because it is not electrified. By the second week you are working so hard by day that you carry the work to your room at night in order to continue the excitement, but you find that you don't work at night after all.
    Carson McCullers was at Yaddo—our rival.[4] Everything's different there. It's free—for instance. We pay 20 dollars a week, all found. At Yaddo where they pay nothing the Penshioners are in a constant state of stormy ingratitude, tho' their food and accom[m]odations are marvellous. At Yaddo they have to lunch together as well as breakfast and supper. This keeps them in a high state of gossip, hatred, love-affairs, and hurt feelings. For some reason, Yaddo has always been associated with coteries who drink gin in lily-cups.

Come to think of it, we occasionally drink strong drinks and from paper cups but while doing we are not glamorous to ourselves or others.

x

To return to FW:

Have you ever found a basic pattern for the rubbishy presents which ALP brings to her children? (I see you've been working on the passage with your Bully Hayes etc). Are they all avatars of the various members of her family? If so, is there a pattern? I can't believe that there is anything in FW which is haphazard or arbitrary. What you [have] there [is] the *succession* of items?

When I get back to Hamden I shall send you an article from a Canadian periodical I never heard of, analyzing The Oxen of the Sun chapter in Ulysses.[5] It reveals to a greater extent than I ever saw it done before the tiny wheels within wheels of JJ's schematic intentions; that's the way his mind worked and I'll bet that kind of goldsmith microscopic filigree underlies every page of FW.—or did he relax and allow himself a certain amount of free improvisation?

I enclose a card taunting me—it is from Edmund Wilson. Destroy it.[6]

When, then, do you think you'll be ready to send me the "book"? I go abroad about October first for a few months.[7] (Not because I *want* to be in Europe.[)] Now that you know the extent to which I am a vulgar chauvinistic American, you can understand that. But to continue—by sheer removal of my body—the hermit-like isolation afforded by a MacDowell Colony.

Cordially ever
Thornton Wilder[8]

---

1. In a letter which has not survived, Glasheen may have sent Wilder information she received in a 14 July 1952 letter (HWS). The correspondent (?Jarmela) enclosed information on Dublin, Georgia, found in a book by Bertha Sheppard, *Official History of Laurens County Georgia: 1807–1941*, edited and published by the John Laurens Chapter, Daughters of the American Revolution, Dublin, Georgia, 1941. See TW to AG, 24 May 1952.

2. The expanding census.

3. Georges Simenon (1903–1989), the prolific Belgian–French writer who created the Inspector Maigret series.

4. A writer's colony on the Spencer and Katrina Trask estate in Saratoga, New York, founded in 1926 by George Foster Peabody, Mrs. Trask's second husband.

5. A[braham]. M[oses]. Klein (1909–1972). His essay, "The Oxen of the Sun," was published in *Here and Now: A Canadian Magazine of Literature*, I, 3 (January 1949), [28]–48. It is reprinted in *A. M. Klein: Literary Essays and Reviews*, edited by Usher

Caplan and M. W. Steinberg (Toronto: University of Toronto Press, 1987, [289]–325). Klein's other essays on *Ulysses*, "The Black Panther: A Study in Technique" (1950) and "A Shout in the Street: An Analysis of the Second Chapter of Joyce's *Ulysses*" (1951) are reprinted in the same volume.

6. Wilson wrote: "Wilder lives laborious days/Dating Lope de Vega's plays/But Wilson, regrettably, couldn't be vaguer/On varied voluminous Lope de Vega" (HWS). The card is postmarked 4 August, sent from Boonville, New York.

7. Wilder sailed for Europe on the SS *America* on 12 September and remained there until his return to New York on 28 April 1953. During these months, he attended a UNESCO conference in Venice and traveled in Italy, France, Germany, Austria, and Switzerland. See TW to AG, 26 August 1952, n. 2.

8. On the back of the envelope Wilder wrote, "MADGE ELLIS" and "MADGE LES," which may refer to FW 369.30, 420.7.

☐

To Adaline Glasheen, Forestville, Connecticut

[MS. APCS—HWS]

26 August 1952
Last days at Peterboro
[The MacDowell Colony
Peterborough, New Hampshire]

Dear Mrs Glasheen:

TNW accepts with please [i.e., pleasure] the kind invitation of Mrs. G. to dinner. . . . . but, alas, at a deferred date.[1] Suddenly I've said yes to pressure to go to UNESCO conference in Venice and will sail Sept 12 and once over there, stay 6–8 months.[2] Woeful interruption to work on book and play.—But will be back eager to see progress on book and all the sons-daughters of so privileged an ascendance.

So that's what the Magicscene Wall saw [553.24]! ¶ Yes, Issy is certainly split in two. I thought it was just narcissism and infatuation with mirror—an unkind judgment on femininity. Start at that place in the movie-script where we see Isabel in her cradle.¶ To think: that by the time I've come back you will have solved all these Tormenters.

Ave Salve Vale
TNW.

1. Wilder and Glasheen had not yet met; they had only corresponded and spoken on the telephone. Their first meeting would be on 16 July 1953.

2. Wilder was one of the official delegates to The International Conference of Artists organized by UNESCO in Venice from 22 to 28 September 1952. The conference was attended by over two hundred delegates from forty-four countries and representatives of eleven international associations of artists. Wilder was the general *rapporteur* of the conference, which discussed among other issues the question of censorship and the artist's relationship to government. Wilder's report is in *The Artist in Modern*, 121–124. Wilder comments on the conference in journal entries 624, 627, and 630.

□

To Adaline Glasheen, Forestville, Connecticut

[MS. APCS—HWS]

6 September [1952]   [50 Deepwood Drive]
In haste   Hamden [Connecticut]

Dear Mrs Glasheen—

Isn't that exciting! I wrote to Edmund Wilson about Rowntree and now I shall write about this. What a catch! And J. J. cunningly buried the allusion in the text. What a fella. And what a detective you are.[1]

Congratulations. "Finds" are now accumulating by geometrical progression. It adds new eagerness to my return to the U.S.

       Cordially
       TNW

1. Reference to a lost letter. Wilder wrote Wilson (16 August 1952, YCAL) about Joyce's use of Rowntree's *Poverty* particularly in the "respectable" passage (543.23–545.12) which Wilson called "a masterpiece of humorous sordidity (especially 'copious holes emitting mice')" in his essay "The Dream of H. C. Earwicker" (reprinted in *The Triple Thinkers and The Wound and The Bow*, 218). See TW to AG, 24 May 1952, n. 14. On 8 September he wrote Wilson again: "That same Mrs. Glasheen who's working with all the concentration possible to a housewife with three children and expecting another, on Finnegans Wake, has discovered plenty.

You remember Issy's babbling to herself before her mirror? . . . Well, that all is his rewriting of a psychopathological creature in Morton Prince's 'The Dissasociation or Dissociation of a Personality'—account of a Miss Beauchamp who was two-girls-in-one. J. J. has cunningly concealed her name and Dr. Prince's in the text and her nurse, etc. But the most interesting thing is that there—or thence—proceeds the letter from Boston Mass" (YCAL). Glasheen's "*Finnegans Wake* and the Girls from Boston" was first printed in *The Hudson Review*, VII, 1(Spring 1954), [89]–96. Glasheen had, of course, only one daughter.

Thornton Wilder and Isabel Wilder on board the SS *Olympic*, July 1954. En route to London for rehearsals of Wilder's play *The Matchmaker*. *Photographer unknown, Private collection*

1953

To Thornton Wilder, Stuttgart, Germany[1]

[MS. TLS—YCAL]

8 March 1953 [22 Carrington Lane]
Farmington, Connecticut

Dear Mr Wilder,

Touring Europe or Africa or the Moon or wherever you do tour, being a Representative American, do you ever say to yourself—and how goes Finnegans Wake? I hope you do because the question so unlikely would add just that touch of fantasy that a writer must have to survive his generation. I often think that Trollope failed here and for this reason does not commend himself to the studied and whole hearted intellectual. In any case, I must assume you to be positively panting for news of FW or my raison de lettre would not exist.

Since you went away, since in a sense Robin Ostler died,[2] FW has really been going great guns. Mr Atherton and I have continued to have bright ideas by the score and we have picked up a new FW player in the person of a Mr MJC Hodgart who once conferred with you during the war about (I think he said) office furniture but like all FW enthusiasts his handwriting is mostly squiggles.[3] He has published an FW article in the Cambridge Journal (I have a copy for you) which is not very exciting but very earnest.[4] He is working on one on Shakespeare and FW which turns up a good deal of Shakespeare stuff that I hadn't suspected was in FW,[5] but then it is an affectation of mine not to know much Shakespeare. He sent Mr Atherton and me his first draft and is almost embarrassingly grateful for our comments. Indeed, his attitude toward Mr A and me is deferential as—well perhaps as my attitude toward you. I expect him to address me as Cher Maitre any day. He and Mr A are going to collaborate on an FW book to be published in a year or two.[6] Mr H. is English Don and Librarian of Pembroke College Cambridge and thinks that just a little good will, will solve all the problems of FW and convert England to the Cause. He also thinks that the "low jokes" in FW are a personal matter. I don't know why he told me. I hadn't made any low jokes.[7] In other words, general sweetness and zeal are Mr H's strong points at present but there is no reason why he shouldn't be very good indeed someday.

Mr Atherton has just written me that something called Memoirs of a Justified Sinner by James Hogg is a prime source of FW. I've not read it yet but he says the hubbub in Edinburgh and much about the twins is from this.[8] He has a note coming out in Notes and Queries which proves, if I understand him, that Dick Whittington in FW is really Cardinal Newman.[9] He has also turned up a great deal of Macauley influence, quotes, etc. in FW and quite rightly it seems to me. But he wants to identify Macauley with Matt Gregory which I fear won't do.[10] I'll tell you all about [it] if I discover I am not in truth writing to a man on the moon.

Me, I had an operation instead of a baby and convalescing finished up the census, which I guess is a useful sort of reference book but eminently unpublishable in its present condition. I do want to hold you to your promise of reading it and advising me about it when you are at leisure—any time in the next ten years will do.

I think I was just reading Morton Prince's Dissociation of a Personality when you went away. I remember mentioning it to you. Prince is unquestionably one of the great keys to FW, although it unlocks many mysteries that I, at least, had not dreamed existed. I think it is fair to say that reading FW without knowing Prince is like reading it without knowing what happened in the garden of Eden. In other words, it is absolutely basic to the book and diffused through it so quietly that on first reading it is almost possible to miss its influence. Roughly all Issy passages and all references to the letter or to Boston, Mass are based on Prince. The greatest influence—I don't know just why—is in the textbook section, though the most extended quotation from Prince is in Issy's monologue in the Jaun-to-the-girl's-school-section. Prince ties in with many of the Alice in Wonderland references because Prince is the prime source of the "grateful sister reflection." Indeed I would not say that I had yet encompassed all the influence of Prince on FW.[11] Only lately I came to realize—and Mr Atherton agrees with me—that the Royal Divorce does not refer to the putting away of an older for a younger woman, but to the shock that split Miss Issy into two girls.[12] This last may strike you as wildly incredible, but if you read Prince and live with him and FW for a while, I don't believe you'd think so. I am very anxious to write you at length about Prince and FW. It's far far more interesting than my census.

You always used to say to me that the census stuff was fine, but that it didn't touch any part of FW that really mattered. I always agreed politely, but didn't exactly think so. But since Prince—well I see it, I see what you mean. But oh oh the new mysteries that Prince poses.

Surely, you have read FW a little in all these months. Please tell me what you've been thinking about it. "Yet confess I always that, as the fertilest ground must be manured, so must the highest-flying wit have a Daedalus to guide him."[13] I wouldn't swear that my wit perfectly soared, but that it needs a Daedalus there cannot be two opinions.

> Faithfully,
> Adaline Glasheen

---

1. Forwarded by Isabel Wilder who wrote at the top of the letter, "This will put heart & spirit into you! Acknowledged."

2. In Shakespeare's *I Henry IV* (II, i) one of the Carriers remarks "This house is turned upside down since Robin Ostler [one of the grooms] died."

3. Matthew J[ohn]. C[aldwell]. Hodgart (1916–1996). James S. Atherton had written to the critic L. A. G. Strong, author of *The Sacred River: An Approach to James Joyce* (New York: Pellegrini & Cudahy, 1951), with a question about Joyce. Strong replied suggesting that he contact Hodgart who was teaching at Pembroke College, Cambridge University. It was Atherton who then put Hodgart in touch with Glasheen. Hodgart's letters to Glasheen are in HWS. During World War II, Hodgart served in the Argyll and Sutherland Highlanders and the intelligence service. It was no doubt in North Africa that he met Wilder, who, from 1943 to 1945, served with the American intelligence service. See "Memorial to Matthew J. C. Hodgart" in Hodgart and Bauerle, xiii–xiv.

4. Hodgart's "Work In Progress," in *The Cambridge Journal*, VI, 1 (October 1952), 23–39.

5. Hodgart's "Shakespeare and *Finnegans Wake*," in *The Cambridge Journal*, VI, 12 (September 1953), 735–752. Hodgart's introduction, "Songs and the Interpretation

of *Finnegans Wake*," in *Song in the Works of James Joyce*, is adapted from this article.

6. The book proposal was rejected by several publishers. See Hodgart to Glasheen, 23 April 1955 (HWS).

7. Glasheen began corresponding with Hodgart in late 1952. The letter she refers to here is not in the Glasheen Archive at HWS.

8. Atherton's letter is not in the Glasheen Archive at HWS. *The Private Memoirs and Confessions of a Justified Sinner* (1824) by James Hogg (1770–1835). See Atherton, *The Books at the Wake*.

9. "Cardinal Newman in *Finnegans Wake*," in *Notes and Queries*, 198 (March 1953), 120–121. Atherton refers the reader to the paragraph in Newman's *Apologia* where he describes the crucial point of his conversion which includes the line "'Turn again Whittington of the chime.'" Atherton writes: "Cardinal Newman, equated from his own statement with Dick Whittington, once shares that hero with the Duke of Wellington" (121).

10. Atherton first discussed Joyce's use of Thomas Babington Macaulay (1800–1859) in a letter of 2 August 1952 (HWS). See Atherton's *The Books at the Wake*, 263–264.

11. See Glasheen, 1954, "*Finnegans Wake* and the Girls from Boston, Mass."

12. "A Royal Divorce in *Finnegans Wake*," in *James Joyce Review*, I, 3 (September 1957), 39–44.

13. Sir Philip Sidney, *The Defence of Poesy*.

☐

To Adaline Glasheen, Farmington, Connecticut

[MS. APCS—HWS]

16 March 1953
Stuttgart, Germany[1]
T. N. Wilder
American Express Co
11 rue Scribe Paris

Dear Mrs Glasheen:

Your (fascinating) letter is headed "Farmington." My sister does not send me the envelope. I assume you have moved; but Forestville can forward. ¶ Oh, what glorious fun that all sounds. I can't wait to get back to Prince and Hogg and if you permit it your letter-file with

Atherton and this new adept.² —Oh, no I haven't brought either FW or the Lope work along. I've had to be outward-bent for speeches to students and then inward-bent for projects of my own.³ Haven't had any of that peculiar kind of fun which is the gratuitous fun of FW and Lope work.

How strange that for so cosmic a myth-formulation as FW we should find him leaning heavily on single non-classic works like the two you mention. And now are we to see that that unengaging figure Macauley is also to play a considerable rôle

I hope you folks have unlocked some rebuses in the pages that are my special project—the broadcast Amstadam [532.6]. I still dream of an explication of them—partly because they are in large part somewhat marginal to the family-situation in the book and can be treated without waiting for the whole to be unlocked. I think, too, that it's extraordinary how little we know of "Anna Livia Plurabelle"—we can all "sing" it, but do we know what's really transpiring?

Anyway, I'll be back in Connecticut end of April and we shall have our long postponed colloquium.

Is spring wonderful over there? Here it's got me beside myself. Now I understand the ecstatic character of all those German Lieder—many regions here scarcely see the sun for four months. Its emergence and the first crocus are like a convulsion of nature. Every day now I'm convulsed.

Vaya con Diós
Thornton Wilder

---

1. Wilder left Stuttgart on 20 March for Baden-Baden where he remained, except for two days in Tubingen, until he left Germany for Strasbourg, France, on 29 March. He arrived in Paris on 4 April.

2. Matthew J. C. Hodgart

3. In the months following the September 1952 UNESCO conference, Wilder gave talks at American centers in Germany and Austria, and was interviewed on Radio Free Europe. In December 1952, Wilder planned and then abandoned an opera libretto about "a woman in love, a woman who seems about to lose her singing voice because something has come between her and the young man of the house" (*Journals* 171–173). In February 1953 he began, and then abandoned, a play, "Illinois, 1905," originally titled "The Heir," about anarchists in Illinois (*Journals* 175–177).

To Thornton Wilder, Hamden, Connecticut
[MS. TLS—YCAL]

4 May 1953 [22 Carrington Lane]
Farmington, Connecticut

Dear Mr Wilder,

How, I ask you, how does a real author like you retain so much as a vestige of common humanity? Having The Hudson Review (a publication on which I have never even laid eyes) accept "FW and the Girls from Boston, Mass" has gone to my head like wine.[1] How false these figures are—wine actually makes me stupid and I experience euphoria only when I am in the hospital on a good codein[e] jag. I mean I have grown conceited and fall into smiles of idiotic self congratulation, tempered only by the conviction that Mr Morgan, one of the editors of the Hudson, took the article not out of admiration for Joyce or Mrs Glasheen but because he fell in love with Morton Prince. He keeps writing me post cards about Morton Prince and which of the multiple mes he thinks he is addressing I could not tell you.

Are you glad to be back from Europe? Did you finish your play?[2] Are you well? Will you come to dinner? If you will, you must set the time. I imagine you deluged with dinners while my social life is the flimsiest and can be patted into any shape at all. Sometime my uncle William is coming to visit me. I have not seen him since I was eight and all I know about him is that he was once Aimee Semple MacPherson's [i.e., McPherson] cemetery manager.[3] I defy even you to have as valuable a relation as that. But he is not coming until mid-summer and perhaps you will want to come while the world is still fresh and cool. We would like your sister to come, too, if she likes dinners. She wrote me such a nice card while you were in Germany.[4]

FW never stands still. Mr Hodgart, the Cambridge one, has had quite a clever idea and discovered that all of the 124 Irish Melodies are scattered like citron through FW, with the name of the airs to which they are sung.[5] As you have "One bumper at parting" with Mrs Molroe in the morning (87.1–2) because the air to "One Bumper" is "Moll Rowe in the morning." Or 104.30–1 works out to "Ne'er ask the hour," air: "My husband's a journey to Portugal gone." You see the kind of thing, and it clears up a great many puzzling sentences. I have a list of these melodies and airs, I have a tentative list of songs in FW that H. is working on, I have his Shakespeare article[6]—all for you. To say nothing of Prince and the census. I'll tell you what, you just give up writing plays—sleep too—and—

I dreamt the other night that Joyce had based the ALP section on A Trip on the Concord and Merrimac Rivers[7] and I got up in the middle of the night and read the book and Joyce hadn't. However he did base 464.36–465.7 or so on Henry James's story "Julia Bride."

The identification of Shaun and Julia's patronizing ex-fiance makes these pages rather clearer and more amusing, I think.[8] Oh and I found out why Old Parr turns up on the first page of FW. Seems that when he was over 100 he got a young girl in trouble. I always say every little [bit] helps and the end is not in sight.

                Faithfully,
                Adaline Glasheen

1. Glasheen submitted her article, "*Finnegans Wake* and the Girls from Boston, Mass." to the *Hudson Review* in early 1953. Frederick Morgan, the editorial director, returned it to her on 18 March and suggested that she try to place the article elsewhere or return it to them in a condensed form. Glasheen made revisions, and, on 13 April, Morgan wrote accepting the article (Morgan letters, HWS). It was published in the Spring 1954 issue of the *Hudson Review*.
2. Wilder returned to the United States on 28 April. See TW to AG 16 March 1953, n. 3.
3. McPherson (1890–1944), the Canadian-born American evangelist, founded the International Church of the Foursquare Gospel (1918) in Los Angeles, California. The Angelus Temple, a five thousand seat hall, opened in 1923. She offered hope and salvation to migrants newly arrived in Southern California and was known for her flamboyant preaching style. McPherson established a radio station to broadcast her sermons, opened a Bible school, and published a magazine.
4. The card is lost.
5. Glasheen had sent to Hodgart a checklist of songs in *Finnegans Wake* that she had been keeping. Hodgart replied to her list on 10 March 1953 (HWS), telling her that it inspired him "to write up my notes into a draft typescript." Hodgart sent her a carbon copy of his list and suggested that they revise their copies together. In their preface to *Song in the Works of James Joyce* (1959), Hodgart and Worthington include Glasheen in their list of "people who have added to our list of songs or who have sung the songs for us" (v).

6. See AG to TW, 8 March 1953, n. 3.

7. *A Week on the Concord and Merrimack Rivers* (1849) by Henry David Thoreau (1817–1862) describes a boating trip to the White Mountains in New Hampshire that he and his brother John took from 31 August to 3 September 1839. The book is a meditation on nature, history, religion, philosophy, and literature.

8. In "Julia Bride" (1909), Julia enlists a social climbing ex-fiancé, Murray Brush, to explain to Basil French, a social conservative whom she would like to marry, her six broken engagements and her mother's three divorces. See Atherton, *The Books at the Wake*, 258–259.

To Adaline Glasheen, Farmington, Connecticut

[MS. ALS—HWS]

18 May 1953
50 Deepwood Drive
Hamden 14, Connecticut

Dear Mrs Glasheen:
 Did you notice that I hadn't answered your last letter?
 Were you aware of it, I mean?
 That one—even more delightful and fascinating than its predecessors?
 I wonder what you said to yourself—that Old Wilder was just proving how *shallow* he was—for anybody whose interest in FW could cool, there's no other word for him than shallow.
 No, ma'am.
 At each letter I rejoice more,—that these studies are now in such brilliant and fiery hands.
 And the more I rejoice the more I see that I can't keep up with the running. {The other morning in New York between the boring chores I always have to do in NY, I spent hours in the Public Library from which I drew Morton Prince, Hogg and the Irish Melodies.}
 I can not, dare not, must not keep up with the running—running in the sense of digging, mulling, collating.
 I don't have to tell you why.
 Tomorrow I go to NY again: see a convalescent sister,[1] meet Austrians whom the State Dept wants me to meet, listen to a warbuddy's

story of distress, meet with a widow who wishes to publish her husband's literary remains, "advise" two former students who want to start a repertory theatre; attend a MacDowell Colony Board meeting; lunch with Dr Bunche, etc.[2]

When I come back I'm going to call you up and ask when you can give me a cup of tea—and when I can read the paper about the "Girls from Boston."

This is not my resignation, but my handing over the books—my tra-dition.

> More anon.
> Ever cordially
> Thornton Wilder

It's maddening the way you never answer personal questions until scoffed at (see envelope); for instance, I *assume* you now live in Farmington.[3]

---

1. Charlotte Wilder (1898–1980), a poet and teacher at Smith College, was the eldest of Wilder's three sisters. In February 1941 she suffered a nervous breakdown and was hospitalized until 1947, and thereafter, with brief exceptions, remained institutionalized until her death.

2. During his stay in New York, Wilder met with the publisher Kurt Wolff, saw his army buddy Dr. Joseph Still, met with Helene Thimig (1889–1974), the widow of the director Max Reinhardt (1873–1943), met with T. Edward Hambelton about theater projects, and had lunch with Dr. Ralph Bunche, a senior member of the staff of the United Nations commission on Palestine, who had won the Nobel Peace Prize in 1950 for his mediation of the Arab-Israeli war in 1949. Bunche (1904–1971) became an undersecretary of the UN in 1955, and in 1969 he was given the title Undersecretary General of the UN.

3. Wilder had asked her about her move from Forestville, Connecticut, in his letter of 16 March 1953. Wilder addressed the envelope to "Mrs. Francis J. E. M. Glasheen" in Farmington. In her next letter she would ask what the "J. E. M." stood for; Wilder replies in his letter of 26 May, "What on earth could I have meant by J. E. M."

To Thornton Wilder, Hamden, Connecticut
[MS. TL—YCAL]

21 May [1953][1]   [22 Carrington Lane
   Farmington, Connecticut]

Dear Mr Wilder,

I think I have genuinely triumphed if I have avoided the personal note. It is so unlike me. Yes, I now live in Farmington, in the village, just about three blocks from the post office on Carrington Lane. My telephone number is 7–2138. My house is practically solid mahogany which I think strikes a grandly gaudy note like E. M. Forster's description of the American women who shoot the hippopotamus with platinum eyebrows.[2] I have a husband who (domestically) is a dead ringer for your Mr Antrobus except that (to my knowledge) he does not pinch respectable girls but that perhaps is owing to our having no servants.[3] I have a daughter, Alison who will be seven tomorrow.[4] She is all too faithful copy of her namesake, even to being gat-toothed. No, as a matter of fact, I think she is something more like what Shakespeare's Cleopatra must have been as a child than the Wife of Bath. None of this, of course, will appear should you come to have tea with us. Which I hope you will. Though I hope you don't mean tea *literally* since I don't really make very good tea.

I enclose Mr Hodgart's list of Moore's melodies.[5] I had a letter from him today all about my census,[6] toward which he is amiably disposed only he thinks I should list all the place names, too. He has made some fairly hot suggestions about the census, particularly one about Toulouse-Lautrec. I will convey them to you when I get them sorted out.

Indeed, indeed I did not think nor will think you shallow in resigning from digging at FW. I think I may give it another six months or a year and then—shh—I, too. I realize that at the age of thirty-three I have a talent for doing nothing but writing people letters about Finnegans Wake. I do not consider it a barren talent, but I would like to see if I have others. I have never had any thought of you but the most respectful and respecting except once when I felt motherly toward you. That was on the occasion of reading that a girl had said to you that she was an awful liar but was trying to correct herself.[7] I don't hold with the rude female attitude of all-men-are-such-little-boys-my-dear, but I fell into it then, and sure 'twas a venial fault of mine.

Please come to tea.

What in the hell does J. E. M. stand for? I can guess the first word.[8]

    Faithfully,
    [unsigned]

1. Dated as a direct response to TW's letter of 18 May 1953.
2. "Mickey and Minnie," in *Abinger Harvest* (1936; rpt. New York: Harcourt, Brace & World Inc., 1964, 50).
3. In Wilder's *The Skin of Our Teeth* (1942), Mr. George Antrobus lives with his wife and children, and their servant, Lily Sabina, in Excelsior, New Jersey. Adaline Erlbacher married Francis J. Glasheen in 1938, while both were students at the University of Mississippi. She earned her Bachelor's degree in 1939, and her Master's degree from Washington University, St. Louis, Missouri, in 1940. Glasheen taught at Wheaton College, Norton, Massachusetts, from 1943 to 1946. When her husband returned from the Army, he took over the job teaching at Wheaton.
4. Alison Glasheen was born in 1946.
5. See AG to TW, 4 May 1953, n. 5. Wilder returned the list in his letter of 25 May 1953.
6. Hodgart to Glasheen, 10 May 1953 (HWS), suggested references to the French painter Toulouse-Lautrec on 531.15, .18.
7. Quoted by Wilder in his "Exploration and Explanation," in *Seventy-Five: A Study of a Generation in Transition* (New Haven: Yale Daily News, 1953, 76–77).
8. See TW to AG, 18 May 1953, n. 2.

To Adaline Glasheen, Farmington, Connecticut

[MS. ALS—HWS]

[postmark: 26 May 1953] 50 Deepwood Drive
Monday Hamden 14, Connecticut

Dear Mrs Glasheen:
    Got home from a rackety week in New York[1] and found your letter and have already copied the Moore-material into my copy.
    So you're going to take the pledge, too![2] Well, as we take our hands from the plough, the Lord continues to raise up new workers. Selah!
    The only abbreviation I ever use is FW. What on earth could I have meant by J. E. M?[3]
    "Tea" was a trial balloon. Orrible.
    I've just had a recurrence of that cold-with-deafness that's been appearing and disappearing since December, so I'm cancelling everything for a while; but I've written down your phone-number.

x

Is there any possibility (i.e. danger) that I could interest you in Lope de Vega studies? If you took *them* up, then I wouldn't have to continue them myself. Weren't we urged by commencement speakers to "pass on torches"?

x

    I hasten to return the Tom Moore list with abounding thanks.

    More anon,
    Yes, faithfully
    Thornton Wilder

1. See TW to AG, 18 May 1953.
2. The pledge to stop working on the *Wake*. See AG to TW, 21 May 1953.
3. See TW to AG, 18 May 1953, n. 2.

To Adaline and Francis Glasheen, Farmington, Connecticut
[MS. ALS—HWS]

[postmark: 20 July 1953] 50 Deepwood Drive
Monday Hamden 14, Connecticut

Dear Glasheens =
 Greetings!
 Selah!
Had a lovely time at your house.[1]
You now owe me a visit down here.
 Unfortunately, my days are numbered here for the present: New York tomorrow; and Cambridge, Saturday. But its for October when I get back from the MacDowell Colony.[2]
 Well, I've spent [a] lot of time of [i.e., on] FW again, whipped up to it by the visit.
 For instance: reread A—L—P—. I adore it; but my heart sank in my boots. A dozen idea-patterns are going on there; and we don't know what they are. I can stand frustration only so long.
 Then I read my "Amstadam"[3]: same suffocation.
 And yet: there is always the pleasure in the progress.
 Delighted with the Arrah-na-Pogue: playing so large a part in the Old Men's Chapter.[4]
 Can't wait to read your Sisters from Boston.[5]
 x
 Now, I'm returning all the material you gave me. {under separate covers.}[6]
 Don't be angry.
 I've copied out every notation.
 I return them so that you can pass them on to other workers.
 Ma'am have you *inoculated* (no, I should say = habituated a new addict) a new enthusiast yet.
 It's like Early Christianity = You're not saved until you've converted a new soul.
 I can't point with pride to you as my catechumen; you were already converted. I have other novices. But *none* as GOOD as you.
 x
 Reunion in the Fall.

Love to Alison. She's at the age when we beaux are just *boring*, but that'll all be changed.

                    Cordially ever
                    Thornton Earwicker

1. Wilder met the Glasheens for the first time on Thursday, 16 July, at their home in Farmington.
2. This reference is misleading. Wilder drove from New Haven to York Harbor, Maine, on Tuesday, 28 July. He drove to the MacDowell Colony, in Peterborough, New Hampshire, on 1 August where he remained until 30 August.
3. See AG to TW, 16 March 1953, n. 3.
4. *Arrah-na-Pogue or The Wicklow Wedding* (1864) by Dion Boucicault (1820–1890) is a political melodrama set during the Rebellion of 1798 by the United Irishmen who sought to reform the Irish Parliament. During their meeting, Glasheen shared with Wilder James S. Atherton's letters, his article "*Arrah-na-Pogue* and *Finnegans Wake*," in *Notes and Queries*, 1 October 1949, 430–432, and a draft of his article, "Islam and the Koran in *Finnegans Wake*," which would be published in *Comparative Literature*, VI, 3(Summer 1954), 240–255. This material is revised in Atherton's *The Books at the Wake*. "The Old Men's Chapter" is "Mamalujo," FW II, iv (383–399). See Wilder, *Journals*, # 648, 181–182, for a summary of TW's and AG's discussions.
5. Glasheen's "*Finnegans Wake* and the Girls from Boston, Mass."
6. The Atherton and Hodgart letters and articles Glasheen had lent him.

To Thornton Wilder, Hamden, Connecticut

[MS. TL—YCAL]

23 July 1953   [22 Carrington Lane
                                                               Farmington, Connecticut]

Dear Mr Wilder,

We had such fun meeting you, Francis and I did. As for Alison—after your letter—I asked her "Were you bored with Mr Wilder?" and she said "I didn't see enough of him to know."

Thank you very much for the books you brought. Shall I return them to you in the fall? The Jung, as you surmised, is full of good things for FW.[1] Joyce used alchemy far more than I'd supposed. In FW it seems to be specially associated with the 4, who as elements are logical for alchemy. The basic process of alchemy—it says—was a 4 stage proposition—birth, marriage, death, rebirth. And there is lots in alchemy about the white light that absorbs the 7 spectrum colors. I read the book very hastily and am going to reread it, but I have the notion that "The Mime" may well be basically alchemical. Glugg is trying to find a magic word or formula that will get him Issy, isn't he? First he guesses at different stones, then at colors—all very alchemical seems to me. I have even been led to wonder if "The Mime" could be about splitting the atom too—modern as well as ancient alchemy. There are—or were—92 elements in the atomic table and this is 29 backward and ... Well, what do you think?

I have also been dashing through the book about the vicinity of Dublin. Joyce never used that book but it has lots in it, of course.[2] Makes me sure I must possess a map—a good map of the course of the Liffey or I never will understand ALP. I also read the Ulysses article in New Directions. Isn't it good, isn't it fascinating?[3] But how can you do it for FW until you know what FW says on the printed page level. Could you, for instance, tell the story of Kersse and the Norwegian Captain? Do you know what insult to Ireland finally caused Buckley to shoot the Russian General? Etcetera.

The day after you were here Hugh Kenner (at my request) sent me an article called "Joyce's Anti-Selves" from *Shenandoah*, [S]pring 1953 (published at Washington and Lee).[4] I have long considered Mr Kenner the best writer of general articles on Joyce that we have around. In this article he does a beautiful job on Wyndham Lewis in FW—lots and lots and lots of Shaun apparently is Lewis, it seems. Comes near scuttling [Oliver St. John] Gogarty as the main source of Shaun which I never did thing [i.e., think] anyway. I will save the article as I think you would want to see it.

I have had a minor ALP idea which I hope you think well of. Who, I have always been wondering were the 2 washwomen? Well, the usual idea has always been that they were Norns, Fates, washers of the shroud and so on—with which I agree. But Mr Hodgart was always saying "Then there should be 3 of them." Well you know, of course there are 3 for Anna Livia is just as present in the section as the washwomen *and* I think that they are the wild Amazia and the haughty Niluna to whom ALP returns or wants to return at the end of FW. "and what is she weird haughy Niluna" [627.29]. Well a weird is a wyrd is a fate is a norn. On 620 [.18] (about middle) the 2 washwomen are described as "those two old crony aunts" of Shem and Shaun, and if they are the twins' aunts they are likely ALP's sisters (I suppose they could be HCE's sisters but let's not spoil the theory) ALP's sister river nymphs and sister fates. I think this is all rather neat.

No, I have never converted anyone to FW, nor am I going to try, but you've no idea the trouble Jim Atherton and I take to chasten and subdue Mr Hodgart's bright ideas and enthusiasms. That ought to count for something. I hope you have a lovely and profitable summer.

     Yrs,
     A. G.

1. Carl Gustav Jung, *Psychology and Alchemy*, translated by R. F. C. Hull, New York: Pantheon Books, 1953. Volume 12 of the Bollingen series, *The Collected Works of C. G. Jung*. The copy Wilder gave Glasheen is in HWS.
2. Probably Weston St. John Joyce, *The Neighbourhood of Dublin, Its Topography, Antiquities and Historical Associations, With Numerous Illustrations from the Author's Photographs. And Sketches and An Introduction by P. W. Joyce* (Dublin, M. H. Gill, 1912). Wilder gave Glasheen a 1939 printing of this book which may explain why she says it could not have been used by Joyce.
3. A. M. Klein, "A Shout in the Street: An Analysis of the Second Chapter of Joyce's *Ulysses*," in *New Directions in Prose & Poetry: 13* (New York: New Directions Books, 1951). Klein argues that the entire chapter is shaped by Joyce's reading of Vico. See TW to AG, 16 August 1952, n. 6.
4. *Shenandoah*, IV, 1(Spring 1953), [24]–41. Kenner's letters to Glasheen are in HWS.

To Adaline Glasheen, Farmington, Connecticut

[MS. ALS—HWS]

25 October [1953]   Until Nov. 9[1]
   General Delivery
   Newport R I

Dear Adeline—[2]

Long since I should have returned to you the Koran paper.[3]

I enclose a letter from George Reavey.[4] He doesn't say confidential, but I think he means it. For me, it's a very lively example of how to go rushing off in 20 directions; but his report on the Buslayev saga hero is valuable.

I had two visits from another FW student—a farmer who does nothing all winter but milk his cows and study FW.[5] Doesn't visit, go to the movies,—8 hours a day on FW. Naturally I was very curious about this. It would take pages to explain the sense one has of his wasting his time; for him FW is a sort of fetish-book; he doesn't so much read it as *inhale* it for its magic powers. (And among other things he was making a sort of little compendium of its pornographic aspect!)

I warned you that I would fail you. Soon I am going south—to disappear for months among the obscurer Keys of Lower Florida and the more desolate sponge beaches of Cuba. Rum there, I hear—tell Francis—is plentiful and cheap. When I return I want to hear of all the wonderful progress you have made and the material you have collected representing the progress of others. I especially want to know, before I die, the structural patterns underlying the A. L. P. chapter [I, viii, 196–216].

   Lots of friendship to you both
   Thornton

---

1. Wilder arrived in Newport, Rhode Island, in mid-October and left for New York on 28 October where he visited with his sister Charlotte and attended a meeting of the American Academy and Institute of Arts and Letters to which he was elected in 1938. On 11 November he drove to Florida where he remained, except for a few days' visit to Havana, Cuba, until he started his return trip on 28 December. He stopped in Washington, D. C., from 30 December 1953 until 6 January 1954 when he returned to New Haven.

2. An accepted spelling of her name. The title page of her 1940 Master's thesis, "Shelley's *The Wandering Jew*," done at Washington University, St. Louis, Missouri, lists her name "Adeline Erlbacher Glasheen."

3. A draft of James S. Atherton's article, "Islam and the Koran in *Finnegans Wake*." See TW to AG, 20 July 1953, n. 4.

4. George Reavey (1907–1976) was a poet, publisher, and translator of Russian and French literature. He probably met Wilder through his wife, the painter Irene Rice Pereira, whom Wilder knew from the MacDowell Colony. See Appendix XIV for Reavey's letter of 26 September 1953 (HWS). See also AG to TW, 28 December 1951, n. 5 for another letter of Reavey to Wilder on *Finnegans Wake*.

5. Lawrence A. Wiggin lived on his family's farm, Rock Ridge Farm, Tilton, New Hampshire. It is possible that Wilder met him at the 14 May 1952 meeting of the James Joyce Society. Wiggin contacted the Society on 5 April 1952 after purchasing the Folkways Recording of the 23 October 1951 Society meeting. "For seven years I have been reading *Finnegans Wake*. I have read it over and over. . . . Now, I am writing a dictionary of the language in *Finnegans Wake*. It is more or less a hobby, something to fill out the long nights here in the country. The dictionary is not another *Skeleton Key* of Messrs Campbell and Robinson. Where they were concerned with the etymology of many of the words, I am concerned with their symbolism" (Berg-Gotham). A copy of Wiggin's "Introduction to 'A Categorical Synthesis of the Words in James Joyce's *Finnegans Wake*,'" dated 4 August 1953, is in Wilder's papers (YCAL). Wiggin's, "The First Thunderword: An Analysis of BABA-THURNUK" [3.15–.17], is in *The James Joyce Review*, III, 1–2 (February 1959), 56–59, and "The Voice of the Frogs: An Analysis of BREKKEK KEKKEK KOAX from *Finnegans Wake*" [4.2], is in *A Wake Newslitter*, N.S., VI, 4 (August 1969), 60–63. Wiggin died in the 1970s in Tilton (letter received, F. Gayle-Twombly, Town Clerk, 6 August 1996).

1954

To Adaline and Francis Glasheen, Farmington, Connecticut

[MS. APCS—HWS]

[Postcard: Hay Adams House, Sixteenth and H Sts. N. W., Washington, D. C.]

6 January [1954]   [Washington, D. C.]
en route home

Dear Friends:
    This is just in time to wish you a merry Christmas next year. ¶ Belated thanks for the letter about Mrs Riddle and H. J.[1] I once had dinner with Theodate P. R. I'm sure I'd be a perfect ninny if I had a million. Ask yourself searchingly before the mirror how you would *fare*. ¶ I've been asked to speak on J. J.'s birthday at the J. J. Society in New York. Maybe my delayed but jubilant yes reached the committee too late.[2] If I do, you both are *barred*. ¶ I refuse to believe your assertion that Hodgart on Shakespeare in FW is definitive. What a word to use about anything in FW at this stage of the game. ¶ I'm just twiddling my thumbs and waiting until someone does discover the formal patterns underlining the A. L. P. chapter; then I shall go to the hospital and expire happily. Mille amitiés

Thornton

1. A lost letter. The information about a Henry James letter may be attributed to the Glasheens' brief period as curators of the Hill-Stead Museum in Farmington, Connecticut, which had been founded by Theodate Pope Riddle (1868–1946).

Mrs. Riddle, who met Henry James (1843–1916) during his American visit, 1904–1905, was a well known architect, social and educational reformer. In *The American Scene* (1907), James describes Hill-Stead, the retirement home for her parents which she helped design (Stanford White is credited as the architect): "Never was such by-play as in a great new house on a hilltop that overlooked the most composed of communities; a house apparently conceived—and with great felicity—on the lines of a magnified Mount Vernon, and in which an array of modern 'impressionistic' pictures, mainly of Manet, of Degas, of Claude Monet, of Whistler, of other rare recent hands, treated us to the momentary effect of a large slippery sweet inserted, without a warning, between the compressed lips of half-conscious inanition" (*The American Scene*, with an introduction and notes by Leon Edel, Bloomington: Indiana University Press, 1968, 45–46). See James's only published letter to Mrs. Riddle, 12 January 1912, in *Henry James Letters* Vol. IV, ed. by Leon Edel (Cambridge: The Belknap Press, Harvard University Press, 1984, 599–600).

2. Malcolm Merritt, Secretary of the James Joyce Society of New York, wrote Wilder on 14 December 1953 inviting him to speak at the Society's meeting at the Gotham Book Mart to coincide with Joyce's birthday—2 February 1954. Wilder received the letter in Key West, Florida, and telegraphed his acceptance on 21 December. A. M. Klein, the other scheduled speaker, was ill. A copy of Wilder's talk, which was recorded (there was a break in the tape) and transcribed is in the Berg Collection. Wilder later adapted the talk and published it under the title "Joyce and the Modern Novel." See Wilder bibliography.

□

To *Thornton Wilder, Hamden, Connecticut*

[MS. TL—YCAL]

8 January 1954 [22 Carrington Lane
Farmington, Connecticut]

Dear Mr W.,

Do you know I don't even know when Joyce's birthday is. Tell me that, tell me what you say to the Joyceans, tell me what a gathering of Joyceans is like. I have always been surprised by the accounts of relative luridity of the proceedings at the Dr Johnson celebrations,[1] but I imagine a Joyce festival will be more subdued. You probably attach yourself to Dr. Johnson out of a fear that you are basically a faun or a maenad, to

Joyce because you know you pass the plate in church, and know it all too well. In any case, please tell me fully about the party.

I feel as though a great deal of FW must have happened since I wrote you and I will presently go through my notes and see what small things have. No, I really do think Hodgart's Shakespeare is definitive in that I believe he has collected every damn WS echo in FW. What he does with them is not, but neither is it offensive as the frameworks of so many J. articles are. I have written another article which one journal has turned down and the other is having the opportunity of doing. Oddly enough, it is on *Ulysses*, not FW and, perhaps just because I am out of my real field, I consider it a most superior production.[2] Doubtless I will feel that I have to tell you all about it one day, if it shouldn't be accepted anywhere. I will only say that, whether my article is itself good or bad, I can prove that there is an undiscovered myth elaborately worked out in *Ulysses* and it explains why the Scylla and Charibdis Scene has to take place in the public library. Jim Atherton is sending us a 36 x 36 17th century oil portrait of a Hapsburg Infanta. Why did I never think of sending you anything like that? He hasn't told me why he is sending it, so I can't tell you. Now it is presumably on the way after a long wrangle with the British customs. When Atherton wanted to sell the picture, he could get nothing; when he wanted to export it they accused him of sending a national treasure out of England. Well, this is one fruit of an FW correspondence. Atherton and Hodgart met each other for the first time at Christmas at the British Museum where they were to look at the FW ms there, only it turned out they weren't ready.[3] H. is going to fix up and have mimeographed his list of songs, of all kinds, in FW and I will bespeak one for you if you like. I saw it in rough form and am going to see it again before mimeographing, but it was quite vast and had lots in it I didn't know. He and I are determined not to make any more lists of anything but actually try to work out what each section says—ha—don't say it. I had a perfectly awful time with the Joycean writer, Hugh Kenner, who sent me a book that he has written on Joyce.[4] Parts of it were brilliant, I thought—he's quite hot on FW and the liturgy for instance—but Kenner's is what I imagine the R[oman] C[atholic] party line is going to be on Joyce and I find it abominable. All hail to technique, damn Joyce's people. Stephen gave up God the Father so as his just desserts he gets Bloom the father—grrrr. I wrote, though politely, what I did think (I had to tear up three letters, as my husband says, you can't accuse somebody you've never met of spiritual pride) but he has not replied. This paragraph, not the most exciting of paragraphs, will show you how one little Joyce clique is making out.

According to Hodgart—J used the following symbols on the FW ms.

⊓	= HCE or 'the wake'
⊔	= HCE interred in the landscape
△	= ALP
∧	= Shaun
[	= Shem
S	= Snake
P	= St. Pat
T	= Tristan
⊥	= Isolde
⊣	= Isolde ?2?29?
X	= 4
O	= 12?
□	= Title of Book

[set off by lines at the bottom of the page]
see 299
    111
    119
    486

I can figure out a few of these like x for the 4, but . . . Do they make sense to you?

44–5—I think the reason HCE is compared to Cromwell is because Cromwell rebelled against his king and then became a tyrant to Ireland as HCE does in this section.

40.15–17 all these three youths seem to be Swift

40.16 and 41.4—Peter Cloran becomes Roche Mongan because the Kloran is the sacred book of the KKK and their traditional meeting place is Stone Mountain, Ga.

49.7–8 Blanco White (d. 1841) was half Irish, half Spanish aristocrat, became an R. C. priest, left church, came to England, became Anglican clergyman; 1834 became unitarian, receiving on this occasion a letter from Newman that he described as "one long moan"

53.1f Quoted from Portrait of the Artist (p. 194 in Mod. Lib) Atherton[5]

53.16 [i.e., .15] "The Peace of the Augustans," by Stainsbury [i.e., Saintsbury]. Hodgart.

54.5 Horace, Ode III, *Favete Ling[u]is.* H[odgart].

56.28–30 "Time and Western Man," "There is not very much reflection going on at any time inside the head of Mr James Joyce." Kenner

57.22 Horace, Ode III, sss. Hodgart

59.14 Pranjapana was the Buddha's wife.[6]

85.23 Maam is a place in Ireland, but Festy, I believe is also a child of M. A. M. of Malicious Animal Magnetism

186–7 All titles in Dubliners in this paragraph. Somebody told Hogdart who told me.

210.07 In Joyce Cary's latest novel it says that Gipsy Lee is the "avenging nemesis" of a play called Maria Martens or the Red Barn, which Yale doesn't have.[7] I gathered GL avenges himself on somebody named William. Did you ever read the play? And what as a novelist do you think of J. Cary?

223.27–33 St Augustine, Confessions, X, para. 9. H[odgart].

241.15 Somebody told H[odgart]. this Plato

458[.]14 in his book Kenner quotes a letter from J. (in Slocum collection) saying this section is in form of a via crucis of 14 stations.[8] I can confidently identify only a few. Issy here is pretty clearly Veronica. On 462.7–8 I think we are at the 8th station: "My children," said He, "weep not for me but for yourselves . . ."

565.8–9 Song by Thomas Heywood, 1608: "In Amsterdam there lived a maid/You mark well what I say . . ."

565.19 according to Kenner who doesn't link it up with this passage there is a tradition that Christ's father was a Roman centurion named Panther. K. cites *Ulysses*, 510 (mod. lib. giant)

611.20 Entis-Onton is, I think, Einstein-Newton.

Well as you see, I can contribute only details and those mostly not by myself. I'm bound to say I am about fedded up with the details of FW and I don't mean to extend myself much on them in the future, except that I have an inextinguishable spirit of competition and would not let my two Englishmen get too far ahead of me. I don't, however, regret one bit the time I have spent on the details of FW. They are quite a discipline in their way. They have led me to read all sorts of fascinating books that I would never have read otherwise. But from now on I must lisp in great things if only the great things will come.

I believe that if I had been born and raised a millionaire I would be a ninny. I don't believe if I became one now I would be a ninny, but . . . but I know too that I always make a silly fool of myself when I feel I am being a success, so maybe you are right. In case you want to know about the end of the James letters. 1) Mr Wm. James, the lit. executor, would not let them be published because last year he let them publish some letters in which H[enry]. J[ames]. referred to a lady as his "tiger kitten," and 2) the bank that controls the school doesn't want anybody to mention Mrs Riddle.[9] I find 2 distinctly odd.[10] What do *you* think of Henry James? I have just been reading "The Golden Bowl" and it struck me that the critics are wrong who harp about H. J. not knowing about sex. He knows about that right enough. What he doesn't know anything about is marriage.

I hope you got done all the writing you wanted to do. Happy New Year and please please tell me about the Joyce affair.

    Yrs,
    AG

Have you ever called a lady a tiger kitten?

---

1. Glasheen would have known about these celebrations from her friend Charles Bennett who worked on the Boswell Papers at Sterling Memorial Library, Yale University.

2. Glasheen's "Another Face for Proteus," was published in the *James Joyce Review*, I, 2 (16 June 1957), 3–8. From her correspondence, it is not clear which journal turned the article down. It was provisionally accepted by *Essays in Criticism*, edited by F. W. Bateson (see AG to TW, [?28 January 1954]), but Glasheen stopped working on the revisions Bateson suggested.

3. See Hodgart to AG, 30 December 1953 and 7 January [1954] (HWS).

4. Kenner wrote Glasheen on 15 November 1953 (HWS) that he would send her a carbon of his as yet unpublished *Dublin's Joyce* (1956; rpt. New York: Columbia University Press, 1987), a revision of his Yale doctoral thesis, "James Joyce: Critique

in Progress," supervised by Cleanth Brooks. He asked Glasheen to "give it a quick read & possibly note errors which have certainly crept in." In the same letter, Kenner comments on the draft of her article, "Another Face for Proteus," which she had sent him.

5. Glasheen is sharing with Wilder information from letters of Atherton, Hodgart, and Kenner (HWS).

6. Buddha's mother Mahamaya, the daughter of Suprabuddha, died seven days after Buddha's birth. Her sister, Mahaprajapati, who was also married to King Shuddhodana, nursed and raised the child.

7. In Cary's novel, *Except the Lord* (1953, chapters 18–19), the Nimmo children are taken to the Lilmouth Great Fair, where they see a play based on the murder of Maria Marten (1827). William Corder was convicted of two murders: he poisoned his child and then murdered its mother, his mistress, Maria Marten. Corder buried her body in a red barn where they frequently met and where she had come, disguised as a young boy, expecting that they would leave for London where they would be married. The murder was discovered after Marten's stepmother, who dreamed on three successive nights of the murder in the red barn, convinced the police that her daughter had been murdered and that the letters she had been receiving from her were written by Corder. During the trial, there were puppet shows depicting the murder, and subsequently a number of plays based on the case appeared in local theaters. Because of British libel laws, names were often changed; in this case, the name of James Lea, an officer in the Lambeth Street division of the London police, who arrested Corder and collected evidence against him, was changed to Gipsy Lee. See Richard D. Altick, *Victorian Studies in Scarlet* (New York: W. W. Norton, Inc., 1970), and *English Popular Literature: 1819–1851*, edited, with an Introduction and Commentary, by Louis James (New York: Columbia University Press, 1976).

8. Joyce to Harriet Shaw Weaver, 24 May 1924 (*Letters I*, 214–215). Fourteen crosses, usually accompanied by images, representing events in the Passion of Christ. The stations are: Christ's condemnation by Pilate; his receiving the cross; his first fall under the weight of the cross; his meeting with Mary, his mother; the carrying of the cross by Simon of Cyrene, a passerby; the wiping of Christ's face by Veronica; Christ's second fall; his warning to the women of Jerusalem; Christ's third fall; the stripping of his clothing; the crucifixion; Christ's death; the presentation of Christ's body to Mary; Christ's burial.

9. See TW to AG, 6 January 1954, n. 4.

10. Two articles, with letters of Henry and William James, appeared in the same issue of *PMLA*: Carl J. Weber's, "Henry James and His Tiger-Cat," *PMLA*, 68, 4, pt 1(September 1953), 672–687, and Burdett Gardner's "An Apology for Henry James's 'Tiger-Cat,'" 688–695. Both articles deal with James's relationship to the writer Vernon Lee (1856–1935, pseudonym of Violet Paget). "Tiger-cat" is the phrase James used to describe her in a letter to his brother William on 20 January 1893 (Weber 683). In "Lady Tal," the first story in Paget's *Vanitas, Polite Stories* (1892) the character of Jervase Marion is a harshly drawn portrait of Henry James. After hearing from friends about it, Henry wrote William on 20 January 1893: "She's a tiger-cat!" and accused Paget of treachery (Weber 683). After reading the story, William James wrote her on 11 March 1893, "the book has quite quenched my desire to pay you another visit" (Weber 684).

To Adaline Glasheen, Farmington, Connecticut

[MS. APCS—HWS]

18 January [1954] [50 Deepwood Drive]
 Hamden [Connecticut]

Dear A. G.
    Fasc—in—a—ting letter. ¶ The ⊓ ⊔ △ ∧ ⌐ etc are in a letter that Joyce wrote to Harriet Weaver—now in the NY Public Library.[1] ¶ Cannot see how 40.16 boys are all Swift. ¶ Yes—lots of Dubliners' titles in 186.7 but where's Araby? ¶ Joyce Cary's novels—brilliant identification with his varied characters, but oh awfully conscious that he's brilliant. ¶ 458 = The Fourteen Stations—*that's* the kind of basic pattern I'm crazy to find—thanks a million. But oh! where is Simon of Cyrene etc. Awfully hard. Maybe that chapter is merely Station VI VII and VIII Exhortation to the women of Jerusalem. Of the three Falls of X I can only find one and maybe another. ¶ The Roman Centurion PANTHER of course I'm horrified but you have certainly placed it right on p. 565.19. Thanks. ¶ I still don't think you should go on to seek the book by book interpretation; I think one should pick up more and more of these chicken-feed items first.
    If you and Francis did decide to go to NY on the 2nd of February (I should try and rise above the embarrassment of your presence in the audience) my sister and I invite you to dinner at 7:00 (cocktails at 6:45) at the Town Hall Club 123 W. 43.
    You ask me about H. James. I believe that about 1904 he suddenly jumped from an intelligent story writer to a great international classic.[2] And of course I have a theory about why.

        Favete linguis
        Cordially
        (T. N.)

---

1. Wilder would have read a copy of Joyce's letter of 24 March 1954, which Weaver had made for John J. Slocum and Herbert Cahoon (*Letters I*, 213). The original of the letter is in the British Library.

2. Between 1902 and 1904, James wrote: *The Wings of the Dove* (1902), *The Ambassadors* (1903), *William Wetmore Story and his Friends* (1903), and *The Golden Bowl* (1904). Although there are numerous references to James in Wilder's *Journals* (see particularly pages 58–68 and 82), he does not explain his theory.

☐

To Thornton Wilder, Hamden, Connecticut

[MS. TL—YCAL]

[21 January 1954] [22 Carrington Lane
Thursday Farmington, Connecticut]

Dear Mr Wilder,

I don't think I ever had a more thrilling invitation than yours to dine with you and your sister and then hear you speak on Joyce. We would like it of all things, but between Francis's classes[1] and Alison's looking-after, it would be as near impossible as makes no difference. I console myself in this my grievous disappointment, by hoping that sometime you will ask us to come to see you in Hamden and that you will still tell me all about the occasion.

40.16. Well Peter Cloran is a "cashdraper's executive." [Jonathan] Swift wrote the Drapier Letters, often called the Draper Letters in FW and they concerned bad money or cash. O'Mara is "an exprivate secretary" and when Swift came to Ireland he was Sir Wm. Temple's ex private secretary. Hosty is an "illstarred" beachbusker and Swift not only wrote ballads but is certainly associated by Joyce with two Esthers with whom he had troubles. Isn't this a classy explanation.

187.11 must, I guess, be "Araby."

Why are you horrified by the Roman Centurion Panther?

I must tell you two other things that I got from Hugh Kenner's book.[2] The first has reference to 470–1, letter from J. to H. Weaver, August 8, 1928: "The Maronite (Roman Catholic) liturgy, the language of which is Syrian is at the back of it. On Good Friday the body of Jesus is unscrewed from the cross, placed in a sheet and carried to the sepulchre while girls dressed in white throw flowers at it and a great deal of incense is used. The Maronite ritual is used in Mount Lebanon. Shaun departs like Osiris, the body of the young god being pelted and incensed. He is seen already as a yesterday (gestern, guest-turning back his glance amid the wails of "Today" from To Marrow—tomaronites wail, etc.). The apostrophe balances the hyphen—gesturn's, To-maronites . . ."[3]

I wouldn't claim to understand all this but I don't find it too exciting as I had already divined that the girls were weeping a dying god like the women weeping Adonis in Fraser.[4] Also bottom 470, top 470 [i.e., 471] is 29 different ways of saying "Peace," as the word was signalled around the world in 1918.

The other quotation concerns Section IV, is from a note dictated to [Frank] Budgen.[5] "In Part IV there is in fact a tryptych—though the central picture is scarcely illuminated. Namely the supposed windows of the village church gradually lit up by the dawn, the windows i.e., representing on one side the meeting of St Patrick (Japenses) [i.e., Japanese] and the (Chinese) Archdruid Bulkely (this by the way is all about color) and the legend of the progressive isolation of St Kevin, the third being St Lawrence O'Toole, patron saint of Dublin, buried in Eu in Normandie."

Once I knew this last I found IV full of references to the windows and stained glass, but I do not think I would ever have happened on it for myself.

The 14 stations are about to drive me off my head. I am inclined to think that Joyce was talking about the first two sections of Book III which might have been one section in his mind in 1924. This would mean that the questions by the ass could equal Pilate questioning Christ. Or/and Shaun's attack on Shem could be Pilate's condemnation of Christ. 426.8f would fit Christ's meeting with his mother pretty well. Look at 409 for Christ accepting the cross, ll. 17–18 and l. 34. But then the letter has to be the cross and in the next section it seems like Issy is the cross. Oh I don't know!

Perhaps it is not a good idea to have Joyce's explanations for things.

Small thing but I have solved W. K., 503.12 and on p. 13 too. it is 1132 backwards.

There is a short story of Eudora Welty's that ends with a small boy screeching at some one "If you're so smart why aint you rich?" and I often ask myself this substantially about FW.[6] If I'm so smart why don't I understand the Museyroom. Why does Wellington get beaten when after all he did win the battle of Waterloo. Why does he make the "royal divorsion" (9.36 [i.e., .35]) when it was Napoleon who did. Why does he have an enemy called "the seeboy"[10.14–.19] when it was Wellington who was known as "the Sepoy"?

And do you know what I think about 16–17? I think the quhare soort of a mahan [16.1] is partly Polyphemus which I can't understand why he is and partly the missing-link which I can understand and wholly the Man Servant Old Joe which I don't understand either.
I know you will give a lovely Joyce speech.

        Faithfully
        AG

1. Francis Glasheen was a professor of English.
2. Glasheen's transcription here differs from Kenner's on page 352 of his *Dublin's Joyce*. Kenner's in turn differs from Ellmann's version in *Letters I*, 263–264. See AG to TW, 8 January 1954, n. 4.
3. *Letters I*, 263.
4. Sir James G. Frazer, *Adonis, Attis, Osiris: Studies in the History of Oriental Religion* (1907) part of *The Golden Bough*, 11 volumes, 1890–1915.
5. Frank Budgen (1882–1971) met Joyce in Zurich in 1918 and became a close friend. He contributed to *Our Exagmination Round His Factification for Incamination of Work In Progress* (1929). His *James Joyce and the Making of 'Ulysses'* was published in 1934. Budgen's autobiography, *Myselves When Young* (1970), contains reminiscences of his friendship with Joyce. Kenner quotes the note dictated by Joyce to Budgen in *Dublin's Joyce* (note 1, page 353). Glasheen quotes the note in *Census II*, lvi. This letter clarifies Glasheen's note in *Census III* (lxviii) that she had forgotten who gave her the letter. The dictated note is in the Slocum Collection (Yale).
6. Welty's "Petrified Man."

To Thornton Wilder, Hamden, Connecticut
[MS. TL—YCAL]

[?28 January 1954] [22 Carrington Lane
Thursdat [i.e., Thursday] Farmington, Connecticut]

Dear Mr Wilder,

I suppose you may well have seen the enclosed, but in case you haven't I do enclose them. Please send them back in a year or two, no hurry.[1]

I love having FW correspondence, I do. Two madly funny letters came in the same mail from [Matthew] Hodgart and [James] Atherton who met and did not like each other and then wrote me letters that[2]—well they *weren't* as good as the letters in "The Ides of March,["][3] but they fitted together the way letters do in novels.

My Ulysses article accepted provisionally by Essays in Criticism, a thing at Oxford, providing I lengthen it and explain why Joyce should want to pile myth on myth in Ulysses. My instinctive answer to this is a feeble—well he just liked to.[4] Do you have any theories on the subject? I would treasure them above rubies at the moment. I think I am a born writer of footnotes, not a born critic.

Happy Joyce's birthday.

        Yrs
        AG

---

1. The enclosures have not remained with the letter.

2. Atherton to Glasheen, 3 and 7 January 1954 and Hodgart to Glasheen, 7 January [1954] (HWS).

3. Wilder's epistolary novel, *The Ides of March*, is a "fantasia on certain events and persons of the last days of the Roman republic" (New York: Harper & Brothers, 1948, vii).

4. Glasheen's "Another Face for Proteus." See AG to TW, 8 January 1954, n. 2.

To Thornton Wilder, Hamden, Connecticut
[MS. ALS—YCAL]

3 February 1954   [22 Carrington Lane
                                               Farmington, Connecticut]

Dear Mr Wilder,

Eureka. In short, the 14 stations of the cross. And while I may have fallen into error over details I am confident that I have the scheme. Hear me before you look at the diagram and decide that it is my substitute for sticking straws in hair or muttering "Tone's a-cold." Though my brain is definitely enfeebled after this effort which I spent all day yesterday on instead of working on my article for *Essays in Criticism*.[1]

> "... a postman travelling backwards in the night through ... written in the form of a *via crucis* of 14 stations..."

J. *begins* with time on p. 403 & the only undistorted numbers are 2, 10, 12. So on an ordinary clock face we are at 2, which is ten minutes after 12 & we are going to move counterclockwise back to 12 because on 427/34 we are told that it is 12 o'clock {on 403 lower down it says it's 12 then but I think this can be explained only I'm not up to it}. III, i, therefore, is the first two stations of the cross, moving from 2 ⇒ 1 ⇒ 12 and so they are. On 409/17–18 you have Station II Shaun accepting his cross {the letter} and below 409/27 you have the condemnation {verdict first, trial after as it says in Through the Looking Glass}. The main part of this section elaborates on these 2 stations. Shaun describes & complains about letter. He condemns Shem, is himself condemned by the sniping questions of the ass {remember he is the property of the 4 who have been identified with Pilate} who shows that Shaun doesn't really understand the letter. 424—ends condemnation.

On 426/30 etc we reach 12 o'clock or the 12th station—Jesus dies on the Cross. I think there is an echo of the missal in the word "weight."

Thus section i ends, as it should with Christ's death at station 12.

Stations 13, 14 do not fit into the clock-time picture & are apparently huddled in at the beginning of the 2nd section, unless indeed they come in at the end of III, ii. I'll come back to them.

At the opening of Section ii, on 429–30 it is apparent that, moving backward in events Shaun is getting down from the cross. On 429, he loosens his bruised shoes. On 430/17–18, he doffs the crown of thorns. This then is station 11.

On 430/26f it is apparent Shaun is naked {in contrast to his elaborate clothes at the beginning of the 1st section}. This then is station 10—Christ stripped of his garments.

He is down or he could not "rise" on 432. So 430–32 roughly is also station 9 the 3rd fall. Station 8, Daughters of Jerusalem, is the bulk of the section 431–55.

Station 7—2nd fall is 455/33–4. Very clear.

Station 6—Veronica, 457–61.

Station 5—Simon of Cyrene is Shem {who also plays the Holy Ghost} whom Shaun persuades to take on Issy {Issy & letter naturally identified—see Mrs Glasheen in Hudson}. Note 463/5 "Bearer," 464/3, "Crozier." Station 5 continues to 468.

Station 4—469. Christ meets with mother—yes because Shaun's mother *is* a running water & he gives himself to the waters {this particular form of the station has to do with, I think, these 2 sections being about the embryo in the womb & birth}.

Station 3—is 471—note he gets up & is off again

Or Station III is on 467 & having gone round the clock we now get 13 & 14. 13 fits with J's interpretation of the Maronite ritual that I sent you[2] & in the Missal the 14th station is all about resurrection like 473. Note in next or Jaun sect. they are waiting his resurrection—birth.

If all this is right it brings up so many questions that I don't even like to think of them. I won't.

       Yrs
       AG

Map of the Via Crucis in FW III, i, ii

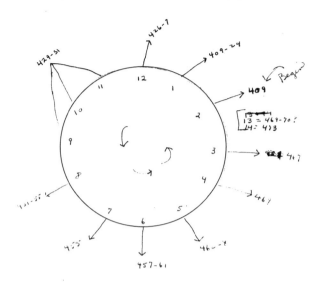

1. See AG to TW, 8 January 1954, n. 2 and [?28 January 1954].
2. Joyce's letter to Harriet Shaw Weaver of 8 August 1928 (*Letters* I, 263–264), quoted in AG to TW, 21 January 1954.

☐

To Adaline Glasheen, Farmington, Connecticut

[MS. ALS-HWS]

Feb. 1954 50 Deepwood Drive
[postmark: 6 February 1954] Hamden 14, Connecticut

Dear A. G. . . . .
 Your fascinating clock-face of the 14 Stations arrives just when I have again given (loaned) my copy to the New Hampshire dairy-farmer. He will be returning it to me in a month.[1] Oh, how smart you're getting

about such complicated things as the time-element. Thanks for the time and work you spent on outlining these stations: I shall be applying them with a microscope when my copy returns.

Well, we had a very good time and you were missed.

Of course, there were more there than just the members,—so many that the usual question and answer period was out of the question.[2] Though we did have some Hot Air from the floor.

Mr. Klein would have been there but is sick.

That day Columbia Univ. Press had brought out Prof. Tindall's edition of *Chamber-Music*.[3] It was boosted and toasted. And the Professor took a bow.

Columbia Press furnished us with one of J. J.'s favorite wines,— Neuchâtel. Enough to go round!

I opened with a short account of the beavers of industry and Klein and Glasheen and Atherton and Ho[d]gart. The non-industrious looked real abashed.[4]

My dinner-party of ten—of which you two were to be Crown and Ornament—was a joy; and after the hour and a quarter in the shop, another gang sat over beer at a bistrow across the street.

Now my remarks contained my attempt at an answer to the question you have put to me,—why does Joyce superimpose myths?

The style which Joyce evolved—the employment of multitudinous formal categories—is an effort to present at the same time one individual and the archetype,—one individual and his orientation towards a total universe of time, place, and the history of the race.

The Twentieth Century man (even the man in the street) is aware (through inventions, communications, and the popularizations of archeology, anthropology, geology, astronomy) as no generation before him of the vast dimensions of time, distance and especially of the innumerability of the humans who have lived, are living, and will live. His sense of identity can no longer take assurance from nation, city, family, locale, the group-mores etc. etc. Frightened among these billions, he has resort to two aids:

(1) To orient himself to the larger dimensions and
(2) To explore his subjective individuality.

JOYCE is the novelist of those two trends: Myself and the Universe; myself in myself (stream of consciousness and depth-psychology.)

Myself-and-the-physical universe is stated by the categories of zodiac-analysis of light (rainbow etc)—analysis of sound (Guido D'Arezzo's scale).

Myself-and-the-human race is done largely by myths. Myths are the dreaming soul of the race projecting its situation. After Freud, Jung declared we all more or *less* consciously follow myths, base our picture of ourselves on myths. Juno—Penelope—Alcestis marries Zeus—Ulysses—Prometheus; their son Oedipus—Orestes—Joseph has to make the choice of Hercules and has to decide whether he will give the golden apple to the Intellect, to Conservative Institutions or to the hedonistic life-force, i.e., to Athene, Hera, or Aphrodite . . . and so in eternal repetitions.

But oh goodness, I said this much better over there.

Rest not. Faint not. Weary not of well-doing.

        Cordially
        (T. N.)

---

1. Lawrence A. Wiggin came down from New Hampshire to hear Wilder's talk at the James Joyce Society of New York on 2 February 1954. See TW to AG, 25 October 1953, n. 5.
2. In an unsigned finding aid of the James Joyce Society Archive in the Berg Collection of the New York Public Library, Wilder's talk is mentioned: "When Thornton Wilder addressed the Joyce Society on Feb. 2, 1954, standing room extended to the sidewalk on 47th Street" (2).
3. *Chamber Music*, thirty-six lyrical poems expressing the feelings of a young poet whose idealized love ends in failure, was Joyce's first published book (London: Elkin Matthews, 1907).
4. This introductory material was not included when Wilder adapted the talk for publication as "Joyce and the Modern Novel." See Wilder bibliography.

☐

To Adaline Glasheen, Farmington, Connecticut

[MS. ALS—HWS]

24 February [1954]   50 Deepwood Drive
                                 Hamden 14, Connecticut

Dear A. G—

It never occur[r]ed to me that you would wish to borrow my copy of FW—most of the notations you gave me; the others I had given you; the rest were from the earliest years of reading it and were mostly nonsense.[1] But you sure can have it when the Farmer sends it back to me.

Rê the enclosed:
About a Trieste novelist called Scipio Slataper.[2]
I vaguely remember that somewhere in FW—I think in the Broadcast—there is a reference to "Slataper's plate" {or tape} [542.33] I thought it might be to some Dublin trade-mark or store. This Slataper however seems to have lived in Trieste when Joyce was there. He wrote a book on Ibsen. His best novel seems to have been *Il mio Carso* {Carso, probably a man's name; I don't find it in my Italian dictionaries}. Appears to have been more a long monologue than a novel, full of tormented sensibility.

    Cordial greetings to all
    Ever
    (T. N.)

1. During a telephone conversation, Glasheen may have asked to borrow Wilder's copy of *Finnegans Wake*, now in the Beinecke Library, Yale University. He had lent his copy to Lawrence Wiggin (see TW to AG, 25 October 1953, n. 3 and 6 February 1954, n. 1).

2. The enclosure has not remained with the letter. Scipio Slataper (1888–1915) was an Italian writer born in Trieste. Arturo Farinelli prepared his *Ibsen* for publication in 1916. *Il mio Carso* is not a novel but a book of description, travel, and social life in the Karst (Carso) region near Trieste, between Yugoslavia and Italy. Slataper wrote regularly for a local newspaper, *La Voce*, from 1909–1910.

☐

To Adaline Glasheen, Farmington, Connecticut

[MS. APCS—HWS]

3 March [1954]   [50 Deepwood Drive]
               Hamden [Connecticut]

Dear Adaline:
  Yes, yes, yes—delighted and eager to read it.[1] Doubt whether I am competent to comment helpfully—but I'm not very shy; I'll speak up anyway.

Of course my FW was off in N. H. when your Stations pattern came: but I'm saving it to write into my copy with all your other glosses.

My students have always called me "T. N"—my first name is so portentous.[2]

Ever
T. N.

1. A draft of Glasheen's "Another Face for Proteus."
2. Niven is Wilder's middle name. In the 1920s he taught at the Lawrenceville School in New Jersey; in the 1930s he taught at the University of Chicago.

☐

To Adaline Glasheen, Farmington, Connecticut

[MS. APCS—HWS]

[THE AMERICAN SCENE
Connecticut Tercentenary, 1635-1935: Historic Houses]

4 April [1954]   Hamden Conn
[postmark: New York, 5 April 1954]

Dear A. G.—

Terribly sorry. I'm ashamed of myself. Delighted with paper—wrote notes on it—then mislaid it in my heaps of papers.[1] Now have found it again but must leave for NY to save a friend from galloping alcoholism—will send it to you first thing when I return.[2]
Forgive my poor old disorganized system.

Cordially
(T. N.)

1. The draft of Glasheen's "Another Face for Proteus."
2. Wilder was in New York from 5 to 8 April. On the morning of 8 April he left for Princeton, New Jersey, where he remained until his return to New Haven on 12 April.

To Adaline Glasheen, Farmington, Connecticut
[MS. ALS—HWS]

[?5–10 April 1954][1] [50 Deepwood Drive
 Hamden, Connecticut]

Dear Adaline—
   Many thanks.
   Fascinating.
   I made some jottings in the margin.
   It's just fine. But you have prepared the paper too quickly—not as writing but as deep digestion.
   Surely, you must find one overt allusion to the Orestes theme. Surely, J. J. has buried them somewhere. None?—Clytemnestra was the sister of Helen. Their mother was Leda (only Helen and Pollux were children of the swan). No allusions to Argos? And the Library—Areopagus no buried double-reference?
   No faintest picturezation of his self-reproaches as Erynner—Eumenides? no snaky locks?
   Remember, Orestes find[s] protection from the Furies by clinging to the Omphalos at Delphi. Any help there?
   At Tauris he steals the image (black wasn't it of Diana?)—does he leave Bella Cohen's with any object that could symbolize his release?
   Has Stephen's sister (heart-rending creation) any momentary relation to either Electra or Iphigenia?
              Weeks later!
          (A thousand apologies)
   The *Girls from Boston* just received.
   Splendid, splendid.
   It makes me see more clearly what is needed in the new paper, and which I have already described above.
   What the editor called 'fat' is really that rambling at the beginning—and you ramble because you have not (as so richly in the *Boston* paper) a handful of very concrete references to make. Your sentence on the top of page 13 "resemblances" is all right—but lordy! we need more than resemblances.[2] Had you written a paper saying that certain aspects of Issy were like the case studied by Dr. Prince it would have been interesting = = but you did lots more

you found Christine and Morton Prince and Boston and the ladder climber right in J. J.'s text.

Mr. Atherton writes me that he's sending you—as he has sent me—a British Museum Ms copied ur-Text of a passage of FW.³ Isn't it fascinating the way that Joyce worked = few internal changes, merely adding new words and phrases.

> Do forgive all this delay.
> Gratefully ever
> (T. N.)

⁴I think one reason that Mr. Bateson thinks that the paper has "stylistic superfluous fat"—is that there is something arbitrary about your selection of literary images. If we let you have Tristan in Pyramus and Thisbe (that little tragedy is not a "solid. . . .all-too-human world";⁵ it would seem that what you need is a "realistic" work of art for your parallel—"into some earlier and vaster Juno and the Paycock") we are really stopped by Trollope's *Autobiography* as an example of the Artist regarding himself as Hero.⁶

Not until the end of the century do you get artists as heroes (exc. for Goethe's Tasso and Hawthorne's Marble Faun and several writers and painters in Balzac) but you get many heroes of Aesthetic Sensibility—Werther, Wilhelm Meister, Childe Harold, Melville, Ishmael and Pierre etc.

I'd cut the allusion to Trollope and pass as [i.e., at] once to Stephen D. Leaving his colleagues to be "understood."

---

1. Wilder began this letter at his home in Hamden and brought it with him to New York. He may have completed it there or in Princeton. Wilder enclosed the typescript of Glasheen's "Another Face for Proteus" with his comments. For publication, Glasheen substantially edited the essay following many of Wilder's suggestions.
2. Resemblances between Stephen Dedalus and Orestes.
3. Atherton's letters to Wilder and his transcriptions from manuscript pages of the *Wake*, with notes by Hodgart are in YCAL. The Glasheen Archive contains a greater number of transcriptions.
4. From here to the end is written on a page attached to the article.
5. The sentence Wilder refers to, which Glasheen cut, is: "Through the solid, comic, all-too-human world of fifty-year ago Dublin, Stephen Dedalus sees himself drifting like an exile from another world, like Wagner's Tristan strayed into 'Pyramus and Thisbe.'"
6. The sentence Wilder refers to is: "The biggest and most fetching imaginative creation of 19th century romanticism was the Artist as Hero, a monstrous superman

who drove Anthony Trollope to write his *Autobiography* and James Joyce to create Stephen Dedalus." Glasheen revised this and used it to open the essay: "*A Portrait of the Artist as a Young Man* traces—if it does not parody—the hagiology of the Artist Hero, that gaudiest and most fetching creation of 19th century romanticism."

☐

To Adaline Glasheen, Farmington, Connecticut

[MS. ALS—HWS]

[postmark: 13 April 1954]   [50 Deepwood Drive
                                                     Hamden 14, Connecticut]

Just back from Princeton

Dear Adaline—
    Rê [Matthew] Hodgart's plan:[1]
    Sure, I believe in letting anybody publish (if we don't have to share the expense—ahem) any *ipsissima verba* of J. J. As you say, those items don't seem to be a great addition, but it keeps the cauldron boiling. And in the unpublished portions there may, here and there, be a spark of light that helps. In fact, I think it's quite droll that you and Jim [Atherton] (how on earth did you arrive at first names with an Englishman short of 40 years' close friendship?!!) don't encourage him. Will [Arnold] Davenport be a worker?[2] all we want now is workers not casual admirers. (Since I've ceased to be a worker I've no right to have penned that sentence.)
    What *could* have shocked your step-mother—I didn't see a word that might have pained anybody.
    The *census*. Do you really feel it's as near done as that? I should think new lights would be striking you every three days. All right: Find a university press that'll publish it. Try Yale first—I'll put a word in there. If they don't take it, try six others. If you still have trouble deposit it in the Yale Library. Keep a careful list of *addenda*—be assured that it will be published some time.
    I hope you got my letter (and enclosures).[3] On the "Recent Accessions" shelf of the Princeton Univ. library I saw a book called *The Secret of Ulysses* (or something like that)—all very esoteric it seemed to

me.[4] I whirled the index and could find no references to Orestes or Clytemnestra. If I had I'd have cabled you. I hope that in that letter you got all my apologies also. I'm a disorganized wastrel.

    But I'm an admiring friend
    (T. N.)

1. The context of this letter suggests that Wilder and Glasheen may have spoken on the telephone. Many of the points raised by Wilder in this letter are given response to by Glasheen in her letter written the next day.
2. In the "Acknowledgments" to *The Books at the Wake* Atherton writes: "My thanks are first due to my friend since schooldays, the late Arnold Davenport, Senior Lecturer in English Literature at Liverpool University, without whose encouragement this book would never have been started, and under whose guidance much of it was written as a dissertation towards the degree of M.A." (9).
3. Wilder's letter returning Glasheen's "Another Face for Proteus."
4. Rolf Loechrich, *The Secret of 'Ulysses': An Analysis of James Joyce's 'Ulysses'* (McHenry, Ill.: Compass Press, 1953; London: Peter Owen, 1955).

To Thornton Wilder, Hamden, Connecticut

[MS. TLS—Private Collection]

[14 April 1954]   [22 Carrington Lane
Wednesday 1954   Farmington, Connecticut]

Dear Mr Wilder,

Of course, Jim Atherton and I are comic over Hodgart.[1] Don't you expect people to be comic? I always do and they nearly always are. Jim and I feel responsible for Matthew because, as it were, we taught him about FW and that we will be thanked by him in a footnote to any article he writes. At the same time, we know he will have swiped some of our ideas and made them happily his own. Again, of course, we all call each other by our first names—after the things about FW we have all discussed at one time or another, formality would be absurd. I don't in truth think any of us wallow in the unmentionable or the obscene (like Tindal[l] in his introduction to Chamber Music, have you seen it?)[2] they are both very nice-minded men and I don't see myself an advanced or unsexed woman. Still, FW is FW and besides we have all told one another the stories of our lives, discuss friends, families, careers, likes and dislikes quite apart from the business at hand. All rather like strangers on a train. I always let myself be picked up by men on trains (so safe) and they almost always tell me the most interesting stories. A private from Brooklyn once told me all about how he and his wife had to try six states before they could find a priest to marry them and they were finally married in a flood in Pennsylvania; and the president of the CIO optical workers union told me all about his wife's psychoanalysis. Fascinating, but I always wonder how real because while I often talk about myself a great deal to strangers, I am fairly sure I don't say anything that really counts. I don't know how I got here. In any case, you are of course right about letting Matthew publish as he will. No point being a busybody, but I still don't approve.

Jim seems to think [Arnold] Davenport will work and has a lot of potential contribution. We can but see. You—but you're not supposed to work on FW exactly. Because you can do what is a million times more important. But giving countenance, beneficence to us, to FW—we feel we rub some of your glamour onto us. You must know how romantically bookish but non-creative people feel about the creative. You walk in an aura of that romance, you know you do. Likely it bores you by now because only a flaming egoist would go on enjoying it indefinitely. But you are nice, you go on being patient about it.

My parents are putting on a good face about FW and the Girls. We don't understand it, dear, but we are proud of you, is the line they've settled on. If you don't think that there is anything in the article to mildly alarm middle-west middle-class middle-brow America you are out of touch with a large piece of the contemporary national scene. My stepmother is a lamb but she was shocked when I told Alison that the kingdom of heaven was within her. My father is a great reader but he read Tess of the D'Urbervilles years ago and was shocked by it and said he meant never to read another Hardy novel. A friend of my mother's said, Give him Jude the Obscure and he'll never read another novel.

As to the census. It is as ready as it can be. It ought to be worked on in a big library for a long time, but this I just can't manage. Imagine asking for a grant or a fellowship so that you could work on a census of FW! I don't think it will be greatly improved by five or ten years of just sitting around here. Of course, I keep finding people—Donnelley on 281, note something [3] is Ignatius Donnelley, The Great Cryptogram (1888), a big Shakespeare was Bacon or rather the other way around man.[3] I don't think the finished product will be grand enough for the Yale Press. I will of course try there first and I would no end appreciate your dropping a good word when the time comes. But perhaps someplace would mimeograph it like the Ulysses word-index.[4] And if no one will I will give it to Yale.

As I see it the major unsolved mystery of the book is the story that is shadowed in the Letter of Sec. IV. A story of Magrath a butcher who slanders a dairyman and so on. It may be an obscure novel. It may be an actual incident that occurred in Dublin. Ah well, if FW lost all its mysteries where would we be?

Oh, I've not thanked you for reading the Orestes article. You are a fine critic. And annoying. Unerringly you put your finger on all the weak points, all the things I hoped I was slurring over, hustling out of sight. I do agree with all you said so I can't very well make entertaining repartee about it. The basic trouble—you hit it—is I don't really know Ulysses, not like I know FW. I will try to improve the thing.

Oh again. I learned from Tindal[l] that Mrs Joyce is dead. When, where, how did she die?[5]

Have you read the new Gogarty? He has the wind up.[6]

Thank you and thank you and thank you again.

Faithfully,
Adaline

1. The opening of this letter suggests Glasheen is responding to a telephone conversation with Wilder the day before. During the course of writing the letter, she may have received Wilder's letter postmarked 13 April.

2. The Tindall edition was published earlier in the year by Columbia University Press. It was "toasted" at the James Joyce Society meeting on 2 February. See TW to AG, 6 February 1954.

3. Ignatius Donnelly, *The Great Cryptogram* (Chicago, New York and London: R. S. Peale & Co., 1888).

4. Miles L. Hanley's *Word Index to James Joyce's 'Ulysses'* was first published in mimeographed form in 1937.

5. Nora Barnacle Joyce died in Zurich on 10 April 1951.
6. Oliver St. John Gogarty (1878-1957), *It Isn't This Time of Year at All! An Unpremeditated Autobiography* (Garden City, NY: Doubleday, 1954). Gogarty was a physician, writer, and, in 1922, became a member of the Irish Free State Senate. Joyce first met Gogarty in the National Library of Ireland in late December 1902. They quickly became friends, and, in September 1904, Joyce stayed with him at the Martello Tower in Sandycove. When Gogarty read Joyce's poem "The Holy Office" (1904), he recognized himself as one of the writers of the Celtic Revival that Joyce was lampooning. He broke with Joyce, and they remained bitter enemies. Joyce alludes to Gogarty in poems XVII and XXI in *Chamber Music*. Joyce modeled Buck Mulligan in *Ulysses* and other characters in his writings on aspects of Gogarty's personality.

☐

To Adaline Glasheen, Farmington, Connecticut

[MS. ALS—HWS]

[postmark: 7 May 1954]   Hotel Algonquin
May 6 or 7 or maybe even 8—a Friday   59 West 44th St.,
                                                        New York 18

Dear Adaline—
    I think it's very invidious of you, ma'am, to address me as Mr. Wilder. Am I not worthy to join that circle of Jim's [Atherton] and other transatlantic converts you have made to 'direct address'? But the fact that I cannot come and speak to the Teachers College is not a reflection of my hurt feelings.[1]
    I simply can do no more. On principle I'm not speaking at this Spring. But the exceptions have already overwhelmed the principle: I spoke to the French Graduate Students, to the playwriting classes at the Drama School; Wed. I must speak to the Seniors Banquet at Davenport college; and to the successor's class to Johnny Berdan's Daily Themes Course;[2] the Tribute to John Marin at the Academy.[3] I can do no more.
    Already you understand.
    Already you have forgiven.
    Addendum: I never accept an honorarium from an educational institution. (Short of a month's course of lectures.)

I just came across the fact that Moham[m]ed's horse's name was something like Chankata—which is in that Rest aisy passage.⁴ But I suppose you had that long ago.

I haven't forgotten that you want the Atherton lectures back. I just got back from a week's hideaway in Newport—will send them to you when I get back to Hamden.⁵

I'm in New York as quasi-consultant and clucking hen over the forthcoming production of Chekhov's Sea Gull.⁶ Oh, Lordy, what diversionary sallies I get into.

Loads of regard to you both
your old friend
Thornton

---

1. Francis Glasheen, a professor of English, invited Wilder to speak at Central Connecticut State College in New Britain.
2. Yale University obligations.
3. Wilder read his tribute to the painter John Marin (1870–1953) at the Spring meeting of the American Academy of Arts and Letters and the National Institute of Arts and Letters on 26 May. The tribute is in his *American Characteristics*, 234–239.
4. FW 24.23. Buddha's horse is Kantaka; Mohammed's horse is Katachanka.
5. Probably drafts of articles by James Atherton. Wilder was in Newport, Rhode Island, from 28 April to 5 May.
6. Wilder's friend, the actor Montgomery Clift (1920–1966), played Constantin Treplev in the Phoenix Theatre production of Anton Chekhov's *The Sea Gull*. At Clift's urging, Wilder, among others, reviewed the translation of *The Sea Gull* that had been made by Mira Rostova (who played Nina Zarechnaya), Clift, and Kevin McCarthy (who played Boris Trigorin) and made line by line changes. The play, directed by Norris Houghton, opened at the Phoenix Theatre on 11 May 1954 and ran for forty performances. Wilder had attended readings of the play at Clift's home in New York before work began on the production, and he attended the rehearsals, dress rehearsals, previews, and the opening night.

To Thornton Wilder, Hamden, Connecticut
[MS. ALS—YCAL]

8 May 1954 [22 Carrington Lane
Farmington, Connecticut]

Dear Thornton,

But it does not come naturally. I feel Jim Atherton[']s intellectual equal and Matthew Hodgart[']s superior but your infinite so infinite inferior. After all, I've told you *The Ides of March* is just a book I adore. And *The Skin of Our Teeth*. So I will continue to feel you are Mister Wilder.

Letters from my Englishmen. Apparently Miss Weaver has stepped firmly on Matthew's project of publishing the drafts for now at any rate. He is even having to excise some quotations from the letters that he had in an article on Songs in FW that was in proof. Because Stuart Gilbert is bringing out Joyce's letters with Faber. Jim has had his Koran article taken by *Comparative Literature*, will come out in the fall.[1] I guess I ought to know what *Comp. Lit* is but I don't. I think it's quite a good article and so am glad. Hodgart's song is good too, I think.

Mr. Bateson after going on about how the Orestes thing must be revised—and me bothering you about it—now writes that it needs almost no revision, Ha.[2] Jim said he sent you that further draft.[3] My emotions about the drafts rises in Bafflement. The drafts show that the obscurity of FW does not lie in the language. Stripped of puns, foreign words, allusions of all sorts—FW is for me not pregnant with meaning and this of course is what FW's enemies have long been declaring.

262. note 7—the "Matthew Bible"—1537—is called "Bugge Bible" because of the rendering of Psalm 91:15 [i.e., 91:5] as: "So thou shalt not nede to be afroyed of any bugges by night."[4]

258.5 Kidoosh = Kid[d]ush the Jewish liturgy—Hodgart.

No, I did not know about Mohamet's horse. Thank you.

Animal life surrounds me. Since I began this my cat Miltess (shall I put her in a book) has had one kitten on the sofa and I guess is going to have some more and while there isn't anything I can do for her, I can't somehow write a coherent letter.

We're sorry you couldn't speak. I will be sorrier in another letter. I think I will have to name this first kitten for you. Should you mind?

                Yrs
                Adaline

1. Atherton's "Islam and the Koran in *Finnegans Wake*," *Comparative Literature*, VI, 3 (Summer 1954), 240–255; revised in *The Books at the Wake*, 201–217.
2. Bateson's letter about Glasheen's "Another Face for Proteus" is not in HWS.
3. Typed copies of draft passages of *Finnegans Wake* made by Atherton and Hodgart from manuscripts in the British Library.
4. An English translation of the Bible by Thomas Matthew printed in 1537. Glasheen slightly misquotes the passage; it should read: "So that you shalt not nede to be afrayed for any bugges by night." A copy of the Bible is in the Beinecke Library, Yale University.

☐

To Adaline Glasheen, Farmington, Connecticut

[MS. ALS—HWS]

[postmark: 24 May 1954]   Hamden

Dear Adaline:
    Have been going through the haystacks of my files.
    Here's an Atherton letter.
    Have I lots more?[1]
    Maybe I lent some to that New Hampshire farmer.[2]
    Anyway, I'll forward them all

                Stout and true
                Thornton

1. Glasheen often sent Wilder letters she received from James Atherton and Matthew Hodgart.
2. Lawrence A. Wiggin, see TW to AG, 25 October 1953, n. 5.

☐

To Adaline Glasheen, Farmington, Connecticut
[MS. ALS—HWS]

30 May [1954]¹   50 Deepwood Drive
   Hamden 14, Connecticut

Dear Adaline—
   Of course, I was downright flabbergasted by your announcement.
   And yet, I understand it—a moment comes when one can not live close to that Old Man of the Sea any longer. What is surprising is the variety of reasons we all give for wanting out.
   Anyway, you've done splendid work and you've fired other workers in the vineyard.
   I hope you have my feeling: pleased expectation of the moment 5–10 years from now when I shall return to FW and see what lights the researchers have brought to the text we once knew so well.
   I hope, Madam, that this does not mean that our correspondence has lost its *raison d'être*. And I should be chagrined to hear that you are going to be a housewife only. If you are thinking of taking up some literary problem, do let me know.
   Does Francis take the PMLA? On the chance he doesn't I enclose a few pages from the new one—a terribly silly paper—but perhaps I don't understand it. No, I do understand it and think it's very silly.²

   Lots of regard to you both
   Thornton

1. This letter was given a date of 1968 in Carolyn France's 1977, "Preliminary Calendar of the correspondence of Adaline Glasheen and Thornton Wilder" (HWS). On the basis of the return address, this letter is clearly earlier than 1968. The

"Hamden 14" was used until 1957. The zip code then changed to Hamden 17, and in the 1960s it became a five digit code. The context also suggests 1954. This letter, perhaps a response to a telephone conversation, is part of a sequence of letters which began in 1953: AG to TW, 21 May [1953] announcing she would give *Finnegans Wake* studies "another six months or a year," and Wilder's response of 26 May 1953.

2. The article has not remained with the letter.

☐

To Adaline Glasheen, Farmington, Connecticut

[MS. APCS—HWS]

[Sculptured and Polychromed Alabaster Relief
Burgundian, XVth Century
Yale University Art Gallery, New Haven]

[postmark: 11 June 1954]   [Newport, Rhode Island]

Dear Adaline—
    Still finding letters I should have returned to you—letters from that era when you too were "beside yourself" in absorption with F. W.[1] I expect to find some more—which however will not be the only subject of our correspondence!

              Ever
              Thornton

Beautiful card? French children playing in the Tuileries still look exactly like these.[2]

1. Probably letters from Atherton and Hodgart to Glasheen.
2. A reference to the image on the postcard.

To Adaline Glasheen, Farmington, Connecticut

[MS. ALS—HWS]

12 July [1954]   50 Deepwood Drive
                                              Hamden 14, Connecticut

Dear Adaline—
    Sailing Friday.
    Long absence. After Oct 1 shall settle down in Aix-en-Provence* to work for several months. Probably back next April.[1]
    Can't answer your questions, of course. Rê Cad with a pipe. If we could find the Dublin newspaper that reported Joyce's father's being held up in Phoenix Park, we might find a MacGrath. (But did it get into the papers.)
    So you haven't yet *eschewed* F. W? Or are you like those cigarette smokers who decide to give up the vice gradually? Sometimes I feel as tho' I'd like to fall into a Rip-van-Winkle sleep and wake up years later and read all that our successors have discovered in the book.
    Anyway, when I return you can report to me what you have learned and learned from others.
    All cordial best to you both—nay, to all three and a happy au revoir

                yr old friend
                Thornton

*Vale Vaucluse, lucydlake in [inserted above: near] the Petrarch-Laura foliation [203.26]

---

1. Wilder sailed on the SS *Olympic* on Friday, 16 July and remained in Europe until 8 April 1955. He attended the premiere of his play, *The Matchmaker*, a rewritten version of his 1938 play *The Merchant of Yonkers*, which opened at the Royal Lyceum Theatre, Edinburgh, on 23 August. The play was directed by Tyrone Guthrie and starred Ruth Gordon as Dolly Levi. Ian Hunter, director of the Edinburgh Festival, asked Wilder to contribute a play for the following summer; this became the major writing project that was to occupy Wilder during his extended stay in Europe. After leaving Edinburgh on 8 September Wilder worked on an idea for a play which he called "The Martians." He abandoned this project, and, on 24 November 1954, turned to *The Alcestiad*, a play he had worked on intermittently since 1937. (See Wilder, *Journals*, 219–241).

1955

To Adaline Glasheen, Farmington, Connecticut

[MS. ALS—HWS]

4 March [1955]   last days at Hotel Sextius,
                                                Aix-en-Provence [France]

Dear Adeline—
   Greetings! Selah!
   Yes, I'm writing the Yale Press at once.[1]
   Fascinating—those items you're always bringing in on FW.
   But what *else* are you doing?
   Didn't you lead me to believe that you'd put FW behind you?[2]
   Where are you "two-plus" going to live abroad?[3] Please ask me some advice.
   I've finished a new play. It's bath-towel-heart-rending. I've stolen a moment of FW from it that only you will recognize.[4] It's too bad that G[ertrude]. Stein weaned [me] from pleasure in this world's gaze because I've become the glitter-boy of international festivals—but pshaw, don't mean a thing to me.[5] Must say I was a little pleased to learn that Mary Martin will be playing Sabina (Lily McGrath) and Helen Hayes Mrs Antrobus (Maggy Earwicker) in Paris. That's one of them convocations that Earwickers only dream about.[6]
   Next week I leave this beautiful little university town (where I've been since October—imagine) to go into Spain. . . . Got no address except an agent c/o John Carrara and Sons P. O. B. 9 Irish Town Gibraltar (YES—I know what you're thinking . . . . I'm going to look for the Molly site)[7] then New York about Holy Week.

You'll make me angry if you talk about pestering me—I TORE your letter open . . . and Hell, I don't do that often.

Liveliest greetings to you all
Thornton

P. S. I've written announcing your MS to Mr. Gene (Eugene, I supposed[)] Davison of the Yale University Press. Forward March.

---

1. Referring to a lost letter in which Glasheen asked Wilder's support for her proposal for *A Census of 'Finnegans Wake'*.
2. Glasheen had suggested this in her letter of 8 January 1954.
3. Francis Glasheen had won a Fulbright-Hays fellowship to teach in the Netherlands.
4. In his letter to Glasheen of 13 April 1955, Wilder explains that "in the closing four minutes of it [*The Alcestiad*] there's a beautiful steal from FW. Not verbal, but in feeling."
5. "Stein had observed Wilder in talk and in action—his attraction to personalities, his wish to please, his fear of being judged, a sense of duty that interfered with his art, his great restlessness. She came to call him community man and company man. . . . But she took him in hand and tried to teach him not to be obliging" ("Introduction," Burns and Dydo, *The Letters of Gertrude Stein and Thornton Wilder*, xix–xx). In addition to the Edinburgh Festival, Wilder attended the Berlin Festival from 21 to 24 September 1954.
6. *The Skin of Our Teeth* was one of the American works performed in the *Salut à la France* festival in Paris. The play, produced by American National Theatre and Academy and directed by Alan Schneider, also included George Abbott as Mr. Antrobus and Florence Reed as the Fortune Teller (a role she played in the original production). The play opened at the Théâtre Sarah Bernhardt, where it was billed as *La Peau des Dents*, on 28 June 1955. When Helen Hayes was offered the script in 1942, she mistakenly thought Wilder was asking her to play Mrs. Antrobus (a part that had been promised to Florence Eldridge, wife of Frederic March who played Mr. Antrobus). When she learned that Wilder wanted her to play Lily Sabina, she refused, claiming that she suspected the part had been written for Ruth Gordon and that she would be "haunted by the way she'd [Gordon] speak every line." It was Hayes who suggested to Wilder, the producer Michael Myerberg, and the director Elia Kazan that they consider Tallulah Bankhead for the role of Lily Sabina. See Appendix VIII in Burns and Dydo, Stein/Wilder Letters, particularly 384–385.
7. In *Ulysses*, Molly Bloom was brought up in Gibraltar, a British colony, where her father, Sergeant-Major Brian Cooper Tweedy, a member of the Royal Dublin Fusiliers, was stationed for more than seventeen years. The "site" probably refers to the place where Molly, at the age of fifteen, had her first sexual adventure with Lieutenant Mulvey. See *Ulysses*, chapter 18, *passim*. Wilder boarded the SS *Cristoforo Colombo* in Cannes, France, on 8 March for a cruise that took him to Gibraltar for 10–11 March and then Malaga, Spain. He traveled in Spain until he rejoined the ship in Gibraltar on 2 April—eventually docking in New York the afternoon of 8 April.

To Adaline Glasheen, Farmington, Connecticut

[MS. ALS—HWS]

[postmark: 13 April 1955] The Graduates Club
Tuesday *in albis* One Hundred and Fifty-Five Elm Street
 New Haven, Connecticut
Written on a telephone book in a room that has no desk or table.
Theory being Yale grads don't write.[1]

Dear Adaline—
 In haste,— but eagerly, to be helpful.
 Yes, yes—you will adore Holland. So right to start the language; it's not hard (*I* don't speak it, but I can see that it's not hard.) And I can just see Gorinchem.
 The surprise of your life will be how small Holland is. I couldn't get over it that from Amsterdam you could get to the Hague or Rotterdam or Haarlem or Delft in much less than an hour.
 So hope for you that Holland isn't expensive—France is wickedly so; Italy ½ French and Spain ⅓ France.
 Trying writing to Elmaman [Richard Ellmann] that WILDER wants to see the lexicon at once.[2] I hate every sign whenever I *do* intimidate people; let's see if to my enjoyment I can intimidate him.
 Francis will go mad about the pictures. I always thought Hals was a sort of slicker J. S. Sargent and then you go to Haarlem and he's the greatest deepest painter. Also so that he reads Sacheverell Sitwell on the baroque and rococo architecture in Holland.[3]
 [Frances] Steloff says A. M. Klein's book on Ulysses will be out soon; I'm still a dazzle about those two chapters he printed first. Oh, I wish he'd give me a few hints as to how to start breaking down the A L P chapter. . . .[4]
 Never heard such nonsense=there's nothing difficult about Heaven[']s My D—.[5] But don't know where (in a letter) to begin talking about it. . .
 The new play is The Alcestiad. (That other title[6] was wrung from me by the Edinburgh committee.) In the closing four minutes of it there's a beautiful steal from FW. Not verbal, but in feeling.
 I have to do a few lectures—but hope to [be] back in Hamden about 2nd week in May[7] and can get my car out—

Have no distrust—you will enjoy your trip wonderfully. . . . Francis is going to teach, I assume; is he also going to work on some project on the side?

Nestorically and devotedly
(T. N.)

1. Wilder received his B. A. from Yale College in 1920.
2. Ellmann had the only available typescript of Glasheen's *Census*. See TW to AG, 4 March 1955, n. 1.
3. *The Netherlands: A Study of Some Aspects of Art, Costume and Social Life* (London, New York: B. T. Batsford, 1948) by Sacheverell Sitwell (1897–1988).
4. Klein never published a book length study of *Ulysses*. See TW to AG, 16 August 1952, n. 5.
5. *Heaven's My Destination*, Wilder's 1935 novel about George Brush. Brush, a traveling salesman, who is a religious fundamentalist and humanitarian, tries to reform society.
6. *A Life in the Sun*. See TW to AG, 12 July 1954, n. 1.
7. On 18 April, Wilder lectured at the Library of Congress under the auspices of the Gertrude Clarke Whittall Literary Fund. On 2 May he lectured at the 92nd Street YMHA in New York, and on Thursday, 5 May he left for Berea College, Berea, Kentucky, where he remained until 7 May. At Berea College he gave a talk and met with students.

☐

Thornton Wilder to Virgil B. Heltzel, Editor, Northwestern University Studies

[MS. ALS-copy—HWS]

[postmark: 14 May 1955]   [50 Deepwood Drive
                                               Hamden, Connecticut]

Dear A[daline]—here's a valentine[1]
Dear Mr. H
     But I saw Mrs Glasheen's Census in an earlier state,—I rejoiced in it—I contributed to it—I have corresponded on aspects of it with its author since.

I feel sure, that like Prof. Hanley's concordance of *Ulysses* it will sell out though slowly and finally become a precious collector's item selling at 10 times its sale price!

My correspondence from strangers shows me how many ardent FW readers there are (in fact, there are no lukewarm readers; there are only the bewildered—defeated and the ardent).

Many thanks for your letter and offer; but I am *amicus curiae*[.]

May you get much pleasure from publishing this work—the publisher's pleasure of serving madly enthusiastic readers.

        Sincerely yours
        Thornton Wilder

---

1. Wilder made this copy for Glasheen of his reply to Heltzel's letter of 4 May asking for an evaluation of Glasheen's *Census*. It was Richard Ellmann, then a professor of English at Northwestern University, who suggested she submit the manuscript to Virgil B. Heltzel, editor of Northwestern University Studies (the Press was not yet formally constituted). Ellmann and Glasheen began corresponding in the Fall of 1954, perhaps after C. G. Bowen, an assistant editor in the trade department at Oxford University Press in New York, asked Ellmann about the quality of Glasheen's "*Finnegans Wake* and the Girls from Boston, Mass." and whether with a few more "discoveries" Glasheen would have a book (Ellmann to Glasheen, 10 October 1954). In her reply Glasheen asked Ellmann for advice on her *Census*. Ellmann replied on 2 November: "You speak of asking my advice about your census. What is your census?" Glasheen must have sent it immediately because Ellmann replied on 28 November with details about publishing at Northwestern. The problem, Ellmann explained, was that the Northwestern University Studies series only published authors with an academic affiliation. Ellmann suggested that if they could not get around this rule an alternative would be to publish the *Census* in the *The Analyst*, a journal published by the English Department in mimeographed form. It was not until February 1955 that Heltzel, gave his permission for a non-academically affiliated author to be published, and Glasheen's *Census* was published in 1956.

To Adaline Glasheen, Amsterdam, The Netherlands[1]

[MS. ALS—HWS]

[postmark: 9 October 1955]   Last weeks to be reached thru
Americ[an] Exp[ress] Co.[2]
11 rue Scribe, Paris

Dear Madam:
 Are you sure it's right for you to be so blithe? Is it *kind*?
Doesn't everybody love Amsterdam? I did.
Went picture mad, especially at Haarlem.
So it's a novel. No harm in being autobiographical—just a little.[3]
 Have a new FW correspondent—a Dublin youth who walks the course of the Liffey over and over again to get the loci of the ALP chapter.[4] But without my volume I'm no good as a commentator, so I must let the correspondence lapse.
 The British critics hated my play at Edinburgh but Shucks—capacity houses and deeply moved silence—Shucks.
 Do you like Paris? I wish I were in Madrid. Leaving Monday for a few weeks in Switzerland, then meeting my opera composer in Rome (we're doing a *grand* opera, not one of these sung short-stories);[5] then home by Thanksgiving.
                              x
 I'm shocked to hear that your Dutch friends are back in the Galsworthy days.[6] Why I spoke at a literary club Der Kuppel (or Turm?) and I tho't they were deeply interested in the "latest."
 Very sorry to hear that Francis has that teaching load—that's not right or fair. You're supposed to live as Exemplary Americans, a light set upon a hill, not be work-laden. Brace yourselves, too, for that mattress of clouds overhead which makes the European winter. (See my classic: The history of European literature in the light of meteorology.[)]
Fortunately Dutch gin is very good and very cheap. You should be getting a lot of good music too.
 Do resolve to enjoy yourselves. Take the cue from your daughter. Don't work too hard on the novel—play with it like a trout on a hook.
 See you in Farmington.

                              Pal
                              Thornton

1. Francis Glasheen was on a Fulbright-Hays Teaching Fellowship in the Netherlands.

2. Wilder remained in France until 10 October when he left for Switzerland. Wilder traveled in Switzerland until just before he departed from Cherbourg, France, on 20 October. Immediately upon his arrival in New York on 25 October, he left for Philadelphia to attend the premiere of his play *The Matchmaker* on 27 October.

3. In a lost letter Glasheen had probably written that she was starting a novel. There are no materials relating to this novel in the Glasheen Archives.

4. Wilder enclosed a letter of 4 October 1955, from Gerard O Flaherty. At the top of the letter he wrote to Glasheen: "Infuriating—the way F. W. correspondents tell you things you've known since the age of 3." Ulick O'Connor, the Irish writer and journalist who sometimes wrote on Joyce, had put Wilder in touch with O Flaherty—probably because of questions Wilder had about Gaelic references and references to Dublin in the Anna Livia Plurabelle section of the *Wake* (I, viii, 196–216).

5. Wilder did not meet Louise Talma, the composer whom he knew from the MacDowell Colony, in Rome. Talma and Wilder first discussed collaborating in the Spring of 1954. While at Aix-en-Provence in February–March 1955, Wilder did an outline for an opera (see *Journals*, 234–236). But after the premiere of *The Alcestiad* on 22 August 1955, Wilder wrote to her suggesting she use that play as her libretto. *The Alcestiad: An Opera in Three Acts* had its world premiere in Frankfurt am Main, Germany, on 2 March 1962. See *Journals*, 240–242.

6. The writer John Galsworthy (1867–1933).

SADE

La Coste, seigneur de   (one of de Sade's titles) 184.30
Saumane, seigneur de   (ditto: with Soude, etc.) 184.36 ; 240-36 (with his splendivous cavalry)
Aguilar, padre   page probably allusion to the imperial eagle (sp. Aguila) on de Sade's crest 184.35

Pelagie   de Sade's wife, Renée-Pelagie de Montreuil, 182.3 (with saddishness)
358.3 and 10 renovations ..... pelaged. (St. Pelagie is also one of the
prisons where de Sade was held)

Drake, Sir Francis (Latin: Draco, dragon — belongs in FW to the "dead hero returns"
motif, with King Arthur, etc., hence "Drake's Drum") 358.28-29

358.28-29   hero ... arthouducks (duck and drake) dragon
316.29   (with Lief 26 and Hawkins 26-27) dragon - to - market
623.35 - 624.1   d...d...d... tattat .... rounding his world of
                    eighty days
469.9-11   quick-quack ... travel the void world over ... 16 mound
(last word)   circus 17 ..... Jerne valing (Jules Verne)

(suspect all drum motives: Boom boom, rataplan, Tow
Tow, tambour, taratara ; and quack-quacks ; and periplus 313.33]

Nelson, Horatia   (d. of Nelson and Lady Hamilton) 329.4

[In FW most of the Horace, Horus etc. are for Horatio Nelson]

Nelson, Horatio, duke of Bronte (!!) So page 328 has battles of Copenhagen and
the Nile 22 Emma 21 House 34
I suspect that FINGAL of victories is an anagram of
Trafalgar won by Nelson on his flagship Victory)
325.   13 chorea 17 horasa ... 22 iron sides (a ship at Trafalgar)
322   17 horsey ; 25. horses ..... 32. (Nelson's flan)
[I suspect as Sea Captain Nelson is all through this chapter:
note p.323.29   oneseyed one-eyed. all everywhere
as cyclops ... monocular ... borgne (french for one-eyed]
so:
273.27 [Napelon between his two chief enemies Wellington and Nelson:]
hitheris poorblond (purblind) hoerse. Huirse.

620-621   cove and haven ... barque ... duties ("England expects
every man to do his duty") .... Bosuns ... Phoenix, dear (Nelson's
battle at Finisterre)

A page of Thornton Wilder's working notes for *Finnegans Wake*
Courtesy, Beinecke Rare Book and Manuscript Library, Yale University

1956

To Adaline Glasheen, Amsterdam, The Netherlands

[MS. ALS—HWS]

13 February [1956]   Naples—Europe's new winter sports resort.[1]
   Bring your ear muffs and hip boots.

Dear Adaline:
   Many thanks for word.[2]
   Wish I could give you a tip about an ideal little Costa Brava village.
   All I know is that they are there: I hear repeatedly at third hand of such places. Will start asking around and will write you if I get any exact addresses.
   Yes, rê the Dutch. But you also describe the people in French-speaking Switzerland.
   Yes, the tide is turning against J. J. It began strong spearheaded on both sides [of] the Atlantic by Pritchett: over-implication of matter to conceal absence of real content etc, etc.[3]
   As to private character: I'm not surprised: I always assumed Towering egocentricism plus a sly analytic view of all friendships except the choicest, and then added to it all that invalidism which in his case did nothing to mellow. But under the less likable traits that ocean-like understanding. But it would probably [be] very easy to write a "life" of him or rather a "character" of him in disparaging tones and there'll be many. For many writing-chaps that kind of writing is such fun. His brother's begun it, I see.[4]
   Is your novel in "chronical" style? Don't tell anybody but I've begun another and it's pretty old style in manner of presentation.[5]

Are you in yours? I'm too old to put myself in any more—and even when I did it was very indirect.

What's this about a cheese for me?

I guess it's waiting there in Hamden. Isabel reported a vast log of cards and messages but I don't remember now about any cheese. Will report.

Today's letter-writing day (just picked up a big bundle at American Exp. including yours), that's why my lines are as dull as the Dutch's.

All my sympathy to you on the weather we're enduring.

But Amsterdam can be ever newly beautiful, can't it? And you are saturating yourself in great painting I hope—Haarlem, that glo-o-o-ry.

And the young, the young—how are the young?

And does Francis find interest in his teaching?

When I get back to Deepwood Drive circa March 1, I'm going to give myself two treats: a week's work in a certain problem in Lope de Vega (I think I've discovered another that'll have to take its place in every biography of both Lope and Cervantes henceforth!!!);[6] and a week on FW. Each of them of joyous absorption 12 hours a day. When I work on those two things I never flag; nor get impatient; nor want to eat; nor to go to bed.

All cordial best to you all—

Your old friend
Thornton

American Exp. Co
Naples until Feb 20

In Rome Louise Talma played me the music she's written for the first scenes of our opera.[7] It's 12-tone technique, but dramatic and eloquent and singable.

(T. N.)

---

1. Wilder sailed on the *Andrea Doria* from New York on 16 November 1955 and arrived in Naples on the 24th.

2. A lost letter.

3. V. S. Pritchett's, "Joyce's *Ulysses*," (*The New Statesman and Nation*, 21 January 1956, 75–76) opens: "It is not difficult to write about *Ulysses*; the difficulty is to read it and to go on doing so."

4. Joyce's younger brother, Stanislaus (1884–1955), an important source for Richard Ellmann's biography, had begun before his death a volume of memoirs. Stanislaus Joyce's *My Brother's Keeper*, edited, with an Introduction and Notes by Ellmann and a Preface by T. S. Eliot was posthumously published by the Viking Press in 1958.

5. Probably a reference to the notes, "Beauty of the World: The European and the American," in his *Journals*, 245–248, 252–256. This project was abandoned; the next novel Wilder published was *The Eighth Day* (1967). No notes for Glasheen's novel have been located.

6. Responding to a controversy about the dating of Lope de Vega's plays, Wilder went back to his notes about the actor-manager Nicolás de los Rios for whom both Lope and Cervantes wrote. See *Journals*, 201–203, 242–243.

7. *The Alcestiad: An Opera in Three Acts.*

☐

To *Adaline Glasheen, Amsterdam, The Netherlands*

[MS. ALS–HWS]

10 May 1956   50 Deepwood Drive
                                           Hamden 14, Connecticut

Dear Adeline—
    Retro Sathanas.[1]
    Your letter fascinating, if a little breathless.[2]
    Yes, why is Fox-Goodman (35.30[)] always tolling the bell throughout.
    Fuit (42.2 and bottom 33[.34]) primarily means Has-been. When anything's failed in my Lope plays they use as a gag FUIT TROIA—all's up with Troy.
    Thanks for the rest.

⟵—————————————————⟶

    Of course, your novel will be published.
    Don't rewrite it *too* often.
    You and Ruth Gordon are the only novelists I know who adore writing. Hers—she says is already as long as War and Peace. I'm in it.[3]
    Mine has been shunted off a while.
    It can be despairingly hot in the valley of the Arno or anywhere—but also in Farmington, so accept your blessings. Passed Vallambrosa on the train and sobbed aloud. Couldn't see those leaves for the snow.
    Learn to make some delicious pasta dishes and ask me up. Fettucine verde, for example.

I'm a little anti-Florence—as having had all the force of the Renaissance drained out of it by being looked at by too many Victorians and Brownings etc. But just the same anywhere there is a glory—enjoy it.

What a big work you did in that census. Yes—addenda and corrigenda for generations, but *you* did it. Are you duly proud?

Best regards to Francis and to the Young Un.

Mid-June I leave for several months in Mexico. Don't be mean—write whenever it strikes you.

Been to see those pictures in Haarlem lately?

Ever cordially
Thornton

1. Maybe "Satanas," variation on "Satan."
2. A lost letter.
3. An unpublished novel by Gordon (1896–1985).

To Adaline Glasheen, Amsterdam, The Netherlands

[MS. ALS—HWS]

13 June 1956

50 Deepwood Drive
Hamden 14, Connecticut

Dear Adaline:

Yes, ma'am. I shall write praises on your behalf for the Guggenheim.[1]

Secretly I will hope that you will be working on the novel and not the Parnell Report—but you'd do any of 'em well.[2]

x

I went back and had a little go at FW. Tried to work out the elements of the GOSPEL (of the Mass) in Anna Livia P.

Don't butt me—hike—when you bend [196.9] is a genuflection, yes. Kicks the Buck. Yes. Allelulia and everything.

But on what holy day is it the gospel passage?

Where is the gradial?

Hell, he would make it as hard as possible. We're probably in some minor Abyssinian rite. It probably works backward.

Isn't Kelleher tiresome in Analysis—merely Lint-picking.³

Isn't Klein splendid in Accent? Every now and then—all right—he's [i.e., he] strings his wire a little too tight, but on the whole he's the best.⁴ Did you notice Kenner's waspish aside about him? ("I doubt whether J. J. was as much a mathematician as Mr. Klein supposes.")⁵ Sheer jealousy.

x

Oh. . . *I* made you angry with my reservations about Florence.

I wish you all joy in "sober-toned" Fiesole.

I beg you to keep a notebook of your gradually accumulating insights into Shakespeare. I mean it. I mean it.

Saturday I start driving to Mexico—to a Doctors' Club, sic, where I shall be at least 2½ months.⁶

Letters (including inquiries from Mr. Moe)⁷ will be forwarded from here,—dilatorily, I suppose.

It's terribly humid-hot in Conn. this day. My brother got a hon.D. from Yale on Monday.⁸ We're very pleased.

All my best to you all
(TNW)

---

1. Glasheen was not awarded a Guggenheim Fellowship.

2. Glasheen's, "Joyce and the Three Ages of Charles Stewart Parnell," in *A James Joyce Miscellany*, Second Series, ed. Marvin Magalaner (Carbondale, Illinois: Southern Illinois University Press, 1959, 151–178).

3. John V. Kelleher, "Notes on *Finnegans Wake* and *Ulysses*," in *The Analyst*, No. X, March 1956, [1]–9.

4. Klein's "The Black Panther (A Study of Technique)" in *Accent: A Quarterly of New Literature*, [University of Illinois at Urbana, English Department], X, 3 (Spring 1950), 139–155.

5. Wilder slightly misquotes from Kenner's *Dublin's Joyce*: "It probably isn't necessary to suppose that Joyce was quite so fantastic a mathematician as Mr. Klein would like to believe" (1987, note 1, 259). Kenner is referring to Klein's essay, "The Oxen of the Sun," in *Here and Now: A Canadian Magazine of Literature*, I, 3 (January 1949), [28]–48. See TW to AG, 16 August 1952, n. 5.

6. A vacation resort.

7. Henry Allen Moe was "the chief executive officer of the John Simon Guggenheim Memorial Foundation from its founding in 1925 until June 1963 (but his title for most of that time—until May 1961—was Secretary General" (letter received 12 May 1998, G. Thomas Tanselle).

8. Wilder's eldest brother, Amos Niven Wilder (1895–1993) was a distinguished New Testament scholar, teacher, and poet. He received an honorary degree of Doctor of Divinity at the 255th Yale Commencement on 11 July. He had received his Ph.D from Yale University in 1933, the same year he received his first honorary degree from Hamilton College, New York.

□

To Adaline Glasheen, Farmington, Connecticut[1]

[MS. ALS—HWS]

3 August 1956

As from: Hamden Conn
Acapulco Mexico.

Dear Adaline:
Your letter delightful but not one damn word about your novel or other work.
One of those Ghirandescas (where did you get that final u?) was in New Haven studying, a friend of my sisters.[2]
Delighted that you're in such delightful situation. Remember: you're learning recipes to glut me.
It's so hot here that all day I groan—others are down on the beaches or out fishing. Next week I'm going up to higher land.
Put in some time on that insidious F. W. Did you find Saturn and Uranus and all their satellites on p. 583; and the brilliant poignant Shakespeare foliation on p. 251—where Angelhood is Angelo in Measure for Measure. I'm near solving the last of the (Walt) Meaghers.[3] Can't wait to follow up on the clue you gave me about ALP and the Ganges.
What strikes me most this week is that the book is burdensomely compulsively dirty. Sic.

Last day at Huasca August 29

Don't know what became of this leaf. Lord! is this now too late to reach you in Florence?
Tomorrow I start driving north. Slowly. I'll be in New Orleans by the middle of next week.

Forgive me. It's late. I've gotta mail this. ¶ I'm shocked that you couldn't see the large role that The Book of the Dead plays in our FW.[4]

>See you in Connecticut—la—bella
>Lotsa regards to you both—I mean to all three
>Ever
>(TNW)

1. This letter arrived in Fiesole, Italy, on 28 August 1956 and was forwarded to the Glasheens in Farmington.

2. In the absence of Glasheen's letter, the reference to Ghirandesca remains unclear. Perhaps associated with Ugolino della Ghenardesca, a 13th-century count whose exile is recounted in Dante's *Inferno*, XXXIII. In *Census II* Glasheen finds Ugolino in the *Wake* at 513.8.

3. In FW Wally Meagher "appears to have inherited a pair of trousers, to have been involved in some kind of 'troth.'" See *Census I* and *II*.

4. For the importance of *The Book of the Dead* in *Finnegans Wake*, see Atherton, *The Books at the Wake*, 191–200; see also John Bishop, *Joyce's Book of the Dark* (Madison: University of Wisconsin Press, 1986).

□

To Adaline Glasheen, Farmington, Connecticut

[MS. ALS—HWS]

[postmark: 26 September 1956] Hotel Algonquin
Wed. 59 West 44th St.,
  New York 36, N. Y.

Dear Adaline—

Just got back from the South.

Been so busy inscribing all your discoveries into my FW that I haven't had time to write to you.

Splendid,—the book in its successive editions will be the classic. English publisher will be after you soon.[1] Wait until you have received the *addenda* of all us beavers—soon your postman will be flooding you with letters from the fellow-workers.

The composer of our opera has just arrived; I drive her up to Peterboro[2]—later, I want to come to tea and bring my "list."
The one glaring omission, dear lady, is
Joyce, Giorgio . . . .
Joyce, Lucia . . . .[3]
But you've done a glorious invaluable work splendidly. And your introduction; what a good writer you are!

> More anon
> Lots of regards to you both
> Thornton

---

1. Glasheen's *A Census of 'Finnegans Wake'* was published by Northwestern University Press on 12 September 1956. Faber & Faber of London published an edition in 1957 and inserted a page of addenda.

2. Wilder drove Louise Talma, the composer of *The Alcestiad*, to the MacDowell Colony in Peterborough, New Hampshire. See TW to AG, 13 February 1956.

3. In *Census II* and *III* Glasheen added entries for the two children of James and Nora Barnacle Joyce: George [Giorgio] Joyce (1905–1976) and Lucia Joyce (1907–1982).

To Adaline Glasheen, Farmington, Connecticut

[MS. ALS–HWS]

[15 October 1956]　　　　　　　　　　50 Deepwood Drive
Monday　　　　　　　　　　　　　　Hamden 14, Connecticut

No, ma'am'—
　I understand the situation perfectly. Three weeks out of every six months I vow never to look into F. W. again.[1]
　And BESIDES: the novel developing.
　Don't let me distract you: you just keep a file of the suggestions from the Infatuates—scarcely without looking at them—until you come to some pause in the novel. Then copy 'em all down on your little cards, and send them on to the printer.

And there's a student at Penn who's ready to build the Tower of Babel of a Lexicon!
For Alluded to, but not named, I tried:
{IAGO} character in Othello: the ancient 281.21 but now I don't think you need the square brackets.
I'd love to find the works all in one place,—for instance:
IBSEN, Hendrick etc, then the line references to him then
> Rosmersholm
> Hedda Gabler
> The Crown Pretenders 252.16 [i.e., 252.15]
> and so on.
WAGNER etc etc.

xx   xx

The subtitle isn't really on-the-nose. "Thornycroft" can't be said to be a character in the novel. But let it stand, though; long subtitles sound pompous.[2]

xx

I hope we can sneak the planets and their satellites in, merely because they're named after mythological beings. Charley's Wain [426.25] and Georgian Mansion [140.30]

xx

I love
GAUTIER, Marguerite, in English called "Camille," in Dumas' play La Dame aux Camelias. 432:21[3]

xx

I think you'll be pleased {see your *Donachie's}[4]
DOLACHUS (DOOLAGH) ST.—church on Malahide Road: Donachie's 624:16

xx   xx

No no,—stay immersed in the novel. Let the rest wait.

Ever
(TN)

I'm not going to the J. J. Society meeting.[5]

---

1. Wilder's response to a lost letter or to a telephone conversation.
2. The subtitle of all editions of the *Census* was "An Index of the Characters and Their Roles." William Hamo Thornycroft (1850–1925) is included in a listing of architects and sculptors on 552.11–.13.
3. Glasheen includes this in *Census II* and adds 334.17.

4. Glasheen's asterisk in the *Census* indicates that she has not discovered the person's identity.

5. Paul R. Taylor, Professor of Philosophy at Brooklyn College, spoke on the philosophical content of Joyce's work at the James Joyce Society meeting on 16 October at the Gotham Book Mart.

☐

To Adaline Glasheen, Farmington, Connecticut

[MS. ALS—HWS]

[18 November 1956] 50 Deepwood Drive
Sunday Hamden 14, Connecticut

Dear Adaline—
  Greetings, Selah, and Mizpah.
  I've just written an encomium of you for the Guggenheim Committee that would be exaggerated for a combination of Mme de Staël, Colette, and Rebecca West.[1] I felt I had to work hard to counteract your ill-judged word in the last paragraph. You don't know those committees: they've never yet heard a candidate recommend his "frivolity." I've told 'em—and with serene conviction—that you are a very beaver of dedicated and sober industry.
  I've returned from wanderings and wanted to come and see you, but have found all sorts of obstacles—I've lost a conspicuous tooth and until it's replaced I look like an old Punchinello; my sister's arthritis has flared up and I answer the phone and the door, and so on.
  So I'm sending you (instead of my bringing you) my Census. Some of my interlinears are items you first told me but which you seem to have forgotten; some are picayune (for instance, some cross-reference entries); some are probably erroneous.
  I'm rather proud of one: 28:35 "samesake . . . . of a salmon = SMOLT = SMOLLETT—hence in the paragraph we get rody random. . . . . pickle. . . . . clinkers.
  Why,—we do not yet know.
  I'm rather proud too of having found Pascal's sister Jacqueline-Euphemia.[2] Wasn't it you who told me the following (no, maybe it's in Kenner[)]. Sts GODARD and MEDARDUS 185.21

Not St. Godard but Giraldus, bishop of Rome, was the brother of St Medard. However it was in 1132 (!) that the Benedictine Abbey there was built under his patronage and two altars dedicated to him.

I withdraw Defoe 30:11[3]
There are a host of conjectures that I don't feel sure enough to urge—for instance, I think "semicolo[u]red stainedglasses" 463.14 is Coelicola Stanislaus.

I still think every quotation from an author should be felt as the presence of the author in the book. That would swell your volume (think of the T. Moore page!) but I think it's within the design of the volume. But it lets us see the relative weight that they played in J. J.'s thought. For instance, opposite this page I've just quoted here is VERDI, G etc.
462: 26 froubadour
462:32 home to mourn mountains (Duet from Il Trovatore: "Home to our mountains")
465:21 "county de Loona" Comte de Luna—rôle in Il Trovatore.[4]

But except to write this letter I haven't looked at FW for weeks. I've conquered my addiction. Congratulate me.

But send my Census back to me after a while—I have another copy, but this is the one I annotate.

I hope you get your Guggenheim: And that you are able to finish the novel on "their" time as well as do the TRIAL for us.

> All cordial best to you all
> Ever
> Thornton

---

1. In support of Glasheen's application for a Guggenheim Fellowship to work on Joyce's use of the trial of Charles Stewart Parnell, Wilder wrote: "Mrs. Glasheen is a very alert, intelligent, inquiring, observant person, indeed. And a very lively and accomplished writer—as the preface to her *Census of Persons Mentioned in Finnegans Wake* shows—an exacting assignment if ever there was one. I was distressed to see her reference—at the close of the accompanying project—to her 'ironic frivolity.' The sheer force of her intellectual vivacity may strike *her* as frivolity, but what has most impressed me is the devoted and even dedicated industry she brings to whatever subject engages her. And I feel certain that she could digest the voluminous report of that famous trial and recreate it brilliantly" (copy of Wilder's letter from the archives of the John Simon Guggenheim Foundation). See TW to AG, 13 June 1956.

2. Jacqueline Pascal (1625–1661), who became a nun, was responsible for converting her brother Blaise Pascal (1623–1662), the French religious philosopher and mathematician. See Pascal in *Census II*.

3. A reference either given to Glasheen during a telephone conversation or an entry he made in the *Cenus*. The identification does not appear in *Census I* or *II*.

4. In Act IV Scene 2 of Verdi's opera *Il Trovatore* the gypsy Azucena is imprisoned with her supposed son, the Troubadour Manrico. As she gradually falls asleep, Azucena dreams of returning to the peace of her Biscayan mountains, "Ai nostri monti ritorneremo."

☐

To Adaline Glasheen, Farmington, Connecticut

[MS. ALS—HWS]

28 November 1956   [50 Deepwood Drive
             Hamden 14, Connecticut]

Do you hate prompt answers?
Dear Adaline =
  Sorry my jottings were so unclear or inaccurate.[1] Here are your itemized answers

p. 3   Bishops Aguilar—merely found them in the Catholic Cyclopaedia = they are of Santiago de Chile and Segorbe [i.e., Segovia], Spain; and a Deacon in Cortez's expedition. What makes them fitting is that the word means Eagle and gives us St John the Evangelist's emblem.

p. 8   Anne of England. Maybe I'm wrong but didn't the prince of Orange and Nassau (135:12) sue for the hand = Anne of Queen Anne?

p. 9   Before I took to counting lines from the top, I was also counting lines from the bottom with a minus sign before it—so Arabin 553:–2 should read 553:35

p. 9   Archer on this page, can't find it myself 34:8.

p. 10   Athlone = correction meekly accepted

p. 13   567:25 What's the difficulty = the colors of the Beaufort Hunt.

p. 24   Cassiopeia 618:12. The star swings around the pole, sometimes upside down, so the legend grew that SHE was tied to a chair.

Also that she was an acrobat!—which may give us 375:28 where she is up in the cirrhus clouds. (Personally I think she is somehow at the top of 59, too—her husband was Cepheus an Ethiopian black, whose star is up there near her.[)] (you remember my sense that the Pleiades and Hyades are on that page—the whole Heavens are talking about the scandal on earth)

p. 26 Duke of Clarence and "Collars and Coughs"—But it was you who told me that Collars and Coughs was the nickname of the Duke of Clarence.

p. 36 Eliphas = I must have made a slip of the pen = it is not on 569.9 but on 244.35

p. 36 Hilton Edwards is 569:–9 = 569:28 {one of the few friends or acquaintances of mine mentioned in the sublime work}[2]

p. 36 Duc d'Enghien = murder ordered by Napoleon I

p. 37 Europa is not 583:36 but 583:3–4; shows that all the planets and satellites mentioned on this page are also being treated as (mythical) persons.

p. 37 Pascal's sister Jacqueline = Euphemia in religion—nun at Port Royal—yes, a wonderful person.

p. 42 Prince Fortunatus = 618:6–7. So you won't buy just a prinche for-tunight-us?

p. 46 Ghost of Sheep's lane. All London agog. Dr. Sam Johnson's common-sense wouldn't give credence.

p. 58 Houghton = for 608:–7 read 608:29–30[.] Stanley Houghton wrote a play called Hindle Wakes {festival in town of Hindle, Lancs} produced by Miss Horniman.

p. 68 Kali = for 128:5, read 128:32

p. 69 Mireille Haven't got my Census here so can't clear this up. Must have been a slip of my pen in the page number.

FW 469:14 some confusion here. Maria Theresa (Teresiam) is on
    p. 538:1–2. Am I wrong: Louis XIV's wife. Joyce is packing in the names of cities here and gives us Teheran.

{Have lost the reference to Schott = it had something to do with the Schottenring in Vienna.}

p. 125 You can have Proust's Swan[n] for 410:3—but the swans on the Liffey (I've seen 'em—scores of 'em) are sufficient for 450:5 and 465:35, seems to me.

p. 128 Tereus—399:32 no . . . must have been some slip of the pen of mine. Sorry

p. 135 Tuskar Light—25:26 and 245:1 (Where it belongs to tusked animals but sets off a foliation of lighthouses.)—all I know

[is] that it's on the S. E. corner of Ireland and my notes say a light-ship.

p. 144 VAL POV DEV hog-latin plus Italian plus french forms Valere to be able; POUVOIR—to be able; DEBERE—DOVERE = Je ne DEVAIS PAS etc.={Sorry that I threw these at you as Latin = they are probably good LOW (late) Latin as they are anyway, they are fully supported by I WILL, I CAN and I OUGHT TO[}] {Will, Conn Otto} [51.12–13]

Thanks for Sweeny Todd.

- - - - - -
- - - - - -
- - - - - -

SOME NEW ONES
{I wish I knew the ballad or legend of Billy with the Bowl 542:35}[3]
135:15 [i.e., .13]

GOULD   American millionaire family 327:28

HARRINGTON, Timothy MP Lord Mayor of Dublin 1904, friend of J. J.'s father coalesced with Sir John Harrington 447:9

HERO   {of the Thelospont} add 135:17

IRENAEUS, St. Bishop of Lyons. 254:10
      {where is MELKARTH or MELCARTH, patron deity of Tyre?}

MONA   viâ Song "boat of my heart" coalesces with the Church: una vera . . . . apostolica p. 449:10

MISPRINT   p. 108 PIGGOTT first page reference should read {not 42:32} 43:32

PRIMROSE   Vicar of Wakefield. insecurely suggested prim rossies 327:16

- - - - - -
- - - - - -
- - - - - -

Your correspondence!! Three years ago I'd have been crazy-eager to read every word of your correspondence on these matters[.]

¶ No, don't you take off a minute from your novel to transcribe any lists for me = just once in a while a postcard with a particularly juicy one.

¶ I read over half of Humphry Clinker. I wish I'd like it more; but I will say that Winifred Jenkins' later letters are the nearest thing in all literature to the style of FW.[4]

My sister's better but my dental woes are worse—(not painful merely humiliating). So I'm in house-arrest which has its compensations.

Since you are absorbed in your novel (and its successor) and about to do the Parnell Trial, why not select from the more ardent of these FW enthusiast[s] (from the more ardent and sensible and capable) a worker to carry on the Second Edition?
By Adaline Glasheen and John Doe

        Ever cordially
        Thornton

1. Some of the references in this letter are to *Census I*. Others are not found there, suggesting, perhaps, a lost letter with itemized questions. Many of the identifications were incorporated into *Census II*.

2. A founder of the Gate Theatre, Dublin. See TW to AG, 2 June 1952, n. 3.

3. Louis Mink identifies this as "Johnny, I Hardly Knew Ye!" an Irish song, in *A Wake Newslitter*, N.S.10, 3 (June 1973), 38–39.

4. Tobias Smollett's last novel *The Expedition of Humphry Clinker* (1771) comprises the epistolary adventures of the Bramble family's expedition through England and Scotland. Winifred Jenkins, a family maid, eventually marries Humphry Clinker.

☐

To Adaline Glasheen, Farmington, Connecticut

[MS. AL—HWS]

[? November–December 1956–I]   [50 Deepwood Drive
                                       Hamden, Connecticut]

CENSUS:[1]
Suggestions for the attention of Mrs. A. Glasheen, the Sorcerer's Apprentice who unforseeingly released a FLOOD.
    {I'm now a little mixed up in the records of our correspondence; forgive it, if there are some repetitions here.}

DESCARTES, René {etc}
                        p. 269 note 2 René(e) goes back to the pack of cards {Descartes}
                        p. 304:[.27–]28 a reborn (René) of the cards {DES CARTES}
                        {and see four line[s] below: cogito ergo sum [FW: 304.31]}
                        ⇒ Probably: 358.3 RENATIONS. . . . . 9. motu propia . . . . . . 15. "I am."

ELLIS, Havelock	{psychologist in the abnormal} 294:8
WHARTON, Thomas	{English anatomist; name to Wharton's jelly} 12:23
POND, cosmetics	add 526:29
MIREILLE	{figure in Mistral epic and Gounod opera} Add 527:28 {My rillies}
LOVELACE	{of Clarissa Harlowe} 527:35
JUBAL-TUBAL	add 305:14, 19.
EUSEBIUS,	bishop of Nicomedia, an Arian, 409:36
VERDI	{remove interrogation point after reference 412:33. His opera "Force of Destiny" is alluded to 4 lines later} [FW: 413.1]
GROTIUS	415:25
LEWIS, Wyndham	415:29
CANTLEMAN	{of Lewis novel} add 165:24–25
MISPRINTS	CENSUS p. 30 under DAGDA and DAGDASSON both AEGNUS should read AENGUS
DAGDASSON	add 374:2 {D's dodges: Aengus was always playing disguise and disappearing tricks.}
DORCAS	associates of St. Paul 470:7
SILAS	470:7
ADD:	TRABEZOND, Lady Rhomba (for Trapezoid, allusion to Lady Rhomba, London Publisher)—after a portrait {perhaps of Lady Rhomba} in quasi-cubist style, by Wyndham Lewis 165:22

FOR CENSUS—continued
CHARMIAN⎱ Cleopatra's maids 528:23
IRIS   ⎰ 527:18 {charmeen}

MORE TENTATIVELY PROPOSED

FLAVIUS—FLAVIAN, Roman imperial dynasty; also tawny colored: 526:25

CLOVIS, King	526:27
CATULLUS	527:1 {I think ATTIUS or an ATTICUS 527:1 and TITUS 527:2 are persons in his poems}
EUPHEMIA	{Jacqueline Pascal} add (?): 528:24 or maybe it's a saint of the Greek church.
PALAMON	Pal of mine 462.18
PRISCIAN	{"break P's head" use bad grammar} 467:32
GOULD	wealthy American family 327:28
JOYCE, Giorgio	here identified with Kevin add 303:17
SKINNER	silk manufacturer his hosiery ? 414:32–33

Very tentative: I think GAUDYANNA 294:29 (so near Shakespeare) is GOETHE as an old Walpurgis witch—don't I see 295.1 the homunculus in Faust? daughter to a tanner to ATHENA? and was G's merchant father in hides?

quer homolocous   QUER German cross, diagonal
CARAMEL?   QUA'ARAN?
I give it up.

The principle to introduce persons into the CENSUS only when their names are actually mentioned results in such illogical situations: whole pages answering or making fun of Wyndham Lewis that your readers cannot be directed to, merely because his name is not specifically mentioned. AND the Shakespeare references. And De Valera!!

Add:

JONES,	{hypothetical Welshman, professor, in parody of Wyndham Lewis} 149:10 160:18
JOHNS	{a butcher} see JONES as Wyndham Lewis 172.5
SILAS, Uncle	{Le Fanu's novel, associated with coaches and *diligences*} Add 167:26–27
WALLAT'S	153.30 —The Wallace Collection—Paintings etc in London.

MELKARTH (deity of Tyre:Baal) 91:13
MENCIUS   159:33 [i.e., 159:34]
PICKETT   Civil war soldier 291:19

see page 3—How I run on

MISPRINT: Census p. 38 FESTY, Pegger 2.6—where dat? [i.e., 92.6]
Add: King Festy: Tykingfest (anagram) 86.13

Later = I can't stop! Help!

GUILBHE who provide[s] the ale that kept Irish Gods immortal 406.33
DEVOY, John: an Old Fenian, ang[l]o-american associate of De Valeria. {Tho' the whole phrase applies to De Valera, the Spaniard} [72.11]
Add Eckermann (Goethe's) 71.8
HUMBOLDT, Alex v. 588.16 [i.e., 588.33]
GAUTAMA "But da.["] etc 338.9–10 [i.e., .13–.14] and sea vast a pool is. also the adjectival form for SIVA {So in those paragraphs but BUTT and TAFF are Buddha's—line 7—every Bodhissatva—a faithful who has become a Buddha—carries a "world umbrella."[}]
CRIPPEN, the murderer 589.16
LELIA George Sand's heroine 340.22 {and I think a contemporary heroine Feydeau's FANNY is probably in 340.25 and 29.}
TAILTE, Queen for whom the Games were founded 344.17
SYNGE, John M. "Seeing" [344.12] I'm sure of this—the parody of Synge's style begins 344.36
ORIANA Queen Eliz—surely 339.14
BESSEMER (I think I gave you this one before—or was it another?) 359.4
PEER GYNT 365.6
COSGROVE, President. Isn't that he on p. 128.20.

Lately I've found [Eamon] De Valera everywhere. And his wife Jane O'Flanagan, his Gaelic teacher who gaelicized her name to SINÉAD Ni Fhlagan and his mother Catharine Coll of Bruree Co. Limerick {the Shamon who married into a family in Spain?}

But J. J. has had to be awfully careful, so most of it is buried very deep. But SHAWN is constantly De Valera. I'll prepare a list for you—and then *you* can be sued for libel.

1. Glasheen put a check mark next to many of these corrections/additions, and they found their way into "Out of My Census," published in *The Analyst*, No. XVII, April 1959, where Glasheen credits Wilder for the information.

☐

To Adaline Glasheen, Farmington, Connecticut

[MS. ALS—HWS]

[? November–December 1956–II]   [50 Deepwood Drive
                                  Hamden, Connecticut]

Dear Ma'am
 Of course, there are going to be lots of editions.
 I wouldn't [let] *Analyst* offer an addenda list.[1] Let them—if you wish—print as a rueful note to the editor, a list of page-misprints; I mean reference misprints. That'll alert some more to buy the book. And the correction of misprints is an obligation of scholarship. At the same time in the note, say that an enlarged edition of the book is to appear, thanking the many readers etc who have contributed toward its thoroughness etc. You might even add, to spice their expectation, a few of the juicy addenda (I love those Descartes ones, I add, licking my chops.)
 Yes, let Faber and Faber and all comers buy ever new copies of this one. It will only make more evident to the publisher that he can (and must) give you an enlarged edition when *you* are ready.

                                  Mizpah
                                  Thornton

1. This letter is a response to a lost letter. Almost immediately after the American publication of *Census I* in September 1956, Glasheen began receiving letters pointing out errata and suggesting addenda. Glasheen must have mentioned this correspondence to Wilder and queried him about how best to present this new material. Faber & Faber bought the rights to the *Census I* from Northwestern University Press on 20 February 1957, and Glasheen must have communicated to Peter du Sautoy of Faber & Faber suggesting the insertion of errata and addenda. On 3 May 1957, Richard Ellmann wrote to Glasheen suggesting that if an errata sheet were

published in the British edition it should be purchased and included in *The Analyst*. In their edition of *Census I*, Faber & Faber published Errata and Addenda on pages xxix–xxx. About the insertion of an errata and addenda page in the British edition of the *Census*, Glasheen wrote that it was dismal: "They made a little bitty silly looking list of about 15 additions and corrections and refused to let me choose the 15 additions I thought most vital. Instead, they were chosen by, I think, a Mr. [George] Painter—anyway, some Proust man at the British Museum, Dick Ellmann knows him—who I do not think knows a great deal about Finnegans Wake. I told them I thought they were making a mistake, but I did not press the point because I don't after all, greatly want to compile the complete list, but it should be compiled" (Archives, Northwestern University Library). Eventually, however, Glasheen did compile an interim list which was published in *The Analyst*, No. XVII, April 1959. *The Analyst*, a mimeographed journal, began publication in March 1953. It was edited by Robert Mayo and published by the English Department of Northwestern University, Evanston, Illinois. It ceased publication after No. XXVI, in September 1971. The first issues were about *The Cantos* of Ezra Pound. Beginning with No. IX, articles were also devoted to Joyce.

☐

To Adaline Glasheen, Farmington, Connecticut

[MS. ALS—HWS]

[?17–24 December 1956]   50 Deepwood Drive
Monday   Hamden 14, Connecticut

Dear Adaline:
    Many thanks.[1]
    I've "posted" them as we used to say in the Army.
    A few comments:
12:23   Wharton: yes, your Wharton is closer; but I believe both Wharton's are intended. Wharton's Folly = Wharton's Jelly. (I think Joyce mainly used the same dictionary I do, Webster's New International, 3210 pages; and I think he didn't only consult it, but *read* it.)
159.34   Mencius: rementious. I gave you the wrong line-reference.
72.11   Devoy. I gave you the wrong etc
588.33   Humboldt " " "   "   "   I must'a been drinking.

Every Giorgia[2] reference ([Peter] Sawyer etc) is it to Giorgio Joyce? Don't dare say. But Shaun fans out into De Valera—Stanislaus Jr—Wyndham Lewis (yes, a Welchman—hence a TAFF{Y}—so we are back at PROTEUS. HCE is Shaun also—and being SHAUN he carries these other avatars often when you least expect it.

Will it be 5 years before we can establish when SHEM becomes SHAUN and vice versa?. . . it's all there in Ox-sheep goat identifications and so many others.

93.35   Bloom, Molly—{yes, but also realize that it's Lever's novel Charles O'Malley.}[3] as your Census tells us.
534.10 Bottomley (your pen slipped—you said was on line 18.)

Oh, so you haven't read any Wyndham Lewis.[4]
Well, the edition of Vortex[5] (I've lost the FW reference to that [150.7]) harangues and capitalizes—165.15 166.16 and pours contempt on his readers 152.4ff

Wyndham Lewis is also the author of TARR[6] 232.36 [AG: 150.12]

Can't wait to read the pages on the Blake's Prophetic books in FW—to appear in one of the Joyce magazines.

I wish someone could tell me what design subtends Anna Livia Plurabelle.

Been reading Letters of Yeats. Not found much new.
Miss Horniman subsidized Abbey Theatre and many others.[7]
540.22 is chiefly policemen, but the Ibsen foliation that follows shows that she is alluded to.

Think this over. The figure of Ulick Dean in George Moore's Evelyn Innes is modelled on W. B. Yeats.[8] Now read 337.36. Is B. U. D. also an avatar of Yeats. OR ARE THEY EXCHANGING RÔLES during that passage!!! Hell, excuse me, hell. How did I ever get drawn into this thing.

>But Merry Xmas
>Ever
>(T. N.)

P. S. A friend on the faculty here is Swinburne-authority. You gave me a reference to a NOVEL by Swinburne and I've lost it.[9]

And isn't the Hounds of Spring buried somewhere?
P. S. II You realized that O. Wilde collected some poems under the title Eleutheria?
See 536.11 and 42.20

---

1. This letter is a response by Wilder to a lost letter by Glasheen commenting on Wilder's list of [? November–December 1956–I].

2. Wilder is playing with Georgia and Giorgio.

3. The Irish novelist Charles Lever (1806–1872); his novel *Charles O'Malley* was serialized in 1841.

4. This exchange between Wilder and Glasheen may be the origin of her research into Lewis's work. Eventually she published "Rough Notes on Joyce and Wyndham Lewis" in *A Wake Newslitter*, N. S., VIII, 5 (October 1971), 67–75.

5. Ezra Pound and Wyndham Lewis edited the two issues of the little magazine *Blast: Review of the Great English Vortex*, 1914 and 1915.

6. Lewis's novel *Tarr* was first published in 1918; a revised edition was published in 1928.

7. Wilder was reading *The Letters of W. B. Yeats*, edited by Allan Wade (New York: The Macmillan Co., 1955). Annie E. F. Horniman (1861–1937) was the daughter of F. J. Horniman, chairman of W. H. and J. Horniman and Co., Ltd., well-known tea merchants. In 1894 she financed a season of plays for the actress Florence Farr. She was a member of the Golden Dawn, and became a friend and admirer of Yeats's. When his eyesight worsened, she acted as his amanuensis. Miss Horniman bought and restored the Abbey Theatre, Dublin, and from 1904 until 1910 she gave the Irish National Theatre Society free use of the theatre and provided an annual subsidy. In 1907 she founded the Manchester Repertory Theatre (see Wade, 262–263).

8. George Moore's *Evelyn Innes* was published in 1898; its sequel, *Sister Teresa* was published in 1901. Evelyn Innes, the daughter of a church organist, falls under the spell of Ulick O'Deane, a composer and poet based on Yeats and George Russell.

9. Since Glasheen's letter is lost, it is impossible to know if she made a reference to a novel by Algernon Charles Swinburne (1837–1909). The "hounds of spring" may refer to a line spoken by the chorus of Calydonian maidens, "When the hounds of spring are on winter's traces," in Swinburne's verse drama *Atalanta in Cayldon*.

To Adaline Glasheen, Farmington, Connecticut

[MS. ALS—HWS]

[?24 December 1956] 50 Deepwood Drive
Monday Hamden 14, Connecticut

—in haste—I gotta tear down
to a dress rehearsal of Bob Sherwood's
last play[1]

Dear Adeline—[2]
    Lookit.
    I vowed never to open that book again.

x

    Everybody asks me about agents.
    I have no agent for "books." Only for plays.
    For children's books (*very*) remunerative I'm told,—esp. in the age group your's implies. There is nothing any more for twelve-on.)—that would be very special and very important. But why not try submitting first directly to the BEST HOUSE in that kind of thing. That'll save you paying 5%–10% forever after.
    Are you in good vein? I've written four one-act plays in 3 weeks. . . . a sudden burst.[3] And the FW weeks didn't stifle 'em at all. They're terrible. I mean they wrench your heart. Why will a merry chap like me go on such woeful journies?
    Couldn't Christmas be postponed somehow?
    Don't begin to dread my big envelopes. I'll stop and save'm up, if you like.

Cordially
Thornton

---

1. Robert Sherwood's (1896–1955) play *Small War on Murray Hill*, produced by the Playwrights' Company, opened at the Ethel Barrymore Theatre, New York, on 3 January 1957 and ran for twelve performances. The play, set during the American Revolution, was directed by Wilder's friend Garson Kanin.

2. Alternative spelling of her name.

3. While in Saratoga Springs, New York, in late November, Wilder began writing a series of "Four-Minute Plays for Four Persons." He planned to write two series of one-act plays for the arena stage illustrating "The Seven Deadly Sins" and "The Seven Ages of Man." In his *Journals* he wrote: "[T]he self-imposition of a schema always seen as an aid, even when as with Joyce one sees it becoming an appallingly exacting discipline" (257). The plays completed at this time illustrated the seven deadly sins: *The Drunken Sisters* (Gluttony, which became a satyr play to conclude *The Alcestiad*), *In Shakespeare and the Bible* (Wrath), *The Wreck on the Five-Twenty-Five* (Sloth), and *Bernice* (Pride). All are in volume I of *The Collected Short Plays of Thornton Wilder*.

1957

To Adaline Glasheen, Farmington, Connecticut

[MS. ALS—HWS]

?11 January 1957[1] [50 Deepwood Drive
Happy New Year Hamden 14, Connecticut]

Dear Adaline:
 I'm worried.
 But don't let me influence you.
 What I'm crazy to see is the Second and Enlarged Edition of the Census.
 If Faber and Faber is sufficiently interested to sell in England 2,000 copies (I assume they are merely buying the sheets of the first edition from Northwestern), I should think they could be persuaded to issue a whole new book. (After all they print scores of books of which they have less hope for 2,000 readers.)[2]
 Of course—the other way to look at it is that the 2,000 volumes of the First Edition in England will bring in tons of correspondence and a world of precious new additions.
 The more one looks at it, the more one sees that so far only the surface has been scratched. I enclose a copy of Kelleher's review of the Key in *Accent*.[3] Please return when you've finished. Had you ever seen it?
 So Caddy and Primas are Lawrence O'Toole and Henry II!!
 I'm not sure I agree with all this; but there must be a lot there.
 And I send of[f] a page of Devalera stuff—but I'm dejected and frustrated about it: that's only scratching the surface too. J. J. had to be very cautious—foxy about references to him.

And on the reverse of this page some more notes. (And again, some of them may be repeats of what I've written before—all my notes are in such disorder.[)]

> Anyway,
> lots of regards
> ever
> (T. N.)

[4]MISPRINTS:
    ✔ [5]SPINOZA reference 611.26 should read 611.36
    ✔ O'TOOLE, St. L. reference 435.5 (Gay O'Toole[)] should read 433.5

ADD
? SIRR, Major	181.2 (surr Chorles)
✔ THALIA, muse	569.29
? { CYMBELINE IMOGEN	162.27–28
✔ SPENGLER, historian	151.9
✔ TURRIDU (in Cavalleria Rusticana)	60.31
✔ MONA	61.1 ✔✔
? PROTEUS	107.8
✔ POLYGONUS, son of PROTEUS *	231.29 [i.e., .30] and ? 339.35

    ✔ Marduk 325.32
        At Marduk add see Bel
        At Bel add see Marduk
[Marduk reference circled and near the bottom of the page Wilder writes: I see you have this under MERODACH—I feel you should have cross references]

✔ BATESON, English biologist	286.24
✔ THEMIS, law, goddess	167.10
✔ Gaea, earth mother	257.5
✔ PAN ("is dead")	340.31
✔ CORE (Pasybone)	220.19

    [* at bottom of page] *Proteus had another son TELEGONUS (married IÔ—both sons killed by Hercules)—is Telegonus anywhere in FW?

⁶De Valera, Eamonn {i. e. Edward}, called "The Long Fellow." Born same year as J. J.; former schoolmates in mathematics, born in New York; collected funds for Fenian Movement in U.S.A; temp. president of League of Nations; allusions to him are associated in FW with Spanish language, oil (Spanish olive oil); berets and the basque country (his father was of Basque descent) and the Dominican order.

✔ 41.12–13	no fella . . . . . . longa. . . .
✔ {82.13	stlongafella . . . .
82.17	Ned {So one of the men in the encounter is identified with De Valera. . . . . the toller man 82.4 and probably El Don de Dunelli 84.36.[}]
✔ 257.8	. . . feller longa . . . again assoc. with pidgin English.
✔ 287.1	D. V
✔ 287.4	Deva
✔ 287.27	demun {EAMONN} Joyce removed in proof a ANAN in line 31 {"pupal anan souaves"}. The passage shows De Valera teaching young revolutionaries. Footnote 3: Canorian: for Canary Islands? Spish from the Doctor. . . Spanish. Over the page is
✔ 288.5	ned . . . 288.8. . . . . math. . . . . . long. . . segund (Spanish) and footnote about the money he collecd [i.e., collected] 288.1 a dillon a dollar {who was this DILLON?. . and footnote 1 an ounceworth of onions FENIANS}. The page is about how DeValera-St. Patrick drove celtic-pagan joy out of Ireland . . . and note 7 Spanish MUCHACHAS = girls.}
✔ 346.4 and 5	H(a)b(a)neros . . . . Ibrahim (via Iberia. . . bella suora (spanish). . . devilances. . . . {The *Alibey* here may help us with all the *albys* etc = charging DeValera with parliamentary evasions.[}]
✔ 347.26	feller. . . longa villa. . . {again pidgin English.[}]
X 358.23–24	. . . deliveried. . . {That is Arthur Griffith 358.21 [i.e., .22]—and is that Tallulah Bankhead?}
✔ 422.28	thelemontary {via Rabelais Thélème} but De Valera is all over this page; and I'd like to see thee—AEMONN—tary here, combined with long 13; and *long* 28 and the association of De Valera with the Dominicans 29, and the Spanish *pueblos* 30.
X 507.15	basque of his beret

x

281.footnote 1	The reference is to Numancia in Spain—where our folk's father came from—that VAL{era} over giddy rex.

234.12   EAMONN is in almonder. (Almoner has become Spanish almond.) We have been in the Spanish p 234.1–5. Shem-Glugg has been Don Quixote: now Shaun-Chuff is Sancho Panza, the practical non-spiritual. He wears the colors of De Valera's Irish Free State lines 9 and 10: green, white and yellow: and he presides over Eucharist Congresses, 20.

1. Wilder's question mark.
2. Faber & Faber of London entered into an agreement with Northwestern University Press on 20 February 1957.
3. John V. Kelleher, "Joyce Digested," a review of *A Skeleton Key to 'Finnegans Wake'*, by Campbell and Robinson in *Accent: A Quarterly of New Literature*, V, 3 (Spring 1945), 181–186. Kelleher writes that *A Skeleton Key* is "[A] hard book to make up one's mind about." He is critical of the authors' "chewed-up version of Joyce's text" (181). "Even a *Reader's Digest* editor [Robinson] ought to know, or be able at least to learn, that Joyce is no nickel-a-word magazine stuffer, and that his labor of eighteen years in freighting language with multiple burden is exactly what can be elucidated, if by any re-expression, only by extended paraphrase. In attempting to condense his text, all they have been able to do is to cut it up into scraps and paste some of the scraps together again in a way that may or may not make sense but never makes Joyce's sense" (181). In addition to faulting the authors' compression of Joyce's text, Kelleher finds many footnotes unreliable, and he cites particularly one relating to Caddy and Primas (185–186).
4. "MISPRINTS" begins on the verso of the letter.
5. The checks, question marks, and Xs are Glasheen's.
6. "De Valera, Eamonn" begins a new page.

□

To Adaline Glasheen, Farmington, Connecticut
[MS. ALS—HWS]

circa Jan 17 1957   50 Deepwood Drive
snowing   Hamden 14, Connecticut

Dear Adaline—
    For all much thanks.

Does Atherton want more for his list? Is it a thesis of some kind.¹
If so—in this section.
Sure

ELIOT, T. S.	65.32–3 is a parody of Eliot's (of Faber and Faber) parody of popular songs in Sweeney Agonistes.
GOETHE	Reinecke Fuchs 480.23
KRYLOU	Fables 159.14
KIERKEGAARD, S.	Enten eller (Danish for "Either/Or") 281.33 [i.e., .27]

x

Went to a dinner for the Bollingen Prize judges. All the American literati are getting Joyce mad. Cleanth Brooks contemplating a book about Ulysses; Robert Lowell agog about anything I could tell him; ditto Dudley Fitts.

x

Very vivacious letter from Kenner. His book on J. J. is very good. Relieved to see that I am not damned among the Gotham Book Mart Joycians but I *am* one of them.² I am sending you a volume of our forthcoming periodical³—did I ever thank you for the Census you sent me? (I wouldn't have loaned it to you, if I hadn't had *another*!)—

x

You sure do allude to money with a world of deprecation and self-minimazation. Ma'am, among the subjects for general conversation, I think that of money is downright bracing. My attention never flags when money, weather, food, and the bringing [up] of children are discussed (when talk turns on psychic research, international affairs, and 'what will become of us,' I wish I were at home with a good book.)

x

Discouragement about a 'work in progress' should be expected by you. It normally arrives when one is about a third through. And what else could one expect? The hovering idea and image—the radiant promises of the imagination—must be brought down to earth and made concrete. Don't be unkind and impatient with yourself; wait a little and you will receive a 'second wind' and will be able to resume it with new afflatus.

x

Ever cordially
(T. N.)

1. There are no extant letters from Atherton to Glasheen dated between 1956 and 1957. Atherton had probably requested information for his *The Books at the Wake*.
2. Glasheen had sent Wilder Hugh Kenner's letter to her of 2 January 1957 and had asked, at the top, for him to return it to her. In his letter he advised her on the sale of the *Census* to Faber & Faber. Of Joyceans he wrote: "I have steadfastly refused to have ANYthing to do with Joyceans: you and John Slocum are the exceptions. He attracts the nastiest disciples. The J. review is so far as I can see just the JJ Society in a new guise: the Levin-Ellman[n]-Colum-Gotham Book Mart axis" (HWS).
3. Wilder's, "Joyce and the Modern Novel," appeared in *A Joyce Miscellany*, edited by Marvin Magalaner. See Wilder Bibliography.

□

To Adaline Glasheen, Farmington, Connecticut

[MS. ALS—HWS]

[12 February 1957] [Winter Park, Florida][1]
c. Feb. 12
a-roaming to cure my deafness

Dear Adaline:
Many thanks for [Fred] Higginson's notes[.][2]
Much splashing in the water, but oh where are the first signs that someone's found one of the 1,000 basic patterns. There's of course a reason why ALP's presents are in that order (or any of the words and sentences and paragraphs in that order) and such designs we've not yet found.

x

I suppose I'm the party contemned for saying we've only scratched the surface. We all go through alternations of vain glory when we think we're "almost there." What more are these notes of his but just such scratching?
Take Pender for example. It must be another Pender. Twice associated with deltoïd [210.8–.9].
And what has he told us of the Dunnes [213.35] etc?

x

I've read the proofs of [Marvin] Magalaner's first publication as a review—I forgot its name, tho' I'm on the "Board." [margin: A JOYCE

MISCELLANY] Saw sadly that there's not much substance in it. Do better next time.[3] I begged them to get another Ulysses chapter analysis from [A. M.] Klein (which would make the volume classic and indispensable) but Klein's been sick. I wish Klein would move over to FW. . . he'd sweep all before him.

I wish the Guggenheim nominees would come out. I've got 4 or 5 recomendees this season but you're my star protegée.

a week later.

This heat—but this humidity.
My hearing is ever worse, but I don't care.
Starting slowly north next Saturday[.]
I must hurry to get this off—already a week delayed—

> All cordial best
> as ever
> (T. N.)

Have read Le Fanu's Uncle Silas (twice in FW) in hope that an episode there is reflected in FW. No signs. Will send it to you for your library. It begins splendidly but loses its grip. Splendid preface by Eliz Bowen[.][4]

---

1. Wilder started driving to Florida on 30 January.

2. It is unclear which notes by Fred Higginson Glasheen sent Wilder. Higginson was working on the drafts of the "Anna Livia Plurabelle" chapter of *Finnegans Wake* (I. viii. 196–216). See his *Anna Livia Plurabelle: The Making of a Chapter* (Minneapolis: University of Minnesota Press, 1960). Another set of notes from Higginson is referred to in AG to TW, 23 February 1957.

3. *A James Joyce Miscellany*, edited by Marvin Magalaner, was published under the sponsorship of the James Joyce Society of New York. The members of the publication committee were Herbert Cahoon, Padraic Colum, Leon Edel, chairman, Malcolm Merritt, Frances Steloff, William York Tindall, and *ex-officio*, Mary Colum, Maria Jolas, and James Johnson Sweeney. In addition to Wilder's essay, "Joyce and the Modern Novel," the miscellany had contributions from: Marvin Magalaner, Padraic Colum, Julian B. Kaye, Alfred Kerr, Leon Edel, Georges Markow Totévy, Maria Jolas, and a letter from J. B. Yeats to John Quinn and "Greetings to the James Joyce Society" by Margaret Anderson.

4. Joseph Sheridan Le Fanu, *Uncle Silas; a tale of Bartram-Haugh*, with an introduction by Elizabeth Bowen (London: The Cresset Press, 1946; New York: Chanticleer Press, 1947).

To Thornton Wilder, Hamden, Connecticut

[MS. TL—YCAL]

23 February 1957 [22 Carrington Lane
Farmington, Connecticut]

Dear Thornton,

We have only scratched the surface as I told [Fred] Higginson. But at times I wonder if FW isn't meant to be all surface? The early drafts are so very shadowy, so very ugly as though they were meant for nothing but layers of verbal enameling. If this is true—and it ain't been proved—a certain sort of critic will say he told you so—nothing there, just nothing but what's the ceiling of the Sistine Chapel but surface? No, I don't like Michelangelo. What's a Goya but surface. Why shouldn't FW be just words with nothing put behind them by Joyce, but whatever behind them the reader finds there. FW was meant to be a book in which the reader participated. I'm clear on that.

Mr. Higginson is not great on FW, but he is the best of those who have written me since the Census has come out. You can't imagine—or maybe you can—how utterly inane most of the suggestions sent me have been. Two ladies have written me such perfectly awful suggestions that I can't bring myself to write down their names. Mr. H. has, however, found a Magrath who was martyred in Clonmel in 1650 and who is known in the Rosary as Father Michael. I wrote asking for more details since I've always had an idea that Magrath and Fr. M. were a pair like Kevin and Jerry.[1]

Jim Atherton has I think solved all the Albert Nyanza business. John Hanning Speke says in Journal of the Discovery of the Source of the Nile "I saw that old father Nile without any doubt rises in the Victoria Nyanza, and as I had foretold, that lake is the great source of the holy river which cradled the first expounder of our religious beliefs."[2] Well, Jim doesn't say so, but I think that the O answer that always accompanies the Nyanza passages is Speke because to speak is to O answer.

I do hope the Guggenheim people have the sterling sense to elect me, but I've never really counted on it. I would, of course, rather succeed.

I have heard very distantly that the Census has been reviewed in the TLS,³ but no one seems to know anything about it and the friend who wrote from Amsterdam congratulating me is something given to fantasy.

I have been writing on my novel (which after sufficient prodding Faber and Faber said could they see when it was finished which it never will be and I begin writing it over in the third person tomorrow) so I haven't had many thoughts about FW. Except 211.35. In Heartbreak House isn't there a Hector Hushaby and a young girl named Ellie?⁴ Also have I told you about the source of "He's the man to rhyme the rann" [44.16]? It's in a piece of Lover's called "Ballads and Ballad-Singers"⁵ I'd better quote it:

"THE RHYME FOR THE RAM"

. . . which rhyme is declared to be a mystery, far beyond the poet's comprehension, hitherto undiscovered, and to be classed only with the philosopher's stone, or such arcana of nature. . . (The given rhyme doesn't pertain to FW. but I'll give it)

> No one could discover
> From Calais to Dover
> The house of Hanover and the town Dunleer.
> Nor they who belie us
> And freedom deny us,
> Ould Mr. M—'s could never come near;
> For no Methodist preacher
> Nor nate linen blacher,
> The keenest of teachers, nor the wisdom of man
> Nor Joanna Southcoat [AG: sic]
> Nor Fitgarild the pote (poet)
> Nor iver yit wrote a fit rhyme for the Ram.

In my spare time I am trying to translate into modern English the Flyting of Dunbar and Kennedy.⁶ It is a lovely lot of scurrility, and I do it very badly, but I am currently in love with medieval poetry.

I hope you are well. I am sorry about your hearing. I hope your motor trip is pleasant. Where do you motor to?

I should love to have Uncle Silas.⁷ But didn't I see that you had written something on Joyce. What is it?⁸

    Yours
    Adaline

1. The information in this paragraph comes from Higginson's letter of 18 February 1957 (HWS) which included "Two Letters from Dame Anna Earwicker" (615.12–619.19): "the first draft and a version made by combining the first two pages of the second draft and the remainder of the third" and Higginson's notes on his transcriptions.

2. See Atherton, *The Books at the Wake*, 171, 281. The Victoria Nyanza and Albert Nyanza lakes are in east central Africa; John Hanning Speke, the British explorer, was the first European to sight Lake Victoria in 1858 while on an expedition to investigate the source of the Nile River.

3. An unsigned review appeared in the (London) *Times Literary Supplement* on 1 February 1957, 64. Titled "A Portrait in Two Mirrors," the review discussed the Northwestern printing of the *Census*, Theodore Spencer's edition of *Stephen Hero*, and a reprint of *A Portrait of the Artist as a Young Man*. The reviewer praised Glasheen for the "clever idea of compiling an index of the characters and hundreds of people mentioned in *Finnegans Wake* with biographical notes on them all, real and fictitious alike." The reviewer went on to praise her Preface as "one of the few sane things that have been written about an eminently sane book."

4. In George Bernard Shaw's *Heartbreak House: A Fantasia in the Russian Manner on English Themes* there is an Ellie Dunn and a Hector Hushaby.

5. Samuel Lover (1797–1868) cites this ballad as an example of the "bard" soaring to "sublime flights" to find a rhyme. See "National Minstrelsy: Ballads and Ballad-Singers," in *The Selected Writings of Samuel Lover in Ten Volumes*, Vol. III, pt. 1 "Legends and Stories" ([Dublin]: P. F. Collier, n. d.), 189.

6. "The Flyting of Dunbar and Kennedie," by William Dunbar (?1460–?1520), maybe the earliest surviving example of 'flyting'—a form of combative alliterative verse popular in Scotland in the fifteenth and sixteenth centuries. Dunbar's target is the poet Walter Kennedy (?1460–?1508).

7. An 1864 novel by Joseph Sheridan Le Fanu.

8. Wilder's "Joyce and the Modern Novel" in *A James Joyce Miscellany*. See TW to AG, 12 February 1957, n. 3.

To Thornton Wilder, Hamden, Connecticut
[MS. TLS—YCAL]

16 March 1957   [22 Carrington Lane
                                  Farmington, Connecticut]

Dear Thornton,

Thank you so much for the books?[1] How are your ears and teeth? Did you go on your motor trip? I liked your piece in the J[oyce]. Miscellany.[2] It's deep and it's living. May I add, it makes the rest of the book look pretty thin and inane.

31.16 I am reading Morley's Life of Gladstone.[3] Gladstone was "short fingered." He shot a finger off by accident when he was fooling with a gun. He wore a black guard over the stump. Also the papers called him Wm. the Conqueror. Did you know he was a devoted friend of Lilly Langtry?[4]

I have been rereading Macdonald's Daily News Diary of the Parnell Commission?[5] Have you ever seen it? In a way, it's one of The sources of FW, though J. uses it specifically only in I, iv and the Yawn section[6], but it so perfectly illustrates the nightmare from which Stephen was trying to awake.[7]

I don't know any Joyce news, I think. The Analyst is projecting a work on section ii by somebody at Northwestern named Staples[8] and by Kelleher, also John Thompson is to amplify the notes he did for Brinnen's [i.e., Brinnin] Modern Poetry on the end of ALP and the last soliloquy.[9] I am fairly confident nothing much will come of this. I am quite discouraged by the people who now work on FW. That is a form of egoism is it not?

Penalties of authorship I am sure you are familiar with. I had one. A letter from a Dubliner named Patrick Byrne, saying would I please send him a free copy of the Census.[10] The answer unkindly is no, but there is a subtle compliment in being asked for a free copy, yes indeed.

I have also been rereading Mrs. Parnell's life of Parnell.[11] Have you read it? It is oh alas but full of interest to the reflective mind. It is virtually impossible to admire a man who addressed a woman as "Queenie" and signed himself "Your King" but after all, we do not have the letters of Antony to Cleopatra, though thanks to you, we have some of her letters.[12] Parnell never read any book except Alice in Wonderland which he said was "curious." Gladstone read everything. Who is more admirable the man who read nothing like Parnell, or the man who admired Wordsworth's late poems like Gladstone?[13]

The story of Parnell is like the source, the raw stuff of a Shakespearean play. I am pretty fascinated. I hope I get my Guggenheim.

This is a pretty thin sort of letter. Forgive that.

        Again thanks
        Yrs
        AG

1. See TW to AG, 12 February 1957.
2. Wilder's "Joyce and the Modern Novel." See TW to AG, 12 February 1957, n. 3.
3. John Morley, *The Life of William Ewart Gladstone* (1904; rpt. 3 volumes in 1, New York: The Macmillan Co., 1921), 185.
4. Mrs. Lillie Langtry (née Le Breton, 1853–1929), the actress/courtesan, met Gladstone at the studio of the painter Sir John Everett Millais. See Langtry's *The Days I Knew* (1925; rpt., New York: AMS Press, 1982), 175–177.
5. Glasheen first discusses the Parnell Commission in her letter of 6 June 1951.
6. In *Census I* Glasheen titles III. iii (474–554) as "Yawn"; in *Census II* and *III* it is titled "Third Watch of Shaun."
7. *Ulysses*: "—History, Stephen said, is a nightmare from which I am trying to awake" (1961, 34).
8. Hugh Staples, then a professor of English at Northwestern University, did not publish an article in *The Analyst*. He did, however, publish articles about Joyce in *A Wake Newslitter* and the *James Joyce Quarterly*. See Deming, *Bibliography of James Joyce Studies*; see also "Thirty-Year Index: *James Joyce Quarterly*, Volumes 1–30," *James Joyce Quarterly*, 32, 2 (Winter 1995). One letter from Staples to Glasheen is in HWS; two letters from Glasheen to Staples are in the Hugh B. Staples Collection, Beeghly Library, Ohio Wesleyan University, Delaware, Ohio.
9. *The Analyst*, XII (April 1957), contains: "Soft Morning, City!: A Paraphrase of the End of *Finnegans Wake*" by John Hinsdale Thompson ([1]-8), and "Notes on *Finnegans Wake*" by John Kelleher (9–15). Kelleher's article continues his "Notes on *Finnegans Wake* and *Ulysses*," in *The Analyst*, X (March 1956). Thompson's

article was a paraphrase of pages 619–628 of *Finnegans Wake* and supplements the notes he prepared for *Modern Poetry: British and American*, ed. Kimon Friar and John Malcolm Brinnin (New York: Appleton-Century Crofts, Inc., 1951), 505–519.

10. The letter is not in HWS.

11. Katharine O'Shea (Mrs. Charles Stewart Parnell), *Charles Stewart Parnell: His Love Story and Political Life* (London: Cassell & Co., 1914; New York: George H. Doran, Co., 1914).

12. Cleopatra's letters in Wilder's epistolary novel *The Ides of March* (1948).

13. "To the great veteran poet of the time [William Wordsworth] Mr. Gladstone's fidelity was unchanging, even down to compositions that the ordinary Wordsworthian gives up" (Morley, n. 3 above, 220).

□

To Adaline Glasheen, Farmington, Connecticut

[MS. ALS—HWS]

[postmark: 4 April 1957]   Newport R[hode]. I[sland].

Dear Adaline =
    This is to say goodbye.
    I sail for Europe next Tuesday.¹
    How restless I've been—always trying to get away from Hamden and those plagued phone-calls about thissa and thatta from N.Y. Or flying to Florida to cure my deafness. (Yes, I cured it. *All* blessings are mixed.)
    I may be back for two months in the summer.
    I'm not taking my FW to Europe—but I'm seeing Samuel Beckett and I'm going to try and dig some hints out of him.²
    The J. J. dinner programme sent me by Eliz. Sprigge the less than satisfactory biographer of G[ertrude]. Stein.³
    The letter by an Irish actor who gets few jobs—and who sent me discs of Joyce readings.⁴
    My address until about June 10 (though I shall actually be mostly in Switzerland) will be American Exp. Co 11 rue Scribe Paris.
    Every now and then write me and tell me how things are going: family and novel and F. W. And slip in one or two newly discovered nuggets "To comfort my sad heart."

{vide The Toys by Coventry Patmore}[5]
The biggest present anybody could make me would be to reveal the structural patterns under the ALP chapter.

        adieu
        your old friend
        Thornton (60 this month!)

1. Wilder sailed on the *Liberte* on 9 April and arrived in Le Havre on 15 April. He remained in Europe until 15 July when he returned to New York. During this trip, Wilder worked on revisions to *The Alcestiad*, which had its German language premiere, translated by Herberth Herlitschka and directed by Leopold Lindtberg, in the Schauspielhaus, Zurich, on 27 June. He also worked on a series of one act plays that he had begun in November 1956 in Saratoga Springs, New York. See *Journals*, particularly: 257–263, 265–266, 270–272.

2. Beckett (1906–1989) met Joyce in October 1928 in Paris. For nearly two years, 1928–1930, he acted as secretary-assistant to Joyce which included taking dictation for *Work in Progress* (*Finnegans Wake*). See Beckett's "Dante. . . Bruno. Vico. . Joyce" in *Our Exagmination*.

3. A dinner of the James Joyce Society on 2 February 1957 celebrating the publication of *A Joyce Miscellany* and commemorating the tenth anniversary of the Society was held at the Kensington Restaurant in New York. A copy of the program is in Glasheen's papers at HWS. Elizabeth Sprigge's *Gertrude Stein: Her Life and Work* (New York: Harper & Brothers, 1957) was criticized by Alice Toklas and by many of Stein's friends. See Edward Burns, ed., *Staying on Alone: Letters of Alice B. Toklas* (New York: Liveright, 1973), 314, 318, 337, 340, 352. Sprigge's notebook, kept while researching her biography, includes reports on her conversations with Wilder in New Haven and is in YCAL.

4. The individual has not been identified.

5. A poem by Coventry Patmore (1823–1896) about his eldest son Milnes first published in *The Unknown Eros* (1878).

To Adaline Glasheen, Farmington, Connecticut
[MS. APCS—HWS]

[Postcard: Am Spazzacalderas (Albigna)]

23 May [1957]　　　　　　　　　　St Moritz Switzerland
　　　　　　　　　　　　　　　　　(as from Americ[an] Exp. Co
　　　　　　　　　　　　　　　　　11 rue Scribe Paris)

Dear Adaline:

I had heard that Kitty O'S[hea] was charged with selling Parnell but assumed it was a smear of those furious contentious times.[1] I'd hate to believe it. Before such problems as the annals of FW 13–14 I get my recurring longing: to fall asleep for 20 years and then wake up and find out "what has been settled" during my slumber. Have been reading Patricia Hutchins's J. J.'s World (a successor to J. J.'s Dublin); how few biographies ask the right questions to say nothing of answering them.[2]

Isabel was with me at a première in Brussels of *La Marieuse*[3] (get it?) then she went off to Amsterdam etc for the first time and was mad about it, as I was. Soon we have another in Zurich. She's going off in the meantime to Corsica with Mrs Robert Ardrey (ARDRHI = High King in FW) [261.L3].[4] I'm fine and working well. We're still having superb snow falls up here.

You don't mention your novel. Alas, apparently only one of my Guggenheim protégés got one—Marcia Nardi the poet.[5] I'm glad for her because she's been in actual destitution for years, but I grieve for my others. Ask your husband to forgive me for your name on the address![6] My mind was wandering.

　　　　　　　Lots of best to you both
　　　　　　　Ever
　　　　　　　Thornton

1. In her letter of 16 March 1957, Glasheen wrote: "I have been reading Mrs. Parnell's life of Parnell." Wilder is either responding to that letter or to a lost letter. Charles Stewart Parnell's career was destroyed when he was named co-respondent in the O'Shea divorce proceedings which began in December 1889. Parnell married Katharine O'Shea in June 1891 and died the following October.

2. *James Joyce's World* (London: Methuen, 1957); *James Joyce's Dublin* (London: Grey Walls Press, 1950). The first full scale biography of Joyce did not appear until Richard Ellmann's *James Joyce* in 1959.
3. Wilder's *The Matchmaker*.
4. Irish for "high king." Helen Johnson Ardrey was the first wife of the playwright and anthropologist Robert Ardrey (1908–1980). Robert Ardrey had been a member of Wilder's creative writing class at the University of Chicago in 1930 and remained a protégé and friend. The Ardreys' marriage was dissolved in 1960, and he married the South African actress Berdine Gruewald.
5. Wilder first met Marcia Nardi (1901–1990) at the MacDowell Colony. In a letter to William Carlos Williams (2 January 1956), Nardi wrote: "Thornton Wilder asked to look at my work a couple of years ago when I was at the MacDowell Colony and became so enthusiastic about it that he personally gave a reading of a group of my poems on the same occasion when he read aloud an act from one of his own plays in Peterborough." See *The Last Word: Letters Between Marcia Nardi and William Carlos Williams*, ed. Elizabeth Murrie O'Neil (Iowa City: University of Iowa Press, 1994), 226. Their letters are in YCAL.
6. Wilder customarily addressed his letters to Mrs. Francis Glasheen; on this card he wrote Mrs. Adaline Glasheen.

☐

To Thornton Wilder, Hamden, Connecticut[1]
[MS. ALS—YCAL]

11 August 1957 [22 Carrington Road
Farmington, Connecticut]

Dear Thornton,

How are you? Where are you? Are you Joycing? Pursuit of the Master leads to strange occasions. An evening with Edmund Epstein and his mamma whom I liked.[2] Lunch today with Mrs. Helen Joyce whom I suppose you know from the J[oyce]. Society.[3] It was like a [Henry] James short story of the middle period.

The place the garden of her house in Cornwall Hollow. We all having eaten her fine continental cooking and drunk her splendid wine. Cars slashing by on the highway. Dogs, cats and parakeets in profusion. Mrs. J—ravaged by her ten years of shock treatments but still alive and female and baffled. My husband and I. A young man named Kevin

Sullivan who teaches at Columbia & is writing a biography of Joyce with Mrs. J.[4] He a non-descript young man, physically indeterminate, assuming a Don Giovanni he has not. Conversation on a hot afternoon.

Mrs. J—I hate these far-fetched interpretations of *Finnegans Wake*. I worked with Joyce on *Anna Livia* and *Tales of Shem and Shaun*.

Mrs. G.—How interesting for you. Why do you think Joyce had the washer women turn into a tree and a stone?

Mrs. J—I think Mr. Joyce took the women from Nora who was a sharp gossip, very clever. She didn't like me because I was almost as old as she was and had a romance with her son before I was divorced from my first husband.[5] I was in some sense Anna Livia or so Mr. Joyce told me. He was very fond of me. They become a tree and a stone because they gossip about Anna Livia—a punishment. Mr. Joyce liked me because I could read FW without ever trying to make sense of it.

Sullivan—(mixing beer and sherry) He liked you because you were a damn handsome woman, ma dear.

Mrs. J—That of course. I once had a cerise velvet housecoat by la Schaperelli with a long dark blue fish tail down the back.[6] I think he could see the color. Joyce adored that housecoat and I still have it somewhere. But things disappear. My husband took everything Mr. Joyce gave me and sold it. Everything is under glass at some damn library even the little gold FW from Cartier that I gave Mr. Joyce and was given back by him.[7] I have one single letter about the marriage of Mr. Joyce and Nora (he handled that so cleverly) and Kevin took it years ago to have it photostated. My housecoat—Maria Jolas[8] spilled wine all over it—I loathe her, great hulk of a thing. Oh in our book we're really going after Maria, aren't we, Kevin?

Sullivan—We're going after a lot of people. These people—bloody bloody fools who think they can write on Joyce when Irish Catholicism isn't the very air they breath.

Mr. Glasheen—Oh are you Irish?

Sullivan—I was born in Brooklyn but the taint is in my blood and bones. My grandfather came from—

Mr. Glasheen—My father came from—

Sullivan—Joyce can have no meaning outside Irish Catholicism. Aquinas.

Mr. Glasheen—If Joyce can be grasped only by Irish Catholics, he's a small man.

Sullivan—When I visited Clongowes two years ago, the rector—

Mrs. Glasheen—Oh what did you find at Clongowes?

Sullivan—Actually they've destroyed the records at Clongowes. But at Belvedere I found Joyce had served in the sodality—a fact which he suppresses.[9]

Mrs. J—Oh he was Machiavellian. He used to sit listening to Nora & Lucia & me gossiping. Always a hand over his mouth to hide his smile. He loved misleading people. Machiavellian. Oh I know he was a very learned man but FW is about very simple things. You know that bit about the toy fair at the end [628.9]. My husband told me about that. He hated Christmas because when he was 4 or 5 he wanted a rocking horse for Christmas and Mr. Joyce had no money. He took his son to the toy fair in Zurich and my husband thought it meant he would get the horse but there was no money. He hated Christmas.

Sullivan—The vital point about Joyce is that he was not a Puritan.

Mrs. G.—He was the last humanist. {Follows a wrangle about what I mean by last}

Sullivan—Joyce was too great a snob to be a humanist. All Catholics are spiritual snobs. Irish Catholics have a sense of doom in whose shadow they laugh and whose Joyce's is the ironic laughter of doom. Pardon my rhetoric. It is an affectation I permit myself.

Mrs J—But Mr. Joyce is hopeful. Things go on and on, round and round.

Sullivan—Joyce pluralizes doom—those bloody thunderclaps. {imitates thunder} Crash crash. Laughter and doom.

Mrs J—Oh he was prophetic. Do you call it extrasensory perception. But he was a hopeful man[.]

Mrs. Glasheen & Mr. Sullivan play at knowing more about Joyce than the other one does.

Can Joyce be right in saying Shem is St. Patrick?

Yrs
Adaline

---

1. Wilder sailed from Europe on 4 July. Until 15 August, when he again sailed for Europe, he stayed at the Century Club, New York. This letter was forwarded to Wilder's attorney in New Haven and may not have reached him until after he had sailed.

2. Epstein was the founding editor of the *James Joyce Review*. Three numbers were published between 1957 and 1959.

3. Helen Kastor Fleischman married Joyce's son George (Giorgio) on 10 December 1930. Their only child, Stephen James Joyce, was born on 15 February 1932. The Joyces separated in 1939 in part because of her mental problems. In May 1940, she returned to the United States under the care of her brother Robert Kastor. The Joyces were divorced in 1954. The Glasheens remained friendly with Helen Joyce until her death in January 1963. See Appendices IX and X.

4. The biography was not written, but Sullivan did publish *Joyce Among the Jesuits* (New York: Columbia University Press, 1958). In the Acknowledgments he writes: "In this country I am indebted to Mrs. Helen Joyce, the daughter-in-law of James Joyce, whose memory of him in his role as husband, father, and grandfather has often confirmed *mutatis mutandis* my own impression of a much earlier Joyce" (247–248).

5. Helen Joyce was ten years older than George.

6. Elsa Schiaparelli, the fashion designer.

7. Many of Mrs. Joyce's possessions are in the Joyce Collection of the State University of New York at Buffalo.

8. Maria Jolas (1893–1987), the American born writer and translator who with her husband Eugene Jolas and Elliot Paul founded *transition* in 1927. She was a devoted friend to the Joyces and was particularly helpful when they left Paris in December 1939 for the village of Saint-Gérand-le-Puy where they remained until they moved to Switzerland in December 1940.

9. In the Appendix to his book ([231]–240), Sullivan publishes documents from the period when Joyce was a student at Clongowes Wood College (1888–1891) and Belvedere College (1893–1898).

To Adaline Glasheen, Farmington, Connecticut
[MS. ALS—HWS]

10 October 1957   Montecatini—Italy

Dear Adaline =
    Acct of your lunch with H[elen]. Joyce incomparable and yet it filled me with rage—that the river-like traditio has now to float so much nonsense on it. My teeth grind.
    Joyce and Lope have had to retreat to a great distance. . . . I've had to work, and hard. Gave in Frankfurt the last speech I'll ever make, and from the moment it ended I was 10 years younger.[1]
    I'm here in this well-known spa because the Garson Kanins are here taking the cure.[2] None of that mud-slapping for me. Laus Deo, I feel fine. We're an hour's drive from 7 of the most beautiful sites in the world but there's nothing here but waiters and waiters and shrieking Vespas in the street and the beautiful lines of Tuscan hills in the distance.
    If I let myself go I'd be writing a cranky letter——about the burden of formalish stuff; letters that my contacts with Germany have gotten me into, and my longing to be on a Swiss or Austrian Alp waiting for the first snowflake.
    Do rest it on your heart that you will write me at once when you learn that someone has found the basic structure-patterns that underlie the A. L. P. chapter.
    I go back to Frankfurt on Nov 14 for a doctorate[3] (thanks, chaps) and am using American Exp. Co. Frankfurt a. M. as my address throughout the Fall.

                     A world of regard to you both
                     Ever
                     Thornt.

1. Wilder returned to Europe in mid-August. On 27 September he acted as master of ceremonies for an evening of one-act plays directed by Lamont Johnson in celebration of the new Congress Hall in Berlin, a cultural and scientific center built under the sponsorship of the Benjamin Franklin Foundation and the West German government. The evening opened with two plays by Tennessee Williams, *This Property Is Condemned* and *Portrait of a Madonna*. These were followed by Eugene O'Neill's *Before Breakfast* and William Saroyan's monologue *Ever Been in Love with a Midget?* The evening ended with three plays by Wilder—the first two world premieres: *Bernice* which starred Ethel Waters and Wilder as Mr. Walbeck and *The Wreck on the Five-Twenty-Five* with Lillian Gish and Hiram Sherman. The final play of the evening was Wilder's *The Happy Journey to Trenton and Camden* in which Wilder played the role of the Stage Manager with an all African-American cast which included Ethel Waters as Ma Kirby and Billy Gunn, Billie Allen, Richard Ward, and Vinie Burrows. See TW to AG, [?24 December 1956], n. 3. On 6 October Wilder was in Frankfurt am Main to receive the Peace Prize of the Association of German Publishers and Booksellers at the Frankfurt Book Fair. He delivered his talk "Kultur in einer Demokratie" (in German) before an audience of two thousand people in the Pauluskirche. In his talk he warned of the danger of leaving cultural activities "in the hands of bureaucrats—of committees, of institutions, of foundations, and of governmental organizations—that is to say, of men and women who sit at desks from nine in the morning until late in the afternoon. The money they dispense comes very directly from the people and they must be attentive to the tastes and wishes of the majority" (68). He also warned against the "insult" that "God and destiny had given to a small number of persons an unearned superiority and that to the majority He had given an inferior lot; that *privilege* is not only in the order of society, but that it is in the order of nature; and in the order of divine governance. This was the feudal lie: that leadership is transmitted in the chromosomes; and that only communities enjoying these mystical privileges can produce and encourage and maintain all that is excellent, true, and beautiful." Wilder then specifically mentioned T. S. Eliot, who, with many others, "still believe that only elites can produce an excellent thing" (70). The speech raised "a little hornet's nest" and Wilder vowed never to speak in public again. The original English text is in Wilder's *American Characteristics*, 67–73. For Wilder's view of the conservative reaction to his speech see *Journals* 266–269.

2. Wilder's close friends, the theatrical couple Garson Kanin and Ruth Gordon.

3. Before going back to Frankfurt, Wilder attended the premiere of his play *Die Alkestiade* (*The Alcestiad*) at the Burgtheater, Vienna, directed by Ernst Lothar. On 14 November he received an Honorary Doctorate from the University of Frankfurt. He then visited Alice Toklas in Paris, and, on 30 November, he sailed from Cherbourg on the *Statendam* arriving in New York on 6 December 1957.

To Thornton Wilder, Frankfurt, Germany

[MS. ALS—YCAL]

30 November 1957   [22 Carrington Road
                                                  Farmington, Connecticut]

Dear Thornton,

To a man writing plays on a mountain top, all this is going to sound far away and under water. Nevertheless, Joyceanism goes on large as life and rather more so.

We met Helen Joyce again at dinner with mutual friends[1]—she had with her a nice boy like a smooth brown brook pebble named Byrne—Cranly's son.[2] He lives with his parents in Brooklyn, decorates windows & prefers Science Fiction & Hemingway to Joyce. His father thinks all Joyceans are "treacherous." Then, Helen Joyce asked us to Thanksgiving dinner—very fine. Kevin Sullivan, the *type* ([Richard] Ellmann says he's an ex-Jesuit) took 200 dollars advance from her for ghosting her memoirs & now says he is being psychoanalyzed & cannot work for her. He doesn't offer to return the advance. Helen wants me to take on the job but being really serious with my eternal novel I refused. All the same, I like Helen's memoirs. They always begin with what she had on & never really go anywhere else but somehow a woman and her carnelian ear drops is what art's about.

My Novel—reminds me. Faber is anxious—anyway they've written me 3 letters wanting to see it. Should I send it to them—about next May I think—or to American publishers first?

They published the Census last week and write me the chummiest letters.[3]

Mitchell Morse of Penn State sent me the m. s. of an article called "Molly Bloom Revisited."[4] He hates Molly because she leaves her underwear around the bedroom & wipes her greasy fingers on the sheet & he thinks Joyce hated her too. I wrote him that he (Morse) didn't like women except as they are high-minded & tidy. He wrote back that of *course* he didn't like women because they were women anymore than he liked negroes because they were negroes. But *I* like men because they're men and I'd never even imagined the abyss of horror—finding oneself involved with a man who liked only individual women.

Ellmann's had a piece in the Yale Review—"Ulysses the Divine Nobody"[5] but as he sees Bloom, he's nobody divine. Oh he likes Bloom of course.

Hugh Kenner came to see us and his wife. As I guess I ought to have guessed from the shirty arrogance of his writing, he is a handsome, stammering *boy* of 35, his nice wife's son. He was amusing & did an imitation of Ezra Pound imitating Henry James (whom he knew) speaking in his last manner. Also he told me all about Bartell D'Arcy's son who's retired from the Dublin P. O. & spends his time checking up on Joyce's originals. D'Arcy Senior was insulted by "The Dead" & spent his last years drinking & insisting he had *so* been in voice at the Morkan's party.[6]

There is an Australian in Cambridge England named Hart[7] who is drawing up a complete word index of FW—*cross-referenced*. He says it isn't very hard.

Oh, Christ, the sheer pettiness that adheres to The Great! Aren't you glad you're on a mountain top?

I don't know anything interesting about FW. Do you think Kersse might be a female?[8]

Merry Christmas! When do you come home?

        Faithfully
        Adaline

---

1. For Glasheen's first meeting with Helen Joyce and Kevin Sullivan see AG to TW, 11 August 1957.
2. The Byrne referred to here is the son of John Francis Byrne who was the model for Cranly, Stephen Dedalus's confidant in *Stephen Hero* and *A Portrait of the Artist as a Young Man*. See TW to AG, 7 December 1950, n. 6.
3. The Faber & Faber edition of *A Census of Finnegans Wake* is identical to the Northwestern University Press edition except for a new title page and the inclusion of a list of errata and addenda.
4. J. Mitchell Morse, "Molly Bloom Revisited," in *A Joyce Miscellany*, Second Series, ed. Marvin Magalaner (Carbondale: Southern Illinois University Press, 1959), 139–149. Morse replied to Glasheen's comments on his article on 25 October 1957 (HWS).

5. Richard Ellmann, "*Ulysses* the Divine Nobody," in *The Yale Review*, XLVII, 1 (September 1957), [56]–71.

6. The character of Bartell D'Arcy, the hoarse singer in "The Dead," was based upon Barton M'Guckin, a tenor with the Carl Rosa Opera Company who sometimes sang under the name of Bartholomew D'Arcy. See Ellmann, *James Joyce* (1982), 246.

7. Clive Hart. With Fritz Senn he edited *A Wake Newslitter*. Among his publications are *Structure and Motif in 'Finnegans Wake'* (London: Faber & Faber, 1962) and *A Concordance to 'Finnegans Wake'* (Minneapolis: University of Minnesota Press, 1963; corrected edition, Mamaroneck, NY: Paul P. Appel, 1974). Hart's correspondence with Glasheen is in HWS.

8. In *Census II* Glasheen speculates that "I get the impression that the Captain is castrated and that Kersse [the tailor] is a female or turns into a female." In *Census III* she drops the speculation, and adds significantly to her earlier identification.

1958

To Adaline Glasheen, Farmington, Connecticut

[MS. ALS—HWS]

9 March 1958 [50 Deepwood Drive
Thursday Hamden 14, Connecticut]
{begun Feb 13}

Dear Adaline:
    Vice versa.[1]
    I thought *you* had given up FW.
    Missed you at the Birthday Party.[2] Heavens, you're our doyenne.
    Every now and then I do 10–hours straight on the Old Book. Then drop it for months.
    Thanks for the Bronte.[3]
    Yes, very likely, Finn dreams the book.
    Yes, from time to time wrote *addenda* into my *Census*, but didn't make a separate list of new ones to send you (thinking you had resigned from the work) so they're all mixed up with old ones.
    Began a new list, for you, yesterday:
So far only:
Charlemagne (of Aix-la-Chappelle) 334.36
Lewis, Percy Wyndham, Perrylewis 352.14[4]
MISPRINT: GOUGH 375.17 should read 357.31
(I think I gave you[)] CONSTANCE LLOYD, Mrs O. Wilde: 350.16[5]
And Lord Alfred Douglas is (but YOU DON'T INSERT PERSON'S NAMES unless they're expressly stated LORD OF CREMATION after the Blue Cremation written about by him?)
[margin: Robert Hickens]

Have a volume about Mallarmé and Joyce (second volume of two).[6] Much of it over-enthusiastic selling of his mania. He claims all big Double M's are Mallarmé MacMullah etc and 4:3–4 has Baudelaire—Mallarmé—Verlaine. Maybe, maybe not.

But in L'Après-midi d'un Faune ONE FAUN is spying on two nymphs . . . and all thes[e] FAUNAGAINS etc are allusions. Also Herodiade (Salome) is mad about her image in the mirror and so, too, my God, is Issy.
Really omnipresent is M's Coup de Dés =
    Ulysses 184–185 [1961, 187] speaks of "the rarified air. . . . . of Mallarmé.
    FW. 318.2 "rarefied air of a Montmalency"
FW. 353.7 bleachin banes (bones . . dice)
    " 8 die and be diademmed
In Mallarmé's poem La Chevelure "Se pose (je dirais mourir un diadème[)]" i. e. became a constellation. The author (David Hayman—the book's in French and reads like a Sorbonne thesis) fails to see that STEPHAN (os) means crown—hence turban—halo
FW 305 right margin COME SI. . . The first words of Le Coup de Dés and repeated later are COMME SI
357:4   But the hasard (spelt French) . . just behind his meddle throw.
    " :15 [i.e., 18] Culpo de Dido (Dido's sin[)] and Coup de Dés.
        perhaps Colpo di Dio—Italian: act of God.
And keep an eye of [i.e., out] for DIE, CUP, BONES, SEVENS(!) ELEVENS, DOMINO
FW 117:29–30 Tumbled down. . . . at all hours like a COUP DE DÉS!! With Mallarmé: existence, literature, engendering is a throw of Dice.

    SINNETT, Alfred Percy {co-worker with Mme Blavatsky who is probably here the Procuratress—but you don't print allusions to persons, unless their name is explicitly stated; author of Esoteric Buddhism} 352.13.
    JESHUAM = mixture of JOSHUA (made the sun stand still) and
    JESHURUN: Biblical for Israel

372.9–10 Isn't that Raoul Le Fevre passage hard. Le Fevre was not a poet, but a romancer, rewrote the Fall of Troy, Jason etc. And represented the Knights of the Round Table as Gods. Cannot trace a single other of those 8 names.⁷ They are not among Bérangers associates. Damn!

Forgive my erratic silences.

In an hour I start driving to Albuquerque, New Mexico for a semi-hermitage to work (in proximity, too of a University library.)

I did Letters A and B of the Phrase and Fable.⁸ Why, oh why, didn't I remember to see if there was anything about the omnipresent Hillery; Hilarion; Hillary Allen, etc.⁹

¶ I'm still somewhat leery of your cat's mother-wood-O'Shea passage.¹⁰

¶ I'm now in a state of being furious, spent, frustrated and disgusted at FW. Spent (wasted) HOURS trying to find a scheme under pp 126–139.¹¹ Why, why, why. I get 389 taunts; but why?

Rejoice in your novel.

- - - - - - -

a world of regards to both of you
Ever
Thornton

Some Letters from W. B. Yeats to John O'Leary and His Sister (New York Public Library; 1953[)]
Note 43: Samuel Liddell MATHERS (1854–1918) ¹²
.... Englishman ... Freemasonry, Rosicrucian .. Founded Order of the Golden Dawn, deposed from its leadership by Yeats. Took name of MacGregor. O'Leary disapproved Yeats's consulting him in connection with founding the Nat'l Lit Society (of Ireland.)
Probably
To the MATHERS in your Census...
Mather 268. left margin

1. This letter is a response to either a lost letter or to a telephone conversation.
2. Wilder attended the 4 February meeting of the James Joyce Society of New York held at the Gotham Book Mart. Leon Edel moderated a panel on Joyce Studies in America—1958.
3. Possibly a reference to the Brontë family in 7.20 to 8.8.
4. (Percy) Wyndham Lewis (1882–1957), the Canadian-born British artist and writer, attacked Joyce in his *Time and Western Man* (1927) and in his autobiography *Blasting and Bombardiering* (1937). Joyce satirized Lewis in *Finnegans Wake*, particularly in the fable of "The Ondt and the Gracehoper."
5. Constance Lloyd (d. 1898) married Oscar Wilde (1854–1900) on 29 May 1884 and bore him two children, Cyril in 1885 and Vyvyan in 1886.

6. Wilder's discussion (from this point to the line separator) of Stéphane Mallarmé (1842–1898) is based on David Hayman's *Joyce et Mallarmé: les éléments Mallarméens dans l'oeuvre de Joyce*. The first volume is *Joyce et Mallarmé: stylistique de la suggestion* (both volumes, Paris: Lettres Modernes, 1956). The work is Hayman's thesis completed for the Université de Paris in May 1955.

7. The names of Alfred Percy Sinnett, Raoul Le Fevre, and Pierre Jean de Béranger are all in *Census II* and *III*. In *Census III* Glasheen identifies Le Febber as "maybe the 15th-century poet, who wrote *Recueil des histoires de Troy*." The seven names in 372.9–.11, in addition to Le Febber, are: Josiah Pipkin, Amos Love, Blaize Taboutot, Jeremy Yopp, Francist de Loomis, Hardy Smith, and Sequin Pettit. In *Census III* Glasheen would identify Love, Yopp, and Smith as "early settlers in Dublin, Ga." Loomis is identified "with the Peers of France"; the identification of Pipkin, Taboutot, and Pettit continued to elude her.

8. Wilder is systematically reading through *Brewer's Dictionary of Phrase & Fable*.

9. Wilder probably means Hilary, one of the twins in the Prankquean episode, 21–23. Glasheen identifies all three names in *Census II* and *III*.

10. Possibly a reference to 223.19–.24.

11. The first of the twelve questions set by Shem and answered by Shaun.

12. *Some Letters from W. B. Yeats to John O'Leary and His Sister: From Originals in the Berg Collection*, ed. by Allan Wade (New York: New York Public Library, 1953; rpt. The Folcroft Press, Folcroft, Pennsylvania, 1969). The information on Mathers is drawn from Wade's note 43 (22–23).

☐

To Adaline Glasheen, Farmington, Connecticut

[MS. ALS—HWS]

[postmark: 15 April 1958]   Taos, N[ew]. Mex[ico][1]
Monday *in albis*

Dear Adaline:
    Thousand thanks. All duly transcribed.[2]
    ¶Your handwriting's (excuse me!) is difficult some times. I can't get what you are writing—wish I could read your words on 10.36 "pigeons pair" "boy and girl—something."
    ¶ 623.23 your mausoleum—Moss is brilliant
    ¶ No, you never told me abt. Lizzie from Blankshire 291.14
    ¶ You mention Pinksir-Whitsun 99.16. Notice that the motto of the Order of the Annunziata is below in initials F(ortitude) E. R. T. All that has to do with Phodes-Neoda-Fert = is feelth.

¶ The Faulkner's dog: named: Adaline! Have you been corresponding with him? Is he F. W. –mad?[3]

x   x

569.29	Not in the Census but I suppose you've collected it since: Melpomene
616.32	Percy's Reliques ("Balladed")
452.36	Is that my friend Nora Waln?[4]
CENSUS:	misprint page 1. ABRAHAM reference 531.19 [i.e., .10] misprint sub LIVINGSTONE 273[.17] should read 283.
416.13	Let's have another KANT
CENSUS.	Misprint sub HECTOR reference "225.16" an error? [i.e., 255.16]
	Misprint sub GELCHOSSA 288[.14] should read 228

{For CENSUS: one often needs first names separated from last; and names isolated from other contexts. So[:]
        Zerubbabel 563.32 [i.e., 536.32]
        Erechtheus 539.3
Query: Edinburgh's famous murderess Madeleine Smith 576.36
[TW margin: Oh yes I see you have it]
Another rainbow-spectrum 568.2–3
   "   JOSHUA 550.2

AGNES   (hat designer in Paris) 548.22
AGNES   (or Agnèse, I forget) minx heroine in Molière's L'Ecole des Femmes, who deceived (French *coiffer*, hence the two ffs; and would certainly [i.e., certainly] made *cocu*, hence the second *c* in coquette, her guardian if she'd married him.[)]

POUND, Ezra (poet, friend etc) 378.24, 26 (os for Ez).
    Page 208 ff. Parody of Hera's dressing up for Zeus Iliad XIV
    Catch Zeus's women:

208.2	Hera
208.9	Zeus visited Danaë in a GOLDEN shower and the result was PERSEUS.
208.18, 19	leadown. . . . swansruff
208.19	hayrope. . . Europa
208.25	siouler's = IO

DESLYS, Gaby   (French revue artist, fleurit 1910–20)
        351.23; 379.17; 184.27 (where her recipe for cooking eggs has been inserted into her name.)

Now something very odd.

In Mozart's *Cosi fan tutte*, two girls Flordiligi [TW correction at margin: FIODILIGI] (fleur de lys) and Dorabella.

Joyce breaks the first name down into Floh and Luse—horrid! but so it is, as he tells us himself = 417.19 [i.e., .17–.19].

Where Biene and Vespatilla come from—apart from entomology, I don't know.

DORABELLA is 432.21 (coalesced with another composer!) and probably 333.29–30 if you allow Dor. . . . . billa. . . . And all the DORA-DORIS PANDORA problems must be worked out later.

MOZART, again

In his *[Die] Entfuhrung aus dem Serail* (I forget the Italian. . . . Seraglio) the majordomo of the Turkish Pasha's house is named OSMIN. He's fat and irascible and the assumption is that he's a eunuch. Anyway, Joyce thinks he is.

Now look at:[5]
205.35
129.16
235.6 (in addition to Osman towels)
and probably 416.30 Tossmania.

PROBLEM:

Shem the penman cooks eggs p. 184. (French *oeufs* relates to *oe[u]vres*, works.[)] He sings incestuous songs, I'm sorry to tell you: *hermana*, sister: and read: *and Amarilla* as and—TAMARILLA, a sad story about King David's daughter.

His four masters—line 33: Aguilar is probably DANTE in Alleghieri-anagram. LUCAS = LUCIAN or LUGAN? Le Père Noble is maybe CORNEILLE (his CINNA is in line 20 and twice on page 173 it is thrown up against him: line 2 and line 20. (Corneille in French means *crow* or rook!!) Where is Shakespeare where is HOMER!—

Then these *OEURFS* he's preparing in the manner of other people. There's Gaby Deslys.

And there's the Marquis de Sade 184.29

Could sowtay sowmmonay [184.30] be Mannanan who ate the imperishable sow of Paradise?

Oh, isn't it awful?

I suspect that Letty van Leven [Letty Greene? 184.25] and B de B. Meinfelde [184.27–.28] were great (allegedly) courtesans like Gaby.

I've got to finish this up and send it off:. . . . . No, I must be an awful mug. . . I can't discover who that STOTTERER [317.18] is and now I've lost the reference.

My brother's[6] got a Guggenheim and the loan of a villa near Florence. Just like you.[7] Wonderful.

>   Gotta hurry
>   a world of regards
>   Thornton

---

1. Wilder left Connecticut on 9 March and arrived in New Mexico on the 15th. He briefly stayed in Albuquerque, Santa Fe, and visited friends in Taos before driving to California.
2. References to a lost letter.
3. There is no known correspondence between Glasheen and William Faulkner.
4. The writer Nora Waln who wrote about social life and customs of China in *The House of Exile* (1933) and about Germany in her *Reaching for the Stars: One Woman's Story of Germany, 1934–1938* (1939).
5. Glasheen wrote a large question mark to cover this list.
6. Amos Wilder, the Biblical scholar.
7. Glasheen was not awarded a Guggenheim Fellowship. When she and her husband were in Europe in 1956, during Francis Glasheen's Fulbright award, they traveled to Florence.

☐

To Adaline Glasheen, Farmington, Connecticut

[MS. ALS—HWS]

[postmark: 28 April 1958] Pacific Palisades, Calif.
soon returning home: April 27

>   a no-good letter—a poor return for your fine crammed one—[1]

Dear Adaline:
 (You're signing your letters so formally now, that I feel I should address you as Dear Sir or Madam.)
 Yours of the 19th devoured.
 Don't hit me, but will you buy this?

AHAB, Captain (protagonist of *Moby Dick*)
see   aabs and. . . . . . . Worse nor herman dororrhea. . . . .
{followed by an imitation of *Huck Finn*.} {and so much for Goethe!}
[283.26ff.]

CENSUS: Misprint: Henry VIII: 133.32–33 ??? [138.32–.33]

Elisa or Elissa: the other name of Queen Dido 291.14
　　　This doesn't prevent it's also being your Eliza of Blankshire;[2] but the footnote 3, shows that Joyce was thinking of Dido. Anyway, both were abandoned by their gentleman friends.

WALPOLE, Horace (author and correspondent) 307.1 and name of Horace in left margin. Also probably 105.28–29 (referring to the death of his eminent father); Maybe 455.6 (referring to his authorship of the first horror-novel: The Mysteries of Udolpho.) All these coincident with their allusion to the Roman poet or Egyptian God.

Robin Red-Breast (long felt to be a symbol of Christ—especially in Middle Ages when the bird was called RUDDOCK—anglo-saxon RUDIC). This is perhaps important for us, when on Page 369.18 it coalesces with Rodrick O'Connor = and can mean that all those episodes of the KING COMING INTO THE INN YARD ("a health to your majesty") are a Divine Visit.
　　　Vide   211.27
　　　　　　　537.9
　　　　　　　563.31 French for Robin Rougegorge.
[AG margin: ?]

KALIDASA (poet and dramatist) lived at the court of Emperor VIKRAMAADITYA (493.12) for KALIDASA 187.7 and, I think that's his play The Little Clay Cart on the preceding page 186.23; and maybe he is in the note on p. 279—the 10th line [i.e., 11th] from the bottom: cooledas.

Vere, Captain.
　　　I accept yours—and suggest another on p. 343 at the end of line 30. I was meditating finding him at 373.30 (but there was a De Vere in the poetry circle around Dobson, Lionel Johnson, young Yeats, etc).[3] I rejected 324.28 and 565.10

I can't get to any books of reference here, but I *think* I have some plums up my sleeve for you involving JUVENAL and CAMOENS.[4]

And not just glancing allusion, either, like those concerning KALIDASA

Who is working on the DANTE aspect? All through the book I can "feel" the circles and *bolgia*'s of the *Inferno* and the terraces and cornices of the *Purgatorio*, and I made a try at co-relating sections, but had to give up. He's too foxy about it.

And BEATRICE must be here a lot—I find some along with the tricksies etc, but I can't nail any down. Dante's wife was named GEMMA (quaem vide).

I had—and lost—a *lateeny*; if you find it, send me a card.

I've always assumed that anybody could quote from our books if the quote wasn't too extended. For that they must ask permission, which is usually granted, if acknowledgment is made. It is felt to be good for business.

Point out to Northwestern that if they don't prepare to make a second enlarged edition of the CENSUS, someone else will—availing themselves of yours (and for the mere *data* you could never prove their indebtedness).

And that this book will continue to have a ever larger sale, which will stop at once unless YOU bring out the enlarged edition.

Oh, how legibly I'm writing since Francis passed an aspersion on my hand. I'm careless with *h* and so are you. Your (George Eliot) Ligger and Liggen look just like higger and Higgen and maybe they are. Incidentally, 228.27 Luogotenente is the Italian Lieutenant.

N. B.   A Brereton 437.6 was one of the men executed for having been thought a lover of Anne Boleyn.

N. B.   You've noticed how J. J. twice runs through the instruments of the passion and events on the cross: 192[.11–.25] crown of thorns—coat—throngs—excrué—to rob you. . . etc and 424–5 root—rude—stick—cane—foresupposed—forceps—last word—cane—thong—minuit (for huggssup) Tale of me shur—convic—vincula—pence. Between indecency and blashphemy,. . . . !!!!

I hope we're ultimately justified for all this slumming.

        Ever
        (T)

1. A lost letter, probably dated 19 April.
2. This identification does not appear in any edition of *Census*. See TW to AG, 15 April 1958.
3. Poets connected to the Rhymer's Club: Aubrey Thomas de Vere (1814–1902), Henry Austin Dobson (1840–1921), Lionel Johnson (1867–1902), and William Butler Yeats (1865–1939). Of the Club, which was devoted to poetry, Yeats wrote: "for some years [it] was to meet every night in an upper room with a sanded floor in an ancient eating-house in Fleet Street called the Cheshire Cheese" (Yeats, *Autobiographies: Memories and Reflections*, London: Bracken Books, 1995, 165).
4. Juvenal (Decimus Junius Juvenalis) (?60–?140), the Roman lawyer and satirist, Luz Vaz de Camõens (1524–1580), the Portuguese poet. Neither name is in the *Census* nor are they included in Wilder's *Wake* notes in YCAL.

☐

To Adaline Glasheen, Farmington, Connecticut

[MS. ALS—HWS]

[postmark: 17 June 1958]   [50 Deepwood Drive
Tuesday June maybe 17th '58   Hamden 14, Connecticut]

Dear Adaline =
    It was great seeing you;[1] and apparently our fanaticisms didn't give the others a bad time.
    On the other side, see some comments.
    But I don't want to think of you re-typing those pages so I'm not sending any more.[2] {I'm beginning a New List, though, for the SECOND PRINTING.}
    There's only one I think you ought to give your reader now: Lloyd, Constance Mrs Oscar Wilde. 326.19 (look at the context!!) 413.5 616.1
        {context} 350.16 {circumstances}
LLOYD'S of London (see also Lloyd, Constance) 373.4 590.5
      THANKS A MILLION for IBSEN'S PLAYS
         "   "   "   for CENSUS-ADDENDA I
         "   "   "   "   "   "   II
         "   "   "   " ATHERTON and the KORAN[3]
Mrs Maycocks d[ied]. a Duchess might sue you = not shady but "fast"

I'm sending the material back—in separate envelopes, so as not to risk all in one accident.

All my sympathy to you on that typing chore,—extra hard with this kind of material. Anyone [i.e., Anyway], don't "reopen" these pages you've already typed. Resolutely refuse new data—and start a new file.

A world of regard to Francis and mil faittes for your and his next visit.

ever
(T)

[on back of letter]

Aldrich 548.35 is already in your Census
Beppy—as this is an Egyptian context, I assume this was "Joseph in Egypt" [415.36]
Sub Butt and Taff your page 19.[4] To *HE* who can.
Byrne, Alfy = didn't I learn from you that he was a friend of J. J.'s father? [568.32]
Charlemagne 334.1 should read 334.36
Disraeli = the reference is already in your CENSUS
Dryasdust—is it worth mentioning that it coalesces with Drogheda? [447.13]
Dunn, Ellie—too far afield for me
Ellis, Alex J   "   "   "   "   "
Edwards, Hilton actor and stage-director in Dublin [569.28]
GLINKA= oh—I *think* that Czar and Zimmerman is by LORTZING [341.17][5]
HAENSLI etc REVERSE the order = John and James
Hugh, Lord etc is already in the CENSUS
MISPRINT in CENSUS   FINN, Huckleberry. Cannot find 364.26 [Wilder misreads *Census I*: 346.26]
NEW CENSUS: LA ROSE 494.24 should read 495.24
NEW CENSUS: LEONE, Paul should read LEON, Paul
"   "   Your NUTTER 16.5 has a mistake in the page [AG: 16.15]
Adaline: 453.32–33 Eliceam élite. . . . land of lost of time ELI ELI LAMMA SABACHTANI

1. Wilder had dinner with the Glasheens on 12 June.
2. Glasheen had prepared an Addenda to *Census I* to which Wilder is adding.
3. Probably Atherton's chapter "The Koran" from *The Books at the Wake*. See AG to TW, 8 May 1954, n. 1.
4. The page reference is to Glasheen's typed Addenda list.
5. The reference may be to either or both Mikhail Glinka's opera *A Life for the Tsar* (1836) or Albert Lortzing's opera *Zar und Zimmerman* (1837).

☐

To Thornton Wilder, Hamden, Connecticut
[MS. TL—YCAL]

19 June 1958 [22 Carrington Road
Farmington, Connecticut]

Dear Thornton,

Thank you for your letter and comments and all. 453. Eli Eli Lamma Sabachtani is one of your master strokes. I'd never have seen it if I lived a thousand years. Right now I'm in a phase of thinking I'll never see another new thing in FW as long as I live, but 'twill I trust past.

I think you are wrong about Ellie Dunn being too far-fetched. If J. was going to put in H. James heroines, why on earth not Shaw heroines? As to Alex J. Ellis, you're probably right, but I have a feeling that J. sometimes just read Encyclopaedias etc and stuffed in names out of hand.[1]

I'm not going to retype anything, but there will be a lot of stuffing in or listing at the end, for Dick Ellmann,[2] who was here yesterday, says he has a lot of Dubliners, family friends, Zurich friends etc. which he'll send me as soon as he gets home. I also expect more from Jim [Atherton] and from Father Noon.[3] We liked Ellman[n] (though our daughter oddly did not and said he was common!) and had a pleasant time with him. I had discovered that "Kathleen Ni Houlihan"[4] Yeats' [play] is one big source (conscious on J's part) for "The Dead" and I gave it to E. because I don't want to be bothered writing it up myself. He says he'll give me credit. But what's more important, I (and you, E. hopes) can, I think, get him to say what we like about FW. He said he realized he really knew nothing about it—too right—and I said well all we knew was still tentative, but then later he said would I (and you) read his chapters on FW later on. I shall. Will you? He may as well have it right as possible, don't you think? He liked the title Out of My Census.[5] I can't say I learned anything very exciting about Joyce except that he was a problem drinker which seems to weigh on E. Incidentally, E. is to edit the second volume of J. letters, the bulk of which will be from Stanislaus's collection and E. says they're long and intimate much more interesting than any in the first volume. I told him you and I didn't believe a word J. wrote to Miss Weaver and he was shocked as if I'd told an obscene story about the pope or something like that.

I'm reading *De Civitate Dei*, a kind of nice book and I've not got very far being still bogged down in St. A's low opinions of the Roman gods, but in the introduction by Sir Ernest Barker, it says: "St. Augustine, taking over the idea from the philosophers of antiquity, distinguishes four grades (or, we may say, concentric rings) of human society. The first is the *domus* or household. Above that, and wider than that, is the *civitas*—which had originally meant the City. . . but had been extended to mean the state in general. Above the *civitas* comes the *orbis terrae*—the whole Earth and the whole human society. . . Finally, and widest of all societies, there is the Universe, *mundus* which embraces the heavens and their constellations. . . and includes God and His angels and the souls of the departed, as well as human society now sojourning upon the earth."[6] Well, no doubt you know all about this, being better educated than I, and I can't work it out off hand in terms of FW anymore than I can work out Vico off hand, but I think it could be done.

I'll fill up the paper with old things I hope I haven't told you.
342.22-23—Mr. W. H.?
347.31 Rome and Carthage
349.20 The R. G. is the Trinity [?.19: wohly ghast]
365.16 Villette again
370.28 The luddites—19th century smashers of machinery
407.4   *lecker* is Dutch "delicious"
430.10 they're playing "Post Office"—didn't you when young?
Did I tell you Noon said 433 and 619 parodied the so called *Ordo*?
432.24 Clive Hart says A Gentleman with a Duster is by Harold Begbie (1871-1929)

457.29 ref. to Heloise?
547.24 Pouilly-Fuisee Latour—Fr. wine firm
563.26 Swift born in Hoey's Court [i.e., 563.27]
566.36 Isn't there a trashy book called Heather of the Mist?[7]
605.4   Jim [Atherton] says Yad is the name of a work of Maimonides, means "code" in Hebrew

Well you can see I'm drained dry of information, no blood from this turnip. Ah but Joyce if no other has promised the return of fruitfulness.

I enclose the rest of the Census,[8] also unproofed which isn't kind of me. They're dull dull dull

       Yrs
       AG

[handwritten]

Sat.
You may well feel sorry for me. Magalaner returned my Parnell piece[9] & wants it all done over after the MLA style sheet & returned by July 1.

1. Both names are in *Census II*.

2. Richard Ellmann and Glasheen began corresponding in 1954. He was helpful in having Northwestern University Press publish *Census I*, and his Foreword appears in both subsequent editions.

3. Father William T. Noon, S. J. His *Joyce and Aquinas* was published by Yale University Press in 1957.

4. Yeats's 1902 play.

5. The title Glasheen gave to her list of corrections and additions to *Census I*; it was published in *The Analyst*, XVII (April 1959), [i], 1–73.

6. Quoted from Sir Ernest Barker's Introduction to Saint Augustine, *The City of God (De Civitate Dei)*, ed. R. V. G. Trasker (London: J. M. Dent & Sons, Ltd., 1950), xii.

7. Glasheen may be thinking of Edward Martyn's play *The Heather Field*, which, with Yeats's *The Countess Cathleen* inaugurated the Irish Literary Theatre (later the Abbey Theatre), in 1899.

8. The addenda which would be published as "Out of My Census."

9. Glasheen's "Joyce and the Three Ages of Charles Stewart Parnell," in *A James Joyce Miscellany*, second series, ed. Marvin Magalaner (Carbondale, Illinois: Southern Illinois University Press, 1959), 151–178.

To Adaline Glasheen, Farmington, Connecticut
[MS. AL—HWS]

[? late June 1958–I]¹   [50 Deepwood Drive
                                          Hamden, Connecticut]

FOR MRS GLASHEEN

ARISTOTLE	{etc etc; the "Stagirite"; the "Peripatetic"; appears in FW accompanied by phrases associated with him: *autokinaton*; *nous*. JJ relishes the middle syllables: Tot'e. In an important place JJ associates him with Father Theobald Matthew—probably because Matthew as evangelist is the supreme man and because (by mistaken etymology) of the syllables Theo—*} [bottom of page: *because he was a tay-totaller.] {Query: Is he also the philosopher of CHANCE—Mayhappy-Mayhapnot and Perh'ps. I put them here for your deliberation}
110.7	Mayhappy Mayhapnot {combined with Mallarmé—whose sigla is two M's—whose most famous poem is about Dice}²
" .17	Harrystotalies
183.34	[i.e., 184.34] Father Mathew (Shaun's Master)
298.24	Perperp
" .Left margin	peripatetic
306.left margin	Aristotle
330.5	Father Matt Hughes. . . . taytotally
343.15–16	noy's totalage (philosophical jargon; allusion to Greek Tragedies)
{393.10	probably oldpoetryck}
394.30–395.2	All Aristotle's terms. His name probably concealed in 395.2 N-ARSTY-
417.16	aristotaller
" .32	veripatetic
440.17	Mrs Trot (with Kant, etc)
484.16	avtokinatown (or: A's definition of God)

614.34–35   veripet— {see autokinaton in line 30 and many Aristotelian terms}

DISCUSSION
Eugenia in James's Europeans? 528.20 [?528.24]
James's Ambassadors: isn't a friend of the hero
    Little Bonham 459.24–25
    351.26 [i.e., .16]
NB. Baggot St = Maunsel and Roberts[3]
Mrs Sanders as O. Wilde
    412.30 intentions
    413.5 Loyd
Cecil
    230.9
    354.14
Coat and Compasses

MENO   {slave boy who is given a geometry lesson in Plato's dialogue of the same name} 294.12 297.6 341.4 615.9

GORGIAS   {Rhetorician, subject and title of Plato's dialogue} 303.17 458.25 562.29

PLATO   {etc. etc. known as the BEE (MELISSA) of Athens. Add:}
    257.11 {plattonem} [AG margin: Had]
    470.20 {playtennis}
    451.23 [AG: 351] {with immoral implications: meelisha's deelishas—with Gaby Deslys.

GIDE, Andre   {French novelist and critic. 1869—? author of *Les Nouritures Terrestes*, 406.31; *Symphonie Pastoral* 409.10; apologist for homosexuality} [AG margin: *Counterfeitors?*]
    408.30 Handy {in transition March 1928: Andy}
    409.7 Guide 409.31 andy
    124.36 {probably Andycox}
    345.22 guidness—two lines above is a reference to Gide's book on the Congo.[4]
    346.9 begidding
    347.27 Gidding

CENSUS: Misprint
          CALIGULA 37–41 (what that) [i.e., years of reign A.D.]; 60.36 should read 60.26

LOWE, Sir Hudson {Napoleon's overseer on St. Helena} 343.17

COMUS   {son of Circe and Bacchus; in Milton's play}
               409.12–13 {with Ital. Candela, a candle}

RIMBAUD, Arthur   {French poet. . . c 1854–1891}
               319.5 rinbus
               407.4–5 aart or

YEATS, W. B. 404.15 {will of a wisp—by analogy with[5]

---

1. This letter and the following letter, dated as late June 1958–II, may have been sent in the same envelope. Glasheen's letter of 2 July mentions items in this listing.
2. "Un Coup de Dés."
3. The Irish publishing house in Dublin that in August 1909 agreed to publish *Dubliners*. For nearly three years, until September 1912, Joyce and the publishers were in negotiations about changes they demanded. Before Joyce could take over the sheets that had already been printed and publish *Dubliners* himself, the printer John Falconer destroyed the plates.
4. *Voyage au Congo: carnets de route* (Paris: Gallimard, 1927).
5. Wilder does not complete the entry.

□

To Adaline Glasheen, Farmington, Connecticut

[MS. ALS—HWS]

[? late June 1958–II][1]   [50 Deepwood Drive
                                          Hamden, Connecticut]

Deer Adaline = =
Addenda CENSUS: O—Z
Oberon   among the satellites of URANUS "one bore one" 583.10
                 {There are two others, but don't soil your pages 41.16

	357.2} so 41.16 is four people: Poet Byron, [Henry James] Byron author of Our Boys, William O'Brien and Oberon!!!
Odet	in Proust Odette de Crécy [200.33]. {a "female" in Proust—yes, begins as a prostitute and ends a great lady in Society.}
PAOLI	Sankt Paoli, waterfront district of Hamburg famous for colorful low-life [117.24]
POBBLE =	also PÖBEL Germ. Mob, rabble. [334.24, 454.35]
PREVOST	If you put this in, put an †² so we can also look for Mohammed's ever-suspended Prophet's coffin. [5.22]
PRUNIKOS =	delighted =
ROBY =	Yes, George ROBEY [156.27]
{Rooney Handy	Andy = 279. note 6th [i.e., 7th] line from the bottom = looks to me like another André Gide = he wrote a novel called Isabelle![}]
TAPPERTIT	do you mean 501.2, 5? [AG in *Census II*: 505.1]
VEDETTE:	also in French means theatrical star, feminine [577.17]
WALDMANN	Haven't you the wrong line number? [345.4]
SUMMANUS =	splendid, remembering JJ's terror of thunder and lightning. Maybe SUMMANUS is also 184.30 egges santés saumoné (not really a French word but very FW. combining Finn eating the salmon of wisdom and Mananaan eating the imperishable sow of Heaven.

TIMON of ATHENS also 184.36
(I forget = did you get MANGAN 184.36[)]
SWARAN (published Census pp 125–126) from OSSIAN—isn't he also
        348.14
        521.1
        524.17

SEVEN: RAINBOW
    There's another 284.28–285.2 (J. J. corrected "Misprint"
REDOR 285.2 to ERDOR, so we seem to lose our color red, but even ard—means burning. Also there is no orange but habby—or mierelin may contain orange in some other language.[)]
    There's another 339.28–29
    There's another: 403.10ff [i.e., .8] ruddled. . . delph (blue). . . . green. . . blue. . . . indigo. . . pansy. . . . violet.
        can't find yellow or orange = but surely there.

They begin by making white in line 8 [i.e., .6] and end by making black in line 29 [i.e., .17]
{N. B. In pages where a chapter begins or in pages where some lines are left blank I think we ought to give line-references as though all 36 lines were there}
There's another (and beautifully in place) 556.3–[.18]
        ivory (yellow). . . peach. . . blue. . orange. . . . apri'cot green. . rose. . . . . mauve.

IN THE CENSUS p. 18 [i.e., 118] column one, the rainbow 285. note 6, you might help your reader by adding. . . orange marmalade. . . . quince.

On Fritz Senn's page[3] you put a question mark—can't find—after Tom Dick and Harry: thane and tysk and hanry. It's 316.5

I find 24 complete or nearly complete SEVEN—COLOR—"run throughs"

        Gotta run (am half thru article on FW!!)[4]
        Return Pages next mail
           TW

---

1. This letter is dated late June because in Glasheen's letter of 2 July 1958 she responds to Wilder's query about Samuel Tappertit, the anarchist apprentice in Charles Dickens's *Barnaby Rudge*. All of the identifications in this letter appear in *Census II*.
2. In the *Census* Glasheen uses a dagger to mean a composite drawn from the names of two or more people.
3. Senn, the Swiss Joyce scholar, and Glasheen began corresponding in 1954; it was Senn who proofread *Census II*.
4. Glasheen in her letter of 2 July 1958 assumes Wilder is writing an article, but Wilder may have meant that he was reading an article on the *Wake*. His first two articles on Joyce were published in 1941 and 1954. Wilder's "Giordano Bruno's Last Meal in *Finnegans Wake*" was printed in October 1962.

To Thornton Wilder, Hamden, Connecticut

[MS. ALS—YCAL]

2 July 1958 [22 Carrington Road
Farmington, Connecticut]

Dear Thornton,
Holed up with my air conditioner & little to do but FW.
When your article is done do I get to see it if I don't tell people about it?[1] Thanks for your letter & information—Tappertit is 505.1

93.34	Sam Weller had to be someplace
6.7	Hubert—who he?
17.14	A hit at Patrick's Latin which they did hit in the saint's time
26.2–3	Pelagian?
27.8–9	Again—devil *in* Jerry, not J the devil—but Kevin *is* an angel
28.1	Nora
28.27	Viv in Mrs Warren's Profession??
28.33	Why is ALP's hair brown here?
29.27–8	Hories—set
29.27	adi = Ida
29.35	Timon?
30.35	Sekskar
31.26	Grania
32.4 [i.e., .3]	Sceptre—horse in *Ulysses*
32.23	Finn is pronounced Fewn
34.1	Umballa in India—as in *Kim*
34.23	Elaine?
36.20	Ko-Ko in The Mikado?
37.14	Eliot?
39.4–5	June 29 = feast of Peter & Paul
40.11	Herman? Melville?
41.2	Lazarus
41.9	Orwell??
41.17	Via Crucis
42.4	Hewitt??

I know you think I have no marbles on the subject of p. 262 being a cipher or something but my playing about has revealed that 262.2—ATLOP is an anagram of Plato—see 286.3

I read "Meno" & consider your find one of the *Great*[2]

No more news. I shall read lots of FW if the heat lasts[.] Saturday we're going to H[elen]. Joyce[3] for lunch with a "terribly dogmatic Irish protestant who married money & thinks he knows all about *Finnegans Wake*!! Ha [line from "knows" to:] His wife knows all about Hieronymous Bosch

     Yrs,
     Adaline

[Wilder has written the following sideways on the page]

sordomatic
florilingua
shelta focal   gardens
flayflutter   foca-Pharos
con's cubane
a pro's tutute   Pyramite
strassarab   Statue-Diana
ereperse   Babylon
anythongul athall

[page reversed from above list]
viola   ram   America
      Europe
      Africa   Fire
      bull   Van'essy'er wide
      Capricorn
      Gemini
roter   Cancer

end to the
r' bow

---

1. See TW to AG, late June 1958–II, n. 4.

2. In the "Supplement" section of "Out of My Census" Glasheen credits Wilder for the references to Meno, a character in a Platonic dialogue (70).

3. See AG to TW, 11 August 1957.

To Adaline Glasheen, Farmington, Connecticut

[MS. APCS—HWS]

[Postcard: Portrait of Jane Avril (drawing)
Henri De Toulouse-Lautrec
1864–1901
Fogg Art Museum, Harvard University
Grenville Lindall Winthrop Collection]

[postmark: 8 August 1958]   [50 Deepwood Drive
Hamden 14, Connecticut]

Dear Adaline:
    I always seem to be on the point of sending you cracking discoveries, and then it goes down the sand. I have collected some trifles = but not until I get a score of trifles do I dare forward them. But I do think that FW 297.31 is very funny for Madame (the titled = = Baroness) de Staël, the exacting friend of Benjamin Constant 297.29.[1]

              Ever
               TNW.

FW 415.11[2]

---

1. Neither Madame de Staël (1766–1817), the French writer, nor Benjamin Constant (1767–1830), the French author and politician, are in *Census II* or *III*.
2. The line in the *Wake* refers to the dancer Jane Avril, whose image is on this postcard.

To Adaline Glasheen, Farmington, Connecticut

[MS. ALS—HWS]

13 August [1958] [50 Deepwood Drive
 Hamden 14, Connecticut]

Dear Adaline =
 As you well know, there are some days when one can't see a thing in FW and you decide to throw it into the incinerator.
 Then other days!
 The SHEM chapter[1] is as full of authors and book-titles as ALP is of rivers and HAVETH of places.
 Tolstoi's name is variously LWOV, LEV, LEO etc 181.6 [i.e., .26] and then on the preceding line perfect of Sniffey: NEVSKY PROSPECT?
 Turgeniev's name is SERGEI, Serge etc 189.18! and 186.3 [i.e., .33]

189.11 s. .catch. . . . man Huntsman's Sketches
 .13 fluctuant Torrents or Freshets of Spring
 .28 nest A nest of Gentlefolk.
190.8 fumes Smoke (J. J. reads Turgeniev in French: Fumée.)
189.29 sleep at our vigil On the Eve. (Fr. Le Vigile)
189.6 sensibility Jane Austen
 sponsibility Manzoni (sposi = sponsi)
 passibility Tolstoi Guerre et Paix
 prostability Proust.
 .11 Mann
 .12 d'arounda Deronda
 .13 for acres H. James' Vereker, again
 d'roods Drood
 .14 Sand
 .16 Chalwador Mrs. Wharton (Cadwallader-Jones)
 honor Honoré Balzac
189.19 sola Zola

 ───────────────

 After months of persistence I'm beginning to see that many words on a M—M—formation are Mallarmé[2]
186.1 Marivaux
 Mallarmé

	Vico
4	Dante
	the s LOW F Tolstoi
8	chagrin = Balzac Peau de Chagrin
23	'Igitur (Mallarmé's play)
	little clots = coup de dés
	mobmauling Mallarmé
[186.25]	Knockmaree (sorry) Méry Laurent M's mistress (beautiful portrait of her by Manet in the Williamstown gallery)
28	Mergyt Mer. . . y. . .
186[.25]	Comty Mea Plato's Timeaus French TIMÉE and there is Diotima as the pigeonesse = Pythoness

---

A thousand thanks for the invitation = from Isabel too.
Wish we could come right now.
Can't budge until we learn when our Aunt Charlotte will or will not come to visit = she's driving (at 74! up from Florida.) Will let you know, well in advance, when we know.

    A world of regard to both.
    (T)

1. FW I, vii (169–195). See also TW to AG, 3 October 1958.
2. See TW to AG, 9 March 1958.

□

To Adaline Glasheen, Farmington, Connecticut

[MS. ALS—HWS]

20 August 1958   50 Deepwood Drive
            Hamden 17, Connecticut

Dear Adaline:
  Is FW blasphemous? ! ? !
  Hold your hat.
  Per Exemplum:

P. 457.4		Apparently this is the St. Veronica Station[.] But it looks like the Magdelene, too
		It's the *I THIRST* from the Cross
		The Spanish for Elizabeth is Isabel. Elizabeth mother of St. John is also at the foot of the Cross
	.5	Biddies = Betties. s'looking - Germ[an] Schlucken = to swallow
	6	stave-stab: German in [?word] for the cross. IS A. Is the sentence both indecent and blasphemous?
	7	Reverse "weighted" and "suaged." On one's hunkers = in a desperate situation. Isn't HUNKER gypsy cant for a whore?
	8	don't you turn pale at *that*?
		Also YE CAN German JUCKEN to itch.
	9	grame: angry, grieved . . . . Jack the Ripper
	10	collect for day's saecula sacculorum?
		blesser: french to wound "as A" = se blesser: have a miscarriage. . . in disgust
	10–11	curly hair I = Hari Kari
	11	Houseman Lightfoot (c) Lad
	11–12	Clo. . . marund Cléo Mérode. . . great ex-actress and beauty in Paris.
		(Ruth Gordon called on her recently in her old age. . . insists she was never a courtesan, but the world has always thought so. . . . all these highwaymen[)]
	12–13	Yoni—Hindu: female sex
		Yan-Yin male and female principle
		METHER (Irish Meadar) drinking cup mother a pimp?
		Best pair = Vesper
	14	calipers = pincers, of the Crucifixion
		creamsourer = lightning.
		Manners = Lady Diana Manners d[aughter]. of the Duke of Rutland—she *would* go on the stage. Better = Betty.
	15	Consuelo Vanderbilt
	16	's a re SARAH. . . fond of ex = Pontifex. . ized
	17	me duty = meadar = drinking cup
		Bruise = brose = a broth. BOLGIA in Dante's Inferno. There's one for harlots
	18	memorias? Dinorah[1]. . Miss. . . . . . Nora (Barnacle?). . . harrowing of hell. . . harrowing weeks of lent?
	[.17]	me duty on = Medusa?
	19	Dolly (Tearduct) Trull-y Nelly. .
	20	my west Mae West

[457.]21   to dine. . . TUDE Danish blow a horn
A tear (sheet)
TOOT Scot to drink
maybe Turridu from Cavalleria Rusticana, elsewhere in FW.
[457.]22   We now come to the crowd watching the Via Dolorosa—as though they were at a smart race-day at Longchamps.
clique cloche cloaca d'off with our cloaks
cynera = shady lady of the poem
silk hats
Maybe the Paris restaurant LARUE's
his ELEGANCE. . If this is Bianconi, there's our Hindu Yoni again.
again: he can lick creation.
Anyway Edward the VII liked those Paris creations.
Will you consider his STELLA—Jonathan? and St John

That's bad enough—but I assure you there are far worse horrors in that kind elsewhere.

We're still trying to get our aunt's schedule.

Burn this letter. It's already SINged.

Ever
T

1. A reference to Giacomo Meyerbeer's opera *Le Pardon de Ploërmel* (1859) later known as *Dinorah*. The phrase in the *Wake* is "me more as".

□

To Adaline Glasheen, Farmington, Connecticut

[MS. ALS—HWS]

11 September [1958]   50 Deepwood Drive
                                       Hamden 17, Connecticut

Dear Adaline:

Aren't those Wilders unreliable and provoking.

Aunt Charlotte went off after 2 weeks.[1]

Then our nephew arrived to enter Yale.[2] Then I was called in on the laboratory-discussions surrounding Eugene O'Neill's play at the Schubert.[3]

Now I gotta go to Boston until Monday.
We still want to come and see you.
But now school has begun and Francis can't be there for lunch—except the weekends and weekends is exactly the time when he wants his rest and there shouldn't be guests. So when I come back from Boston I'll call up and ask what day we can come for the tea-hour, suggesting Thursday or Saturday.

x   x

Almost nothing to forward about F. W.

But one thing which I haven't got time or "contacts" enough to explore:

The TV play on shooting the Russian General is *on one level* an insurrection of Russian authors against Tolstoi

TOLSTOI is LYEV 338.6 and 19 340.2 341.9 and elsewhere. Is a Count and Graf 353.10, 339.23 349.2. He wrote Sevastapol 338.14[.] In autobiog. novels he gave himself the name Polikushka 339.15 and DUBROUSKI 340.1. His ANNA lives in the highest 340.22. His play is The Living Corpse = TOD-LEBEND 339.21 and his novel in French is PAIX ET GUERRE POR DAGUERRE 339.23. Many Confessions and Memories 339.15 348.7[.] A novel Resurrection 346.13 [TW margin: The plot of Resurrection is in 352.3–4]; a story Hadji Hamid 347.19 357.7[.] The Two Hussars 348.27. The Cossacks 350.21 with Pierre in War and Peace he takes on a Mason's uniform 352.1–2. Wrote Kreutzer Sonata 353.28. A story LUCERNE (French for window in the roof = skylight etc[)] 338.5–6 358.1.

Alex Pushkin preceded Tolstoi but seems to get into this he was a mulatto ebony boy 341.9 354.10[.] Wrote Mozart and Salieri 346.9–10. The Fisherman and The Fish 339.1 = 25 fish's. . . allasundery. Eugene Onegin 348.5. The Pique Dame (Queen of Spades): 338.23 344.2.

GOGOL Two great stories The Coat and The Nose. All Russian Fiction said to have fallen out of the sleeve of The Cloak 339.29 GIGLS 341.7 permits us to see gurg in the gorge in line 2 and 343.3 {349.29ff gives us GOGOL Noses and GORKI "Mother" and what-others in succession.[}]

MAXIM GORKI (his birthtown Nitzhiä-[i.e., Nizhni] Novgorod is now called GORKI)—"Mother" 340.16. 342.2 GMAX; KNOX Nikolai GOGOL and the GMUGGIES—several Russian masters have Mikhail in their names.

But most of all Dostoievski—but mostly in Russian and I can't find the Russian spelling Pronunciation of Crime and Punishment,

Brothers K. . . . etc nor of War and Peace. But there's something to start on.

> Call you when I get back
> Lots of regards to both
> (T)⁴

1. Charlotte Tappan Lewis Niven (1882–1979), his mother's sister.
2. Amos Tappan Wilder, son of Wilder's brother Amos and his wife Catharine Kerlin Wilder.
3. Wilder was in New York from 3 to 8 September to attend rehearsals for the American premiere of Eugene O'Neill's *A Touch of the Poet* which opened at the Helen Hayes Theatre (not the Schubert) on 2 October 1958 and ran for 284 performances. The play takes place from the morning to the night of 27 July 1828 in the dining room of Melody's Tavern, situated in a village not far from Boston. Wilder's friend Helen Hayes played Nora Melody; also in the cast, directed by Harold Clurman, were Kim Stanley and Eric Portman.
4. With this letter Wilder enclosed a postcard he had received from a friend, Harry [?Levin], who was visiting Ireland. The image on the card is Bachelor's Walk and the Liffey River from O'Connell Bridge, Dublin.

To Adaline Glasheen, Farmington, Connecticut

[MS. ALS—HWS]

[postmark: Friday, 3 October 1958] 50 Deepwood Drive
Sunday [28 September 1958] Hamden 17, Connecticut

Dear Adaline:
    First: thanks for the delicious meal and delightful time.¹ And everything. And for the loan of the two vast typescripts.² Naturally I copied everything in at once.
    Atherton's all well as far as it goes but it's always seeming to claim that it's gone much farther than it has. It *tends* to give the impression that it's found all the allusions to authors and to the sacred books, for instance. Reading FW is such a despairful job that

I'm amazed at anyone so blithely implying that they've just about cleared the matter up.

Take his nonchalant lines about the MASS. Golly! His brilliant discovery Qui Tecum vinit et regnat 414.13 should have alerted him to the fact that other phrases from the missal are all over the place.

Isn't that the Protestant vision of the creed:
498.27   forgiveness of sin
  30   communion of saints
499.1   resurrection of the body
  2   life everlasting.

All the trisagions Hagios etc—(NINE TIMES—given or implied) buried in the HIC-HA[E]C-HOC 454.15

And look at it buried in 423.10–11—after the tryone, tryon triune on the previous page 422.26 (we are in the Improperia where this has to be rung after each of the Reproaches.[)]

I keep looking for Systems, so I haven't any new identifications for you[.]
408.6 454.13–14 the ASSEMANI, a family of Maronite scholars who wrote on that
    RITE.
The page which has 37 lines is page 528

Do I imagine it—or are all those droll or nasty objects in SHEM's house, an author?³

P. 183.11	telltale stories = TOLSTOI	
[12]	bouchers BOURGET. . . . . McAlmon	
14	Mahaffy (who lisped)	
17	Herman Broch ly jars Léger (again)	
18	scapulars CABELL breeches Robert BRIDGES	
19	GIDE WILDE (author of INTENTions)	
20	UNDSET STEIN	
22	POUND	
23	SADE	
24	INGE	
25	JUNG. . . . . WASSERMANN	
27	Supervielle	
28	FORSTER	
29	clippings = German SCHNITZler.	
30	RILKE (Czech who lived in Switzerlet [i.e., Switzerland][)]	
30–31	Hebrew Aleichams.	
32	Léon Blum. . Anne Grubbe (isn't that a famous Danish novel?)	

32–33   Wyndham Lewis.
33   Gottfried Keller
35   Glenway Westcott

    I GUESS I ONLY IMAGINE IT... but if we could show a few more as likely as the GIDE and the WASSERMANN and the WYNDHAM LEWIS—what an ingenious page it would be!! I have to drive to Amherst one of these days and will leave the vast TYPSCRIPTS with you. WORLD OF REGARD AND THANKS to BOTH and Does Alison[4] remember her OLD FRIEND

THORNTON

Isabel shouts down the hall—"give her my love—"

1. Wilder saw the Glasheens for lunch on Thursday, 25 September.
2. Probably Glasheen's "Out of My Census" and James S. Atherton's *The Books at the Wake*.
3. See TW to AG, 13 August 1958.
4. The Glasheens' daughter.

1959

ISABEL WILDER:

To *Adaline Glasheen, Farmington, Connecticut*

[MS. APCS—HWS]

5 January [19]59   50 Deepwood Drive
Happy New Year!   Hamden 17, Connecticut

Dear Adaline—
    I'm sending your envelope to T. as air mail.[1] He's in Vienna for a week & perhaps Zurich after that. His work goes well—hope yours does, too. I'm RELUCTANTLY off to Florida Thurs. to an ailing aunt.

          Love
          Isabel

1. Wilder sailed for Europe on the SS *Vulcania* on 14 November 1958. During this trip, which lasted until 26 March 1959, he continued work on plays for the cycles on the seven deadly sins and the seven ages of man.

To Adaline Glasheen, Farmington, Connecticut

[MS. ALS—HWS]

4 February [1959]   Until Feb 25
                             Neues Posthotel St Moritz
                             [Switzerland]

Dear Adaline:
    Horrified—not only to return you this late—but with one page missing.[1] I feel sure it's in my chaotic papers and will turn [up]. As this has just done.
    Had some exhilarating hours with Fritz Senn in Zürich and will have some more. (Zürich is turning up everywhere.)[2] They are the nicest couple you can hope to meet.
    Also I've found a lot of new stuff—for some reason most of it is shady or worse. Francis will put his foot down. Shall I send you a horrid mess of such stuff. I'll wait til I get back.

                    x

    It's glorious sunlight here.

                    x

    Forgive me.

            a world of regard to both
            (T. N.)

Almost all references to Bruno are shady because of his play Candelaio[3]—hence candle: chandler
Stendhal wrote a novel "Armance";[4] here "Octave" impotent or
        eunuch.—French word is Babelan [i.e., Babilan] (hence all
        Babel—Babylon including Nebuchadnazzar.)
Stendhal wrote Mérimée[5] that he heard that Isaac Newton and Swift
        were Babelans.— and it's in FW.
Two great tennis champions underwent scandals in court for
        homosexuality
Hence Count SalmSalm[6] (and all Psalms—hence David)
¶ All use of Camp. . . . Campbell. . . camel . . . . All cocus[7]. . . . . .
    In fact, I begin to think the book is mostly about just such unwholesome matters.

If it weren't for the beauty of the Resurrection chapter,[8] I'd be fed up to the gills. Even the ALP chapter[9] is "riddled" with it: 214.2 marigold = maricom—marical = homosexual smear. Cobbler = cablen etc = Bruno = who wrote a CABALA[10] and a candlemaker. 214.5 kneebuckle = Nabucco = Verdi's opera, Italian for Nebuchadnazzar. To hell with it.

1. Reference to the unidentified material mentioned in Isabel Wilder to AG, 5 January 1959.

2. Wilder saw the Senns several times during the ten days, 17 to 26 January, he was in Zurich.

3. Giordano Bruno (1548–1600), the Italian philosopher. After being forced to leave the Dominican order because of his unorthodox views—he supported the ideas of Copernicus and was against Aristotelian logic—he traveled widely in Europe lecturing, teaching, and writing. His play, *Il Candelaio*, was written in 1582 while he was in Paris. Bruno was arrested for heresy by the Inquisition in 1592 and burned at the stake on 17 February 1600. Joyce was sympathetic to Bruno's ideas and his tenacious character, and references to Bruno appear in *A Portrait of the Artist as a Young Man* (chapter V), *Ulysses*, and *Finnegans Wake*. Bruno's theory of the coincidence of contraries underlies the Shem-Shaun relationship in the *Wake*. See "The Bruno Philosophy," Joyce's review of J. Lewis McIntyre's *Giordano Bruno* (1903), in *James Joyce the Critical Writings*, ed. Ellsworth Mason and Richard Ellmann (New York: Viking Press, 1964), 132–134. Wilder is collecting material that he would use in his article "Giordano Bruno's Last Meal in *Finnegans Wake*" (1962).

4. *Armance, ou quelques scènes d'un salon de Paris en 1827* (1827). Octave de Malivert, the hero of the novel, is a delicate, gloomy young man who is impotent.

5. Stendhal to Prosper Mérimée, 23 December 1826, in *Armance*, ed. Henri Martineau (Paris: Éditions Garnier Frères, 1950), [249]–253. Although Stendhal mentions Jonathan Swift, Newton is not named in his letter.

6. Wilder's reference here is obscure. "Count SalmSalm" does not appear in *Finnegans Wake*.

7. French for cuckold. In his letter to Mérimée, Stendhal writes that the true Babilan cannot be cuckolded

8. FW I, i (3–29).

9. FW I, viii (196–216).

10. *Cabala del cavallo pegaeso* (1585).

To Adaline Glasheen, Farmington, Connecticut

[MS. APCS—HWS]

[Postcard: Kaiser's Reblaube
und Goethe-Stübli, Glockengasse 7, Zürich 1]

3 March [1959]　　　　　　　　　　Zürich [Switzerland]

Dear Adaline =
　Three friends of yours have had dinner together—lots about FW. We wish you and Francis were here because the eats are good and the shadow of Goethe is over us.

　　　　　devotedly
　　　　　Thornton–

　We are very happy to have been able to spend another delicious evening together.

　　　　　Best wishes
　　　　　Margrit & Fritz Senn[1]

---

1. Although Glasheen and Senn had been corresponding since 1954, they had not yet met.

To Adaline Glasheen, Farmington, Connecticut

[MS. ALS—HWS]

[? April 1959] 50 Deepwood Drive
April Something Hamden 17, Connecticut

Dear Madam =

Enclosed please find a draft of [Fritz] Senn's paper.[1] He is very diffident and sends it with a world of deprecation.

I told him to weed out the less salient and certain items and to concentrate on the big point—that J. J. found a most valuable image of his death and rebirth theme in the Sechselaüte and worked it for all it could give. Senn hasn't had time to insert the other important point—Joyce's similar frequent allusions to the Zurich Zunfthäuser[2]—or ancient guilds.

I too haven't time to draw up all the Virginia Woolf—Sackville-West matter. I'll try later.

Have also been looking into the Roughhead trials. Apparently a man name[d] William Burke Kirwan (who kept a second menage with seven children!) succeeded in drowning his wife Maria Louisa on a pleasant all day picnic to Ireland's Eye[3] (and of course I've failed to index all allusions to that small watering-place) but there's ireglint's eye on page 6.35.

I do my spiel here on the evening (8:00 pm) of April 23—I'm not sure where. Isabel and I'd like you to come to cocktails here at 6:30ish; then dinner at the [Graduates'] Club. The Romance Club has invited the Germanic Club the Slavic Club etc!! The title is Finnegans Wake: The Polyglot Everyman.[4] Popcorn sold; Bring the Kiddies. The listeners will hold a mimeographed sheet with selected passages.

We hope that Francis is progressing as well as Isabel is =

Regards to you all
Thornton

---

1. Senn's "Some Zurich Allusions in *Finnegans Wake*," was published in *The Analyst*, XIX (December 1960), [1]–22.
2. The meeting halls of the ancient guilds, many of which had evolved into restaurants.
3. An island near Howth.
4. See Appendices III and IV.

To Adaline Glasheen, Farmington, Connecticut

[MS. ALS—HWS]

3 May 195950 Deepwood Drive
Hamden 17, Connecticut

Dear Adaline =
Here are some jottings.
I thank you for all your suggestions in your last.[1]
And of course the supplement is a great gift.[2]
Now be thinking of a new format for the nex[t] FULL PRINTING of the Census.
I think you can leave out the *dagger*.[3] It now looks as though it's remarkable if any name does *not* allude to two or more persons at the same time. But I think you might consider indicating that a supporting allusion is in the vicinity. Say you used a dagger to indicate justa for instance—"next" or "near by"
As in my penultimate note on the adjoined leaf

> SEB, in early Egyptian theogonies Father of Isis and Osiris. . etc etc
> 486.1 sob († Tattu, THOTH)

> TAMAR, incestuous daughter of King David, 2 Sam xiii
> 184.20 d Amarilla († hermana, sister)

Hope Francis is coming on fine—as Isabel is. Isn't Spring wonderful?

Tutte Buone Cose
Ever
Thornton

[4]Woolf, Virginia, born Stephen.
Allusions under LUPUS and variants
Under ORLANDO (in the Renaissance interchangeable with RINALDO
and ROLANDO—hence REYNALDS) [i.e., Reynolds, 26.1]

Under variations of VIRG'
Under FLUSH, her book about E. B. B.'s dog.
   "   SPANIEL.
   "   WAVES, GUINEA,
[AG margin: 4 old latkes in Waves][5]
And almost constantly associated with her friend
SACKVILLE-WEST, Mary Victoria—called VITA (or VIDA) whose grandmother was a GYPSY, named PEPITA (i.e. JOSEPHINE) who lived at the ancient house KNOLE (now at its gate-house) SISSINGHURST and whose photographed portraits in male and female dress were used in the first editions of ORLANDO,—in which the hero-heroine changes sex and is therefore a HERM— (APHRODITE).[6]

No REFERENCES are given here unless at least two of these allusions are in near vicinity.
I begin with some of the more obvious

514.24	Sackville-Lawry and M*orland*-West
74.4–5	Wulverulverlord. . . roll, orland, roll.
26.12–4	[i.e., 13] Shewolf. . . . . .Virgo
192 =	3 LUPO; 4 Virgin; 5. . . lector general = Common Reader; 14 Reynaldo; 29 Flush.
444 =	28 lupitally 32 Wolf 36 Luperca {35 doll yarn = Dalloway?} and see the Lupita Luperca 67.33–36
385.17	vita(ls). . . Wulf! Wulf!
442.	5 Kno(w)l(ing[)]; 9 wolf—; 12 West . . . wave

Many, many more, that'll come out "clearer" with more work.

Pilkington, Laetitia (divorced by Rev. Matthew P)—Dict. of Na. Biog. calls her "adventuress"—friend and valuable writer about Swift—in her memoirs.
   born VAN LEWEN

184.23–25	Pinkingtone. . . . .Litty fun Letty fan Leven.
144.29–30	live on, the rubberend Mr Polkingtone, the. . .fleshmonger. L in her MEMOIRS[7] she claims her husband threw her at the heads of other men. .
203.29–30	Letty Lerck's lafing {LEWEN} light. There are a number of other Letties, but these are all I vouch for so far.

415.36	BEPPY: Fritz Senn: citizen of Basel; and Swiss-German for Father: also Italian nickname for Joseph or Hosepha. Also Budge[8]: Book of the Dead LXIII quotes a pyramid text of King PEPI I: "if the name of NUT {or OSIRIS. . etc} flourisheth, the name of Pepi. . . shall flourish and this his pyramid flourish. . .["] Also BAPPY 499.4
416.1	HAPI = child of Horus, present at the Last Judgment of the Negative Confession—in a later text of the Book of the Dead represents the NILE, BOOK OF THE DEAD, Budge, page 605. ALSO at the JUDGMENT SCENE (climax "My heart, my mother" 493.34)
494.25	TCHATCHA (Budge: Book of the Dead 25, 150) Heads or chiefs of the trial. Probably also 485.36 (with THOTH and SEB)
494.35	AMAM or AM-MLT—eater of the dead — Habasund—HUND, BARKING—dog comparison of THOTH, who helps weigh the souls.
495.6	ANPU = Egyptian ANUBIS (see Budge idem index) ANYPOSS
486.1	Sob = SEB, father of Isis and Osiris (lord of Tuttu 486.14 and see Tuttu and THOTH on preceding lines 485.35, 36.
488.20	MUT = in Thebes, supreme goddess, wife of AMEN, mother of all the Gods including OSIRIS (488.19)—Here "MUT'S deeply beloved."[9]

1. A lost letter.

2. Glasheen's "Out of My Census" filled all but one half of the last page of *The Analyst*, XVII (April 1959). It began with a statement by Glasheen [i] and had two parts, the Census: 1–64 and the Supplement, 64–73.

3. In *Census I* "A dagger means a name is made up of two or more people" (1); in "Out of My Census" she used the mark # to indicate the same principle.

4. From here to the end is written on a piece of three hole loose-leaf paper.

5. Titles of works by Virginia Woolf (1882–1941): *Orlando: A Biography* (1928), *Flush: A Biography* (1933, Woolf includes aspects of her own spaniel in this imaginary biography of Elizabeth Barrett Browning's dog), *The Waves* (1931), and *Three Guineas* (1938).

6. Woolf's novel *Orlando* is dedicated to Victoria Sackville-West (1892–1962). Three of the photographs in the book (possibly taken by Woolf) are of Sackville-West: "Orlando on her return to England," "Orlando about the year 1840," and "Orlando at the present time."

7. *Memoirs of Mrs. Laetitia Pilkington, 1712–1750, written by herself*; first published in London in 1748, a new edition with an Introduction by Iris Barry appeared in 1928.

8. We have not been able to identify the edition of *The Egyptian Book of the Dead* Wilder used.

9. On the envelope Wilder has written:
144[.14]–turkish
144.17 Pepita
279 notes
49.28 Shewolving
~~WOLF~~
~~FOWL~~
WOOLFE
Waves–203.31, 204.23
　　　　373.8

☐

To Thornton Wilder, Hamden, Connecticut

[MS. ALS—YCAL]

5 May 1959　　　　　　　　　　[22 Carrington Road
　　　　　　　　　　　　　　　Farmington, Connecticut]

Dear Thornton,

Yes isn't spring lovely, but it is always undermined for me by the threat of summer in which season I opine and droop like a wistful flower and quail beneath the lightning's flail.

I am fascinated with V. Woolf, Orlando et al and mean promptly to reread *Orlando*. (By the bye shouldn't somebody read Yeats' *A Vision?*) I don't know what I think. I don't mean I doubt most of your identifications, but I don't know how far they go. Are they mere decoration or more? If more I would like them to tie to Issy who I still think at times changes herself or her other into a man. And if I could find echo[e]s of *Orlando* it would pretty well prove the change, wouldn't it?

144.17 & 147.33 are surely Pepita.
144.14—Do I remember a Tur[k]ish avatar of Orlando's?
279 note—Has Rolando & viginity

281 rt. margin Virginia?
304[.25] Virginia? ?
49.28 Another She-wolf but why V. W. should tie to K. O'Shea I don't know
67.33 V. Woolf killed herself too late for this?[1]
All this wants vast thinking of, but what fun to think.

An infuriated letter from Mrs von Phul[2] who says she sent me 54 identifications & was only credited with 28 because A) I didn't use some B) I ascribed them to you. All of which of course. It was strictly first come first serve and I didn't take anybody's suggestions entire. She—RvP—goes on to accuse me of bad faith and of preferring your initials to hers and says she will never tell me any FW thing again. Untrue, unreasonable, my intentions were good, but I think little of good intentions & so have written her a letter meant to soothe. If my method has infuriated everyone only time can tell. If I sound half-witted in this letter it's because after 3 weeks I've finally gotten a minor scene in my novel straightened out & I am wrung out like a rag. Why are minor scenes, paving-the-goddam-way scenes always the hardest to write? I see, I see why you took to the theatre. A play is clean & concentrated. A novel is a sloppy lummox, a cross between Caliban & Tony Lumpkin.[3]
F[rancis]. progresses. I'm glad Isabel does.

    Yours,
    Adaline

I've been reading Pound's *Cantos*. Very easy reading I must say.

[Enclosure]
260.16   [i.e., .4] will = Y[eats]'s[4] technical term & William himself
 .left margin—face = phase
 .20 [i.e., .8]   wheel Y's term
[AG margin: I'd question these but for what comes after]
261.8   maker mates with made—steadily figured as Leda thereafter
 .9   cones—Y. Term
 .21   Yeats Hunchback is The Multiple Man
262—   Anagrams of Yeats
263.18   M[aud]. Gonne
 .22   Hermes = one of Y's masters
264.30   Tower
264 note 3— Porphary [line drawn to reference 263.22 above]

266.19	will / 27 Leda
.note 2	I think parodies Yeats though not in Vision
267.1	Leda
.24–25	may parody Y's astrology / ?284 & note 1 all over roses
268 left m-	Mathers Y's hermetic master
269.17	More maker & made stuff—these are the 4 elements
.29	[i.e., .28] eggs all over Y
?271.18–19	M[aud]. Gonne
272.2	Leda / .4 Will / "Love & war come from the eggs of Leda"
?274.31	face = phase
275 left m-	Mrs. Yeats used to smell cats {in 1st ed?}[5]
276.note 3–	Yeats & moon
?277.6	will? / .9 Yeats was a member?
277.9	Are the Mikes & Michaels—M. Robartes?[6]
277.19	I think Y uses "Order" technically but am not sure
280.6	Gonne
.34	I think may echo "When You are gray" etc

{Hey I just noticed 281.23 = Jane *Eyre* & *Thornfield*. Mr. R[ochester]'s evil house—both wives—Ra begarrese}

283.23	May or mayn't be significant—Y. says he got his geometry all wrong at first
?285.3	Y. went in for table turning / .4 eggs
.15	Yeats an M. P. ?
.note 5	all Yeats
286.5	primary tincture = Yeats term .17 wheel
287.18	husk, spirit, spir{al} / Barkeley /
288.8	Mather again /?.5 eggs & note 2
?289.33	[i.e., note 2] spirit?
293.3	Shift / 293.11 Y's "Lapis Lazuli" is too late
294.27	Byzantium & stylistic imitation
295.10–12	Dreaming backward & telescope / .24–5 [i.e., .23–.24] gyres
296.21	Mather again
297.11	Cones / .12 vortex
298.3	egg / .17 gyre [i.e., .16] / .28 sphere / .32 stylistic imitation
300.20–27–	Other / creative mind (2 times) / mask (mess mass) Body of Fate (2 times) / "own" may be Owen Aherne / spirals
??302.31–2	possible quote / note 2 William
303. left m.,	3rd gloss—I think a quote / ditto gloss 1 left m. on 304
303.7 & 8	Named
306.4	will & Nobel Prize which to sweeten his betters (as you told me long ago) ALP gave WBY

I also think the men in the margins 306–7 were probably suggested by Yeats. Aside from them, I think J. takes over in this section most, if not all, historical examples from *A Vision*.

With understandable hesitation I proceed. Do you know the passage in *Portrait of the Artist*, Stephen says Michael Robartes wants to embrace the beauty that's faded from the world, while he (Stephen) wants to embrace the beauty that's not yet come into the world?[7] Well up to 272.9 where the past is dead, Leda (a faded out beauty) has dominated. Now we move on to Shem creating new or modern beauty.

I've found all Yeats' important technical terms *except* Celestial Body and Passionate Body which go with Mask & Spirit as Creative Mind & Body of Fate go with Will & Mask. I bet they're there. Will you look for Celestial Body & Passionate Body?

Is it all trimming or does it go farther?

    Yours AG

1. On 28 March 1941 Woolf drowned herself in the River Ouse.
2. Ruth von Phul, a Joyce scholar and professional crossword maker. Her letters to Glasheen are in HWS. In "Out of My Census" Glasheen used initials to identify individual contributors (see Glasheen Bibliography for the list of contributors).
3. Caliban, in Shakespeare's *The Tempest*. Tony Lumpkin, in Oliver Goldsmith's *She Stoops to Conquer*, is described as "fond of low company" and as "an awkward booby, reared up and spoiled at his mother's apron-string."
4. Glasheen abbreviates Yeats as Y throughout this list.
5. *A Vision* was first published in 1925. In 1937 Yeats prepared a new version with substantial deletions and additions; the major addition was selections from *A Packet for Ezra Pound* (1929).
6. A character in Yeats's work.
7. See chapter 5, 251 in *A Portrait of the Artist as a Young Man*, ed. Chester G. Anderson (New York: Viking Critical Library, 1968).

To Thornton Wilder, Hamden, Connecticut
[MS. ALS—YCAL]

20 May 1959 [22 Carrington Road
Farmington, Connecticut]

Dear Thornton,

I can't answer your letter because I lost it in the excitement of my relatives and the trailer. They were good as gold and excessively dull and stayed a week. Now they're gone. I am nursing my boss at the library whose back has failed.[1] It doesn't really matter because I can't write on my novel when there are thunder storms. Miss Muse flees shrieking.

Did I tell you Mrs von Phul is soothed and Mr Higginson doesn't mind his name being spelled wrong & it saying "he teaches *as* the University of Minnesota[.]"

280–1	later Lammas = never
297.31	a "bare" = a tidal wave
303.5	"Bold Stroke for a Wife" = a play by Mrs. Centlivre.[2] Why don't modern plays have titles like this?
483.14–15	In the Reynard cycle,[3] the leopard = Fyrapel
516.12–14	Reynard claimed to have a (nonexistent comb) made of Patherais bone, irresistibly perfumed & to make one merry of heart.

The brilliant aboves are from a Reader's Handbook by Brewer[4] that I am glumly reading through, I daresay I found a few more bits & will find a few more. What have you found? How are you & Isabel?

Yours,
Adaline

---

1. Glasheen occasionally worked at the local library in Farmington, Connecticut.
2. *A Bold Stroke for a Wife*, a comedy by Susannah Centlivre (?1667–1723), was produced in 1718. Centlivre was the author of eighteen plays between 1700 and 1722.

3. *Fables* by Jean de la Fontaine (1621–1695) appeared in three separate volumes, in 1668, 1678–79, and 1693.

4. The Rev. Ebenezer Cobham Brewer (1810–1897), his *Reader's Handbook* was first published in 1880.

To Adaline Glasheen, Farmington, Connecticut

[MS. ALS—HWS]

[postmark: 27 May 1959] [50 Deepwood Drive
Begun: May 21 Hamden 17, Connecticut]
Finished in Haste
25 May

Mona 502[.12]
Rhoda [466.19]

Dear Adaline:
    Thanks as always.
    Whenever your "references" send me to a page I read the whole page.
    But I keep finding so many I'm not sure of—or where the allusion is to a book or person but doesn't not mention the proper name.
    You send me to 303.5 for Mrs Centlivre.
303.17   George {Lees, really Hyde-Lees} Mrs William B. Yeats[1] doing
        the Vision by automatic writing, line 19
          {I have a great deal more about that [?turn]
          table-tipping, Round-table hence Merlin chair—
285:2–3 but it'll have to wait until its comes clearer.[}]
[AG margin: George Gaman]

    You send me to 483.14–15 for Fyerapel—for which much thanks. Yeats all around.
483.5–6   Yeats: Reveries over Childhood and Youth
      → Did you note "Point Counterpoint" 482.33–34?

482.1   Eddy's = for Aldes Christi—name for Christ Church College ("The House") where Lewis Dodgson lived [i.e., Charles Ludwidge Dodgson].

Keep your eye open for MADGE WILDFIRE, gypsy girl in *The Heart of Midlothian*. She may be[2]

can you trace down an old song about
".... Rhoda... lived in a pagoda.... where she sold... tea... and soda["][3]
It's 466.19
{all very confusing: there's a very popular cheap novelist in the German-speaking world named Roda-Roda[4] 434.7 478.13 78.17 (as ALP) 81.9 266.21–22 469.34 478.13 (viâ "ready road")[}]

72.4   Paul Rutledge: hero—fanatic pacifist—of Yeats's play "Where There is Nothing"[5]—killed by a mob—(with a bomb?)

BE thinking this over: MAUD is short for Magdalene—Madeline but MADGE and MAGGY are only short for MARGARET.
[AG margin: Margit]
J. J. shows that he knows this: and separates the two:
    p. 586.6–7 Maid Maud
           12 Maudlin river
    Then separating the two.
         .13 muddle me more about the maggies
         .14 Madge Ellis and... Mag Dillon.
    I think –next time!—you should have separate listings of Madeline-Mauds and Margaret-Maggies.
    I think that Maud Gonne is all over the place—the most romantic love-story in Joyce's world.[6]

After her exile in France and marriage to and separation from Major John MacBride, Maud Gonne was always called Madame MacBride.
    451.3   madamaud.

When Yeats did table-rapping etc at séances, his "familiar" was LEO AFRICANUS. (I don't know if he "used" Leo when he and Georgie did a "Vision"); but just above this long quote from A VISION see *leo* on p. 300.16
    Also 466.6

love apple, for Leas {G. Lees, Mrs Yeats} and love potions {and that gland operation} for Leos. . . . (NB) line 9 "boiling." One of the last things Yeats wrote was a sort of pamphlet "On the boiler."[7]
  notice 300.16 I read
      .17 you write. . . all your horoscopes
 ¶ I think groping for words on a ouija-board makes James Joyce think of Jacob's letter-crackers and Jacob's alphabet soup-cracker. See him spelling in 300.12?
    and 303.16

LATER: Again in Rare Book Room: Yeats: A Packet for Ezra Pound.[8] Describes how A Vision was made. Wife, first, automatic writing: later talking in her sleep, etc. No table-tapping or ouija. But J. J. may have thought it was table-ouija which Yeats certainly did in London days. Yeats says dictated by "various" masters—names none

    Had a lovely time at your house[9]
    Ever
    (TNW)

P. S.
 I suppose your learned English correspondents have pointed out that *aureoles* 306.1 is probably
  Philippus Aureolus Paracelsus—né Theophrastus Bombastus von Hohenheim[10]

---

and that FW 299.14–15 the gheist that stays forenenst is Mephistopheles in FAUST. der Geist der stets vernint who always denies.

---

p. 300 left margin =
 STURM, Dr. F. P. Yeats' friend and correspondent on oriental mysticisms.
  Probably we are to read also S'TURM Tower because 300.30 Thur = THOOR gaelic tower Yeats' house—as you know—was called THOOR BALLYLEE

My next letter to you will be very exciting!! I'm getting hot on something. You'll have to triple the size of the Census.

(T)

1. Yeats married Bertha Georgie [George] Hyde-Lees on 20 October 1917. Four days after their marriage Mrs. Yeats began the automatic writing experiments that became the basis for *A Vision*.

2. The sentence is not completed by Wilder. *The Heart of Midlothian*, a novel by Sir Walter Scott, was published in 1818.

3. Glasheen quotes Wilder in *Census II*. Hodgart and Worthington identify it as "Rhoda and Her Pagoda" and add a reference to the song on 478.13 (199).

4. Alexander Roda Roda, the pseudonym of the Hungarian born writer Sandór von Rosenfeld (1872–1945), who emigrated to the United States in 1938. His work describes pre-World War I Austria and is filled with humor and satire. His best known works are the light comedy *Der Feldherrnhügel* (1910, in collaboration with C. Rössler) and *Roda Rodas Roman* (1925).

5. A play in five acts completed by Yeats in 1902.

6. Maud Gonne (1866–1953) was the daughter of an English army officer posted in Dublin. Yeats met her in 1889, and in 1891 he made the first of many marriage proposals to her. Gonne became active in the Irish Nationalist cause and was a founder of Sinn Féin (1906). She was a popular speaker at meetings and fundraising events in Ireland, France, and the United States. In addition to founding revolutionary organizations and journals, she acted, most notably in the title role of Yeats's play *Cathleen Ni Houlihan* (1902). In 1903 she married Major John MacBride. Their marriage ended in divorce. Major MacBride was one of those executed in the aftermath of the 1916 Easter Rising.

7. *On the Boiler*, a collection of short essays was posthumously published (Dublin: The Cuala Press, 1939, 46pp).

8. *A Packet for Ezra Pound* (Dublin: The Cuala Press, 1929). When first printed it contained: "Rapallo," "Meditations upon Death," "Introduction to 'The Great Wheel,'" and "To Ezra Pound." When Yeats revised *A Vision* in 1937, he omitted portions of the 1929 text.

9. Wilder had visited the Glasheens on Saturday, 9 May.

10. Glasheen had, in fact, made a query about Paracelsus in 1952—see Glasheen Bibliography. Philippus Aureolus Paracelsus (?1493–1541) was a Swiss born alchemist and physician who argued that diseases are specific entities and can be treated by specific remedies. Jonathan Swift refers to him in *A Tale of a Tub*.

To Thornton Wilder, Hamden, Connecticut
[MS. ALS—YCAL]

31 May 1959 [22 Carrington Road
Farmington, Connecticut]

Dear Thornton,

You would laugh but we can't. Alison is giving a report on you at school, not saying she knows you, not pretending she has read you. On us she practices—"This ever—versit-*ilé* and deeply American..." "... attended Purdue and Yale[1]..." Did you? I strongly suspect some of her information is wrong. Mind, you never tell her I told you about it.

Come come tell me what your new great thing is!

Wonderful things in your last. AS to George Yeats[2]—where does it say "Gam on George"? I mean in FW, I can't find it. [599.18]

Childhood Reveries—good
Aldes Chréstre—good
What's Roda-Roda about?
There is a distinction between Maud & Margaret but I have a vague recollection of a footnote in Don Quixote saying Margit (or whatever the Spanish for Margaret is) means whore in Spanish. Would you know?

Yes I think M. Gonne is all over
Aureoles—lovely
Faust quote "
All is lovely I wish I had something good to give you back.
O (letter in alphabet L M N O) used to mean the Virgin. As in O tell me about Anna Livia? [193.1–.3]

I kind of think that *The New Art of Punning*[3] may be 184.24. The Misses Barry at l. 24 [i.e., .21]. Infanta at .34. I'm not awfully sure.

Watching baseball this afternoon I sort of read at 104ff. Noted a few things & puzzles.

?104.18–19	[i.e., .6–.7] Billy Budd?
.22	[i.e., .10] Isaac
105.3	Abraham
.8	Marlborough?
.14	Noah & possibly 104.24
.26	Abigail—who she?
106.9	I guess this is R. L. Stevenson who wrote *The Master of Ballantrae*—Polynesiona<u>l</u> Entertaine<u>r</u> Exhibit<u>s</u>. Really!
.17	Last of Mohicans—see Hawk Eye line 24
106.23	It doesn't make sense to me but is this Alyosha Karamazov? I've always known the Brothers had to be there.
.28	Isaac
105.35	Terriss and 111.6—Who he? I keep groping for someone named Roy Terriss who I associate with ugh Hemingway.
[111].20	Catullus
112.30	Is teasy Yeats?
116.36	I have an idea that "will be" always means W[illiam]. B[utler]. Y.[eats] Anyway here because we go into maker mates with made stuff at top 117.
[117] line 2	Here = Hera

{Is "Insult the Fair" Iseult Gonne—or was her name MacBride?}[4]

.3	lightning = Zeus to Danae
.3	bird " " Leda
.16	Anne Bol[e]yn & Henry VIII?
118.20	S[inclair]. Lewis
119.9	Who said that about "The Excursion"?[5]
122.19	I often worry because I can't find Kipling's Kim who went looking for a river. Could K. M. O'Mara be Kim O'Hara?
123.24	I suppose this refers to that damned Parable of the Plums[6] in *Ulysses* which I do not understand.
123.15	Somebody named Millicent
	I start getting pretty confused on 124[.] I think "but" in line 1 = Butt[.] line 9 says the letter (which below seems to be a female) was pierced (O'Reilly?) by ∧ , ⌈ which according to my list (maybe I copied wrong) is Shaun and Shem's mark ⌈ is at line 11. But, if I have the signs right, Shaun is here Time punching a hole in Space which is backwards. Why don't you explain this page to me?

      Yours,
      Adaline

1. Wilder attended Oberlin College, Ohio, from 1915 to 1917; he then transferred to Yale College where he earned his B.A. in 1920. (Wilder took eight months off for military service in the Coast Artillery, Fort Adams, Rhode Island, in 1918–1919.)

2. Bertha Georgie Hyde-Lees, Mrs. William Butler Yeats.

3. Thomas Sheridan (1687–1738), *Ars pun-ica, sive Flos linguarum = The Art of Punning, or, The Flower of Languages: In Seventy-Nine Rules: for the farther improvement of conversation and help of memory/by the labour and industry of Tom Punsibi* [i.e., Jonathan Swift] (1719).

4. Gonne had an affair with Lucien Millevoye, a French baker, and bore two children. The first died shortly after birth, the second was Iseult, born in 1895. In August 1917, while visiting Maud Gonne in Normandy, France, Yeats proposed marriage to Iseult but was rejected.

5. A poem by William Wordsworth that was to be the central section of the never finished *Recluse*.

6. The story of two "Dublin vestals" who "purchase four and twenty ripe plums" to take on an excursion to the top of Nelson's pillar is told by Stephen Dedalus in episode 7 of *Ulysses*. Stephen names the story "*A Pisgah Sight of Palestine or the Parable of the Plums*." The title is repeated in episode 17. See *Ulysses* 1961: 145–146, 149, 685.

□

To Adaline Glasheen, Farmington, Connecticut

[MS. ALS—HWS]

1 June [1959]   50 Deepwood Drive
    Hamden 17, Connecticut

Dear Adaline. . . .
   Not important, but "may quietly amuse"
615.5–6   paraidiotically[1]
    and here are the Periodicals
614.28   Criterion
   29   Calendar
   {31   "Work in Progress"}
   {31   "Faber and Son"[}]
   32   probably The Egoist
   33   Dial and Little Review
   36   Transition

615.1	Leader
.2	p-Loon-ey, maybe Adrienne Monnier of Navire d'Argent[2]
.3	Margaret Anderson[3]
	{The Italian for hyacinth is GIACINTO—feminine in—
	a = means "already pregnant"—who is that?
.4	il-lyrical = Poetry

620.5   That's Yeats's poem *Baile and Ail[l]inn* (and the song "Eileen Aruna." ¶ Perhaps in Gaelic they often turned words about ["]Purseproud Baile."

  I already gave you
378.23 [i.e., .24] propound[e] as Ezra Pound but I didn't see *parsonifier* alluded to Pound's book PERSONAE. (How often one kicks oneself in this work.)

540.30   Maud Gonne—pretty cute, eh?

131.33+   is Ezra Pound has—his: read EZ. . . EZ. . . he reverses the Chinese for Confucius: Kung-Fu-TSE. Taishan = sacred Mt of China. Pound[']s head: very "sugarloaf"—hair is wild Kangaroo's beard in shanty-land Ashanti-land = E. P.'s admiration for Fenellosa's work in Africa[4]
For Chin(chin) = mountain see Yeats's letters p. 250[5]

. . . . unimportant, but may quietly amuse.

       Cordially
       Thornton

---

1. The identifications Wilder gives for 614–615 are of periodicals in which Joyce published or with which he was acquainted. Faber and Faber were London publishers of fragments of "Work in Progress" in booklet form: "Anna Livia Plurabelle" (1930), "Haveth Childers Everywhere" (1931), "Tales of Shem and Shaun" (1932), "The Mime of Mick Nick and the Maggies" (1934). They also brought out the first British edition of *Pomes Penyeach* in 1933. For Joyce publications in journals and magazines see Slocum and Cahoon; for a history of British journals see *British Literary Magazines: The Modern Age, 1914–1984*, ed. Alvin Sullivan (Westport, CT: Greenwood Press, 1983).

2. Adrienne Monnier (1892–1955), the owner of La Maison des Amis des Livres, on the rue de l'Odeon, was an important figure in French letters between the two World Wars. In her journal *Navire d'argent* she published pages of what would

become the Anna Livia Plurabelle chapter of *Finnegans Wake* (I, viii, 196–216). She also published Auguste Morrel's French translation of *Ulysses* in 1929.

3. Margaret Anderson (1886–1973) founded *The Little Review* in Chicago in 1914. In 1916–17 Jane Heap (1887–1964) became co-editor. The European editor of the review was Ezra Pound. Between March 1918 and September 1920 *The Little Review* published installments of *Ulysses*, resulting in a trial and conviction for printing obscene literature. Anderson lost her case in December 1920 and paid a fine of $100. Anderson and Heap moved the review to Paris in 1923, and its last issue was in May 1929.

4. Ashanti is a kingdom in Ghana. Ernest Fenollosa (1853–1908) was an orientalist who became a practicing Buddhist. Educated at Harvard University, he was Curator of the department of Oriental Art in the Boston Museum of Fine Arts (1890–1897). He taught in Japan from 1878 to 1886 and then again from 1897–1900. Ezra Pound was his literary executor.

5. *The Letters of W. B. Yeats*, ed. Allan Wade (New York: The Macmillan Co., 1955).

To Thornton Wilder, Hamden, Connecticut
[MS. APCS—YCAL]

8 June 1959   [22 Carrington Road
                                                               Farmington, Connecticut]

Dear T.—

Frazer[1] tells a story—Isis wanted to know Ra's great secret name so she gathered up his spit (FW 38[.10]) & made it into a serpent which stung him so badly that he finally had to tell it[2]—I don't suppose it was Persse O'Reilly [44–47ff.]—story doesn't say what. We can be *sure* J. used this story for what do you think Frazer footnotes—*Tom Tit Tot* by E. Clodd![3] Clodd's around, isn't he? I would like to see the book.

I wrote a long informative letter to Senn this morning and I am going to write a long informative letter to somebody or other this afternoon. I hope you're pleased.

                         Yours,
                         Adaline

I am v[ery]. touched by your calling up to show me the way I should not go. Love to Isabel.

1. It is not known which edition Glasheen used of Sir James G. Frazer's (1854–1941) *The Golden Bough: A Study of Magic and Religion* (1890–1915). Her citations have been keyed to the 1980 edition published by the Macmillan Press in London.
2. *The Golden Bough: Taboo and the Perils of the Soul*, part II, "Names of Gods Tabooed," 387–388.
3. Edward Clodd (1840–1930), *Tom Tit Tot: An Essay on Savage Philosophy in Folk-Tale* (London: Duckworth & Co., 1898). "Tom Tit Tot" is the name of a group of stories derived from oral transmission. Frazer mentions Clodd in *The Golden Bough: Balder The Beautiful: The Fire-Festivals of Europe and the Doctrine of the External Soul*, vol. 2, "The External Soul in Folk-Tales," note 1, 96–97 and in the general bibliography. See also AG to TW, 22 June 1959.

To Adaline Glasheen, Farmington, Connecticut

[MS. ALS—HWS]

[?11–18 June 1959]   [50 Deepwood Drive
Thursday   Hamden, Connecticut]

Dear Adaline =
    Just some jottings to keep your morale high.
    Yes, I think that's the beautiful role for you: to keep your whole chorus producing.
    And then finally bringing out a volume called *Readings in FW*—of which you are the high editrix. Demand of each of us a resounding paper. {No paper hitherto published can be included unless you can guarantee that it has been enriched and doubled in matter since its first publication.}
    First some trifles
MAUGHAM, SOMERSET 115.14–16
JEWKES, MRS (old procuress in *Pamela*)[1] 456.31
LITTLE BROWN, Boston publishers 114.31

On pages 289 to 292 JJ is basing himself on the PAOLA-
FRANCESCA passage in Inferno V
Dante: verse 100   Amor ch'al cor gentil ratto
                      s'appre[nde]   FW 292.1–2
   {and the suffering sinners are being whirled about onto Moore's
     song in 2–3.[}]
Dante: verse 142 e caddi, come corpo morto cade   FW 289.15
              and fell as a dead body falls
              NOW Dante's sample lustful sinners
Dante 54–60 Semiramis ?
       61–62 Dido and husband Sichaeus   FW. 291 note 3
                 Elisa = Dido   FW 291[.]14
       64   Helena   Nell   "   14
       63   Cleopatras Cliptbuss   "   14
       65   Achille   ?
       67   Paris   ?
       67   Tristano   passim = 290.2
and I forgot to add
       61 [i.e., 62] SICHEO   subsequious   FW. 291.8
_____

         OLD IRISH OGHAM FANGER LANGUAGE[2]
Graves's White Goddess 204, 305[3]
FW 283.19 Forefingers surmounted by LUIS (rowan) here maybe
           from Italian LUIGI and LEAGUE
           NEXT FOOL-Finger
           NEXT LEECH-Finger
           Maybe Little Finger—little ear = is in archer = harkers
_____

   Now—just for *your* interest—don't circulate it yet.
   T. S. Eliot and Pound *all over the place*. [TW at margin:
confidential] Joyce had to conceal it hard, because they were beautifully
his benefactors and they were reading the material as it came out.
FW 191.12 possum
       13 gumtree = a possum tree {The whole class of trees
           including licuidanber![4] and eucalyptus are interrelated—
           and *so* Eliot is also Australian by all the Marsupials—esp
           Kangaroos—}
       26 reverse ELIOT you get TOILET (which J. J. uses only
           once I think in the book, because he had read too often
           that he had a "cloacal obsession")
   Now .10 No VENA   no blood
            No VARA   Latin etc. staff

9	Amidah = standing prayer = benediction in Hebrew service
21	Tom
21	bing = Bang not whimper
24	possum. . . . .like muck. . .
22	[i.e., .23] edify.
30	possum
	I'll bet there's lots more there, from the poems. A very distasteful passage

FOR POUND FW 65

This is a take-off on that imitation of musical comedy that Eliot wrote—is it Sweeney Agonistes? So it mixes Pound and Eliot.

65.1	Bruised stone = Boston
2	waste lands
7	viv = Eliot's first wife Vivian
12; 19; 20; 23	Pound's nickname was GRAM or Grampapa.
28	Pound's A B C of Reading. Faber and Yale Press 1935
32	Faber.

Courage up, young lady
(T)

1. *Pamela, or Virtue Rewarded*, a novel by Samuel Richardson (1689–1761) published in 1740.

2. Ogham or ogam is an ancient British/Irish system of writing. It was probably developed in the fourth century, and it uses an alphabet of twenty to twenty-five characters.

3. Wilder is referring to the first edition of Graves's book (1948). See pages 200, 235–236 in the amended and enlarged Noonday Press edition (1975).

4. Wilder is probably referring to licuala lauterbanchii, a type of Australian fan palm.

To Thornton Wilder, Hamden, Connecticut
[MS. ALS—YCAL]

22 June 1959   [22 Carrington Road
                                                      Farmington, Connecticut]

Dear Thornton,

They sent me the 2nd Joyce Miscellany today and 50! offprints.[1] I have a kind of fondness for my article which I will send you but in the book (which is nicely bound & printed) it partakes of a pervading and lowering harmlessness which cannot but nauseate.

Ruth von Phul's "Joyce & the Strabismal Apologia" is clear & certainly right in the main (not about FW) but the wonder is that anybody should think it worth writing down. Best—at least useful—is Walton Litz "The Making of FW" which charts when what part of FW was written. I was going to work it out roughly & am glad to be spared the trouble. I wrote Mr. Litz to thank him.

I don't think I told you about "The Dead" whose hero, as you may know, is Gabriel Conroy. Gabriel Conroy is the title hero of Bret Harte's only full-length novel which needless to say isn't in Farmington so I mentioned it to [Clive] Hart who says the book opens with Gabriel lost in the middle of a snow storm.[2] Joyce's early trashy reading ought to be thought of, I suppose. Hall Cain[e] for instance?[3]

The 2nd paragraph of FW detains me. It goes from violet (*viole* d'amour) to red (rory—In red-see J to Miss Weaver). I never saw till now that Jhem or Shen = Jameson. But J. tells Miss W. there's *a reference to Sir B. Guin[n]ess*[4] which I'm damned if I see & I don't understand him about the *Anglo-Irish no bloody he business.*
?FW 9   Frazer says in Ireland on Midsummer Eve people leaped through fires. Also had a wooden frame 8 ft long with horse's head & white sheet concealing frame. Man carried it through fire. Shouts of "The white horse." The horse explained as meaning "all the cattle[.]"[5]
13.36   Balfour—he was stern as Viceroy

111.20   Catullus?
   Frazer says at Beltane in Skye they have a ritual Cake called
CONNACH MICHEIL or St. Michael cake[6]
?112.30   Yeats?
117—top of page—Zeus & his women again—Here l[ines] .2 /.3
     lightning = Danae
   .3   birding cry = Leda, Yeats possibly 116.36. Is W[illiam]
B[utler] Y[eats] indicated in all "will be"s?
—175.36   ancients called ripe corn "Yellow Demeter"
—196—   Brewer[7] says by false analogy Dublin is derived from
     dub{ious} lin{en}
226   Forsaken girl common in May Day rites
249   "   lad   "   "   "   "   "
289 [i.e., 269.left margin)   Dante—lovely
290.note 7— man named J. Curtin wrote *Myths & Folklore of Ireland*
     Frazer mentions[8]
328[.28–.29] Bride & Breed both forms of Bridget
403.25 [i.e., .13]   Oberon
   .29 [i.e., .16–.17]   Song to Titania[9]
   .30 [i.e., .18]   Bottom's "Methought" speech IV, ii [i.e., i] 200 /
     Methought repeated by ASS on 404[.4]-5[.7].
     Shem = Ass = Bottom. Shaun = Moonlight.
     ALP = Titania HCE = Oberon
407.35   rag up—Moonshine is batching forth at Globe Globe is
     mentioned somewhere in this section
407.4   *lecker* = Dutch "delicious"
405.33   Bacon—to show this fake Shakespeare? 406.3, .15
406.10   Botherhim = phonetic[al]ly Dutch "sandwich"
408.6   Ton—Iosal—very heavy Fianion—Osséan

| 412.31 | MSND III, i, 189 ? |

414   Anybody read Terence's Formio [i.e., Phormio]?
     I noticed in J's letters he speaks of "The *Mouse* & the
     Grapes." Is this a different fable?[10]
425.13   Playboy killed his pa with a "loy"[11]
426.17   Felix culpa
427.19   Did Yeats write play "The Twisting of the Rope"?[12]
431.34   See footnote 279
455.32   MSND III, i, 195
466.17   Starveling played Moonshine[.] If Shaun is Starveling
     maybe why he eats so much?

527.29 etc— Brewer[13] says before Eve expelled from Eden she was called "Ishah" because taken out of ISH or Man
I wrote Ruth von Phul & irritated & she responded like an angel. But not to much point. She will not give up theorizing about Joyce.

I hope you are well. I am not. I am sick—not fatally in bed and filled with all sorts of odd substances. How is your sister? Whom we like so much. And you?

Yours,
Adaline

1. Glasheen's "Joyce and the Three Ages of Charles Stewart Parnell," in *A James Joyce Miscellany*, Second Series, ed. Marvin Magalaner (Carbondale: Southern Illinois University Press, 1959), 151–178.

2. Joyce alludes to Harte's description of snow in the opening of *Gabriel Conroy* (1875) but not the characters and plot. See "The Dead," last paragraph.

3. Sir Thomas Henry Hall Caine (1853–1931) wrote popular novels, many set on the Isle of Man.

4. Joyce to Weaver, 13 January 1925 in *Letters I*, 224–225.

5. *The Golden Bough: Balder the Beautiful: The Fire-Festivals of Europe and the Doctrine of the External Soul*, vol. I, "The Midsummer Fires," 1980, 202–206.

6. As above, *Balder the Beautiful*, "The Beltane Fires," 149.

7. Glasheen is reading Brewer's *Reader's Handbook*. See AG to TW, 20 May 1959, n. 4.

8. In the General Bibliography of *The Golden Bough* Frazer mentions this title (London, n. d.) and Jeremiah Curtin's *Myths and Folk-tales of the Russians, Western Slavs, and Magyars* (London, 1891).

9. In Shakespeare's, *A Midsummer Night's Dream*, I, ii, 83–84: "I will roar you as gently as any sucking dove" is spoken by Bottom at Quince's house and not sung to Titania, the Queen of the Fairies. In the reference to 412.31 below, the box and question mark are Wilder's additions.

10. The Mookse and the Gripes, *Finnegans Wake*, 152.15–159.18, is derived from Aesop's fable "The Fox and the Grapes."

11. In Act I of John Millington Synge's (1871–1909) play *The Playboy of the Western World*, Christopher (Christy) Mahon announces: "I just riz the loy and let fall the edge of it on the ridge of his skull."

12. A one-act play by Douglas Hyde (1860–1949) based on the character of Red Hanrahan in Yeats's story of the same name.

13. Brewer's *Reader's Handbook*.

To Adaline Glasheen, Farmington, Connecticut

[MS. APCS—HWS]

[postmark: 25 June 1959]   Stockbridge [Massachusetts]
returning home Sat'dy

Dear Adaline =
Just a word to thank you and to express sympathy on your indisposition = be a good patient and rest completely so the medicines can work.

Haven't got my FW up here but hope to send you a series of allusions soon to the Tarot pack in FW.[1]

[Fritz] Senn wrote, sort of dejected, can't finish his Zurich paper.[2] Yes, it's terribly hard to finish anything on FW.

He began finding so many allusions to the Böögy—Secleselante [i.e., Sechseläuten] Festival that he came to doubt his own judgment. Just to cheer up his morale I sent him some rough-notes stuff that I couldn't finish on Eliot and Pound.

Very eager to get back to my copy to trace your Midsummer Nights Dream allusions in it.

Your question: Not Yeats but either Dr Douglas Hyde or Ed. Martyn wrote a play The Twisting of the Rope[3]—but before that, that is the title of a folk-song ballad.

Get well =

         Cordialest to all
         (T)

1. There are references to the Tarot in Wilder's "Giordano Bruno's Last Meal in *Finnegans Wake*." See Wilder bibliography. There are also notes on the Tarot in Wilder's *Wake* notes (YCAL).
2. See TW to AG, [? April 1959], n. 1.
3. See AG to TW, 22 June 1959, n. 12. Edward Martyn, the playwright (1859–1923).

To Adaline Glasheen, Farmington, Connecticut

[MS. ALS—HWS]

[postmark: Wednesday, 1 July 1959]　　50 Deepwood Drive
Tuesday?　　　　　　　　　　　　　　Hamden 17, Connecticut
Wednesday?

Dear Adaline =
　　Gracious sakes alive.
　　You would go and select the most tightly-packed be-riddled paragraph in the whole book.[1]
　　I'll make no comment but add a few things that may help or confuse you:
　　Try the signs of the Zodiac then: two to a clause
[following references are to page 3]
.5　　ARIES RAM scrag = neck of a ship (isthmus is neck in Greek)
　　　Wielder = Widder = German for RAM
21 [i.e., .9]　　Bellow TAURUS
21 [i.e., .9]　　Brigid = Virgo? or 22 Venus Virgo
23 [i.e., .11]　kidd. . . butt Capricorn. Scad = Pisces?
24 [i.e., .12]　sosie. . . twin GEMINI
　　　nathandjoe = CANCER—crabs go backward.
26 [i.e., .14]　AQUARIUS. And EL NATH is a star in TAURUS

　　　CONTINENTS must be there
[3.9]　　AFIRE = AFER Africa
[3.8]　　hen Gypsies Georgio and mumper for Egypt-Africa
　　　What nicknames has Australia other than "down under"?
[3.9]　　Bellowsed = OST = German for East and OSIA (OSTEN)
COLORS =
　　　damned if I can find a blue unless it's in Bland-Blind [3.11]. . .
　　　he uses IND many times for Indigo.
　　　lots of reds

The MAIN THEMES of the Book.
　　　You told me that REGGIN [3.14] tried to kill his brother FAFNIR in the Volsunga saga[.][2] But where are the THREE and the FOUR?

Stray items = Letters p. 225 Sir Benj. Lee Guinness of the Brewery is Dublin's Noah.[3]

I always felt that the paragraph "not yet. . . not yet" meant that the sun had not yet set and the constellations appeared. . . . . 32 [i.e., .20] sol-id man.

.16 [i.e., .4]   FROVER Old English = comforter, God, Holy Ghost.

Why the spelling Jhem or Shen? [3.13]
    He. . . she. . . ?
    Hen?
By arclight = Barkley? [3.13]

    I don't see fully yet that the Rota music applies. [466.19, .21][4]
    And I need more confirmation for the analogy with the waste land.

        In haste
        Cordially
        (TN)

1. In her letter to Wilder of 22 June 1959, Glasheen announced she was working on the second paragraph of the *Wake*.
2. The Scandinavian prose form of the German epic poem the *Nibelungenlied*. The hero Sigurd is brought up by Regin, a smith, and at his instigation Sigurd slays the dragon Fafner.
3. Joyce to Harriet Shaw Weaver, 13 January 1925, *Letters I*, 224–225. Mentioned in AG to TW, 22 June 1959.
4. This and the following sentence may refer to a telephone conversation or a lost letter.

To Adaline Glasheen, Farmington, Connecticut

[MS. ALS—HWS]

11 July 1959 [50 Deepwood Drive
Hamden 17, Connecticut]

Dear Adaline:
Many thanks for letting me see Mr. Jarrell's *Swiftiana in Finnegans Wake*.[1]

It's a splendid example of what we should have more of: *Blake in FW, Swedenborg in FW, St Augustine in FW*[.]

There are two aspects of Swift's biography and legend that he has not touched on: his supposed impotence[2], and the often-denied conjecture that he was Hester Johnson's half-brother.[3]

The first charge is often hinted at. I shall write you about it later. It crops up in plays on Babylon and all its many variants (French = BABELIN, an impotent man), an Enoch—Eunuch, and in association with others in history, literature, etc, Sir Isaac Newton, Osmin (Mozart's Seraglio), Stendhal's Octave.

Here are a few notes about the Incest-theme.

First, an additional lexicon.

The bird SWIFT is related to the SWALLOW. {Maybe that's one reason Shaun eats so much 404–407; maybe; it's a part of the name CHIMPDEN[4] and all the other chimney = a chimneyswift.} Joyce uses all the forms of Swift and Swallow in many languages—as noun and as verb. After all, he called himself Presto,—Italian swift. We see the two words together: 449.3–4. . . . . "swift. . . . . swallow."

Swallow, verb: ingurgitate, gurgle 406.12 "gurgle. . . . swallying." French, Avaler 406.9. Gober, elsewhere. GERMAN schluck, schlund.

SWALLOW, bird, French, hirondelle 359.27 [i.e., .28], Italian Rondine, Rondinella 359.28–29 German, Schwalbe, 542.21.

Now, for this INCEST factor, Joyce uses among others TAMAR—AMNON 2 Samuel XIII. LORD BYRON and AUGUSTA LEIGH, and the brother and sister in Ford's Tis Pity She's a Whore = Annabella and Giovanni Florio. {I suspect the Tutenkhamen, Egyptian and Cleopatra bear this insinuation also.}

So it must be shown that the SWIFT—STELLA couple is juxtaposed to any of these,—as children of TEMPLE

184.19–20   . . . blanca hermana {white sister}. . and Amarilla = TAMAR. Followed by Swift's Asther, Huster and Laetitia van Leven Pilkingtons[5]
378.20   Tiemor[e]. . . tis. tis. . . badday {Tamar. . . . tis pity.}. . The plague will soon be over. {Follow Pound, Shaw, Casey, Ibsen and GURGLE—SWALLOW—SWIFT and .26 tub.
404.26–27   Tamagnum. . . DAMASKER. . . . . .29 brotherd . . . . .30 M.D. (for Stella)
   TAMAR—jumbled with AMNON. Note the Swiftian shirt and surplice.
561.21   {after .16 brooder's. . . . . bride . . . thimble—Temple—Dean} d amaranth—24 Enameron. . .
107.18   stellates—vanessas from flore to flore. Going on to Byron: . . . herou. . . . 22 giaours.
352.7   {after a Van Hoveigh} odious the fly-fly-flurtation.
359.35—360.2ff   Moore-parque, swift. . . floflo floreflorence. . . tisshad {Tis pity}. . . 19–20 [i.e., .14–.15] flourish. . . flourish.
364.14—ff   . . . beflore their kin. . . . Ears to hears. {Esther. . . whores}. . . park your FORD in it. Very funny!
512.4   "man. . . . in his shirt" . . . 7 Crestofer = Presto. . . . .10 Annabella {ALP is HCE's sister as well as Izzy being SHEM's!. . . . . 31 O'Ford.
305.   A VERY COMPLICATED ONE. The German for Incest is BLUTSCHANDE {Blood-shame.} Now in lines 23–24 there are six Shanty-Schandes, and I find above two bloods .5 bleating 16 bloater's.* There is Byron twice .3 giaour .33 pilgrimage. And .8 Celbridge was Vanessa's[6] house. Byron is next page 7. Mizpath for his Mazeppa.

* Add another in note 1 = bluedye—which could give us another .15 blue in the shirt.

288.19–21   Mr. Dane. . . bloodshot {Blutchande} of that other familiar Temple.
290.2–3   belle. . . . . tompull.
407.19   Moore Park. . . . open secrets. . Scotias {Greek: darkness} l' ist' ing sister. . .

   I suspect there's one last delicate allusion to this matter in ALP's closing speech.

621.20–20 [i.e., .21]   quotation from Mozart's *Don Giovanni*
{Giovanni Florio, here.} "Give me your. . . . .hand."
22   . . . in the language of flows.
30   . . . florizel.
34   . . . timpul. . . . . bells (for Annabella)
13   . . . blug. . . . . 36 . . . . .shindy.

There seem to be a great many more, but these are all I dare submit, lest you tell me that I'm imagining it.

You may wish to send these notes on to Mr. Jarrell with my compliments and thanks.

            Your old friend
            (TNW)

---

1. Mackie L. Jarrell, "Swiftiana in *Finnegans Wake*," *ELH* [*English Language History*], XXVI, 2 (June 1959), 271–294. Throughout this letter Wilder assumes that Ms. Jarrell is a man. Glasheen sent this letter to Ms. Jarrell and wrote at the top: "Dear Miss Jarrell—Please Return AG."

2. See TW to AG, 4 February 1959.

3. Baptized Hester, Esther Johnson (1681–1728) is the Stella of Jonathan Swift's poems and the *Journal to Stella*. She was born at Moor Park, Surrey, the home of Sir William Temple, a diplomat and author. Her mother, a widow, was Temple's housekeeper. She was probably the daughter of Ralph Mose, Temple's steward, who married her mother. Swift (1667–1745) worked for Temple at Moor Park from 1689–1699. Irvin Ehrenphreis in *Swift: The Man, His Works, and the Age* (Cambridge: Harvard University Press, 1983, 3 vols.) writes: "I do not believe that Swift ever went through a marriage ceremony with Esther Johnson, any more than that he ever had sexual relations with her" (III, 405, n.1).

4. The hero of *Finnegans Wake*, Humphrey Chimpden Earwicker.

5. Laetitia Van Lewin Pilkington, the daughter of a Dublin physician, was married to a clergyman, Matthew Pilkington. She was introduced to Swift in December 1729. See TW to AG, 3 May 1959.

6. Esther Vanhomrigh, Vanessa, a mistress of Swift's who died in 1723.

To Adaline Glasheen, Farmington, Connecticut

[MS. ALS—HWS]

22 July [1959]   50 Deepwood Drive
                                                   Hamden 17, Connecticut

Dear Adaline—
  Just a few line[s] for adieu.[1]
  Ed Clodd's TOM TIT TOT 1898.[2] He glosses an English old nurse's story with chapters of parallel stories like the Golden Bough and often quoting the Golden Bough.
  T. T. T. is a little devil with a long black tail who spins skeins for a queen—who will be beheaded if she doesn't get the work done. T. T. T. does it for her, but at the end she must guess his name within 9 tries or else he'll have her. . . . i. e. her soul. She learns that his name is
        Nimmy nimmy not
        My name's Tom Tit Tot.
  Clodd finds parallels charmingly. He also wrote a book on the Alphabet.[3]
  I suggest: {all except the first *Tom* were added by J. J. later[}]
178.27   tom
   30   T out
   31   cloud
   32   Incer tit ude
344.17   tailtottom
   23   clouds
   30   tob tob tob. . . . .patom.
505.1
315.25–26   tilt too't (t)aut. . . tammy. . . with his {tail} tucked up.

  Probably there are more in this *tit* for *tat* uses, but I've not got them listed.

  Clodd, p. 222 quotes an old saying (people whose surnames begin with the same letter should not marry) "If you change the name and not the letter, You change for the worse and not for the better."
  Doesn't Izzy say that first line somewhere? [419.17–.18]

Queen Anne and her dear Sarah, Duch[ess] of Marlborough used to address one another as Mrs Freeman (Marlböo) and MRS MORLEY Sarah was much caricatured as in 291.note 6

Mitchell Morse's book shows us that John Scotus Erigena[4] had bold ideas about the sexes joined etc etc
279.3   {and see the gloss in the right margin.)
431.35

Donald Gallup is a close friend of Eliot.[5] He was scandalized and amused by page 191—but acknowledged it[.]
Did you know that long ago Eliot wrote an unprintable ballad called BOLO and his black African queen.[6] It now grieves him.
p. 151.8   neoitalian E. O. I. . T. . . L.
    14   bo. . . ll. . . .o. . .
    18   tom
    20   Morte d'arthur of Waste Land . . . . communion
    21   waste . . . toes T. E. S.
    22   overpast. . . .passover
    23   Bolo.

These trivia are just to keep galvanized for your flock.

            Best to all
            (T)

---

1. Wilder left for Newport, Rhode Island, on 24 July; until the beginning of September he traveled in New England. In August he played the Stage Manager in *Our Town* in the Williamstown Summer Theater's production directed by Nikos Psacharopoulos. On 2 September he went to New York and returned to New Haven on 9 September.

2. See AG to TW, 8 June 1959, n. 3.

3. Edward Clodd, *The Story of the Alphabet* (1900).

4. J. Mitchell Morse, *The Sympathetic Alien: James Joyce and Catholicism* (New York: New York University Press, 1959). See particularly Chapter III, "The Erigenal Sin: Irish John."

5. Donald Gallup (1913–2000) retired in 1980 as Curator of the American Literature Collection, Beinecke Rare Book and Manuscript Library, Yale University. He was the author of the standard bibliography of Eliot.

6. See Eliot, *Inventions of the March Hare: Poems 1909–1917*, ed. Christopher Ricks (New York: Harcourt Brace & Co., 1996), 31, 305, 315–321.

To Adaline Glasheen, Farmington, Connecticut
[MS. ALS—HWS]

[25 September 1959]   50 Deepwood Drive
Friday   Hamden 17, Connecticut

Dear Adaline

I wish I had a voice persuasive enough to urge you to keep off those first paragraphs of FW; they are the most *farci* of all and should be unravelled last. "That way madness lies."

In a few days I'll send you the "Reading F. W." by Frances Motz Boldereff.[1] Should be called "Some Allusions to Irish History in FW." No index. Pagination iii–xiv, 1–210, i–viii, 1–284 (that's enough to drive you crazy). Amateurish through repetitions, and thinks [i.e., things] like this (in her idioglossary):

> as you honour and obey the queen 488 see: judyqueen.

so

> judyqueen   207   Ireland
>   [arrow from Ireland]
> 30 listings   and that's all! for the 30
> sublistings
> including
> Where is that
> Quin but he
> [s]knows it knot 305[.20]

Nevertheless there are things that we can copy out and lay beside the others.

It's funny to read her so-called translations (she offers a "translation of these opening paragraphs"—in her Part I p. 155)[2]—where all these paragraphs we agonize over are read *solely* in the light of Irish history. It's like having a "copy" of the ceiling of the Sistine Chapel with only the values in *green* reproduced.

But I think she's right that Humpty Dumpty in the Ballad is British Rule—that will presently crumble—that brought us all those evils.[3]

	Punch is also England.
	So we see that one aspect of the Ondt is British Rule.
415.15	H'ty D'ty sat for awhile but Timmy Irishman will arise.
415.18	nobodies (little clouds—NUBES NUBECULA) surround his belly—PAUNCH, like the rings about SATYR—SATURN (line 14[)]
415.19–20	he is by Grace of God King of England Dei gratia and by barratry (barheated) and by bribes (gratiis)

I'll soon send of [i.e., you] Ellmann's Life of J. J.[4] an enormous book.

I wonder what you'll think.

The books have *got* to be great to justify such towering and withering egocentricity.

I sail for Europe Oct 16,[5] leaving FW interests behind me. but you'll hear from me before then.

worlds of regard to ALISON
FRANCIS ADALINE

Thornt

For your index of places[6]

MONS,	Belgium—prison where Verlaine spent 2 years for shooting Rimbaud[.] He did it in Brussels near waterloo etc. The little statue Minnikin Pis (which makes refined ladies blush is in Brussels.)
so 17.2	Minnikin pass. . . brookcells. . . riverpool (Paul Verlaine)
318.32	Alpyssinia {Rimbaud spent the last years of his life in Abyssinia}
375.27	Hawthorne's story Maypole of Marymount or Merrymount I forget its spelling—now Walliston, Mass.
582.28 [i.e., .29–.30]	Those concords are really American.
419.28	hellas. . . .harrowbred. . . Shelley went to Harrow
131.33 [i.e., .35]	Taishan—sacred mountain of China in Pound's Cantos too
508.28	I suspect Pranksome Quaine is Branksome Hall (of Lay of the last minstrel—see .22 minnestirring.

The Walk to Howth
619.23   I think this is Findaly's wood—verify.
    28   I suppose that's Merrimack—and—McMonroryles,
           Kings of Ulster
620.11   Raheny (pron: Rahenny = ancient Rath Enna)
622.3   Kinsaley village on Malahide Road
622.35   Delvin a river bounding the district Finglas in the
           Annals—no longer there I think
623.23   Dollymont on road to Clontarf and Howth
623.31   The Main Drain
624.16   Donachie = Church on Malahide Road
           St Doolagh (Dolachus—DUILECH)
    18   St. Finton's Terrace
    19   Bailey Light
    21   Shelmartin Hill—slopes of Howth
    26   Nose of Howth
    27   Aston Quay
625.15   signal you—Fern (German Fernsprech Telephone)
           Telegraph Hill—and Martello tower on Dunhill.
    22   knock = Battle of Cruchra = Castle Knock.
626.6   So called Whip of the Waters where Howth Rd
           descends to the sea.

I have a feeling you know all this—maybe *you* gave it to me

---

1. *Reading 'Finnegans Wake'*, Frances Motz Boldereff (Woodward, Pennsylvania: Classic Nonfiction Library, 1959). The book is divided into two: "Part One: Bluest Book in Baile's Annals," "Part Two: Idiogloassary He Invented." The second part of the book is "a glossary of those words and phrases pertaining to the life of Ireland to be found in Joyce's poem" (i).

2. Boldereff: "Translation Part I. Sections 1 & 2 (pp. 3–55)," 155–181; see also "Translation Part II, Section 2 (pp. 260–264)," 182–210.

3. Boldereff, Part I, 157.

4. Richard Ellmann, *James Joyce* (New York: Oxford University Press, 1959).

5. Wilder sailed on Thursday, 15 October, on the SS *Bremen* and remained in Europe until his return to Florida on the SS *Amerigo Vespucci* on 13 January 1960.

6. Glasheen was contemplating a place index for *Finnegans Wake*. She would contribute to the work compiled by Louis O. Mink, *A 'Finnegans Wake' Gazetteer* (Bloomington: Indiana University Press, 1978).

To Adaline Glasheen, Farmington, Connecticut

[MS. ALS—HWS]

11 October 1959   [50 Deepwood Drive
                                                Hamden 17, Connecticut]

Dear Adaline:
    I'm writing you with a mixture of sorrow and relief.
    I'm *giving up* Finnegans Wake.[1]
    Thursday I sail for Europe[2] and I'm not taking a FW page nor a note nor a thought about it with me.
    The straws that have been breaking this camel's back are the increasing realization that it's TOO DIFFICULT. It's not fair. The list of association with Nora which you pointed out from—Ellman[n], for example, doesn't help; it only makes it worse; because Nora never comes alone.
    For instance, again, for your PLACE-INDEX
BRABANT, former dutchy of Netherlands; now provinces in both
    Holland and Belgium; capital, Brussels. BRABANÇONNE,
    National anthem; BRABANÇON, breed of draught horses,
    138.12. ELSA of BRABANT, heroine of LOHENGRIN.
    COUNT PALATINE SIEGFRIED of MAYENFELD 264.24
    falsely repudiated wife GENOVEVA ossia GENEVIEVE,
    "called of BRABANT" 266.27. Connects with BRUSSELS
    theme of Verlaine's shooting RIMBAUD, hence Mannekin
    Pis 17.2–6 (brookcells)
    brueburnt 384.28
    browbenders 130.2

    You saw, in Ellman[n], J. J.'s astonishing behavior in trying to publicize John Sullivan (twice shouting out and making a public scene in the Paris opera!).[3] Strange goings on. Nora in consternation. Looks like half-jokingly J. J. added the tenor to the SULLIVAN-SULLY-THUG group. One of Sullivan's big roles was in *The Masked Ball*.
    Reread 622.23–24
    PPs 434, 435 In Masked Ball, witch Ulrica mixes a poison 434.29 next page is that SULLIVAN 435.29, his role in Debussy's Pelléas line 24. . . Debussy. . . Nocturne's. . . Bagatelles. John Chine-John

Pinkerton. . Chine. . . throws over Japan,—Madame Butterfly. . . is on the prowl—RAOUL in *Huguenots* as in 133.20 456.25 (side by side with Verdi's Nabucco .22 and Eric .22 in *Flying Dutchman* and probably ROMEO—roomiest .27) and 495.15 (Pelléas) 495.16 Raoul.[4]

    I'm sick of accumulating Allusions that don't add up to patterns—though I know that the strictest patterns are there.

    So I'm retiring for five years.

    I may rejoin the factory when some wider roads have been made through the jungle. There always will be room for one more worker.

    This sounds kinda like a goodbye. But it's not a goodbye to you—only to that old boa-constrictor FW.

    For a while I kept on, because I felt that at any moment one of us would light upon one of the bigger guiding patterns. Then would be the moment when the rest of us—those who had read each page at least one hundred times—could leap forward and help, and make other connectives and speed the work along. But that moment has not come. Everybody's still delighted—myself too, until recently—if he finds one new identification.

    Anyway, you will be there USHERING IN THE DAWN. When I "return" in five years, many more articles and books will have been published: we will know why any one sentence follows any other sentence in the adorable but skeletonless A. L. P. chapter; why there is a Brontë half-paragraph and a Smollett half-paragraph in Book I and many many other things. And yet = I think it'll take more than five years. . . I fear that in 1964 we'll be much where we are. . more allusions to Irish history and The Koran, but still merely spotty footnote elucidations. Maybe I'll better re-open my copy in 1969 D. V.

    Yet I suspect that if next year one worker actually plotted the Stations of the Cross in III 2 or the course of the Liffey in ALP—everybody talks about 'em but nobody can demonstrate 'em—I'd probably come feverishly back. Because I'm sure of one thing = the minute we get *one* of these bigger organizational patterns straight, it will be much easier to find the others superimposed or subtending it.

    I hope Isabel will join me abroad about Xmas time. In any case I'll be back towards February and March. Don't let my defection diminish your zeal. And it's always a joy to hear from you (so far I have no address abroad—letters will be promptly forwarded from here.)

    Best to Francis and Alison—and a world of regard to you

    Ever
    Thornton

1. Despite his claim, Wilder proceeded with three years of his most intense work on the *Wake*.

2. See TW to AG, 25 September 1959, n. 5.

3. John Sullivan (?1877–1955) the Irish-French tenor who at Joyce's suggestion changed his name from O'Sullivan. Joyce first heard him sing the title role in Richard Wagner's *Tannhäuser* at the Paris Opéra in the autumn of 1929. When Joyce met him, shortly thereafter, he found out that Sullivan came from Cork, Ireland, the home of Joyce's paternal ancestors. Joyce's devotion to furthering Sullivan's career became an obsession. During a performance of Rossini's *Guillaume Tell* at the Paris Opéra on 30 June 1930, Joyce twice shouted out after hearing Sullivan sing the role of Arnold. The first time he declared that a miracle had happened because for the first time in twenty years he could see the light. After Sullivan sang the fourth act aria "*Asile héréditaire*," Joyce shouted "*Bravo Sullivan! Merde pour Lauri-Volpe*." Joyce's 1932 essay, "From a Banned Writer to a Banned Singer," is a tribute to Sullivan written in the word-play style of *Finnegans Wake*. Joyce reviews Sullivan's principal roles, he compares him to his contemporaries, and he complains that an Italian lobby is keeping him from access to roles in the great opera houses of the world. The title of the essay reveals the shared sense of persecution that Joyce felt. For the essay, see *The Critical Writings of James Joyce*, ed. Ellsworth Mason and Richard Ellmann (New York: The Viking Press, 1959), 258–268. See also Ellmann, *James Joyce*, 1959: 632–641; 1982: 619–626; see Hodgart and Bauerle, passim, for Joyce's relationship with Sullivan.

4. Operas associated with the tenor John Sullivan: Giuseppe Verdi's *Un Ballo in Maschera* and *Nabucco*, Claude Debussy's *Pelléas et Mélisande*, Giacomo Puccini's *Madama Butterfly*, Giacomo Meyerbeer's *Les Huguenots*, Richard Wagner's *Der Fliegende Holländer*, and Charles Gounod's *Roméo et Juliette*.

1960

To *Adaline Glasheen, Farmington, Connecticut*

[MS. ALS—HWS]

21 March 1960   50 Deepwood Drive
                   Hamden 17, Connecticut

Dear Adaline =
   Greetings.
   Delighted that you are thus signalled out by Central High School[1] and am glad that any leaf of mine finds its place in your garland. You have done a superb and lasting work and I shall not tell Evansville that every now and then you have faltered and inveighed against.
   I no longer work on FW but I am fascinated to read anything about it and long for the first paper that will [be] describing you-know-what, my old song, the "patterns."
   Had some lovely hours with the Senns their new little boy will carry my first name as his middle name.[2] I am very proud.
   [James] Atherton's book is much better than the typescript I saw.[3] Though I am still amazed at the nonchalance with which he tends to give the impression that he has just about explored all Dante, Rabelais* etc etc.
   All joy to your novel.
   Alison must be a Big Young Lady now. And so travelled. Give her our best.
   And to Francis.
   It's a special pleasure that this engarlanding came to you from Evansville while your father is there. It's *that* the [i.e., that] enhances all such recognitions.
                   Devotedly ever
                   Thornton

I always saw [Henry Morton] Robinson as a man in a rage.[4] He raged so at me, and then redoubled it when I didn't answer. Pooooor man.

*There's a Rabelais quote 118.16 Bacbuc is the Divine Oracle—Battle of Pantagruel

1. Glasheen, who had gone to Central High School in Evansville, Indiana, was chosen to be included in their permanent hall of fame, and a letter which Wilder wrote detailing her accomplishments was requested.
2. Wilder saw the Senns during his visit to Zurich in November 1959. Wilder was the godfather of Beda Thornton Senn.
3. *The Books at the Wake*.
4. Shortly after *The Skin of Our Teeth* opened in New York, on 18 November 1942, a two-part article by Henry Morton Robinson and Joseph Campbell (who were collaborating on *A Skeleton Key to 'Finnegans Wake'*) appeared in the *Saturday Review of Literature* in which the writers, while not directly accusing Wilder of plagiarism, charged that the play was "not an entirely original creation, but an Americanized re-creation, thinly disguised, of James Joyce's *Finnegans Wake*." They accused Wilder of knowingly "quoting from and actually naming some of his characters after the main figures of Joyce's masterpiece." They further charged that "Important plot elements, characters, devices of presentation, as well as major themes and many of the speeches, are directly and frankly imitated, with but the flimsiest veneer to lend an American touch to the original features" (I, 3). Campbell and Robinson, "The Skin of Whose Teeth?" Part I, "The Strange Case of Mr. Wilder's New Play and *Finnegans Wake*," 19 December 1942, 3–4; Part II, "The Intention Behind the Deed," 13 February 1943, 16, 18–19. When *The Skin of Our Teeth* won the Pulitzer Prize for Drama, Campbell and Robinson protested to the committee in a sharply worded telegram, parts of which were printed in *PM* (New York), 5 May 1943, 22 and quoted widely elsewhere. They demanded that Wilder pay Mrs. Joyce royalties, not knowing, of course, that Wilder had been instrumental in raising the financial guarantee required by the Swiss authorities before they would permit the Joyces to enter Switzerland in December 1940. Nor did they know that Wilder actively pursued Joyce's nomination for the Nobel Prize in Literature. Campbell's and Robinson's anger at Wilder continued to surface over the years. In "The Curious Case of Thornton Wilder" (*Esquire*, March 1957, 70–71, 124–126), Robinson dissected Wilder's *The Matchmaker* in relationship to its sources in Nestroy's *Einen Jux will er sich machen* and John Oxenford's *A Day Well Spent*. Wilder never responded to Campbell and Robinson, and refused several offers of the James Joyce Society of New York to provide a setting for a discussion. Wilder's only public comment on the charges comes at the end of his "Preface" to *Three Plays* (Harper, 1957, xiv): "The play [i.e., *The Skin of Our Teeth*] is deeply indebted to James Joyce's *Finnegans Wake*. I should be very happy if, in the future, some author should feel similarly indebted to any work of mine. Literature has always more resembled a torch race than a furious dispute among heirs." See Burns and Dydo, *The Letters of Gertrude Stein and Thornton Wilder*, Appendix VIII, "Thornton Wilder: January 1942 to May 1943."

To Thornton Wilder, Hamden, Connecticut
[MS. ALS—YCAL]

30 March 1960 [22 Carrington Lane
Farmington, Connecticut]

Dear Thornton,

Thank you so much for your letter. I have dispatched the earlier letter to Evansville, may it flourish there.

I have had a break through a bit on the 4 damned things on 13–14[1] which I am tired of & don't want to think about any more. I suppose it extends & means a lot, I dunno.

You remember a while back I was playing round with the 4 things being Zodiacal.[2] Last night I was studying the article on Zodiac in the 11th Britannica (because of a poem somebody writes in my novel) and it came out like this:
    1. The stranded fish (Month Adar 13.24–5) = fish god EA or HEA who gave us the sign of Pisces in modern Zodiac. Adar = EA's month to the Babylonians[.]
    2. Joyce associated the month Nizam with the poor old woman and Nizam = sign of Ram Aries. I can't see any references to names on 13–14 but I bet one's there. Nizam was the month sacred to Bel & he's there in the Beltane fire.[3] And the old woman suddenly created like Sarah & creation began in Aries. However this is still my weakest item.
                    Silence [14.6]
    3. Virgo—Ishtar grieving for her Tammuz—as I saw long ago.
    4. This is what I saw last night. One's natural impulse is to make the twins Gemini and elsewhere (or also) they are, but look at 13.28 "A penn no weightier nor a polepost." They are Libra or the Balance, which really describes as well as Gemini does.

At first I was thrown by the E. Brit. saying Marchesvan = Scorpio[.][4] But it turned out that Scorpio and Libra were after the same sign, even printed with the balance held in Scorpio's claws. I think probably J. means The Balance to = the twin's considered together and then broken down into the net 2 signs of the Zodiac 1) Scorpio or Shaun as Serpent 2) Sagittarius or Shaun as archer or shooter—drilled all decent people, shot the R[ussian]. General.

But for the moment let the 4 things simply equal:
1. Pisces—Feb. 18 → March 20
2. Aries March 20 → April 20
Silent
3. Virgo August 23 → Sept. 23
4. Libra Sept. 23 → Oct. 23

Well the Zodiac—you may remember—goes like thus

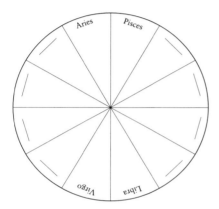

Pisces is followed by Aries and the break between them is the spring equinox[.] Then between Aries & Virgo is a big gap which silence represents 4 skipped or missed signs[.]

Then we take up again with Virgo which is followed by Libra, the break between them being the autumn equinox.

I'm sure I'm missing all hell, lots of things. But it's the birth of the year & the death of the year that will never fail in Dyfflinarsky [13.22] until smoke and clouds shut out the sight of the sky and the Zodiac[.]

I will not ask you if you make anything of this but it would be lovely if you did.

        Yours,
        Adaline

[Arrow drawn from "I'm sure I'm missing. . ."] Or is the year born & deaded at the Solstices?

Is it too much to presume that Silence [14.6] does *not* mean the end of a cycle but a break in the cycle like Joyce says on 14?

But for the moment let the 4 things simply equal:
1. ~~Aries~~ 1. Pisces – Feb. 18 → March 20
2. Aries   March 20 → April 20
   Silent
3. Virgo   August 23 → Sept. 23
4. Libra   Sept. 23 → Oct. 23

Well the Zodiac – you may remember – goes like this:

Pisces is followed by Aries and the break between them is the spring equinox. Then between Aries & Virgo is a big ~~silent~~ gap which Silence represents ~~equally 4 skipped~~ skipped or missed signs.

Then we take up again with Virgo which is followed by Libra, the break between them being the autumn equinox.

I'm sure I'm missing all hell, lots of things. But it's the birth of the year + the death of the year that will never fail in Dyffinarsky until smoke and clouds shut out the sight of the sky and the Zodiac.

I will not ask you if you make anything of this but it would be lovely if you did.

Yours,
Adaline

✓ Or is the year born & deaded at the Solstices?

Is it too much to presume that Silence does not mean the end of a ~~cycles~~ cycle but a break in the cycle like Joyce says on 14?

~~As~~ Are the 4 items Tim Finnegans Wake?
1. TF on his bier
2. ALP. Mrs. F. carrying on – calls for lunch etc
3. The lamentation for the lost
4. Primas the fighters at the Wake
   Lastly the maker of the ballad about the wake.

Are the 4 items Tim Finnegans Wake?
1. TF on his bier
2. ALP. Mrs. F. carrying on—calls for lunch etc
3. The lamentation for the lost
4. Primas the fighters at the Wake
    Caddy the maker of the ballad about the wake.

1. FW 13.4–14.27. See Glasheen's discussion of the Four in *Census II*, xxiv–xxv, and in *Census III*, xxvii.
2. See AG to TW, 5 May 1959, and TW to AG, 1 July 1959.
3. See AG to TW, 22 June 1959.
4. In the Assyrian and Babylonian zodiac system Marchesvan, the eighth month, was known as "the month of the star of the Scorpion."

☐

To Adaline Glasheen, Farmington, Connecticut

[MS. ALS—HWS]

2 April [1960]   50 Deepwood Drive
                                  Hamden 17, Connecticut

Dear Adaline =
  Many thanks. I'll meditate those Zodiac signs. You do fasten on the hardest *cruces*!
                    x
  Don't tell anybody but I reopened FW for a single afternoon.[1]
  Came on this:
  Bach's cantata WACHET AUF is sung in England as SLEEPERS AWAKE.[2]
  597.26
  Italian corrente d'aria = a draught of air.
  CORRANTO = Italian, a dance form in BACH's Suites, next to the ARIA there. There's BACK—BACH

smalls = schmaltz German colloquial for sentimental music (from the word for grease.) [597.27]

>That's all!
>Best to all
>Ever
>Thornt.

1. Wilder was working on two plays, "Ira" and *Childhood*, each of which were to have dream sequences. In a journal entry of 24 March 1960, he speculates on "what takes place in dreaming" and discusses Freud, Joyce, and Kafka. Of the *Wake* he writes: "*Finnegans Wake* is a vast compendium of techniques to reproduce dream life, but I do not find there several on which I intend to lean heavily" (*Journals*, 275–276).
2. Johann Sebastian Bach (1685–1750), Cantata BWV 140, "Wachet auf, ruft uns die Stimme."

☐

To Adaline Glasheen, Farmington, Connecticut

[MS. ALS—HWS]

27 July [1960]   [50 Deepwood Drive
                           Hamden 17, Connecticut]

Dear Adaline:
   To whom it may concern:
   Legendary Kings of Rome
FW 467
.32 prisckly   Lucius Tarquinius Priscus
.33 numan   Numa Pompilius
.33 ancomartins   Ancus Martius
.35 n'ormolus   Romulus
.35   Lucius Tarquinius Superbus
.36   Servius Tullius
.36–468.1   Tullius Hostilius

Probably 467.31
tiptop [FW: tiptoe] Titius Tatius.

You see the Feast of Lupercalia[1] on 444.36ff
Men in goat-skins ran around the foot of the Palatine Hill lashing women with goat-hide thongs.

In haste—leaving today for 2 weeks at Algonquin Hotel, NY[2]

Best to all
(T. N.)

1. Festivals in honor of Pan held in Rome on 15 February.
2. Wilder returned to New Haven on 10 August and the next day left for the MacDowell Colony in Peterborough, New Hampshire, where on 13 August he was awarded the first Edward MacDowell medal.

□

To Adaline Glasheen, Farmington, Connecticut

[MS. APCS—HWS]

[postmark: 29 August 1960]   Martha's Vineyard
[Massachusetts]

Dear Adaline:
  Believe in it enormously.
  But always deferential to Francis's wishes.
  Have begun a long letter to you. Only worth doing it if you accept that editor's plan to make it big and to adopt a new mode of cataloguing.[1] I have easily more than 200 new items.
  Be patient. Will mail letter soon.

Best to all
Thornt.

1. Robert Armstrong, Director of Northwestern University Press, approached Glasheen in early July about preparing a revised *Census* with an expanded outline of *Finnegans Wake*. *Census II* was published on 17 July 1963.

☐

To Adaline Glasheen, Farmington, Connecticut

[MS. ALS—HWS]

[postmark: 20 September 1960]   Hotel Algonquin
 59 West 44th St.,
 New York 36, N. Y.
 home again on Wednesday[1]

Dear Adaline:
 It's awful the way I promised you a letter and then fell silent.
 To answer your question correctly it needed that I justify my notion that there are double the number of entries for your Census and that a new method must be found for entering them.
 Because about 20 days ago I "returned" to FW and how!—12 hours a day. I took up name after name: Carroll (almost all the carry me back to CARLO, and broke the bank at Monte CARLO)[.] Hamilton and Lady (Finisterres and Copenhagens) and then found in a paper back (accessible to the public!) a selection from the Marquis de Sade with preface by Simone de Bea[u]voir and a chronology of the chief events in his life.[2]
 You know and [Fritz] Senn knows and I know how bewildering it is to get hold of ONE theme in FW: presently *one seems* to see it on every page.
 But there is no doubt that Sade is one of the most important "sources": Joyce says so himself.

 Page 184 Shem's manner of working:
 de Sade was Seigneur de Sauman[e] and Seigneur de La Coste.[3]
lines 29 Sulphate de SOUDE {all the soda sore SADE-SODOM[}]
(He wrote a book called 120 Days in Sodome)[4]
30 sowmmonay {sauté saumonné in French; but saumarre à la Monseigneur (Fashionable restaurants in both London and Paris.[)] [}]

35 [i.e., .36]   coste Satan = Sade of La Coste

He fed prostitutes aphrodisiacs of candied anis (they almost died and he had to run away to Italy; he was condemned to death and his effigy was hung in Aix—pronounced by the French AKES line 33 [i.e., .13]) so Licorice—Anisette and Fennel all alude to this line 21 and 32. And throughout all FW. his coat of arms included an imperial eagle—Padre Aguilar (Spanish for eagle) 35.

He seduced his sister in law[5] (and she went to Italy with him) she was a Chanoinesse Canoness. {French prounce <u>shan</u> → 27.[14] Essie Shanahan has let down her skirts shan'n'esse}

211.9 Nancy Shannon a Tuami brooch {The Canoness's name was ANNE—Prospère}

213.32[–.34] same brooch of the Shannons was married into a family in Spain.

There's something I miss here but at Tuami or the Shannon there is a "Spanish bridge" and TU—AMI is good hoglatin. And the next line [.34–.35] *Dunders in Markland*

Sade's first name was Donatien and all the DONs and most of the Mark (for Marquis) are de Sade.

Another reason I hesitated to write you after my promise is that the material is all so hideous. Don't ever try to *read* de Sade.—but certainly J. J. did and Flaubert called him the *divin Marquis* which J. J. remembers in several places.

Returning to pps 184–185

The Latin for Ink is Encaustum 185.25 and one of de Sade's titles is Seigneur de la Coste. And these get all mixed up so in page after page you get shady—costly—ink—stink until—as I say—you see Sade everywhere. Now take a page we always knew was Sade: The Lupercalia custom of whipping girl.[6]

Page 444[.35]   Mark
Page 450 [i.e., 445]
 1 Nesbo = the tendon of an animal used in whipping
 .4 [i.e., .5] the closet = La COSTE
 7 budd—probably and omnipresent—his most famous book Philosophie dans le BOUDOIR
 8 Sad. . . .
 9 Rodeo 16 [i.e., .17] rhoda. Line 17 [i.e., .18] calor
  {One of his most pitiable victims was a certain ROSE KELLER—she made her deposition to the police under the spelling Ka[i]lair}[7]

line 11 Pimpernella is of the anise = liquorice family.

Poor Rose is all over the book in all languages[.] Those Rhidarhodas [434.7] and the celler-keller—cave—underground.

And his poor wife! Renée-Pélagie!!
And the mother-in-law who so justifiably hounded him into prison from which he was always escaping.

Now your Census-readers wouldn't believe that the tiny word just page 445 line 14 was an allusion to Sade's most read novel JUSTINE unless you could show them that there are at least 8 indubitable allusions to de Sade within 18 lines[.]

And it gets worse when J. J. plays a verbal game that I call Catenation.
On page 496 we see line 20 peeping tom. . . Mama etc Madas Sadam . . .
He has set up Midas. . . Sade . . . Sodom. . . .
And Page 482 line 4 we have Midas's long ears as a discovered eavesdropper and his relation to gold
4   Me das has or oreils and Sade was Lt. Govenor of BRESSE {Breeze softly .3[}] (and breeze passim!!)
So I'm not surprised to find spreadeagle in line .15 because in heraldic lore that's what was on his crest (Two headed—wings and feet out.)
I wish I had time to show you the extent of some less repulsive material (Nelson etc) but I choose this because it's easier to illustrate the immense amount of Sade material and the necessity of finding a new way to present it.

Should you do the new Census?
I think so. Tho' just now I'm sick to death of the nauseatory aspect of the Sade <u>and</u> the L. Carroll treatments.
At all events prepare the Editor of Northwestern that it would be a big book and would take time.
Somewhere I had a letter started to you saying that I don't think that the performance by women of exacting scientic [i.e., scientific] or literary disciplines necessarily harm her role as wife and mother. . . . .
They certainly interfere with novel-writing, as *I* know only too well.

> a world of regard to you all
> Ever
> Thornton

1. Wilder was in New York from 15 to 22 September meeting with, among other people, Louise Talma, with whom he was working on an opera, *The Alcestiad*.
2. *The Marquis De Sade* (New York: Grove Press, 1953). Simone de Beauvoir's "Faut-il brûler Sade?," translated by Annette Michelson as "Must We Burn Sade?," was first published in *Les Temps Modernes*, December 1951 and January 1952. The selections in the book were chosen and translated by Paul Dinnage who also compiled the chronology and bibliography. The book was/is on the open stacks of the Sterling Memorial Library, Yale University. Much of the information in this letter comes from De Beauvoir's essay and Dinnage's detailed Chronology (211–228). Donatien Alphonse François, comte de Sade (1740–1814).
3. Following his father's death in January 1767, the Marquis de Sade inherited his father's estate and offices.
4. *Les 120 journées de Sodome ou l'École de libertinage* (1785) was posthumously published in 1881.
5. The Marquis married Renée-Pélagie Cordier de Launay de Montreuil on 17 May 1763. His wife's sister, Anne Prospère de Launay, was a witness to the marriage contract. Although she had lived in a religious community, she had not taken vows.
6. See TW to AG, 27 July 1960.
7. For the deposition, see Dinnage, 211–216.

To Thornton Wilder, Hamden, Connecticut

[MS. ALS—YCAL]

21 September 1960
[22 Carrington Lane
Farmington, Connecticut]

Dear Thornton,

Well it was a letter worth waiting for and madly coincidental since I've begun to make motions at my novel and at precisely the part about Sadism-Masochism in the female. I have read, incidentally, Sade's *Justine* and, you know, when I read, just lately [Lawrence] Durrell's *Justine* & sequels, it seemed to me that Sade had a basis in nature, perhaps even an innocence, at least a straight forwardness whereas Durrell (who as an artist or craftsman is gloppy) is really crooked and snide and contra nature.

Anyway, I first may say I have signed a contract with Northwestern (10% on the first 1000, 12% thereafter—what after?) to deliver the enlarged 2nd ed. on Jan. 1, 1962. Which gives me time—Christ I hope so—to finish my novel this winter—spring & then start on the 2nd ed. It also gives you time, please, to make clear to me (it still isn't) how you think I should present the material.

For yes, of course, I agree with you. About there being twice—oh 3 or 4—the number of people and about mad subterranean rivers like de Sade or Nelson. But dear heaven, can I deal with them, can I even adequately allude to them by Jan. 1, 1962? I can't write a novel while breasting the flood of FW. The two processes are incompatible. I'd say they were both mainly subconscious, but not the same kind of subconscious. No, when you're in the proper kind of doze for writing, FW is a horror like eating bananas with a martini.

Why bother you with problems I have to solve? What I want from you, when you can spare time, is all your FW material and your practical suggestions.

Where are you going now? What are you doing?

> Yours,
> Adaline

Wouldn't you think the Madas-Sadam = Sade & Masoch? Without thinking of FW, I found I kept using Sadmas to express the two in the notes I'm making for the chapter I'm writing.[1]

I can't enter into the Sade & Carroll stuff in FW nauseating you. Sexual obsessions in literature only nauseate or titillate me at the start. Then, their inevitable repetition goes flat & tiresome. I only mean in literature. MY sexual obsessions don't get tiresome but—last 2–3 years—they are beginning to seem comic. Which is I suppose the beginning of the end for intensity.

You surely don't mean my revisions will be so drastic that I abandon the alphabetic progression?

---

1. A chapter in her novel.

To Adaline Glasheen, Farmington, Connecticut

[MS. ALS—HWS]

[25 September 1960] [50 Deepwood Drive
T'home. . . . Sunday night[1] Hamden, Connecticut]

Dear Adaline:
To whom it may concern and may quietly amuse:
It looks to me as though every time we get the rainbow motif (Light) we get the Guido d'Arezzo[2] scale (sound) also. I can't find it every time, but maybe that's because it's so deeply hidden. But here are some of the more obvious examples:

68.30	[i.e., .20] iridescent hue
68.30	[i.e., .20] down right mean = Do re mi fa so la si do
227.16–17	The girls colors.
227.29–30	do-ve. . . Ry-all; Beg (B-M); C Sundy FA MacFearsome {the scale is gamma-nt-Do; A-Re; B-mi; etc} C-Fa-ut.
C-Fa-ut.	By the way on the preceding page, the girls are singing *Sur le Pont d'Avignon*
	226.34 avignue is the old name for Avignon AVENIO and the song goes *font comme ça; font comme ça*. i.e. .35 does like so; does like so.

An ancestor Hughes de Sade is by tradition (but wrongly) supposed to have built that famous bridge.

260.25 [i.e., .12–.13]   and margin do-re-mi is obvious

267.13 [i.e., .14]   There are the colors (N. B. flogs = for flags = IRIS[)]
But   13 ray = re
             15 domisole DO MI SOLE
             16 flash FA
             17 silent SI

407.27   does she lag = descending scale Do si la etc

432.30   there are the colors and there is GUIDO in guidance .28

433.1   ignitious red. . . . purple. . . . ultramarine
    .2   GAMMA (gam-et) .3 [i.e., .4] Do-re-mi

---

now you're ready for
66.14   seven stages of ink preceded by
66.13   gummi = gamma.

We can't say that the spectrum is *only* the Feminine principle of hope, because 590.7 and elsewhere HCE is chameleon—rainbow.

Nor can we say that the Musical scale (ladder-laddy) is the masculine principle. Oh, no, J. J. wouldn't make anything that easy.

There's lots more dirt for you but I scarcely dare to point it out to you. With Francis's permission, however:

Walt Whitman did a lot of poems about the calamus plant, identifying it with the male organ.

Now Joyce permits himself a change of syllable—so almost all them camels fall under suspicion—And the dove-colombs!!

The calamus is also a reed or a cane or a pen.

So: 128.28–29 Donation Sade & calamus.

Now to get a little wholesomer:
359.1   Pelikan is a fountain-pen ink used all over Europe
                 and there is also ball-pen.

Post script: Guido's scale was taught on the fingers of the hand:
                Look at 519.16 guide 519.11ff can you work it out?

Mrs Glasheen, are you listening?

In Pound's Cantos—Canto XXII—he tells a mediaeval [i.e., medieval] story about how God looked around to find a companion for Adam—and he took the fine bush of a fox. . . and that's why she's *una* fuRRia. . .

So woman's a VIXEN

And in the Reynard legend her name is HERMINE

I think she's
114.30   t erminal and maybe 114.29 t'adam 'stained
and
339.29   Erminia—accompanied by her raindow: and if she's also Emania, the old capital of Ireland, that's all right. Do you want her at 480.21? where she's certainly among the foxes.

Really, there's no end to it.

It's enough to make you despair.

And I still haven't found the basic patterns—not ONE.

The things that make me go on with it are (a) that I like puzzles—

which is a tiresome and pointless liking and (b) the great charm and ingenuity and brilliance of some of these wordplays.

Like I said before: maybe they'll show us some day that it's a great book by reason of its ideas and its philosophical inclusion of the cosmos (if that means anything) but so far I think it's a great book because it can be very funny and because it has an awe-inspiring way of superimposing the trivial on the universal myth—that's his way of making poetry and it's full of *that* wild poetry.

If you feel something like that—then do your vast concordance (because that's what it will be) and assure me (and Francis and yourself) that you will—along with all the hard work—get a great deal of enjoyment out of it, too.

x x   x x

Mr and Mrs Brendan Behan came to lunch with me in New York. Mrs B B was 1¾ hours late!! and made not one word of allusion to it. B B began by eating two apples and a peach which the hotel had sent to my room. Then he had two sirloin steaks and most of his wife's which was reposing in a portable heater. It was all very earthy and popular but from one to four-thirty was enough for me. I get sick to death of the straight jacket of civilization; but now I'm cured for a while: punctuality, decorum and self-constraint is all I ask—for a time, anyway.

A world of regard to you both
Ever
Thornt

---

1. Wilder was in New York from 15 September until 22 September. Brendan Behan was on his first visit to New York to attend the opening of his play, *The Hostage* which opened at the Cort Theatre on 20 September. The lunch described in this letter was at the Algonquin Hotel the afternoon the play opened. In *Brendan Behan's New York* (London: Hutchinson, 1964), Behan writes that he was introduced to Wilder by James Thurber (119).

2. The Aretinian syllables, ut, re, mi, fa, sol, la, used by Guido d'Arezzo in the eleventh century for his hexachord, or scale of six notes. The seventh note was introduced in the seventeenth century.

To Thornton Wilder, Hamden, Connecticut

[MS. ALS—YCAL]

10 October 1960[1]   [22 Carrington Lane
                     Farmington, Connecticut]

Dear Thornton,

A couple of things I noticed. Page 143. I read an article on glaucoma in some Dr's column in the paper & he said the first symptom of glaucoma = a nimbus around objects which I think is 143.20 because of the stars that follow in line 22. You know J's letter about the Germans calling the stages of blindness after stars. Are the stars the 7 Plei[a]des— Seven is ll. 15–16 whiles *even*. I looked up stars in German & they're stern which may account for the pairing of Swift & Sterne[.]

I read yesterday a biography of New Haven's own Delia Bacon[2] & I read part of Kierkegaard's *Either/Or*.[3] I'd like the "dowce little delia looked a bit queer" 208.29 to be D. B. who went very queer, but I can't quite make it, despite "poaching" & "Shake" 209.14.[4]

Delia's biography sent me however to reexamine p. 281 because of Ignatius Donnelly in note 3.[5] I guess wilfulness line .17 ties to shillum in left margin to make William & I guess Shakespeare comes in on the top of 282 because his writing for Bacon—the boor [282.4] works for the lord—or taking credit for Bacon & it's a logical introduction to Shem doing Shaun's homework[.]

To go back to *Either/Or*, I'm sure you know one section is about *Don Juan*—Mozart's[6]—& its left margin up above [281].

How're you? My novel goes good.

                                        Yrs.
                                        Adaline

1. The material on the Grail Quest, Delia Bacon, and Shakespeare that preoccupies Glasheen in the remaining letters of 1960 and into the letters of 1961 become part of her article, "The Strange Cold Fowl in *Finnegan's* [sic] *Wake*," in *Spectrum*, V, 1 (Spring 1961), [38]–64. See Appendix VIII. For Joyce's letter mentioned in the first paragraph, see *Letters I*, JJ to HSW, 20 September 1928, 266–269.

2. Delia Salter Bacon (1811–1859) was born in Tallmadge, Ohio, and later lived in New Haven. She was a proponent of the theory that Shakespeare's plays were written by a group headed by Francis Bacon which also included the participation of Walter Raleigh and Edmund Spenser. She also believed that a system of thought was concealed in ciphers in the plays. She was encouraged in her efforts by Ralph Waldo Emerson and Thomas Carlyle. Nathaniel Hawthorne contributed a preface to her *The Philosophy of the Plays of Shakespeare Unfolded* (London: Groombridge & Sons, 1857), and he wrote of her in "Recollections of a Gifted Woman," in *Our Old Home: A Series of English Sketches* (Columbus: Ohio State University Press, The Centenary Edition of the Works of Nathaniel Hawthorne, Vol. 5, 1970, 90–119). Glasheen also read *Delia Bacon: A Biographical Sketch*, compiled by Theodore Bacon (Boston and New York: Houghton, Mifflin & Co., 1888). At the end of her life she was violently insane. See Schoenbaum, *Shakespeare's Lives*, "Delia Bacon," [385]–394.

3. *Enten-eller* (*Either/Or*) (1843) by Søren Kierkegaard (1813–1855).

4. According to an anecdote Shakespeare was imprisoned and whipped for deer poaching. See Schoenbaum, *Shakespeare Lives*, "Shakespeare the Deer-Poacher," 68–72.

5. Ignatius Donnelly (1831–1901). In his *The Great Cryptogram* (1888) he claims to have found indisputable evidence of Bacon's authorship in cryptic utterances in the plays attributed to Shakespeare.

6. There are numerous pages devoted to Mozart's *Don Giovanni* in *Either/Or*.

☐

To Adaline Glasheen, Farmington, Connecticut

[MS. AL—HWS]

[?12–14 October 1960][1]   [50 Deepwood Drive
                              Hamden 17, Connecticut]

F. W.
VARIA for Adaline Glasheen

546.23   "Abide with me" was written by LYTE[2] 546.21
40.3   "Abide with ..." see 6 my horse delayed: My heart's DeLIGHT

NINETEEN SIXTY 263

	Beautiful example of Tom Moore's name added to one of the melodies:[3]
600.12	more..... 13 team (dick and Harry)..... 15 "Tis believed that this harp"
484.	The quote from The Night before Xmas 19 has its author Moore in line 15 meer.[4] (But not the quote on 606.15.)

	ASSASSINATION OF LINCOLN
26	10 jackboots {John Booth}. . . 14 as you were born {you're in Kentucky} . . .loamsome road to Lafayette is ended {FORD Theater is near Lafayette Sq. Washington.} Drop in your tracks, bABE..... 19 abramanation {The White House is *on* Lafayette Sq.[}]
245[.10]	simhath Torah {Feast of the Law} and. . . anTARGUMends {PENTATEUCH for Abraham} in Liffeyetta's bowl. . . . giggling about JONAH and the whale-whalk-WILKEs

In that very funny passage about ELIOT[5] 191.9–33 the crowning insult (after all the references to his being a banker 10 [i.e., .18] counterleaf and Lottery {E. . L. . . E. . O. . . T}) is the word 16 [i.e., .26] TOILETTES {E. L. I. O. T} but it's a stinger that he lives at
    No vena lodge = No blood
    No vara Avenue = No rod {Ital. male organ}.
The passage is addressed to SHEM as UNWISHED SAVAGE for the following reason

The poet Richard Savage
sued Lady Macclesfield (née Anne!) 381.14 claiming he was her son by LORD RIVERS (himself a Richard Savage) and he wrote a book called the BASTARD[6]
586.12   river
    15   ditcher's {Richard's} dastard
    23   riviers
I guess that's the mother
[289.]25   Ainée Riviere as well as Lady (Anne Rivier) Bishop

And you can't put that in the CENSUS because it doesn't happen to mention the last name SAVAGE!!!

> So you see why SHEM 191.11 is addressed as an
> UNWASHED—UNWISHED SAVAGE i. e. BASTARD?

1. This letter is placed here because Glasheen's letter of 15 October responds to material Wilder raised.
2. Henry Francis Lyte (1793–1847), an Anglican clergyman and hymn writer.
3. Thomas Moore (1779–1852), the Irish-born poet. His *Irish Melodies* (1808), with music by Sir John Stevenson, adapts many of the airs first published by Edward Bunting in his *General Collection of The Ancient Music of Ireland* (1796). Wilder is in error in his identification; Hodgart and Worthington in *Song*, and Hodgart and Bauerle in *Joyce's Grand Operoar*, identify this as "The Moon Hath Raised Her Lamp Above" (Act I scene 1) from Julius Benedict's opera, *The Lily of Killarney* (1832).
4. Clement Clarke Moore (1779–1863). His poem, "A Visit from St. Nicholas," appeared anonymously in the *Troy Sentinel* (New York) on 23 December 1823.
5. See TW to AG, 22 July 1959.
6. In his poem *The Bastard* (1728), Savage (?1696–1743) claimed he was the illegitimate son of the fourth Earl Rivers and Mrs. Anne Mason Brett, once the wife of the second Earl of Macclesfield.

To Thornton Wilder, Hamden, Connecticut

[MS. ALS—YCAL]

15 October 1960   [22 Carrington Lane
                                    Farmington, Connecticut]

Dear Thornton,

Oh joy all around & I can't wait for your letters. Meantime—I do wish *I* had thought of J. W. Booth but no repining, you are clever[er] than I & there's an end on it—meantime, I'll put down a few things I've found.

I reread Miss Weston[1] & dareswear J J did not. That is, I think he heard about *From R— to R—* from Eliot or somebody and I suspect he read Miss W's article on The Grail in the 11th Brit.[2] So did I as you shall see.

As yet I'm far from proving Sect. I = Grail Quest but I think I maybe can. Absolutely, however, I can prove that the Grail Quest theme is a very fairly developed theme in, at least, in the first five sections of Book I[3] which as far, as in my plodding way I've gone: I still haven't made up my mind about whether some things count as Grail Quest or not.

Clearest evidence is on 43–4. 43.31 & 35 = Percival the Grail Knight & 44.3 "companions of the chalice." 44.9 "piersified" again, but then how can you fail to take the further step and say that piersified leads directly to Percival = Persse O'Reilly. And this I don't quite want for I want to make Persse O'R—HCE into the Fisher King. {*That's* easy} & Shem, say, the Grail Knight.

It would of course be Joycean to make HCE—POR both Fisher King & Grail Knight.

Struggling with this has, at any rate, led me to question what we have all taken for granted. Listen Mr. Wilder. *Can you prove that HCE is Persse O'Reilly.* I really think he is but 44.10–14 *can* be read as referring to Hosty—after all, Shem & Shaun are also named Earwicker. Shem-Joyce became frenchified & might have changed his name to POR. It certainly could be Shem on 175.28. In short, The Ballad of, means The Ballad *made* by Persse O'Reilly [44–47].

Next thing I noticed 44.19–21. What the hell *is* it they break? I always assumed they broke a window or a glass house with their stones—as happens later on—or possibly a statue of HCE. Well it doesn't say that on 44. The companions of the chalice sing & 44.19 "It's cumming, it's brumming! The clip, the clop!" It really is exactly like Miss Weston's descriptions of the Grail coming to the waiting knights. (J. puts in a Cambronne ref. to make like it's a potty but nevermind.)[4] It *can* be read: "It's coming. It's brimming. The cup, the cup." And the chalice, being in this case, glass falls & crashes[.]

What makes this seem a little more possible is p. 31[.11–.12]—his majesty is drinking from a goblet & this scene remains, you know static, throughout FW[.]

I won't go into HCE as a fish or Fisher King because I'm collecting it in my now go through FW for Census.

In *11th Brit*. Miss W. says of the earliest forms of the Grail Story ". . . exhibits a marked affinity with [the] characteristic features of the Adonis or Tammuz worship; we have a castle on the sea-shore {Howth}, a dead body on a bier, the identity of which is never revealed, [mourned over with solemn rites,] a wasted county {for FW a flood-wasted}, whose desolation is. . . connected with the dead man. . . weeping woman. . . food providing, self acting talisman of the feast [i.e., of a common feast]["] {HCE}. . .

J. could of course have been mutating Tammuz[5] on his own book, but look at 13–14.
    1. A dead fish—fisher king
    2. A crone & one of the Grail Stories = *Diu Crône*
    3. Weeping girl is in all the Grail Stories
    4. The Grail Knight's born?
Merci, FW gets me to the place where I don't know What *is* evidence!

529.20 Miss W. mentions Anglo-Norman romance, *Histoire de Fulk Fitz-Warin*. Ever heard of it?
    She also mentions an Irish poem of *Owain Miles* who went to St. Pats' Purgatory & was resurrected.[6] Ought to be in FW.

222.28 kelchy = Gar kelch, cup or chalice

John Pope = Union General at 2nd Bull Run[7]—He's at 78.28 & 84.6[.] Grant[8] is 78.28 & 29. {You have noticed Shem = a negro?}
78.36—   Could be Garrison??
83.15 & 21   Able & Cain
84.2   Jubal Early?[9]
84.7   Civil War battle—Pea Ridge[10]
85.6ff   Clearly modelled on Billy Bones[11] & Treasure Island
                But—oh godamn Joyce—we have
                line 6 [i.e., .8] bone ⎫
                  " 14 bare   ⎬ or Praisegod Barebones
                  " 17 praisegood ⎭

I am collecting Bacons. He & W. S. *must* be a pair. Is a Bacon 85.18

89.18–19   Eng. children sing: "Londonderry, Cork & Kerry. Spell
              me that without a K [i.e., R]."[12]
I told you? Silence, exile, cunning = 98.2, 98.5 & 99.22
104.22 [i.e., .10] & the l. following = Exact people & order of 7 in par.
    2, p. 3
108.21—I told you the [i.e., that] [Ruth] Von Phul solved as Da Da
            Less—Dedalus.

112.3 & 4   Kipling's "Brushwood Boy"—I know I shouldn't but I love the story. I've often wondered if the Constable in FW is like Policeman Day?[13]
117.2   Hera (her)

And so. I was going to copy names onto FW cards & all I've done is write you a letter this afternoon and listen to my daughter who is entering true female sanity (perhaps the only female sanity) of taking a boy friend who offers himself instead of mooning over rare & far off beauties. The end of female idealism and good riddence.

Keep on.

      Yours,
      Adaline[14]

---

1. Jessie Laidlay Weston (1850–1928), *From Ritual to Romance* (1920; rpt., Princeton: Princeton University Press, 1993). In T. S. Eliot's notes for the first book publication of *The Waste Land* (1928), he acknowledges Weston: "Not only the title, but the plan and a good deal of the incidental symbolism of the poem were suggested by Miss Jessie L. Weston's book on the Grail legend."

2. *The Encyclopaedia Britannica: Eleventh Edition* (New York: The Encyclopaedia Co., 1910).

3. *Finnegans Wake*, 3–125.

4. Glasheen suggests an aural connection between 44.19–.20 and 9.27 where Joyce uses the name of Comte Pierre Jacques Étienne Cambronne (1770–1842), one of Napoleon's generals who said *merde* in public at the Battle of Waterloo.

5. The tenth month of the year in the Jewish calendar; it is also the name of a fertility god.

6. Weston, *From Ritual to Romance* (1993), *Histoire de Fulk-Fitz-Warin*, 181, 183; *Owain Miles,* or *The Purgatory of Saint Patrick*, 184–185.

7. Bull Run, a stream in Virginia, about thirty miles southwest of Washington, D. C., was the scene of two of the most important battles of the Civil War. In the first battle on 21 July 1861, the Confederate forces under General Thomas "Stonewall" Jackson forced the Union forces to retreat. In the second battle, a year later, 29 and 30 August 1862, Major General John Pope's troops were forced to retreat northward to Washington after a flanking maneuver of Generals Robert E. Lee, Thomas "Stonewall" Jackson, and James Longstreet. The two battles are also known as the Battles of Manassas.

8. Ulysses S. Grant (1822–1885), commander (1863–1865) of all Union armies in the American Civil War and 18th President of the United States.

9. Early (1816–1894), an American Confederate general who played a role in the Second Battle of Bull Run and in the battles of Chancellorsville and Gettysburg.

10. Battle of Pea Ridge (also known as the Battle of Elkhorn Tavern), 7–8 March 1862. The Union army forced the retreat of the Confederate army thus preventing them from regaining control of Arkansas.

11. The pirate who steals the treasure map in Robert Louis Stevenson's *Treasure Island*.

12. An Irish riddle. The answer is "T-H-A-T."

13. In Rudyard Kipling's "Brushwood Boy" Georgie and Miriam find out that since childhood they have dreamed the identical dream about Policeman Day.

14. At the bottom of the page Wilder has written: Tristan Tom Bridget Isaac Esther [?are]

To Adaline Glasheen, Farmington, Connecticut

[MS. ALS—HWS]

[16 October 1960]   [Stockbridge, Massachusetts]
Sunday night

Dear Adaline

Looks to me as tho' J. J. has placed an allusion to T. Moore[1] in the vicinity of all those first line citations from the Irish Melodies. I haven't been able to find this every time, but I suspect it's always there at least once—(some of the Irish Melodies are given three or four times).

The obvious ones are 468.27 (where he covers two Melodies)[2]

184.16 and 15	moromelodious {This is not in the Census. The O is there to bring in the third of Sade's titles into this paragraph: he was Governor-General of Valromey: moROMElodious. Almost all the Romeos and even the ROMES of the book take a glance at that because he is omnipresent.}
326.30	"brought your summer with us and TOMkin["][3]
488.36	The harp that once[4]. . . . 489.1 MOURNE 489.2 more
477.33	How sweet the answer[5]. . . 29 myrrh of the moor

304. note 4   J J has changed "I'd mourn the hopes" to MORE in
17.24 [i.e., .23]   Let Erin rember [i.e., remember]⁶. . . . . . 25 [i.e., .24] MEARmerge
316.2   "   "   "   the proud invaders.
                4 [i.e., .5] thane (from Tom Dick and Harry) 6 [i.e., .7] moor. . .to mear. . .
                All these MOORES because 3 melodies are quoted on the page⁷
338.32   Let Erin remember. . . . . . 26 tom. . . 29 thumb
362.22   Like the bright lamps. . . . Thamamahalla⁸
398.22   . . . loves young dreams⁹. . . 23–24 Mor. . . another more
446.14   meeting waters¹⁰. . . .15 part no more

MOORE'S WIFE was Betsy [i.e., Bessy] DYKE: hence
617.31   I wish I was by that dim lake¹¹. . . . TYKE
528.32   minstrel boy¹². . . . moreen. . . . 33 TYKE
517.10   Sublime was the warning¹³. . . . . . 15 DYKE

    And Moore's mother was ANASTASIA(!) CODD
91.24   "The dawning of the morn"¹⁴ . . . 22 CODDLING doom
427.17–23   Two melodies:¹⁵ with 20 mornings: 20 cod: 23 more.

    And for Mangan¹⁶
338.36   The fair hills of Erin. . . 32 ching lew MANG
                (J. J. twice calls this green hills of Erin)
387.17   long long ago is the refrain of Mangan's The Time of the Barmecides.
                Do you think that Mangan is MOMONIAN 18?
                _____

    And my favorites: Oft in the Stilly Night¹⁷ (Not in the Irish Melodies)
136.20   the light of other days. . . . 21 TIMOUR!!
                And he twists the spelling of his quotation from Dante¹⁸
292.3   This life is all chequered¹⁹. . . . . 1 lamoor
568.13   It is not the tear²⁰. . . . 15 much much more
                _____

There are a great many more I don't give you more because you are ever more more *sceptical*

I have an increasing list of addenda for Hodgart-Worthington SONGS. Don't tell them yet, because I haven't time to draw it up—but let me know if you hear that they are preparing a new edition.

The chief addendum for that book is for the preface—pointing out that certain songs are stamp-allusions to certain people.

Yankee Doodle is always POE (born in Boston and wrote Diddling as a Fine Art)

Also Hi diddle diddle (which they failed to catch in their book.) Also Polly wolly doodle[21]

All the many Rockabye. . are a glance at Whitman because of that "CRADLE endlessly rocking") as you can see in 104.18—(which incidentally may also be Billy Budd[)][22]

Almost all the many songs about BELLS are directed at Poe, including The Ding Dong for *Sachsdente* [i.e., *Sechleläuten* or *Sächsilüte*] that [Fritz] Senn is working so hard on.[23]

It is extraordinary the role that American literature[24]

Here I was interrupted.
Am enclosing another leaf[.]
Oh—how eagerly I await your new Census = that big book with wide margins = and on good paper.

        All best to you all three
        Ever
        (T. N.)

[Enclosure][25]
        Foliation of Schiller's plays:[26]

32.9 The Robbers	.29 Wallenstein; maybe 33.8 well entitled = William Tell {Schiller's here because J. W. Booth played the Robbers and this page is the Assassination of Lincoln: Boots 24 SEMPER 29 Washington etc.}
514.19	Schiller and his play .23 *Demetrius*
514.24–25	Virginia [Vita] Sackville-West, her portrait in ORLANDO 24.

Who are J. J.'s (SEVEN) HEROES who RETURN? I think they are many times in the book; I choose the places where the[y] are most clearly seen.

499.28	Roland-Oliver-Charlemagne: Oliver and his horn 500.13
500.15	chareman = Charlemagne
499.35	LINCOLN. 500.13 linklink. 11 Lancs for Lincolnshire; independence 14 freedman 15
499.30	Hart = Arthur
500.1	Drake's drum. Drake's ship the Golden (aure 19) Hind 12

500.4	Finn.
500.7	[i.e., .6] Oliver Cromwell
500.3	[?500.15] Christ. {Perhaps all the Words from the Cross are here.}
{Later: I see that Charlemagne should be combined with Roland-Oliver} And where is Barbarossa? "dead giant" 500.1	

74.3	*the heroes return*
74.4–5	horn. . . roland-orlando 2. Roncesvaux means vale of Briers. [inserted above: paladin 73.35] ⇒ Charlemagne
74.6–7	Lincoln. . . allprohome. . . (bis)
73.36	Arthur. . . 74.2 crested head!
. . . . .	Drake??
74.1	Finn Finn.
74.4	olver lord Protector
73.35	Herr {Christ} 74.6 Deyes. . . . . . Deyus. . . .

358.28	*nine and thirty hero-heroin[e]s! 359.27 Lets All Wake*
359.26	Orland (for Charlemagne) As constellation the BIG BEAR = Charles Wain [358].30
358.20	{Lincoln} aboarder? 359.22 a ham. . . a ham pig?
359.15	Arthur-round table. . . camelot. . . 358.29 arthou
358.29	Drake. . . ducks draken.
358.19	Finn. . . . 23 Finn.
. . . .	? (Cromwell?)
358.19	Christ. . . . Messiah. {MESHIA in Aramaic}
358.22	Barbarossa is under the KYFFHAÜSER
Looks like Documents I and II are the old and new testaments 358.29 [i.e., .30] 359.12 (look at all the Bibles here!)	

Surprising I can't find a clear Heroes Return in the Resurrection Chapter!! You'd think it [would] be around Heroes' Highway 607.12 (you can always find a few of those heroes on any page.)

You are certainly right that SHAW is all over 161ff {for 161.27–32 remember that SHAWS means greens, the tops of beets and potatoes etc

.30 green leaves.[}] An early word for this kind of shaw was SKOG which may be behind 28 sprog.

On page 62 [i.e., 162] he's doing *too* many things at once:

Shakespeare's Pericles—Per-c-l-e-s .12 prince of TYRE .1 and his daughter Marina .16 (and 163.1 reverse arinam) thought by her father to be coo-coo (bastard) oafsprung [162.14]. (I don't know why we go to the Caucasus 14 to find Tobol[o]sk in the Ural 12.)

Shakespeare's Julius Caesar. It was a mistake to have Caesar knived and removed in the First Act, but the twin conspirators come back to the deserted battlefield [162].11 at FLOP AS 9 = Philippi. Caesar in the play is said to be the cynosure of all eyes .14[.] And it is Sh-pre not Shaw who is mocked as a half-baked military strategist from Sandhurst [.8] and West Point.

Good luck to you on the Graal. Sounds right.

It may be useful to you to the broken chambers to note 353.36 [i.e., .35]–354.1

Eliot is certainly associated with the Weston-Arthurian-Graal motif on page 151	
151. . . .	.17 cup 24 couple 20 communion .30 hydro. . .pneumo water and spirit .22 overpast = pastover = Paschal {all the words about drinking} 20 Morte d'Arthur
151.18	tom tom 21 waste toes = TSE {foes 11} BOLO (Eliot's ribald poem never reprinted about BOLO KING of the something isles [151.23].
.17–21	Eliot trying to fashion queer faiths for himself
.18	crevises and crevasse comes from *crever* to shatter, break
Note for the Census .23 Looswallawer Anita Loos	
	Lewis Waller, the ranting actor Wyndham Lewis who was starting a magazine called the TYRO[27] (23) CRITIC (and tyro is Greek for cheese)
.21	*waste* may be Weston

1. Thomas Moore, see TW to AG, [?12–14 October 1960], n. 3.

2. Moore, "One Bumper at Parting" and "Farewell!—But Whenever You Welcome the Hour."

3. Moore, "Come, Send Round the Wine (We brought the summer with us)."

4. Moore, "The Harp that Once through Tara's Halls."
5. Moore, "How Sweet the Answer Echo Makes."
6. Moore, "Let Erin Remember the Days of Old."
7. Moore, 316.2, "Let Erin Remember the Days of Old," .21–.22, "How Oft Has the Banshee Cried [The Dear Black Maid]," .35, "Oh Where's the Slave So Lowly." Hodgart and Worthingon in *Song*, Hodgart and Bauerle in *Joyce's Grand Operoar*, and Bauerle in *Picking Up Airs* identify other references to music on this page.
8. Moore, "Erin, Oh Erin," ["Like the Bright Lamp, that shone in Kildare's Holy fame (Thamama Halla)"].
9. Moore, "Love's Young Dream."
10. Moore, "The Meeting of the Waters."
11. Moore, "I Wish I Was by that Dim Lake."
12. Moore, "The Minstrel Boy" ["The Moreen"].
13. Moore, "Sublime Was the Warning."
14. Moore, "The Dawning of the Morn."
15. Moore, .17–.19, "How Dear to Me the Hours when Daylight Dies" ["The Twisting of the Rope"] and .20 "In the Morning of Life."
16. James Clarence Mangan (1803–1849), the poet and translator, "O, The Fair Hills of Eire." His poem, "The Time of the Barmecides," first appeared in the *Dublin University Magazine* in 1839, and a year later a revised version appeared in the same magazine.
17. Moore, "Oft in the Stilly Night."
18. FW 292.1–.2, Dante, *Inferno*, V, 100: "Amor, ch'al cor gentil ratto s'apprende," "Love, that can quickly seize the gentle heart" (Allen Mandelbaum, translator, Bantam Classic, 1982).
19. Moore, "This Life is All Chequered With Pleasures and With Woes."
20. Moore, "It Is Not the Tear at this Moment Shed."
21. Edgar Allan Poe (1809–1849), "Diddling Considered as One of the Exact Sciences." The tale opens with "Hey, diddle diddle,/The cat and the fiddle." Stephen Foster (1826–1864), "Polly Wolly Doodle."
22. Walt Whitman, "Out of the Cradle Endlessly Rocking." Herman Melville, *Billy Budd Sailor (An Inside Narrative)*.
23. Senn, "Some Zurich Allusions in *Finnegans Wake*," *The Analyst*, XIX (December 1960), [1]–22.
24. Starting here, three lines are crossed out.
25. This enclosure was probably begun at an earlier date as notes for Glasheen; Wilder added notes on information in Glasheen's letter of 15 October 1960, with its references to Jessie L. Weston. For the assassination of Abraham Lincoln, see TW to AG, [?2–14 October 1960]; for notes on Virginia Woolf, see TW to AG, 3 May 1959, and AG to TW, 5 May 1959; for notes on T. S. Eliot, see TW to AG, 22 July 1959. Glasheen mentions George Bernard Shaw in her letter to Wilder of 19 June 1958.

26. Johann Christoph Friedrich von Schiller (1759–1805), the German historian, poet, dramatist and translator. The plays Wilder mentions, with their dates of first production, are: *Die Räuber* (The Robbers), 1782; the Wallenstein trilogy: *Wallensteins Lager* (Wallenstein's Camp), 1798, *Die Piccolomini* (The Piccolominis), 1799, and *Wallensteins Tod* (The Death of Wallenstein), 1799; *Wilhelm Tell* (William Tell), 1804; *Demetrius*, an unfinished tragedy written in 1804/05 and published in 1815.

27. Lewis was the editor and did most of the writing for *The Tyro: A Review of the Arts of Painting, Sculpture and Design*. The review, published by Harriet Shaw Weaver's The Egoist Press, had only two numbers, the first in April 1921; the second was published in March 1922.

◻

To Thornton Wilder, Hamden, Connecticut
[MS. ALS—YCAL]

18 October 1960   [22 Carrington Lane
                                          Farmington, Connecticut]

Dear Thornton,

I could screech on two counts & *you* are to blame for both.

First, I found a passage about Savage yesterday.[1] That is—somewhere in Book I I came on Savage with a capital S. & said to my husband What was his first name. And he said Richard & there wasn't any Richard so I reluctantly decided RS wasn't meant. 1 hour since your letter came & I still can't find it.

Second, I'm in a spell of finding—ah Everything in FW & so my novel's gone to hell.

I forgive you & will put some things down. I am going through FW, picking up themes. One big one is going to be Will & Bacon[.][2]
p. 31 has *all* the King Williams of England, including Gladstone
31.11—   Sailor King, Wm IV
  .14—   Wm. I the Conk & Wm. III who did really come and
                 conquer Ireland
  .25   Our red brother = William Rufus[3]

36.4	Hokusai[4]
37.14	Eliot?
37.17 [i.e., 39.17]	Packenham—Bacon & Ham—WS's poaching[5]
40.13	Wilde[6] & Eros
40.14	Arthur Hallam[7]
41.13	Bacon
44.11	The name of the priest who broke the chalice in *Dubliners* = Flynn.[8]
Note	
	d*u*b him Llyn & Phin. I think so
49–50	I think plays with TSE's[9] Waste Landers melting together

There are dozens of Charlottes. Who she?

52.3	Am I right in thinking tutu = Fr. for pox?[10]
55.22	Cyclops—.27 Circe—.28 Bloom[11]
59.5	Dante because of his passage about Rachel & Leah the Mirror Girls
59.4	Aida[12]
.20	Bacon / Hamlet .31 / Ham & Hamlet = indistinguishable
.21	Kevin—Lorry below [.26] must be Jerry
62.9–10	Mrs. O'Shea, called Queenie whose husband certainly haltered Parnell
62.10 [i.e., .11]	Lot, .12 [i.e., .13] tol 63.22 Lot / 65.17 tolloll—with Lard Tolloller Yum-Yum is below
63.29	Poe?
63.33–34	Hammering on gate = Macbeth & Hamlet. See Jocasta (Gertrude) above / Soliloquy of drunken Porter line 20
64.1	Was there a Shakespearean critic Tilyard?[13]
.3	Rognar
.7 & 9	Harris other name = Canaan = Mulling*can Inn*
63.4	Pistol
66—	Will (Shakespeare? Yeats? ?Other) all over—l. 10, 18 (bis), 21, 22
66.28 [i.e., .29]—	Arp (bis)
Who's Hock or Hicky? 64.6 / 67.18, 20?	
68.27	Dagon
87.26	At Puck Fair in Killorgin, Kerry, male goat (called Puck) wreathed & paraded, chased etc. Was King of Fair
91.1	Joyce and his Gretta

> More, I fear, anon
> Yours
> Adaline

1. Richard Savage, see TW to AG, [?12–14 October 1960].
2. William Shakespeare and Francis Bacon.
3. Glasheen suggests that this is King William II or William Rufus (1056–1100). Beginning with the reference "p. 31" until "Rufus," Wilder has boxed this material in in red pencil.
4. The Japanese artist (1760–1849).
5. See AG to TW, 10 October 1960, n. 3.
6. Oscar Wilde.
7. Arthur Henry Hallam (1811–1833), chiefly remembered as the subject of Tennyson's "In Memoriam."
8. The Reverend James Flynn, formerly of St. Catherine's Church, in "The Sisters."
9. T. S. Eliot.
10. Tutu is French for a ballet skirt. Pox, in the sense of a disease, would be a form of *vérole*.
11. Leopold Bloom, Joyce's *Ulysses*.
12. Opera by Giuseppe Verdi.
13. E. M. W. Tillyard (1889–1962) wrote extensively on the literature of the sixteenth and seventeenth centuries. Among his most well-known books are: *The Elizabethan World Picture*, *Shakespeare's Early Comedies*, and *Shakespeare's Problem Plays*.

To Thornton Wilder, Hamden, Connecticut

[MS. ALS—YCAL]

24 October 1960   [22 Carrington Lane
Farmington, Connecticut]

Dear Thornton,

Great fun to see you.[1] I'm sorry your sister wasn't there. By the time we got home I had thought out Abraham Lincoln and accepted it like Mgt. Fuller.[2] But I haven't—dreadful—even unfolded the paper of names you gave me.[3] I'll tell you why. The use of Shakespeare in Sections ii, iii, iv of FW[4] so overcame me, and its further extensions everywhere at all, that I sat up all Sat. night thinking it out and yesterday and today working it out roughly. And roughly I'm going to write it out for you. It's going to be awfully long, even rough, incomplete, and limited to those 3 Sections. By the nature of the use of WS, it must go on. Also I've massed a lot because I know little about S., had to read the Brittanica yesterday, really don't know S's plays well (except *Lear, Antony & C & Love's LL*).

It's going to be so long that I'll keep interpretation to a minimum. Indeed it's incomplete & rather overwhelming so I don't know I can interpret yet. I can say it is some sort of rewriting of Scylla & Charybdis[5]—lots more odd parallels there than I've gotten down and I am not for a minute going to try to work out who people are, beyond saying Shem *seems* to be Bacon and Shaun, the Baconian version of Shakespeare—the Butcher and/or Butcher's Son.[6] But who exactly are Hamlet *pere* and *fils* and the real Shakespeare and Stephen etc. I don't even want to think about yet. One more thing, I am going to shove in a lot of S. references that we've all known for ages & ages because it's the aggregate that's so impressive. Oh yes, & there are loads of S. critics, his fellow actors etc.—I've caught a few & will hunt them out sometime.

It is so complicated. So too much.

Here we go. It starts quiet but builds[.]

Well, this is the rough lot for the moment. If I wanted to write an article on J J & W S I guess I'd be happy because if I find this much (you predicted it long ago) in this little FW there's likely a whole lot more, though this may be the main bout with Shakespeare. Certainly the S.-Bacon theme must turn up whenever plagiarism's in question—and homosexuality?—brother battles? theatre? I guess it is announced in my eternal paragraph on p. 3—"will be seen"[7] = William—Bacon seen or scene.

I assume The Letter is, among other things, WS's works and I assume that there as [i.e., is] a cryptogram someplace in FW, but I am not going to dig it out. You can be okay sure of that. It is now 9 a. m. Tuesday & I have worked 20 hours a day since I saw you. I still have to make a typescript of the allusions & send it [to] lots of people to establish my rights to B & S—I now believe in dowce little Delia [208.29]—because I'm not going to write an article & I don't want it swiped by Matt Hodgart in the next year.[8]

    Yours,
    Adaline

1. Wilder and the Glasheens had dinner in New Haven on 20 October.
2. Wilder discussed Abraham Lincoln in his letters of [?12–14 October 1960] and 16 October 1960. "I accept the universe," is a remark attributed to Margaret Fuller (1810–1850) to which Thomas Carlyle reportedly commented, "By God, she'd better."
3. A list that has not survived.
4. Book I, ii (30–47), iii (48–74), iv (75–103).
5. *Ulysses*, episode nine.
6. One anecdote about Shakespeare was that he showed a particular talent as a butcher.
7. The phrase on 3.14 is "was to be seen."
8. Matthew J. C. Hodgart's "Shakespeare and *Finnegans Wake*," in *The Cambridge Journal*, VI, 12 (September 1953), 735–752. The essay was adapted and is in Hodgart and Worthington, *Song*, "Songs and the Interpretation of *Finnegans Wake*," [24]–58. Glasheen did write an article. See Appendix VIII.

☐

To Thornton Wilder, Hamden, Connecticut

[MS. Typed—YCAL]

[?October–November 1960–I]

NOTES ON SHAKESPEARE IN FW,

BOOK I, SECTIONS 2, 3, 4—A. Glasheen

FW 31— *all* the King Williams of Eng. here—including Shakespeare (here-after S.) by way of *Ulysses* (U) 201 [1961: 204], where S. is identified with Gladstone: "The people's William." Hereafter, as far as I go, S. is comprehended in every William, Willy, Will, Bill, Billy, Belly, and in most Wells and Walls

35.14   S. wanting [to] be country gent?

39.16–17   Treacle (Sweet) Tom is Tom the Piper's Son.[1] Stole pork from Kehoe, Donnelly (Ignatius), Packenham (Bacon-Ham). The pun on Hamlet-ham is early as Saxo G[rammaticus]. 11th Brit. says.

.29	wild (Oscar) and woolly (Willy) haunts—note initials WH. Begins homosexual theme.	
?40.23–4	Hamlet[2]	
?41.1	Later on Will-well does *somewhat* melt into Wellington vs Boney[3]	
.13–14	bakenbeggfuss. . . shinkhams	
.18	hamlet—the theme is awfully quiet, underground as yet	
?42.11	I think Bacon melts into Buck-Buckley but am not yet sure	
?43.2	Hamlet / .5 Ham	
44.13	Will / S. wrote a bitter song against Lucy[4]	
50.1	Baxters and Fleshmen are Bacon and Shakespeare, and if this seems uncertain, remember Cain-vegetarian, Abel-meatman and see FW 162.6–10 [i.e., 172.5–.10]: "John's (S's father John a butcher)[5] is a different butcher. . . John's is now quite divorced from baking" [172.5, .7] I don't mean that "butcher" always means S. senior. It's just Shaun is the Butcher, Shakespeare, and Shem the Bacon that gets butchered. The relation of John Joyce and John Shakespeare is yet unclear to me.	
52.4–5	S. quote[6]	
53.1–3	Scene-seen (all dramatic terms and refs?) seem to bring in S. Also arras and Mother suggest Hamlet here. (I never knew till yesterday that "He was the first to bear arms" [5.5] was *Hamlet*.)	
.36[7]		
54.22–7	Commercial S.? Billy and Belly interchange	
55.1	S. a schoolmaster Aubrey says[8]	
.10	S. quote / .24 Bacon? /31 S. quote[9]	
56.16	ghost—is, becomes always King Hamlet	
.22	wearywilly /.27 baccy	
?57.4	I think the *real* Shakespeare whoever he may be, is the Father of the race as in "Scylla and C[harybdis]."	
.6	ghost / 15 pork	
59.20	Kevin-Shaun eats Bacon as he does 405.33, 406.2, 406.5	
.31	Hamlet	
60.8	Well / 10 bard / 26 "The Brut" is an analogue of the Hamlet story	
62	"Scylla and C" emphasizes S. as an exile	
.5–6	leaving Stratford for London theatre? In Stratford his father fined for a dunghill[10]	
.8	things in ear—Hamlet	
.15	franchisable—Francis B.	

.17	ghost
62–64	so filled with allusions I can't begin to untangle
62.19	ear in garden
.26	We *seem*
.34	11th Brit. mentions some legend about S's crab-tree.[11] What?
63.2	A loaded Hobson is the same as Scylla and Car[y]bdis
.4	Pistol[12]
.10	gentlewriter
.15	Chambers—S. critic[13] (practically all of them probably in FW)
.16	Butcher
.19ff—	the knocking at the gate in "Macbeth"—Drunken porter's soliloquy (see line 20). Hammering takes in Hamlet—Biblical Ham who's been put out of family—Ham-Bacon. Also, I think, somebody named Sir T. Hanmer[14] (see below)
63.30	lameness of Oedipus who ties to Hamlet, lameness of W. S. as in Sonnets. Jocasta-Gertrude 1. 31.
.34	Richard Savage[15]
.35	Swan / .36 Bib. Ham
64.1	Til[l]yard—critic?[16]
.7–8	hammering-pig
.9–10	Mullingcan is Mulligan / allower is Oliver—he shut Stephen out of tower, was present in S[cylla] and C[harybdis]. 18 butcher and baker
65.1 [i.e., .2]	Actium? (Incidentally, the Cream Puffs [.11], wardrobe [.14], ideal may be from Kierkegaard's banquet piece[17] where they sit around as in S and C
66. 10, 18, 21, 22, 25—will	
67.15	Butcher
.23, 24	(and later) Hamlet a woman by way of Mrs. Palmer and Vining in *Ulysses*—see below[18]
68.32	will
69.3	Wilde's and S's homosexuality.
.3	P[adraic]. Colum same quote as "S and C"[19]
.3	MSND [*A Midsummer Night's Dream*]—fairies, Bottom—prepares for Shem's later becoming gray ass
.7–9	more MSND—Wall a character in
.22	pig
.28 [i.e., .26]	porter
71–72—	many forms pork-pig—fatmeant [72.15] etc. in names
72.34–5	Butchering
73.16	biting thumbs in Romeo and J[uliet][20]

.21	Bach turns into F. Bacon later on
75.27 [i.e., .15]	3 wills / 33 [i.e., .21] belly
76	HCE-Noah segregates Ham, makes him a negro, criminal, servant. I think that in some way Shem-Ham has got to be the Man Servant pore old Joe—cf. Joy and Ham line 5
.10, 33	same pun on good and best and Mr. Best in "S and C"[21]
78.3	stage / .8 hall—S's daughter named / .13 bought land
.14	spearway
	Note all the Fs and Bs in this paragraph. I *guess* that freeing the slaves is associated with Bacon because Francis-Frank—means free.
.24	gruntens—grunts-pigs and Ulysses Grant—Grant freed slaves, Ulysses freed pigs from Circe
.11–12 [i.e., .7]—	BBB as in Bacon / WW as in William
79.1	ham / 8–9 S. quote[22] / 18 Venus / 20–21 bare bodkin
.22	Every Man in His Humor? S acted in[23]
.23–4	Wells. . . wills—see stuff in "S and C" about Anne Hathaway being the one who wooed S
.27ff	This paragraph almost all S, whose initials are everywhere—just look and see—will in overplus. They even occur in "Widow *Strong*" which seemed kind of senseless, but 1) Ulysses 188, 200 [1961: 191–192, 203–204]—passages about how Anne and all the S. women outlived their men. U., 209 [1961: 212–213] says AH weakened S's will—compare 79.33 2) U. 188–9 [1961: 192–193] Stephen associates Kate the Shrew with Anne Hathaway[.] That Kate in FW is somehow ALP I have long known. Perhaps she keeps the museum because she is the great man's eternal widow, guarding and innaccurately recalling him—like Katy O'Shee's [i.e., O'Shea] biography.[24] Remember will-wellington do melt together later on, and maybe are already together in "The Museyroom," [8–10] to some extent[.]
79.30	John Shakespeare's dunghill again—I guess maybe it is the basic dunghill of FW
.33	her weaker—Earwicker
.35	Hamlet—dane
80.1 ff—	Just mark the Ws, the Ss, Fs, Bs—
.8	butcher
.14–19—	almost a literal quote from "S and C," U. 192.8 [1961: 195]. The critic [Georg] Brandes is in U, becomes brandihands, l[ine]. 14[25]

.15 lost is Perdita / Ma is Marina. (You really have to put them side by side)
80.13 In the S. bibliography in 11th Brit. gives—P. Capell *The Castrated Letter of Sir T. Hanmer*, (1736). Who he?[26]
M. J. Wolff is S. critic[27]
.20 Initials—A—S / propag*ana*—AH and her faithfulness which Stephen questions
.20 ff faintly follows gravediggers in Hamlet

Foregoing aspect of S. now given up—move from his female to his male love and to the stealing of *Hamlet* from Bacon (or the other way around, but I think from Bacon)

81.2–3 plots—one person doing work, other getting credit
.5 mausoleum—Ophelia's grave—heterosexual love
.6 [i.e., .10] Romeo JUL.'s " " "
.11 Capitalized initials—WH
.16 MSND—dreams, Puck, juice in eyes
.17 This is where the Liffey (ALP-A. Hathaway women) turns into the Oscar Wildean sea. (Salt for Sodom and Gomorrah). See "S and C" about WS leaving world of women for world of men
.17 Francis Meres S. contemporary praised S.[28]
.23 A. Michele, mid-19th cent. took a very bad cast of S. bust
81.28 *U*, 196 [1961: 199–200]—swearing by St. Patrick
.30 *well let* [the] *blubbywail ghoats out of him*—Will, ghost, Hamlet
.34–35 W fighting B—Wellington and Bonapart[e]
82.5 bully (Billy—Bully Bottom—is Bull also always to suggest S?)
.29 Billi
.9, 11 *Let* me go... younger *him* of the same *ham*
.12 Was *six*
.14 *foul b*ehind
.31-2— W H
83.5 [i.e., .3] *w*ell *h*ave, boy Baches—WH and Willy Hughes. *Bache*, Skeat says, is MHG for a flitch of bacon. It's German "boy" too, isn't it?[29]
.5 Heart alive. The Harts, descendants from S's sister are still alive. In T. Brooke's *Shakespeare of Stratford* a paragraph ends "Hart alive."[30]
.23 grace is Anne... will
.28 Bully Bottom. Stephen says S. made in Germany
.29 Compare *U*, 185 [1961: 187]—SD on WS: "Not for nothing was he a butcher's son, wielding the sledded poleaxe and spitting on his palm."

84.4	danegeld—blackmail and Hamlet is, in a sense, a gelded dane
.34	ear pierced
.36	Donnelly
85.8	*belly*bone / 10 Wellington? / .14 will / .18 Bacon / .28–9
86.13, 27—	Anthony and Francis Bacon
.14	pig / .15 Hyacinth as object of male affection
.21–2	Is a connection between Hamelet [i.e., Hamlet] and Ireland—see below
87.9, 10	pig, ham / 20 Lewes—S. critic / 22 "S and C" S a fox[31]
88.15	Robert Greene jealous of S[32] / .33 William
[87].20	Lewes a S. critic / 22 "S and C" makes S a fox—a christfox
89.3–4	Comedy of Errors—is it also at 62.25?
.34.	pig / 36 handkerchief
91.6,7	Cleopatra, pig
92.14	willingly—note this is Shaun
.15	swine
.20	woolywags—and all that sweetness ascribed to S.
93.1	Same verdict as "S and C"
.8	vinesmelling is Vining, man mentioned in "S and C" who thought Hamlet a woman. Note 92.4, 67.23–4, 93.18–19[33]
.18	Bottom [*A Midsummer Night's Dream*]
94.3	Merchant of V[enice]?
94–5	Other men having Anne Hathaway before and after marriage. Of course the 4 are SD's judges in "S and C"
96.2	"Love's LL"—they hunt roses in park
.4	Mrs. Nial is fun.[34] Hamlet's name occurs in Annals of 4 Masters, in a stanza by Irish Queen Gormflaith who laments death of her husband Nial Glundubh, killed at "battle of Ath Cliath," 919. Can read about in "Hamlet," 11th Brit.
96.33	The real S. our ancestor, father of the race—S and C—played poss[u]m, is an unknown quantity which saves him from horrors on the biographical side, unless, of course, S. Dedalus is after him
97.21ff	things done S's works
.22, 34	will
.34	"Julius Caesar"
98.5	S. as exile in S and C
99.19	Pig is Piggot who—like Bacon really wrote the letter that passed for somebody else's[35]
.29–30	S's coat of arms?[36] him—him / don't you like "left him lion," which I think, means that there was nothing biografiends and others can do to S. which will keep him from being the

	king of the beasts or Lion, which is, we all know, the name Joyce gave to this section
100.6	pig / .28 Bacon?
101.3	See S and C—at last he comes back to Anna Livia—Anne H.—Molly Bloom. In S and C they say tell us about Mrs. S.
101.9–10	pig
.22	Hamlet
.24	Francis—Baconian heresy, B and S scandals in private life
102.21–22	S's epitaph—banes is bones and curse[37]
.27	Willy Hughes—*hue*moures. . . .*w*hilko *h*er *w*hims (hims)
103.5	Willy Hughes again
103 last paragraph—cf. U. 204, [1961: 206] about AH "loosing her nightly waters on the jordan"	

1. The thieving hero of an old nursery rhyme, Tom the Piper was one of the characters in the fifteenth century morris dance.

2. Cheng, *Shakespeare and Joyce*: "The description of Hosty's state seems much like that of Hamlet's" (117).

3. The Battle of Waterloo (1815) where the Duke of Wellington defeated Napoleon Bonaparte.

4. See AG to TW, 20 November 1960, n. 11.

5. John Shakespeare (d. 1601), William's father, was a glover and a dealer in agricultural products, primarily hides and wool, not, as was alleged, a butcher.

6. *Macbeth*, V, i, 47–48: "all the perfumes of Arabia will not sweeten this little hand."

7. Possibly "Upkingbilly," a reference to King William III (of Orange).

8. John Aubrey (1626–1697), in his *Brief Lives*, first published in 1813, claims that as a young man Shakespeare was a schoolmaster in the country. Aubrey's information on Shakespeare came primarily from William Beeston, whose father Christopher was a fellow actor in Shakespeare's company.

9. Line 10 echoes *Macbeth*, IV, i, 80: "The power of man, for none of woman born." Cheng finds in line 31 an echo of Mark Anthony's speech at Caesar's funeral, *Julius Caesar*, III, ii, 79.

10. On 29 April 1552, John Shakespeare, together with Adrian Quiney and Humphrey Reynolds, was fined for keeping an unauthorized dunghill on Henley Street where all three men lived.

11. In [?October-November 1960-II] Glasheen writes that Shakespeare, after a drinking bout, left Stratford and was found asleep under a crab-tree.

12. Falstaff's ensign in *2 Henry IV*. In *Henry V* Pistol has married Nell Quickly and is the host of the Boar's Head Tavern.

13. Sir Edmund K. Chambers (1866–1954). Among his books are: *The Medieval Stage* (2 vols., 1903), *The Elizabethan Stage* (4 vols., 1923), and *William Shakespeare: A Study of Facts and Problems* (2 vols., 1930).

14. Sir Thomas Hanmer (*c.* 1676–1746) published a six-volume edition of Shakespeare's plays in 1743–1744.

15. See TW to AG, [?12–14 October 1960].

16. See AG to TW, 18 October 1960.

17. Perhaps a reference to two sections of *Either/Or*, "The Tragic in Ancient Drama Reflected on in the Tragic in Modern Drama" and "Silhouettes Psychological Diversion" both of which are "Delivered before the [Fellowship of the Dead]." See *Either/Or*, Part I, ed. Howard V. Hone and Edna Hong (Princeton: Princeton University Press, 1987).

18. Mrs. Bandmann Palmer, an actress, played *Hamlet* in Dublin. Edward Payson Vining (1847–1920) wrote *The Mystery of Hamlet: An Attempt to Solve an Old Problem* (1881) in which he argued that Hamlet was a woman who dressed as a man to secure the throne of Denmark for her family's lineage.

19. Glasheen is hearing a connection between "wilde erthe" and the line in *Ulysses*, "Yeats admired his [Colum's] line: *As in wild earth a Grecian vase.*" See *Ulysses* (1961), 198.23–.26.

20. An exchange I, i, between Sampson, a servant of the Capulets and Abram, a servant of the Montagues.

21. Richard Irvine Best (1872–1959), assistant director and then director of the National Library of Ireland, is frequently mentioned in *Ulysses*, Episode 9, "Scylla and Charybdis."

22. See note 9.

23. Shakespeare's name is included on the printed list of actors in Ben Jonson's play in 1598. He is also included in the cast list for Jonson's *Sejanus: His Fall* in 1603. It is generally thought that Shakespeare played Elder Knowell. See Schoenbaum 16–19.

24. Katharine O'Shea (Mrs. Charles Stewart Parnell), *Charles Stewart Parnell: His Love Story and Political Life* (London: Cassell & Co., 1914). See AG to TW, 16 March 1957.

25. Georg M. Brandes (1842–1927), the Danish scholar and critic whose *William Shakespeare: A Critical Study* appeared in two volumes in 1898. It is one of the principal sources used by Joyce in *Ulysses*, "Scylla and Charybdis."

26. Glasheen here is in error. The bibliography cites P. Nichols, actually an error for Philip Nicholas. Just above this entry is one for Edward Capell's *Notes and Various Readings to Shakespeare*. For Sir Thomas Hanmer, see note 14.

27. Max. J. Wolff (1868–1941), *William Shakespeare: Studien und Aufsätze* (1903).

28. Shakespeare is mentioned in Francis Meres's *Palladis Tamia* (1598) in the section "A Comparitiue discourse of our English Poets, with the *Greeke, Latine, and Italian Poets.*" Mention of Shakespeare helps date Shakespeare's early plays and his sonnets.

29. Walter W. Skeat, *An Etymological Dictionary of the English Language* (Oxford: The Clarendon Press, 1910). "Bache" is Welsh, not German, for boy.

30. Tucker Brooke, *Shakespeare of Stratford: A Handbook for Students* (New Haven: Yale University Press, 1926), 2. Joan Shakespeare (1569–1646) married William Hart (d. 1616) and had four children only one of whom, Thomas, had issue.

31. Probably an allusion to Percy Wyndham Lewis's *The Lion and the Fox: The Role of the Hero in Shakespeare*.
32. Robert Greene (1558–1592), the playwright, poet, and novelist who attacked Shakespeare in his *Groats-Worth of Wit* (1592).
33. See note 18.
34. In *Census II* Glasheen claims Nial might be one of the Nine Hostages who ruled Ireland in the fourth century or "A later Nial who was perhaps slain by Hamlet."
35. Richard Pigott (1828–1889), who forged letters that became the basis for a series of newspaper articles implicating Charles Stewart Parnell in the Phoenix Park Murders and the violence connected with the Land War. He escaped from England and committed suicide in a Madrid hotel. In 1621, while Lord Chancellor, Bacon was charged before the House of Lords with bribery. He confessed, but denied he had ever perverted justice. He was removed from office, denied the right to sit in parliament, and briefly imprisoned.
36. In 1576, Shakespeare's father, a prosperous businessman and landowner, applied to the College of Heralds for a coat of arms and the right to call himself a gentleman. Perhaps because of financial problems his petition was either dropped or denied; it was not until twenty years later that it was granted.
37. The verse on Shakespeare's gravestone in Holy Trinity Church, Stratford, which ends: "AND CURST BE HE THAT MOVES MY BONES."

☐

To Thornton Wilder, Hamden, Connecticut

[MS. TYPED—YCAL]

[?October–November 1960–II]

Shakespeare and FW by AG

?104.30 [i.e., .18]   My husband's a journey etc—S. off to London?
   .32 [i.e., .20]   Cleopater's—including Pater
105.1   Merchant [*of Venice*]
  .18   Ophelia Culprints. . . old Danish—I daresay all "danes" must be scrutinized for Hamlet
  .22   S. quote[1]
  .34   bed?
106.2   Hue
  .11–12   Entered as the Latest *Pig*tarial and my Pooridiocal etc

.17–18	See "scylla and C"—AH seducing S. and getting pregnant	
.30	Will	
107.15	belly	
108.1	mountbank... partywall?—I begin to suspect back is Bacon but am not sure	
109.1	quest—see "S and C" 1961: 195]—cryptogramers on their Great Quest	
110.13–14	quote²	
.17	Harry—I think S's Henries sometimes	
.18	will...back	
.23	quote?³	
110–113	For me, at least, it makes a difference that basically—or at least, on some level the dump-dungheap in FW is the dump-dungheap of John Shakespeare. (John and Mary Shakespeare, John and Mary Joyce—J. S. and JJ both prosperous fathers, fell into decline at about the same stage in their sons' careers. Both sons exiles from birthplace. I think John Shakespeare is one of HCE's main roles, may be even more than that.) Anyway, since the dump (which got sold in Mutt and Jute in the first section of FW, and, probably got sold in Stratford, near as I can make out) is John and William Shakespeare's dump (father and son proved identical in "S and C") it becomes extremely probable that the hen that dug up a letter from America is, none other than *Delia Bacon* or *Biddy Doran*. The passage 110–113 comes clear, for me, is a lot funnier, makes good comic sense if you read it in this light.	
111–112	Biddy turns right into Kate, both being aspects of ALP-Anne Hathaway-widow of the great, falsifying his story and personality. But Kate is just the ignorant exhibitor of part truths and wild innocent mistakes, while Biddy seeks to warp the thing from highest motives.	
	I haven't of course gotten a chance to read DB's book on S.⁴ Joyce may or mayn't have used it, but in ALP, 205 you notice HCE has been slandered and ALP is out to do something about it, so I think the dowce little Delia on 208.29 may very well be poor mad Delia Bacon. J. may have used her book or just known it was an American female who started the Baconian heresy.	
110.30	sunseeker—son seeker or Bloom-Shakespeare—back	
111.5	*Belin[d]a...Dorans*	
.11	well...well	

	.13	born gentleman
	.16	well... well
	.26	Well... will
	.28	well... well
	.30	masses (foresees translation to ass)... Well... freely
112.1		back?
	.5	quest—see above
114.16–17		thit[h]aways... hithaways
	.18–19	oldsemetoneplace (Old Place /Shem / cemetery) and jupetbackagain (Japhet, Bacon) from tham Let (Ham-Hamlet-pig) Rise till Hum Lit.
	.23	seen / .30 mummer / .35 will be
	.34–6	—see "S and C"
116.21–2		waiting Kate's will—AH home in Stratford keeping her wrath warm (note Scotch) like Kate, Tam O'Shanter's wife
	.25	born gentleman
	.36	will be
117.4–7		iordanwater.. a fore marriage... will... plucked out whiskers in Lear
118.1–2		deciphered / .3–4
	.13	cf FW 86[5]
	.16	will... baccbuccus
	.19	will / 20 wall will hue
	.22 [i.e., .23]	dump
	.22	changing molecules in "S and C"
	.25	anticollaborators—what S and B / .26 will
	.28	hyacinth—see above—in FW I 4
	.32	dungflies
119.5		will begin
	.7	will... pigs
	.9	this will never do—ringing in Will Wordsworth
	.10	farmfrow (AH—see S and C)... flayful foxfetor—butcher and fox, see "S and C"
120.6 [i.e., .5]		middle—midden?
	.8–9 [i.e., .7–.8]	bullsfooted bee (Bacon)... dumpshow— "Hamlet" and the dump
	.9	born gent again
	.11	Hamlet quote[6]
	.15	errors?
	.27	S. return home—see S and C
	.35–36	AH in S and C
121.1		Claudius—plus Roman emperor[7]

.2–8	obviously somebody's description of some actor acting Hamlet, maybe Lichtenberg on Garrick as Hamlet:[8] . . . the Ghost is seen standing motionless. At these words Garrick turns suddenly about, at the same time starting with trembling knees two or three steps backward; his hat falls off; his arms, especially the left, are extended straight out, the left hand as high as his head etc etc[.] I guess maybe this is the passage J's working from but there may be others.
121.11–12	Hamlet's madness
.20	frank / .27
.31	last with first—see S and C—S goes back where he began / 31–32
122.7	bellical
.9ff	
.10	porter
.11–12	S holding horses—did he hold them in front of the Temple?
.12–13	Arson—in the sagas and Belleforest Hamlet burned everybody up in the end. Drink? S. was supposed to have left Stratford after a drinking bout, after which, I found out, he went to sleep under a crab tree.
.16	God and Shakespeare have created most? All the red stuff and William Rufus tie to p. 31[9]
.19	pigsking
.28	[i.e., .23] Tunc—I put here because I saw something lately—have forgotten what—which tied tunc to S or Bacon. I somehow associate it with Middle High German
.31	Dark lady? or Bacon-Ham being a negro
.33–4	S. a woman?
123—melts into Ulysses	
.19	wellinformed
.32	quote Hamlet[10]
124.2	stabs like in Hamlet that play by William Shakespeare
.6–7	wall of a singleminded men's asylum—Hamlet's madness, Joyce's, and the madness of Baconian fanatics or anybody else you like to name
.13—Him is Ham	
.23–24	
.27	honey a word not infrequently applied by his contemporaries to the swan of Avon
.32	Wm. IV—see 31[11]

Of course W. S. comes in on 31 also as Wm the Conk—see that story about Wm the Conk in "S and C." I don't know just why J. associates him with Wm. Rufus, but he does. Probably all the King Wms on 31 are W. S.
125.11–12
   .21–22 notesnatcher—

1. *Macbeth*, II, iii, 126: "Look to the lady."
2. *Hamlet*, III, i, 56: "To be, or not to be—that is the question."
3. Cheng does not cite an allusion for this line in his *Shakespeare and Joyce*.
4. *The Philosophy and Plays of Shakespeare Unfolded* (1857). See AG to TW, 5 November 1960.
5. "Coccolanius" may be a reference to *The Tragedy of Coriolanus*; the connection Glasheen sees to page 86 is not clear.
6. *Hamlet*, III, ii, 399: "Very like a whale."
7. Claudius ursurps the throne after killing his brother, King Hamlet, in *Hamlet*.
8. Glasheen is paraphrasing Georg Christoph Lichtenberg (1742–1799). See *Lichtenberg's Visits to England: As Described in his Letters and Diaries*, ed. Margaret L. Mare and W. H. Quarrell (Oxford: The Clarendon Press, 1938), 10.
9. King William II. See AG to TW, 18 October 1960, n. 3.
10. *Hamlet*, I, ii, 180–81: "The funeral bak'd meats/Did coldly furnish forth the marriage tables."
11. William IV, "The Sailor King" (1765–1837).

To Thornton Wilder, Hamden, Connecticut

[MS. ALS—YCAL]

1 November 1960 [22 Carrington Lane
Farmington, Connecticut]

Dear Thornton,

Nothing is clearer to me than why they had to put Delia Bacon away.[1]

{You know why she borrows Shaun's lamp in I i [27.6]and Alp [198.31]? Because Delia is Artemis—moon who was also good to little chickens.}

You are likely in a privileged position. At least Nathaniel Hawthorne, who was also a novelist, felt *he* was singularly privileged in watching Delia on her quest, and I should be surprised if your reactions were less fine & sensitive than his. In short, I am wrung out like a rag by Joyce and Shakespeare and Bacon, they should drop dead. I guess I also hear Joyce laughing in heaven and feeling another American hen, one of those coincidences he well loved.

Annoying, I have not been able to get a good biography of Bacon. But a piece of mid-19th century hagiology[2] revealed the fact that Bacon was an old man with a child wife named Alice, which I guess accounts for the use of L. Carroll & Alice[.]

I read a pretty bad book *The Poacher from Stratford*[3] (1958) about Anti-Stratfordians & their candidates. Unscholarly, the author mentions a larger survey of the subject, but doesn't name it. I imagine Joyce used some such book. For work upon work sounds like FW are a couple of removes like. Examples[:]
FW 34.15 Parker Woodward, *The Strange Case of Francis Tidir* (1901)
404.15   *Will o' the Wisp, or the Elusive Shakespeare*, George Hookham, (1922)
335.32–3 Sir George Greenwood, K. C., MP—about 1900 had a big WS fight with Andrew Lang[4]

A lot more familiar-sounding names, but no use going into it all if Joyce used a particular book. Where, by the way, is the passage about the Amenities?[5] One Anti-S book = *A Minute Among the Amenities* lovely title.

2 things however I guess are sort of close. A Mrs. Ashmead Windle[6] believed all WS'[s] wonderful titles could be made into poems—were meant to be. Example:

> *OTHELLO*
> A tale, oh! I tell, oh!
> Oh, dell, oh! What wail, oh!
> Oh, hill, oh! What will, oh!
> What hell, oh! What will, oh!
> At will, oh! What at well, oh!
> I dwell, oh!

Wadsworth is rather sniffy about this, but I kind of like it and I think, yes, that it inspired the beginning of ALP. I had already figured out

Othello there because of his getting the water black, etc & the French opera being pronounced O-Tell-o.[7]
So I would kind of like to see Mrs. Windle's book—published in the 1880s.

{You notice I don't say why Othello should begin ALP. Such me [i.e., Search me].} Maybe because he's so black it really gives them something to wash. Black & White are to be taken quite literally[.}]

Then there's a 1926 book. {When did J. publish I ii?} by Brig. General SAE Hickson, *The Prince of Poets and Most Illustrious of Philosophers*:
> Dedicated to the mother of Shakespeare, that is, to Queen Elizabeth. . . In Memory of one of the Greatest of Men Who Had No Name of His Own But Who May Be Called by a Whole Library of Names—Gascoigne—Laneham—Immerito—Lyly—Broke—Gosson—Webbe—Puttenham—Watson—Lodge—Daniell—Greene—Nash—Peele—Marlowe—Spenser—Cervantes—Montaigne—Bacon—and Shakespeare.

Now this seems to me pretty close to FW 44[.10–.14].

I am not thank God called on to lay down law & prophets on the extension of the S-B theme in FW. I'm really just trying to corral the evidence, letting chips fall where they may. In utter irresponsibility I may say that Joyce's serpent—symbol S—seems to me to be Shakespeare and that logically free ought to equal Liberator[.]
But these things are not proven[.]

I have torn—but *torn*—through FW, clutching Wills—Belly's—Wells—Frees—& all pertaining to pork[.]

I have not refined. I have no balance, no perspective. I try not to see the extensions or even the old references we have known & loved so well.

[(]I *suppose* Joyce is working from S & C [Scylla and Charybdis]—W. S[.] is the father of his race. Reading that Delia Bacon biography I was struck by a remark of hers about "Love's Labor"—"All the world was walking through the park that day.")

Well, I *think*—and I don't for a moment expect you or anyone to accept it at this point—that there is a possibility that, in a way, FW is a dream of Shakespeare's & that FW follows Shakespeare's life and works as *Ulysses* follows Homer and his works. In "S & C" Joyce set up WS as identical with Stephen—Bloom—Everyman. (By the way, I am certain that the word "crown" in FW always means Stephen.) [inserted above "crown": Helmet = William]

The attempt to get at Shakespeare the man—the source—the answer is compared to man's attempt to track down his beginning & the answer to the riddle of his universe—and is just as futile.

Shakespeare played Adam in *As You Like It*.

I am still totally flummoxed by little things like the identity (in FW) of Mr. W. H.—of Hamlet etc etc.

Did you know that the Shakers (I was looking up Shake & Spear in Webster unabridged) believe in a male & a female principle & the female principle is named Mother Ann.

I hope this doesn't all come out as confused as it is in my mind. I am, of course, afraid of seeing Shakespeare (whom I really must read) everywhere. And yet you are—*suppose you are*—supposed to see him everywhere. Take Phoenix {& Turtle} Yes? No?

Take 19.12–19—Is there or is there not a light touch of Cleopatra's death scene. She gets a snake—a worm—in a basket of fruit. Pretty farfetched, but then why does Charmian occur at the top of the next page? Maddening, but—Joyce does this for you—Cleopatra's death scene takes on another layer of meaning for me. *Was* Shakespeare thinking of Eve & the Serpent?

19.15. that reminds me. John Pomfret (1667–1702) was a poet & young clergyman who got in trouble with his bishop over a poem called "Choice" {here you see its Joyce Choice & free-will. In I, vi HCE gives the heinousness of choice} in which he said he didn't want to marry (he *was*) but wanted an occasional sprightly female friend[.]

    Yrs,
    Mrs. Hen

Did I say the Quest is Weston's in the form of the cryptographers as in S & C

1. See AG to TW, 10 October 1960, n. 2.

2. Glasheen had probably read James Spedding's commentary in *The Letters and the Life of Francis Bacon* (7 volumes, 1861–1874).

3. Frank W. Wadsworth, *The Poacher from Stratford: A Partial Account of the Controversy Over the Authorship of Shakespeare's Plays* (Berkeley: University of California Press, 1958).

4. George Greenwood, a barrister and member of parliament, wrote *The Shakespeare Problems Restated* (1908) in which he argued that Shakespeare's plays were written by a barrister. Lang wrote a defense of Shakespeare, *Shakespeare, Bacon, and the Great Unknown*, which was published after his death in 1912.

5. *Finnegans Wake*, 502.25–.26. William Thomson (1819–1883), a Scottish-born Australian medical doctor, was the author of *A Minute Among the Amenities* (24 pages, Melbourne, 1883). His books are mentioned in Wadsworth, *The Poacher from Stratford*, 39–40. Among his other books, which argued the Baconian theory of authorship are his *On Renascence Drama* (Melbourne, 1880), *William Shakespeare in Romance and Reality* (Melbourne, 1881), and *Rejoinder to the Shakespeare, Not Bacon by J[ames]. S[mith].* (Melbourne, 1881) .

6. Catharine F. Ashmead Windle, *Fallings from a Lady's Pen* (1849). See Wadsworth, *The Poacher from Stratford*, 42–53; on pages 44–50 he quotes verbatim from Windle.

7. Both Rossini's *Otello* (1816) and Verdi's *Otello* (1887) had Italian libretti.

☐

To Adaline Glasheen, Farmington, Connecticut

[MS. APCS—HWS]

[Postcard: Hotel Claridge, Atlantic City, N. J.]

[?3–4 November 1960]   [Hotel Claridge
                                           Atlantic City, New Jersey][1]

Dear A—
    You asked about the "amenities" line.
    It's 502.25
    In haste. More anon.

                     Greetings etc
                     T. N. W.

1. Wilder was in Atlantic City from 1 to 8 November. The date on postmark is obscured. Wilder is responding to Glasheen's letter of 1 November which Isabel Wilder had forwarded to him.

☐

To Thornton Wilder, Hamden, Connecticut

[MS. TL—YCAL]

5 November 1960   [22 Carrington Lane
                                                  Farmington, Connecticut]

Dear Thornton,

If you're in a phase of not being inarrested with FW, I sure must be boring the hell out of you, but still, let's see it out, sticking for heaven's sake, as closely as possible to pp. 111–112.

I guess you know Hawthorne wrote an introduction to Delia's book. He also wrote a short piece, "Recollections of a Gifted Woman" which is in *Our Old Home*.[1] It's an awfully nice essay. It gives me a kind of confidence in Hawthorne, in what I guess you have to call his human sympathies. He didn't believe in Delia's theories, he wouldn't rather be wrong with her than right with Samuel Johnson (as a disciple of hers declared) and yet NH is deep-down bone sweet about Delia, treats her with respect and dignity, and judges other people by how they treated her. I am pretty sure Joyce read Hawthorne and J. too comes out well.

Maybe you've got the piece there, but I'll quote from it and comment.

First, H. uses the expression "those treasures from the tomb" to describe the papers Delia expected to find in S[hakespeare]'s tomb, and he repeats the phrase or idea. This ties, I think, to the whole Tut-ankh-amen, curse and treasure business in FW. Remember, it is a letter that's the treasure in FW.

Then H. says "Miss Bacon imagined herself to have received (what is certainly the greatest boon ever assigned to mortals) a high mission in the world, with adequate powers for its accomplishment. . . she had faith that special interpositions of Providence were forwarding her human efforts.["] FW 112.13–14; 369.27.

"I was sensible to a lady-like feeling of propriety in Miss Bacon, and a New England orderliness in her character, and, in spite of her bewilderment, a sturdy common-sense." 112.16; 112.11–12.

?"A doubt stole into her mind. . . she was afraid to hazard the shock of uplifting the stone (on the tomb) and finding nothing." ?112.27.

(English critics on Delia's book) "A few persons turned over one or two of the leaves, as it lay there, and essayed to kick the volume deeper into the mud." 370.2 ?

". . . it has been the fate of this remarkable book never to have had more than a single reader. . . since my return to America, a young man of genius and enthusiasm has assured me that he has positively read the book from beginning to end, and is a complete convert to its doctrines." 120.13–14; 112.21–22—the disciple.

(This disciple was William D. O'Connor, who wrote a novel *Harrington: a Story of True Love*, supporting Delia. He was also author of "The Good Gray Poet."[2] I doubt J. knew about him or he'd have ringed Whitman in with Delia. He was the one would rather be mad with Delia, so he could be faintly shadowed in 370.4, 10, 13.)

To go back to pp. 111. I guess Belinda brings in "The Rape of the Lock"[3] because of 110.16, 111.8, 112.35. and ties to Delia's wanting to rape the lock on the tomb. There's more than that, though, cf. "The Rape,["] I, 16–17: "And sleepless lovers just at twelve awake: / . . . the slipper knocked the ground." which is echoed 111.8. Then also I, 37:

> Some secret truths from learned pride concealed,
> To maids alone and children are reveal'd.
> What tho' no credit doubting Wits may give?
> The fair and innocent shall still believe.

Also I, 117–118:

> 'Twas then, Belinda, if report say true,
> Thy eyes first opened on a billet-doux.

FW 112.26–7

So I decided that if Joyce wanted this deep a going into "The Rape" in order to understand his attitude, the feeling of the passage, I had better look into Lydia Languish and so I read *The Rivals*.[4] I hadn't of course read "The Rape" or "The Rivals" since college and was absolutely enchanted with both of them.

Lydia Languish has got several meanings here. She's in because of the Miss Beauchamp aspect of the letter from Boston.[5] ". . . last Thursday, I wrote a letter to myself to inform myself that Beverely was. . .paying his addresses to another woman. . ."

Then in *The Rivals* Mrs. Mal[a]prop is corresponding with Sir Lucius O'Trigger who believes it is Lydia who's writing to him. And—how inevitable Joyce is—of course the letters are being signed—you guessed it—Delia.

Mrs. Mal[a]prop: (of Lydia) There's an intricate little hussy for you!

Sir Anthony: . . . all this is the natural consequence of teaching girls to read. . . I'd as soon have them taught the black art as their alphabet.[6]

Letticea in her greensleeves [161.30]—wherever she's at—is Letitia Greene about whom I don't suppose anybody knows anything except that she and her husband lived with Anne Hathaway while S. was away. She had a son named William.[7]

    Yours,
    AG

[written by hand]

Bacon incidentally, did get mixed with the hen on a cold day in early spring & Macaulay says he remembered the hen even on his death-bed, announced that the snow had acted as a preservative[.][8]

And, having writ the above, I see that the Hen *was* indeed preserved and so lived to dig up the letter.

---

1. See AG to TW, 10 October 1960. Delia Bacon's book is *The Philosophy of the Plays of Shakespeare Unfolded* (1857). Hawthorne, *Our Old Home: A Series of English Sketches* (Columbus: Ohio State University Press, 1970), 90–119. The passages Glasheen quotes are on pages 107–109, 111, 115, 116.

2. William D. O'Connor (1832–1889). His novel *Harrington: A Story of True Love* was published in 1860; *The Good Gray Poet: A Vindication* was first published in 1866.

3. Alexander Pope (1688–1744), "The Rape of the Lock" (1712–1714).

4. Lydia Languish, a character in Richard Brinsley Sheridan's (1751–1816) play *The Rivals*.

5. See Glasheen's "*Finnegans Wake* and the Girls from Boston, Mass."

6. Quoted from Act I, scene ii.

7. Thomas Greene, whose family was distantly related to Shakespeare's, married Lettice Tutt with whom he had six children, one of whom was named Anne (b. 1604) and another, William (b. 1608). This may be an indication that the Shakespeares served as the children's godparents. In 1609 (*Census II* and *III* say 1608), the Greenes lived with Anne Hathaway Shakespeare in New Place while waiting to move into their own house.

8. In his essay "Lord Bacon" (1837) Lord Macaulay notes that "In the last letter that he ever wrote, with fingers which, as he said, could not steadily hold a pen, he did not omit to mention that the experiment of the snow had succeeded 'excellently well.'" See Macaulay, "Lord Bacon," in *Critical and Historical Essays Contributed to the Edinburgh Review*, ed., F. C. Montague, 3 volumes (London: Methuen & Co., 1903), II, 194–195.

To Adaline Glasheen, Farmington, Connecticut

[MS. TELEGRAM—YCAL]

6 November 1960   Atlantic City [New Jersey]
PM 11:21

FORGIVE SILENCE YOUR WORK SPLENDID WILL HAVE SOME STUFF SOON REGARDS = WILDER.[1]

1. Presumably sent after Wilder had read through Glasheen's letters of 1 and 5 November.

To Thornton Wilder, Hamden, Connecticut
[MS. ALS—YCAL]

20 November 1960   [22 Carrington Lane
Farmington, Connecticut]

Dear Thornton,

For anything I know, you're off to Europe or anywhere lovely and sans your copy of *Finnegans Wake*.[1]

I tag after you to say, what I guess you saw coming, I have unalterably concluded that FW *is a book about Shakespeare*[.] He is the dreamer.

In *Ulysses* Joyce established S. as "the father of all his race" equal to Stephen—Bloom—Ulysses, and Stratford = Dublin and Molly = Anne Hathaway. I suppose Joyce was planning it even then.

And so this vapid later Joyce, surrounded by absurd parasites was Joyce living under-ground, under the motto of Exile Silence & Cunning / And maybe there's cunning below the cunning I have observed[.]

Once committed, like Childe Roland,[2] to the plain, you—or I—see endless signs—finger-posts pointing, impishly, I fear. Look at J's letters. He sends a list of signs to Miss Weaver,[3] including S as in snake, he says, but who of us has made out a separate character called Snake in FW? And in the same list a ⊓ which there or elsewhere he says is HCE if you turn it around. Well it makes an E or letter E but not an H or a C that I can see, but it does make ⊔ as in William. Thus I take it ⊔ is HCE (father) interred or Shakespeare dead & S = Shakespeare up and alive as Shem or Snake or Satan.

Or take *Our Exagmi[nation]*—the last letter by Vladimir Dixon is supposed to be by Joyce and it ends (after hen references) "or is there really in your work some ass pecked which is Uncle Lear?"[4]

Or take every key to a passage that he sent Miss Weaver. They always contain a reference to S. or Bacon. In the one about the 1st and 2nd paragraph. He glosses "Willy Brewed a peck of malt." Well, sweet God in heaven, Willy Shakespeare *did*. He got in trouble for having corn & being a Maltster in famine-time in Stratford. And in the same paragraph—look at the venison which was what S. stole.

And in the key about Jaun dying. J. quotes "at my *frank* incentive."

It's everywhere and—for me at least—pretty overwhelming though I miss the old FW we knew & loved so long.

It will of course, invalidate a great many books about FW including obviously my *Census*. But the great thing is what it does to the reminiscences of those who knew him in those seemingly inane underground years, (Archibald McLeish has risen in my opinion by having sensed there was something dangerous under the gentle (imitating S. I suppose) public figure[5] & I remember Helen Joyce telling me of Joyce listening & laughing behind his hand.)[6] But anyway, that mountain of biographical glop, crowned by Ellmann, will come tumbling down.

I want to see it happen, but I don't, frankly, much want to do the tumbling. I want, oddly enough, to finish my novel & make a little money. I hate fussing. I am no crusader. I do not feel called upon to resurrect James the Jester. Oh I love puzzles. I will love helping to puzzle it out, but such attention as I may get will not gratify me when other people will get the fellowships to work on Joyce. In short, the prospect entertains me highly and exasperates me thoroughly and in certain moods I would like to resurrect James Joyce—and shake him!

If you can't go along with this, tell me why.

I have gotten so far along I can hardly bring anybody up level with me, so I'll just jot up the page with little things that I can remember off hand.

Look up John Lane in *Census*.[7] He was sued by Susanna Shakespeare Hall[8] for saying she was carrying on with Rafe Smith. Note eldest daughter & pansying. I can't go into all of why but "Casting her perils before our swains from Font[e]-in-Mont[e] to Tidingtown & from Tidingtown tell havet [i.e., tilhavet]" [202.8–.10] breaks down into casting her pearls (Margarets—I have identified Margaret with Maggy & Gretta of "The Dead") before our swan & our swine (S. & Bacon) from the fount in the mountains (maybe a place name) to Tidingtown &

from T—to *havet* = Nor. "sea." (& Hamlet?) Tidingtown is v[ery].
interesting. Is none in Ireland but is one—Tidington—near Stratford,
where a girl named Katharine Hamlet drowned in the Avon & has been
suggested as the original of Ophelia. Because you see when you get to
dowse little delia (oh dear I haven't told you about Artemis—or have
I?)[9] she's pretending to be mad like Ophelia—they tell her to mind the
puddle (or Poddle river) and not fall in the sea [208.29–.31] & then she
goes on to distribute presents, like Ophelia & flowers [209–212]. She is,
as Joyce said, Pandora = All-giving & this puns on Hawthorne (Nathaniel
means Gift of God) & his "Recollections of a *Gifted* Woman." Joyce
didn't, incidentally, use Delia's book.[10] So you don't have to read it,
though it's rather well written. (Delia beat Poe in a short story contest)
& very fair criticism, if simply nuts & distinctly disingenuous.

I hadn't known S. wrote a ballad about Sir T Lucy's[11] being a louse like
Hosty did about HCE & the earwig.

Have you read Macaulay on Bacon's death?[12]

Look at 112 [.26–.27] Biddy is a hen (elsewhere a guinea hen) &
she's "how palmy date." Artemis or Delia was worshipped as a guinea-
hen & as a date palm—born under one. Reading about Artemis in
Golden Bough, Robt. Graves[13] & Britannica 11th, clears up a lot
about ALP generally.

Keeping Kevin is Lord Keeper Bacon. When he was a child Eliz. called
him her "Young Lord Keeper."

I am near the end of my paper, I hope you go well. I hopes to soon hear.

Yours, Adaline

---

1. When Wilder left Atlantic City, New Jersey, on 8 November he went to New York; he did not return to Hamden until 26 November after having spent the Thanksgiving holiday with his sister Janet Dakin in Amherst, Massachusetts.

2. Possibly an allusion to Edgar's speech at the end of *King Lear*, III, iv: "Childe Roland to the dark tower came;/His word was still 'Fie, foh, and fum,/I smell the blood of a Britishman.'" Childe Roland, a young knight not yet dubbed Sir, was Charlemagne's nephew and the chief Knight in the Charlemagne epic cycle.

3. Joyce to Weaver, 24 March 1924 in *Letters I*, 213.

4. The last section of Beckett, et. al., *Our Exagmination*, is titled "Two Letters of Protest": "Writes A Common Reader," by G. V. L. Slingsby ([189]–191), and Vladimir Dixon's "A Litter to Mr. James Joyce," ([193]–194).

5. Glasheen is referring to a 1954 letter from Archibald MacLeish (1892–1982) to Richard Ellmann quoted by Ellmann in his biography of Joyce. See page 610–611, note (1982: 598, note).

6. See Appendices IX and X.

7. In *Census I* there is only an entry for Sir Hugh Lane, an art collector who was Lady Gregory's nephew. John Lane is not in "Out of My Census," but there is an entry for him in *Census II* and *III*.

8. Shakespeare's elder daughter (1583–1649) married John Hall, a physician, in 1607.

9. See AG to TW, 1 November 1960.

10. See AG to TW, 10 October 1960, n. 2.

11. In slightly differing anecdotes, Shakespeare was accused of deer poaching by Sir Thomas Lucy of Charlecote. He was whipped and imprisoned. In revenge he wrote a bitter lost ballad that so enraged Sir Thomas that Shakespeare was forced to leave Stratford. See Schoenbaum, 68–72.

12. See AG to TW, 5 November 1960, n. 8.

13. Sir James G. Frazier's *The Golden Bough: A Study of Magic and Religion* (1890–1915), Robert Graves's *The White Goddess: A Historical Grammar of Poetic Myth* (1948; rpt., New York: The Noonday Press, Farrar, Straus and Giroux, 1966).

☐

To Adaline Glasheen, Farmington, Connecticut

[MS. ALS—HWS]

[postmark: 23 November 1960] 50 Deepwood Drive
Wednesday Hamden 17, Connecticut

Dear Adaline:
 Yes, Shakespeare's all over the place.
 No doubt about that.
 But there's one group-of-associations that beats the Shakespeare-group all hollow: that's the Christ-story and the Mass. *There* is the central CRUX of the book. These other interests merely feed it.
 Take JAUN's last words.

Sure those are Shakespeare's, too. *The Tempest, Prospero*
468.23   Will. . . . my last on any stage.
     24   witchcraft
     29   Tempest
     30   storm {In German: The Tempest is *Der Sturm*.}
     33   Androcles had a lion not a collie—so it's CALIBAN
469.4   air = Ariel
   7   break my staff (becomes STABAT Mater = German = STAB = staff

all crowned by = A TEMPEST of good things 471.24
{In the meantime we have the DEAD HERO'S RETURN 469
        DRAKE: quickquack 9
        .18 Jules Verne—Drake—around the world 11
        CHARLEMAGNE, buried sitting in his chair 35
        and his famous standard: Romaine 25
        That CARL of CARLS 32
        and the Charlemagne-Roland-Rencesvalle frogmarchers = fall = front the defile 12–13}[1]

BUT:
        over and above all
        is the Requiem Mass
469.2   Lux in Tenebris [light in darkness]
        and the last benediction in the Mass:
469.23   Benedict vos omnipotens Deus. [Almighty God bless you]
     24   I bless all
470.21   mis[er]ere nobis [have mercy on us]

But no doubt Shakespeare's EVERYWHERE
And especially—appropriately A Midsummer Night's Dream:
How devilish Joyce can be:
    All the "For he's a jolly good fellow"[2] quotes are for PUCK = Robin Goodfellow
278.5   wild pansy = dove-in-idleness—the flower Puck squeezed in their eyes
  .13   Puck
   .6   pussy in the corner: an Irish hobgoblin like Puck
left margin tinctunc = Quincecunet = Quince
   "   "   "Dear Brutus" by [James M.] Barrie has LOB = Puck grown old
note 1 grim fellow = good fellow
  "   2 bottom.
    {Yet note the ANGELUS

     Fanciulla [278.8] = Italian: girl
     F/ANCILLA = Latin: handmaid of the Lord
     and then line 11 [i.e., .12]}
463.35–36 {Hodgart-Withington [i.e., Worthington] missed this}
     jolly. . . .goodfilips. . . then above 15 full = Phil the Fluter
     .21 quince .31 snug
596 [i.e., 569].25 jolly. . . . hellow. . . {It would be brilliant if all these
     actors were also the "mechanics" of Athens; I can only find
     the JOINER 21[}]

 You are certainly right about Nuvoletta on page 159 [.5–.6], but everything in FW is always something else, too, and she is also Salome.
 We are in a[n] Oscar Wilde foliation
158.15 & 16 de profundis
  25, 32 "A Woman of no Importance.["] "Importance of
     B. Earnest"
   {with that collect for the B. V. M.³ from the Song of Solomon:
     Nigra sum sed formosa. . . . . Black 26 comely 33. I insist
     that Xity is the ground theme of this book and A. L. P. is
     ultimately the B. V. M.}
159.15 harrods—Herod. In Mallarmé's poem Salome is *Herodiade*.
     and here is her dance of the seven veils: cancelled her
     engagements 8 dancing 12 (is HOPE = 15 Speranza?)
     maybe 16 waS A Leaptear and 18 so SILLY.
     and probably: in Strauss's opera she asks for the head of
     Jokanaan = 14 who are so keen on. and maybe 18 no canna
     stay.
  .14 Fan Lady Windermere's

Incidentally Ezra Pound Canto XXIX
Deh! . . .nuvoletta. . . . drifts. . . drifts. . . drifts.

 Incidentally, Hodgins-Withington [Hodgart-Worthington] missed the whole point of Joyce's use of songs. They are *always* a label for a person or theme.
 The dingdongs are [Edgar Allan] Poe or Ariel
 The drum—ratatats are [Sir Francis] Drake—as so beautifully:
   tattat 623.35
 prepares for (Dead Hero's Return) rounding his world of ancient days (623.36–624.1)
 There's another BIG SEVEN in the book: Traitors =

That's Guy Fawkes 624.12 giddy. . . .plotting (Guy is short for Guido) In this beautiful section of reconciliation the villains have become harmless = Judas = Jesus 620.26

It may be that Fox Goodman is often Guy Fawkes = see him turned to beneficent on 621.35

There's no end to it.
Must give it up.

>   Best to you both
>   Ever
>   Thornton

1. In *The Song of Roland* the oriflamme, a scarlet banner, receives the name Romaine and is the golden banner of the city of Rome. Carles and Carle are forms of the name Charles (Charlemagne), the Frankish emperor. Rencesvale or Roncevaux, a town and a mountain pass where Roland died after a battle between the Frankish rearguard and the Saracens.
2. A drinking song.
3. Blessed Virgin Mary.

☐

To Adaline Glasheen, Farmington, Connecticut

[MS. ALS—HWS]

29 November [1960] 50 Deepwood Drive
  Hamden 17, Connecticut

Dear Adaline =
 Returned for your files—which must be voluminous.[1]
Answered Graham[2] briefly.
 I dare not add a word about you-know-what, or I'd never stop.

The Swedish Ambassador to U. S. is interested in FW.[3] Was formerly a professor of Oriental languages, Sanskrit—to Modern Turkish. What a help he'd be to us—bring his Scandinavian too!

Best
T.

---

1. It is possible that Wilder is returning either one or both of Glasheen's lists, "Notes on Shakespeare in FW, BOOK I, SECTIONS 2, 3, 4" and "Shakespeare and FW" here dated ?October–November–I and II. Copies of the lists, without a single commentary, are in his archive at the Beinecke Library. Wilder's copies are not in the Glasheen archive. However, Matthew J. C. Hodgart's annotated copy of "Notes on Shakespeare in FW, BOOK 1 SECTIONS 2, 3, 4" is. It is possible that Glasheen sent Wilder two copies of each list and asked for one to be returned with notes and comments. Although she was careful about saving Wilder's correspondence, it maybe that after adding notations to a master copy Wilder's notes were not preserved.

2. Philip Lamar Graham, a friend of the Glasheens.

3. Wilder met Gunnar Jarring at Yale University in either October or November where they discussed *Finnegans Wake*. On 15 December 1960 (YCAL), the ambassador wrote Wilder that he had purchased the *Wake*, ordered the other books Wilder mentioned in his letter of 28 November, and sent Wilder some preliminary notes on possible uses of the Swedish, Magyar, Turkish, Persian, and Arabic languages on the pages Wilder mentioned.

□

To *Thornton Wilder, Hamden, Connecticut*
[MS. ALS—YCAL]

1 December 1960 [22 Carrington Lane
Farmington, Connecticut]

Dear Thornton,

If Mr. Graham does write you about the Marx Brothers (is it true?) do be nice and write him.[1] He & his wife came to see us Tuesday and well in a way they're sort of dopes, but basically very sweet. They bring out the mother in me.

How are you?

I have hardly anything to say because I see so much that it can't really be said. Still, I'll try with little things.

In "Ondt & Gracehoper" [414.16–419.10] the Grace (is it?) has two nymphs named Delia & Peonia who are, I guess, Delia (as the Moon) & Peon[i]a [415.2] who is the devoted sister of Endymion in Keats' "Endymion," a few bits of which are used in FW, specially in the description of Yawn asleep[.]

I put this in to show you I am capable of functioning on other than Shakespearean levels.

I guess I haven't told you William Rufus—as on p. 312 in I, v, is identified with W. S. sort of complex & not v[ery]. interesting. Ben Jonson wrote Poetaster & Dekker & som[e]body wrote something called *Satiromaster* laid in reign of Wm. Rufus & people have suggested Wm R = W. S[.]²

J[onson]. and W S are a so liberal refresher course. I read all kinds of things I never would read—like "Endymion" which struck me as a hell of a lousy poem. I am also struck by how extraordinarily varied stories about W S are. Not in a class with Washington & the cherry tree.

All refs. to Hercules may or must be scrutinized in light of Hercules with Globe on shoulders being sign of The Globe.

Considering Gaping Gill [36.35], I am made rather nervous by S. having a brother, Gilbert.³ To say nothing of the fact that Susanna (& Susie is around a lot) means Lily. And that Judith S. married a man named [Thomas] Quiney whose name is steadily spelt in legal documents & in Aubrey (I adore Aubrey) as *Queeny*. There's a judyqueen in ALP.

Did I tell you about "Casting her perils"? [202.8]

Can you get hold of the Swedish ambassador?⁴ I can think of a million questions.

I got v[ery]. interested in W. S.'s biography. If I was a playwright like people who shall be nameless I would write a play about his last years with those distinctly sinister daughters.

The silver-gilt bowl S. left Judith is in that song title in "Burrus & Caseous."—164.20–21, 26[.]

I had a letter from Clive Hart madly enthusiastic about my Quest stuff & broken chalice, rather skeptical about W S until toward the end of the letter he started finding a lot of new & good stuff in I iii, & iv, whereupon he said, "It's a lot more convincing when you find it for yourself." Now this, I do, of all things believe about S, & FW. It is a new sort of thing. It is so basic that each person has to work it out for himself and I will accept the denial of no one who hasn't gone over every "will" (at least) in FW. My husband keeps saying Don't be Dogmatic. And I would not be. I don't really care. But I won't be refuted by off-hand readers.

W S. played-acted-in B. Jonson's Sejanus—which accounts for Tiberius refs. I am mildly a B. J. fan but not *Sejanus*[.]

W S. played in *Everyman in his Humour*—part of old Knowell[.] May account for "well humours"—W. K.'s etc.[5]

All the woodman spare stuff. 1758 Rev. Francis Gaskell cut down mulberry tree S. planted.

S. supposed to've writ scene of ghost in *Hamlet* in a house next to "Charnal-house & church-yard"

John S. was a petty constable—

391.21	*Alls Well* taken from Boccaccio's story of Gillette of Narboune [Giglietta di Nerbone]
127.1—	"many-headed"—quote *J. Caesar*[6]
187–193	Portia on Justice-Mercy[7]
502.29	Sir George Somer's fleet scattered by tempest, driven to Bermuda. Pamphlet about used in *Tempest*
	Kind of fun to know Humphrey Mosely 1653 registered plays "By Will Shakespeare"[8] among which are:
	The History of King Stephen
	Duke Humphrey, a Tragedy

Nothing more known of them

I am tired of copying . .

        Yours
        Adaline

---

1. Philip Lamar Graham, an attorney and close friend of the Glasheens, was also interested in Joyce. He thought he saw reference to the Marx Brothers in *Finnegans Wake*.
2. See AG to TW, [?October–November 1960–I] and AG to TW, 18 October 1960, n. 3.
3. Gilbert Shakespeare (1566–1612).
4. See TW to AG, 29 November 1960, n. 3.
5. See AG to TW, "Notes on Shakespeare in FW" [?October–November 1960–I], n. 23.
6. The line in *Julius Caesar* is "Sleek-headed men, and as such as sleep a-nights" (I, ii, 193). The exact phrase is in *The Tragedy of Coriolanus*, "the many-headed multitude" (II, iii, 15).
7. *The Merchant of Venice*, IV, i, 184–205.
8. Humphrey Moseley (1627–1661). On 9 September 1653 Moseley did enter in the Stationers' Register a play by Shakespeare. The two plays which Glasheen mentions, however, were registered on 29 June 1660—in addition to a play "Iphis and Iantha." None of these plays is extant.

☐

To Adaline Glasheen, Farmington, Connecticut

[MS. APCS—HWS]

[Postcard: KIYOHIRO. La récolte des coquillages (béni-é)]

[postmark: 19 December 1960]   [50 Deepwood Drive
                                                      Hamden 17, Connecticut]

Dear Adaline:

Last Thursday I mean[t] to start driving to New Orleans, but Isabel caught an awful cold. Maybe I'll start tomorrow.[1] This delayed departure prevented my shopping so regard this as a Merry Christmas card. I could hardly send you a transcript of Finnegans Wake page 52 as an edifying message for the Feast. Give my affectionate greetings also to Francis and Alison. The New Year (May it be Happy) will see the completion of your novel we hope[.]

                your old friend
                Thornton

---

1. Wilder left Hamden, Connecticut, on 20 December and drove south, traveling in Mississippi, Louisiana, and Florida. He returned home on 21 February 1961.

1961

To Thornton Wilder, Hamden, Connecticut

[MS. TL—YCAL]1

9 February 1961 [22 Carrington Lane
 Farmington, Connecticut]

572.21	Honuphrius. The Encyclopaedia Britannica Research Service did me a report on St. Onuphrius, which is not very revealing: St. Onuphrius (Humphrey), his day June 12, d. c. 400. An Egyptian who lived as a hermit for 70 years in the desert of the Thebais. Patron saint of weavers, he was dressed only in his own abundant hair and a loincloth of leaves. Type of the Hairy Anchorite.
514.11	Hephaestus = Vulcan
63.36	Barra, a wife of Mohammed
133.2	Moran. . scurve of his shaggy neck: Moran's Collar. Moran the counsellor of Feredach the Just. The collar strangled the wearer if he deviated from the strict rules of equity. 102.18?
133.2	Kinsella? Kingsale, the premier baron of Ireland, Lord K. is one of the two British subjects who claim the right of wearing a hat in the presence of royalty. 32.7
16.11	pleasurad: Sura in Vedic myth the goddess of wine, produced at the Churning of the Ocean in the Kurma avatar. [S]ura in Sanskrit = god. Surid: pre-diluvial ruler of Egypt, who is stated to have built two great pyramids and to have caused the priests to deposit in them written accounts of their wisdom and science, and records of the stars, their cycles and chronicles, both of the past and for the future.

	Asura: in the Vedas a name of the ruling families of the Naga (perhaps 554.6 nag and . . . pleashadure) civilization, who were defeated by Hindu invaders. The Brahmans attributed to them wealth and luxury, use of magic, superior architectural skill, and the ability to restore the dead to life.
7.27 / 286.27 / 173.28	Ninni = Innana, early Babylonian mother goddess
239.18	*a scold*erymeid Ascold, the Russian (310.16)
413.34	winkerling: Very likely the Swiss legendary hero Winkelried: in a battle he sacrificed himself by gathering several spears of the Austrian knights into his breast and thus making a breach in their ranks. "None whomsoever["] 413.32. . . "rawcawcaw romantical" .35. . . . "ex-voto" .36 echo "stimm her uprecht for whimsoever. . . romance catholeens" 239.19–21, this is partly about Switzerland. Fry, 413.35 is German *frei*.
379.34	Armitage. A bookseller named Armitage was the last "King of Dalkey." This refers to a society, called The Kingdome of Dalkey (87.25). They used to elect a king, Stephen the First, King of Dalkey, Emperor of Muglins, Prince of the Holy Island of Magee, Elector of Lambay and Ireland's Eye, Sovereign of the Illustrious Order of the Lobster and Periwinkle. (All this from Fitzpatrick's *Dublin*).[2]
612.29	sympol: St. Paul
148.24	Christopher Marlowe?
148.21	George R. Sims, English journalist and dramatic author. He wrote a play The Dandy Fifth: 473.10 "dandyforth," and he worked on a newspaper "Fun" 473.9 "fun":
460.11	"he stalks to simself louther and lover. . .For fun"
438.26	"unleckylike intoxication." Joyce owned Lecky, "History of European Morals," see Ellmann p. 788, n. 25 [1982: 779, n. 30].[3]
185.24/5	Orionis / O'Ryans, perhaps Oriani, who wrote "Gelosia," Ellmann p. 788, n. 25 [1982: 779, n. 30]
186.1	marryvoising: Pierre de Marivaux, French writer, 1688–1763.
185.29	nichthemerically Homer
12.26	Bergin's is a Dublin pub (Ellmann 376n) [1982: 366n]
5.18	Titus, Roman emperor
583.9	John Lyly[4]
468.36	Orc, a seamonster in "Orlando Furioso" that haunted the seas near Ireland. Orlando dragged it to the coast where it died[.]

118.28   Petault: 1) Petaud, king of the beggars in whose court no-one acknowledges any authority of laws. A French proverb: "'Tis the court of king Petaud, where everyone is master." 2) Charles Perrault, 1628–1703, French writer who wrote fairy tales for children
4.1   Wills: might be James Wills, who wrote "Lives of Illustrious and Distinguished Irishmen" 1847
548.26   peltries piled: Pontius Pilate?
4.36   eyeful: Gustave Eiffel, French engineer who built the Eiffel tower

1. This list may have been accompanied by a letter that has not survived.
2. Samuel A. Ossory Fitzpatrick, *Dublin: A Historical and Topographical Account of the City* (London: Methuen, 1907). Fitzpatrick's name is mentioned on 133.27. For Joyce's use of Fitzpatrick's chapter VIII, "Dublin Theatres," see Fritz Senn, "Notes," in *A Wake Newslitter*, 2(April 1962), 5–8.
3. In his biography, Ellmann publishes a list of books Joyce bought from the Trieste bookseller F. H. Schimpff between 1 October 1913 and 9 May 1914 (1959, 788, n. 25; 1982, 779, n. 30).
4. John Lyly (?1554–1606), playwright and writer of prose romances.

☐

To Thornton Wilder, Hamden, Connecticut

[MS. carbon-TL—HWS][1]

13 April 1961   [22 Carrington Lane
                                 Farmington, Connecticut]

Dear Thornton,

May I trespass? Will you listen while I say why I think FW is about— in some manner—William Shakespeare? You and I know that we know next to nothing about FW, but we have hung around it so long that we have one faint virtue—we know what is in the damn book. So maybe do twenty-odd people on earth. Maybe twenty more people would like to know. Nobody else gives a damn and I don't know why they should.

In the following, I mean to push my heresy as far as it can be pushed, farther than indeed I could, if challenged, defend. The principle of uncertainty dominates FW and Joyce has taken care that nothing shall be certain. For me, this principle is embodied in Anna Livia's words "he will come to know good" [615.16–.17]. I am vividly aware that all I say must be qualified over and over again, but I haven't got time here and besides I want to make it as strong as possible, like a government agency asking for lots more money than it expects to get.

It seems to me there are 3 possible ways of indicating that FW is about S[hakespeare]. a) by arguing from Joyce's other books, his hints, his general character—this is very risky, likely to land you in a sort of Baconian stupidity and be a matter of mere opinion—so I don't mean to do it here anymore than I can help, but I will insist on saying that a good superficial case can be made out by this means. There is nothing in Joyce's character that would make it impossible he should write a book that was secretly [inserted above: double bluff] about Shakespeare. b) by taking line upon line, word upon word from the start of FW to its finish and showing that S. dominates—this is the only way of real proof and I think it can be done, but it is a fairly endless job and an extremely boring one. I think it will have to be done sooner or later and it will make FW sound a feeful [i.e., fearful] bore. So again, I'm going to avoid this now as well as I can, though some small phrases will seep in I don't doubt. c) by dealing with the larger characters and the general outline of FW, showing their relation to Shakespeare as seen by Joyce in "Scylla and Charybdis"[2] or by Shakespearean biographers that Joyce is known to have used. This is what I want to do here, and I know some of the likenesses I find will be more apparent than real or, at any rate, not strong and certain. How much importance, for example, can be attached to the fact that HCE's wife and S's wife are Anne? Anne is a common name, it is perfectly accounted for by the Anna Liffey. [margin: Avon] Why then haul in Anne Hathaway, not as mere decoration but as the basis for the name? And in respons[e], I can only argue in a circle—because FW is about Shakespeare, Anna Livia is Anne Hathaway, because HCE's wife is Anne that makes it more certain that FW is about Shakespeare.

Or take something to which I attach great importance. HCE keeps a suburban inn on the banks of a river which flows out of a great city. This I take to be Joyce's equivalent for Shakespeare keeping the Globe on the bankside in a suburb of London. This seems to me an equivalent like the Homeric equivalents in Ulysses and so strong does the parallel strike me that I can't even admit the uncertainty principle here, but it mayn't strike you as so certain, and my very certainty may falsely embolden me to go on to less certainties.

Anyway

    I William Shakespeare kept a playhouse on a river outside London. HCE keeps an inn on a river outside Dublin. In this inn plays are put on—see FW II, iii [309–382]. Actor, author, theatre owner, audience / Rival children
    II Shakespeare came up from Stratford to London. HCE came from elsewhere.
    III No one knows exactly when and where either were born
    IV Both died of drink
    V Both were outlived by their wives
    VI Both were resurrected—I refer to Brandes[3] (J's main Shakespearean source) "He was hardly laid in his grave when he rose from it again." And this notion is echoed by almost all who write on Shakespeare. [margin: D. Bacon[4]]
    VII Both had a wife named Anne who, according to S. Dedalus, was S's muse [margin: Kate]
    VIII Both had 3 children, both had twins. This is thin ice perhaps for J. gave Bloom-Ulysses a daughter. S. did not have twin boys, but Stephen says that if Hamnet Shakespeare had lived he would have been Prince Hamlet's twin. Isa is of course two girls. Anyway they both had 3 children and I am in no position to disentangle the like and unlikenesses.
    IX The world has taken a frantic interest in the details of both lives, always ending in a haze of conjecture and uncertainty which parallels the same interest we take in the origin and explanation of Man. The strength of this like uncertainty can only be appreciated if you read any two or three books about Shakespeare—Chambers, Lee, Dowden for instance. I say theirs is the same kind of uncertainty, conjecture, brave guesses etc etc as FW. Personal & unwarranted assumption[.] T. Brooke omits documents about soldier, Dragoon[.][5]
    X The world has held the most opposite opinions about Shakespeare. The Victorians—from whom Joyce got his Shakespeare feeling—were concerned on the one hand to make him a saintly soul, the Baconians to make him a heel, the poacher [inserted above: "hind—31"; i.e., 241.31] from Stratford. The strength of this also depends on your having read the available literature, but I don't think I exaggerate.

It seems to me that there is no great writer or great figure who fits as closely to the outline of HCE, his wife and family as Shakespeare does.

I probably have any number of blind spots—but who else who is of any importance in FW? Not Swift or St. Patrick or Mark of Cornwall, or Parnell, Noah, Isaac. Adam does but that is a different problem. The obvious objection is, of course, that HCE doesn't *have* to be anybody but Adam and Everyman and all I can say is that Bloom didn't have to be Ulysses in order to be (in a sense different from FW) Everyman.

I must add that I don't think HCE is to Shakespeare as Bloom is to Ulysses. I think HCE is Shakespeare's dream self and that HCE-Shakespeare stands to Adam (and God of course) as Bloom stands to Ulysses.

I don't think you would ask How can Shakespeare go to sleep and dream about Ireland in the 20th century, but it is the obvious question people do ask. It would be easy enough to talk metempsychosis or Viconian recurrence, but the fact is that he is Everyman and Everyman is not Everyman if he is at all bounded by time and space. We don't question the Everyman of the old morality about his knowledge of astro-physics or the Easter Rebellion, but if to any degree we question his knowledge—poof he's not Everyman any more. Joyce actually has taken care of the thing by stating that Shakespeare was his grandfather—the past—and his unborn grandson the future. (Actually S. did have born grandsons, but Stephen has forgotten them, only means Susanna Hall had a daughter who didn't breed, and that the whole line did die out in a couple of generations.[)][6]

I'd like to talk about the granddaughter, Elizabeth Hall, first Mrs Nash and then Lady Bernard. The name Elizabeth (and for the dear lords sake variations) occurs 70 odd times in FW which equals just about the Stella-Vanessas-Stars and then she is always comprehended in the words Lamp and Lump—Shaun says "the moon hath rays her lump is love" [338.30–.31, 411.27–.28]—because she is grampa's [inserted above: Hathaway] little lump of love. She also accounts for all the "nieces" because in his will S. calls her his "niece," apparently uses "niece" for grand[d]aughter in his plays too. Aunt was Elizabethan whore so it's S. who begets an aunt that became his niece. Lizzy, Stephen says inspired S's later heroines—Marina a child of storm, Perdita that which was lost, Miranda, a wonder.[7] Look at 363.70 [i.e., .20]. The whole passage is about S's change from the dark plays to the last plays, but I'll only quote a little: ". . . the wild whips, the wind ships, the wonderlost for world hips . . . plumptylump piteousness. . ." [363.22–.24]—the wild ships are Marina in the storm, wonder is Miranda, lost is Perdita, and of course there's also the world well lost which is how most biographers interpret S. giving up London and going back to write his last plays in Stratford. Perdita and Miranda are on 270.20–.22 "Wonderlawn's lost us for ever. Alis, alas. . ." For Lizzy accounts for all the Alice-alas and combines with Issy, who Joyce in his letters always calls Izzy. I didn't mean to get into particulars, I only wanted to say there's a big lot of Lizzy-lump-lamp theme in FW. It explains why Mildew Lisa is a person. It explains the Father or Old man's love for a young girl.

I don't think S's love for his granddaughter is very good Shakespeare. All S's biographers assume it was a young girl brought him out of the shadows. [Georg] Brandes, as I recall, doesn't name her. Frank Harris and Lee grab at Judith and Susanna.[8] The baby girl seems to be Joyce's own idea, but the passage in which he discusses it, is confused, deliberately, I think, so that Lizzy is not distinct from Susanna or either of them from Anne Hathaway who has already been substantially identified with the Dark Lady. And this indistinctness persists, as you know, in FW. Lizzy is the little Alice figure right enough, but she takes Susanna's place with the elders on 399. (I haven't had time to see if the confusion can be worked out.) Lizzy is, however, distinctly one with the Elizabethan Muse, Elizabeth—the moon hath rays her lump is love [411.28]. I can see this, even prove it, but I haven't worked it out either. Thus, Shakespeare—by Stephen's definition—fits to the old man-young child or girl theme, and since Marina, Perdita, Miranda are all taken from their fathers by young lovers, S. fits the Mark-Tristram-Isolde pattern too. I've got these girls listed and I think I can show all or some of J's joins. Jim Atherton accepts them, accepts in fact all my Shakespeare stuff, but says that the presence of a great deal more Shakespeare than we ever thought existed in FW, still does not prove FW is *about* Shakespeare. Very true. But I think there will come a point—when for who?—at which so much of FW will be seen to be Shakespearean. The point is not for me to decide and there are vast areas I can't begin to deal with, or rather vast areas in which I see Shakespeare but cannot for the life of me guess what Joyce is doing with him. However, to more solid things.

I think I can count on Shakespeare's side that so very very much is made of plays and the theatre in FW. HCE is steadily called Michael Gunn. 32–33 speak of his theatre. "The Norwegian Captain" and "Buckley" are shown at his inn. In the Mime, the children stage a play at the Phoenix which was a rival playhouse to the Globe. At 48.15 [i.e., .3] the production of the Mime is associated with Blackfriars which was where the children's company—S's rivals—played for a while. Burrus and Caseous [161–167] (not a play but a Shawlike preface to) is a play of Shakespeare's. Buckley is essentially *Hamlet* [inserted above: *Macbeth*?]. The characters switch roles, move from one to the other. All these things are obvious, we've known them for just about ever. It seems to me there is almost nothing in FW but 1) theatrical performances and 2) searches into the facts about HCE and those two things *are* Shakespeare. What else?

I think there is no important element-theme-person in FW who is not somehow linked to Shakespeare—or at least to Stephen Dedalus's Shakespeare, not a very honest Shakespeare. At the same time, rethinking FW in Shakespearean terms is successful only by fits and often lands me with a whole set of new problems.

Take Cleopatra. In FW she is usually Cliopatra or Cliopatrick and she is a sow. As to the sow, I don't get it, I guess she has something to do with Robert Graves's white sow goddess of the moon, especially as she's Ni*luna* at the end and Amazia is too because Amazons were "Moon women." But I think that Niluna is Cleopatra, Serpent of Old Nile and Hippolyta, the Amazon queen of MSND [*A Midsummer Night's Dream*]. Well, once "serpent" crossed my mind I could see why Patrick, at least a little why Patrick—because he cotched those creeps [19.16] in a paragraph that mentions Charmian too [20.3]. And then Nile. I decided all the Nile references were to Cleopatra—nihil nuder under the closing moon and all that [493.18–.19]. I think Joyce is saying that history is like Shakespeare's Cleopatra, full of cunning corridors and philosophically meaningless, leading after all to nothing more than Victoria and Albert, HCE-ALP, Adam-Eve. But why Cliopatrick, princess of porkers who ate somebody's windowsill or doorway [91.6–.7]? Oh maybe I see. Pig Cliopatrick could be the particular muse of Irish history, made up of the serpent wisdom of the Druid past and the Christian wisdom of Patrick. But why should she eat a windowsill [490.33]?

Take the end of the book. I am rather in love with this. When Anna Livia dies she goes back to her father, the sea, right—well she's Cordelia returning to Lear. Yes honestly. The daughter who always went off with the young one comes back. In "Scylla and Charybdis" Stephen associates King Lear with the Irish sea-god of the Tuatha de Danann. He isn't just a sea-god but the sea itself, so AE says, and the Irish word for sea is *lear*, middle Ir. ler, Welsh llyr. Also in "S and C" Cordelia is associated with It. *cordoglio*-sorrow and with T. Moore's "Silent O Mayle," the phrase about "Lir's lonely daughter." She was enchanted into a swan.

Well, look at the end of FW how they all come together at the end—bleary...the seahags...Loonely in me loneness...sad and weary...cold mad feary father...near...mere...moyles and moyles... [627.26–628.3] You can even bring more in if you like because there's roaring back on 626 and silence up above on 627 and "springing to be free" is the lonely swan wanting to be free of the enchantment, and they're the whitespread wings [628.10], if you like. I hate to write about it and tear it up for it's too beautiful, but it means a lot to me that Cordelia's return to her cold mad feary father should be here.

I feel sound enough on all I've written you in this letter—all my goodness it's enough, but there are a thousand points that baffle me. It's why, I wish, when you're not being glamorous or writing books or anything important at St. Moritz, you'd think about Shakespeare and FW. Without masculine advice and skepticism, I'm going to get nowhere. I haven't any piety for Joyce's memory. I just would kind of like to know.

Fritz Senn says you're coming to see him. How long do you stay abroad?[9]

    Faithfully,
    AG

---

1. In the Glasheen archive there are handwritten and typed notes for this letter. The copy she sent to Wilder has not been located, and this transcription has been made from a carbon-copy.
2. *Ulysses*, Episode Nine.
3. See AG to TW, [?October–November 1960–I], n. 25.
4. Delia Bacon. See AG to TW, 10 October 1960 and 5 November 1960.
5. Sir Edmund K. Chambers (1866–1954), *William Shakespeare: A Study of Facts and Problems* (2 vols., 1930). Sir Sidney Lee (1859–1926); among his books are: *Stratford-upon-Avon from the Earliest Times to the Death of Shakespeare* (1885, new edition 1906), *Life of William Shakespeare* (2 vols., 1898, rev. ed., 1915), and *Shakespeare and the Italian Renaissance* (1915). Edward Dowden (1843–1913), *Shakespeare: His Mind and Art* (1875) and *Shakespeare Primer* (1877). Dowden was also the editor of many editions of single plays. Tucker Brooke, editor of numerous plays and the sonnets in The Yale Shakespeare series and of *Shakespeare of Stratford: A Handbook for Students* (New Haven: Yale University Press, 1926) written to accompany the series.
6. Shakespeare and his wife Anne Hathaway (1555–1623) had three children. Susanna (1583–1649) married John Hall (1575–1635); they had one child, Elizabeth (1608–1670), who was childless in her two marriages. Hamnet died in childhood (1585–1596). Judith (1585–1662) married Thomas Quiney (1589–?1655); they

had three children who all died without issue: Shaksper (1616–1617), Richard (1618–1639), and Thomas Quiney (1620–1639).

7. Marina, the daughter of Pericles and Thaisa in *Pericles*; Perdita, the daughter of Leontes and Hermione in *The Winter's Tale*; and Miranda, the daughter of Prospero, the Duke of Milan, in *The Tempest*.

8. Frank Harris (1856–1931) in his *The Women of Shakespeare* (1911) relates Shakespeare's mother, wife, daughter, and mistress to characters in the plays. For Sir Sidney Lee, see note 5.

9. Wilder sailed for Europe on the *Leonardo da Vinci* on 1 March 1961 and returned to New York on the *Statendam* on 24 May 1961. He traveled in Italy, Switzerland, Germany, and France. He spent the *Sechseläuten* festival, 17 April, with the Senns. The next day he left for Dusseldorf, Germany. When he returned to Zurich on 24 April, he saw the Senns frequently until he left for Frankfurt, Germany, on 3 May.

☐

To Adaline Glasheen, Farmington, Connecticut

[MS. ALS—HWS]

[?12–16 June 1961] RED LION INN,
Returning home Sat'dy[1] STOCKBRIDGE, MASSACHUSETTS

Dear Adaline:

You're certainly right about the LEAR-CORDELIA allusions on pp 627–628.[2] I wish one more direct quotation from the play could be found to clinch it.

Did you notice this:
Revelations XXI, 10–15 "angel coming down. . . . having a key. . . (to bind the devil) (3) thousand years
      XXIX 10 [i.e., XIX, 10] "and I fell down before his feet to worship him" [628.10]
      XXII (8) "I, John . . . . fell down to worship before the feet of the angel. . ."
      XXII (?) "Yea: I come" 628.11 Yes 628.13 coming.[3] Can't read my own notes.
So this probably gives 628.15 Lps = Apocolypse—as 626.5

On their walk to Howth Head—all the places successively marked—they have reached the highest point which is called BLACK LINN 626.33 duv = DUBH = BLACK. . . . . . linn.

And the lighthouse is BAILEY Light = 626.34–35 for which she wishes the glances-glasses were better.

You have another Shakespeare queen: Titania 627.1 [AG margin: 583.17]

In Purcell's Dido and Aeneas, Dido going to her death sings a famous aria ("When in underneath I'm lain") with two poignant "Remember me" 628.14

Have you ever verified that remark (in the Robinson *Key*?) that the Earthmother in some Finnish epic dying, to be reborn, bears *one leaf* with her? 628.6–7

Later:
465.16 "Corsican Brothers" Dion(ysius) Boucicault after a novel by Alexander Dumas. Their names were Louis and Fabien dei Franchi[.] So I guess you have for your census: Franchi, dei 465.12 (isn't J. J. a devil?)[4]

(I'm indebted for that material to Gilbert Troxell[5] who knows everything about the stage. I wish he'd tell us the name of the heroine that presumably these brothers were both in love with.)[6]

I'd better put these leaves in the mail or I'll never get them off

        Best to all,
        (T. N.)

---

1. Wilder was in Stockbridge, Massachusetts, from Saturday, 3 June 1961 until Saturday, 17 June 1961. This letter was not sent until Wilder returned to Hamden; he included it with his letter of 20 June 1961.

2. Cheng lists allusions to several Shakespeare plays on these pages but none to *King Lear*.

3. *The Revelation of Saint John the Divine*, XXII, 7, 12: "Behold, I come quickly" XXII, 20, "Surely I come quickly."

4. Alexandre Dumas's *Les Frères corses*, a long short story in three parts, about a vendetta and the telepathic communication that exists between twins. It was adapted for the French stage by Grangé and de Montépin; that version was adapted by Dion Boucicault (1820–1890) as *The Corsican Brothers*, which opened in

London at the Princess's Theatre on 24 February 1852. The play is published in *Selected Plays of Dion Boucicault*, chosen and with an introduction by Andrew Parkin (Gerrards Cross, Bucks., England: Colin Smythe, and Washington, D. C.: The Catholic University Press of America, 1987), 98–133.

5. Gilbert McCoy Troxell (1893–1967), a college friend of Wilder's and former curator of the Yale Collection of American Literature.

6. In the French version the young woman is Émilie; in the English version she is Emily.

☐

To Adaline Glasheen, Farmington, Connecticut

[MS. ALS—HWS]

[20 June 1961] 50 Deepwood Drive
Tuesday Hamden 17, Connecticut

Dear Adaline:

I have another letter, unfinished, lying around; if I find it in the haystack of my desk I'll enclose it.[1]

(Only just returned; when I called you it was from Stockbridge)
Your questions:

Only thing I know about *tutu* is a ballet-girls skirt.

MOOKSE[2]

I've always thought that MOOKSE was also FOX, tho' there is (so far) only one "fox"-word: "lowrie" 154.2 (short for "laurence" a fox, Scotch[).] BUT Gripes is certainly the crow-raven of the old fable ("La Fontaine: Le Renard et le Corbeau")[.] The Raven in Barnaby Rudge[3] is called GRIP. And there's lots of Poe-allusion in the area.

Incidentally, you catch all the Wilde assoc's at the end of that fable [159], culminating in Salome: dance of the seven veils (gauze. . . . .8. . . dance .12. . . . Herod .15 silly .18. . . Jokanaan. . . . who are keen on. . . 14)

CENSUS: who is who
Leave most of it: it's valuable for those newcomers.
.

But since SHAUN and SHEM switch about, it is rash to say that SWIFT or PARNEL[L] or PIGGOTT (isn't it SHAUN who mostly hesitates?) are one or the other.

CAPEL, Earl of Essex.[4] No opinion.

My dictionary gives LIA FAIL

Yes 493 has Caesar, two Niles, and Cleopatra's "nothing left remarkable under this visiting moon" [493.18–.19].
Have you caught your second Bishop Percy of the ballads in 493.3?

Now some stray pickings:
Don't you think that's the Surface brothers in School for Scandal 465.1 [i.e., .2–.3] (languish etc)[5] Julia is also in Rivals[6] and maybe Honor = Homer in The Country Wife = Horner .14 [i.e., .4].[7]

You won't believe me when I say that some form of Thomas Moore's name or his family's is in the near vicinity of all those quotations from The Irish Melodies. (I can't find them all, but I'll bet they're there.)
How about other poets:
MANGAN: poem: Time of the Barmecides 387.21 its refrain "long
  long ago" 387.17[.] One of Mangan's nom de plume MONOS—
  (with Greek MOMOS: a fault or blame) 387.18.
LYTE. . wrote Abide with Me. 546.23 and "light" 546.21[8]

Could it be that the Ganymede of 269.18 is Rosalind's name in the forest of ARDENT 269.17[.]
Certainly 556.17–22 is As You Like It. . . . Act I ii [21–22] "sweet rose. . .dear Rose["] for 556.17. . . . Rosalind's "come woo me, woo me and I'm like enough to consent"[9] Act IV i 62; and all that wildwood.
But two pages later
ALIENA (Celia's name in exile) 558.8
Adam (role we know played by Shakespeare) .10. . . will. .11 honeymeads .19 for Ganymede?

---

also cordial best
(T)

---

1. Wilder's letter which we have dated [?12–16 June 1961].
2. "The Mookse and The Gripes" passage in *Finnegans Wake*, I, iv, 152.15–159.18.

3. A Charles Dickens novel published in 1841.

4. Arthur Capel, Earl of Essex

5. In *The School for Scandal* Richard Brinsley Sheridan contrasts two brothers, Joseph Surface the hypocrite and Charles Surface the good-natured spendthrift.

6. A subplot in Sheridan's *The Rivals* is the love affair of Faulkland and Julia Melville. The name in the *Wake* is Julia Bride, and this may also refer to the Henry James story "Julia Bride." See AG to TW, 4 May 1953, n. 8.

7. In William Wycherley's (1640–1716) *The Country Wife* (1675), Mr. Horner, a young libertine, spreads a false report that he is a eunuch to allay the suspicions of jealous husbands.

8. Wilder gave the Moore, Mangan, and Lyte references in [?12–14 October 1960] and 16 October 1960.

9. Wilder slightly misquotes Rosalind's speech: "Come, woo me, woo me; for now I am in a holiday humour and like enough to consent."

☐

To Adaline Glasheen, Farmington, Connecticut

[MS. ALS—HWS]

[?1–5 September 1961] 50 Deepwood Drive
September something 1961 Hamden 17, Connecticut

Dear Adaline =
   You remember that both the James novels *Golden Bowl* and *Wings of a Dove* are about poor men winning American millionairesses.
   So Joyce plays them off together:
VERVER, Maggy marries Prince Amerigo—last name not given but
   James hints that it is the Roman prince of the Borgias and Joyce
   accepts it. His affair with Charlotte etc.
           GOLDEN BOWL
   179.31   Borgia; 32–33 [i.e., .33–.34] sewerful of guineagold; 33
            Georgie-Borgie (as in 152.27); Maggie .21; Ver. . . Ver 24
 ⎧161.15   Prince Royal 22 Roman history; 32 split. . . . bowl. 36
 ⎨   *Caesar aut nullus* [either Caesar or no one] motto of the
 ⎪   Borgia family.
 ⎩162.34   (Prince) Charming; 35 king off duty. . . i.e. a Prince

{458.18   Maggy; Borgia = gorgiose [458.25]
{460.12   Prince 26 Margrate
 164.20   bowl . . . . gold. (It was of silver-gilt; had a crack in it, and was bought in a high-class antiquity shop:
 164.23   pawnbreaking
    26   streak. . . yellow silver
    27   bowl
           Now in
THE WINGS OF A DOVE
           The rich
THEALE, MILLY is courted by a newspaper correspondent MERTON DENSHER while he is still attracted to KATE CROY
 439.3   DANCER-DANGER-DENSHER
    36   ETHEL-THEALE
 457.19   wing
   .27   DOVE
   .28   male corrispondee
 458.16   mercy—for Merty
    18   Catty
    21   pigeon
    23   Ether = Ethel-Theale
    27   Mrs STRINGHAM is Milly's companion
There's another
           JULIA BRIDE[1]
 433.11   bride
    12 [i.e., .19]   Murray (BUSH, the ex-fiancé)
    35   St Swithin is on JULY 15.
 207.16   bride
   .24   Julia
   .34   bush
    There are two more As You Like It allusions to add to those in 556.1–22
           The courtier in Act I is Le Beau; here we have la Belle 9–10
           After the song Under the Greenwood Tree .15–17 we now see Blow, blow Thou Winter wind .20

Isn't Joyce a devil? In the Anna Livia chapter he gives us (all) Ibsen's heroines; but of course he's got to hide them[.]

He's [i.e., He] doesn't give the title "Lady, be good" to go with SAY (Dublin = sea) for *Lady from the Sea*. Oh, no. It must be Missus be good and don't (Fol = river in Turkey) make a fool of yourself [208.30–.31]: which the poor woman does anent the sea.

In Proust the courtesan Odette de Crecy married first Charles Swann and last the Prince de Guermantes. She then became related to Oriane de Guermantes, the duchess.

Now the name Oriane probably derives as it did for Oriana, Queen Elizabeth, from a Renaissance fancy about the rising sun; but maybe it came—and J. J. seems to imply so, from the Royal house of Orange—German and Dutch: Oranien.

And the nickname which Oriane gives to her husband the Duke is BASIN.

Now ALP is both these fascinating women:

207.19   bassein. . . . . 27 oddity
(I suspect the Duke's brother, the appalling Baron de Charlus—often in FW—is here too—his first name was PALAMÈDE. . . . .calamity 207.8 [i.e., .28]. Irish-P, as your Census calls it.)
208.15   orange. . . garment-Guermantes
.19   swan
200. . . 24 [i.e., .25] garments. . . . . 33 Odet! Odet! and I suspect that COMBIES .35 is Combray.

Will you take the following? (Everybody knows how *mean* and *incredulous* you are; I cry for hours when you won't buy my blooms.)
185.14   Prosator-Proust. . . .24 Orion. . 25 O'Ryan. . . . . .24 Cocteau. . . . 31 Ourania. . . .
Then: very beautiful is .33 gallic acid (ink is made from gall nuts); Proust is oh! gallic acid on iron ore = ORIANE. Will you buy that?

You can be an angel, too. Will you be an angel and send this letter on (when you've finished *despising* it) to Fritz Senn, with my deep regards to him?

> And all devotion
> Thornt

---

1. A short story by Henry James. See AG to TW, 4 May 1953, n. 8

To Adaline Glasheen, Farmington, Connecticut

[MS. ALS—HWS]

12 September 1961   Quebec [Canada][1]

Dear Adaline:
    I've been very remiss.
    For one thing I was very cast down by your last question: don't we go all over the map reading things into FW? Yes, we do; and every now and then I simply despair—but dammit, I've got to come back to the work. Without fumbling we'd never get anywhere. ¶ And I love to *contribute*. I'm probably too late for your Second Edition; but here are some suggestions for your files:

Page 423 has a quote from *Twelfth Night* .11–.12.[2] But also a FOLIATION
    TOBY 33 BELCH 13
    FESTE .6 fast a
    17 jawache = ague-cheek
    Maria 30
    Malvolio 35 mis-(cross)-gartered.
    And I suspect the two REASONS .26 .32 of being ORSINO
    On the same page is A WINTER'S TALE .23–.24 and Oedipus: false-feet 28–29 complex 29
    And it was Portia who said "by that same token" .32[3]

    JAUN started out on p. 431 giving all that low advice to his sister as St. Benedict. But he's still a Benedict on p. 450 where he quotes a number of songs from the Lily of Killarn[e]y—composed by Sir Jules Benedict and based on Collegian .15 by Griffin 14 and the French for Benedict is BENOIT (450.16) [?.17] just as the traditional English is Benet 430.2[4]

    Have you a section for J. J.'s play with initials?
454.24   The Salt of the Earth = TSE Eliot
454.27   Tone be Silent. Engagements TSE = Eliot
   .8   [i.e., .9] he probably lived in Westminster = wESTminster
   .9   stenorious STE

Page 191 initials of the paragraphs: top to bottom:
S. . . . T. . . . E. . and the whole page crammed with Eliot.
The gumtree of line 13 is also called the Opossom Tree. and
I pointed out to the idiotic anagram .26 toilettes = Eliot.[5]

I am sure that one of the most important pillars of the book is Arrah-na-Pogue. Including the last lines: man receives the key to life from the *lps* of a woman [628.15]. But the last distinct allusion I find is 626.6.[6]

And while we're talking about Boucicault have you caught all those Eily[7]—Colleen Bawn—Lily of Killarney?

110.35   heily
144.10   Eilish assent
192.26   Airish and (her beau) na Coppaleen[8]
410.33   eilish with her beau Myles na Coppaleen.
464.4 [i.e., .5]   coppy is Myles na Coppaleen because of the proximity of napper Tandy [464.24] (Wearing of the Green)

Father Noon's paper[9] tells us that the Jesuit church in Dublin is in Gardiner St. So I think it's very funny that we read:

p. 446.36 ignite (Loyola)
    .34   garden

and Joyce knew it well:
569.7
601.21

I got so many addenda to make to Hodgart / Worthington SONGS. I think it's awfully funny they couldn't see *The Charge* of the Light Brigade:

87.10
188.12
256.36
334.26
347.14
348.26
349.11 [i.e., .10]
474.28 [i.e., .16]
567.3

There's an awful lot to share with Fritz Senn, but that's not for a lady's ears: but here's the chain of association Griffin wrote the Collegians—hence Colleen Bawn and Lily of Killarney. The joy-house where O. Wilde's crowd hung out was on College St. So all the Lily of

Killarney associations are tainted by that jump of association. Isn't that damnable?

Father Noon sent me an off-print of his admirable article in the PMLA. I wrote him and thanked him and sent some of the above material.

Thank Francis for all the patient work he did in proof-reading—and through our killing hot summer—

I think I've got an exciting new lead: . . . .
more anon
Best to you all, including Alison

    Yr OLD friend
    Thornt.

I wish that astronomical paper would come out.[10]

---

1. Wilder arrived in Quebec on 6 September and stayed until 17 October.
2. Sir Toby Belch's question to Malvolio: "Dost thou think, because thou art virtuous, there shall be no more cakes and ale?" (II, iii, 104–105). The names are characters in *Twelfth Night*: Feste, a clown; Sir Andrew Aguecheek; Maria, Olivia's woman; Malvolio, the steward to Olivia; and Orsino, the Duke of Illyria.
3. In fact, this line is spoken by Cressida to her uncle, Pandarus, in *Troilus and Cressida*: "By the same token, you are a bawd" (I, ii, 264).
4. Dion Boucicault's *The Colleen Bawn; or, The Brides of Garryowen* was first produced in New York on 29 March 1860 at Laura Keene's Theatre and then on 10 September 1860 at the Adelphi Theatre in London where it ran for 278 performances—a record at the time. It is based on Gerald Griffin's novel *The Collegians*. Sir Jules Benedict (1804–1885) based his opera, *The Lily of Killarney* (London, Covent Garden, 8 February 1862), on an adaptation of Boucicault's play done by John Oxenford. According to Hodgart and Bauerle (198–199), the references on page 450 are lines 12, 28–29.
5. Wilder discusses Joyce's references to Eliot in a number of letters. See particularly TW to AG, 22 July 1959, [?12–14 October 1960], and 16 October 1960.
6. Dion Boucicault's *Arrah-na-Pogue, or The Wicklow Wedding* was first produced on 7 November 1864, at the Princess Theatre, London.
7. The main action of Boucicault's *The Colleen Bawn; or, The Brides of Garryowen* concerns the love affair and secret marriage of Hardress Cregan, from the Big House, and Eily O'Connor, from the thatched cottage. See TW to AG, [17 September 1961].
8. In the play Hardress Cregan bemoans that he is being pushed into a marriage (he is secretly wed to Eily O'Connor). Danny Mann, Cregan's devoted servant, misinterprets a conversation and thinks Cregan wants him to kill Eily. Mann takes Eily

out to the lake and pushes her in. At that moment, Myles na Coppaleen (Myles of the little horses), a poacher, arrives on the scene. He shoots Mann and dives into the lake to rescue Eily. In the last act Myles and Eily marry.

9. William T. Noon, S. J., "James Joyce: Unfacts, Fiction and Facts," *PMLA*, 76 (June 1961), 254–276. See particularly 272.

10. It is not certain what paper Wilder is referring to.

☐

To Thornton Wilder, Quebec, Canada

[MS. ALS—YCAL]

15 September 1961   [22 Carrington Lane
                           Farmington, Connecticut]

Dear Thornton,

All I know about Quebec is that you and the remnants of Hurricane Carla are in it. I owe about 5 other people FW letters, but am of course writing you. I know a little how out-and-out gold-diggers feel for I am mining John Kelleher.[1] Today I learned from him that *Cearc* is Ir[ish] "hen." It's my impression that the word is all over FW but I can't imagine where. Morse says twice Mrs Hen is a Baroness Hahn Hahn who wrote Ger[man]. novels.[2]

I guessed and J[ohn]. K[elleher]. confirmed in Irish that the reason the ass goes around with the 4 is because it's the "missing fifth" or "lost province" of Ireland, Meath (Midhe).[3] What I'd learned from Clive Hart[4] & J. K. also told me again was Yawn lies on Uisnech which was the very middle of the missing 5th & the very middle of Ireland. I guess since it's the ASS's land & Asnoch, that's why the Ass interprets & becomes in fact Yawn (I guess). Also Patrick's name Cothraige = "Servant of 4 Masters." The Ass then is the symbol of dispossession (and a lot else). [474–476]

I also made out from the Britannica & J. K. confirms—the Auna-Aven-Avon part of *Anna* Liffey is the same word as Avon in Stratford-upon.

Jim Atherton sent me a lot of stuff out of *Fanny Hill*. He & [Fritz] Senn are both quite sure it's used in FW. I see it on 204.8, 13 but for the rest, I think you must have to read the book to see the relevance. There is an unshockable Mrs Cole and Jim thinks she's in most "coal" references are erotic & to her.[5]

Jim has also found out about 101[.15]. Who Struck Buckley was a 19th century gibe at an Irishman, for, as you might guess, Buckley, in a story, struck himself. Jim also has latched on to a dictionary of French argot which Joyce must have used.[6] He sent me 10–15 examples (I'll send the letter to you if you want it). Clears up a lot of words. Jim gave a lecture on FW at Cambridge to a mess of Serbs-Croats who were madly enthusiastic about Joyce, said the translated *Ulysses* had swept them all off their feet & was a best-seller.

Matthew Hodgart is being at Cornell this year. He hopes to meet me.

Walton Litz sent me his book.[7] Useful for knowing when Joyce wrote what. Nothing much else.

Jim and Senn say *The Classical Temper* is verbose & nothing special.[8]

I am trying to get [Richard] Ellmann to let me see his ms of the 2nd volume.[9] Bound to have some help for the *Census*. I hope he does.

Ruth von Phul is back writing her Joyce book[10] after a long interruption of taking care of grandchildren whose mother was remarrying & moving to West Germany.

I guess this is all my news of Joyceans.

I would not for worlds have asked a question to make you despair. No, I meant to flatter you by saying you had taught me how to step onto new levels of FW[.]

There are fine things in your letter, but the Wilde-Collegians—that's a lovely one[.]

Are you going to Europe?

    Yours,
    AG

1. John Kelleher, professor of Irish History and Literature at Harvard University where he co-taught a seminar on Joyce with Harry Levin. Kelleher to Glasheen, 13 September 1961 (HWS).

2. J. Mitchell Morse, then a professor of English at the Pennsylvania State University. His correspondence with Glasheen is in HWS. Gräfin Ida Hahn-Hahn (1805–1880) was a poet and writer of social novels. She converted to Catholicism in 1850 and, in 1854, founded a convent in Mainz, Germany, where she lived and continued to write novels with a strong Roman Catholic influence.

3. Kelleher to Glasheen, 9 September 1961 (HWS). A discussion about "The Auna-Aven-Avon" is also in Kelleher to Glasheen, 10 August 1961 (HWS).

4. Undated letter to Glasheen (HWS).

5. John Cleland (1710–1789); *Fanny Hill, or Memoirs of a Woman of Pleasure* (1748–1749) tells the story of a prostitute's rise to respectability. Mrs. Cole keeps a brothel where Fanny Hill works. Atherton's and Senn's letters to Glasheen are in HWS.

6. In his article, "French Argot in *Finnegans Wake*" in *A Wake Digest*, ed. Clive Hart and Fritz Senn (Australia: Sydney University Press, 1968), 41–42, Atherton identifies the book as Olivier Leroy's *Dictionary of French Slang* (London, 1935). The Leroy book is in the Joyce collection of the Lockwood Memorial Library at the State University of New York at Buffalo.

7. *The Art of James Joyce: Method and Design in 'Ulysses' and 'Finnegans Wake'* (London, New York: Oxford University Press, 1961).

8. Samuel Louis Goldberg's *The Classical Temper: A Study of James Joyce's 'Ulysses'* (London: Chatto & Windus, 1961).

9. Ellmann was working on revising Stuart Gilbert's one volume edition of Joyce's letters and editing two further volumes of letters.

10. For many years von Phul planned a book about Joyce. In *A Wake Newslitter*, No. 4 (July 1962), it was announced that her book *The Individual Passion: a Study of James Joyce and his Work* was completed (9). The book was never published.

□

To Adaline Glasheen, Farmington, Connecticut

[MS. ALS—HWS]

[17 September 1961]   Quebec [Canada]
Sept ? 1961
Sunday

Dear Adaline:
    Just as the mother's initials are A. L. P. so the daughter's are A(lice) (Pleasance) Liddell.[1]

This gives us a wide play with Apples (and Eve and the Garden)
On p. 314 his daughter, line 33 is the lappel of his eye.

On page 276 bodge-Dodge-son in line 25 gives us footnote 7 "A liss in hunterland"; and note 5 gives us the girl (who writes the notes) in her A—P—L's creed-cradle—rather than in his APL-pied bed.

On page 7 [i.e., 57] (with all that Carroll material 23–29) we get both mother and daughter in .11 alplapping and cool of her curls .12 carrolls.

106.24	seen Aples and thin dyed
113.16	apple. . . little. . . .apple and .34 [i.e., .35] a Christmas CARROLL
126.29 [i.e., .17]	lapapple
184.14	(old proverb: apple does not fall far from the appletree = like father like son:) APL. . and Humpty dumpty and .17 Dodgson.
175.16–17 [i.e., .19–.20]	Humpty-Dumpty and ALICE = APL again
296	.9 hump .21 dump. . . 24 A. . L. P. E/A. L. P. [296.26]
406.11–12	mockturtle Appelredts [406.9].

In the *Colleen Bawn* and *Lily of Killarney*, the heroine is Eily[2]: hence Eileen = Helen = NELLY
and LILY = French LYS old French LIS; and an Iris is a Lily.

And however nice she is in the play she's certainly one of those temptresses down in the hollow in the park.

After reading page 34.19–23
We get

34.32	nelly. . . . 33 lilyth. . . allow (Eily!) and probably in malers, her beau Myles.
102.11	lilly (bolero) and the other fellow Hardress 12
{410.33	eily and .34 mires.
{411.26	ily. . . lamp. . . gloom. . . lamp is love {a song sung in *The Lily of Killarney*}[3]
428.8	Eily Mamoureen. . . 21 Myles.
426.15	eyle. . . 16 oogling around = Eileen aroon 17 Li's = lily.

NOW YOU CAN GET BOTH THE GIRLS TOGETHER

57.28	ALYS
270.20	Alis. .
276. note 7	A liss
359.32	Alys! Alysaloe!

508.29	silk A. P. L... ALUS
30	(Big and little) LIDDEL
32	Colleen
34	Liszt = LYS

I'm especially pleased about the reading here = about every two years I get one more speck of light on that crucial passage on p. 184[.] This week I saw APL 184.14 and Dodgson 17 and Gaby Deslys .27 of the LILY's[.]

Has anybody traced those ancestral GLUES and GRAVIES and Sidleshome?? [30.6–.8]

I always feel that with a little bit more work I can GIVE UP Finnegans Wake!

                Best to all
                Thornton

1. Lewis Carroll's *Alice in Wonderland* (1865) and *Through the Looking-Glass* (1871) were written for a child, Alice Pleasance Liddell.
2. See TW to AG, 12 September 1961, notes 4 and 7.
3. "The Moon Has Raised Her Lamp Above" (I, i).

To Thornton Wilder, Quebec, Canada

[MS. ALS—YCAL]

20 September 1961   [22 Carrington Lane
                                                    Farmington, Connecticut]

Dear Thornton,

I think *Alice Pleasance Liddell* is brilliant.

There is a very obvious point about FW that I don't understand.

Who was the Eve who tempted Adam to eat the apple? Was it Anna Livia or was it Issy? Or was it sometimes one, sometimes the other? *Is* there a distinction between Eve and the apple?

It's not always true that ALP is older, Issy younger. In "ALP" Anna Livia is young & then a child when she seduces Father Michael? What do you make of 203.9–10?

Could Anna Livia be Eve, offering Adam the apple—Issy—as a lure? Is it true to masculine human nature that a man will risk a fall to get a daughter?

Of course I think Alice-Alys-Lily-Lis-Lissy-Lizzy-Izzy form one theme or idea—the young thing on whom an old man dotes. I would add Susanna since Lily means Susanna & Susanna & the Elders[1] is pertinent. Joyce in "Scylla & Charybdis" linked Susanna Shakespeare & her daughter Elizabeth. As Alice or Lizzy, she's grampa's lump of love. She gets older and leaves him for a yong man as 1) Shakespeare's late heroines—Perdita, Miranda, Marina leave their adoring fathers 2) as the Dark Lady left W. S. for W. H. Now when she leaves the older man enters a voyeurist stage, becomes the Sycomores [203.21–.22] or Elders and watches the young people, as, it is fair to imagine, Shakespeare (who had Othello in him) watched the D. Lady & Mr W. H. Not literally watched but intensely imagined. WS-WH-Dark Lady = Finn-Dermot-Grania = Mark-Tristan-Isolde = Arthur-Lancelot-Guinevere.

In time, I think, all things cycle & the daughter now Cordelia returns to her father Llar-Lir-sea. Note when the daughter goes (II, iv) [383–389] there is a sea connection as when she returns. Elsewhere the 4 are old men of the sea[.]

Mr. Bonheim[2] sent me a list of additions, solid dull or I had them mostly. 611.28 is Helmholtz who wrote on color vision. Mr B. also pointed out Eccles [567.27] wasn't just a street (who *was* it named for?) but a composer[3] who sounds rather fun.

Did I tell you [John] Kelleher gave me Irish month names.[4] February has 3 names, one means "month of Brigit" which I guess ties up the Biddoes-Bridgets being February daughters in the Jaun Section.

Oh yes, I read a memoir of John MacCormack by his wife,[5] a very junky book, adoring, but if you read between the lines Jaun is there all right.

I think the postal-Boucicault uniform on 404 is the equivalent of MacCormack's uniform as Papal Count. The pictures of him as Papal Count are comic beyond comic.

Did you know Woodrow Wilson asked J. Mc. to stay on the home-front "to keep the fountains of sentiment flowing."

Friend of mine Iggy [Ignatius] Mattingly is starting FW. Suggests Auburn Loveliest village of the Plains[6] memorializes ALP. Why not?

        Faithfully,
        Adaline

1. The *Story of Susanna*, one of the books of the Old Testament Apocrypha, tells how Susanna was accused of adultery by two Jewish elders because she would not sleep with them. Her innocence was proven by Daniel and the elders were put to death. Many painters of the Renaissance and later periods produced works on this subject.

2. Helmut Bonheim to Glasheen, 12 September 1961 (HWS). Among Bonheim's books are: *Joyce's Benefictions* (Berkeley: University of California Press, 1964) and *A Lexicon of the German in 'Finnegans Wake'* (Berkeley: University of California Press, 1967).

3. John Eccles (?1668–1735) was a composer of songs for plays, two 'all-sung' masques, and operas.

4. Kelleher to Glasheen, 13 September 1961 (HWS).

5. Lily McCormack's *I Hear You Calling Me* (Milwaukee: Bruce Publishing Co., 1949). For Joyce's complex relationship with McCormack (1884–1945) see Hodgart and Bauerle, *Joyce's Grand OPEROAR*.

6. The phrase, as such, is not in *Finnegans Wake*.

To Thornton Wilder, Quebec, Canada

[MS. ALS—YCAL]

25 September 1961   [22 Carrington Lane
                                           Farmington, Connecticut]

Dear Thornton,

I don't seem to have made clear—what I question in your identifications is what I question in myself and not only in you and me but generally. Take Jim Atherton. He has found undoubted *Fanny Hill* references. Therefore he wants the author of F. Hill, John Cleland.[1] This he says is "Shamrogueshire" [472.1] (wherever it is), Shamrock = Cle; shire = land. It is perfectly possible, but it is *as possible* that it just means Ireland is the land of shamrocks, shams, rogues. And yet no doubt Joyce memor[i]alized Cleland somwhere—why not in any reference to Ireland?

Now I think—and I *know* I'm being tedious—that very much the same thing applies to the Golden Bowl on p. 164.[2] A broken golden bowl is Biblical, it is Poe ("Broken is the golden bowl, the spirit flown forever"), it is H. James, about a Maggy. The countrymaid M., Margarine certainly is Margaret or Maggy. Take William Shakespeare. He left a "silver-gilt" bowl to his daughter Judith. It is conjectured in one of J's main sources (Brandes or Lee—I forget which) that W. S.[,] B. Jonson, Drayton caroused out of his bowl at Judith's wedding.[3] Now Judith is not mentioned on p. 164, nor Shakespeare, and breaking is not associated with WS's bowl. But the reference occurs in "Burrus & Caseous"[4] & they are Shakespearean characters[,] lines 20, 21 "left" "will." [margin: Neither specifically fits in context.]

Now, my sense of evidence is no great shakes & it has been vitiated by too long a swim in you-know-what. I can't see that your James or my Shakespeare is any more possible. Either, both, neither may be intended[.] This is how much of what you've sent lately strikes me. It is how much of my Shakespeare stuff strikes me. Who is to judge? That's the wicked thing. Joyce is a devious devil and there is nobody competent to say that you are wrong or I am wrong. If we made articles out of it, we could get them in print but who could judge us? It makes me yes sad. But what I hope won't happen, is your thinking I reject or don't want or don't think deeply—or at least lovingly—about what you send. But yes it is sad.

I just had a letter from Fritz [Senn]. I cannot get the 2nd volume of Joyce's letters out of [Richard] Ellmann. He says they're not in ms yet. Fritz & Clive [Hart] offer to read proof[5] for me. Brothers in FW is the only truly amiable international organization[.]

You must not think I think your path less sound than mine. I worry about the system of equivalents in my little forcing house. I *think* HCE keeping on him where plays put on, in a suburb of Dublin, on Dublin's rivers is a strong equivalent of the Globe & Shakespeare. Stronger, it seems to me, than well—Bloom's cigar being Ulysses' burning brand. Is it? And if it is, do I carry on equivalents rightly? No, a long time ago I thought of *A Royal Divorce*[6] = *Henry VIII*. Yesterday I realized Queen Eliz. I is a Shakespearean character, a babe-in-arms and—read the end of the play—a reconciling babe like Lizzy grampa's lump of love.[7] I already thought Lizzy & Eliz. I identified in the lamp-lump-moon-muse theme so I am delighted they should both be Shakespearean babes. But if you think I am surer of this than of Maggy Verver, you are, my good man, wrong. I question you because I question myself.

?? 7.4, 13 Jack Falstaff. In *I Henry IV* J. F. dies & is resurrected—V, iv, 112–113 Falstaff rises from the dead & says, "I['ll] give you leave to powder me and eat me too to-morrow."

Do you go to Europe? How are you?

           Faithfully
           Adaline

1. See AG to TW, 15 September 1961, n. 5.
2. See TW to AG, [?1–5 September].
3. Anecdotally, Michael Drayton (1563–1631), who was born in Hartshill, Warwickshire, was a close personal friend of Shakespeare's and, with Ben Jonson (1572–1637), attended Judith Shakespeare's wedding to Thomas Quiney.
4. Identified by Glasheen as Brutus and Cassius in *Julius Caesar*, but also "In FW they are Shaun and Shem. . . .The Burrus-Caseous episode is a burlesque Shavian preface. 161–168, *passim*." (*Census II*, 38)

5. For *Census II*.
6. W. G. Wills's play about Napoleon's divorce from Josephine and his subsequent marriage to Marie Louise. See Atherton, *The Books at the Wake*, 161–162.
7. At her christening Archbishop Cranmer says that Elizabeth shall be: "A pattern to all princes living with her/And all that shall succeed" (*Henry VIII*, V, v, 22–23).

□

To Adaline Glasheen, Farmington, Connecticut

[MS. ALS—HWS]

11 December 1961
T' home[1]
[50 Deepwood Drive
Hamden 17, Connecticut]

Dear Adaline:

Fritz Senn is going through his period of discouragement that we all go through. Don't tell him I mentioned it to you. Oh, what a labyrinth of a book.

If you *will* attack that first paragraph [3.1–.14]:

Note that there seems to be a linking-arrangement (as in old Irish poetry) as in 142.31.

We begin with the Earl of Howth, but his family names extend into the second clause: Laurens = St. Lawrence.

Then we go to Dublin, Georgia. You tell us it was founded by Jonathan Sawyer, but I think Joyce decided it was founded by a Peter Sawyer* and he uses it to mean Peter = Rock = Papacy. Now *Tu es Petrus* is the motet, or whatever, sung as the Pope enters to perform the office: = Thu art peatrick drags in St. Patrick as a secondary illusion.

So in Clause Two we get ROCKS with Peter Sawyer = and in CLAUSE Three we get "Tu es Petrus." So I read that: Not yet had Pagan Ireland (Brigid) been converted to Catholocism.

The next clause is probably Parnell-Jacob and I cannot see that there is a linking with Clause Three, but there seems to be a similar juxtaposition on p. 291 (Parnell and Kitty are among Dante's adulterous lovers {290.1 Shee 24 Arklow-Wicklow, Parnell's home at Avondale 25 "get my price" 291. note 1 O'Shea O'Shea. 26 sussex home (their house in Brighton)}: and there is your Tauft-tarf. que TU ES Pitrë again (French for piteous foolish fellow). 291.24

You notice that both the family names of the Earl (Jarl) of Howth are in the Grace O'Malley story.[2] Just as Tristan can turn his name around so can Laurence—St. Lawrence; and the Boy HILARY of 21.36 becomes the LARRYhill of 22.19 on a laurency night (22.12)[.] And we meet the Howth twins again 92.6–7 hilaro-Larry and Tristi

---

We haven't given enough attention to the Earl of Howth = (the "head" of the sleeping HCE). The first Sir Amory-Amories won Howth at the battle of the Bridge of IVORA: 4.36 hoyth—4.31 ivoroiled .34 roundhead. (next page 5.3 lots of those *Lawrence* O'Toole's also serve by side swipe as of the family St. *Lawrence*).

And 619.25 man of the hooths .36 your iverol.

One of the themes of the book is the mating of Irish girls with the successive Norse-Norman-English invaders.

I think we see Eva Mac Murrough (who married Strongbow in) in MAKMERRIERS 619.28 and EVA in JAHWEH plus HAWWAH Heb. for Eva 619.34. (Strongbow is 626.2.)

In the new CENSUS give all the names because J J plays with them all:

STRONGBOW, Richard Fitzgibbon de Clare, Earl of Pembroke and Clare, Lord of Leinster. (There's another title in there that I've lost... A Duglad, or something like that.) I suspect he is in most of the "A was for Archer" [80.9] and in 622.18[.]

It looks as though *any* Peter will serve for the Papacy.

Thus on page 205.34 are Peter the Great and Peter Stuyvesant but .33 the pope's triple tiara and .28 St. Peter was crucified upside down.

Shaun's ribald sermon [429–473]: "Girls, don't have anything serious to do with those Vikings and Normans and Black and Tans[3]; but play 'em for all they're worth."

To return to the Earls of Howth (both Sir Tristram and the Hill personified):

HOWTH, Earl of, family names gradually acquired, Sir etc etc. Arms: crossed words and roses; crest, sea-lion, motto "Qui pense" or "Que panse."*[*] Associations in FW: Grania O'Maley, door open at mealtimes, Bailey Light, Ireland's Eye, rhododendrons, Benn Eder, and frequently all forms of "head[.]"

(I suppose it would make your volume too long if you appended to the persons a list of such "associations," e.g. . . . PARNELL- - - - - - - - owner of quarries where he made and sold setts.) How it would help!! (Setts 61.14)

SITRIC = since we see on p. 353.14 that J J combines KNUT with Sitric at Clontarf,[4] we can add

80.1–2	sidetrack. . . . . Bryant (Brian Born)
313.24	sixtric (vincinity of Ragnar Ladbrok. 15. . . . 24.[)]
221.34	is Silken Thomas Fitzgerald, but the spelling surely gives us Sitric too
376.8–9	Clontarf. . . . Brian. Born. . . . Norse. . . Knut. . . .31 slick of the trick. . . If you believe the Encounter with the CAD is also the Battle of Clontarf, you get
84.2	Bull's run. . . . . 23 knut.

NOW

BRIAN O'LINN is a ballad about a shiftless tramp who wore his clothes inside out but it serves J J to allude to Brian Born

17.9	clontarf. . . . . . Brian. (note all the Clontarf material on the opposite page)
338.28	You have cited Bruyant for Born—note the O'LINN ballad is quoted line 18
51.27	clontarf. . . . 29 Bryn.

Did I call your attention before to FEBRUARY saints in the Sermon?

Feb 1	St Brigit	430.2
Feb 5	St Agatha	" .35
Feb 7, 13, & 16	Three Spanish St. Julianas 430.36	
Feb 12	St. Eulalia	430.36
Feb 10.	St. Scolastica	431.23
Feb 2	Feast of the Presentation of Christ. 431.30	
Feb 9	{? Oh Phoebus = St Apolonia}	" 36
Feb 12	Feast of the Seven Servites (? sick server 432.34 [i.e., 430.33])	
Feb 3	St. Blasius (for Pascal 432.30?[)] charming?	

And maybe the beginning of the Lesson Chapter [260–308] is the Month of March.

264.4   roaring month ("comes in like a lion. . .")
262.15 [i.e., .16] St. Lucius March 4
"   "   [i.e., .16] St Perpetua (in "lux perpetua luceat eis") March 6
"   note 6   Mary Achinhead (Aquinas) . . . beautified Tommy ??? St
              Thomas A = March 7
              (St. Thomas *ought* to be at the beginning of the Lesson
              Chapter, shouldn't he? with his {SAME = 263.1}
              {SUMMA = 263.2}

You have Isaak Walton on 76.27–28
I think you have him again 61.19 WALT. . . . 24 PISCMAN = Piscator

HAPPY HOLIDAYS TO ALL THE GLASHEENS AND THE FINEST NEW YEAR

                your old friend
                Thornton and Isabel

*

211.28   Thou art Peter and on this rock I shall found my church:
           conditus in Latin: Conditor Sawyer.
372.6   Tuppeter Sowyer: Tu PETER = Tu es Petrus.
549.24   sankt Pioter. . . . 25 sawyer
580.4   Peter's sawyery.
           Similarly though no relation to Sawyer: we have p. 449.10 One
True Apostolic Church and 449.16 Peter the Rock {Oh, forgive me, I
see you have that in the Census[}] Twoways (TU Es) Peterborough 442.11

---

*[*]
    I forgot the crest also has a "sirène" (I got it from a French book
of heraldry "St Laurence, Comte de Howth")—a mermaid gazing at
herself in an oval mirror!! This may be mixed up with other things—
546.5 frish .6 devoiled (the mermaid is *nature* in heraldic diction: i. e.
naked). 9 lances . . . crossed. .18 merfish. 547.8 undine 548.31 the
mirror: and 547.14 ff it does look as though she were a fish and would
have the "Torture of the boots" 548.30

---

1. After his return from Quebec, Canada, on 3 October 1961, Wilder remained in Hamden making brief trips to New York, Washington, D. C., and Atlantic City.
2. Grace O'Malley (?1530–1600), a pirate in the time of Elizabeth I. She was also called Gráinne Mhaol Granuaile. See *Census II* and *III*.

3. In 1920 Eamon de Valera campaigned to dissuade young men from joining the Royal Irish Constabulary. Faced with a shortage of men, the British government advertised for recruits—many of whom were out of work veterans of World War I. They were called Black and Tans because of their mismatched uniforms: khaki trousers from the British army and black RIC belts. They were the most feared and hated group of British forces in Ireland.

4. The victory of Brian Ború (Bóroime), king of Munster, over Máel Mórda, king of Leinster, and his Viking allies at the Battle of Clontarf, on Good Friday, 23 April 1014, ended Danish rule in Ireland. Ború was killed by a fleeing Viking. As Glasheen notes in *Census II*: "there are a good many Norse King Sitrics in Irish history." Here the reference is to Sitric Silkbeard, king of the Dublin Vikings, who was defeated at the Battle of Clontarf.

☐

To Adaline Glasheen, Farmington, Connecticut

[MS. ALS—HWS]

[?12–14 December 1961] 50 Deepwood Drive
 Hamden 17, Connecticut

Dear Adaline
POSTSCRIPT
 rê Joyce thinking the founder of Dublin, Georgia, was a Peter Sawyer.
 See Scribbledehobble p. 129 {it's the worst edited book of the decade: do you suppose Joyce or Connolly wrote those words *"First Paragraph"*?}
 Tristan
 S Peter Sawyer
 St Patrick
 ──────────────

 Do you suppose this another EVA—STRONGBOW?
494.15 The Italian volcano is STROMBOLI—Joyce writes—BOLO. Does he want (with another weapon) Strongbow—to juxtapose with EVA in line 17 and heva heva in line 26 and maybe dick (Richard de Clare) in line 23?

311.12   does he turn Meat-safe around so we can get EFA to juxtapose with strongbowth in line 15

and 293.28 [i.e., .18]   Do we hear A is for Archer, so as to get the Eve takes a fall in line 31 [i.e., .21]?

> But you're busy
> All best
> ever
> Thornton

[attached sheet]

SHEM's ancestors 169.16 [i.e., .4]
    Note that p. 444.5 Joyce combines
        Harold Harefoot (k. of Saxons 1035–1040);
        and Ragnar Lodebrok
    Aren't they here (altered) on 169.16 [i.e., .4]?
    And if—for some reason—he associates—Lodebrog with Bluebeard, don't we get it again
        p. 332.22 Lord, me LAD, he goes with blowbierd. ?
          373.29 beerd. Lodenbroke. . .
       {Incidentally two more R. Lodebroks
          19.4 ragnar
          440.29 the lad who brooks}
And if SHEM (by 444.5) is descended from Harold Harefoot, doesn't that throw light on the fact that his alternate name is HAROLD (p. 30.14 [i.e., .2])? which CENSUS refers to HAROLD II. And if his ancestor had a HARE FOOT it may have something to do with Shaun's omnipresent shoe-trouble (which associates, too, with Byron and Oedipus.)

                       x

    Oh, Lord, has anyone found out anything about the GLUES and GRAVEYS and ANKERS etc [30.6–.7]?

To Thornton Wilder, Hamden, Connecticut

[MS. ALS—YCAL]

14 December 1961 [22 Carrington Lane
 Farmington, Connecticut]

Dear Thornton,

Yours was a wonderful letter. Look, would you read my expla[n]ation of Par. 1 & 2 if I sent it? I'll send the carbon so I wouldn't have to have it back by Jan. 1, deadline.[1] My husband read it & said it was clear "if one knows your mind and how it works." Also that it was "charming and funny." Since I aimed at total clarity and an audience of intelligent people *about* to read FW, I am not wholly consoled by this.

I won't talk about the passage since I may send it—if you've time. I've gone on to do a S[keleton]. Key of "The Wake" which is finished to the Prankquean.[2] Just before your letter came the P. Q and I broke off violently with the realization that its plot is the same plot as the Circe episode in *The Odyssey*. It's reversed (but everything's reversed in "The Wake"). She comes ashore & enchants his children (Odysseus' men) & then is overcome by Odysseus. Is it true? If so, what does it mean?

Your discovery of the mermaid in the mirror on the crest is dazzling. It would add another level to the P. Q. wouldn't it? And help account for the looking-glass girls I shouldn't wonder. If, as I can show, everything in "The Wake" is reversed, is it mirror reversal?

After doing the opening paragraphs I'm convinced that in all "The Wake" we have a Noah-Mystery Play level everywhere. And the fact I can't always find and/or explain the Noah level doesn't change my mind—I can *find* it at the end of the Prankquean but I can't help feeling I would follow the plot if only I knew who the "dummy" was. Because the P. Q. ends up with the "dummy" & may have been after it all the time.

I am sorry about Fritz [Senn] being unhappy. I will say nothing. I am in the opposite state—so much comes in that I can't deal with it.

Did I say the February saints were brilliant, but then what in your letter is not.

Questions:
About when did they blow up King Belly's equestrian statue? I think that's the end of the Museyroom [8.9–11.28]. Is it referred to in 3.35 [i.e., .23]?

p. 9—How do you translate (in German, French & into English) the letters?[3]

I never realized. Napoleon does not write Wellington. The Jinnies[4] write W. a letter, signed "Nap" [9.6] & W. sees through it & addresses his letter to the Jinnies [9.13–.14]. See H[orace]. Walpole & Infanta Gunning.[5]

Something also I never noticed till yesterday. 9.31[-.32] Willingdone has thundered-defecated & "me Belchum" collects "the crapes" in his cannister. Well it's repeated 19.15–16.

10—When Wellingdone picks up the ½ hat, does he change to lipoleum? If not, why is he the lipoleum at 10.35?

12.31   According (apparently falsely) to G. Cambrensis[6] Olaf, Ivor, Sitrec = 3 brothers, Vikings, who built Dublin, Limerick, Waterford.

16.35 [i.e., .36] *Who* was poached, Brian or Sitrec?

As you can see, my main care is reading lines[.]

31[.6]   I never knew why anyone would want to pothole a road, but the IRA did to stop the Black & Tan's machines
33.1   cuckoospit = snake spit. Also Cockpit Eliz. theatre
34.15   Woodwards & Regarders = officers of a forest who saw no hurt done to vert or venison
     In an Irish book, *Army Without Banners* an Irish nurse ended fairy-stories: "They put on the kettle and made tay, and if they were not happy, that you may." 332.2–3[7]

Vico's stuttered syllables "pa-pe" always occur around the 100 letter word[s].[8]

Merry Christmas I hope you will read my thing

Yours,
Adaline

1. See TW to AG, 26 December 1961, n. 1.
2. For *Census II* Glasheen substantially revised and expanded the synopsis of *Census I*. The Prankquean in *Finnegans Wake* (20.19–23.15) is based on the sixteenth century pirate Grace O'Malley.
3. See TW to AG, 19 December 1961.
4. Two girls, also called Cherry Jinnies, who are at war with HCE and Wellington in the Museyroom episode.
5. Glasheen expands the Gunning family entry in each *Census*. In a letter of 18 June 1751 to Sir Horace Mann, Horace Walpole writes of them: "These are two Irish girls of no fortune, who are declared the handsomest women alive. I think their being two, so handsome and both such perfect figures, is their chief excellence, for singly I have seen much handsomer women than either: however, they can't walk in the park, or go to Vauxhall, but such mobs follow them that they are generally driven away" (*Horace Walpole's Correspondence with Sir Horace Mann*, IV, ed. W. S. Lewis, Warren Hunting Smith, and George L. Lam (New Haven: Yale University Press, 1960), 260).
6. The priest and historian Giraldus Cambrensis (?1146–?1220).
7. Ernie (Earnâan) O'Malley (1898–1957), *Army Without Banners: Adventures of an Irish Volunteer* (1930; rpt., Boston: Houghton Mifflin, 1937; published in London and Dublin as *On Another Man's Wound*). The book is "an attempt to show the background of the struggle from 1916 to 1921 between an Empire and an unarmed people" (ix). O'Malley begins Chapter I of the section "Flamboyant": "Our nurse, Nannie, told my eldest brother and me stories and legends. Her stories began: 'Once upon a time, and a very good time it was,' and ended with 'They put on the kettle and made tay, and if they were not happy, that you may'" (23). The last line of the memoir is: "Put on the kettle now and make the tay, and if we weren't happy, that you may" (403).
8. "It thunders a good many times in *Finnegans Wake* and on ten occasions (pp. 3, 23, 44, 90, 113, 257, 314, 332, 414, 424) thunder speaks a hundred-letter word, which I shall call, hereafter, a Cletter.... The first nine Cletters contain 100 letters, the tenth Cletter (424) contains 101" (Glasheen, "Part of What the Thunder Said in *Finnegans Wake*," *The Analyst*, XXIII (November 1964), [1]).

To Adaline Glasheen, Farmington, Connecticut

[MS. ALS—HWS]

[postmark: 15 December 1961]   [50 Deepwood Drive
                                  Hamden 17, Connecticut]

Dear Adaline =
    You sure said it: Noah's everywhere, and usually joined to the Guinness family (explicit in 549.34)
    That big funeral on 497–499 is Noah 496.30–31 and Guinness
    Greek and German for Ivy = Epheu 498.13–14 his sons IVEAGH and Ardilaun.[1] So, too, we get HCE's house:
560.9   ark 16 ephort {and hence I think: line 8 "porter when it is finished["] = guinness'd.[}] {Noé 561.5 is french for Noah[}]
    Now ALP is Noah's wife, too.
622.1   doves and ravens. . . 15 40 days etc
619.20   folty and folty. . . nights and 36 comforter {"And God said I shall call him {{Noah}} comfort. . . } See also 136.32
The motto of the GUINNESS family is SPES MEA IN DOMINO [i.e., Deo]
485.19 and 21 IVY-IVEAGH: across the page your RAVEN and DOVES gets 484.32 PORVUS CARRIO = corvus = crow = traitor CAREW.

    Now in our generation a Guin[n]ess girl married a (Russian?) MIHAIL ESSAYAN (I think I copied that down correctly in Burke's Peerage and Baronetage) and was living in Paris (surely to the fascinated interest of Joyce) and isn't she in 7.4 (with her father all around 6.27 and 7.15)
    And in the Gertrude Stein circle (that Joyce was very aware of) was a (lady) Noel Guinness who is probably 490.23 (as rainbow, too 490.30)
    Maybe 351.1 Nowell. . . 5 arc. . . 26 ham, shem and Japheth
         393.11. . . 15 shims {beautiful sisters[}]
         588.27 opposite is the flood passage 589.25
    Apparently JJ foists upon Noah (sin of drunkenness and indecent exposure) the sins of LOT (incest with daughter and imputed homosex'y in Sodom); and on Guinness, a bankruptcy.

¶ The Deucalion-Pyrrha² are interchangeable with NOAH add 94.34 197.3 and in line 28 he b'ark'ed it.
   506.25 There's Pyrrha but not her name and on the opp page 507.33 the arc of covenant
YES = NOAH'S all over the place—anyway Shem—Joyce is Noah's son.
   But I'm getting in the way of your holiday enjoyments.

> Again =
> best to all
> Thornton

1. Sir Arthur Edward Guinness (1840–1915), eldest son of Sir Benjamin Lee Guinness (1798–1868), was created Baron Ardilaun in 1880; the youngest son, Edward Cecil Guinness (1847–1927), was created a baronet in 1885, in 1891 was named Baron Iveagh, and in 1919 he became Earl of Iveagh.
2. In Greek mythology Deucalion, a son of Prometheus, with his wife Pyrrha built an ark and floated in it to survive a deluge sent by Zeus in anger at the irreverence of humans. They survived, and later an oracle told them to cast behind them the stones of the earth. The stones became the repopulated human race.

☐

To Adaline Glasheen, Farmington, Connecticut

[MS. ALS—HWS]

[postmark: Tuesday, 19 December 1961]   50 Deepwood Drive
Monday   Hamden 17, Connecticut

Dear Adaline:
   In haste.
   Yes,—gladly read the explication, but I still say *it's all too soon to attack that.*
   In the Museyroom, you realize all those bullsfoot [8.15]-bullseye [10.21] are for the greatest battle of all: CLONTARF[.]¹ Through most of Ireland's rebellions all the men had to fight with where [i.e., were] *pikes and forks* (against—as Swift said "men in armor") especially at Clontarf: 8.15[.]

Did I tell you the insign[ia] of the Volunteers (and Tom and his friend Hamilton Rowan) was a liberty cap on a pike[2] {liberty cap called a corsican cap because of *that* 18th Century revolt 403.20 [i.e., .8][}] {there assoc. with Emerson's Concord Hymn because the Americans were trying to free themselves too}[.] This may be at the back of all those hats on poles—which, alas, was indecent, too.

Translation of letters
- 9.4   Ja. . . .5 Lieber (dear) Arthur (pron. Artoor) Versuchen = try or attempt. Wie gehts (how is) deine—deine Frau? (your wife). Hochachtung = deepest respect.
- 9.7   Si is yes in Italian; but in French it is a stronger oui = i. e. "oh *yes*, it is."
- 9.13   chéries (dear) maybe *jeunesses* (young ladies)
  victoire. . .ça ne (for damn) fait rien?—"That doesn't make a damn bit of difference" "Your."
- 9.27   frequent German oath: Donnerwetter! (thunderweather ?) Gott straf (punish)
- 32   Pour la paix = for Peace.
- 34   Sauve qui peut ("escape who can")
  assoc with one of the regiments at Waterloo
- 10.19   German Besucher = visitor
- .19   Usted, Spanish formal: you.

Don't understand *one* word about Lipoleum   [10.1ff]

Just think! You have a Brittanica in your home and kind [i.e., can] find out the names of the battles where Vercingetorix and Caractacus were defeated.[3] Lucky you

> In haste
> Again: happy holidays
> Thornty

1. See AG to TW, 11 December 1961, n. 4.

2. The Irish Volunteers, a paramilitary group formed on 25 November 1913 under the leadership of Eoin MacNeill (1867–1945), Patrick Pearse (1879–1916), and Thomas MacDonagh (1878–1916). Pearse and MacDonagh were executed by a firing squad for their participation in the Easter 1916 uprising.

3. Vercingetorix, a Gallic (Celtic) leader, chief of the Arverni, revolted against Rome in 52 B.C. He was defeated by Julius Caesar at Aleisia and brought to Rome where he was executed in 46 B.C. Caractacus was a British chieftain of the Catuvellauni. He was defeated by Ostoriius Scapula in A.D. 50 and sent as a captive to Rome.

To Adaline Glasheen, Farmington, Connecticut

[MS. ALS—HWS]

26 December 1961 50 Deepwood Drive
 Hamden 17, Connecticut

Dear Adaline =
It's fine.[1] There's a great deal of new in it that I'm very glad to learn. But:
Is it in its right place as the Preface to the Census?
You're first preface was delightful—and not too long—and now with enormous vitality you analize [i.e., analyze] two paragraphs in the greatest detail, as though the CENSUS was not a Census but a line-by-line examination of the text.

It's all too much; it overwhelms; and it bogs down in digressions, and finally it's so back-and-forth that it lacks charm and persuasion, and that fairest quality of prefaces which is: to introduce. Nay, it discourages.

What I feel is this:
That when we really know FW, it can be done much more succinctly; you are (rightly) forced to use so many words because there are certain clues not yet in hand.

I suggest that you put this in an appendix; use most of your old Preface and then get on to the new enlarged enriched beautiful Census.

But if you do decide to use this material in this way here are a few suggestions

page 1	bottom: don't you feel a definite characterization for HCE and ALP etc? I do, J J has such a grasp on individuation that through all the fog-transformations I "hear" *that* man, *that* woman. . . .
page 2	paragraph 1. . . don't you think one could add: all the people from history and fiction are superimposed *upon* the Chapelizod family?
Page 2	bottom: rephrase "wretchedly understood"
page 9	"Fr' over"—I have a dim feeling that there is an Anglo-Saxon word like *faode* that means something "leader" a confessor that could be identified with Christ. Maybe I'm wrong.

page 11   Aren't you going to include that Wellington is in the Peninsulate War?

page 12   avois = latin AVIS bird is certainly there—maybe St Patrick "Dove without gall" Later: MOSES?

page 5   "twitters" page 12 bottom "mad about" you have a splendidly vivacious style; once in a while you run away and get too vivacious.

page 28–29   seem to me to be just joyous galloping around the pasture—suppositions, and free associations and sheer fun but quite unsuitable for an efficient functional preface—I'm sure most of it will ultimately be shown to be true but it will be integrated and confirmed elsewhere by Joyce, so that there won't have to be this continual tone of *supposition*. He is terribly systematic and when we get the system the exposition can be concise and almost mathematical. (Klein's papers on Ulysses.) Imagine you saying that he turned Jonathan around to Nathanjoe *just in order to get another Bible figure in*! Joyce doesn't work that way, he doesn't put a significant name in just to make "another" name. (You remember my feeling: the Zodiac: sosie—Twins are GEMINI and the reversed name is CANCER that goes backward)

I still think that paragraph is "out of bounds."

It's admirable stuff but it's for another book—the book you will write next.

However I may be all wrong; do as you think best and all cordial greetings to you all; and thanks

Ever
Thornt'

[new page]

For Adaline

The Census gives us JACOB 89.15. Esau is there in .13 (and a dish of lentils .4)

104.22 [i.e., .10]   is certainly ISAAC followed .23 [i.e., .11] by Jacob's birthright

106.28   Icyk. . . all the Patriarchs are here. . . . GUINNESS .30 is interchangeable with NOAH. . . and

106.33	HOFED is Danish for HEAD-HOWTH and Manorlord Hoved is Earl of Howth.
312.19	Earl (St) Laurence. . . 20 of Howth. . . and his wife LAURETTE feminine of Laurence who is also Grace O'Malley 22
545.32	All the Patriarchs are in this proclamation—if we could only find them: {a dome 541.5 JACOB 542.30} but surely this is MOSES the LAWGIVER as well as Dr Mosse the (LAV = wash) giver. {next page: 546.14[}]
552.30	similarly our MOSES in mossy is confirmed by "here is holy ground" line .9 from EXODUS III 5 and the Passover 553.8 (with MATZOS)
307.	Do you notice how Joyce—after identifying NOAH with GUINNESS in line .1 identifies MOSES with St Patrick in lines 22–23? does that add anything to the VOICE from the Burning bush fire in 3.21? [i.e., .9] ¶ notice 326.2 commandments. . . . as .3 Paddy. . ¶ 491.11 Patrick's . . . 26 Tara's thrush . . . .29 Mo.
81.3	At Battle of Lake Trasimene, 2nd Punic war. 217 B.C. Hannibal def. Romans under FLAMINIUS.
301.29	since ISAAC means LAUGH I think you get it in laugh. . sack. . .
69.9	You'll give us MOSES for Deacon Moses, in view of the context?
11	Since we have ISAAC in line 35, won't you give us REBECCA in .11 beggybaggy . . . bickybacky. SARAH (Sally .17[)] laughed .33 when she heard she'd have ISAAC .35 ¶ There is SARAH laughing again 293 footnote 2 at Laugh—Isaac's birth SARA ISAAC = line 27
359	Look at all the Patriarch's families. . . . it's really about (unnamed) NOAH: You have the HAMS 22; but JAPHET: jeff 18

LOT = Twice 16 and his wife in SAULT [.17].
SALLY = Sarah 18 probably meets Abram in a ham .22
Swing low, sweet chariot .19 is felt as the death of Moses

446.1   Abraham meets Sally-Sarah .6 (This is probably in your Second Census but I've mislaid it for the minute.)

If you asked me the whole Fracas on pages 69–70 takes place among the Patriarchal families from MOSES 69.9—Eden—Adam-Eve 69.10–11 to Rebecca 70.12 heeltapper-Esau 70.22 and his porridge-stirabout 70.25

263.   Just as that is NOAH in line 1–3 and the ark-Zoo footnote 1.—and the ARK in line 30; and ADAM in line 21; so we have LOT (French spelling Loth) in line 23 and its footnote LOTHARIUS = "gay" in slang has come to mean "of sodom." ("You can tell by their extraordinary clothes!!")

240.13   The juxtaposition of henessy shows that Allbigenesis contains GUINNESS

Yes, Joyce is mad about all the MAYORS of Dublin—not least Sir Abraham Bradley King who is also in 307. ABRAHAM (l. 7 "we love.... Lord Mayor") and 568.16 mayour.... 23 DOM KING.....34 Sir.... KING {and next page, for 569.23 for Old Finncoole, read Old KING Cole.. and naturally all the bells of Dublin celebrating his knighting[2]

---

1. In this letter Wilder comments on Glasheen's detailed notes on the opening paragraphs of *Finnegans Wake*. See AG to TW, 14 December 1961 and TW to AG, 3 January 1962. Glasheen accepted Wilder's suggestion and kept the Preface from Census I in II. The essay, however, became a quarry for Glasheen. She used parts of it in her five part article about the *Wake*, "The Opening Paragraphs," published in *A Wake Newslitter* in 1965–1966, and she incorporated ideas from this article in the revised introduction she wrote for *Census III*.

2. Abraham Bradley King was Lord Mayor of Dublin from 1812–1813; he served a second term from 1820–1821 by which time he had been knighted. In *Census II* Glasheen uses a list of the Lord Mayors compiled by James Atherton from Thom's *Dublin Directory* of 1851 and 1951. In *Census III* she added names gleaned from Joyce's workbook (Buffalo Workbook #28). The most complete listing of Mayors and Lord Mayors of Dublin from 1229 to 1983 was prepared by Jacqueline Hill for *A New History of Ireland*, ed. T. W. Moody, F. X. Martin, and F. J. Byrne, Vol. IX, *Genealogies, Lists. A Companion to Irish History Part II* (Oxford: Clarendon Press, 1984), [547]–564.

1962

To Adaline Glasheen, Farmington, Connecticut

[MS. ALS—HWS]

3 January 1962   50 Deepwood Drive
                                   Hamden 17, Connecticut
                    Letter 2^1 =

Dear Adaline =
     It's all very stimulating for those who have worked some time in FW,
But put yourself in the place of someone in his First Year.
     It is a work of High Enthusiasm. I don't often find myself deploring enthusiasm, but the character of enthusiasm in a work of literary analysis is very different from that in a work of fancy. Here enthusiasm skips transitions—alights on a supposition (I never read so many "perhaps," "maybe" "possibly")—blithely skips over enigmas—pursues digressions that obscure the issue—assumes that a crux has been solved when it has merely been stated in other terms.
                           x
     Oh, give us a preface that is really a preface,—the real excellence of your book lies in the fact that it is a much-needed CENSUS[.]
                           x
     And save this* for your next book which it is incumbent on you to write.
     Sorry to take this tone, but though I can't ever claim to be right, I can claim to say what I think.

                     Ever cordially
                     Thornton

* or boil it down considerably and add it as an appendix: Aid to reading the first 30 pages.

1. A continuation of Wilder's letter of 26 December 1961.

◻

To Adaline Glasheen, Farmington, Connecticut

[MS. ALS—HWS]

[postmark: 16 January 1962]   [50 Deepwood Drive
                                Hamden 17, Connecticut]

ADALINE
    a few notes for fun to keep the kettle boiling
                             T. N. W.
    I've copied most of these out for Fritz [Senn]

Giraldus Cambrensis's first name is SILVESTER: I think you have him
    388.26 (in all that old history and with Saxo Grammaticus .31).
You have it in Census Sylvester.[1]
    and probably 473.3 where it also means New Year's Day.

    Since 549.13–16 gives us (Electric supplier) Kettle. . . . . . lamping limp. . . . ampire; I think I see its echo 137.23–25. . . kettle. . . . lymphyamphire. .
    {Incidentally do you think that is [T. S.] ELIOT? . . 549.15 WASTE. . . .Tarred Strate. . . Elgin?}

    As DINAH was the daughter of Jacob. . . seduced . . and revenged by massacre (Genesis XXXIV) I think we see her in 175.35; in 328.14 (Joyce has changed Dona Marqueza to DINA); 170.3; and it might well be DINAH speaking in 457.29, talking to her "brother Benjamin." (141.29) 476.1

    We know from Scribbledehobble that Joyce placed FATIMA as Mohammed's daughter;[2] but our western tradition remembers her most

as the last—and alert—wife of BLUEBEARD. (And Bluebeard is an ancestor of SHEM p. 169.16 [i.e., 169.4].)
  I think they are in 72.15. And maybe 205.31; and maybe both girls in 389.15.

  Joyce was very interested in the mayors of Dublin which extended to all mayors including Dick Whittington,[3] and Peter Sawyer[4]—founder and presumably mayor of Dublin, Georgia; but most of all Guinness.[5]
  We see a collection of them in 371.35 [i.e., .36] Dick Whittington and 372.1 bowe bells and his mauser-cats; where he is 372.2 lord mayor of Dublin. . . then Van Howton—ples [372.3] Earl of Howth and the Prankque[a]n.[6] Then Peter Sawyer, line 6. and then Guinness: line 7 Benjamin Lee (liefest) =
  now, dear Adaline, can those next twelve be Mayors of Dublin?[7]
  I suspect all the Hosty Kings are Mayor Abraham B. King[8]—and there he is 372.23. so soon after 372.17 Turn again, Whittington.

Sir Abraham B. King again:
  Once before Joyce gave us an APRON for Abraham 570.19 Now: 11.31 Lord and Lady Mayoress—34 naperon 34 kickin KING. . . sair. . . solly. . 35 Isaac

---

  Since you are bespelled by the second paragraph of FW I call your attention to something: You remember that on seeing the identification of St Patrick with Moses on 307. left and .22–23, I suggested that the "voice from the fire" 3.21 [i.e., 3.9] might be Moses's burning bush? Well, milady, what did the voice from the bush say? Exodus III 4? it said "Moses, Moses" and in Hebrew MOSHEH, MOSHEH, Doesn't that give you pause?

  Several of those MISH-MISHE'S look like MOSES to me:
416.7   mouche mothst. . . . with ikey [416.6].
433.10 {Shaun has just been saying 432.26 that he's urging the ten commandments, and is about to give a series of them: 433.27–28 thou shalt not}—so I think the miss. . . . . mass in 433.10 is Moses; and Issy-Veronica will address him as Meesh Me[e]sh 457.25
505.20 Mushe mushe. . . . 21 shrub. . . stone of law. . . . stile = stele. . . There are a good many more but I don't wish to defend them until I'm surer; but also take
455.36 Matzos (Passover food) is spelled MOZOS. . . for {St} Moses, the whole passage is Exodus XII "not boiled but roast," etc

You remember I pointed out Beppy as Italian dim[inutive]. for Joseph, in 415.36[.][9] There he is again in 277.18 "Bappy... we dream" ... and there are the fat and lean cows of Pharaoh's dream = .14 cows of Drommhiem (*Drimin* Gael[ic]. name for a cow; Ireland = "silk of the Kine."

Referring to DINAH: she was half-sister of Joseph; so those Dinas and Joes probably include Joseph of the coat 170.3 175.35

262. note 1 is Yussef = Arab Joseph, too, but I don't know why. Don't you think that Joseph the dream-interpreter:
   397.2 oneirist. . . .3 Jo. . . . 11 jo

---

1. The name Silvester is not mentioned by Glasheen in *Census I*, "Out of My Census," nor in *Census II*.

2. Joyce's *Scribbledehobble: The Ur-Workbook for 'Finnegans Wake'*, edited, with notes and an introduction by Thomas E. Connolly (Evanston, Ill.: Northwestern University Press, 1961), 110.

3. Richard Whittington (d. 1423) served three terms as Lord Mayor of London: 1397–1398, 1406–1407, and 1419–1420. According to legend, while in the service of Mr. Fitzwarren, a London merchant, he sold his cat for an enormous sum to the king of Barbary, whose land was plagued by rats and mice. Before he learned of his fortune, he ran away because he was ill treated by a cook. On another occasion, listening to Bow Bells, the bells of St. Mary-le-Bow, in London, he thought he heard them pealing: "Turn again, Whittington,/Lord Mayor of London."

4. Jonathan Sawyer, not as Joyce thought Peter Sawyer, was the founder of Dublin, Georgia.

5. In his letter of 26 December 1961, Wilder began discussing Joyce's naming the Lord Mayors of Dublin. See note 2. Sir Benjamin Lee Guinness (1798–1868), of the brewing family, was Lord Mayor of Dublin in 1851.

6. Wilder's references here are unclear. A "Mr van Howten of Tredcastles" is on 414.4. There is no Van Howten listed as a Lord Mayor of Dublin; however, a Bartholomew Vanhomrigh was Lord Mayor of Dublin from 1697–1698. His daughter, Esther (1687 or 1688–1723), was passionately in love with Jonathan Swift and is Vanessa in his writings. There is no listing for the Earl of Howth as Lord Mayor of Dublin.

7. In lines .9–.11 there are eight names. Three of them, Amos Love, Jeremy Yopp, and Hardy Smith, were early settlers of Dublin, Georgia. The other names on these lines were either unidentified by Glasheen or were clearly not Lord Mayors of Dublin.

8. For information on King see TW to AG, 26 December 1961, n. 2.

9. See TW to AG, 3 May 1959.

To Adaline Glasheen, Farmington, Connecticut

[MS. ALS—HWS]

5 February 1962   50 Deepwood Drive
                                             Hamden 17, Connecticut

Dear Adaline:

Am preparing a modest item or Two and will send it before I leave on the 13th.[1]

Your latest list is a honey;[2] but it only makes the horizon retreat farther. Novels one has never heard of. Items about James J's marriage that even historians have forgotten. Anyway, it calls attention to his method—and also his use of the dictionary—he simply explored every ANNE in the encyclopedias; every Potter in the manuals.

I devour ever item you send me

         More soon
         Best to all
         T. N.

---

1. Wilder sailed to Europe on the *Ryndam* to attend the premiere of *The Alcestiad*, the opera composed by Louise Talma to a libretto by Wilder. The premiere was on 2 March 1962 in Frankfurt am Main, Germany. He returned to the United States, on the *Bremen*, on 2 April.

2. A lost letter.

To Adaline Glasheen, Farmington, Connecticut
[MS. ALS—HWS]

[11 February 1962] [50 Deepwood Drive
Hamden 17, Connecticut]

FOR ADALINE

You agree with the fact that the MOYLE is associated with LER-LEAR whose daughters were changed to swans there, and gives us King Lear on 628.2–3 (and Manaanan, another Celtic-Neptune called Mananam ((etc)) Ma-Lin.[)]
428.21 [i.e., 428.18]   Don LEARy. . . . Moyle. . and as Dunleary (Dun Laoghaire) is now KINGSTON (No, the Irish Free State has changed it back to Dunleary) we get it again in 582.35 Leary. . . . Kingsto[w]n. . .[1]

Father JOHN MURPHY and his brave Shelmaliers led a remarkable campaign "'98" against Lord Mountjoy. . . successful at Hill of Oulart, Enniscorthy, New Ross, Wexford, Gorey, Fern[s], Vinegar Hill, Tubberneering.[2] Aren't they together:
333.12   [i.e., .31–.32] gory. . . . . . 13 [i.e., .32] Murphy's. . .
446.30–31 (insurrectionists) Murphy, Henson and O'Dwyer
           (of the Glens).
529.25   Hansen, Morfydd and O'Dyar

TRAITORS
O'Donovan Rossa's Fenian Brotherhood Insurrection in '64[3] was betrayed by NAGLE, MASSEY, CORYDON and TALBOT (O'LOCHLAINN's Irish Street Ballads, no 34)
    Page 516 has SIRR .15 SWANN .18—as you report—and now you can add:
516.12   NAGLE
516.27   TALBOT

359.16   LOT is in camelottery and lyonesslooting:
359.10   he must be naclenude = Na Cl = Salt and so SALTY or
          saults and Sallies .17

　　　　　　　　　To the other patriarch here Jacohob gives us
　　　　　　　　　HIOB = German for JOB
　　　　　　　　　SAL = Salt
　　　　　　　　　So we must look at all the SALLY's for this possibility:
364.30–31　sally berd. . . . 35 lots wives.
　　　　　　　　　Note it in 579.23–24 Gomorrha SALong (for Sodom) Lot
　　　　　　　　　MAYBE 19.27 nick and larry NACL. . 27 [i.e., .28]
　　　　　　　　　SOD. . . 29 SALLY
　　　　　　　　　The French for LOT is LOTH and I suspect 627.[17–.18]
　　　　　　　　　loth loth loth. . . 628.4 saltsick
Note 596.2　sod on .7 solas (phosphate of SODA) .12 lands LOTS
146.13　　　sourdamapplers = apples of Sodom 17–18 lanka LOOT

　　　　　　　　Sunday night.
　　　　　　　　Sailing Tuesday.
　　　　　　　　I meant this list to be larger. Sorry.
　　　　　　　　Best to all.
　　　　　　　　Will be back end of March.
　　　　　　　　(T)

1. King George IV visited Ireland from 12 August to 3 September 1821. To commemorate his departure from Dunleary Harbour, and to mark the completion of a new east pier, the borough, on the south shore of Dublin Bay, was renamed Kingstown. The name was changed by the Irish Free State to Dun Laoghaire in July 1930.

2. Sites associated with the May-June 1798 rebellion by the United Irishmen against proclamation of martial law in March and the excessive brutality of government troops. Fearing a French invasion in Wexford, the government sent the North Cork militia, known for its barbarity, to disarm the population. Father John Murphy, a Catholic clergyman, led a contingent of Wexford men in rebellion. After initial victories, the insurgents were defeated at Vinegar Hill, near Enniscorthy. Father Murphy was arrested and executed on 26 June 1798. A second Catholic clergyman, Father Michael Murphy, also took part in the insurrection and died in the Battle of Arklow on 9 June 1798.

3. Jeremiah O'Donovan Rossa (1831–1915). In 1856 he founded Phoenix Literary and Debating Society in Skibbereen. In 1858 his group became part of the Fenian movement, the Irish (Revolutionary) Republican Brotherhood, founded by James Stephens, among others. There was no specific Fenian insurrection in 1864. In August 1864 James Stephens declared 1865 to be the year for Fenian insurrection.

☐

To Alison Glasheen, Farmington, Connecticut

[MS. ALS—HWS]

[postmark: 6 April 1962]   50 Deepwood Drive
                            Hamden 17, Connecticut

Dear Alison
    It's Spring!
    I've just got off the ship from a stormy crossing and some cold weeks in Germany[.][1]
    So you see I've gone crazy with delight.
    And I was delighted to read your sweet generous letter.
    If your parents do take you to New York and you still want to see the *Plays for Bleecker Street*,[2] please let me (or my sister Isabel if I am away) know when you want to go because I'd be outraged if my dear friends in Farmington did not go to see them as
    GUESTS OF THE AUTHOR.
    Please tell your mother that I am very grateful for her letter[3] about old Irish languages and will write her soon.
    And my best also to your father.

        Ever cordially
        TH—There I go again—ornton Wilder

---

1. Wilder arrived in New York on 2 April and spent two days there before returning to Hamden.

2. Three one-act plays, from the two cycles of plays Wilder was writing, collectively titled *Plays for Bleecker Street*, opened at the Circle in the Square Theatre in New York on 11 January 1962. The plays, *Someone from Assisi*, *Infancy*, and *Childhood*, were directed by José Quintero.

3. Either a lost letter or a copy of Glasheen's "*Finnegans Wake* and The Secret Languages of Ireland," in *A Wake Newslitter*, No. 10 (February 1963), [1]–3.

To Thornton Wilder, Hamden, Connecticut

[MS. TL—YCAL]

8 April 1962 [22 Carrington Lane
 Farmington, Connecticut]

Dear Thornton,

How Alison—and we—loved your letter! You are a nice man.

I am a woman in a tizzy. Who would think a university press would go to press promptly. I never heard of such a thing so I sent them the bulk of the book and prepared to have a lovely spring planting rosemary thyme sage basil and catnip. Suddenly, Northwestern wrote they were going to press in England this summer and would I get them the rest of my copy by May 15! I am glad to say I got them to let Fritz Senn do a preliminary proofread and subsequent and get paid for it. That's the only bright side to a chaotic and gloomy picture. But never mind me and my ruined spring. Listen and advise.

1) They want to call it A SECOND CENSUS OF FINNEGANS WAKE: An Index of the Characters and Their Roles, Revised and expanded from the First Edition. Well, at least it's true, but can you suggest a zippier title?

2) I am going to let my first ed. Preface stand—few v[ery]. minor changes—not 20 words and then add a short—half page note saying this is a second edition. Then thank yat yat yat. Do you approve of this?

3) I am going to cut out Who is Who[1] because it is wrong in ways I cannot mend, at this stage of my knowledge of FW. Approve?

4) I am going—at [Richard] Ellmann's suggestion—to rewrite the Synopsis, a page, page and a half for each section. I've done this through I, iv. V[ery]. interesting but I don't know [if] I'm going to be able to do a good job in time. Worries me. Think the synopsis will be useful in the long run, not popular in the short. Any comments?—Any help?

4) [i.e., 5] They say I can include a map of Dublin and environs if I want. I said I can't do that by May 15. If they give me the time, do you think it worth doing? I've got someone who can draw a map for me—that's all right. But if I do it at what date should I take Dublin? Do you have a map of the right period? Do you know one I could send to Yale and get?

Seems to me the map must include the Liffey from her source to Dublin Bay, and it must include all Dublin Bay—Howth to Dalkey. What do you think?

No really, the map just seems too much, doesn't it?

I am open to all suggestions, criticisms. I can put stuff in till May 15, and, obviously as long as Fritz has the ms. I hope he'll be able to do it.

Sorry, sorry to write so dull, but I am dull, trying to get it done and keep half in the subconscious—you do have to keep one foot in the subconscious to work on FW, and it's fine when the foot can slip in, not be forced in. It's like trying to dream for a psychoanalyst, I fancy.

When do you go deserting?[2] Oh, I think I found out about the white patch—see under "Deer" and "Mamals" in the 11th Brit.—fits perfectly on p. 93, less well elsewhere. Do help me if you can

       Yrs
       Adaline

1. Per Wilder's suggestion (TW to AG, 20 April 1962), Glasheen kept "Who Is Who When Everybody Is Somebody Else" in *Census II*.
2. During an interview given at the time of the premiere of *The Alcestiad*, Wilder announced his plan to "retire" to the Arizona desert for two years.

To Adaline Glasheen, Farmington, Connecticut

[MS. ALS—HWS]

[postmark: Special Delivery, 20 April 1962] [50 Deepwood Drive
Hamden 17, Connecticut]

Dear Adaline:
Here are my suggestions—for what they're worth. Yes, Preface stand.
1) I think you should use their title: A SECOND CENSUS.
2) If you include "and their roles," you should include the Who's Who.
3) Don't trouble about the fact that it cannot be definitive now.

You and I suspect that ISSY is often Lucia Joyce but frequently the ISSY-column, put (in the Adam row: ISSY = young Eve and Lilith and ALP = surely Older Eve.[)] (EVE-ALP sinned too)

NOAH-row Noah's wife COBHA = COVE, is it worth putting = but she's ancestress of the Irish race (Keating).[1] {501.26}

OMIT BUDDHA-MOHAMMED-FALSTAFF-CROMWELL-WILDE-HAROLD-NORWEGIAN CAPT- and add a Note at the bottom of the Who's Who saying simply: HCE is frequently identified with those persons. (and O my God with MOSES)

RUSSIAN General column: I think you should reverse BUTT and TAFF = it was SHEM-TAFF who hadn't the heart to shoot the Russ. Gen. 345.2–3. But as they change places throughout the chapter I may be all mistaken.
4) SYNOPSIS

>The ballad[2] accuses HCE of offenses as various as being all the invaders and exploiters of Ireland—Scandinavian and English—of homosexuality, indecent exposure, seduction of girls in the park, and of Noah's drunkenness. (The last sentence is pretty glib, ma'am. . . . presents FEW difficulties??)

>MAP? No, indeed. What does a map add to PERSONS? Your next book will be PLACE-NAMES, PEOPLES, and Languages in Finnegans Wake. I have two maps; DUBLIN (ordnance survey 1:25,000 revised to 1959,—bought at Gotham Book Mart.) and DUBLIN and ROSCOMMON, John Bartholomew & Son Ltd, Edinburgh, Revised 1961—bought at Hammond Map Store 1 East 43rd NYC 17.

My copy of your Census is falling apart—and oh—there's not enough Margin-space.

The craziest index ever made is surely Mrs Boldereff's in "Reading F—W."[3] Imagine because of one among 25 allusions having to go to WHOOTH to find HOWTH and she does that all the time.

I suspect that most of those characters are also COROTICUS King of Strathclyde (also given as CERETIC) against whom St. Patrick wrote an outraged epistle. The pirate-King having killed some of Pat's missioners

85.33 Karikature. (K. K. K. is for the raiding Ku-Klux-Klan) that little prisoner in the Dock is partly St. Patrick 86.2 padder. . . . tripartite. . . with [h]is pig (86.14) and all "paddie whacks" (Dear Patrick) .17 and his trifling = French: triefle = shamrock.

Have you found out any more about that Mr. Cornwall[4]—caught in the homosexual scandal in the Mansion House Castle—Vice-regal set? I suspect it's all over the place (St. Ives in Cornwall; look at the repulsive pages 523 ff—523.8.

The early lives of St Patrick said that he resembled Moses in four ways, as you found in 3.21–22 [i.e., .9–.10]. Fritz Senn had been working on the paragraph 4.18 ff—so full of Noah and Moses. Did he see the St. Patrick:

4.24 vipers met their exodus
.30 mitre
.31 St. Pat wrote a (lost?) treatise DE TRIBUS HABITACULIS.

LATER:

I keep my letters to you for days—always hoping to find more items to submit. But to work on FW is to get paralysis of uncertainty—an incapability to finish anything—always it seems that one is hot on the point of discovery. ¶ The Newslitter[5] has arrived. Some delightful items, but some unhelpful overchoked pages, too. I'm going to send them some dough.

Have a happy Easter—all.
Thornton

1. *The General History of Ireland* by Geoffrey Keating (1570–1644), written in Gaelic, was first translated into English in 1723. Keating's *History* extends from the earliest times to 1172.

2. "The Ballad of Persse O'Reilly" (FW 44.24–47.32).

3. Frances Motz Boldereff's *Reading 'Finnegans Wake'* (Woodward, Pennsylvania: Classic Nonfiction Library, 1959).

4. In *Census II* Glasheen identifies him as an Irish post-office official who was accused of homosexuality by Charles Stewart Parnell in the *United Irishman*.

5. *A Wake Newslitter*, edited by Fritz Senn and Clive Hart, No. 2, April 1962.

☐

To Adaline Glasheen, Farmington, Connecticut

[MS. APCS—HWS]

[postmark: 26 April 1962][1] 50 Deepwood Drive
Wednesday Hamden 17, Connecticut

Dear Adaline:
    Cobh-Cove may not be named after Noah's wife but her name in Keating[2] is given as COBHA. . . his three sons you know. . . his three daughters OLLA, OLIVIA, and OLIBANA. . . Keating vol. I 77.
    Did you know that Adam began CAIN and his sister COLMANA
                                   ABEL "   "   " DELBORA
(from the Welsh Polychronican: Keating I 76.[)]

    Look at 108.26 Shem Ham and Jophet. . . .27 COVE
    Maybe 382.21 transition to that ship departure 382.27 and all the ark on 383.21 [i.e., .9]
    I don't urge 501.26 but maybe ¶ 528.31 is certainly the Munster Town.

    There's so much of the NOAH family in ALP's last speech (622.15) that I'd certainly look on Page 620 as the family: line 15 SOM. . . . SIM. (via Tom and Tim, but you can't get away from those

Esses) and COVE as you point out in line .35 [i.e., .34], which justifies in re-examining many of the Copenhagen.

I open your letter greedily

ever
(T. N.)

P. S. I don't think Adelina Patti (Census) sang Madame Butterfly. She was 60 in 1903![3]

1. This letter is probably a response to a lost letter which Glasheen had written in reply to Wilder's letter of 20 April.
2. Geoffrey Keating, *The General History of Ireland*.
3. The first performance of Puccini's *Madama Butterfly* was given in Milan on 17 February 1904. Adelina Patti (1843–1919) retired from opera in 1897; she made a famous farewell tour in 1903 and continued to give concerts until 1914.

☐

To Adaline Glasheen, Farmington, Connecticut

[MS. ALS—HWS]

5 May 1962
50 Deepwood Drive
Hamden 17, Connecticut

Dear Adaline =
    You scare me when you ask me a question.[1]
    I'm never tired of saying "I know nothing about FW."
    Your question never occurred to me.
    Look at how confusing it is:
    626.4   Wrhps. . . . 626.6 She's at the "The Whip of the Water" where Howth Road descends to the sea. (But that would be right under Howth Castle by the enclosed Harbour—not likely to have much "whip about it." (See it J. Joyce pages 254, 319)

626.33	"Inn this linn." Linn is the highest point on Howth Head. The previous lines show it was where HCE proposed to her.
626.7	The comma after island frees us from reading Island Bridge (which is way back—a bridge and a region and a park opposite the Liffey from Phoenix Park.) In which case the island would be Ireland's Eye just north of where "whip of the waters" is, but there could be no bridge here!
626.34	.. It is reasonable that on the Linn she could wish for "better glasses" to see him in the day-light and Bailey Light.
627.3	so she's swimming or flowing. . . . . toward
628.3	The Moyle. . . the name given to the portion of the sea outside Dublin (her son goes there, too, in 428.21)

I don't think she jumps—commits suicide; I think Joyce would have gone to some length to render that (though you can consider 627.32 "we spring to be free.").

I think she flows into the Moyle. As the river Liffey. And that the walk to LINN is combined with it merely as a reminiscence of the earlier betrothal walk.

{Notice: I can give no explanation of 628.12 which I chiefly read as: like Alice, we pass through glass—to Heaven ("now we see in a glass darkly. . . later. . .face to face" 434.31–32 St. Paul, Corinthians somewhere)[}]²

x   x

Now, maybe she's blown off the top of Howth Head:

626.1   ["]I feel I could near faint away. . . . Into the deeps. Annamores leep." Which is so spelled that it is more a SLEEP than a LEAP. . . . . that WIND (626.4) as out of Norway.

x

Wouldn't Joyce give us more of consternation and drama if she were blown off?

x

Where is the evidence that she (like the girl that follows her 627.11 or like her earlier self. . . once a cloud 627.9) will now go up into the sky as moisture-absorption? We see her at once as the river by Eve and Adam!

x

So you see I can't help you one bit. I can only make it harder.

x

But I'm damned sure of one thing. This passage 619 to the end is far more a WALK to the LINN than it is a river-course to the sea. If it were the Liffey flowing to its extreme mouth we'd look for Alexandria Basin, Ringsend, Pigeonhouse, Bull Wall, Fool Beg Lighthouse, North Bull Lighthouse.

When you come to write PLACES in FW I can give you various sites on this walk (which I took myself—and a beautiful walk it is.)

Additionally puzzling is that the last pages are filled with allusions to the last pages of the Bible (and Christian entering Heaven at the close of Pilgrim's Progress?) And one might think that ALP were, like Moses, to be "lifted up" and so become a cloud—but . . . if so why the sudden forlornness of . . . ". . . a love a last. . a loved. . etc" [628.15–.16]?

x

So I've not been a particle of use.

But I rejoice that the volume is going to appear.

I will be far away by then. I am gently intimating to many friends that I shall be reading few letters out there; but Yours are among the few that I shall open with eagerness. (Address: via Deepwood Drive—with your name on the envelope. I don't know my future address yet.)

> Cordial best to all
> Ever
> (T)

[enclosed sheet]

457.32 s, engine. St. John in England is pronounced Sinjon. (see Mont St Jean 274.2[)]
193.11 Swift's lampoon on Godolphin: Sid Hamet's Rod[3]
   .15 Swift not only called himself CADENUS—but Vanessa and himself used CAD frequently (Quintana's Life).[4] So Cadbury gives us the fact that they both lived in BURY St. Don't you think—previous page [arrow to Montjoy]
192.35 {Esther}. . . . . Johnson[5] (spelt with a y to get in Montjoyhison)—supposed daughter of TEMPLE. . . Swift born. . . 36 in hay HOY St.
        I'm now sure that it was Swift who is [arrow to "Divinus, below]
 14.13 Caddy went to Winehouse (Divinus) and wrote a farce.

---

1. A reference to a lost letter or to a telephone conversation.

2. Wilder slightly misquotes from *I Corinthians*, 13:12.

3. Jonathan Swift's "The Virtues of Sid Hamet the Magician's Rod" (1710). In 1708, Swift represented the clergy of Ireland in their effort to get a grant of the first-fruits from Sidney Godolphin, the Lord Treasurer and first Earl of Godolphin. The title plays on Godolphin's first name and his staff of office. Swift borrows the name, Cid Hamet Benegeli, from the suppositious author of Cervantes's *Don Quixote*.

4. Ricardo Quintana, *The Mind and Art of Jonathan Swift* (1936; rpt., London: Oxford University Press, 1953), 221–225. In his poem "Cadenus and Vanessa" (1713), Swift tells the story of his friendship with Esther Vanhomrigh (Vanessa).

5. Swift's Stella in his poems and *Journal to Stella*. See TW to AG, 11 July 1959, n. 3.

□

To Adaline Glasheen, Farmington, Connecticut

[MS. ALS—HWS]

[? 18–20 May 1962][1]   Hotel Algonquin
59 West 44th Street
New York, 36, N. Y.

Dear Adaline =
   I want to try something on you.
   Joyce loved the chapter-titles of Ulysses and puts them over and over in FW.
   Take ALP's farewell

1 Telemachus	(can't find it.[)]
2 Nestor	624.6 [i.e., .26] nasturtls.
3 Proteus	626.18 [i.e., .19] sealsker (In Homer, he lives surrounded by seals.)
4 Calypso	can't find
5 Lotus eaters	[620.3] the very lotust
6 Hades	621.26 burnt in ice. (That's CAINA, the lowest part of Dante's inferno)
7 AEOLUS	621.6 windbags
8 Lestrygonians (cannibals)	621.5 [i.e., .25] hugon (Ugolino—ate his sons—and in The Inferno is eating his enemy).
9 Scylla and C.	620.33 dogging you round cove and haven (SKYLAX means little bitch.[)]
	620.34 [i.e., .35] swishbarque waves or
	621.15 woolpalls
10 Wandering Rocks	623.4 [i.e., .24] rollcky roll-rock
11 Sirens	622.32 "stick this in your ear,"

12 Cyclops	can't find!!
13 Nausicaa	can't find
14 Oxen etc	621.15 [i.e., .14] Oaxmealturn
15 Circe	can't find.
16 Eumaeus	can't find
17 Ithaca	" "
18 Penelope	622.9–10 antilopes. . . penisoles = antisoles. . . penilopes.

Look what he does elsewhere with Calypso = (nymph of KALPE[)] Gibraltar

5.27	collupsus
229.13	Ukalepe
297.10	fillies calpered
193.31 [i.e., 197.31]	smell of her kelp. She lived on the island of Ogygia—hard g's = So probably
206.14	O gig goggle of gigguels
363.36	Meggy Guggy's giggag.
{363.20	fellows culpows
{363.32	I am incalpable
79.18	Venuses were gigglibly temptatrix

Certainly the same catalogue must be in The Shem The Penman Chapter[2]

	1.	176.36 telemac or 179.11 [i.e., .17] dedal
	2.	177.14 nobookishoNESTER
Proteus	3.	
	4.	176.34 collapsed
Lotus	5.	
	6.	177.10 Sheols or 183.35 Hades
	7.	175.33 Niscemus Nemon (because in 229.13 Joyce calls this section Nemo in Patria)
Lestry.	8.	
Scylla	9	
Rocks	10.	
Sirens	11.	
Cyclops	12	[174.19] onewinker..
Nausicaa	13.	
	14.	175.31 misoxenetic

Circe	15	176.28 scented curses of. . . . belles. {Bella Cohen}
Eumaeus	16	182.15–[1]6 "sharing a precipitation["]. . . etc scene from Ulysses.
Ithaca	17.	
Penelope	18	

See what he does with Proteus: 324.8
encient. . . . murrainer. . .wallruse. .merman. . . seal. . . Thallassa.

Another Seven Rainbow 59.2–14
    russets [.2]
    orange [.8]
    lemon [.8]
    virid [.11]
    climatitis, blue "all branches of["]—hence indigo [.12–.13]
    pansie [.14]

Got a fine letter from our Zürich friend.[3]
Do you think that's Madame Marian Tweety—40.23 or is it merely Oscar Wilde, the caterpillar sitting on his mushroom?

                My "article's" getting on.[4]
                Best to you both

                Ever
                (T)

---

1. Wilder was in New York for several days before beginning his drive to Arizona.
2. Joyce's title for FW I, vii (169.1–195.6).
3. Fritz Senn.
4. "Giordano Bruno's Last Meal in *Finnegans Wake*."

To Adaline Glasheen, Farmington, Connecticut
[MS. ALS—HWS]

[postmark: 12 July 1962]   Address: General Delivery
                                      Douglas
                                      Arizona

Dear Adalina =
    Here's a little piece I've sent on to Fritz [Senn] for the *Newslitter*.[1]
    "May quietly amuse"—and horrify.
    I'm doing another for the PMLA[2] which I'll send on to you when it's ready.

x

    The desert is glorious.
    And silence and solitude is just what I needed.

x

    Do I have to remind you that I rejoice in hearing from you?

              Devoted best to you all—
               Ever
               Thornton

---

1. Enclosed was a draft of Wilder's essay, "Giordano Bruno's Last Meal in *Finnegans Wake*."
2. Wilder did not publish an article in *PMLA*.

To Thornton Wilder, Hamden, Connecticut
[MS. TL—YCAL]

14 July 1962 [22 Carrington Lane
 Farmington, Connecticut]

Dear Thornton,

Beautiful, beautiful, beautiful. Oh my dear man, what a lovely, what a model explication of FW!!!!! Not one imperfection. Sheer goodness.

What are you writing on for PMLA?

I did not write because I'd nothing to say. After getting the 2nd ed finished I went into a healthy enough trough where FW is concerned. A distinctly grousing envy of your Bruno piece is not going to bring me out. But twill pass.

And oh the joy of Fritz [Senn] and Clive [Hart][1] who have been beefing over the poverty of mind of those who would contribute to the Litter. The best things they got were at best, mild. Now!

But, as I say, I've not anything to say about FW, bar the Ulysses bit I sent you,[2] was it yesterday? The summer is not bad here so far. My husband teaches summer school. I slut around the house. Alison works in the Emergency Room at Hartford Hospital and loving it, makes it sound not like literature but the rankest TV—Ben Casey, do you watch Ben Casey? Like that—switch-blade knives and women who drank ammonia. Our dog has maggots, our cat will soon kitten.

Till I do have something to say worth your hearing, I remain in deepest admiration,

 Faithfully,
 A. Glasheen

---

1. The editors of *A Wake Newslitter*, where Wilder's essay was published in No. 6, October 1962.
2. What Glasheen sent is not known.

To Adaline Glasheen, Farmington, Connecticut

[MS. ALS—HWS]

[? July 1962][1]   [Douglas, Arizona]

PS
    I expect that's pretty import[ant] that the Margaret-Margot is the Magpie-Dominican. (They are "pied" french *pie* magpie—piebald nag etc)
    So the Mime of the *Maggies* does not primarily mean the girls— they are the "Floras" and the Jennies[.]
    Must we think all those "Majesties" over again?

T N W.

1. This undated letter is a "postscript" to Wilder's letter of 12 July 1962. Attached to the note is a revised and expanded typescript of Wilder's "Giordano Bruno's Last Meal in *Finnegans Wake*." On top of the typescript Wilder wrote: "For A. G. expanded version—fun, eh? TNW new stuff on pages 2 and bottom of p. 8." This draft includes minor corrections made in Wilder's hand and several marginal comments by Glasheen. The references in this note are discussed in his article.

To Adaline Glasheen, Farmington, Connecticut

[MS. ALS—HWS]

[postmark: 6 September 1962]   General Delivery
Labor Day [3 September], 1962   Douglas, Arizona

Dear Adaline =
    Well, well, milady, it's time to assemble the workshop for Edition FOUR of the Census.
    I'm too far away for you to throw your typewriter at me.

I think it's time you can drop the Census dagger.¹ There are darn few names that don't mean someone else also. I think you might use a sign that means "identification supported by related material in the context." People who haven't worked years in FW can scarcely believe the extent to which Joyce can make a syllable relate remotely to a person. E. G. Every "Pop" in "Pop goes the weasel" refers to Amalia Popper of Trieste²—Sez I.

But today:

Joyce's identification of himself with John Sullivan,³ the tenor-he-might-have-been, was boundless. It's Sullivan and not Stanislaus who was his *semieuse*⁴ *twin*. And the opera roles are all over the place. Imagine anyone shouting out in the Paris Opera as Joyce did twice! Shocking! (Ellmann p. 638) [1982: 624–625]

VASCO da Gama in L'AFRICANA [i.e., *L'Africaine*] (Meyerbeer) Chief aria: O Paradiso.

{Vasco means Basque. By Grimm's law: B = V. The Bay of Biscay is in Spanish Vizcaya.} [margin: The basque allusions may also be de Valera who came of basque stock.] [{]So all the "basques" I can find refer to this explorer and his role in the opera, and Sullivan who sings it.}

Hamlet: It appears that because of Sullivan's singing the role in Ambroise Thomas' opera, the opera takes precedence over Shakespeare's play.

ROMEO ditto Gounod's opera.⁵

RAOUL in Huguenot's.⁶ But you haven't scratched the surface. It appears to me that every damn "roll" in FW goes back to the Huguenots.

POLLIONE in NORMA.⁷ Called Pollio. Related by a false etymology to POLLUX

NABUCCO (Nebuchadnezzar) I doubt Sullivan sang this in Paris. J J would have heard it in Italy. One of its choruses played a big part in the Italian risorgimento⁸

SAMSON and Delilah; Forza del Destino; Carmen = Don José;⁹ Pelléas; Nemorino in Elixir d'Amor; Duke in Rigoletto; Tristan¹⁰ Hoel-Dinorah CALAF in TURANDOT Des Grieux in Manon¹¹

ARMAND = Traviata Pinkerton in Butterfly Ottavio in Don Giovanni¹²

MASKED BALL AIDA TRAVIATA¹³

First some easy ones that you've marked mostly already.

512.10 (Masked Ball) 15 Vasco da Gama 16 Hugenot 17 caecodedition = blinding of Samson: 18 Don Alvaro in

	Forza del Destino takes the name of Don Frederico HERREROS. 13 Hussif = Arab. Sura 12 YUSUF: Joseph = Don José Carmen.
465.16	Cork (Sullivan and J J's father from Cork); Manrico as Conte de Luna-Trovatore; 21 Nebuchadnezzar—first vegetarian (only worse!);[14] 22 have a hug (Huguenot!!) a pullet, 24 (I think this is POLLIO because of the mistletoe in .27 "Norma" opens with herself as Druid priestess holding the golden sickle to cut the mistletoe. 32 Ophelia—Hamlet 35 swansway = Lohengrin.[15]
456.8	gimme = GAMA; [.10] Oliviero = Alvaro = force of Destiny 14 Huguenots 22 Naboc. ERIC (tenor role in Flying Dutchman);[16] 25 RAOUL. 26 TAMINO in Magic Flute 27 roomiest-Romeo;[17] 30 Thaddeus = Bohemian Girl; [.31] Jukes = Duke Rigoletto[18]
32	Marshalsea = Marcel in Huguenot sings the ever famous Piff Paff aria and the opera contains a Ratatatat chorus .36.[19]

Now some stranger and harder:

5.30	Walhalla = Siegfried's Rolls-Raouls[20] 31 stonengens (Joyce said Sullivan's voice was like Stonehenge[)] = (Ellmann page 633) [1982: 620] Tramtrees = Treestam = 35 in Cavalleria Turridu bites the ear of Alfio in challenge over a woman.[21]

133.19–20 add ELEAZAR (Halévy's La Juive) and SULIKA-sulka [i.e., Selika] in L'Africana.[22]

143.3	BASK = VAXO AROMA = ROMEO
5	gouty = Goethe = Faust
7	Hamlet
10	(make a note of: the answer to Turandot's[23] first riddle was SPERANZA-hope[)]
11	d egregiunt = Des Grieux in Manon
15	Hoel in Dinorah
19	poignings = blessing of the Poignards = Huguenot
24	Pale = palls POLLIO
26	Violet = Violetta = Traviata

530.	2 blind to the world. . 3 Hebrew for Samson = SHIMSHON. . 16 J J said Sullivan looked like a member of the Dublin Metropolitan Police (Ellman[n] 633) [1982: 620].

93.29 [i.e., .30]   Even though another Sullivan wrote "Tramp Tramp Tramp"[24] it's the Tenor here—

I have so many notes I don't know what to pick next but I'll show how these roles are distributed through the final pages:
- 620.1   Yore Tales of Hoffman[n]: He has his shadow stolen from it [i.e., him] but gets it back.[25]
- 7   flying Dutchman.
- 621.11   maybe GAMES = GAMA 13 RADULLY = POLLIONE Rolly Polly
- 14–15 [i.e., .24–.25]   The famous blessing of the poniards in Huguenots begins "GLAIVES PIEUX";[26] here is the glamis and the Hugon
- 36   Tristan
- 622.9–10 ANTI-LOPE x PENI-SOLE = I suspect D'Indy's Penelope put on at the Paris Opera in the 20's
- 23   SULLIVAN!
- 24   MASKED BALL and OSCAR is the Page in M'd B'l.
- 25 x 28   NILE and or AIDA ing
- 622.30 x 31   pole . . . poll = POLLIO
- 33   I think all the HU and CRY s are "Huguenots"
- 623.1   Eric in Flying D—man
- .12   I think most of the Chinese interjections are from TURANDOT which is all about riddles.
- 16   "Remember Bartholomew's Eve" = Huguenots
- 624.19–20 One of the days = Butterfly Un be[l] di
- 625.3–4   Aida 35 Agata = Der Freischutz[27]
- 626.2   I take most of the STRONGBOWS for Tell[28]

TELL = see
- 343.1   Those poignards. . . Sagitarius Bowman = Strongbow
- 3 [i.e., .4]   strangbones. . . camp camp camp. = Tramp etc by Sullivan
- 6   marshalled = Marcel Huguenots Hail = Hoel
- 8.   Tell

Sullivan did not sing the role of Tell in the opera but that of "Arnold."

> Incidentally there are 3 characters in Turandot named PING, PANG, and PONG! And the tenor hero is a rash youth named CALAF 426.13 and the son of the exiled TIMUR of TARTAR 136.21 (which Joyce first printed and then corrected to TORTUR[)]

The NEXT DAY, Sept 4.

As always many thanks.

Yes,[29] the editors of *Newslitter* made a mistake in dumping those two over-lint-picking pieces into their magazine.[30] They'd had them stored in the ice-box a long time, anyway, and in the first enthusiasm of editorship they stuck them in.

[Fritz] Senn wrote me that they planned *not* to have longer articles in the future. So I was chagrined to send my number,[31] because I think that principle of briefer query-and-answer is right.

So please don't write Senn.

Did he tell you he's going through a time of unsettlement and dejection? Don't mention it unless he mentions it first.

Lord knows, anybody who gets hooked with FW goes through dreadful hours, but I think he's got it worse than the rest of us.

Thanks for the items.

I am disappointed in Sullivan[32] on 184. You know how I wrestle with that important paragraph. Did you give him my Sade-Soda-Saumanne readings.[33] I'm delighted though with *ab ovo usque ad mala* [.28].[34] Oh, oh, if someone would tell me who B de B Meinfelde [.28] is ([Thomas] Moore wrote Lalla Rookh [.16] at Mayfield Cottage, but it's not enough for me here)[.]

Now a little marshmallow to end the meal.

You know J J's absurd infatuation for Martha Fleischmann[35] of Zurich {Ellmann 462ff} [1982: 448ff]—that piteous comical and sleazy and wet-firecracker amour—oh how I dislike Joyce as a person any way!

Well while that was going on in Zurich he was living in Seefeld Street.

So read

"Siegfield follies and or a Gentlehomme's Faut Pas" 106.12

Don't you think that's funny?

          Best to all Glasheens—
          Ever
          Thornton

1. In *Census I* and *II* Glasheen used a dagger to mark "a composite drawn from the names of two or more people"; in *Census III* a plus sign (+) replaced the dagger.

2. Amalia Popper (1891–1967) was a student of Joyce's in Trieste in 1907–1908. She is the "Who?" of the opening page of Joyce's *Giacomo Joyce*, a series of sketches completed in 1914 but not published until 1968. She is the model for Beatrice Justice in Joyce's play *Exiles*, she contributed to the Southern European looks of Molly Bloom, and she may be included in Issy's character in the *Wake*. See Vicki Mahaffey's "Fascism and Silence: The Coded History of Amalia Popper," in *James Joyce Quarterly*, 32, 3/4 (Spring/Summer 1995), 501–522; see Richard Ellmann's introduction and notes in *Giacomo Joyce* (London: Faber & Faber, 1968).

3. See TW to AG, 11 October 1959, for a similar discussion of the Joyce-Sullivan friendship and *Finnegans Wake*.

4. There is no such word in French; this may be an error for *Siamois*.

5. Charles Gounod's *Roméo et Juliette*.

6. Giacomo Meyerbeer's *Les Huguenots*.

7. Vincenzo Bellini's *Norma*.

8. In the second scene of the third part of Giuseppe Verdi's *Nabucco*, a chorus of Hebrews, on the banks of the Euphrates River, sings "Va, pensiero, sull'ali dorate" ("Fly, thought, on wings of gold"). This chorus became popular with the Italian Risorgimento movement.

9. Camille Saint-Saëns's *Samson et Dalila*; Giuseppe Verdi's *La Forza del Destino*; Georges Bizet's *Carmen*.

10. Claude Debussy's *Pelléas et Mélisande*; Gaetano Donizetti's *L'Elisir d'Amore*; Giuseppe Verdi's *Rigoletto*; Richard Wagner's *Tristan und Isolde*.

11. Giacomo Meyerbeer's *Dinorah*; Giacomo Puccini's *Turandot*; Jules Massenet's *Manon*.

12. Giuseppe Verdi's *La Traviata*; Giacomo Puccini's *Madama Butterfly*; Wolfgang Amadeus Mozart's *Don Giovanni*.

13. Three operas by Giuseppe Verdi: *Un Ballo in Maschera* (*A Masked Ball*), *Aida*, and *La Traviata*.

14. Characters in Giuseppe Verdi's *Il Trovatore* and *Nabucco*.

15. Richard Wagner's *Lohengrin*.

16. Giuseppe Verdi's *Nabucco*; Giacomo Meyerbeer's *Les Huguenots*; Richard Wagner's *Der Fliegende Holländer* (*The Flying Dutchman*).

17. Raoul in Meyerbeer's *Les Huguenots*; Tamino in Mozart's *Die Zauberflöte* (*The Magic Flute*); Roméo in Gounod's *Roméo et Juliette*.

18. Michael Balfe's *The Bohemian Girl*; Verdi's *Rigoletto*.

19. Giacomo Meyerbeer's *Les Huguenots*: the "Piff Paff aria," a battle song of the Huguenots, is sung by Marcel in Act I; in the ensemble that opens Act III, the soldiers sing "Rataplan, rataplan" (the phrase is not translatable), a call to war.

20. Valhalla, the home of the gods in Wagner's *Der Ring des Nibelungen*. Siegfried is the hero in *Siegfried* and in *Die Götterdämmerung*. Raoul de Nangis is a Protestant gentleman in Meyerbeer's *Les Huguenots*.

21. Pietro Mascagni's *Cavalleria Rusticana*.

22. Fromental Halévy's *La Juive*; Meyerbeer's *L'Africaine*.

23. Princess Turandot in Puccini's *Turandot*.

24. Timothy Daniel Sullivan (1827–1914). His song, "God Save Ireland," written to the tune of "Tramp, Tramp Tramp, the Boys are Marching," is about the execution of the Manchester Martyrs of 1867.

25. Wilder probably means 359.24–.25. In the "Giulietta" section of Offenbach's *Les Contes d'Hoffmann* (*The Tales of Hoffmann*), Hoffmann discovers he has no reflection when he looks into a mirror.

26. In Act IV, three Monks bless the pious blades of the "poniards" or swords of the Catholic soldiers who are about to massacre the Huguenots.

27. Carl Maria von Weber's *Der Freischütz*.

28. Giacomo Rossini's *Guillaume Tell*.

29. In this section Wilder seems to be responding to a lost letter.

30. *A Wake Newslitter*, No. 4, July 1962. It is difficult to determine which articles Wilder means.

31. Wilder's "Giordano Bruno's Last Meal in *Finnegans Wake*" was published in *A Wake Newslitter*, No. 6 (October 1962).

32. Possibly a reference to Philip B. Sullivan made by Glasheen in her letter.

33. See TW to AG, 20 September 1960.

34. "From the eggs to the apples: from start to finish" (McHugh).

35. Joyce first saw Fleischmann (1885–1950) in December 1918. She appeared to him to look like the young girl he had seen wading in the Irish Sea in 1902. He followed her, and, without knowing her name, sent her a letter. According to Ellmann in *James Joyce*, she claimed that theirs was a platonic relationship. At the time that Joyce met her she lived with her lover, the engineer Rudolf Hiltpold, at 6 Culmannstrasse and the Joyces were living at 29 Universitätstrasse. The Joyces had lived in two different apartments in Seefeldstrasse from March 1916 to October 1917. The relationship lasted until the Joyces left for Trieste on 16 October 1919. Martha Fleischmann (Ellmann alternates between Martha and Marthe) is, according to Ellmann, a prototype of Gerty MacDowell in *Ulysses* and in part the prototype of Martha Clifford, to whom Bloom is always careful to write with Greek *e*'s, as Joyce does in his letters to Fleischmann. Joyce's letters to her, and an essay on her relationship with Joyce by Heinrich Straumann, are in *Letters II*, 426–436.

To Adaline Glasheen, Farmington, Connecticut

[MS. ALS—HWS]

[postmark: 24 September 1962]   General Delivery
                                 Douglas, Arizona.

Dear Adaline:
   Like I always say: we know nothing about FW.
   So you're back at the Museyroom.[1]
   Well, I think there's one person in the book we haven't given enough attention to. And it's hidden deep deep deep. That's Lucia Anna Joyce[2] = LUC'AN.
   It's Folletta L A Jambe [422.33]. As she's often talking to herself in the mirror she's two girls.
   Now the Museyroom isn't about Waterloo and all those battles—that's just sly and cautious eyewash. The passage is toweringly obscene and scatological. You concede that! And it's subject is fancied sexual aggression on daughter and son. Sic!
   I think that's why it's preceded by the Brontë family:[3] the Rev. Patrick's overpowering shadow on those gifted daughters.
   LUCIA = Lucy = assuredly called LOO in the home. The IRIS is called Flower de Luce, by a popular but erroneous etymology.
   As we approach the museum we are in
   8.3–4 [i.e., .2–.3] waterloose 8.4 prettilees 8.14 Saloos. . "Up with your pike and fork!" 8.15 a PIKE is a LUCE
   9.2 looted 9.26 too loose.
It's perilous ground and Joyce has to play it with great circumspection
   71.9 lacies in loo water = LUCIA at Waterloo
And he reverses her initials =
   106.13 Jealesies = J.' A. L
   and from this I take all the Jack and Jills 211.15
318.10 jilt. . . with 318.14 glowworld lamp = French for a glowworm is
       LUCIOLE!
So here I read 9.7 jillous for Lucia.
                    x   x
   LUCIA is LILITH-LILY, and the way a LOO-LOO becomes a LILY is shown us on Page 58.6 LOU LOU .18 lo! lo! .30 Lili

So you've got all your Lily's of Killarney into one picture; and a-lis, a-lys.

There are hundreds of references!

No wonder the girl went insane in that psychic atmosphere.

I wish I could write you a less malodorous letter. I hope to next time. I rejoice in *your* letter.[4]

   Cordial best to all
   Thornton

[verso]
OVER Read the other page first

MUSEYROOM; odd data I can relate
8.36	Since this is King Arthur's EXCALIBUR—with the Arthur to come 9.5—9.26 may it be that the JINNIES of 8.3 which is firmly singular could be here JENNY for JENNIFER—GUINIVERE?
9.6	Fontenoy St was the last residence of the "Joyces" in Dublin[.] The Pfauen Peacock Restaurant in Zurich[5]—where he ate so often—is in the RENNWEG 9.35
8.28	The Delia is a compliment to A. L. P., but the ear hears the Julian Alps which overhang Trieste
8.20–10.18	with all this Copenhagen around I can't rid myself of seeing Hans Christian Andersen everywhere: Inc: The GOLUSHES of Distance (so suitable for FW.—you can travel anywhere in time); and The Tinder Box and The Little Match Girl.[6]

Branler 9.34 is a sexually indecent expression which I've only seen in the novels of Genet where one sees everything: foutre 9.14–.17–.20 used to be expressed by an asterisk but is now used everywhere.[7]

9.20 Best read Joyce the old lecher after his 100-days indulgence of fancies about Amalia Popper; and Martha Fleischmann in marathon merry 9.33

9.21 Tarra's widdars (He doubles the "R" also tarrascone 227.35 and Tarra water 319.25.) The blessed-Blessés are maybe girls = Terra's widowed relicts.

1. FW 7.20–10.24.
2. Lucia Joyce, the second of Joyce's children, was born in Trieste on 26 July 1907. As early as 1920, the signs of mental illness that were to plague her had begun to become apparent to the family. In May 1932 she was hospitalized for the first time. When World War II broke out, Joyce was unable to arrange to have her released from the hospital to take her to Switzerland. After the war, she was transferred to St. Andrew's Hospital in Northampton, England, where she remained until her death on 12 December 1982.
3. FW 7.20–8.8.
4. A lost letter.
5. The restaurant where Joyce and Frank Budgen used to meet in 1918.
6. Hans Christian Andersen (1805–1875) the Danish writer. Wilder cites the titles of three of his tales; however, the first is generally translated as "The Galoshes of Fortune." Joyce visited Copenhagen from the end of August to 11 September 1936.
7. Joyce's word is "branlish"; in French *branler* is to "masturbate." *Foutre*, which does not appear, per se, on the pages Wilder cites, means "to fuck."

☐

To Adaline Glasheen, Farmington, Connecticut

[MS. ALS—HWS]

[?25–30 September 1962]   [Douglas, Arizona]

POSTSCRIPT = LUCIA

Joyce had to go far afield to find allusions to his daughter that were not too easily decipherable.

He found: The Nightingale = genes LUSCINIA:
So we get that whole complex: Florence Nightingale and Jenny Lind the Swedish Nightingale:

What is there in that passage 359.31—360.16 to connect all those nightingales with LUCIA?

Well, there's 359.32 Alys (if you are now conceding the connection Lucia—Lily.)

  359.34   waldalure—Waterloo—Mont St Jean (if you are now
            conceding a connection Lucia—Waterloo)
  359.35   allies (if you are now conceding a connection Alice-in-
            wonderland—Lucia)

{Note: Moore Park 359.35–36 wraps in Hester-Stella-Swift to the nexus—long thought to be a quasi-incest relation}

{360.2   Floflo floreflore—I've long thought that the brother-sister business of the two FLORIOS in *'Tis Pity she's a whore* of Ford was present here.}[1]

360.3–4   Prima and secunda—the girls in the boat with Dodgson. To cap it: 360.13 LOU must wail.[2]

Antiquity disagrees as to whether it was sister Procne or Philomela who became the nightingale—but Joyce takes Ovid's Philomela. It was then Procne who's [i.e., whose] tongue was pulled out by Tereus:

248.2   Philomel, Tereus
248.10   Tereus became the hoopoe and sang POU
248.8   lingua 248.20 tongue for luncheon
248.17   so that's Flo-Florence nightingale.
        NOW is LUCIA here? I suggest
248.10   Allysloper[3] (with a reference to Miss Sloper—the father-bound daughter in H. James's Washington Square.[)]
248.18   beetle. . . .fly. . . firefly = fr. LUCIOLE (see 29.7)

And MAYBE the much-sought HELITROPE is the SUN-DAY-LIGHT-LUX-LUCIA. 248.13 "The FLO over that stars the day."

Anyway, if almost any FLO can stand for a Nightingale and any nightingale for a LUSCINIA-LUCIA we see Lucia in two forms on page 417.17–18 Floh and Luse and .29 Floh and Luse (and Bienie [.30] is Bee, Beatrice—Dante's—which is a whole other story.)

And can we dare say that most Jennies are the Swedish Nightingale—and hence again LUSCINIA-LUCIA.

Which brings us back to the Museyroom.

Look at the birds = 8.31 Leghorn hens 8.33 doves 8.34 ravens.

Suggestions:

[4](2) Hans Christian Anderson was shyly in love with Jenny Lind.

(3) She completely identified the song Home Sweet Home with herself.

(1) The epithet for Philomela is DAULIS—she of DAULIS. See 337.26 solowly = Russian for nightingale. 378.26–27 [i.e., 337.26–.27] dauliubs = daughter from Daulis.

I said my next letter would be of less distasteful a tone—this is not a letter.

(T)

1. John Ford (1586–1639), the English playwright. In *'Tis Pity She's a Whore* (published in 1633) Ford writes about the incestuous relationship of Annabella and Giovanni, the daughter and son of Florio, a citizen of Parma.

2. In "All in the Golden Afternoon," the prefatory verse in Charles Lutwidge Dodgson's (Lewis Carroll) *Alice's Adventures in Wonderland*, Dodgson recalls the afternoon when he and the Rev. Robinson Duckworth took the three Liddell sisters rowing on the Thames. "Prima" was the eldest sister, Lorina Charlotte (13), "Secunda" was Alice Pleasance (10), and, while not mentioned by Wilder, the Joyce line includes a reference to "Tertia" the youngest sister, Edith (8). Wilder includes her when he expands on the Lewis Carroll allusions in his letter, ? December 1963.

3. A "grotesque disreputable figure in the late 19th century paper. Also a brand of pickles and a sauce" (*Census II*).

4. Wilder crossed out the first sentence and added it to the end of the list.

☐

To Adaline Glasheen, Farmington, Connecticut

[MS. TELEGRAM—HWS]

6 October 1962   Douglas, Arizona

REMEMBER A GUINEA HENCE GUINNESS IS A GEORGE AND THE GARTER EMBLEM IS A GEORGE HONI SOIT TIP[1]

WILDER

1. This telegram, a response to a letter from an unknown correspondent that Glasheen sent to Wilder, is referred to by Wilder in his letter to Glasheen, [?October–November 1962–II].

To Adaline Glasheen, Farmington, Connecticut

[MS. ALS—HWS]

[postmark: 11 October 1962]   [Douglas, Arizona]

Dear Adaline—
The Post Office can't yet give me a numbered box; so they make me use my street address =
>   757 12th Street
>   Douglas
>   Arizona

I had an item for you from "Variety" but I've lost it—a ballet group is preparing to do one called "The Coach with the Six Insides"[1] [359.24] [.]

I can't understand people wanting to go on with such projects—at this stage of our knowledge.

¶ Isabel saw the Portrait of the Artist,[2] however, at the off-Broadway Theatre and thought it absorbing and very well acted.

>   Cordially
>   (T. N)

---

1. *The Coach With Six Insides*, a comedy written, choreographed, and staged by Jean Erdman based on *Finnegans Wake* opened at the Village South Theatre, New York, on 26 November 1962. After it closed on 17 March 1963, the production went on tour. *The Coach With Six Insides* won Vernon Rice and Obie awards in 1963. Erdman, a pupil and later the wife of Joseph Campbell, played the role of Anna Livia Plurabelle.

2. *A Portrait of the Artist as a Young Man*, adapted by Frederic Ewen, Phoebe Brand, and John Randolph from Joyce's novel was presented from 28 May 1962 until 17 February 1963 as part of a double bill with *The Barroom Monks*, a play about Irish-Americans by Joseph Carroll, at the Martinique Theatre in New York.

To Adaline Glasheen, Farmington, Connecticut

[MS. AL—HWS]

[? October 1962–I] [Douglas, Arizona]

(This was written in Tucson; I decided not to send it: but I returned to Douglas to find your letter.¹
 I wouldn't have suggested this LUCIA-line, if I hadn't accumulated pages of it[.])
 Then there are pages of GEORGIOS.²
 N. B. The children called their father BABBO.
To whom it may or may not concern =
 James Joyce—our hero of candor and modesty—pretended that he had scarcely glanced into Freud. Molly Colum was quite right to have told him scornfully to "come off it and stop posing." The fact is that he was crammed up to the neck with Freud. Hence, all the dream-distortion. Mildew Lisa³ is LUCIA (O'Deavis 41.3 Joyce first printed O'Dara; and
 in confusion with the other Isolde her mother she's 388.4
 mild Aunt LIZA is as loose as her neese LUCIA-LUCIA)
 Well, in the dream fantasy she dressed as a man and became
 an AMBREE (127.36) a girl who becomes a soldier in men's
 clothes. . . . here there are 3 of them, another allusion to the
 effeminate character of the soldiers three[.]
49.2 "His husband" (LISA O'DEAVIS O'DARA) A'Hara. . .
 "down at Heels" (like mud-heel-dy Isolde-Wesendonk
 230.12)⁴ she went off under the name of Blanco-Blanche-
 White-FUSILOUNA (note the Russian feminine form)
 Bucklovitch. Well, Adaline, LUCIA de Lammermoor
 married BUCKLAW (killed him on her wedding night and
 went musically mad);⁵ she's both a DOVE and RAVEN and
 so she was missing from the Colunbarium; and her sister-self
 the Cornix (Raven = Vasileff from Basil-Greek-Russian for
 King) also died with some remarks I don't understand,
 ((but I keep my eye on that "papal" 49.14))[.] So it
 seems that maybe POE's raven saying "nevermore"
 can be also saying LAMMERMOORE. Hold it.
Now among PANDORA's gifts Joyce first wrote = 210.7 [i.e., .10]
 O'Hara (and connected it to MacFarlane); in 210.12 I see

a marriage for Isabel, Jezebel, LOOO-ellen and in 210.13–14 Joyce first wrote[6] "a papal flag of the saints and stripes for Keveneen O'Dea." Flag is IRIS = Flower de Luce and O'Dea is our friend O'Mara-O'Hara-mild and LISA-O'Dara. (He changed *papal* to *papar* to get in the river Pharphar—139.6 where it's among the rivers of Babylon that Naaman preferred to Jordan.

I'm going to twist your arm until you see that the JOYCE family is in the forefront of this book:

211.28 an oakanknee for Conditor Sawyer = we know from 3.19–20 [i.e., .7–.8] that <u>everything</u> that has to do with GEORGIA U. S. A. (or USSR) is an allusion to GEORGIO JOYCE, and here's his sister, too, because MUSQUODOBOIT may be a river in Nova Scotia but a MUSKY is a MUSKELINQUE (I haven't got my dictionary here) which is a PIKE or LUCE. Georgio gets a wooden leg and Lucia gets some boots = shoes and boots have a uniformly sexual implication in FW.

You've seen the place where Joyce gives the full scientific name for PIKE-LUCE 525.12 Esox LUCIUS and combines it with that LOOOLIE-LILLY-LOLLY combination I pointed out to you before—525.14[.] And Esox—sends him off into oceans of bad taste with ESSEX-SUSSEX etc.

But wait until I shiver your timbers with the whole Francesco CENCI and Beatrice business.

It's time we all got back to Louisa May Alcott (except the very word LOUISA has got me scared.)

This note is UNSIGNED[7]

---

1. A lost letter.
2. George (Giorgio) Joyce (1905–1976).
3. The reference is to Isolde's aria, "Mild und leise," in Act III of Richard Wagner's *Tristan und Isolde*.
4. Mathilde Wesendonk (1828–1902) and her husband Otto, who lived in Zurich, became Richard Wagner's patrons. Wagner fell in love with her and set five of her poems to music in 1857–1858, the *Wesendonk Lieder*. Their relationship is also echoed in *Tristan und Isolde*.
5. In the third act of Gaetano Donizetti's opera *Lucia di Lammermoor*, based on Sir Walter Scott's novel *The Bride of Lammermoor*, Lucia Ashton, who is secretly in

love with Sir Edgardo Ravenswood, the mortal enemy of her family, kills her husband Lord Arturo Bucklaw and goes mad.

6. Pages 196–216 of *Finnegans Wake* were first published in *transition*, 8 (November 1927), 17–35. The pre-publication history of *Finnegans Wake* is discussed in Michael Groden's essay "A Textual and Publishing History" in *A Companion to Joyce Studies*, ed. Zack Bowen and James F. Carens (Westport, CT: Greenwood Press, 1984), 71–128.

7. Wilder's sentence.

☐

To Adaline Glasheen, Farmington, Connecticut

[MS. ALS—HWS]

[? October 1962–II][1] 757 12th St
Sat'day Douglas Arizona

Dear Adaline =
    Some other work is going to pull me off FW for a time; but *don't* let that mean that I'm off your mailing list.
    So I can't now assemble the massive demonstration rê *The Cenci*.
    I append a leaf I've been saving for some time.[2]
                       x
Now your letter:[3]
    I thought you agreed long ago that there is really only ONE girl—but that J. J.'s theory about girls is that they are of dual nature—narcissistic—talk to themselves in mirrors.[4] SWIFT was beset by two, but it served J's purpose that they both had (about the same name[)]. One is a goody girl and one is bad. And there they are 27.11–21 Esther-Jane-John. . . and Esther-Sean-John.
    And being mirror-images they look alike and are SOSIE, French comedies after the Greek comedies are full of identical twins called SOSIE and it's a current word in French usage.
    SO = there she is in that first (or pseudo-first) paragraph where you complain that you can't find her. You can't find her by express name as you can the rest of the family because LUCY is the hot-box of the book = JOYCE couldn't risk sharp readers excavating certain material too soon. And it's taken years to excavate SOSIE (3.24

[i.e., .12]—SUSIE-LILY-LUCIA) and who are these two-in-one girls wrathy at? The father-lover image in Dean Swift who is himself split—twone—into the Duple-Shem-Shaun.

x

I can't find any quotes from *Lucia di Lammermoor*. She wanted to marry Edgar of Ravenswood[.][5]

x

I'm returning this letter (from whom?) Do assure him that my odd telegram to you was not irresponsible mystification. I'd hate to be thought of as one further clouding the waters.[6]

x

If you really wanted the "I am" "YAM"—they are 253.24 304.8 455.23 481.35 604.23. I was brought up to believe that it was a "signature" of God.

x

The stolen cotton gloves are 434.5–6

x

Terrible old Cenci's name was FRANCESCO.[7] Joyce doesn't want to bring it to the surface and he goes very far afield to introduce him. The Old Norse for goat is GEIT. . . 71.11 Goldy Geit = Rich old goat = Golden Gate = San Francisco.
Now read 433.32
(and a little flick on 433.1 and all those Beatrice-Bees Buzzing on 430.20[)]

x

I'm almost ready to do a piece on the opening of the sermon;[8] but the material is obnoxious.
(1) A station of the cross
(2) St Benedict to his sister.
(3) Claudio to Isabella (German for *Measure for Measure* is *Mass für Mass*) (433.10)
("Let your story be brief" 433.24 etc. . .)
(4) And now the Cencis.
And always dodging under the surface LUCIA—

x

I'm going to close FW for 6 weeks; but you know whom you can make grateful with nuggets of discovery.

x

Most of your letters will go to the Yale Library—yes, but let's make an arrangement that certain ones really too full of clinical stuff we will silently destroy. I think we should be proud to be in the first generation of FW workers. There was an honorable generation before

us [Edmund] Wilson and Harry Levin[9] but they did over all—cartoon—
we're the first ones to sift, sift, sift.

>Best to all
>Ever
>Thornt.

A rich friend discarded an air-cruise trip to Spain to Isabel. . . .
she's in Madrid today. A guided cruise but for and by specialists in
painting etc. I'm awfully happy for her.

[attached sheet]

TOWARDS NEXT EDITION OF CENSUS

St. EXUPERANTIA   (maybe EXUPERANTIUS; confer St. Exupéry!)
 martyr saint, buried with SS. REGULA and St. Felix in the Old
 Munster at Zurich.
 612.3 EXUBER. . . . .5 SUPEREXUBERABUNDANCY.
 (see 610.8 fenicitas = concealed-Felicitas = Felix; 610.9 [i.e., .10]
 rugular = Regula)
 58.8?

DERBY—DARBY: (the hero Lionel in the opera MARTHA[10] will
 inherit the title of Earl of Derby and marry LADY HARRIET-
 Henrietta. The allusions are to Martha Fleischmann.)

180.15	dearby darby— {Hodgart and Worthington tell us that 180.6 contains an allusion to the aria M'appari from MARTHA. Also 180.5 squealed. . . squall is the aria *Squilli* from *Il Trovatore*[11] and "sponiards" 180.11 is the "blessing of the poignards["] from HUGUENOTS.}
454.16	{Hodgart-Worthington give *M'appari* from *Martha*}. . . 32. Derby
433.10–11	{Hodg-Worth} *Last Rose of Summer* from *Martha*}. . . 16 Dar Bey
?49.27	Last rose. . . . 24 upsomdowns = Derby is at Epsom Dounes
?	(On page 371.15–16 puts the "LAST ROSE" together with its tune "The Groves of Blarney)["]. On PAGE 472.6–7 we have the Groves of Blarney (indirectly from MARTHA and across the page 473.9 Darby).

SIMMONS, founder of KU-KLUX KLAN.[12]
  367.13 Simmence {25 invisible empire; 8 mask. . . mask. . . etc.[}]
  (.11 Kallikak = KKK)

Verify: In Goethe's Wilhelm Meister[13] = MIGNON 268.10 and Philine 268.18

EON, d CHARLES Chevalier (hermaphrodite) b. at Tonnerre, called Maid of Tonnerre
585.1 eons. . . . 11 paratonnerwetter (Par[a]tonnere, Fr. lightning rod etc)
291.28 nEONovene babe. . n.8 Charles
  I suspect many more, but tremble to submit them to you

---

1. This undated letter, of either 20 or 27 October, follows Wilder's previous letter, [? October 1962–I] where he promised to write about *The Cenci*.
2. This "leaf" did not remain with the letter. It is possible, however, that what Wilder sent was a typed sheet, with corrections and additions in his hand and titled "TWINS." See Appendix VII.
3. A lost letter.
4. This theme is explored in numerous letters written in 1961. See also, TW to AG, 24 September 1962.
5. Referred to in Wilder's previous letter.
6. Wilder's telegram of 6 October 1962. The unknown correspondent may have been Philip L. Graham, a close friend of Glasheen's who was engaged in explicating material in *Finnegans Wake*. Wilder's next letter to Glasheen, 29 October, begins with a mention of Captain Francis Grose's *A Classical Dictionary of the Vulgar Tongue* (1785). Graham discusses Joyce's use of this book in his articles: "re'furloined notepaper (419.29)" in *A Wake Newslitter*, No. 7 (November 1962), [1]–4 and "More Groseness," No. 9 (January 1963), 7–8. See Graham to Glasheen, 11 and 17 October 1962 in HWS.
7. Beatrice Cenci (1577–1599), with her step-mother Lucrezia and her brother Giacomo, plotted to have two men murder Francesco Cenci because of his cruelty to his wife and children. During her trial, her lawyer accused her father of attempting to commit incest with her. Beatrice, her step-mother, and brother were executed on 10 September 1599. Another brother, Bernardo, too young to have been involved in the murder, watched the killing of his family and was then killed. The story has been a theme in poetry and art. Shelley's verse-tragedy, *The Cenci* (1819), was sparked by his viewing the Guido Reni portrait of Beatrice (1598–1599).
8. *Finnegans Wake* 431.21–457.24. "Jaun's sermon or letter on female chastity is the 'savingsbook,' dedicated to Swift's chaste, dead Stella, which he promised in the First Watch (412.30–413.26)" (*Census II*, xlix).
9. Edmund Wilson (1895–1972) wrote a number of articles about Joyce. Joyce is also discussed in a chapter of his 1931 book, *Axel's Castle: A Study of the Imaginative*

Literature of 1870–1930. Harry Levin (1912–1994), a professor of English at Harvard University, wrote *James Joyce: A Critical Introduction* in 1941, and in 1946, *The Portable James Joyce* was published by the Viking Press. Wilder was a friend of both men.

10. *Martha*, an opera in five acts with music by Friedrich von Flotow (1812–1883) and a text by W. Friedrich.

11. In Verdi's *Il Trovatore* (II, ii), the Count di Luna and Ferrando, his captain of the guard, are preparing to abduct Leonora before she can take her vows. As they await her arrival, a bell sounds and the count sings "Qual suono! Oh ciel!" ("That sound! Oh heaven!") to which Ferrando replies, "La squilla/Vicino il rito annunzia" ("Its tolling/announces the approaching rite").

12. The original Ku Klux Klan was founded in Pulaski, Tennessee, on 24 December 1865. The Klan was disbanded in 1869, and in 1871 President Ulysses S. Grant issued a proclamation calling on members of illegal organizations to disarm and disband. The new Klan, organized by a former preacher, Colonel William Simmons, was incorporated in Georgia in 1915.

13. Two novels by Goethe: *Wilhelm Meister's Apprenticeship* (1795–1796) and *Wilhelm Meister's Wanderings* (1821–1829).

☐

To Adaline Glasheen, Farmington, Connecticut

[MS. ALS—HWS]

29 October 1962   757 12th St
                                                      Douglas Arizona

Dear Adaline =

The U. of Arizona has an "original" Grose[1] which I made notes on as far as M.

Those compendia are wearisome reading. Dandruff-covered antiquarians run them up—enough material to be of interest for six pages; the rest they fill out with the self-evident, the irrelevant, and the dubious. As tho' I made a list of American words.

> Bull's eye: center of a target—hence an accurate guess or answer.
> skirt (pej[orative]) woman.
> Zowie: expression of happy surprise (see: "What do you know!"[)]
> fest: party (Ital: fiesta?)

x

Rê: obscenity.

I'm not sure I understand your question.[2]

Years ago I asserted to you that FW was a toweringly indecent book,—that was only the first step in appraising it.

(1) Indecent: allusions to the physiology of excretion and generation,—a legitimate expression of human communication and literature, grave and comic, relative to situations and intention. Aristophanes and Rabelais are constantly indecent.

(2) Obscene: the indecent with a heightened element of insistance,—the will to revolt, disgust, or offend.

(3) Pornographic: the indecent designed to arouse impure emotion.

(4) I cannot find a name for it: it is the desire on the part of the author (and, in life, the conversationalist) to give expression to unharmonized neurotic drives within himself—in relation to excretion and generation—and in so doing to make the reader-listener an accomplice to his action,—i.e. to "de-grade" the reader.

Joyce is strong in (1) and (2). I cannot imagine anyone being "aroused," so he can be absolved of (3); but oh! he beats everything in No (4).

He was arrested at an infantile level, not only with the famous cloacal obsession but with some complications of it that are not only rare in life but are rare even in the subconscience [i.e., subsconscious]. (It is rare in life that boys are bent on killing their fathers and marrying their mothers but I can believe it when the Viennese school says that it is universal in the subconscience—and hence has a rightful place in literature.[)]

Are you still in the Museyroom:

Don't forget that the Chevalier Charles d'EON was the "maid of Tonnerre"

Napoleon = may conceal Napoleon = EON[3]

FigTreeyou = may conceal Victoria Sackville-West who dressed up in men's clothing for V.Woolf's Orlando[4]

(You can't overemphasize the *transvestism* in this book.)

My Webster gives ARMINIUS, germ. Herman {and the Hermans here like the Post pillar boxes are Herms = Hermaphrodi[t]es in your Museyroom Lipol EONS.[}][5]

On page 433 [i.e., 443] LUCIA dresses up as Charlie (Chaplin and Charles d'EON) in his great film The Floorwalker .18 and .21 with tooth brush mustache and baggy slacks. . . and is also WOLL (Virginia) the Ganger. . . .who is also ROLLO-ROLAND-ORLANDO consorting with OLAF-OLIVER. . . 30[.] {Incidentally he is also MANGAN who said "I am grinning through a horse-collar" . . . had an ill fitting set of teeth. . 25. . . .several attempts .28 were made to reform him by Father Mathews, and in his Barmecide poem .7 says "My eyes are filmed". . . 34 and 36.[6]

Read any good books lately?

faithfully
T

[attached sheet]

ADALINE

SHEEHY, Judge Eugene. (Ellman[n] 52, n. **[1982: 51n]). Somewhere I remember reading that Joyce wrote to Miss Weaver that he identified Judge Sheehy[7] with the "four old men"—(partly because they are SHE-HE epicene.)
395.15 shee shee (plus chichi); 395.25 Shehusbands 390.20

O'DARA, Lisa.[8] Joyce first wrote 41.3–4; then Lisa O'Deavis. it is a part of the Mildew Lisa—. O'Mara 40.16–17 A'Hara 49.3— probably associated with LUCIA

See 395.34	o'dears (and "deaf with love"—Lieb[e]stod—395.29 "mild und leisse"
392.12	Ah dearo (Note: no comma)
386.15	heladies
339.20	[i.e., 389.20] Ah, dearo 339.31 [i.e., 389.31] Ah, dearo

---

CARROLL, Lewis

We know from 361.21 that Joyce associates Dodgson with onanism. He feminizes the mathematician and gives us 211.12 Elsie = L. C. Hairpin is a phallic harpoon as elsewhere. fractions are frictions as 385.12.

I think the ugliest thing (*so far*) in FW is the passage where he makes fun of LUCIA's squint, at the same time placing her in the anatomical sex demonstration: 294 [i.e., 295].17 strabisnus. . . . . . .19 (French: Loucher "to squint". . . [)] 20 LUCC-an .33 LUCIhere. {567.29 Squintina}

> I probably imagine it = but look at the following:
>> Joyce hated Virginia Woolf[9] (London's most influential critic who had been cool about *Ulysses*[10] [)]; he took a low view of her; illustrating *Orlando* with pictures of VICTORIA MARY (VITA-VIDA-The Gypsy PEPITA's daughter (granddaughter?) SACKVILLE-WEST as a man. It comes fully to the surface in 514.24 but is present in the book in all the ORLANDO-ROLAND-RINALDO-OLIVER passages.
> 300.   right margin   SICK. . . .SOCK. . . . . SAKE (Sackville[)]
>   12   M. A. . R. . . I. . . A. JACOB'S ROOM
>   16   Leo (Leonard Woolf)
>   17   . . . Spanish (Pepita)
>   18.   ravenosTONNORiously = Earl of Tonnerre dressed as a woman—man alternately.
>   29   waste-west. . . .noland for orland (next page 301. n. 3[)] OLIVER n. 1 Stephen—Virgina Woolf was née STEPHEN[)]
>   n. 4 [p. 300] elephant {Roland's Horn. . . The Oliphant[}] DO I IMAGINE IT?

> PAGE 279 note 1
>   .14   ROLANDO-Orlando
>   .15   "FLUSH" Woolf's book about Mrs Browning's dog (housepets-28 [i.e., .18])
>   .15   Virgin-woolf
>   .16   -T always = Dalloway
>   .16   year. "The YEARS"
>   21   vicking = Vicky-Victoria Sackville-West
>   21   Oliver-Roland's "girl-friend"
>   .32   anegreon: Anagor EON
> Pshaw! I only imagine it.

    Don't print that *Don Giovanni* was a favorite rôle for McCormick or Sullivan. That's a baritone rôle. They sang Octavio;— but the rôle is not large enough for a leading tenor so that [i.e., they] sang in concert his aria *Il mio tesoro* 462.22[.] I still think that he began superimposing the image of SULLIVAN on that of McCormick and with far more enthusiasm from the Fall of 1929.

A striking omission from Hodgart-Worthington is the fiery anti-Catholic song from Les Huguenots—called The PIFF-PAFF song. It precedes the St Bartholomew's Massacre in the opera.

["]POUR les couvents, c'est fini! Les moines à terre."[11]

12.11–12 (note remonstrancers 12.14[)]
15.10 [i.e., .11] (note KILLALA. . . . where the French forces landed)
199.29–30
337.1
341.16
349.24
439.15–17 (with Valentine 439.17 heroine of les *Huguenots*[)]
529.30 (assoc. with St. Bartholomew's massacre . . . 34)

x

Still more surprising is the failing to associate all the "cannons to the right of them" etc with The Charge of the Light Brigade[.] They have only ONE allusion to the "Charge" there are at least ten more.

---

[12]Beggar's Bullets—stones 79.31
Black a-se—a copper or kettle, pot calls the kettle black a-se 251.12
   [i.e., .11] (note pot just above)
Bog or Bog House—necessary house ?8.24; ?262.n.7 etc
Bonnet—concealment, pretext ?9.10
Bowman—thief (cant) ???198.30
Bull Beggar or Bully Beggar—you scare children with him like Raw
   Head, Bloody Bones 82.5; ?135.15 [i.e., .13]
Caterpiller—soldier 63.24 [i.e., .29] (does this all tie onto O. Wilde and
   soldiers?) Story of the name involves an innkeeper, who during
   war said soldier was pillar of nation, after war said caterpiller
College—any prison ??228.32–33; 385.9 [i.e., .8]; 388.35—someplace
   the 4 called gallow-birds [385.25] ???
Colt's Tooth—old fellow who marries or keeps young girl is said to have
   colt's tooth 534.8
Crack—whore 221.35???
Dangle—to hang 534.36—practically all words around here in Grose
Earwigging—snake-in-the-grass, one who tells tales about his employer,
   whisperer (Father Whisperer??) [96.10]
Shouldn't FW contain "Eve's Custom House where Adam made first
   entry" but I don't think it does
Fake—to do, make 311.27?
Fat as a hen in the forehead—said of a meagre person 275.13
Flash—knowing, Flash cant / Flash of lightning—glass of gin
   ?426.29–30

621.6–7 If soldiers meet a hunch-back on a march, they say, "The gentleman is on his march too, for he has got his knapsack on his back." (I had divined the rucksack was HCE's hump—sins—and I think this proves it)
Impure—whore 234.30 (but aren't there impure Sss in Latin or something?)
Merkin—"counterfeit hair for the monosyllable" 387.28
Mizzle—elope, run off 468.26
Miss Molly—effeminate fellow 360.28
Morning Drop—gallows 210.28
Prig—thief 563.26 (also Shakespearean)
Prigging—lying with woman 163.10
Quim—monosyllable 383.4 [i.e., 283.4] (m———e also in FW, no?)
Reverence, sirreverence—excrement ??334.17
Roratorios and uproars—oratorios, operas 41.27 [i.e., .28]
Salt—lecherous 210.14 and elsewhere?
Silent Flute—penis 43.33 [i.e., .32] (I guess all flutes)
Spice Islands—privy, fundament 263. note 2
Stark Naked—gin ?264.n.1
Siff one—dead man 462.5
Upright Man—head or vilest rogue in band ?261.23 etc

Now follows a partial list of things I'm sure are in FW but cannot pinpoint. Perhaps it's not worth while to try since the coming concordance will do it[.] But if you know their place out of hand. . .
Ask or Aix my a-se—common reply to any question[.] In FW is like "Ask you ass if he believes it"
Botheared or Both-eared [156.23]—talked [to] in both ears by different people at the same time, Irish
Bowled Out—in FW something like "he was bowled out by judge and jury" [AG: 337.2]
God's Head [233.16]—fool
Oh yes Common Garden is Covent Garden FW 224.32
Craw Thumper—R. Catholic
culp [322.35]—blow, kick
Draggletail [436.26]—slattern
Fraters—crooks who beg for charities
Heavy wet—beer
Jark—a seal / FW "amen says the Jark" [AG: 558.17]
Jury Leg—wooden leg FW "God forgive his jury leg"
Latitat—an attorn[e]y [AG: 50.17]
Looking-glass [459.4]—chamber pot (I don't think J so uses) [AG: Yes I do think so—eg. Madge my looking glass girl]

Maggoty—capricious
Marrow Bones—knees [AG: 391.32]
Max—gin Museyroom?
Nancy—the posteriors—I don't think J so uses
Park-paleing—teeth
Pig—policeman
Quill Driver—clerk
Scragged—hanged
Shot—poxed
Tittup [576.27]—gentle gallop, canter
Tom Sawyer—master genius of any profession
Three-legged Stool—gallows
Tub Thumper—Presbyterian parson
Twiss—Irish for Jordan because Richard Twiss libelled the Irish in his travel book
Wagtail [377.14]—whore / FW "witty witty wagtail"
Wedding—the emp[t]ying of necessary houses by Nightmen ??

1. Captain Francis Grose, *A Classical Dictionary of the Vulgar Tongue* (1785). See TW to AG, [? October 1962–II), n. 6.
2. A reference to a lost letter.
3. Also discussed in TW to AG, [? October 1962–II].
4. See TW to AG, 3 May 1959.
5. The words: "lipoleum," "Lipoleum," "Lipleumhat" "lipoleums," and "Liploeums" appear frequently in the Museyroom section of the *Wake*, 7.20–10.24.
6. Wilder is quoting from John Desmond Sheridan's *James Clarence Mangan* (Dublin: The Talbot Press, Ltd.; London: G. Duckworth & Co., Ltd., 1937). Mangan (1803–1849), the Irish poet and translator, is quoted by Sheridan: "I occupy the laughable office of Grinner-General to the public at large. I am grinning night and day like a mountebank through a horse-collar. I now begin for the first time in my life to understand that the great business of my existence is grinning" (36). Sheridan also quotes from W. F. Wakeman, who had worked with Mangan as a copyist in the Ordnance Survey Office in Dublin: "His teeth were an ill-fitting set, as evidenced by the fact that the wearer was for ever fixing them with his fingers lest they should fall from his gums" (56). Father Mathew was a temperance evangelist who tried to help Mangan overcome his alcohol and opium addictions. "My eyes are filmed, my beard is grey," is the first line of "The Time of the Barmecides" in the 1840 edition. See *The Collected Works of James Clarence Mangan: Poems 1838–1844*, Vol. II, ed. Chuto, Holzapfel, Mac Mahon, and Mangan (Dublin: Irish Academic Press, 1996), 168–169. Joyce admired Mangan's poetry and wrote about him. See Joyce, *The Critical Writings*, "James Clarence Mangan" (1902), 73–83; "James Clarence Mangan" (1907), 175–186.
7. The Sheehys were a well-known Dublin family with whom the young James and his brother Stanislaus often played. Eugene Sheehy, later a judge, was a year behind

Joyce at Belvedere College. He wrote about his friendship with Joyce in *May It Please the Court* (Dublin: C. J. Fallon, 1951). Portions of his reminiscences are reprinted in *The Joyce We Knew*, ed. Ulick O'Connor (Cork, Ireland: Mercier Press, 1967), 15–35.

8. Wilder discussed this material in his letter to Glasheen, [? October 1962–II].

9. For Joyce's references to Virginia Woolf and Vita Sackville West, see TW to AG, 3 May 1959, AG to TW, 5 May 1959, and TW to AG, 16 October 1960.

10. Woolf discusses *Ulysses* in "Modern Novels" first published in the *Times Literary Supplement* (London) on 10 April 1919 and reprinted in *The Common Reader* (New York: Harcourt, Brace & World, 1925), 150–158.

11. "It's all finished for the monasteries! Down with the monks."

12. What follows is three typed pages drawn from Grose's *A Classical Dictionary* with possible references to the *Wake*. There is some overlapping between this list and Philip Graham's list published in *A Wake Newslitter*, No. 7, November 1962, [1]–4. Because of the unique way in which Wilder reads the text of the *Wake*, we have supplied page and line references only when there could be no doubt. In two instances minor typographical errors have been corrected.

☐

To Adaline Glasheen, Farmington, Connecticut

[MS. ALS—HWS]

[7 December 1962]   [Douglas, Arizona]

I do less and less FW.[1] Here are a few jottings. But I love to receive news.

FOR ADALINE: NOTES

BEAUFORT:
Somehow some girls and the FOUR old men-as-women have a modern name which is BEAUFORT 393.22–23
And a few pages later, ISOLDE has
"her beaufu mouldern maiden name" 396.36–397.1
Elsewhere we are told that the BEAUFORT HUNT (fox-hunting pack) has the colors:
"In blue and buff of Beaufort the hunt shall make" 567.25
"In bufeteer blue" (The Beefeaters are in scarlet.) 511.10

It might be a good idea to look up the family name of the Dukes of Beaufort.[2] (I think the British pronounce Beaufort "byoo-fer"—which gives more closely this wordplay with beautiful.

THUNDER—OAK TREES—ZEUS
After Delphi the most important oracle in Greece was that in the oak-grove at DODONA. Thunder is very rare in lower Greece (Athens has only 16 overcast days in the year I'm told); so the priests at Dodona beat bronze gongs to imitate thunder and the sounds were read as Zeus speaking. I'm puzzled not to find DODONA anywhere in the book.
N. B. some of the many Phila-Delphias may be Delphi

MARINERS—NAVAL BATTLES—PIRATES
Shall I write up a piece asking readers of the NEWSLITTER to contribute of their lore to the following subject? At the close of the Old Man's Chapter we pray for "oremus" for NAVIGAN(TIBUS) and PEREGRINANTIBUS 398.12; 15–16—includes discover[er]s:

383.33 [i.e., .19]	CORTEZ MANDEVILLE'S TRAVELS (mandibles 385.21[)]
385.32	(He changes Mrs Heman's "warrior" to Morines-Foreigner) 385[.35]–.36 quotes Byron's stanza[3] which is about waves rolling over sunken battleships
386.22	prostituent = Themistocles 392.24 was PROSTATES TOU DEMON of Athens and was buried at MAGNESIUM 397.27
386.24	the BOOTERS—is derived from Freebooters 388.19, 386.31 GOTO = Togo
386.35	Polo 387.5 Arctic SCOTT
387.6	jaypee = John Paul Jones
387.10–11	Crusoe Travels = Yahoo. . . horses Houyhnhnms

BATTLE OF LEPANTO: Don Juan of Austria 387.14 AUSTERIUMS. . . 15 Johnny
Andrea DORIA 395.9 steamadories. . fumadory. . 22 chambadory 398.18 dorion
Grand Pasha Ali 394.25 passion grand

387.20	wreck of Norman's Woer 26 red sea etc 388.1 crossing of Wm the Conq[ueror].
388.3	SCAPA flow 11 Armada 17 naval siege of Copenhagen
388.19	Battle of Helgoland 23 Battle of the Nile
390.8	Drake 392.25 kid = Captain KIDD!!!??
392.19	Perry or Peary 392.33 (wasn't there an explorer Shakelton?[)][4]

393.8	Eric (Soteric) the Red. . . Jason's Argo. . . . . Jean BART
394.7	(Capt) Cook's (Voyages) 393.26 kook
396.19	Hagia = Holy Cross = Marquis of Santa Cruz—Battle of Lepanto

Joyce used up Columbus [512.7], Vasco de Gama [512.15], Cabot [512.18] etc on Page 512; but where are Raleigh, Harry Morgan, Dewey, Medina-Sidonia (the Armada); Nansen, Stefansen, Lewis and Clark; Livingstone and Stanley.

SIAMESE TWINS = Twice in the TAFF and BUTT scene we are told that they are SIAMESE TWINS
344.8   scimmia(Ital. monkey)ianised twinge. . . 10 chang—
354.24
Their names were CHANG and ENG
{Enge is a section of Zurich and its branch post office.[}]
So all I can find is that doubtful *chang*—in 344.8 [i.e., 344.10] Other Siams are 66.20 108.26 329.2 408.27 235.30 425.16 x 22 ENG' 328.25 537.12 and host of ENG-LANDS.

I'll bet you there must be some closer treatment of the Siamese Twins somewhere.

This is my chance to wish you all a Merry Christmas

>from
>your
>Western cowboy
>Thornton

---

1. Wilder had begun work on his novel *The Eighth Day*, which would be published in 1967.

2. The family name is FitzRoy Somerset.

3. *Childe Harold's Pilgrimage*, Canto 4, stanza 179: "Roll on, thou deep and dark blue Ocean—roll!"

4. Sir Ernest Harvey Shackleton (1874–1922), British polar explorer.

1963

To Thornton Wilder, Douglas, Arizona

[MS. TL—YCAL]

6 March 1963 [22 Carrington Lane
Farmington, Connecticut]

Dear Thornton,

Washing dishes tonight I began to think that, living in seclusion with sandpipers and being deprived, like all of us, of the New York papers, you mightn't know Helen Joyce died about two months ago.[1] She died quietly and with little pain, her brother Al Kastor told me. He asked us to come to her memorial service in New York, but my husband was having a mess of tests to which the correct answer was diabetes on top of his anaemia for goodness sake, so we did not go.

Helen had given me a copy of a v[ery]. fine photograph of Joyce and I'd promised never to use it for anything while she was alive and might write her memoirs. When she was dead, poor dear, I sent it to Northwestern press which is going to use it on the 2 Census jacket and / or the frontispiece.[2] I've always said it was the only picture of the mature Joyce that doesn't make him look like a booby.

Then Mr Dalton (yes, your Mr Dalton)[3] wrote me he'd known Helen a little at Joyce Society meetings and she'd told him she had noted in her copy of FW all the phrases that echoed domestic sayings, tag phrases, etc. of the Joyce family.[4] Mr D. said that in the aggregate the notes might be interesting and, in any case, ought to be seen by scholars. His notion was that he and I try to get the book for ourselves. Well, I decided he was probably right about the existence of the notes, for Helen used to tell me things like "the Fleshmans may they cease to bedivil us" [50.1] referred to her first husband and "Mamalujo" referred to Mamma-Lucia-Giorgio. So I wrote Al Kastor (who I like very much) and said I thought the book and Helen's papers ought to be given to one of the Joyce collections, preferably Buffalo because so many of her things were at Buffalo already.

Al responded by calling up and inviting us to lunch on Washington's birthday at Helen's house, which he owns, in Washington Depot, Conn. He said David Fleischmann, Helen's oldest son,[5] had all Helen's books and papers and he would be there for lunch, too, since he was coming to discuss the division of the furniture in the house—division between him and Al who had bought some of the furniture when he bought Helen the house.

So we went but did not, in fact, get any lunch because Mr and Mrs Fleischmann had turned up with a moving van and by the time we arrived most of the furniture and all the kitchen equipment had vanished into the van. Oh Thornton such a scene. Al Kastor stood in the middle of the floor, denouncing David Fleischmann at length and in terms that should have led to a calling out. D. F. only looked unhappy, Mrs. F. spurred the movers on. Mrs Kastor, a foreign lady hung with diamonds, sat in a corner, said, "Notting in dis house I have, not if you pay me," and kept divinely aloof from the moving scene. There were also two youngish lawyers with deadly eyes, exactly like secret service men in a scene with the president. I don't know who they represented but oh they represented. Socially at a loss, I dithered over to a stacked up table and picked up one of those right fun paperweights that you shake and it's a snowstorm. Instantly at my elbow a lawyer, saying it was better not to touch *anything*. My husband was better employed in fraternizing with Al Kastor's coal black chauffeur—the only beautiful person in the house—and this samaritan (for we were after all damn hungry) detached us and in a deserted garage shared his lunch of coffee, tuna-fish sandwiches and jellyroll. After we ate we left. I doubt if anybody saw us go, for all the furniture was now in the van and that left Mrs Fleischmann free to tell her husband's uncle Al what she thought of him. And for a woman I know to be a Den Mother in Newton, Mass. she had a very fair flow of invective.

I did, in all this todoing, manage a few words with the Fleischmann's. David and Stephen Joyce—who didn't come from Paris—are the heirs except for a mental health clinic in—in—well in a New Jersey town beginning with an M—Montorse—no—Monmouth seems right. Mrs Fleischmann said Helen's books and papers would be given to the Joyce Society or Buffalo. Mr F. said to Harvard, but they'll go where Mrs F. finally decides.[6]

Oh mercy what an occasion.

I suppose I must know a lot of FW news. The Analyst's taken something I wrote on the C-letters.[7] Fritz [Senn] gave a Joyce lecture which I hear was very good. Miss Worthington[8] got an AAUW scholarship to collect Irish folksongs.

How are you? I am fine, my husband poorly. I think it ungraceful to be one of those American women in better health than her husband. My daughter's been accepted at the University of Michigan nursing school and is reading Proust.

Have you noticed there seems to be a Wilder revival in England?[9]

        Yrs
        Adaline

1. Helen Kastor Joyce, the daughter-in-law of the Joyces, died on 9 January 1963. See AG to TW, 11 August 1957, 30 November 1957, and 20 November 1960. See also Appendices IX and X.
2. The photograph was not used.
3. Fritz Senn and Clive Hart, editors of *A Wake Newslitter*, published verbatim in No. 7, November 1962, a letter by Jack Dalton about Wilder's "Giordano Bruno's Last Meal in *Finnegans Wake*" (*AWN*, No. 6, October 1962). In their "Editorial Comment" (6), Senn and Hart responded only to Dalton's (7–9) comments on the accuracy of quotations from the text of *Finnegans Wake* and misprints in the *Newslitter*. The editors did not defend Wilder's reading of pages 316–321. A note on Wilder's article by Edward E. Kopper of Temple University, "The Two Saint Lawrences in *Finnegans Wake*," was published in *AWN*, No. 8, December 1962, 6. Dalton's second letter, "Re Article by Thornton Wilder (Litter No. 6)," published in No. 10, February 1963, 4–6, continues to take issue with Wilder's article and responds to Kopper's comments.
4. Dalton's letter is not in HWS.
5. Helen Joyce's son by her first marriage. George and Helen Joyce's son, Stephen James Joyce, was born on 15 February 1932.
6. Helen Joyce's papers went to the Harry Ransom Humanities Research Center of the University of Texas at Austin.

7. "Part of What the Thunder Said in *Finnegans Wake*," *The Analyst*, XXIII (November 1964), [1]–29. See also Ruth von Phul's "Thunderstruck: A Reply to Mrs. Glasheen," in *The Analyst*, XXIV (March 1965), 23–28.

8. Mabel P. Worthington (d. 1977), a professor of English at Temple University in Philadelphia. In the 1960s and early 1970s she planned a revision of *Song*, the volume she and Matthew Hodgart had published in 1959. She divided the work between herself and her former student, Zack Bowen. She was unable to complete her work on *Finnegans Wake*. Bowen's work is *Musical Allusions in the Works of James Joyce: Early Poetry through 'Ulysses'* (Albany: State of New York Press, 1974). Worthington published a number of articles on Joyce's use of song including: "Irish Folk Songs in Joyce's *Ulysses*," *PMLA*, 71 (June 1956), 321–339; "American Folk Songs in Joyce's *Finnegans Wake*," *American Literature* 28 (May 1956), [197]–210; "Nursery Rhymes in *Finnegans Wake*," *Journal of American Folklore*, 70 (January–March 1957), 37–48; "The World as Christ Church, Dublin," *A Wake Newslitter*, N.S., 2 (February 1965), 3–7; "Whip Jamboree," *AWN*, N.S., 4 (April 1967), 37–38; "'Old Roger': Death and Rebirth," *AWN*, N.S., 4 (December 1967), 121–122; "More Songs at the *Wake*," *Joycenotes*, 3 (December 1969), 4–9; "Not for Joe (170.03) and *Ulysses* (160.32)," *AWN*, N.S., 10 (December 1973), 91; "Antony Romeo," *AWN*, N.S., 10 (December 1973), 93. She was the general editor of the *James Joyce Cassette Series: Songs and Commentary*. See Ruth Bauerle, "Hodgart and Worthington: From Silence to *Song*," in Dunleavy, *Re-Viewing*, [200]–215.

9. Glasheen's meaning is unclear. There is nothing to suggest a "revival" of Wilder in England in either late 1962 or early 1963.

□

To Adaline Glasheen, Farmington, Connecticut

[MS. Telegram—HWS]

29 March 1963   Douglas, Arizona

FORGIVE SILENCE STOP WORKING STOP LETTER FOLLOWS READY YET FOR SOME ADDENDA QUERY SORRY TO HEAR OF FRANCIS NOT BEING WELL AFFECTIONATE REGARDS TO ALL THREE

THORNTON

To Adaline Glasheen, Farmington, Connecticut

[MS. ALS—HWS]

[postmark: Special Delivery: 29 April 1963] P. O. Box 144
11 March 1963—26 April 1963 Douglas Arizona

Dear Adaline =
    Many thanks for your letter—oh, how I tear 'em open.
    Very sorry to hear that Francis is not well. At least the tests showed where you are and can take measures. The worst of all physical ills is to *not* know what's the matter with you.
    Give Francis all my sympathy and urge him to be a good and obedient patient.

x

    Northwestern sent me the galleys and I've sent them a publisher's encomium.[1] I hope you like it. They have written me that they do. You must wait to see it in print.

x

    I hadn't looked into FW for quite a while.
    When the galleys came I plunged into them like a channel swimmer. Crammed with good things I didn't know. Many thanks.
    As I went up page and down I found all sorts of other items for the THIRD CENSUS.
    I won't send them on until you're rested.

x

    Got a nice letter from Fritz [Senn]. Praise the Lord, his spirits have risen.

    Oh, DEAR! Have you my bad habit of starting letters and leaving them unfinished and unposted? I hope not[.]
    Here I begin again.

April 26, 1963

Dear Adaline:
    And now thank you for the letter which I received this morning.[2] Glad to learn that Francis is better. I hope that Alison—the slim and lissom Alison—enjoys the training in Michigan as much as another girl

I know as a student nurse—right in New Haven—who says that every day of it is wonderful.

(I'm going down your letter paragraph by paragraph.)

Yes, I've sent for the Concordance.[3] I hope it has big margins!

Now, don't you go and make me a present of the new Census. Purchase is a real, tho' not the chief, way in which I can show my appreciation. My copy of the proofs is all written over already (since I use it as a sort of pro-tem concordance.)

You ask my suggestion as what you should do about writing to the editors of *Newslitter*. Ma'am, you can be sure that they've been getting a barrage of discontent from readers. (One can gather so from occasional editorial remarks. You and I, Adaline, are the two most equilibrated FW workers!) I don't think there's any danger of its being discontinued; but I don't think there's much promise of its getting to be excellent. In the meantime I'm grateful enough for the Grose items. The Japanese and Swahili.[4] Any day someone *may* reveal 1132 or one of the other dozen basic cruces.

I was paid 48 dollars for the reprint of my piece in the *Hudson*[5] which monies I have just sent off to Senn. (I was first told I would get 35. Tell that to any young intellectuals who are planning to earn their living writing articles for the more intellectual reviews!)

As for your KAMA SUTRA, I find in my footnotes to 93.22 "Four ends of life: success, pleasure, duty, enlightenment"—and I could swear that I'd received that information FROM YOU.

Ma'am, I have no suggestions about the C letter—I'll look forward to your note about it in the Newslitter.[6]

Is it too soon to send you these suggestions for CENSUS III? Stash 'em away for future consultation. The fatigues of planting primroses will be well rewarded[.] I hope they come up in their fragrance.

ALL CORDIAL BEST TO YOU ALL.

Adaline—remember—I rejoice in hearing from you.

        Your old friend
        Thornton

[attached sheet][7]

        STRAY NOTES

DESOSSÉ, Le is a man [415.11]

D'OBLONG
OBLONG, May (Ellman[n] 379) [1982: 368] also 315.32–33

GERYON 594.7 Pertinent to add that he carries Dante on his back for a time in the *Inferno*

GORKY in Russian means "bitter" bit gorky. Do you think Gorky and his "Mother" are also in 228.15–16 MUM's for his MAXIM? (what Joyce won't do!?)

HERCULES   maybe 458.33 it is HER COLOUR (In French: Hercule)
                "   567.27 a common oath in Latin comedy is mehercle (it's among the footnote of my Webster International)

HESPERUS   38.14

HILDA   The composer of "Sigurd" is REYER
HONE, Joseph   representative of Maunsel & Co, biographer of Yeats and G. Moore. see Ellman[n] p. 277 footnote [1982: 267n].[8]

MOUNTJOY   192.35 mount joynstone

NASO   see OVID, Publius Ovidius Naso
OVID   add 166.11 avid. . . . ovid (very funny; as the author of the Ars Amatoria—all about "it")

NABUCH   add to Nabuchadnezzar: in Italian NABUCCO, Verdi's opera which contains a beautiful chorus paraphrasing "By the waters of Babylon" = 103.9 [i.e., .8] 103.11–12 [i.e., .10–.11]
Probably Nakedbucker 139.6 (he lay in filth and ate grass)
{He is in 465.21 with other Verdi personages.}

SCHRATT, Kathe   I suspect another in KATEY SHERRATT, *bis* 380.1–2 to tell us of Mocked Majesty 380.4–5
The last Emperor. . . the last King of Ireland.

Shop-Sowry   221.34 surely repeats Shauvesourishe 221.33 "Chauve-Souris" bald-mouse = bat. Paris-organized Russian troops of entertainers ("March of the wooden soldiers.")

SHAW   It may be that SHAW is
               290.17 wush
                  .20 wash
                  .21 washawash
           Note 7 POTEMKIN.⁹ SHAW wrote The Great Catherine
Rê WUSH 290.17 In [Wyndham] Lewis chapter on E. Pound in Time and Western Man there is talk of an editor Mr. WUSH¹⁰ (Didn't I get that from you?)

SMYTHE, Dame ETHEL,¹¹ composer author "Impressions That
               Remain"—fierce crush on Lili von Herzogenberg
               166.7 ETHEL. . . . . . SMYTHE-SMYTHE [166.16]. . . . .
               28 s mites.
               She wore mannish clothes: read . . . 24–26
               So Lady Smythe 178.22 (Dames of the British Empire are
               addressed as Your Ladyship.[)]

HERMES,   Lat. Mercury, son of Zeus and Maya, god of eloquence,
               boundaries and roads; a messenger, and as *psychopompus*
               conductor of the souls of the dead; also god of commerce,
               trickery and theft. His statue, called a *herm* was set up
               at streetcorners and boundaries. Joyce plays on his name
               in the word *hermaphrodite*, bi-sexual, also the word for
               a brigantine or two-masted ship. All forms of HERMAN
               (and Dorothea; Melville) and HEREMON and
               HARMAN (Knickerbocker) are susceptible to
               these[.]

[attached sheet]

JORUM   316.18 {not .19} For what it may be worth, there is
               a JORAM of OMER and JORAM, Draper, Tailor,
               Haberdasher, Funeral Furnisher (these designations were
               not made plural when Joram married Miss Omer and
               became partner), Yarmouth, in David Copperfield. Little
               Emily is apprenticed here as a dressmaker. His coffin-
               making may apply here in association with "Davy's
               locker." Two lines later 316.20 [i.e., .21] *Mortimer* is the
               name under which Mr. Micawber hid from his creditors
               in Canterbury. It reappears in Dickens foliation 434.32
               five lines after a reference to Dav. Copperfield.

STEVENSON, R. L. a quotation from.   [AG margin: In JSA][12]
    He advised young writers to play the "sedulous ape"
    466.21 so sedulous to singe   SINGE, FR. ape

TEIRESIAS   114.29 ?   [AG margin: Halper article][13]

ULIKAH's wine   434.29 In Act II Forza del Destino a wise woman or
    sorceress ULRICA stirs a cauldron with a prophetic brew.

VERA   didn't O. Wilde write a play Vera (? "or the Nihilists")
    348.23 [AG margin: In JSA][14]
    532.18 =
    Wilde also wrote a Duchess of Padua 59.1; 463.4 ?

PLIMSOLE, Australian, a canvas shoe 397.17

ALTOID 210.9 {Alas, only makes the passage harder: confer[}]
    210.[8–]9 sulky Pender. . . deltoid   531.5–6 dilltoyds
    sause-pender . .

ARTAHUT   43.23 where did I find that this was the name Buddha
    gave to himself?

ASTON   quay (in A. L. P. chapter) 205.13

ASTRID   208.23 astride

ASTROPHEL   (Sir Philip Sidney) 223.22 his trifle

ATLAS   add 49.26

[attached sheet]
STRAY NOTES

BOTTOM   wouldn't you want to add 48.30 [i.e., .18]: (since the page
    already has Blackfriars. . 15 [i.e., .3]. . . bard 19 [i.e., .7][)]

WEDGWOOD   72.18 for your interest: the reason the long suffering
    "passive resistant" 72.19 didn't put in a word edgewise
    was because the WEDGWOOD family are well known
    Quakers. Strange to say so are the LUBBOCKS who may
    be in 72.21 [i.e., .26] BULLOCKY

PIGEON   you've got another PIGEONHOUSE 444.24, and probably 129.23

RIGADOON 236.23 if you want it—the dance said to be named after a Marseille dance-master RIGAUD

BARD   another 277. n.3

BROOKS, Maurice 236.25 272.25
STIRLING, James 236.24–25 272.27   ⎫ Politicians ELLMAN[N]
LYONS, Dr. Robert J. 236.25 272.26 ⎬ p. 15 [1982: 16–17]
and GUINNESS 236.25 [272.27]   ⎭

WHISTON   359.23 I read in TRISTRAM SHANDY Book II chapter 9 to be dreaded are "the *worst* of Whiston's comets." [AG margin: Wm—see EB][15]

SAVAGE, Richard. . . . add: author of The Bastard
586.15 ditcher's dastard {Richard's Bastard}. . . . .
23 riviers

FRICK'S FLAME, UDEN 537.30 ODIN's wife FRIGG or FRIGGA in Wagner's "Ring" is named FRICKA. She seems here, with lightning, through her husband, to punish erring husbands, "married goats."

TRAVERS, Mary . . mistraversers 538.6–7 Miss Travers sued Sir William Wilde for just such an offense as is under discussion here.[16]

SUVAROV, Alexander, Russian General 346.11

TEAQUE add 337.30 176.13 408.20 [i.e., .23] (Irish for Thaddeus) [AG line to 408.20: can't find]

Johannes: ger. John: St John's FIRE = Johannes fever. German pagan survival: Play by Sudermann.[17] (Here it is Sächselente: where dressed as Arabs they ride like John around the burning Böög) 346.7

MYRTLE   291.n. 4 I think it would be helpful to add that Esther-HADASSAH means Myrtle. here: M . . . ESTER with STERNE-DEAN SWIFT plus STERNE-STAR-

TWINKLING-STELLA.
Perhaps 147.17 346.28 [i.e., .27]

BEAR in Russian: I suppose many have now told you
'MYEDVYED' (That apostrophy = for a sort of lingering palatalized sound like n in onion.[)]
A truck is Myedvyedka.

MAN-SACKERSON I think there's another p. 315.30–31 ["]sutchenson. . . fraimd of mind . . ." he may be all through here. . . "hiberniating" 316.14–15 [i.e., .15–.16] and maybe 317.2 SAN SAKI = SAKI SAN

HYACINTH add 92.16; 281.14
SINCE GREEK AI = alas = is written as the hyacinth, it is probably 141.32 sTAIn—Joyce originally published "Arthwrgraff stain on the flower of the liloleum"

O'FLAHERTY the full name in *House by the C.*[18] is Hyacinth O'Flaherty—I think it is reflected ("A I") in 80.8 oh . . . 80.9 ah is for archer.

[attached sheet]

MAMERS oscan for MARS 85.36 Mamertime = Roman prison. Note this trial is taking place on the calends of MARS'S MARCH 85.27

MARS why did you drop out MARS 85.27 from your First Census?
Add: 366.29–30 thides or marse
494.12 ares Mars and Mercury.

MARTIAL Marcus Valerius Martialis. I've long wondered why— with so much Horace, Virgil and Ovid-Naso around, he isn't here.
Examine 149.8 349.2 577.4 64.13 martial. . . . mars
? 541.23

ARIEL can't find your 28.8 [?449.30]. Add 77.7 99.10 Maurois' Life of Shelley is called "Ariel." All Ariel's should suggest "see Shelley" and vice versa

416 LETTERS OF WILDER AND GLASHEEN

MISPRINT: FAWKES, Guy your 547.36 should read 574.36

FAWKES   suggest 300.9. . . 3 gayet. . . . fakes

CHARLOTTE   add 51.35 {suspect Thackeray's parody of Goethe's *Werther*:[19] when from her window she saw her lover carried by a shutter "went on cutting bread and butter."

BABAU   stet. add 576.27 where BOBOW is linked with Fr. nightmare: cauchemare
BABBO   (Joyce's nickname in the family[)]: {Ital. grandfather?} {ELLMAN[N] 685, 687 etc [1982: 672–674]}
BABOU, Henry {friend and publisher ELLMAN[N] 641 [1982: 628]} {N. B. Mangan called his father the boa-constrictor.} Suspect all Babels and Babylonians: e. g. 417.12 Papylonian *babooshkees* Papillon *plus* Babylonian *plus* Pappy.
19.22   starting off with a big boaboa
29.2   buaboabaybohm
126.24 [i.e., .12]   buaboababbaun
415.8   boubou
466.1   Babau and Momie
481.20   Hel[l]ig Babbau
   Not suspect all Baa Baa blacksheep 133.25 300.n. 3 301.6
   E. G. 279.7–8 Ah ah athclete. . . ba'. . . . ba'

BIGOD   add 285.28–29 (he plays on it on the next page: 286.4 bagdad . . . 6 begath[)]

CYRUS   add (among Bagdad. . . Medes. . . Persians) series a XERXES

CULLEN   is that cardinhard. . . . . culliman = Cullen 286.13–15 with maybe (Red Cardinal) McCabe in redmachree 286.14

A NOTE TO TORMENT YOU, ADALINE.
286.3–24   PLATO is all over these paragraphs. (Why, oh, why?) (The Arabs because they started geometry? Plato because we're approaching the Meno dialogue?)
              Anyway: ON PAGE 307.1 PLATO is equated with CLUBS. The CARD-SUITS are in 286.15 Culliman diamond; pike

= PIQUE french spade; clubs—French Trèfle also means clover, three-leaf; hearts.

So PLATO is a CLUB and a CLOVER (not forgetting that he is also MELISSA the Bee of Athens 414.30)

Are other Philosophers or GEOMETRICIANS here in the card-suits?

Should the fact that on page 262.1–2 we have HCE and ALP *AND* Plato inwoven with ALP give us pause?

[attached sheet]

LETTER 'I'

IBSEN 252.16 obscind / with his play "Pretenders to the Crown" 252.15
68.33 obseen. . . . Theirs = Thea in Hedda Gabler. . . .
34 allearth's = Eilert Lövberg. . . 34 Tacho is spanish for Turkey = Gobbler-Gabler.

IDA-IDA ? 35.2 chloerEYDES and hYDRophobe.
348.35 Rhoda Cockardes. . . raday (The ear hears RIDA a cockhorse)
There are (single) IDAS in 227.14 and 504.22 (Excuse me: I see you have these)

IMOGEN maybe 162.27 sim (Cymbeline) . . . miss .28 S EMAGINE.

INDRA 208.22 windrush. (among all those gods and goddesses?[)]
leda 18 f'royal = freya. . . 19 Europa .20 civvy:SIVA. . . 25–30

IO Do you see on Page 182 line 12 simul = Semele. . . . chronic = Chronos. . . pann = PAN. . . IO scriobbled = IO? Maybe not.
IO = p. 208. . . 25 with Leda, Europa
Maybe 264.7 AmnIOs = because HATHOR 264.6 also a cow-goddess
(in 583.10 she is present as a satellite of Jupiter)

IRIS with Charmian = Cleopatra's maids: I forget—is her name IRAS?
IRIS 528.23 ⇒ CHARMEEN 527.18
CHARMHIM 288.10 ⇒ IRIS 285.27

? Isherwood = thistlewords 169.34 [i.e., .22]

ISSY   28.20 ASSOTTED Issotta is an Italian form is Iseult

IVANOV   Russian existentialist philosopher, lived in Paris, or hero of early play of Chekhov ?595.24 evenif

IXION
    of the wheel 343.18 erixtion. . . in 22–23 tragedies of the ancients (there was a (lost) play about him by Aeschylus.[)]
    377.24 crucifixioners.
    603.29 iction   } all to represent torture
    604.15 gallaxion

Mac Carthy, Denis Florence, author of a Life of Shelley.[20] We see in
    452.9 that Joyce "thinks" "tennis flonnels" :so
214.26–27 [i.e., .27–.28]   tennis. . . flannels
59.33–34 tennises. . . flannels.
    I suspect Joyce is using him because of the Life of Shelley = another Shelley who testified against WILDE[21]. . . Note 231.12 shelleys . . . . . 15 dense floppens mugurdy.

DENIS   (French St Denis "San' Denee.")?
             361.10
             492.2 Sandy nice.

MARLEY, also dead in 242.2 "diseased, formarly"

---

1. Wilder's statement about *Census II* was printed on the front of the dust jacket: "Mrs. Glasheen's book is indispensable to all students of *Finnegans Wake*, and the material is presented with much charm and vivacity."
2. A reference to a lost letter.
3. Clive Hart's *A Concordance to 'Finnegans Wake'* was published by the University of Minnesota Press in 1963; a corrected edition was published in 1974 (Mamaroneck, N.Y.: Paul P. Appel).
4. The "Grose items" refers to two notes by Philip L. Graham in *A Wake Newslitter*. See TW to AG, [? October 1962–II], n. 6. The "Japanese" refers to Graham's notes, "japlatin, with my yuonkle's owlseller (467.14)" in *AWN*, No. 5 (September 1962), [1]–2; "Addenda (No. 5)," unidentified, but probably by Graham in No. 7, November 1962, 4, and a further "Addenda (No. 5)" by Graham in No. 9, January 1963, 6–7. "Kiswahili Words in *Finnegans Wake*," by Philip Wolff, in *AWN*, No. 8 (December 1962), 2–4.

5. Wilder's brother Amos showed his friend Frederick Morgan, an editor of the *Hudson Review*, the issue of *A Wake Newslitter* with Wilder's Giordano Bruno article. Morgan reprinted it, but no mention was made to its prior publication. Fritz Senn, because of Jack Dalton's scathing attack, reviewed the article before it was reprinted with emendations in the *Hudson Review*, XVI, 1(Spring 1963), [74]–79.

6. A reference to Glasheen's "Part of What the Thunder Said in *Finnegans Wake*," in *The Analyst*, XXIII (November 1964), [1]–29.

7. At the top of this sheet Glasheen has written: "checked for 3rd census—Dec. 1969." Beside many items in the following lists she either puts a check mark, a question mark, or writes "yes," "no," "have."

8. The Dublin publishing house, Maunsel & Co., was founded in 1905 by George Roberts, Joseph Maunsel Hone, and Stephen Gwynn. As early as 1907 they had expressed interest in publishing *Dubliners*. A contract was signed with Joyce in August 1909, but negotiations for changes in the manuscript dragged on until September 1912, when it was proposed that Joyce publish the collection himself. Before the already printed sheets were given to Joyce, they were destroyed by John Falconer, the printer. Maunsel & Co. was liquidated in 1925. Joseph Maunsel Hone (1862–1959) wrote *William Butler Yeats: The Poet of Contemporary Ireland* (Dublin: Maunsel, 1915); he edited and wrote *J. B. Yeats: Letters to His Son W. B. Yeats, and Others* (London: Faber & Faber, 1944). Hone wrote *The Life of George Moore; With an Account of His Last Years by His Cook and Housekeeper, Clara Warville* (London: Victor Gollancz, 1936); and he wrote a book about George Moore (1852–1933) and his family, *The Moores of Moore Hall* (London: Jonathan Cape, 1939).

9. Sergei Eisenstein's 1925 film, *The Battleship Potemkin*.

10. Lewis mocks Ernest Walsh, editor of *This Quarter* magazine, as "Mr. W-sh."

11. Dame Ethel Smyth (1858–1944), the English composer whose two-volume autobiography, *Impressions that Remained*, was published in 1919. She met Elisabeth "Lisl" von Herzogenberg (d. 1892), the wife of her composition teacher, in Leipzig, Germany, in February 1878. Their relationship ended abruptly in May 1885 when Elisabeth learned that Smyth was romantically involved with Harry Brewster, her sister Julia's husband. Smyth was strongly identified with the women's suffrage movement, and her *March of the Women* was played during meetings and demonstrations.

12. James S. Atherton's *The Books at the Wake*, 282.

13. Nathan Halper discusses Homeric parallels in his essay "The Boarding House" in *James Joyce's 'Dubliners': Critical Essays*, ed. Clive Hart (London: Faber & Faber, 1969), 72–83. Halper, an art dealer, did graduate work at Columbia University and published a number of articles on *Finnegans Wake*.

14. Wilde's first play, *Vera: or, The Nihilists* (1883). Atherton, p. 97.

15. William Whiston—see Encyclopedia Britannica.

16. Mary Travers accused Wilde's father, the physician Sir William Wilde, of giving her chloroform and raping her. See Ellmann, *Oscar Wilde*, 14–15.

17. Wilder refers here to two plays by the German playwright Hermann Sudermann (1857–1928): *Johannes (John the Baptist)* (1898), a retelling of the Salome story, and *Johannisfeuer (St. John's Fire)* (1900), a drama set in East Prussia in the 1860s.

18. Joseph Sheridan Le Fanu's novel *The House by the Churchyard* (1863).

19. William Thackeray's "Sorrows of Young Werther," a sixteen-line poem, originally published in the *Southern Literary Messenger*, 19 (November 1853), 709.

20. Denis Florence MacCarthy (1817–1882), *Shelley's Early Life from Original Sources. With Curious Incidents, Letters, and Writings, Now Published or Collected* (London, J. C. Hotten, 1872).

21. Edward Shelley.

☐

To Adaline Glasheen, Farmington, Connecticut

[MS. ALS—HWS]

[? April—May 1963] [Douglas, Arizona]

FOR ADALINE

RÁKÓCZY, Franz II, Prince of Transylvania, Hungarian patriot—gave his name to the Rákóczy March (used by Liszt and Berlioz) which is here being danced to at the Bal Tabarin) 415.10 (rockcoach)

DÉSOSSÉ (i. e. skeleton-thin, "flayed") his billboard name was VALENTIN-LE-DÉSOSSÉ 415.11

McCaper 415.10 the ear hears Danse Macabre (by Saint-Saëns and others)

PHOEBE 415.10 NINTH SATELLITE OF SATURN (415.9)
RHEA (in retrophoebia) Fifth Satellite of SATURN. 415.10 Both Satellites are also p. 583.17 (rhean) Phoebe .19

Catherine, Ste. Patron saint of dressmakers' and milliners' assistants—"Les Catherinettes"—who have an annual ball in Paris on her day 415.9

MYRMIDON son of Zeus, eponymous leader of the Myrmidons who accompanied Achilles to Troy. Also Greek for "ants" 415.13

		357.30 manmade
MYRMIDONS	also I suspect in	358.3 murmurrandoms
		596.14 . . . mermauderman

ZAN 415.26 old Doric name for Zeus who is probably (with Saturn) in 415.9 soturning = Zeus SOTER. This is all a dance of joy over Zeus's killing Cronos-Saturn. (i. e. killing time 415.24).

PEPI, King.   415.36 Budge's Book of the Dead LXIII quotes the pyramid text of King Pepi: "If the name of {NUT or OSIRIS} flourisheth, the name of Pepi. . . . .shall flourish and this his pyramid flourish."

BA   415.31 The soul, eternal and finally divine, preserved in the mummy. Atherton says in Middle Egypt also the God of Sluggards (415.32 sloghard)

NEFER-TEM   Budge Book of the Dead (I think pages 370 and 595), the God addressed in the negative confession. He is the lotus in the nostrils of RA

Nefersenless 415.33

HAPI   416.1 dog-headed, one of the four AMENTIS, child of Horus—Budge says in a later text personification of the Nile

LATER

Your letter received.[1] THANKS

SORRY: My pen slipped. I gave you the wrong reference for Mehercle.
567.27[2]

NEBUCHADNEZZAR = Verdi's Nabucco (beside the character from Trovatore) is [AG margin: Cain is fine] 465.21, Nebuchad' "ate grass"—the first vegetarian.

You could not read my writing and now I can't read yours: "Altpeid[3]—I don't understand yr. note—who he?"

ASTON, Sir Arthur, Catholic veteran, wooden leg, had fought against Cromwell at Edgehill; now defended Drogheda against Cromwell. Lost, and was battered to death by his own wooden leg.

BEAR   in Russian   Alas, I've lost and forgotten the page reference.[4]

SEAGULL   Yes, if *chaka* is seagull in Russian 424.10 *gabbiano* is seagull in Italian

You ask can I explain Shelley's relation to Festy King. No, but remind you that an Edward Shelley was one of those witnesses against O. Wilde—and that's omnipresent.

N. B. The Marquis of Queensbury was known as "Old Q" or "Lord Q"
Let someone else work out for us all that business.
"Mind your pees and queus." "Come down to Kew in Lilac Time" etc.

Have any of your correspondents ever given you the names of the chambermaids at the Savoy Hotel who testified against Wilde and Douglas?

You realize that all the Gilbert and Sullivan operas are Savoyard operas?

And that "fortitudo eius Rhodammum Tenuit" [515.9] is of the royal house of SAVOY?

I fear there's a connection.

TOLSTOI, Leo = Russian LEV
all through pages 339–346 is a foliation of titles from Tolstoi.
It's not a REVOLUTION 338.6 but a RE-LEV-UTION of the Lord—LIEVtonant 338.19 340.2 LYEW

This is in haste cordial best to all
(T)

1. A reference to a lost letter.
2. Wilder had, in fact, given this page reference in his previous letter.
3. There is no such name in *Census II* or *III*. Wilder's handwriting is quite clear; perhaps Glasheen was commenting on "Altoid" in Wilder's previous letter.
4. Discussed, with no page cited, in Wilder's previous letter.

To Adaline Glasheen, Farmington, Connecticut

[MS. ALS-HWS]

[postmark: 19 May 1963] P. O. Box 144
Sunday morning Douglas, Arizona

Dear Adaline—
  Enclosed several Sunday mornings fun.
  Isn't it infuriating how slow FW-work goes!
  Twenty-four years—and we're still picking up pieces of lint, not mapping the book!
  I have my Hart-concordance. It's a great help—and the "Overtones" will someday be three times its present size—or ten, when foreign languages are included.[1]
  I dream that some wonder worker—like Mr. Klein of Ottawa[2]—will suddenly arise and clear up a lot of the jungle; and then there'll be plenty left for us to do—with refreshed fervor—each with our own contribution.
  Your account of the house dismantling at Washington was glo-o-o-rious.
  I'll bet Giorgio [Joyce] is the world's brainless—the biggest kind, the kind that fancies itself as the most intelligent.

      all best to all
      Thornt'

[attached sheet][3]

FOR ADALINE

SUI 570.36 on your journey in the BOOK of the DEAD.[4] There is a chapter (i.e., amulet. . . incantation) called Beating back the crocodile 570.34; it immediately follows the Chapter of Not Letting the Heart be taken 570.35. And the crocodile's name is SUI.—right next to TEFNUT which you already have.

APOPHIS =	your APOPI is the same as your APEP = I feel your entry should read APOPHIS (APEP or APEPI)
	WE OUGHT to leave the Egyptian gods until some expert comes along (because the gods change and coalesce down the dynasties but until then we must bumble as best we can.[)] {AND: vowel changes are permitted between consonants = {AND: in cultus rites the name is often reversed.}
HEP, HEPPINESS etc. see APIS	
APIS	(HEP, HAPI, Greek SERAPIS, embodiment of Ptah) a Bull headed god HEP 26.9 (lines 20 to 24 Book of the Dead) HEPPIS reign 416.1 443.10 478.23 Hep!} note p. 479.32–33 {sektet Hetepui and Hennu} 480.18 Hep}
PTAH	198.17 Phwat Phwat 593.36 [AG: .24] TOHP
MERCURY	add 261.25

THOTH

Now to make you very uneasy. THOTH is also pronounced TOT (esp. in France and Italy where Joyce was swatting up the subject, and where they can't pronounce TH-)[.] I know he is in 26.18 TOTUMCALMUM because the words in the Book of the Dead are: "Get thee back, Hai. . . . .Thoth hath cut off thy head and I have performed upon thee all the things which the company of my gods ordered concerning thee in the matter of this work of thy slaughter.["]

Since you have reminded us that Joyce wrote that Shaun in III ii was Hermes Trismegistus—THOTH, I see him already in the second line: Joyce coalesces cothurnus and co-terminous:

429.14	[i.e., .2] the first cot—HERM's- THOTH is IBIS-headed: so is his sister:
452.8	SISSIBIS

In 457.31	you give us thoud as THOTH—why not 457.21 Toot; 22 toot toot

From Hermes you send us to Mercury and then back again. So you lost the apt farewell to Hermes Trismegistus in
    470.2 hermetic prod

[attached sheet]

FOR ADALINE

TEAGUE
    Webster "often equated with THADDEUS and TIMOTHY["] (Tiger Tim 210.15)

176.13	forky theagues
210.20	Teague {important here as I think that all the 12 disciples receive gifts of Pandora = Thaddeus.[}]
281.n. 2	Note: Teague. . . . Thaddeus
337.30	Donn, Teague and Hurleg. [AG margin: ?Dante] {The Three Soldiers : one is Irish one is Welsh: Teague and Harlech (in Wales.) see also 34.17 Ted. . . Tam. . . Taffyd}* see below
369.30	I suspect it in Madges Tighe
408.23	Old Tighe
622.24	again: foxy theagues Query: 607.17 tigh tigh

THADDEUS	SINCE TEAGUE = Irishman = Thaddeus I suspect it in "carry me along, taddy" 628.8
	QUERY: tig for tag ? 351.17
THADDEUS	add 326.3
	add to Thaddeus, hero of Bohemian Girl,[5] Prince of Poland that 281. n. 2 where he asked to "poliss" it off. Maybe an allusion to a once very popular novel "Thaddeus of Warsaw" by Miss Porter.[6]

TO PONDER:
    NORA / NORAH
    maybe derived from
    HONORA
    LEONORA = and the whole LION etymology
    ELEANORA = and the whole HELEN etymology.

TOLSTOI   LYOW = LEV   181.26 (Does your ear hear NEVSKY PROSPEKT behind "perfects of the Sniffey"? 181.25 If this is Tolstoi would you take "your honour" 181.25 as Honoré Balzac?— in the Shem chapter?

GORKI   and his "Mother" again.
    443.34 MOTH'R. . . . 35 corky-
    {can you find Hester Prynne there = MOTHER OF PEARL?}

CHAKA   (chayka) yes = seagull. But it was also the secret Russian police (the terrible office has changed its OGPU name twice since) and on 332.7–8 you see it combined with GESTAPO. (The other chaka is 424.10)
    And OGPU and CHAKA = 442.35

Just a fancy:[7]
Seeing that Joyce went out of his way to introduce into the "Anna L. P.—" chapter the Duke of Clarence and Avondale, his "May" and his brother, the Duke of York. . . . .

Could it be that Joyce is giving us all the children and descendants of VICTORIA and ALBERT 202.20–21

Edward VII was called "Bertie" berths 199.2 Prince of Wales (hotels in Paris are named after him as Prince de Galles Gullaway 197.6 Galawater 206.31

One daughter married the Kaiser: Julia sees her CAESAD = KAISER [207.24–.25]

But I don't find an Alexandra*[*] of Denmark[8]

Or a Duke of Connaught

Daughter Victoria became Queen of Spain "married into a family in Spain,["] 213.34; did she marry the Infante and become Reina later? 211.22

There are two concealed GEORGES half a crown 200.26 [i.e., .27] and Star and Garter 211.1

There's an Eddy Lawless who abdicated 210.33⁹
(and he was known in the family as "David" 210.29)
There's a Wally (Simpson?) 211.11
Victoria's youngest LOUISE just died in London: neither QUEEN nor QUEAN {102.10 and I assume you accept that paragraph as an annex to the "A. L. P." book.}
There are Mary's enough and Lizzy and Bett and Pegs etc {He did not live to see the Snowdon 205.21!}
Also I cannot find Victoria's son the Duke of Connaught = but Joyce would be likely to use the nicknames in the family ("May" "Bertie" "David" or the sobriquets "Collars and Couffes.")
"Wharenow are alle her childer, say?" [213.30]
Is it worth thinking over?

---

* from above
    8.23. . . inglis. . . . scotcher. . . . . . davy (i. e. taffy = Welsh)

*[*]The city of Alexandria in Arabic is ISKANDERIJA—dare we derive ISKER AND SUDA 213.4?

[attached page]

FOR ADALINE

BOLEYN-BULLEN, Anne
  {575.6–7 Ann, Ann   11 BOLLION
  {576.6 Hal Kilbride v UNA BELLINA Donizetti's opera on her is called ANNA BOLENA

TRISTRAM TANTRIS,	add T. 235.228 [i.e., .28] the name Tristam took when he fei[g]ned madness 235.8 [i.e., .28] first ANTRIES 480.4 {see .1 Iseult's black signal[}] 571.7 tantrist (which you already have)
PILATE, Pontius	I think all the Punch and Judy's should be examined narrowly for Pilate. Tradition assigns to her the names CLODIA / CLAUDIA and PROCULA or both. (She dreamed a dream, remember.)
255.26	Joyce first published Punch my and above .15 procul (Latin for "at a distance," "hence," I think.) Already in 133.23 you have given Punch and Judy

	as Pontises and Judas.
	so I think we have the trial of Christ also:
454.35	S. . P. . . Q. . . R. . . . ditto 455.28
455.1	cohortyard. . . . 2 puncheon jodelling. . .

LIZZYBOY	530.21 It may quietly amuse A. G. to know that on p. 178 in "Scribbledehobble" we read "Lizzyboy (bear)" {Why?} and here it is associated with Sickerson-Sockerson [AG margin: Has been explained]

LUG: LAMHFADA
        191.34 great. . . . landfather. . . . {who long armed tried to reach. . . }

DIGRESSION: You ask me what that thing is ASTRIDE ALP's nose.
102.13   a circusfix riding her Parisienne's cockneze
208.22–23   a clothespeg tight astride on her joki's nose
[TW margin: 423.22–23 barnacled *up to his eyes*]

    A BARNACLE (via bernicles) is an instrument for pinching a horse's nose! {It's also used for spectacles, but he's already given her those in 102.12 specks on her eyeux. . . 208.9 glassy. . . cycles.
    Incidentally, nothing will dissuade me that he is alluding to Henri Becque's play La Parisienne: 102.12–13 s-pecks. . . . . Parisienne.
    Well—look at the picture in the dictionary: It looks like a clothes-pin, doesn't it?—and for Margaret Earwicker: a clothes-PEG.
    That snaffle sat a-stride a-straddle on her nose as that blasphemous Danish Queen Astrid sat herself ("chilly bum bun") on the altar in 279. note 1 (line 27 by my counting) and 552.29–30.

    Damn it, French and Breton and Scandinavian and Gaelic (seafolk) speakers must have their dialect words for "Barnacle"

---

1. Hart's *Concordance* is divided into three sections, "Primary Index," "Syllabifications," and "Overtones."
2. A. M. Klein, who wrote mainly about Joyce's *Ulysses*. See TW to AG, 16 August 1952, n. 5.
3. At the top of this page: "checked for 3rd Dec 1969 AG."
4. For the importance of *The Book of the Dead*, see TW to AG, 3 August 1956, n. 4 and TW to AG, 3 May 1959.
5. Michael Balfe (1808–1870), his opera *The Bohemian Girl* (1843).

6. Jane Porter (1776–1850). Her novel *Thaddeus of Warsaw* (London 1803) went through numerous printings throughout the nineteenth century.

7. In the discussion of the descendants of Queen Victoria and Prince Albert which follows, Wilder is not always clear about which generation he means. A simplified chart of the children and grandchildren can be found in Giles St. Aubyn, *Queen Victoria: A Portrait* (New York: Atheneum, 1992), Table iii.

8. Queen Alexandra (1844–1925), the wife of King Edward VII.

9. King Edward VIII abdicated on 11 December 1936, after a 365 day reign. On 3 June 1937, he and Mrs. Wallis Warfield Simpson were married.

☐

To Adaline Glasheen, Farmington, Connecticut

[MS. ALS—HWS]

[?8 June 1963]   [Douglas, Arizona]
SUNDAY, early June 1963

Dear Adaline:
　Your book's come. I'm crazy about it. I hope you are. I blush with pleasure when I see my name on the wrapper.[1]—And speaking of wrappers, on the back one I read that you taught at Wheaton. So did my sister Charlotte, long ago. Now I'm all agog about the Third Census.
　If I could find time I'd straighten out all my notes about Mrs Noah—alias COBHA—alias Lady Guin[n]ess.
　And about GRIP, the raven in Barnaby Rudge[2] who says "hello" and "no popery" and what else does he say?
　If there is a famous fable about the FOX and the GRAPES there is one no less famous about The FOX and the RAVEN (GRIP).[3] "Let me hear your beautiful voice in song."
　Since you have a word for *Peg o' my Heart* you can find room for another play—long run in London; I don't think it came to New York: *Paddy-The-Next-Best-Thing*[4] 452.20–21　505.27

MAURICE BROOKS　　　　　｝　ELLMAN[N] 15 [1982: 17]
Dr Robert Dyer Lyons　　　　　FW 236.24–25　272.25–27
Sir Arthur Guinness
James Stirling

NOAH in French is NOÉ
    NOES for NOES 114.2 {See below 114.18–19 sem. . . . jupet. . . .
Hum} {And for my money BULGARAD = Benj Lee Guinness-City
(Russian[)], but more of those Bulge-Bilge-BeLGu later}
    Noeman's Woe 321.14–15

    It begins to look as though Noah and his liquor and nakedness
and family were everywhere.

Nuah-Nuah 590.17 (his rainbows shot 590.10) {Noa-Noa, Polynesian:
non-sacred, profane = name of Gauguin's diary.}

    Just to give you a hint of the treats in store: COBHA—
pronounced CÔVA is of course the Ark of the COVE-nant.

    I wish you were doing the "Place Names and PEOPLES in F—W."
It's so logical that it should accompany your immense work and
assembled apparatus. But, even though you aren't you'll be amused
that Joyce alters the latin ploughman ARATOR to ARATAR 59.24
to give us the anagram for Mt Ararat. And how delighted he must
have been to see that Blanche Ring's great song Ta Ra Ra Boom De
Ay = gave us the mountain in reverse.[5]

x

Sorry there isn't more in my mailbag this Sunday.
    A lady who just got a Phd in Columbia under Tyndall [William
York Tindall] is sending me her thesis: "Scandinavian Material in
F—W—."[6] She wrote that she found things that Joyce felt sure
wouldn't be discovered for 100 years. Has she sent it to you?
I'll urge her to, when I've DEVOURED it. I wonder if she'll
concede me the Knut Hamsun foliation on p. 188.
    You must get fascinating mail!
    Remember how I tear open any letter from you.
    Does Alison go to the middle west for training now or in
September? That girl I told you about who is entranced by nurse's
training is the daughter of the second Mrs Thew Wright, Jr. (now
Mrs Thorne.)[7]
    All best to you all. I wish this were a more exciting letter.

(T)

---

1. The official publication date of *Census II* was 17 June. A statement by Wilder appeared on the front dust jacket. See TW to AG, 29 April 1963, n. 1.

2. A novel by Charles Dickens published in 1841.
3. Fables by both Aesop and La Fontaine.
4. This comedy by John Hartley Manners (1870–1928) which starred Laurette Taylor opened at the newly built Cort Theatre in New York in December 1912 and ran for 692 performances. A song of the same name, with words by Alfred Bryan and music by Fred Fisher, "written around" the character of Peg, was interpolated into the *Ziegfeld Follies of 1913*. Bauerle in *Picking Up Airs* identifies four references in the *Wake* to the song: 143.1–.2, 290.3, 490.31–.32, and 577.16. Gayer Mackay's and Robert Ord's *Paddy The Next Best Thing*, based on the novel by Gertrude Page, opened at the Shubert Theatre in New York on 27 August 1920 and ran for fifty-one performances.
5. Blanche Ring (1877–1961), a star of vaudeville and musical comedy who encouraged the audience to sing along with her, sang Henry J. Sayers' "Ta-ra-ra boom-der-é" (1891) in her vaudeville act.
6. Dounia Bunis Christiani. Two of Wilder's letters to her have been located and are printed in Appendix V.
7. A friend of the Wilders.

☐

To Adaline Glasheen, Farmington, Connecticut

[MS. ALS—HWS]

[? June 1963]   [Douglas, Arizona]

Dear Adaline:

I hope Miss (or Mrs) DOUNIA BUNIS CHRISTIANI will send you her thesis "Scandinavian Elements of Finnegans Wake."[1]

I've skimmed off the Names of Persons in her LEXICON-section for your fun—fun, I hope.

more anon.
(T)

4.15   [2]In Norse mythology ASK (sic) and EMBLA are elm tree and first man and woman.

11.3   (GRIMNISMOL 54 an edda) Now am I ODIN /, Ygg was I once / Ere that did they call me Thund.

[AG margin: 607.25]
  {In *Voluspo*³ 18 LOKI is mentioned under his old name of LOTHUR as giving heat to the first man and woman.}
14.20 DAN {acc. to YNGLINGA sag[a] in HEIMSKRINGLA Danes got their name from *King* DAN.} [AG: In 2 Cen]
69.6   BLYANT D[anish]. pencil
91.25 [i.e., .30]   J J. changes Gaelic TIR-country to TYR, Norse God of War. [AG margin: Tyre city?]
97.17 MIKKELRAVEV is in D[anish]. Reynard the Fox
100.25 IVAR BEINLAUS and OLAF the White (HVIDE)
124.29 Both ODIN and JORTH (Earth) are called FJORGYN This is Finn M[a]cCool⁴ in mock Gaelic and Old Norse MacCumhaill = CAMHELS. . . . SON.
130.5 SAERÍMNIR, the boar perpetually served at feast to heroes in Valhalla.
137.7 Sw[edish] KANTARELL Fr[ench] Chanterelle = first string on the violin.
154.23 THOR is also called ORLÖGG [AG margin: 77.13]
173.15 maybe TOMMELISE, H. C. Andersen's Thumbelina
   See 244.30
  {Re son of Sorge 189.18 The Pictish ruler DRUST was called DRYSTAN or TRYSTAN in the Welsh version—influenced, south, by French word Triste.}

P. S. I But I found Strindberg's third wife—29 years younger than he—
  Harriet BOSSE 221.30 [AG: Lovely]
P. S. II Your letter just rec'd—thanks as always.⁵
  THE only place I find the Hebrew alphabet is
  107.34 Aleph-Ox beth-House Gimel-CAMEL = HUMPER = appropriately on the OXUS-river.
TORDENSKJOLD   228.36 (thundershields), name given to Danish naval hero Peder Wessel (1691–1720)
TOMMELISE   244.30 (Hans C. Andersen's THUMBELINA) See 173.15
OELSVINGER   221.6 (Miss D. B. C. thinks ADAM OEHLENSCHLÄGER, Danish poet, author of play ALADDIN) [AG: What mean?]
YGG   267.19 ODIN
FANDEN 282.25 The Devil 315.28 FAND devil, pronounced FOND [AG: Have+516.19 617.31]
BARNUM 288.17 P. T. Publikums see prence di Propagandi 289.2
EYEINSTYE   305.6 ?EYSTEIN one of the two sons of OLAV the White King of Dublin. OR EYSTEIN, St Olav's archbishop. [AG: ?]

CULSEN	310.32	In Danish or Norwegian form MacCool—son of Cool
FRAM	317.9	The famous ship—Nansen's and Amundsen's. [AG: Have]
UGLYMAND	317.28	?YGG = Odin Mand—D[anish]. Man.
Wolving	318.33	VÖLVA, the seeress of VOLUSPÁ [AG: ?]
Kersse of Wolafs	319.27	D[anish]. KORS cross CROSS OF St OLAF or Order.
ERIEVIKKINGR	326.7	Earwicker in OLD ICELANDIC
THOKKURS	326.22	Loki disguised as woman THOK or THOKK refused to weep for Balder the Good so condemning B to remain with HEL goddess of the underworld, LOKI's daughter
AANDT...		(spirit, intellect)... KROP. body 331.15–16 (a reversal!) [AG: ?]
BIL		331.26 333.30 BIL, girl and her brother HJUKE always accompany the moon—they were taken from the earth when they were going to the well BYRGER carrying on their shoulders the bucket called SAGER and the pole SIMUL. Their father is named VIDFIN (HUIDFINN 99.15) a LILLEBIL is a taxi. HCE is an OMNIBIL 337.19 (From the *Prose Edda*.) [AG: ?]
	339.3	Iggs, YGG ODIN?
	344.3	TYR Norse God of Battle [AG: EN TN ?]
	360.23	Bulbul—adulatory pet name given to Ole BULL, Norw[egian]. violinist (1810–1880) [AG: X Nightingale]
	383.22 [i.e., .20]	KAEMPER D[anish]. giants [AG: 332.18]
	387.8 [i.e., .9]	{add to your SWEYNE} SWEIN FORKBEARD son of Harold BLUETOOTH and father of King Canute—KNUD—of England. [AG: + Boneless]
	424.20	ULL Norse archer God. TOR a/e NVEIR (typescript illegible) [i.e., Tordenveir] stormy weather; MIDGARD earth GRIMNIR, ODIN; URD a Norn, "the Past"; MJOLLNIR Thor's hammer. Fenrir wolf, son of LOKI. . . . BAUGE the giant; ODDRUN sister of ATLI; SURT, ruler of the Fire-world; HRIMGERD, a giantess from the "Prose Edda" [AG: ?Tyndall]
	425.28	paa tryk D[anish]. "in print"
	443.21	Snorri says ROLF The Ganger was so called because "he was so big no horse could carry him and he had to walk everywhere"
	443.30	St Olav called OLAV DIGRE, thick set stocky
	444.11	MISFORSTAAELSE = misunderstanding!!

479.35   ORMIRINN LANGI The Long Serpent (dragon or worm) most famous of all Viking ships built for OLAV TRYGVASON (969–1000)
482.7   VÖLVA The seeress who foretold Ragnarok
494.34   ASKKEPT. Dan[ish]. Cinderella. (Joyce by changing one letter gets also ASKAPOT giant to Sir Bevis.

{WÊN CHANG Chinese god of literature 322.6 130.35[}]
513 [?.25] BIL see above
516.19   FANDEN The Devil.
520.24   .. BIL—maybe here a taxi
565.5   VÖLVA, The sibyl
597.31   CELSIUS Swede invented this thermometer

Note.
         628.13 FAR calls FAR Danish Father [AG: 244.22]

1. Christiani's thesis was published by Northwestern University Press in 1965. Glasheen reviewed it in *Criticism: A Quarterly for Literature and the Arts*, IX, 1 (Winter 1967), 104–105.

2. Throughout this letter Wilder summarizes key points of Christiani's thesis. For example, for 4.15 Christiani writes: "elms ... askes *Aske*, ashes; *ask* or *asketroe*, ash tree. In Norse mythology Ask and Embla, or Ash and Elm are the first man and woman: Adam and Eve" (90).

3. While reading Christiani, Wilder probably also read *The Poetic Edda*, a collection of poems which tell of Scandinavian and German gods and human heroes (9th to 12th centuries) translated by Lee M. Hollander (2nd ed.; Austin: University of Texas, 1962). Joyce would probably have known the 1923 translation by Henry Adams Bellow. Hollander translates the opening poem as "The Prophecy of the Seeress: Völuspá." Stanzas seventeen and eighteen present the creation episode (Hollander's spacing): "To the coast then came,   kind and mighty,/from the gathered gods   three great Aesir;/on the land they found, of little strength,/Ask and Embla,   unfated yet./Sense they possessed not,   soul they had not,/being nor bearing,   nor blooming hue;/soul gave Óthin,   sense gave Hoenir,/being, Lóthur, and blooming hue" (Hollander, 3). A second collection, *Prose Edda*, or *Younger Edda*, is the work of Snorri Sturluson (1178–1241).

4. "(Irish, Fionn MacCumbhail)—giant hero (fifteen cubits) of the southern (or Fenian, or Ossianic) cycle of Irish legend" (Glasheen *Census III*).

5. A lost letter.

To Adaline Glasheen, Farmington, Connecticut

[MS. ALS—HWS]

20 June 1963   P. O. 144,
                                           Douglas Arizona.

Dear Adaline:
    Yes, that's very sad, the letter from Fritz [Senn].[1] It's a real melancholia, and could be very serious. I wish you knew the little dark-eyed wife who's had to bear all this—it was hard enough for her to bear the years of his fanatic pursuit of FW—spending all his hours away from the printing-office in the Zurich University Library, reading the Dict'y of Nat Biog—you remember his notes.
    As to what to give him: my instinct (not an infallible counsellor by any means) tells me that one shouldn't send money.
    Patients under psychoanalysis do have those alternations of elation and depression. Write him of your sympathetic concern and since he's not answered (three times!) to your offer of books on FW tell him that when he's better you wish to send him those—or any other books he expresses a wish for. You've then made your gesture of sympathy and of repayment—you can do no more against a stone wall of melancholia.
    I assume that he looks at our letters with a lacklustre eye—but just the same our will-to-write-to him *does* penetrate—*even if he doesn't open the envelopes*—or tells his wife to open them.
    Let's hope he's in the hands of a good doctor.
    He undoubtedly had a predisposition to melancholia, but I have no doubt that the frustrating jungle of FW plays a large part in it. I feel it sometimes—just rage and contemptuous rage.
    Do you want a copy of The Texas Quarterly Winter 1961 (ELLIOT COLEMAN: Heliotropical Nough[t]time: Light and Color in Finnegans Wake)?[2] Worth very little; but your library should have all these items. You probably have it.

                I enclose some *nugae*.
                Cordial best to all. I'll write Fritz today
                Thornt'

[attached sheet]

FOR ADALINE

{GUINNESS}	372.2 {Lord Mayor of Dublin. . . . 7 *Benjamin Lee*[}]
TARTAN—FEADHA,	son of Tartan: first person to die in Ireland (Keating I 86)
TAMMANY	131.8 {New York versus PARIS}

Adaline: don't you think in a future edition you could employ a symbol to denote that a PERSON is intended though not named? Illustration: On one page.

131.13	PROMETHEUS
131.14	FRANKLIN
131.18	MOHAMMED
131.33–34	Ezra Pound {translator of Confucius—it would amuse your readers if you gave the full name KUNG FOO TSE}. Look at the portrait in ELLMAN[N] [3] and you'll see comical hair-on-him and the chin-chin. Taishan mountain comes into the CANTOS. I suspect "chinchin of Ez is Like" [131.34]
134.4–15	(see below) DEVCALION, CADMUS [AG: Yes Parnell]

GENESIUS, St.	Census II Is that a dig at me![4] Why, Sartre's book about Jean Genêt is called by a pun: GENET, SAINT ET COMÉDIEN
TYLTYL	105.10 Isn't that the little girl in The Blue Bird?[5]
SATURN	97.33 Saturnalia 264.5 saturnine
MERCURY	261.25 mehrkurios
TYPHON	325.14 Greek equivalent of SET (Rose: A Handbook of Greek Mythology p. 60)[6]
CADMUS	(see CADMUS: "Should Spelling?" 307.25) A false but popular etymology derives Academy etc from Cadmus. He sowed dragons teeth, not stones like Deucalion, but I think I see him: 494.20–21 writing academy. . . . . 24 pebble-dropper 25 spelling bee.

He is associated with DEUCALION 134.4–5. pebbles
[AG: Snake-letters]

ATH   Don't scholars prefer spelling *TWRCH*? Joyce has distorted it to suggest TRUTH.

ILYA MUROMETZ   legendary hero of Russia 55.3–4 Ilyam. . . mournomates.
ILIA?   REA SILVIA d. of NUMITOR King of Alba—coalesces with RHEA SILVIA, mother of Romulus and Remus by Mars. Some say she was a daughter of AENEAS, hence "Ilium Ilium."

LUPA   nickname ("prostitute") of ACCA LAURENTIA w[idow]. of Faustulus. She lived in the LUPERCAL. Found the twins Romulus and Remus and took care of them. Since LUPA also means she-wolf it gave rise to the wolf suckling them. 67.33 LUPITA LORETTE—LAURETTE—LAURENCIA in French a shopgirl etc is a Lorette, proverbially free-and-easy.

    Joyce here, as elsewhere, is sneering at Vita Sackville-West author of PEPITA—LUPITA and her buddy (via *Orlando*) Virginia WOOLF. Vita's grandmother ("Pepita") was a Spanish gypsy. 68.9 a la Zingara

    I think by sheer chance (in Douglas—on the second-hand stall!) I've picked up a book that Joyce may have used: "A Handbook of Greek Mythology including its extension to ROME" by H. J. Rose of St. Andrews. Its footnotes are full of curious lore that I think he uses. Joyce likes the most far-fetched! [AG: First 1928 Second edition 1933]

    Cont'd. For instance in DuCaye GLOSSARIUM. . words in medium and low (infinae) Latin Troy is TROGA—which fits very well in 74.9

    Adaline, do I imagine it?
We can see Lars Porsena 83.7–8 of CLUSIUM 84.15
Who did he fight at the Bridge? HORATIUS COCLES
84.2 HUROOSHOOS 83.15 COCTABLE 84.11 COCCYX
    All of these except COCCYX were added after the first printing in *Transition*.[7]

It *might* effect something in Joyce's devilish mind that
PRISCA 494.11 is the name that St Paul gives over to Prisilla in
2 Tim. IV 19[8] (it means "primitive" to balance "NOVA" ARDONIS—
a new star—and tho' feminine maybe ADONIS[)]
    Is she 513.20 where PALIED may be St Paul.

FABIUS MAXIMUS   Left margin 278.

JEREMIAH   575.9

---

1. In a lost letter Glasheen must have mentioned a letter from Fritz Senn. Senn's letter is not in HWS.

2. *Texas Quarterly*, IV, 4 (Winter 1961), 162–177. The title phrase comes from *Finnegans Wake*, 349.6.

3. Ellmann in his *James Joyce* (1959) on plate XV prints a photograph of Ford Madox Ford, James Joyce, Ezra Pound, and John Quinn in November 1923 standing in front of an unidentified building. In 1982, Ellmann prints a photograph of the same men, but this time in Pound's Paris apartment (plate XXXVI).

4. In the entry Genesius, St. in *Census II* Glasheen writes: "I was told by a playwright that he is patron saint of actors but *The Listener* says St. Blaise (q. v.) is. 219.21." Glasheen changes the entry for *Census III*: "Roman martyr, patron of actors who played at being a candidate for baptism, but God touched him and under torture he did not recant. 219.9."

5. Maurice Maeterlinck's 1908 play *The Blue Bird* (*L'Oiseau Bleu*) is a symbolic fairy tale. Mytyl and Tyltyl, children of a poor wood cutter, fall asleep after a disappointing Christmas Eve and dream that Berylune, a fairy, sends them to find "the bird that is blue."

6. H. J. Rose, *A Handbook of Greek Mythology Including Its Extension to Rome* (1928, reprinted and revised at various dates). The page reference corresponds to the 5th edition, revised, London: Methuen & Co., Ltd.

7. Pages 75–103 of the *Wake* were published as "Continuation of a Work in Progress," in *transition*, 4 (July 1927), 46–65.

8. *The Second Epistle of Paul to the Apostle Timothy.*

To Adaline Glasheen, Farmington, Connecticut
[MS. ALS—HWS]

[postmark: 22 July 1963]   P. O. Box 144
July something 1963   Douglas, Arizona

Dear Adaline =
    Love your letters. "Papa Westrey!"—Arthur's dog. Sheer delight.
    Much relieved that you've heard from [Fritz] Senn in a more congenial mood.[1]
    Have been in correspondence with [Jack] Dalton. He sent me drafts of two very good papers.[2]
    How often I've been deceived but I think I'm beginning to see a pattern in The Questionnaire 126.[3] Feel the need of knowing so much more about the Finn M[a]cCool legend.
    I feel ashamed of sending you these *nugae*.
    However, I have a feeling that we—the first generation of FW-workers—are at last getting "hot." The big pay-dirt is just around the corner. (And, alas, lots of it will be just plain "dirt," too.)

                Best to all
                Thornt'

Later:
    I sent two Texas Quarterlies—
    The first with a Joyce article the second with one on Yeats and Politics.[4]
    I hope the first didn't go astray.
    Now I'm sending a Kenyon with Mercanton on Joyce—the first of two articles; I've never seen the second.[5]

[attached sheet]

FOR ADALINE

BLADUD, mythical king of England; father of King Leir, supposed
        builder of BATH.
    553.7 bledded or bludded

BUTT, Isaac.   I suspect that Zackbutt/Sackbut 552.28 is spelled so, to remind us Isaac Butt: Dictionary: IZAK var. of Isaac.

SALISBURY = called NEW SARUM. I suspect—see the political setting—that OLD SARUM [552.1] is Lord Salisbury (as prime minister; was he connected with Ireland's history?)

Theophil   163.25 [Giordano] Bruno in the five dialogues of the *Cena* gives to himself the name of Teofilo, filosofo, and is quoted here.

HONE, Joseph,—the firm of Maunsel and Co {Maunsel may be 240.12}.
382.21   See Ellmann index. Author of books on Yeats and George Moore, I seem to remember.[6]

LOYOLA   will you accept ignite 446.36 considering the context?

PRUE, Miss, type of ingenue—isn't she in The Beaux Stratagem? [AG: NO *Love for Love*][7]
337.27
241.5 with Polly Peacham   386.24 prumisceous.

AIMWELL   (the other is ARCHER) one of the two beaux in The Beaux Stratagem 40.1

GUNNE, Selskar. You know that Pervenche—Periwinkle that goes through the book accompanying S. Gunne.
Well, she's also a 14.36 cornflower and 15.9 paxsealing buttonhole = bachelor's button
And don't you think that 14.16 [i.e., 15.16] Elskiss is Selskar = Joyce also omits the S-in Selskar in 388.6 per wenche is Elsker woed.
And to drive us mad if you look up VETCH in the dictionary you will see after its derivations: "cf. PERIWINKLE; earwig"

PALAEOLOGOS   family descended from the Byzantine emperors. Representatives in diplomacy right down to our own day. New French I think. A historian, member of the French Academy. Paleologue[8]
349.23 [i.e., .22]; 470.9; 555.23. Maybe 73.1

TEMORA   of OSSIAN (man or woman?) 87.8. Perfect
anagram of AMORET 350.[.5]
[section of sheet cut out by Wilder: about four lines]
LEDA   620.31 Mother-A. L. P.—LEDA is talking of
           Daughter-Issy-Helen.
           In *Troilus*: of Helen: *Then she's a merry Greek, indeed.*
           620.30[9]

POPINJOY   = Trolloppe's [i.e., Trollope] IS He Popinjoy? (a late
           novel.)[10] I see that Hart page 497 interprets 621.15 cuppinjars
           as poppinjay.[11] If you're really out to collect Trolloppe, try
           Duke of Omnium (omnium-gatherum 186.25); Arabin (both
           a hospitable horse-racing millionaire near Dublin; and the
           character in Trolloppe) 553.35.[12] I hope to have some more
           for you soon: Lawyer Prendegast [144.6], Lawyer Honeyman
           Tudor Plantagenet [504.2, 516.24]; Eustace [535.6]; Harding;
           Carbery; etc etc
[AG: No Arabin is a Dublin Lord Mayor][13]

GODARD, St   (of the tunnel and monastery in the Alps[14]—not a
             brother of St. Medard)[15] The altar was dedicated to him up
             there in the snow—185.25 *frigore*—in 1132!

O'Ryans   185.25 Surely there is an O'Ryan's Ink in the British Isles?

KING NOBLE   another: 187.11–12
COLUMBIA, St   324.26 Columnfiller predicted: Columnkill's
                prophecies (50.9–10)

[attached sheet]
                        FOR ADALINE

SOLOMON } [176.8, 307.21]
BALKIS} [543.14]
11.34–35 her sabboes. . . . . so solly.
          She's kicking ARIAS because she's singing in Goldmark's
          opera La Reine de Saba[16]

   I rather suspect CRESSIDA on this page. During an armistice
11.13 and truce .15 she crosses from Troy. . 36 to the Greek side .35
and is kissed by each of the Greek chiefs in turn.[17]

.27 KISS. KISS CRISS. . CROSS. . CRISS. . KISS. CROSS {CRESS}
But I won't insist.

PANDARUS   279. note line 18 (pimp and pamper = PANDER)
              531.5–6 sausepander (This deltoid business becomes
PENDER 210.8–9!)
The whole PANDORA complex maybe an allusion to
PANDER'ing. See 369.25–26 Pandoria. . . solicitor general.
    ¶ Vide this note on p. 279. Line 10 "Love oh love" isn't that
Pandarus's song?[18] 28—illion for Troy. Doesn't Shakespeare say that
Cressida knows "the rules of the game"?[19] (line 19); then 18
plentyprime could be Priam.

AMPÈRE 137.24   also associated with Electric-system Kettle on
549.13 x 16 (So you can add 549.13 to Kettle, Lawrence.)
    There's a very complicated pun here: AMPHIRINE = having a
double nose; so Joyce gets his NOSE connection with the *other* Kettle:
Kettle (itself by a pun) Kettle [i.e., Ketil] Flatneb.

VANNA, Monna   (Maeterlinck's play)[20] a captain will spare a city
    if Monna Vanna (Giovanna) will come to his tent naked under
    her cloak.
    138.8 wanna. . . . flesch. . . . nue. . . . maid
    Maybe I imagine it.

OHM   {Hart: Concordance p. 493. Thanks 301.3: "Oh he must"[}]

WATT   594.10 if you warm water you get Watt's steam

    Damn it: there's a novel by Trolloppe called "*The Struggles of Brown,
Jones and Robinson.*" Look at: 594.11 "Smud, Brunt and Rubbinsen."
    Forget it.

GORKI and his "Mother":[21]
    Suspect- - - 126.22 [i.e., .10]: "myther. . . . . maxim. . ."

---

1. Wilder is responding to a lost letter. Senn's letter to Glasheen is not in HWS.
2. Dalton probably sent Wilder two articles which were to be published in *A Wake Newslitter* No. 16 (September 1963): "Music Lesson," [1]–5, and either the first or both parts of "One and Thirty" (7–9), Dalton's response to a query by Clive Hart about the phrase "ever youthfully yours" [283.F 1]. At the end of the article Dalton

writes: "A closely related paper will appear in the January issue of WN. It is, in fact, a second part of this paper." The second part of this article, "More Numbers," was published in *A Wake Newsletter*, N.S., I, 1(February 1964), 5–7; and Addendum to "More Numbers" and "One and Thirty" were published in *AWN*, N.S., I, 3 (June 1964), 10. The only letters from Dalton to Wilder in YCAL are from 1964–1965.

3. Book I, section vi (126–168) which Glasheen titles "Twelve Questions" in *Census I* and "Questions and Answers" in *Census II* and *III*.

4. Elliot Coleman, "Heliotropical Noughttime: Light and Color in *Finnegans Wake*," *Texas Quarterly*, IV, 4 (Winter 1961), 162–177; Roger McHugh, "Yeats and Irish Politics," *Texas Quarterly*, IV, 3 (Autumn 1961), 203–216.

5. Jacques Mercanton's recollections of Joyce, "Les heures de James Joyce," was first published in *Mercure de France*, 348 (1963), 89–117, 284–315. A translation by Lloyd C. Parks was published in the *Kenyon Review*, "The Hours of James Joyce, Part I" 24, 4 (Autumn 1962), [700]–730; and Part II in 25, 1(Winter 1963), [93]–118. The essay is reprinted in *Portraits of the Artist in Exile: Recollections of James Joyce by Europeans*, ed. Willard Potts (1979, rpt., New York: First Harvest/HBJ, 1986), 205–252.

6. See TW to AG, 29 April 1963, n. 8.

7. *The Beaux' Stratagem* (produced in 1707) by George Farquhar (?1677–1707); *Love for Love* (produced in 1695), a comedy by William Congreve (1670–1729). In Congreve's play Sir Sampson Legend has arranged a marriage for his youngest son to Miss Prue, a country girl. In Farquhar's play Aimwell and Archer are two friends who have run through their money and are in search of ways to restore their fortune.

8. Maurice Paleologue (1859–1944), French diplomat and director-general of the French Foreign Office from 1921 to 1925. He was the author of *La Russie des Tsars pendant la Grande Guerre* (3 vols., 1921) and *Un Grande Réaliste* (1926), a biography of Count Camillo Benso di Cavour, the Italian statesman and a founder of *Il Risorgimento*, an Italian nationalist movement.

9. Cressida in Shakespeare's *Troilus and Cressida*, I, ii, 103.

10. Anthony Trollope (1815–1882), *Is He Popenjoy?* (1878).

11. In the "Overtones" section of Clive Hart's *Concordance*.

12. Racing is the downfall of the Duke of Omnium's sons in Trollope's *The Duke's Children* (1880).

13. What Wilder is suggesting in this note is that Joyce may have made allusions to characters in Trollope's novels. Some of the names are actual characters; some of the names are Wilder's guesses at Joyce's intentions. Glasheen is correct that John L. Arabin was Lord Mayor of Dublin in 1845. There are, however, several Arabins in Trollope's Barsetshire Novels: Francis Arabin, a vicar, and a fellow of Lazarus College, Oxford; Eleanor Bold, born a Harding, married Arabin after the death of her first husband, John Bold; and there is also a Rev. Septimus Harding.

14. The Saint Gotthard Pass in the Lepontine Alps in south central Switzerland between Airolo and Andermatt. The chapel, dedicated to a holy hermit who had his cell there, was erected about 1300. Some Church histories attribute the name to the early hermit, others to St. Gotthard (Godehard), Bishop of Hildesheim. The Pass,

made accessible in the thirteenth century, is the central pass through the Alps separating northern Europe and Italy. The St. Gotthard Road was built from 1820 to 1830, and the St. Gotthard Railway tunnel was built from 1872–1882.

15. Medard, the Bishop of Noyon and Torunay, was born in about 500.

16. Wilder gives the French title of Karl Goldmark's 1875 opera, *Die Königin von Saba* (*The Queen of Sheba*).

17. Shakespeare's *Troilus and Cressida*, IV, v.

18. Pandarus's song, "Love, love nothing but love, still love, still more!" in *Troilus and Cressida*, III, i, 105–116.

19. In response to Nestor's comment about Cressida, "A woman of quick sense," Ulysses attacks her, ending his speech by saying "And daughters of the game!" meaning whores (IV, v, 54–63).

20. Maeterlinck's tragedy (1902) is set in fifteenth-century Italy.

21. *Mother*, a 1907 novel by Maxim Gorki (1868–1936).

To Adaline Glasheen, Farmington, Connecticut

[MS. APCS—HWS]

[Postcard: Wild Life In Southwest Desert]

24 July [1963]   Douglas [Arizona]

Dear Adaline =
   You're a crackerjack. That Sumerian material is grand.[1] You win the "Annie" for 1963. Yes, indeed, write it up for The Litter. Makes me crazy-greedy for more.

             Congrat's
             Ever
             (T. N.)

1. A reference to a lost letter. Glasheen's note, "Dilmun," *A Wake Newslitter*, No. 15 (August 1963), 2–3.

To Adaline Glasheen, Farmington, Connecticut
[MS. ALS—HWS]

[? August 1963] [Douglas, Arizona]

Dear Adaline =
  This is a poor show but I send it on anyway.
  Still dazzled over the Sumerians.[1]
  Next week I fly to New York for five days—and to search out some papers in my files at Deepwood Drive that I need. I'm going to stay "covered up"—but oh won't it be great to eat something fit to eat, for a change. And oh if I could just see flowing water and feel real rain on my face.
  Will be back here by August 15.

> Don't forget your
> old friend
> Thornton.

Best to Francis and Alison

[attached sheet]
[AG: Probably shouldn't be done till I see 11 / 916 notes in Buffalo ms. again (AG) checked Dec 1969]

FOR ADALINE

DE VALERA, AEMON.[2] (His father's name "de Valerie") The variant VARELA is not merely an anagram, but a vowel interchange frequent in Spanish. See also ORLAND x ROLANDO. Notice Joyce's delight in identifying him with the DEVIL—Devil era, 473.8—hence with the Grimm's law changed B x V = DIAVOLO. And De'il which leads in turn to the DAIL EIR[E]ANN.[3]
  Associations: his father was BASQUE. . . . Bay of BISCAY. . . by B x V change in Spanish: VICSAYA. . . Vasco da Gama = is a BASQUE.
  He resorted to the political maneuver of PLEBISCITES. Took pride in instituting a Eucharistic Congress in Dublin; and in his work for the League of Nations.

By anagram and consonant shift we get a De Lavera = Delivery, and the LAVAR = leads us into washing and laundries and a near anagram LAVENDER = Spanish laundry = LAVANDERIA.

We do not pronounce the L in ALMOND = AEMON... ¶ This D. V. seems to be a Diva because of his spell-binding oratory.

9.36 Davaleras = for battle of Calavera 255.14
24.6 delivered. . . . amain
51.13 Dev (corroborated by .7 lavaleer = Valera)
{233.35 baskly {much Spanish here: carnisa: uricana: criado: suspect much basque[}]
234.3 {all Spanish; but I suspect cabaleer: he had his "lavalier on" as 51.13
.8 candid = white auri = gold virid = green: IRISH FREE STATE
.12 ALMONDER = ALMONERS = AEMON .20 euchoristic congress}

ECONOMICS, POLITICS, UTOPIAS SECTION
{272.9 Dark ages. . . . 14 A. D. Aemon De Valera. 20 chamber of errings = DAIL = Chamber of Eirann.
273.11 NED LEFT basket = BASQUE .23 (the old windbag) 26 NOD = NED

{287.1 D. V. . . 4 DEVA = (Zoroastrian Devil): footnote .4 Basque. This shows that the pages following are related to De Valera. Joyce originally printed .31 pupal anan souaves.[4]
288.1–10 {picture of De Valera's oratory}
.5 NED .8 MATH HOUR . . . 9 [i.e., .8] LONG as he's broad.
306.8 dial-devil = DAIL and footnote 1 Divvy D-V: Emma EAMES = AEM'
331.17 Plebiscites. . . ALEMON . . . . . 24 divvy. 27 lavvander. {.18. . 19 mount of De Lord: mount of Deluge: mount of Ante (deluvian) = delavera.[}]

KATE has something to do with De Valera: because she is Cathleen ní Houlihan?[5]

In 79.23 [i.e., .33] the phrase ["]her weaker had turned him to the wall" is a play on the song OLD UNCLE NED:[6]

Here she calls on him 333.31 O moan and wants him to take her to bed 334.5 de Marera

---

347. (19 annam dammias = ANNO Domini = Aemon Devalera = ANNAM = AEMON
(26. long. . fellow.

I suspect 358.23 deliveried . . . . 27 Basque. . . . 32 "dear Jane" = Mrs De Valera: SIOBHAN or SINÉAD (female: John) ni Flanagan.

(374.17 [i.e., .16]   Boy-Bishop = Bay of Biscay 18–19 Bay of Biscay. Look at the context "Our Island, Rome and Duty" and there's that chinaman speaking who usually talks about longfellow: 374.34–35. Damn')

[attached sheet]
                DE VALERA (cont'd)
466.19   ED. . . . 19–20 DIAVOLO. . 20 DIVA
473.8   you already have the "devil era"; there is .25 AMAIN.
523.22   asseveration = asseveralation = EVERALA = VALERA =
   .23   [i.e., .24] Plebiscites
   .24   [i.e., .25] BOSQUET = BASQUE

{NOTE = 555.22 [i.e., .10] Balearic islands = Consonant change. The (Spanish) BALEARES = VALEARES.
(for the Island IBITZA = the dictionary gives also IVITZA.)[}]
These maybe De Valera's islands because 555.30–31 [i.e., .18–.19] there are the colors of the Irish Free State Creamywhite = orange = cabbage green!
    595.31 [corrected by Wilder: .28] There is the song: Old Uncle *Ned* how about DEEPERARAS = Delaveras?[7]

O'Connor, T. P. (little misprint = Mainly about People should read 260. Left margin.

NEWTON, Isaac. author of the PRINCIPIA
    483.19–20   alpybecca's . . . ikeson. . . . imprincipially.
{Newton was thought by his contemporaries to be impotent or eunuchoid: hence 106.28–29 Ikcy Neuter. . . common sex [}] {Adaline, I think that there BRAHM TAULKED = TYCHO BRAHE[8]. . . but I don't insist.}

⁹ORIEL, Lord of, John VERDUN. . . his son Nicholas killed in 1271.
is it this family that built the ORIEL House in Dublin.
310.27   orel orioled
552.27   oriel house
—
105.11   Orel Orel
609.20   see other oriel
613.15   orielising
{Boldereff: part II p. 266 *sub* Verdons[}]¹⁰

COPALEEN, Miles na {Yes, present day journalist: I read his
brilliant column every day when I was in Dublin. Check the
following because I can't read my own notes. Besides I have
a feeling that I obtained this information from you.} Myles
na gCopaleen alias Flan[n] O'Brien; real name Brian Ó
Nualláin[.] Didn't he write a novel called Last Summer's
Mass 433.10?¹¹

MORMON   a (supposed!!) 4th Century prophet. 64.4–5 199.1 253.35
{Latter day saint 455.5. See Brigham Young.}

TOM, DICK and HARRY   126.29 [i.e., .17] {HEINS = HANS}
{Henry = Harry} 30 [i.e., .18] dick. . . Two marries = Harry

JANUS   126.29–30 [i.e., .17–.18] heinousness: JANUS would
be pronounced in Latin YANUS. . . choice of war or peace.
         JANUS seems important to Joyce because of the Earl of
Howth—Grace O'Malley compact to keep HIS DOOR OPEN
         HENCE 133.16–17 peace. . . . war. . . . 19 open for war
{Polemas}
         {N. B. Joyce's scatology everywhere: chest o d-rawers.}
[{]CESSO: Italian for watercloset}
         Because of Joyce's identification of Howth—open door—
JANUS, I think it would help future students if you included the
JANUARY—Janus' month allusions with JANUS.
         The encounter with the Cad in January 332.25
         The dire event in 1132 in January 420.20
         The Temptation in Eden? (date palm of SUMER) in January
112.26
         The hen found the letter in January 112.26
         Buckley shot the General in January 105.22

SPENSER, Edmund don't you think that in 133.10 (sponsor) he balances RALEIGH. . 11?

BOMPART, Admiral, commanded the French flagship HOCHE (552.31–34) sunk destroyed by the English under Sir John Warren in Loch Swilly—Wolfe tone's "last stand,["] Oct 11, 1798 133.21 Boomaport

---

BABO-BABBO-   if you're using that JOYCE-Babbo identification—notice the
    133.25 Baabaa
    133.28 Babu
Some day I hope to show that these riddles are a chain—each one (often cryptically) linked to its predecessor, like 142.31 ff

---

MATIETO, La 257.7 narrative poem in provençal by MISTRAL[12] (see 256.27 {langue} d'oc .28 {langue} d'oil and 29 Provence. It looks like 257.7 DARIOU is a provençal character in the poem coalescing with loup garou, hero of La Matieto or Mireille?

CURTISE   little hound in Reynard Cycle   } 480.30
ERMINE x HERMINE Reynard's wife   } 480.21

CURTIUS   Verify—wasn't there a Brutus Curtius or Curtius Brutus who kept silent while a fox or wolf—as here 480.30 BOOTH's COURTEOUS—was eating out his vitals?

KNICKERBOCKER   —to be consistent—and because you never can tell what Joyce is up to—add:
98.21
208.15
611.34–35

---

1. See TW to AG, 24 July 1963, n. 1.
2. Eamon de Valera (1882–1975), the Irish revolutionary and politician. He served as President of the Executive Council of the Irish Free State (1932–1937), and Taoiseach (prime minister) of the Republic of Ireland (1951–1954 and 1957–1958). From 1959 to 1973 he served as the first president of the Republic of Ireland.
3. The Irish Legislative Assembly.
4. "A Continuation of A Work in Progress," in *transition*, 11 (February 1928), 7–18.

5. W. B. Yeats and Lady Gregory in their play *Cathleen Ni Houlihan* drew on the stories and poems about Cathleen Ni Houlihan that had begun to appear in the 18th century.

6. An 1848 song by Stephen Foster.

7. "Deeperas" is on line 31. Hodgart and Worthington identify lines 31 and 32 as referring to Stephen Foster's "Old Uncle Ned."

8. The Danish astronomer (1546–1601) whose opinions drew on both the Ptolemaic and Copernican systems.

9. From here to the end, the letter is written on the verso of the first page of notes about Eamon de Valera.

10. Frances Motz Boldereff, *Reading 'Finnegans Wake'* (Woodward, PA: Classic Nonfiction Library, 1959).

11. The Irish writer and journalist, Brian O'Nolan (1911–1966), was, for most of his life, a civil servant. Under the name Flann O'Brien he wrote novels and stories; under the name Myles na gCopaleen he wrote his *Irish Times* column. He used a great many other pseudonyms including John James Doe, George Knowall, and Brother Barnabas. O'Brien did not write a novel, Last Summer's Mass. In the line Wilder cites, the references are to Lady Harriet Durham's aria, "'Tis the Last Rose of Summer," from Act II of Friedrich Flotow's opera *Martha* and to Myles-na-Copaleen, a character in Dion Boucicault's play *The Colleen Bawn*.

12. Frédéric Mistral (1830–1914), a member of the Félibrige movement which revived Provençal as a literary language. His best-known work is the verse romance *Mirèio* (1859). Mistral shared the 1904 Nobel Prize for Literature with José Echegaray, the Spanish playwright.

☐

To Adaline Glasheen, Farmington, Connecticut

[MS. ALS—HWS]

15 August 1963   P. O. Box 144,
                                          Douglas, Arizona

Dear Adaline =
     It was a delight to talk to you on the phone. Was away from Arizona only a week. Had to get some papers in Hamden that no one could find for me. Saw some shows and ate something good, for a change. Glad to get back to Douglas, tho'.

x

Yes, I certainly think that H. C. E. is Ash—ash—Ygdaissil.[1] But he's also Howth Head... i. e. stone. I think you sound so worried because you keep narrowing your image of H. C. E. He is many things—all things—everybody—except a god. As Finn McCool he is many kinds of tree 126.24 [i.e., .12].

If, as you write, the Cross was the Lord's steed—so was Ygdassil both a tree and a horse.

x

Medieval churchmen found religious symbolism in Everything. It was like a game of ingenuities they played, however devoutly. And Joyce has that kind of mind. I think it's too early to ask whether his blasphemies are destructive (i. e. satanic fouling of sacred things); we don't know yet. He's working on an enormous cosmic scale—I think we shall see that the whole range of the life-force from eroticism to spirit will be comprehended.

But oh golly I wish our work went faster.

I'm on a new line now: the Albigensian-Cathar heresy which Denis de Rougement finds behind the Tristan story.[2] But most of my "new lines" get lost in the sand, like the streams in Arizona.

But chins up.

Courage.

I wish Mrs von Phul's book were out, if it is about the Joyce family in FW.[3]

Notice in Hayman[4] that Joyce cut out many things that too directly alluded to Lucia—Dalcroze method and the picture of her in the house.

Greetings to Francis. And to Florence Nightingale Alison. I hope she likes the Middle West it's different. I spent 17 years there (Wisconsin; Oberlin; Chicago)[5] and loved it.

        Ever
        Thornt'

[attached sheet]

SUGGESTIONS FOR ADALINE

CAREY, James.   Betrayed the Invincibles.[6] 132.32–33 "quary was he invincibled."
    Lat[in]. *quà ré*—for what reason! Lat[in]. *cur?* why. Was there a Kerr or Carr among the invincibles?
[AG: Lovely Lovely]

DRAKE, Sir Francis—circumnavigator. Terror of the Spaniards because he raided their ships and colonies in the new world—doubly terrifying because his name for them was DRACO—DRAGO... dragon. Spanish children still threatened that DRAGO will come and devour them. 480.25–26 child's dread for a dragon...
    Important to Joyce because he is one of the Heroes Return Myth. (His ghostly drum (rat-tat-tat) will come to England's rescue[.]
    {N. B. Is that a misprint in your DRAGON MAN 112.7??} Page 316 has only 35 lines: should your dragon the market read: 316.29?[7]
    I think many of the Dragon Man can be *also* Drake

- 197.14   for my duck I thee drake. (all the sea-captain stuff here.)
- 316.29   [i.e., .30] Dragon-the-market... see LIEF 26 [i.e., .27] HAWKINS 26–27 [i.e., .27–.28]
- 343.2   Draco. This is astronomical = constell[ation]. Draco. But also ... 3 corsair. (And 342.36–343.1 TIMOR is in MAYLAYSIA.. on Drake's route[)].
- 358.29   *Drachen.* ger[man] dragon. 28 HEROES ... 29 ARTHUR.... DRAKE {and Magellan is ... 14[}]
- 364.34   ? drakes me druck
- 469.9   (for your interest) "quickquack..." 10–11 "I'll travel the wide world over." [AG: I don't understand][8]
- {479... {9 dragoman} {32 Draken}
- 480... {26 dragon vicefather}
- 486. .8 dragoman 13 manDRAKE
- 500 {for your interest} (The dead stirring to life) .1 the snare drum. .12 white hind (for Drake's The Golden Hind?) Hind is also 499.21
- 577.1 {note manDRAGON = Drake .. and DUCKY.}
- 623. (for your interest) .. 35 tattat ... 623.36–624.1 rounding the world:

---

123. great sea voyagers 16 Ulysses... 17 Drake 26 Jason 32 Hanno NOW I HAVE THE FEELING THAT I SUBMITTED THESE TO YOU BEFORE. FORGIVE IT.)

PRIMROSE, Olivia 361.18 and 22[9]

    For your pleasure: Finn McCool *made* the Isle of Man and LOUGH NEAGH by plunging his hand into the earth and scooping out the earth and hurling it into the sea. [AG: Lovely]
    hence: 76.21–23

310.32 COOL'S SON: CULSEN .33 {pulled up great gob of Loch Negi}
   .32 [i.e., .31] ale of man.
  It is probably at 287.7 mud. . . . Mam and 287.13 because HAYMAN 160.23–24[10] gives "Dump it at a point of coast.—"

[attached sheet]

FOR ADALINE

CHAPLIN, Charles. CHARLEY 443.18 {"The Floor walker" .21 "The Kid" .30 baggy pants 27. hobo "The Tramp" .31[11] {]}
HENCE
NORMAND, Mabel 443.33[12]

COPPÉE, François. (I think he's here because he wrote *Le roman d'un jeune homme* [AG: 416.36] *pauvre*[13] which certainly applies.) Verify.

GROOS, Karl. German philosopher 417.11

JUNG[14] 143.13 recon-JUNG-ation.
  I read that in the London MSS this paragraph begins with the sign of the MANDALA[.]
   Jung introduced the therapeutic drawing of mandalas; he started the theory of the ANIMUS and ANIMA (307.3–4) which is here 143.8–9 exANIMA-tion; and wrote much on the alchemist's problem of CONJUNITO—reconjungation.

NARCISSUS add 522.30–31

FRANKY: should you list a FRANK here 282.8 because Joyce first wrote "A great dab was Franky at the manual arith."? I think it would be a great help to future scholars.
OH, EXCUSE ME I SEE YOU HAVE IT.

HADDING, King. (Thank you for finding that.)
   140.1 Whaddington. (You will find in HAYMAN 94.8[15] that Joyce first wrote Haddington.

CHUDLEIGH, or CHUDDLEY, Miss = cuddley = 4.8.
  Don't I remember a beauty of this name—Boswell's Life and Walpole's letters—who came to court, like the Gunnings,

and married into the peerage?[16] Was she Irish? WHAT THEN of 88.24?

QUERY: re your list. Aren't I right in remembering that GUINNESS was the *first* LORD-Mayor?[17]
CRAMPTON, Sir Philip.   I think 88.31–32 sirphilip a surgeon. . . . When the time comes you include "unnamed allusions to" in the Census CRAMPTON gets 162.32 135.4–5

LIBERTY's—London silk goods firm (see dictionary "liberty" a silk named after the inventor)
179.33 226.24 548.19

NEREUS   (Handbook of Greek Mythology by H. J. Rose, p. 25)
"Nereus. . . Hesiod declares . . . he is called the Old One. . . Homer speaks of him as 'the Old One' (gerwn). . ."
267.18   Adamman: footnote 5 "skewer that old one"
267.22   Vetus (latin: old one.)
267.24   Nereids.
There may be nothing to it, but I think Joyce used this "Handbook."
Thetis (and Galatea) were Nereids. I find no Nereids in astronomy.

VIRGIL   270.25. That O'MARA in the left margin completes his name VIRGILIUS MARO.
But there was another VIRGILIUS MARO in the middle ages or renaissance—a grammarian who is probably being referred to here, *also*, in this grammatical section.

SAMUEL, Hebrew Judge and Prophet. On page 242, Joyce is running through some books in The Old Testament. Judges, 27; Kings, 27; Psalms 30; {Song—of Solomon .30[}]; Proverbs. . 12; {Chronicles? 241.7}; apocrypha, 242.30 Revelations. . 30; Ecclesiastes .11; Numbers. . 5:
Will you accept SAMUEL: 242.20 samhar?
[AG: Well it's bog latin]

VARIA = not for the Census but for your interest, meditation, and annotation.
267. lower left.   in Denmark the YWCA is KRISTELIG FORENING FOR UNGE KVINDER
282.5   Dan[ish]. BùN prayer BEGYNDELSE beginning.

Think this over: In your next CENSUS, maybe you should include names of persons in the early drafts but discarded. They certainly would be an aid to future students. You would mark them Hn = for HAYMAN and give his page-references. Examples from a number: TROYES, Christian de, 12th century. . . . Tristan. HN 161.21–22 SMITH, Adam . . . etc. Hn 194.6 [i.e., .26]
Think it over

URIZEN
THAMUZ (?)   } from Blake Hn 318 (they got as far as print in the *Transatlantic review*)[18]
LUVAH
UTHON (?)

On the phone I asked you about the boroughs of Dublin in SHEM I remembered wrongly. Joyce started out to identify the parts of Shem's body with the wards of Dublin. Apparently he gave it up. HAYMAN bottom of p. 301.

[attached sheet]

ADALINE I find this page at the bottom of a bureau drawer. I *think* I sent these to you before. . . . forgive it, if so. TNW

ASKAPART or ASCOPART 494.34, a conquered giant, then follower. "Sir Bevis of Hampton" old romance

---

ATREUS   49.26 [AG: I can't find it]

ATTILA   ? 100.2

HATHOR   Egypt. Aphrodite; cow-totem: 264.5–6 Horn of Heathen ? 566.[36] I am hathar {mist-heathar! one would expect THOTH of Ku Red}

—Just a suggestion: "Tea for Two" comes from "No, no, Nanette," music by Vincent Youmans:[19] 567.4 yeoman's. . . . . . 9 tet-at-tet. . . . 15 Nan Nan Nanetta.

SCHRANK   (presumed a German botanist)[20] Just to show you how devilish Joyce can be: 238.8–9 "next to our shrinking selves we love sensitivas best."

	The Sensitier Rose is called the *Schrankia uncinata* 527.27 Their sinsitives shrinked
GODOLPHIN,	Yeats went to Godolphin School[21] 563.26–27 the godolphing LAD 300.28 in a passage from Yeats' Vision.
LILY	I don't see the application here but we should bear in mind that Yeats's sisters SUSAN (Lily!!) Mary and Elizabeth Corbett were known as Lily and LOLLY. They ran the CUALA Press or DUN EMIR Press[22] at Dundrum 331.27 ? 352.21–22 396.25–26 etc!! 365.12 lolly. . . . . . .16 Don Amir. !!Damn.
JOVE George	"by Joge" 594.35
[23]*AVELING	. . . 613.30 AVELLAN jilbert or hazel . . . . . "berry". . . .orchard
HOLMES	. . . . 581.10 wendelled . . . . 12 home ? MISPRINT: your HULME 310.24 {do you mean HUMMER 310.19?} Oh, no, you mean 130.24
Fox-Goodman	403.32 vixen. . .33 chimes . . . . .church. . . . 34 goodman.
GOODMAN	Is there one in Pilgrim's Progress, like Christian, "pack on back" 428.22?
*CUCULLUS	"That cry's not Cucullus." [248.15–.16] CUCULUS, lat[in]. cuckoo [AG: hord or cowl]
CLANRICKARDE	367.32 should read 376.32
BRUCE	add 228.10
HODGES FIGGIS, bookseller in Dawson Street 347.19	
COXEY, Jacob S.	347.29 Boxer Rising and Coxey's Army.[24]

1. In *The Poetic Edda*, "The Prophecy of the Seeress: Völuspá," Yggdrasil is Ygg's (Óthin's) horse. Stanza 19, with Hollander's spacing reads: "As ash I know, hight Yggdrasil,/the mighty tree moist with white dews;/thence come the floods that fall adown;/evergreen o'ertops Urth's [fate] well this tree" (Lee M. Hollander, *The Poetic Edda*, 4).

2. Denis de Rougement, *Love in the Western World* (translated by Montgomery Belgion; 1940; rpt., Princeton: Princeton University Press, 1983), see particularly the chapter "'Tristan' as the Account of a Mystical Experience" 143–151.

3. In issue number 4 of *A Wake Newslitter* (July, 1962) under "Notice of Publications" there was an announcement: "R. Von Phul, *The Individual Passion: a Study of James Joyce and his Work*. This large study (*c.* 180,000 words, of which less than half is about FW) is now completed. Further details later" (9). The work was never published.

4. *A First-Draft Version of 'Finnegans Wake'*, edited and annotated by David Hayman (Austin: University of Texas Press, 1963).

5. Wilder was born on 17 April 1897 in Madison, Wisconsin. In September 1915 he entered Oberlin College where he remained for two years before transferring to Yale College. In April 1930 he accepted the invitation of Robert Maynard Hutchins, a friend from Oberlin and Yale appointed in 1929 as president of the University of Chicago, to teach part time. Wilder taught writing and classics in translation. He remained in Chicago for six years and returned again to the University in 1940 to teach a summer course.

6. The Fenian group responsible for the assassination of two British officials, the Chief Secretary, Lord Frederick Cavendish, and the Under-Secretary of State, Thomas Burke, in Phoenix Park, Dublin, on 6 May 1882. Based on Carey's evidence, Joe Brady, Tim Kelly, and Michael Kavanagh were arrested and hanged. A fourth man, James Fitzharris, who drove a decoy get-away cab, was sentenced to prison and paroled in 1902. Carey himself was assassinated while sailing to asylum in South Africa.

7. In *Census III* Glasheen expands her entry to explain 112.7: "The ass-as-dragoman fits with 112.7, where the Four are said to 'own the targum.' A targum is an interpretation of the Old Testament." Glasheen is correct, page 316 has 36 lines.

8. Ruth Bauerle in *Picking Up Airs* identifies this as "Old Rosin the Beau" a folk song from the 1830s.

9. The eldest daughter of the Rev. Dr. Charles Primrose and Mrs. Deborah Primrose in Oliver Goldsmith's novel *The Vicar of Wakefield* (1766).

10. Page reference to Hayman, *A First-Draft*.

11. Films by Charles Chaplin (1889–1977): *The Floorwalker* (1916), *The Kid* (1919), and *The Tramp* (1915).

12. Mabel Normand (1894–1930). In 1914 she made twelve films with Charles Chaplin for Mack Sennett's Keystone Film Company. See Chaplin Filmography in David Robinson, *Chaplin: His Life and Art* (New York: McGraw-Hill, 1985).

13. Wilder probably means Coppée's *Toute un jeunesse*, translated as *A Romance of Youth*. It was published in a volume *A Romance of Youth* together with two stories,

"Restitution" and "The Cure for Discontent" (New York: Current Literature Publishing, 1910).

14. Carl Gustave Jung (1875–1961), the Swiss psychologist and psychiatrist.

15. Page reference to Hayman, *A First-Draft*.

16. Elizabeth Chudleigh (*c*. 1720–1788) married Augustus John Hervey, the third Earl of Bristol in 1775. The Gunning sisters, described by Horace Walpole (see AG to TW, 14 December 1961, n. 5) as "two Irish girls of no fortune, who are declared the handsomest women alive" made extremely successful marriages. Mary Gunning (1732–1760) married George William Coventry, the 6th Earl of Coventry. Her sister, Elizabeth Gunning (1733–1790), married twice. Her first marriage was to James Hamilton, the 6th Duke of Hamilton; her second marriage was to Col. John Campbell, the 5th Duke of Argyll. There are extensive references to Elizabeth Chudleigh and the Gunning sisters in the correspondance of Horace Walpole published by Yale University Press.

17. In the absence of Glasheen's letter, it is impossible to know to what list Wilder refers. Benjamin Lee Guinness was Lord Mayor of Dublin in 1851.

18. The first published fragment from *Finnegans Wake*, "From Work in Progress," appeared in *The Transatlantic Review*, a journal edited by Ford Madox Ford, I, 4(April 1924), 215–223 (the *Wake*, 383–399).

19. The musical, which opened at London's Phoenix Theatre on 11 March 1925, had lyrics by Irving Caesar and Otto Harbach.

20. Franz von Paula Schrank (1747–1835). An important work was *Fauna Boica* (Nürnberg, 1789–1802).

21. Yeats was a student at the Godolphin School in Hammersmith from 1877, when his family moved to London, until 1881 when they moved to Dublin. Godolphin is also a reference to Sidney Godolphin, the first Earl of Godolphin whom Jonathan Swift satirizes in his poem "The Virtues of Sid Hamet the Magician's Rod." See TW to AG, 5 May 1962, n. 3.

22. The press was founded in 1902, the year Yeats met Joyce.

23. Why Wilder put an asterisk before this word and before Cucullus below is not clear.

24. The uprising known as the "Boxer Rebellion" began in the late 1890s as a series of local rebellions against foreigners and Chinese converts to Christianity. In 1900 the Boxers laid siege to the foreign diplomatic legations in Peking. After a bloody fifty-five day stand-off, they were defeated by an allied military force made up of troops from eight foreign countries. Jacob Sechler Coxey (1854–1951) led marches on Washington, D. C., in 1894 and 1914. His "army" was comprised of unemployed workers who demanded emergency legislation to produce work.

To Adaline Glasheen, Farmington, Connecticut

[MS. ALS—HWS]

[? August—September 1963]   [Douglas, Arizona]

Dear Adaline =
 Just some chicken-feed; but I'm very pleased with the Dante—Aguilar. But who are the others of the Four Masters: Homer. . . . Ibsen. . . . Shakespeare. . . . Rabelais. . . .?
 Lucian?
 I'm preparing something very cute for you next time: the word rake is derived from rake-hell—and that's why Rachel Lea Varian-Kate has a stiff steaded RAKE 211.18
 Rachel was the greatest of all French actresses.[1] So there are some more Rachels and Leahs.
 Ah—! won't the house be quiet without Alison!

>   Best to all
>   Thornton

[attached sheet]

FOR ADALINE[2]

COKE, Sir Edward, Lord Chief Justice of England
 98.30 cope. (The ear hears "cock and bull")
O'HAGAN, Baron Lord Chancellor of Ireland.
 98.30 Hogan {Joyce is fooling for the hundredth time with Copenhagen.[}]
 Eminent jurists are deliberating over that phallic symbol. You may find there are some more eminent jurists named Beattie. . 29. . Hare (Heer—Joyce corrects this to capitalized word) and BULL—BALL—BAYLE—BAILEY [99.32–.34].

SIMPSON's "on the Strand," restaurant in London 43.7

FESTY
HYACINTH } 94.29–31 ["]Festives and highajinks and jintyaun. . . . . .
GENTIAN not to forget now a'duna o'darnel."

HAYMAN'S book³ 78.[.13–]14 reads "Festy and hyacinth and gentian and & not to forget a'duna o'darnel"

This damned GENTIAN pops up in the HAYMAN UR-Text several times. Please notice Mrs Glasheen that one form of Gentian is the LUTEA! That whole trial is a headbreaking process. I'm not going to try to work at it.

Denis   361.10 another "Dennis, don't be threatening.["]

DANTE, ALIGHIERI
    238.3 dandy dainty (the context; will explain at length later)
    233.30 aleguere. . .alaguerre.

And, Adaline, who was one of SHEM's "four masters"?
AQUILAR = Alighieri = beautifully combined with Spanish for the EAGLE of St John. 184.34 [i.e., .35]

Dante   (but this should be on my other page "Dubious suggestions.")
    283.24 ALEGOBREW = because 283.7 (divine) comedy; and 283.8
    eloquent: De Vulgare Eloquentia.

MINNIE, Goddess of Love of the ancient Germans. Gave her name to *minna*, the courtship of the (Troubadour)—Minnesänger. By an incorrect etymology these have been identified with MINSTRELS
267.3   . . . minn': the passage is about this Cult: Kings and Tinkers shall aspire and [in] this note 2 Mannequins' Pose = all those Mannikins = Minnikens!
    508.22 music minnestirring.

There are a great many more. I think I'm going to work it up. In the German version, Gottfried of Strassburg, TRISTAN was a musician and precisely a *Minnesänger*. As in the French he was a *Trouvère*.
    [AG: I can't find Minne as Goddess Not E. B. Web]⁴

ISOLDE of the White Hands 494.21

SALOME, step-daughter of Tetrarch etc 497.33 {Hayman's page 238.34:
    Salame, the tetracha ¶ Oh! Forgive me! I see you have it!! Pardon

MODJESKA, Helena[5] Polish actress. {Joyce has been running a mixed Polish and Bohemian background since Kate entered 333.1–5 (as Catherine of Russia with her Potemkin?) It continues to Paderewski 335.24. HAYMAN (his page 180.15) shows that
    335.2 madjestky was first written "modjestky." [AG: Played Lady Macbeth in Evansville Ind.][6]
    {She played in English, *Maria Stuart* of Schiller, at Tombstone, 50 miles from Douglas. I assume she also played *Camille* 334.17, which might draw in *midgetsy* and *madgestoo* [334.18].}

BERNHARDT, Sarah[7]
    432.21 {Camille}. . 22 {Understudy}. . {Sarah}

SCHRATT, Katie   380.1–2 and her "man" is "mocked majesty" poor Emp[eror]. Franz Joseph [AG: TW gave before]

For your interest
(1) The first Marquess of Dufferin and Ava was the son of the poetess.[8]
(2) Was it you or Mrs Cristiani who told me that POULSON, Valdemer 326.26, a Danish engineer who invented a gramophone?

[attached sheet]

    FOR ADALINE = Some Dubious Suggestions:

SALE, CHICK, American vaudeville monologist and author, wrote "The Specialist," on the construction of outhouses[9]
    149.17 dispoSALE. . . . .19 spatialist. 19 sh. . . t. .
see 240.3

ROWE, Nicholas; I like to think his name is beside his play
    569.33 a fair penitent[10]. . . . bROUghton. . . rho'. . . . ro. . . sy.

LEE, Nathaniel;[11] ditto effect. If, as I'm beginning to think, these riddles are linked each to the one before and after. Then
132.8 sLEE
132.10 Rivalry Queens

WALLACE, The (Sir William) Among those great military men
    133.21 Bompart; Bonapart; Wallace; Lee, Wellesly-Wellington. . . .
etc

RAPHAEL, Archangel. We know that "St Michael Killing the Dragon" by Guido Reni[12] [AG: I don't know it] is on the wall of the Earwicker bedroom (599.11–12) [AG: 559]
here he is again 13.9 Mitchel. . . 10 wornout engraving. Well, I think the other archangel is there, too, both engaged in making music: 13.13 Farrelly—RAFFELLI

MAUSOLUS, King of Caria. His tomb at Hallicarnassus was one of the Seven Wonders of the world, and is so used by Joyce. He. . . .it. . . gave his name to all mausoleums. Would you feel like entering it?
13.14   261.13
56.14   553.10
81.5

Tam o Shanter.   As 229.26 shows Joyce is thinking of the hero of [Robert] Burns' poem, whose adventure took place by the river DOON
227.22
229.21 and 26
315.25. . . 26 tail tucked up. Witches seized The Tail of his horse MAGGIE (!)

De Foe, Daniel. The Ency. Brit. says he signed his name De Foe or Foe until the end of his life indiscriminately.
Would you care to read 540.35 FIREBUGS as also FAUBOURGS? If so, would you care to read a "run" on Defoe's works?
"A political (540.26) History of the Devil" 540.29
He wrote a life of Jack Shepherd 540.27 and Jonathan Wild 540.28
mallsight = 540.33 Moll (Flanders).
[TW margin: foreburghers 543.19]

LAMOS.   King of the cannibal Lestrygonians.
327.33 {see 600.1}

LAPLACE, Pierre-Simon. ("Celestial Mechanics"). He's gotta be in this section somewhere. I suggest he is
299.13–14 the. . . palce (footnote 2: scumhead = his comet.)

JACK THE RIPPER   Wedekind's two plays *Erdgeist* and *Box of Pandora* together make the opera "LULU." In the last act Lulu as a prostitute in London is killed by Jack the Ripper.
211.10–11 Dora RIPAR-. . . . Pan.

PETRARCH   Don't you think that PETRARCH 269.24 in the vincinity of Dante (left) and the quotation from Dante "And that your master knows well" 269.25[13]

1. Élisabeth Rachel Felix (1821–1858) made her debut at the Comédie-Française on 12 June 1838 as Camille in Corneille's *Horace*.

2. Glasheen wrote at the top of this sheet: "checked Dec 1969 AG." Next to some entries she has used a check mark, has written "yes," or inserted a question mark.

3. David Hayman, *A First-Draft Version of 'Finnegans Wake'*. The reference follows the page and line in Hayman's book and not the *Wake*.

4. *Encyclopedia Britannica* or *Webster's* dictionary.

5. Helena Modrzejewska (1840–1909) was a star of the Warsaw Theatre from 1869 until she emigrated to the United States in 1876. She changed her name to Modjeska and toured with her own company making occasional visits to England and to her native Poland. She was well-known for her Shakespearean roles.

6. Glasheen was born in Evansville, Indiana.

7. The French actress (1844–1923) played Marguerite in *La Dame aux Camélias* by Alexandre Dumas, fils (1824–1895).

8. Wilder is confusing the genealogy. The mother of the first Marquess of Dufferin and Ava was born Helen Selina Sheridan, the daughter of Thomas Sheridan, eldest son of the playwright Richard Brinsley Sheridan. The "poetess" was the Marquess's great-great-great grandmother, Frances Sheridan (1724–1766), novelist, poet, and playwright.

9. Charles (Chic or Chick) Sale (1885–1936). *The Specialist*, the story of Lem Puti, "the champion privy builder of Sangamon County," was published in 1929 and sold more than two million copies.

10. Nicholas Rowe (1674–1718). His play *The Fair Penitent*, based on Philip Massinger's and Nathan Field's play *Fatal Dowry*, was produced in 1703. Rowe was also a biographer of Shakespeare.

11. Nathaniel Lee (?1653–1692). One of his best-known plays was the verse tragedy *The Rival Queens* produced in 1677.

12. The painting, completed in 1635, is in the Church of Santa Maria della Concezione in Rome. Numerous engravings were made of the painting. See D. Stephen Pepper, *Guido Reni: A Complete Catalogue of His Works* (New York: New York University Press, 1984), entry 154.

13. Dante, *The Divine Comedy: Inferno*, V, 121–123.

To Adaline Glasheen, Farmington, Connecticut

[MS. ALS—HWS]

[?] September 1963   P. O. Box 144
                            Douglas [Arizona]

Dear Adaline:
    I suspect you're going through a phase of repudiation of F. W. (who doesn't.)
    I won't forward any more suggestions until I hear that you're interested.

x

    The latest *Litter* with your piece in it hasn't reached me.[1] I've long suspected that Mr. Hart takes a dim view of me. He probably thinks I owe my dues, too, because Fritz [Senn] while he was in dejection, wrote me that he had still not cashed and forwarded my $50 check—four months after he received it!

x

    But I'd hate to think that you'd relinquish your place as the Directress and Egeria of us all.
    Now that, alas, Alison is away, do resume your eminence.
    Keep stirring us up with your findings. Forwarding the best of mine (without naming me) to the others; and the best of theirs to me.
    Be the Lord High Lady Hub of the Wheel.
    Any day now one of the Governing Designs will crack.
    I think the first to crack will be The Heroes' Return motif. There are probably Seven of them: Barbarossa, Charlemagne, King Arthur, Rip van Winkle; Finn, The Second Coming of Christ. . . and? Oliver? Drake?
    To catch an allusion you have to know so much about their private life—for instance Barbarossa or Charlemagne (I'm not stopping to look at my notes now) won the titles of Basileus—assumed the Iron crown of Lombardy and had conferred upon him the honor of Patrician of Rome. It all fits; but there must be many more such "flecks of the whip." I can dimly see all those heroes among the Old Men in The Hospice for the Dying.
    Resurrection is the theme of the book.

Anyway.

If the latest NEWSLITTER has long since been circulated and *missed me*, will you lend me yours for a few days. It also has the Lithuanian words—and a contrib from Fritz, I think you said.²

I'm eager to hear a word from you—and how you both are—and news of Alison's enjoying her school—and is Farmington beautiful these days?

> ever
> your old friend in the desert
> Thornton

[5 cent stamp attached]
 I don't give a tinkers d—n about the zip number. I only encircled it so that it would look prettier

1. *A Wake Newslitter*, No. 15 (August 1963) contained a number of Notes by Glasheen, see bibliography.

2. *A Wake Newslitter*, No. 15 (August 1963) included "Some Lithuanian Words in FW" by Matthew J. C. Hodgart (6–7). No. 16 (September 1963) included "Some Lithuanian Words in FW: correction and addition" (7). Neither issue had contributions from Fritz Senn.

☐

To Adaline Glasheen, Farmington, Connecticut

[MS. ALS—HWS]

[postmark: 14 October 1963]   Old Douglas
Late October 1963   [Douglas, Arizona]

Dear Adaline =
 Many thanks.
 As I telegraphed you mine just arrived.
 I'd hoped you'd keep the stamps to write me some more gorgeous letters (they'll go ultimately to the Library of Congress where a few of them, like the one of the Washington, Connecticut Fleischman-Joyce mêlée, will have Marines guarding it.)¹

But don't write me a word until you've got the novel² well in hand—all hearty best wishes to it.

And greetings to Francis

Ever
Thornt.

Did you know that HEGEMONE 573.32 was one of the Charities, or Graces, that attend upon Aphrodite?

It's always bracing to recover even *one* of the 110,000 places where Joyce seems to be printing blithering irrelevancies.

TW.

1. A lost telegram. Wilder is probably referring to issue No. 16 (September 1963) of *A Wake Newslitter* which included Glasheen's "Instances Perhaps of the Tetragrammaton in *Finnegans Wake*" (5–6). The letter Wilder refers to is AG's of 6 March 1963.

2. It is not clear whether Glasheen had begun a new novel or had returned to one she had begun a few years earlier.

☐

To Adaline Glasheen, Farmington, Connecticut

[MS. ALS—HWS]

[postmark: 24 October 1963]   [Douglas, Arizona]

Dear Adaline =

A graaaand letter.¹

Mr. Dalton has asked me to recommend him for a Guggenheim on the Buffalo material.²

I told him I'd be glad to; but that Mr. Moe and the committee had often thanked me for the detailed particularity of my reports (they receive 1000s of letters about "fine chap. . . gifted poet. . . . conscientious["]. . . . and they grasp at a specific word); so I've asked Mr. D. to send me some personal data to render my commendation more vivid. He replied that he would; it has not yet come. Poor man,

from Mr. Graham's letter I learn that he hates to reveal any fact about himself.
———But SWEAR you won't tell a soul.———
I hope the novel is going great

              Ever
              (T. N.)

1. Glasheen's letter is lost. With this letter to Glasheen, Wilder returned a letter to Glasheen of 10 October 1963 from Philip Lamar Graham describing a dinner he and his wife had with Jack Dalton at their home in Bronxville, New York.
2. Dalton received a Guggenheim Fellowship for 1964–1965. His project included transcribing the almost 13,500 pages of Joyce's *Finnegans Wake* notebooks in the Library of the State University of New York at Buffalo.

☐

To Adaline Glasheen, Farmington, Connecticut

[MS. ALS—HWS]

[31 October 1963]   [Douglas, Arizona]
Halloween—1963

Dear Adaline =
    Your letter hit me just when I was having a bad day on my novel.[1]
    Anyway, I had a good one yesterday and can hope for others.
    I read that Madame [Nathalie] Sarraute—queen of the new French "anti-novel"—makes scornful fun of the use of "he said" "she replied." Well, she never was a dramatist.[2] I think they are extremely valuable as a sort of rhythmic punctuation. And then the effect of swiftness you can get when you eliminate them for a while.
                  x
    Don't tell the authors of the enclosures[3] that I didn't get much profit [from] them. Why on earth did they undertake an article on precisely those eighteen lines when they found so little coherence in them—?

Do you suppose it's possible that they did that without submitting it to [a] Czech-speaker! The Czech allusions go on all the way to [333].28 Praha = Prague and .36 Marienbad.

I'll bet [333].14 weerpovy. . dreevy drawly. . 28 ropeloop. . . 35 dauberg and lots of others are reflections of Czech words.

But don't let my words discourage you from enclosing anything like that. I devour't.

> On with the novels.
> Ever
> (T)

1. A reference to a lost letter. Wilder was working on his novel *The Eighth Day*.
2. Saurraute, the Russian-born (1901–1999) French writer, had started writing plays, at first for radio and then the theater in the 1960s.
3. The enclosures have not remained with the letter.

◻

To Adaline Glasheen, Farmington, Connecticut

[MS. ALS—HWS]

[postmark: 16 November 1963, Tucson]

P. O. Box 144
Douglas, Arizona
As from: 50 Deepwood Drive
Hamden Conn mid November

Dear Adaline—

Arizona stay coming to an end.

Have written Isabel that I'm not ready to return to Urban civilization yet—want one more year's hideaway. May be in Europe by the end of January.

Am closing FW for a year or two. When I return to it I hope the next generation will have made much progress.

Before I sail I'll send you a sheaf of items—without selections from them—some trivial, wrong, repetitions, maybe some good.[1]

And two books: White's The Godstone and The Blackymore.[2] On page 66 an account of "Queen" Gracia O'Malley's meeting with Queen Elizabeth and the words of Irish she gave the Queen as a sample of her tongue. I called J[ack]. Dalton's attention to it and he's rustling up a translation. Also O'Donovan Rossa's daughter's book[3]: It appears that her father's name was alternately given as Diarmuid or Jeremiah. So JERRY = Diarmuid. What a wall covered with books closely or remotely related to FW you must have. And what filing cabinets!

It may be that someday you'll get a long distance call from Switzerland or Samoa wistfully asking you if there have been some sensational discoveries in you-know-what.

Send my best to Alison.—(My, I was shocked to hear that the preparation at the Farmington High was poor!)

Cordial best to Francis.

My letter's beginning to sound like a last farewell—I don't mean it so.

All power to the novel. Plan to take a year and a half to it. I always do. It's harder for us than for the Victorians; we have to invent the form as well as recount the action. Sez I.

       your old friend
       Thornton

1. Probably the listing we have dated [? December 1963].

2. T. H. (Terence Hanbury) White's, *The Godstone and the Blackymor*, illustrated by Edward Ardizzone (New York: G. P. Putnam's Sons, 1959), is a narrative of White's travels in western Ireland. It details Irish social life and customs. White writes: "Elizabeth, interested by her savage rival, made inquiries about the Irish and their tongue. An illustration of the barbaric language was given to her, thus: 'D'it damh dubh ubh amh ar neamh.' She thought it sounded very peculiar—not so peculiar, however, as Gránia O Mhaille considered a similar English sentence: 'Beg a big egg from Peg.'" The book is not in HWS.

3. In TW to AG, [? December 1963] the book is identified as Margaret O'Donovan-Rossa Cole's *Cead míle fáilte (A Hundred Thousand Welcomes): A Visit to Ireland* (New York: Exposition Press, 1953). Her father, Jeremiah O'Donovan Rossa (1831–1915), was a political activist and writer in the cause of Irish independence. The book is a record of her journey to Europe to participate with members of her family at the official unveiling of the O'Donovan Rossa memorial and park in Skibbereen. As Margaret O'Donovan Rossa she had written *My Father and My Mother Were Irish* which details their lives and political struggles (New York: The Devin-Adair Co., 1939). The copy of *Cead* Wilder sent is in HWS.

To Adaline Glasheen, Farmington, Connecticut

[MS. ALS—HWS]

[? November 1963]   [Douglas, Arizona]
Last days in Arizona

Dear Adaline =
    You sure have been cookin' on all burners.[1]
    Cheers.

x

rê "Imperial City" 130.35 my WEBSTER Int. says "a city that is or was seat of an empire, as, esp. ROME."
    I assume you see he's working on identifying Dublin with other cities all over the world
130.27   24 Dublins in the U. S. A.
   .29   LUBLIN, Poland x Dublin
   .30   rose BUD. . . NIL (French spelling of Nile): so you have
           two NILES
   .34   U and I and in BLDNS = D (U) BL (I) N.
So Erin's free port in the British Empire.
    Query = . . . 35 pelhaps. . . did Pelops found Sparta?
    213.5–6 Ho = sorrow. . . great

x

Mrs Dounia BUNIS CHRISTIANI
    born a Russian in Russia.
    m. a Dane lived only 2 years in Denmark.
    lost her husband in a very short time
    brought up two daughters
    Teaches. Did that Joyce thesis at a professor's urging, though
        confessing to limited knowledge of Scandin. languages
        (but is obviously a bright alert woman)
    is nearing 50.
    big ambition is to be a dramatist. Translated some short
        passages from *Master Builder* in her thesis very
        beautifully, as I told her.
    Her first letters sounded discouraged doleful and self-pitying;
        then she got into correspondence with Isabel, also, and
        her letters became very engaging.

I urged her to do a *Hans Ch. Andersen in FW* paper. She said she thought she saw the *Little Mermaid* all through the closing pages. I pointed out *goloshes* and *matchbox* in the Mewsy room. *The Goloshes of Time* should be a FW theme, eh?

I fear she desponds easy.

I urged her to send you her thesis, maybe she's shy.[2]

Why not try yourself? It certainly contains enough good notations to make up a better number of *Newslitter* than we generally see.

In your role of muse and Egeria, would you like to goad and stir her up?

    Mrs D. B. Christiani
    9 Carstensen Road
    Scarsdale,
    New York.

Just sent you two books.[3] When *I* wrap a parcel that means devotion. I have closed my FW for 2 years.

    all power to you
    (T)

---

1. A reference to a lost letter.
2. Glasheen reviewed Christiani's book for *Criticism: A Quarterly for Literature and the Arts*. See Bibliography, 1967.
3. The books by T. H. White and Margaret O'Donovan-Rossa Cole referred to in his letter of 16 November 1963.

To Adaline Glasheen, Farmington, Connecticut

[MS. ALS—HWS]

[?22–27 November 1963][1]   50 Deepwood Drive
                                          Hamden 17, Connecticut

Dear Adaline =

What's this? They're not 1001—MI—but 101—or have I missed something?— CI—[2]

x

I'm probably telling you things you know already or things that *you* told me—but I go ahead just the same.

In 23.6 GREMITO is a groan

90.31–32 (Bella Cohen's was corner of Mecklenberg and Mabbot Sts—Mecklenberg St later called Tyrone St later Railway St [)] (445.2)[3]

    hure [445.4], Germ. whore

    whore

    scortum—lat. harlot

    strump [530.14, 556.30]

    . . . putta (Italian (formerly a respectable word)). puttana (583.9)

414. [.19–.20] a cough = German Husten.

    French tousser

424 [.20–.22]: all those elements in Norse myth that you taught me

    TYR

    MOLNIT

    FENRIS

    LOKI

    SURT

    . . . . Thor

It must have been awful for Lucia to live in Italy because they cross themselves and run when they see a person with a fault in the eye: Malocchio—Maldocchio—gettatura = the evil eye. I think the Malachy's—*Let Erin Remember*—play into this.[4] It must have been no less a terrible experience for the parents.

I can find only one (upset) cross the eyes and dot the t's: 542.14; I'm sure there are more.

                x

I don't feel the need of bringing "Lucias" to "Elizabeths."

I remember the Belisha beacons during the blackouts in London:[5]

267.8 [i.e., .12] follow me up to Carlo {Carlino: Charlie Chaplin} with unspeaking—pantomime nods for gestures (Lucia studied the Dalcroze Eurythmic gesture school)—our Persephone (margin = CID = DIS ran off with her for half of every year). . . . spells peace, being a rainbow Be LUCIA—tower of light—green-orange-red blue etc. . . . flag-flog-iris = fleur de LUCE.

    [(]footnote 4 Lucia-Anna loves; Anna loved; Anna loved (annaba) Pa.)

    It's all over the book

Oh, yes, the LU works in as a W. C. but that's a part of the GIODANO—Jordan-pot too—that why Shem is so consistently LOW. His lowness is at its worst in 171.25–28 where it's no accident that she is an Arch duchess—rainbow less—as is confirmed by 171.16[.]

This is one of the letters to destroy. . . or block out this nasty paragraph.

Yes, indeed, interchange K and C. . . Hell, that's child's play to what we are permitted. Grimm's Law permits us to exchange P and K 120.2 and V and B and L and R.

"Why do I look like. . . .Porter-plesse"[21.18–.19, 22.5–.6]— undoubtedly LUCIA to her father. . . some family-joke-riddle.

—But I do feel we're getting closer than we've been for years

Happy Thanksgiving to all
Thornton

---

1. After eighteen months, Wilder left Douglas, Arizona, sometime during the week of 17 November. He returned east to attend a White House ceremony and a celebration of his brother Amos's retirement from the Harvard Divinity School. On 4 July 1963 President John Kennedy announced that thirty-one Americans would receive the newly established Presidential Medal of Freedom. The ceremony was scheduled for September, but it was canceled after the death in August of the infant son of President and Mrs. Kennedy. It was rescheduled for the end of November, but was then postponed because of the assassination. The ceremony took place in the State Dining Room of the White House on Friday, 6 December. In addition to the thirty-one individuals previously named, two posthumous medals were awarded: one to President Kennedy and one to Pope John XXIII. The citation for Wilder read: "Artist of rare gaiety and penetration, he has inscribed a noble vision in his books, making the commonplaces of life yield the wit, the wonder and the steadfastness of the human adventure" (*New York Times*, 7 December 1963, 1, 14).

2. A reference to a lost letter in which Glasheen may have discussed the ideas that developed into her article "Part of What the Thunder Said in *Finnegans Wake*" which was published in *The Analyst*, No. XXIII (November 1964), 1–29.

3. In the "Circe" episode of *Ulysses*, Stephen Dedalus, Vincent Lynch, and Leopold Bloom visit a brothel run by Bella Cohen.

4. The line, "torcs of tomahawks aglitter on their breasts, when Malachi wore the collar of gold" (*Ulysses* 1961: 45.12–.13), refers to Malachi (948–1022), a high king of Ireland who fought against the Scandinavian invaders and took the "collar of Tomar" from the neck of a Danish chieftain he had defeated. Joyce quotes "When Malachi wore the collar of gold" from Thomas Moore's "Let Erin Remember the Days of Old."

5. Black and white posts with an amber colored light (now usually flashing) on the pavement at each end of a pedestrian crossing. They were named after Leslie Hore-

Belisha, Minister of Transport from 1931 to 1937. Wilder made one war-time visit to London, 10 September to 18 October 1941, when he substituted for Archibald MacLeish at the Seventeenth International Congress of P.E.N. For a detailed account of the congress and Wilder's post-congress activities, see Burns and Dydo, Stein/Wilder letters, 296–297, note 1.

☐

To Adaline Glasheen, Farmington, Connecticut

[MS. Autograph Lists—HWS]

[? December 1963][1]

FOR ADALINE

PACKENHAM, family name of the Earls of Longford. Very literary family. The present Earl, very obese, has run the Gate Theatre for many years. Assoc. [AG: Drake's wife] here with ham and bacon manufacturers. 39.17 603.1

PATHÉ, French inventor and motion picture producer of news-reels. As on 602.7 [i.e., .27]
Patathicus = the funeral games of Patroclus in Iliad (602.22), the dragging of Hector's buddy (.26–.27) around Troy, and "overheard" pathic = homosexual partners, a sneer at Achilles and Patroclus.

In the poem that opens the Alice books the three girls are PRIMA, SECUNDA, and TERTIA. Alice Liddel is PRIMA (I don't know the names of the other two)[2]
360.4 prime and secund. . . terce.
361.22 primerose (and two Isas Boldmans.) ISAS because they went rowing on the ISIS river in Oxford. {The Thames in Oxford is called the ISIS}
CONSIDER:
    248.3   nude her (photographed so) in her prime. . . . Angus Dagdasson (Dodgson)
    10   Allysloper = Alice-lover {.8 pallet: P. . A. . . L pleasure Alice Liddel}

287.10 prisme = rainbow-girl. . . second. {Note 1. "Will you walk into my."
in *Alice* becomes "Will you walk a little faster." [}]

MacPherson, Aimée S. {Verify: wasn't her church in L. A.—I went there once—called The Four Square Tabernacle?}[3] If so: 584.31 till amie. . . Tubbernacul.

STELLA-ESTHER   That's an important ESTHER 22.2
Not only the King Mark and the Finn-Fingel and the Earl of Howth families are being interfered with, but Mayor Bartholomew Van Homrigh's [21.13], too. First there were "falling angles" [21.25] and then there were STARshootings 22.12

BRANGWAIN, Wagner's BRAGÄNE, responsible for the whole Tristan-Iseult passion 21.15
She may not be present in all the Prankqueen allusions, but she certainly is here.

GRANIA (GRAINNE) Surely, that's she taking charge at the wake of her husband Fin 7.9. . . Fin-7.15
7.9 GRINNY sprids the boord.

The oldest son of the Earl of Howth would be, in every generation, would be a Sir Armory Tristam St Laurence. Joyce has Grace O'Mall[e]y steal not one but TWO babies; he splits the baby's name: so add: Hi-LARY 21.12, 21.36 LARRYHILL 22.19.

GUINIVERE (JENNIFER, GINEVIR)
112.26 Janiveer. . . . 28 majesty, 29 mistress of Arthur. Maybe 406.20 {Fingerhut: German for thimble; Genever: German for GIN but he's toasting another girl Daphne in 406.25 whose name is also the name of a liquor.[}]

MISPRINTS: JESUS 349.20 should read 349.24 Schaffi Fritz should read SCHEFF
Your CUCHULAIN 35.22 should read 35.32

NOISE, son of USNECH, lover of DEIDRE[4]—in Yeats' and Synge's plays NAISI, dict'ry says pronounced NOI-SHE.

290.28 Nash (Joyce—see Hayman p. 162[5]—first wrote NASHE. This is in the passage, after Dante, Inferno V, treating of guilty lovers.)

GOTOBED, Senator. Trolloppe's "The American Senator"[6] 370.17

[attached sheet]

FOR ADALINE

BARRYMORE, John. American actor. There is a "Barony of Barrymore" and a song with that title.[7]

399.[28]	fourth stanza (in the "John" stanza.)
373.5	Moherboher. Here is John again in fourth place, with his "sailalloyd donggie." 373.4. The "celluloid art." 534.25, is the movies.
	"lloyd" [373.4] may well be Harold Lloyd, the American screen comedian.
24.21	Bower Moore, again as John in fourth place, following *Luke* Wadding, in third place.
5.36	{Mark lives at Powerscourt, passim. Here we jump Luke and arrive at John, the bore the more.[}]

WADDING, Luke. add 24.20. See above.

NESTLÉ, Swiss milk products manufacturer 243.23; maybe 136.16

Isolde of the White Hands   ? 157.17 Blemish

FABER and FABER, English publisher of FW and of the Criterion Miscellany which contained portions of FW; of booklet edition of Anna Livia Plurabelle and Haveth Childers Everywhere.[8] T. S. Eliot was one of the directors.
65.32 (The page is a parody of Eliot's *Sweeney Agonistes*.)
150.27 F— and Father (publisher of Criterion 150.4)

I think you'd do well to make the following careful distribution in nomenclature. I cull these from Fritz Senn's paper. I leave the other names there to you, esp DAMMAN[9]

FINGAL—add, son of COMHAL and MORNA (q. v.). ¶ Oscar Wilde was christened FINGAL

CUMHAL, see BELOW

MORNA, in OSSIAN's poems, wife of COMHAL, mother of FINGAL
or Finn MacCool.[10] (In the Irish cycles his mother was ???).
MUIRNE or MORNA means "a woman beloved by all."
189.25 597.33

OSSIAN or OISIN or (in Yeats's poems USHEEN), son of Finn etc;
husband of EVERALLIN q. v; and father of OSCAR
add 243.12 is OSSIAN USHEEN

ORRERY, etc should you mention: wrote a memoir on Swift[11] from
which Joyce frequently quotes? inventor of a portable planetarium—
"hurling stars["] 144.8

CUMHAL, name in OSSIAN's poems for the father of FINGAL or
FINN MACCOOL.
In the Irish cycles his name was CUMMAL q. v.
124.29 Fjorgn Camhelsson

FINN   The above FJORGN for FINN shows that Joyce likes to
relate his Finn to Norse sources, so he gives a reading to an Irish
patriotic lodge (probably FIANNA originally): FJORN 622.6

PASSE PARTOUT   (master key). Phogg's valet "80 Days Around the
World."[12] 25.5

DIARMUID—DERMOT: "Turn back the Virgin Page"[13] 270.26
[i.e., .25] is sung to the tune of "Dermot" 270.26 "two muters."

[attached sheet]

FOR ADALINE

NARCISSUS
    475.10 [i.e., .9–.10] {daffodils. . . . flowers of Narcissus}
    522.30–31 narcissism. . . . 33 nursis sym/

PETERSON (of Kapp and Peterson, tobacconists)
529.30   rooking (Germ. *rauchan* to smoke) the pooro
    (*puro* Sp. the best cigar). . . puffing at his Paterson.
420.31–421.1   Buy Paterson's matches.

Probably: 428.13–14 . . . glow luck to your bathershins (Paterson's matches).

SAMSON (Heb. shimshon) 530.2–3 blind. . . . shamshem

PRETORIUS, A. W. (if you care to use it) Dutch pioneer—founded Transvaal; gave name to PRETORIA 542.2 (Geographical section; suspect in same line Liberia and Thailand.

Query: Isn't there a Robert W. Service ballad The Shooting of *Dan Mcgrew*? 494.26 Dan Magraw. {Joyce first wrote Magrath. Hayman p. 238 [.20][14]}

QUERY: Could Joyce be combining two Lefanu novels[15]
470.7   SILAS "Uncle"
        DORCAS heroine of Wylder's hand
Or: As your Census suggests are these St. Paul's associates to whom can be added TABITHA 470.8 tappyhands

       Belial 175.5
       Bellydull 194.17 [AG: can't find]

[attached sheet]
FOR ADALINE

PRUFROCK, Alfred
 166.15 brieffrocked
 236.13—frufrocksfull {You don't accept this after ELLMAN[N] p. 510, footnote?} [1982: 495]

VESTA   234.15

CHARLES II   King of England 112.35 Halley suggested a constellation: robur
   Caroli = Charles' Oak. (Charles I executed before Halley was born)

GEORGE IV   King of England. [William] Herschel proposed naming the newly discovered planet URANUS the SIDUS GEORGIANUM = estate, mansion. 140.30

CHARLEMAGNE   426.25 Charles's Wain = the Dipper; Ursa Major.

HAMBONE   177.21 Negro figure in American comic strips {SHEM is Negro-Ham here: 177.4 nigger 19 interlocutor in a Minstrel show; 27 eenie meenie miney moe, catch a nigger.[}]

[sheet pasted onto existing sheet]

FOR ADALINE

CAIRBAR
   After reading Fritz's [Senn] note for Ossian—probably more detailed than the contribution he is sending to Newslitter,—following suggestion occurs. Since two of the three references to this CAIRBAR appear in Ossian context, it might be best to use Ossian's spelling and cross-reference the other spellings to it. (Maybe later many other references will appear from Irish-cycle texts—in which case it must be reconsidered.[)]
CAIRBAR, Lord of ATHA, 194.5 in Ossianic poems. As despicable as his brother CATHMOR (q. v.) was noble. In Irish text his name appears as CAIPRE or CARPERY
144.5 194.2 228.18 390.35

CARBERY   see CAIRBAR

CARPERY   see CAIRBAR

EITHNE   add 318.12

ULERIN   in Ossian's TEMORA, Ul-erin, "The guide to Ireland,"
   a star

DIARMUID
JEREMIAH
   I picked up a book by the daughter of Diarmuid O'Donovan Rossa ("Cead mile failte" by Margaret O'Donovan Rossa Cole—I'll send it to you). She resolutely calls her father Jeremiah O'Donovan Rossa—and so he probably called himself during his years in America. So I assume that it is correct: all those Jerry's can be read Diarmuid and Dermot.

ONDT AND GRACEHOPPER[16] 489.4 grapce. . . . .upper. . . . .end

1. This is probably the "sheaf of items" mentioned in Wilder's letter of 16 November 1963. At the top of the first page Glasheen writes "checked for 3rd Dec 1969." Glasheen uses check marks, question marks, and "no" as part of her review of these lists.

2. See TW to AG, ?25–30 September 1962, n. 2.

3. McPherson founded the International Church of the Foursquare Gospel in 1927.

4. Both Yeats's *Deirdre* (first performed in 1906, published 1907) and John Millington Synge's *Deirdre of the Sorrows* (1907–1909, left unrevised at his death) are based on the Ulster, or Red Branch, cycle of Irish mythology. In Yeats's play Naoise is a young king and Deirdre is his queen. In Synge's play Naisi, the son of Usna, is Deirdre's lover.

5. A page reference to Hayman, *A First-Draft*.

6. Anthony Trollope's novel published in 1877. Wilder consistently misspells his name as Trolloppe.

7. Neither Hodgart and Worthington in *Song* nor Bauerle in *Picking Up Airs* identify this song. Ruth Bauerle has suggested that this may be a reference to *Barry of Ballymore*, a 1911 play by Rida Johnson Young, which starred Chauncey Olcott (1860–1932), an actor and singer of Irish ballads. During the play Olcott sang three songs, one of which, "Mother Machree" (words by Rida Johnson Young and music by Ernest R. Ball), later became the theme song of John McCormack. "It's certainly one of the songs JJ made fun of McC for singing" (email received, 22 July 1998).

8. For information on Faber & Faber, see TW to AG, 1 June 1959, n. 1.

9. Senn had sent Wilder and Glasheen a draft of an article that would be published as "Ossianic Echoes," in *A Wake Newsletter*, N.S., III, 2 (April 1966), 25–36. His article argues "that Joyce not only drew extensively on the Ossianic text, but also made use of information supplied in Macpherson's notes, as well as of the etymologies of some names" (25).

10. Fionn mac Cumhaill is the hero of the Fionn or Ossianic cycle of medieval Celtic tales.

11. John Boyle, Earl of Orrery, *Remarks on the Life and Writings of Dr. Jonathan Swift, Dean of St. Patrick's Dublin* (Dublin: George Faulkner, 1752).

12. Jules Verne, *Around the World in 80 Days* (1873).

13. A Thomas Moore song.

14. Page reference to Hayman, *A First-Draft*.

15. Enclosed with this letter was a review by Naomi Lewis, from the *New Statesman* of 8 November 1963 (663–664), of new editions of Joseph Sheridan Le Fanu's: *Wylder's Hand* and *Uncle Silas* (both originally published in 1864). At the top of the second page of the review, Wilder wrote: "How well they write these English weeklies!"

16. *Finnegans Wake* (414.16–419.10), an episode based on La Fontaine's "The Ant and the Grasshopper."

1964

To Adaline Glasheen, Farmington, Connecticut

[MS. ALS—HWS]

[postmark: 29 June 1964]¹ [50 Deepwood Drive
Sunday afternoon. Hamden 17, Connecticut]

Dear Adaline =
    Rê Hermes as black. That is some by-legend. He was born on Cyllene, (modern Zeria), highest mountain in the Peloponnesus. He certainly was not black to the Greeks. (Nor were the Egyptians thought of as black.)
    All the characters pass into a black phase (ALP is a turf-brown mummy—mammy 194.22) and, of course, SHEM is HAM—the "nigger bloke" and hambone p. 177.4, 21[.]
    409.14–15 "mower O meeow"—yes, is Romeo. But here it's the Italian version of the "How are you my dark fellow". . . . *signor Moro,* (moor) *mio.* Perhaps the ear hears another reference to the great tenor, Mario, Prince of Candia 408.10 [i.e., .11]. . . . and Candia is in candylock 409.13, and the favorite tenor aria, *Ecco ridente* ("Barber of Seville")² 409.12 {See Dictionary: Candy, form of Candia, Crete, in herbs etc} So: *Signor Moro mio* could also be *Mario mio.*
    456.23 Don't go too fast on those girls being oxen, being eaten. . . . the word in Greek also means cabbage.

    443.34 Mother. . . . 35 corky: Gorky (? again)

    Consider: Mangan by John D. Sheridan: quotes (p. 36) "I am grinning. . . through a horse-collar["] {443.25 [i.e., .26]} and p. 56 "his teeth were an ill-fitting["] see {443.25 ["]jawcrockeries"}, several attempts made to get him reformed by Father Mathews {443.28 "Father Mathew's bridge pin"} and from Mangan's poem about the Barmecides, "My eyes are filmed["] {443.33 [i.e., .34] filma. . . 443.36 "eyes a bit scummy."}[3]

Don't see what it adds up to, but it appears to fit.

After all these years no one has decided what that "tree of life" is composed of? {504.20ff}

Am sending you the "Winter 1964" Sewanee Review—3 Joyce papers.[4] ("Oh Lord, how long!")

       Best to all in your house
       ever
       Thornton

De Valera—
See 307.13 "Our Allies the Hills." The left margin associates this with SAMSON

Now see *Scribbledehobble*[5] p. 112 line 3: "our loyal allies the hills["] (De Valera)

Why should he associate De Valera with Samson?

But he does—very complicatedly: viâ SAMS and SAMUAELS 341.36ff Slippery SAM. . . . was slooching about. . . Tomtinker TIM (Healy)[6] his faithful retainer. . . the (eyes) are the (eyes) of SAMAEL but the (ears) are the (ears) of TIMOTH. . . 342.11 De Valera's Dominican (asses). . . . . .13 the Governor-General.

HERMES-THOTH-MERCURY-CHRIST MAILMAN AND THIEF
I enclose a rough work-sheet for the Sermon
As a Thief, he is the Knave of Hearts who stole the Tarts:
$$\begin{cases} 459.33 \\ 430.7 \times 25 \end{cases}$$
and all famous highwaymen 457.11 (In a card pack knave in French is VALET in Germ BUBE pron[ounced] boob)

Sloffella   As mailman he is postillion, French, *facteur*, 451.9

In Athens a HERM stood at street corners—shrine, phallic symbols, and street-sign: Joyce identifies it with a British mail-box ("pillarbox") {66.26 "halpbrother of a herm, a pillarbox" and note too connection with THOTH's IBIS 66.25}. 471.7 and 17

436.6 *la Gazza Ladra* (opera by Rossini) means "the thieving blackbird or magpie."
444.31 Why isn't there more about Patch Purcell?
NOTE: on reverse of sketch-sheet the important gnostic identification THOTH with Christ.
Does that motivate the Stations of the Cross?

For your meditation:
LUKE-TARPEY-HEALY
The Tarpeian Rock in Rome—after Tarpeia who betrayed the city—is type word for Traitor. Do you find betrayal-motifs gathered about the THIRD OLD MAN?
I find 390.13 Tom ("doubting Thomas") Tim (Tim Healy) Tarpey. And no doubt about the Roman Traitress: 526.30 Tarpeyan.

[attached sheet]

HERMES IN SERMON 429—   valet coem Bub
First Sketch—in the hope that something will be useful

429.14 [i.e., .2]   COTHURNUS—has been changed to: CO-T-HURM-
430.25   *Tartlets knave 30 pouch 20 post* 10 allo posto (Play Post Office)
432.25   furtive: (Lat. furtum = theft)
433.12   {? knife. . . = knave (of hearts?)} . . .14 heart.
434.24   heartsies
435
436.6   *ragazza ladra*   21 thief 22 [i.e., .7] smuggling
438.14   postequities
440.20   hearts 27 robbing [line drawn to "robbing" citation 453.18]
442.33   pillarbox
444.31   parcels
445
446.8   hearts— uniter of U. M. I. hearts   28 post
449.10   girl of my heart's
450.12   heart's delight
451.9   factor (Fr. facteur = postman)
452.10   th'auth 13 th'oth th'eth 8 SISSIBIS = IBIS (IBIS = over) .28 patch (Purcell)
453.36   postilium (Postillion) 18 robbing
454.20   swifter as mercury 16 geepy, O = G(eneral) P(ost) O(ffice)

455.11   Postmartem [454.]4 letterman
456.29   postages 24 posthaste .{26 LETTERS} 28 understamp
457.11   Duval. . .12 Turpin (thieves = Highwaymen)
458.36   heartless awes
459.33   masterthief of hearts
460.17   stele our harts   25 hearz'waves   21 posts
461.
462.22   post 5 stafetta [stafetta is circled and a line drawn to "staffet" in 469.7]
465
467.35   rhearsilvar
469.29   postludium   7 staffet
470.2   hermetic prod   29 mailed a letter 26 post
471.17   herm   7 pillarbosom
472.22   postanulengro   34 postexilic
473

IBIS: *Graves: The White Goddess*:[7] p. 241 "THOTH the God whose symbol was a crane-like white ibis."
   IBID p. 249 "THOTH who invented hieroglyphs was symbolized by the ibis."
N. B. IBID p. 311 "in the word which was THOTH, Hermes, Mercury and, for the Gnostics, *Jesus Christ* was said to dwell."

1. There is no extant correspondence since Wilder to Glasheen, [? December 1963]. Wilder and his sister Isabel sailed on the *Cristoforo Colombo* from New York on 4 January 1964 and arrived in Naples, Italy, on 12 January. By leaving when they did, they avoided the publicity attending the opening of *Hello Dolly!*, the Jerry Herman musical suggested by Wilder's *The Matchmaker*, which opened in New York on 16 January 1964. During the six months he was in Europe (Isabel returned to the United States in late February), Wilder traveled in Italy, France, and Switzerland and continued work on his novel *The Eighth Day*. Wilder returned to Miami, Florida, via Curaçao on 27 May 1964. He remained in Florida until 11 June when he left for Stockbridge, Massachusetts, where he remained until 15 June when he returned to his home in Hamden, Connecticut.

2. In the opening scene of Rossini's opera, Count Almaviva, who is in love with Rosina, the ward of Dr. Bartolo, arrives at her home just before dawn with his servant Fiorello and a group of musicians. He serenades Rosina in the aria "Ecco ridente in cielo," "Lo, in the smiling sky." The reference to "Mario, Prince of Candia," is probably to John McCormack. See Hodgart and Bauerle, *Joyce's Grand OPEROAR*.

3. See TW to AG, 29 October 1962, n. 6. This is an instance where Wilder, working from his notes, repeats almost verbatim information he has already given to Glasheen.

4. The *Sewanee Review*, LXXII, 1 (Winter 1964), published three articles on Joyce grouped together in a box on the cover: Mary T. Reynolds's "Joyce and Nora: The Indispensible Countersign," [29]–64; Robert Scholes's "Joyce and the Epiphany: The Key to the Labyrinth?" [65]–77; and William Irwin Thompson's "The Language of *Finnegans Wake*," [78]–90.

5. Joyce's *Scribbledehobble: The Ur-Workbook for 'Finnegans Wake'*, ed. Thomas E. Connolly.

6. Timothy Michael Healy (1855–1931), the Irish Nationalist leader and first governor general of the Irish Free State (1922–1927).

7. Wilder is quoting from the 1948 edition. In the amended and enlarged edition of Robert Graves's *The White Goddess: A Historical Grammar of Poetic Myth* (New York: Noonday Press, 1966) the quotations appear on pages 227, 233, and 286.

To Adaline Glasheen, Farmington, Connecticut

[MS. ALS—HWS]

[postmark: 16 July 1964]   [50 Deepwood Drive
                                      Hamden 17, Connecticut]

Dear Adaline =
    Some notes gleaned from an article in the Yale Library.[1]
    He speculates about WHERE and WHEN of the dream.
    Thinks 1132 may be a "bloomer" [i.e., blooper] for 1172 when Henry II granted Dublin to Bristol.
    (J. J. he thinks, made the mistake—it was printed in *transition* and he didn't deign to alter it thereafter.)
    Speculates about the only years when a Sat-Sunday night came on the eve of Michaelmas.
    He feels that J J returned to his religious faith in FW.
    Denis Johnston—author of Plays—"The Moon in the Yellow River" "The Old Lady Says No"—both produced by Abbey Theatre and in New York—has been in this country a long time. I met him a moment when he was heading the Provincetown Theatre. Now teaches at Amherst or some college in that area.[2]

                Best to all
(T)

P. S. I find no passage that could refer to an "Anglers Rest."[3]

Place of FW house = either a MULLINGAR Inn (in photos of Chapelizod.)[4]
p. 264
    BRISTOL Inn or bar (not identified in Chapelizod) or Anglers Rest walk from Strawberry Beds in the direction of a place called The Wren's Nest
Phoenix Distillery (Joyce's father once a director)
~~St. Lawrence's Episcopal Church of Ireland~~
~~Isolde's Garden~~
Shirley
~~Buona Vista~~
Glenburnie
~~Santa Rosa~~
Glenmaroon
Mt Sackville Convent 375.12

    half a mile from Chapelizod Bridge is a grocer's shop and public house Anglers Rest. built in 1870 by a certain Gibney
    about the same time as the Mardyke Mills opposite (at one time a distillery)
    Here too—across the stream—is an abandoned Ink Works: "the haunted inkbottle" and an early site of the Phoenix Laundry.
    So we direct our feet up St. Martin's Row toward the Anglers Rest
    Furthermore on the south side of the Liffey and probably visible from it (—? the Anglers Rest?)
~~Glenthorn~~
New Holland Iron Works
~~Orchard Lodge~~
Riversmount
~~Bellgarve~~
*~~Ardeevin~~
Mulberry Hill (now the Drummond Institute) and
~~Glenaulin~~ (Tim Healy's home until his death)

*not built until 1916 after J J's last visit to Ireland—suggests that J J also worked from the Ordnance Survey

[on side of paper]
    The Massachusetts Review Winter 1964

"Clarify Begins At": The Non-Information of Finnegans Wake by Denis Johns[t]on

[attached sheet]⁵

FOR ADALINE

O'MALLEY, Grace 317.36   gragh knew well {Hayman, p. 36,⁶ shows that J J first wrote Granmaile}

For your interest: many have felt that 234.6ff pictures, among others, De VALERA; but I've always wanted further confirmation.

So: *de Valera and the March of a Nation* by Mary C. Bromage (N. Y., The Noonday Press, 1956) p. 75 Healy first met de Valera: "The ebullient Sinn Feiner could not, as Healy noted, pronounce either the thick or thin "th" and his "dats" and "turks" grated on the ear."

Now read 234.16. . . "and dem dandypanies knows de play of de eyelids."

Bluetooth, HARALD is maybe 323.4 Bloodooth and the Harald as given in the CENSUS on the next page 324.28

Dolly Varden⁷ is a trout of the Salvelinas genus.

PICKWICK PAPERS: probably just a coincidence:
Opening of Chapter II (Pick-Pps):
That punctual servant of all work, the sun, had just risen, and begun to strike a light
FW 41.9—the bustling tweeny-dawn of all works. . . . .had not been many jiffies. . . polishing

---

1. The article, which Wilder mentions later in this letter, is Denis Johnston's "Clarify Begins At: The Non-Information of *Finnegans Wake*" (357–380) which was part of a special section, "Writers of Twentieth-Century Ireland," in *The Massachusetts Review*, V, 2 (Winter 1964). Richard M. Kain's "James Joyce's Shakespeare Chronology" (342–355), was the other article in this section which dealt with Joyce. Throughout this letter, and the first attached sheet, Wilder draws on Johnston's article and its detailed discussion of places mentioned or alluded to on pages 264–265 of the *Wake*.

2. Denis Johnston (1901–1984), the Irish playwright. In 1928 his first play, "Shadowdance," was rejected by Lady Gregory for the Abbey Theatre. A year later it was presented by the newly formed Dublin Gate Theatre Studio (later the Gate

Theatre) at the Peacock Theatre on 3 July 1929. The title of the play was changed to *The Old Lady Says 'No!'*, to reflect Lady Gregory's rejection. The play became a staple of the Gate Theatre and in February 1948 it was included in a festival of three Irish comedies produced by the Gate Theatre in New York. The American premiere of the play was at Amherst College in 1935. The first production of Johnston's *The Moon in the Yellow River* was at the Abbey Theatre, Dublin, on 27 April 1931. It was produced in New York by the Theatre Guild in March 1932. Johnston, who had earned a law degree from Harvard Law School, practiced law in Dublin from 1926 to 1936. He moved to the United States in 1947 and worked for the Theatre Guild. He taught at Amherst College (1950), Mount Holyoke College (1950–1960), and was the head of the Theatre and Speech Department at Smith College (1960–1966) in addition to being a visiting professor at other institutions.

3. Johnston refers to a public house known as Anglers Rest (360).

4. In his article Johnston makes reference to photographs of Chapelizod and the Mullingar Inn in William York Tindall's *The Joyce Country* ([University Park:] The Pennsylvania State University Press, 1960). Tindall's book reproduces seventy-eight photographs of Dublin and its vicinity to illustrate Joyce's works. He identifies The Mullingar as Earwicker's pub (148–149).

5. The items on this sheet are not connected to the previous discussion of Denis Johnston's article.

6. The reference is to Hayman's *A First-Draft*, his page 173.16.

7. A character in Charles Dickens's *Barnaby Rudge* (1841).

☐

To Adaline Glasheen, Farmington, Connecticut

[MS. ALS—HWS]

[postmark: 23 July 1964][1] [50 Deepwood Drive
SAT NOON Hamden 17, Connecticut]

Dear Adaline =
 Forgive silence.
 Progress o.k. here.
 When I don't answer your questions you can be pretty sure the reason is: DON'T KNOW.
x
 Rê: 270.1 ff [i.e., 271.1 ff]

Don't see what can be done with ANTHEMY except "flower-cluster" and maybe anthem = psalmsinging Malthus [271.6].

         x

 Is it worth notice that TORSK [271.4] is Dan[ish]. and Swedish Codfish and that the right hand glasses read C. C. C. C. O. O. O. O. D. D. D. D. P. P. P. That lapidated [271.6] was STEPHEN. That the hero of Bellini's Norma POLLIO (maybe in right column: polar principles) was torn between two Druidesses [271.4]² (which would bring in another of [John] Sullivan's opera tenor roles, Vasco da Gama in *L'Africaine* = Gamely Torskmaster [271.3–.4].) I assume you've found another Hermes-Mercury in n. 5 quicksilver. 271.17 [i.e., .16–.17], the ear hears "do you any harm". . . . HERM. . *

         x

 I must confess that the publication of Hayman's book³ revealed that the LESSONS chapter [FW II, ii, 260–308] was a mosaic of apparently irrelevant bits and pieces that after giving it a score or two of hours I vowed never to dip into it again until you Young Ones had mapped out some of the main lines.

         x

 [Alec] Guinness a born actor—hence a man "without characteristics"—I feel no 'person' in him—just the projecting imagination multi-form.⁴ Irene Worth,⁵ who's played in his company, says he is [a] superlatively nice modest coöperative person. I can't imagine a girl being infatuated with W. Wilson! The girl's *souper* at Luchow's⁶ must have been gorgeous. I love the place.

         x

 I enclose a few notes. I wanted to hold them up longer to get more, but I couldn't find a thing.

         x

 Did you ever see those two articles about de Valera in FW by Andrew Cass: Sprakin Sea Djoytsch in "Irish Times April 26, 1947" and something in "*The Envoy* Vol 5, 1951"? Said to be "brilliant."⁷

    BEST TO ALL
    Thornton

---

*Note: We are in the CLIO—HISTORY section [271.upper left]. There's Suetonius, and maybe 271. lower left column. . . hyper-APE mink he = Monkey = GIBBON. In the Mathematical sections he gives a foliation of mathematicians' names why not here GROTE—MOMSENE [271.bottom left]—etc etc? ¶ You notice that MUTUA [271.10] = AUTUM [271.12] in reverse and may take all from the Egyptian: spitter [270.19] ATEM on the previous page.

[attached sheet]

FOR ADALINE

CENSUS—ERRATA
    For IAGO: for + 412.2 read 41.2
    For MATHER, read
        MATHERS, LIDDELL MacGREGOR, member of
Madame Blavatsky's circle in London, author of The Kabbalah Unveiled.
        (from HONE'S "W. B. Yeats," London, 1942 p. 71)

SUMNER, John S. {Ellman[n] p. 517–19 [1982: 502–504]}
    Don't you think he's Goodboy Sommers with "bluenose" (Mr) 453.16?
    Query: with all of Shaun's circling the world (and with the proximity of S. America BOLIVAR 453.13) could that be MAGELLAN 453.19? {He's Portuguese, but gave his name in Spanish to the Straits = MAGELLANES.}

RAGNAR LODBROKE
Add:
    343.31 lewdbrogue
    440.21 [i.e., .29] the lad who brooks no breaches.
Note: By a real or false etymology LODEBROKE is taken to mean Leatherbreeches (so in your 22.36 ladbroke breeks ["breeks"circled and line drawn to "breaches" above which is also circled]: so I suspect Leatherbags Reynolds 26.1 and Leathertogs Donald 71.24

MALONE   215.34 [i.e., .33]
    You notice that Frank Budgen ("Making of Ulysses" p. 303)[8] seems to know that in Chapelizod, on the bank of the Liffey there is a "Mr. Malone's garden."

---

1. This letter was probably begun on Saturday, 18 July but not mailed until Thursday, 23 July.

2. Bellini's *Norma* is set in Gaul in the first century B.C. Norma, a priestess of Irminsul, has been in love with Pollione, the Roman Proconsul, and has borne him two children. In the opening of Act I, Pollione confides to his friend Flavio that he no longer loves Norma but is, rather, in love with Adalgisa, a novice in the temple, who returns his love.

3. David Hayman, *A First-Draft*.

4. Alec Guinness played Dylan Thomas in the Sidney Michaels play *Dylan* which opened at the Plymouth Theatre, New York, on 18 January 1964. Either in a letter or in conversation Glasheen must have told Wilder about seeing the play.

5. The actress who played Alcestis in Wilder's *The Alcestiad* in the world premiere Edinburgh Festival Society production in August 1955. She had become a close friend to Wilder.

6. A German restaurant located on East 14th Street between Third and Fourth Avenues. It no longer exists.

7. The Cass article in *The Irish Times* (p. 6) takes its title from the *Wake*, 485.13. *Envoy: An Irish Review of Literature and Art* (Dublin, Vol. 5, No. 17) published a special James Joyce number in April 1951. Andrew Cass's article was "Childe Horrid's Pilgrimage" ([19]–30). Other contributors to the issue were: Brian Nolan, Patrick Kavanaugh, Denis Johnston, Niall Montgomery, Joseph Hone, and W. B. Standford. The issue included photographs of Joyce, fourteen previously unpublished letters, and a "Recollections of the Man" section with the three obituary memoirs which appeared in *The Irish Times* on 14 January 1941. A Folcroft Library Editions reprint of the issue was published in 1973.

8. Frank Budgen, *James Joyce and the Making of 'Ulysses'* (1934; rpt., Bloomington: Indiana University Press, 1960). The reference is to the *Wake*, 215.33.

□

To Adaline and Francis Glasheen, Farmington, Connecticut

[MS. ALS—HWS]

[postmark: Friday, 14 August 1964]   50 Deepwood Drive
Maybe Wednesday   Hamden 17, Connecticut

Dear G's =
   It was a lovely time with you.¹ Isabel asked me to recount it in detail and I did—and she was filled with even greater regret.
                      x
   Tell Alison I loved the cookies.
                      x
   I return Fritz's letters.² I wish he didn't refer to his uneasinesses of mind so often, so woebegonely, and—I can't help feeling—with a touch of odd satisfaction. (It's awfully UN-SWISS, too.)
                      x

I've got part way through the book[3] you gave me (again, thanks) and picked up a thing that probably you've always known: the distribution of the various senses among the Old Men. J. J. has run into difficulties—distributing 5-plus senses among four persons.

If you take 92.27 as the four VISION, HEARING, TASTE and TOUCH, you get into conflict with
88.6 HEARING, VISION, SMELL, TASTE
305.n 3 (maybe giglamps are = flaring ears look like the side-lamps on an old fashioned buggy) hence
 HEARING. . . (?). . . SMELL, TASTE (good Italian = GUSTO)
160.26f underHEERD. . . thereover = Thurifer = SMELL be—EYED. . . . .
368.30f <u>MARK is EYES and LUKE</u> is NOSE

My novel's boiling over, or I'd drop everything and go back to those OLD MEN = the four areas of the human body, also ?—etc.

    Vayan con Diós
    Thorny[4]

---

1. Wilder and the Glasheens met for lunch at the Lawn Club in New Haven on Saturday, 1 August and again on Saturday, 8 August.

2. With this letter, Wilder returned (1) a copy Fritz Senn had made for Glasheen of his letter responding to Jack Dalton's criticism about how his recent article in *A Wake Newslitter* had been titled (23 July 1964) and (2) Senn's letter to Glasheen of 5 August 1964.

3. Which book is not known.

4. On either side of the closing and signature Wilder pasted two Italian stamps, one for 100 lire and one for 30 lire.

To Adaline Glasheen, Farmington, Connecticut
[MS. ALS—HWS]

31 August 1964   50 Deepwood Drive
                                               Hamden 17, Connecticut

Dear Adaline =
     Please forgive =
     I've never been so long before in returning treats that you've sent me. "The Envoy"[1] is in the same post under separate cover.
     Gee, you certainly are favored; my Newslitter New Series #3 (June) arrived at about the same time as you got No #4 (August).
     I've been getting cheerful letters from [Jack] Dalton. (He's trying to apply the gimlet-eye to details in my works. I pull boners about "lat[itude]." and "long[itude]." in *Our Town* and put days of the week wrong in 1904, etc. . . . I try to correct such things in later editions, but I care so little for that kind of precision that I forget to.)
     He's put himself on a time-schedule. Must transcribe all those thousands of pages of J. J. notations in one year (plus add his commentary, I assume) and has to do x pages a day; says he's ahead of his schedule. It must be killing work. He likes self-punishment.
     I enclose some not very spirited suggestions for Census III.
     Isabel says you phoned about my health. Many thanks. I'm very well. *IT* has healed up. I go for my final medical look-see next week.[2]
     Please don't punish me for being so long in returning these enclosures.
     All best to Francis and Alison.
     Still all delighted with the good time we had at the Lawn Club (my permission to enter it is withdrawn tomorrow.)[3]

                 All cordial best
                 Thornt'

[attached sheet]

FOR ADALINE

CENSUS
    addendum : EIFFEL 541.6
            : SHACKLETON 512.28
{It looks very much as though SHACKLETON was a Dublin baker famous for his brown bread. Clear enough in 392.33. For 393.1 Joyce first printed SHACKLETON. Clear also in 397.17}
    {Your CENSUS *sub* SHACKLETON directs us to "see Shekleton" which we seek in vain,—tho' it is the above 512.28.}
    Erratum: DINAH, "16.19" should read "116.19."
    McGillycuddy of the Reeks, The: a title—i.e. a man. He was present at an important meeting of the Seanad called by de Valera.
    ("de Valera" by Mary C. Bromage p. 237.)[4]
    92.26 518.9

HUNKER 65.17
{You'll hate this}
    This is a goose-gander: HONKER
    We've just been told he was a geeser 65.5 (not a "geezer," as it should read.)
    It's Joyce himself and those young girls in Trieste and Zurich.[5]
    Joyce married (ho-hum) Norah Barnacle.[6] The barnacle goose—and on the continent—a wild goose. (197.13–14 "and by my wildgaze I thee gander["]) and thereby became his dear goose's gander,—hissing and honking.
    Quod erat demonstradum.
    GOOSE, Mother: add 428.7 "Mery Loye" Ma Mere L'oie (old French L'oye)

FRY, Joseph. {*Scribbledehobble*[7] p. 101 (in Notebook p. 541): "Joseph Fry made cocoa 1728"
    Query:
            413.35 rawCAWCAW. . . . how is Mr. Fry?

CENSUS. BLOEDAX, "One of the Northmen of Dublin"—I don't know where I found this note. (see this character next to Sitric the Blind[)] (maybe a misreading for the "blond") in *Scribbledehobble* p. 7 (MS p. 3)
    bloedaxe 323.4

COPERNICUS, Nikolaus (Ger. KOPPERNIQK; Polish KOPERNICKI)
   On p. 55 "they" behold the constellations going around the great lifetree—(pretend that the North Pole is a wooden-tree-pole)
   55.16–18 "with a bow to a NAMECOUSIN of. . . . Coppinger.["]
   55.33 "in this new reading of the part. . . . 34 because of Dyas in his machina. . ." {DYAS, Sanskrit Jupiter, as you give in the Census. . . but particularly "God of the shining sky. . . . ." i. e. the heliocentric. .
   56.1 you give, with an interrogation, "copycus" for Copernicus.
   Now I think Copernicus is linked with Coppinger in one other place. 294.2 (and footnote 1. CARPENGER)
   copyngink is a passable anagram-play with KOPPERNIGK

Ptolemy—the astronomer. I think it would be advisable to add that his first name was CLAUDIUS.
   It may be in 55.25–26 the clad. . . the cladagain.

POPPER, Amalie = should read AMALIA. (See your own reference ELLMAN[N] 353) [1982:342]
Now (you'll hate this) at that collidabanter in the park 82.15, the altercation wasn't only about a loan of money or a distillery worm but about a young girl—82.19–21 in ribbons and pigtail.
Well: I see 84.17 x 20 POPPY. . . .mAMmALIA)

1. See TW to AG, 23 July 1964, n. 7.

2. In June 1964 Wilder had a malignant growth removed from his face. In July and August he underwent radiation therapy.

3. Wilder and the Glasheens had lunch there on Saturday, 1 August and again on Saturday, 8 August.

4. Mary C. Bromage, *De Valera and the March of a Nation* (London: Hutchinson, 1956).

5. Amalia Popper and Martha Fleischmann, see TW to AG, 6 September 1962, notes 2 and 35.

6. Joyce and Nora Barnacle (1884–1951) left Dublin together on 8 October 1904; they were married at a registry office in London on 4 July 1931.

7. Thomas E. Connolly, ed., *James Joyce's Scribbledehobble*.

To Adaline Glasheen, Farmington, Connecticut
[MS. ALS—HWS]

13 October 1964   50 Deepwood Drive
                                   Hamden 17, Connecticut

Dear Adaline =
   Thanks for letting me see the enclosures.
   I've returned from Quebec.[1]
   Fritz [Senn] sent me pages of one-word readings in FW. We'll all go mad soon if we can't find some more large patterns in that book. I hope that German publisher's project of putting Fritz at the head of a translation of Joyce's complete works (*except* FW) goes through. Mrs Senn is now working in a nearby cinema. I don't think he confided that to me in confidence; he rather likes to broadcast his woes and self-reproaches.
   I thought the doctors had done with me, but they asked me to show up for one more check-up on the 22nd.[2] I don't know what I shall be doing after that.
   Saturday I rec'd my August *Newslitter*—the one you so kindly let me see a month ago!—no, well over a month ago.
   I'd been working too closely on the novel[3] and when I returned I planned to do a blood-warming week's work on FW, but I found that I needed some new ray of light from outside to do that. I've trodden that thorn-patch too often. So I turned to a little notion of mine about *Twelfth Night* instead and have been quite cheerful about it.
   Hope everything's fine with you all.
   I predict that [Barry] Goldwater's showing at the polls will be sensational! Sensationally small. But how feebly the Republicans have behaved all along.

                    EVER
                    Thornt.

---

1. Wilder was in Quebec, Canada, from 13 September until 9 October. The enclosures are not known
2. See TW to AG, 31 August 1964, n. 2.
3. Wilder's *The Eighth Day*.

To Adaline Glasheen, Farmington, Connecticut

[MS. ALS—HWS]

[postmark: 22 October 1964]   [50 Deepwood Drive
                                    Hamden 17, Connecticut]

Dear Adaline =
    You get me all wrong: I love those lists of "little items."[1] All I meant was that there's something frustrating about them also. One hopes eagerly that each new little item will unlock a big door.
    Rê 320.14. Sanskrit tailor-poet.[2] Note also above 320.3 another appearance of that hindoo Shimar (or Shinar) Shin of 10.6 and 18. Maybe he is also 339.15.
    You ask what GITA means. I assume Bhagavad Gita = of the Blessed One / Song. *Gitter* is German for lattice-gate or window. *Schimpf* for insult or word of contempt

481.21   Yes, he's fooling with the Seven cities that claimed to be Homer's birthplace. He does it 129.23 SMYNA (Merrior); Rhoebok (Rhodes?) Kolonsreagh (Colophon) Seapoint (Salamis?) Quayhowth (CHIOS?); Ash town?; Ratheny (Athenai) = where are Argos, Ithaca, KYME, Pylos, Sparta....

481.21   Chivitats Dei = Chios?
           Rhonnda = Rhodes
           Salem, Mass = Salamis
           Argos.

                    Maddening.

544.1   The Marquis of Zetland was Chief or Head or whatever they call it of the Dublin Masons.

498.19   I assume you also know that Pani is Polish for "Mrs." as in 334.3 = thanks for this Russian *melost* grace. = where A. L. P. upstairs is the "Gracious Mrs Costello."—the end of the Polish and Czecho-Slovakian foliation that begins on the top of p. 333.

                  Off in haste.
                  Best to all
                  (T)

1. A response to either a lost letter or to a telephone conversation. The subject of "lists" may refer to a comment made about items in A Wake Newslitter.

2. In the absence of a letter, it is impossible to know whether the Sanskrit tailor-poet was a response to a comment about B. P. Misra's work. See TW to AG, 29 October 1964, n. 1.

☐

To Adaline Glasheen, Farmington, Connecticut

[MS. ALS—HWS]

29 October 1964   50 Deepwood Drive
                                               Hamden 17, Connecticut

Dear Adaline =
    Greetings.
    Thanks.
Mr. Misra:[1]
    We're glad to have him.
    But in his eagerness he offers his material so helter-skelter.
    He would have strengthened his case by saying that the Kathopanishad is generally known as the KATHA. Of three GANAS, TAMAS is "inertia."
    And to have called attention to WILLINGDON as you have done in the Census.
                        x
    Is the Pranquean = from PRANA = life-breath?
                        x
    However, best to leave to Editor [Clive] Hart to curb him while encouraging and editing him.
                        x
    If only SRI MISRA would quiet his fervor to go all-metaphysical and, for a while, merely furnish the Sanskrit vocabulary.
                        x
    No news here. Doctor found me all right; said to return to him in June 1965.
    I'm lingering around because we have an aunt fairly ill in Florida.[2] May be summoned. But soon I'll be off somewhere.

Typist at work on the first part of my novel.³ It's always scary to release one's handwritten lines to what must be considered as a last and final draft.

Yes, wouldn't it be bracing, if Mr. Jenkins⁴ found as fruitful a source for man-servant and Captain as you did for Dr Prince and Miss Beachamp?⁵

All cordial best to all—and again: thanks!

(T)

1. It is not clear what work by B. P. Misra Glasheen might have sent Wilder. Fritz Senn, in "One White Elephant," in *A Wake Newslitter*, N.S., I, 4 (August 1964), 1–3, mentions Misra's unpublished thesis, "Created Conscience: An Approach to James Joyce," and his pamphlet, *Indian Inspiration of James Joyce* (Calcutta: Agra, Gaya Prasad & Sons, n.d., 60 pp.). There is no copy of the pamphlet in HWS. Misra's "Sanskrit Translations" in *A Wake Newslitter*, I, 6 (December 1964), 8–10, and continued in II, 1 (February 1965), 9–11, discusses Joyce's use of Sanskrit words and philosophical concepts on pages 593–628.
2. Charlotte Tappen Lewis Niven (1882–1979), Wilder's mother's sister.
3. Wilder's *The Eighth Day*.
4. William D. Jenkins, who had recently begun writing on Joyce.
5. Glasheen's 1954 article, "*Finnegans Wake* and the Girls from Boston, Mass."

□

To Adaline Glasheen, Farmington, Connecticut

[MS. ALS—HWS]

7 November 1964

50 Deepwood Drive
Hamden, Connecticut 06517

Dear Adaline =
    Again = a world of thanks.
    I think your Emeth-Theme-Math discovery is brilliant,—esp. "the trim triste truth letter"* [120.3–.4].

x

Is it reported that Joyce had a Brittanica always with him—toted all those volumes from apartment to apartment? Certainly he didn't—couldn't—frequent the big libraries in Paris. Maybe "Shakespeare & Co"[1] had a Brittanica and he'd carry home volume after volume.

x

Tomorrow I go to secrecy-silence-solitude in Newport for about 20 days (the novel is in its last draught and the typist—from Fitchberg, Mass—receives and sends back material all the time). Then I go to a dear Aunt in Florida—pretty old and in and out of hospitals—then some southern route boat to the Mediterranean.

So, again, my FW addiction must rest on the shelf.

But if there's some dazzling break-through let me know.

x

Your memo just received.[2] I didn't get your excitement that the Ballad of FW[3] is running like an undertone beneath I i [3–29]... you'd already practically told us so in the Census.

x

I'll probably be abroad by Xmas. Don't want to, exactly—but various courtesy-demands of the New Haven-New York axis are increasing.

    Best to all
    Old Hump

*You realize that Joyce arrived at that late: he first printed in *Transition* August 1927... "the truth letter"—which presumably would be Greek TAU = the cross.

What order is J. J. following!?? The previous clause is Hebrew. PE = Mouth, fooling with Greek PI and Kappa acting under Grimm's law.

---

1. The Paris bookstore founded in 1919 by Sylvia Beach (1887–1962).
2. A reference to a lost letter.
3. "The Ballad of Finnegan's Wake," a nineteenth-century Irish ballad from which Joyce derived the title and themes for the *Wake*. The ballad tells the story of Tim Finnegan, a hod-carrier who falls from a ladder and dies, but is resurrected when one of the wake guests spills some whiskey on his head: "Then Micky Malone raised his head/When a noggin of whiskey flew at him,/It missed and falling on the bed,/The liquor scattered over Tim;/Bedad he revives, see how he rises,/And Timothy rising from the bed,/Says, 'Whirl your liquor round the blazes,/Thanam o'n dhoul ["Your souls from the devil"], do you think I'm dead?'" (Ellmann, *James Joyce*, 1959: 556–557; 1982: 543–544).

To Adaline Glasheen, Farmington, Connecticut

[MS. ALS—HWS]

[Christmas Card]

[postmark: 16 December 1964]   [50 Deepwood Drive
Hamden, Connecticut 06517]

Happy Holidays
To all

sez
Thornton

going south tomorrow to have Christmas with my mother's sister—then take a slow slow boat to Italy—"for the ride"—will be back soon.[1]

---

1. Wilder flew from Miami, Florida, to Curaçao on Monday, 4 January 1965. On 10 January he sailed on the SS *Rossini* which, after a leisurely cruise to some Mediterranean ports, arrived in Genoa on 26 January. Wilder traveled in Italy, France, and Spain before returning to Curaçao on 4 April and then on to Miami. He remained in Florida until 29 April when he left for his home in Hamden, Connecticut.

1965

To *Thornton Wilder, Hamden, Connecticut*

[MS. ALS—HWS]

[January–February 1965]¹   [22 Carrington Road
                                             Farmington, Connecticut]

For Thornton from Adaline

Disjointed notes on II ii or the 10th section of FW [260–308]. They don't tack on to anything or get anywhere, but they could fit in some day.

260² you remember I said Joyce made it clear in footnote 1 {not that I got it till J. pointed it out} that the footnotes are by a girl—"quoshe with her girlic teangue." And I thought it must be made equally clear in the glosses that they are by males and I think which twin is which gloss should be equally clear.

I also pointed out that the twins are identified by the opening letters of their glosses
     260 With   Unde
     293 (where J. says they changed sides[)]
         Uteralterance   Why

It now seems to me the 260 glosses emphasize their identity as 10 for
     W = U{V}U = 10 and
     Unde et *u*bi = 10

That's plain but this is risky—is W = VV = sign ^ or Shaun's sign
and UU = [[or Shem's ???

Left gloss on 260 definitely establishes a male voice just as notes to
feminine
    "With his" gloss
    "with her" note
    *Men*ly

But I can find no sex indications in right gloss, till 293 when the sides
change

Rt gloss 293 "Whis His" echoes the "With his" of 260[.] Is their
[i.e., there] another echo at 271, last line [.29] "Wide hiss"?
{Kindly don't ask me why}

Note 1, 260 echoes the left glosses on 260 in a way I don't get
Rawmeash = retch meat [AG margin: Is Ir rubbish see OH³]
~~quoshe~~ with her girlic teangue. . . beaver beard = With his broad
and hairy face
Note 1—Cromwell {his men} killed innocent babies in Ireland and so
ties to Herod. Would Cromwell's eczema be Cromwell's so famous
wart? And if wart, is Joyce playing with "warty" as a mark of virility
which Yeats says in a footnote was on Irishmen: ". . . all those warty
lads that by her body lay."?[4]

Herod didn't first slaughter innocents, he watched the dance of the
7 veils & there 260–261 is the girl in 7 colors. The 7 girls have
danced for HCE in "Mime."

Notes 1, 2, 3 progress
    1) nine months of pregnancy
    2) nursing baby
    3) divorce
Since above in text talk about marriage, the footnotes = girl's remarks
on marriage
Left gloss 3—according to 11th Brit "Jehova" one meaning of
Yahway = "sinks down" so "lard sinks down" = Lord Yahway!!!
{Don't ask me why}

Mr Tumulty is a character in Gogarty's play *Blight*.[5] I've not read it.
[261.19]

293–drawing is of woman by men

308 drawings are of men by woman

Is it significant that the woman is drawn mechanically, with compasses, while the men are done free-hand {308.n.1}

Another geometric portrait of woman on 165

Regard drawings on 308. First drawing goes with note 1, 2nd with note 2. Note 1 is attached to "Cush" {5} above & the Cush is echoed in "Kish." Note 2 "Geg" {10} is echoed in "gags."

Drawing 1—What is balanced on the hand but a V or 5
    "   2—Crossbones = X = 10
Drawing 1 also = 10 since the V or 5 is balanced on 5 fingers
So drawing 1 *may* = 5 + 5 & echo Rt. Gloss 1 on 260 V *and* V
Whereas crossbones = X = 10
{obviously more Vs can be found in both drawings}

It is my impression that Issy is giving something to each twin, to the first she gives her hand. The second gets merely the drawing {Where's the skull?}

One twin {which?} gets the hand of a living girl
  "   "   "   " art

This present-giving must {how?} echo or opposite the present-giving of 193, 195. ALP gives
    Shaun a deathbone [193.29]
    Shem a life-wand [195.5]

On 308 both presents or drawings are bones, though I don't know who gets what
    1) a hang bone or bones of hand & nose
    2) Crossbones—dead bones
{?Does skull (missing) & crossbones mean she gives him poison?}

Well the above is all I know about II ii and I'm not sure I know a lot of it and I draw NO deductions from any of it.

308-Letter-they send Yuletide greetings so there's a general gift-giving??

Just jottings
In *As I Was Going Down Sackville St.* (oh what a lousy prose-writer Gogarty was, though a much better poet than Joyce.)
p. 33
 "I cannot see a grain of hope anywhere," I said sadly.
 "Hope, is it? You might as well be looking for an earwig in the Phoenix Park."[6]

32.4–5	megeth ?emeth
52.17 [i.e., .16–.17]	List[e]ner Jan 7, 1965[7]: says James Ussher, Archbishop of Armagh (1580–1656) said earth was created 4004 BC, 9 in the morning of Oct. 23
57.8 [i.e., .7–.10]	Blake, "Jerusalem" I, 36 : ["]And the Four Zoas, who are the Four Eternal Senses of Man"—see 305.n.3
64.23	Astraea (Gr. "starry") goddess of justice who became Virgo
73.32–33	J. Atherton identified Hugh Miller, *The Testament of the Rocks*. Miller is source of that sentence about "dappled sea-born clouds" in *Portrait*[8]
74.9	*Truga* = low Latin "Troy"
? 108.27	Webster "hate" comes from Arab *alud*, meaning the piece of wood
112.6 [i.e., .8]	old, did I tell you "all heal" = mistletoe, Frazer says
112.33	*Ari* = Heb. "lion"
113.36	*Peabody—who he?
75.1	[arrow to entry 112.33] Gee I just realized—*Ari*uz, *Ari*oun
? 116.2	EB [*Encyclopedia Britannica*][9] "Heb. Lang." says tradition Ezra introduced the Assyrian character
143.5–6	EB "Religion"—in Vedaa *Vac* = speech
146.17	Without ref I have note: La Belle Isabeau = ["]*petits prophets* of Camisards."[10]
147.21	EB "Lamech": No'man = a name of Adonis
? 156.22	Macha founded Emania
? 157.4	Ungulae—Roman torture—barbed hooks
162	I told you the Finnic-Ugric stuff here?
? 165.28	Ebah = MHG "ivy"
167.16	"The Psalms of Solomon" exist—see EB "Apocalyptic Literature"
169.30–31 [i.e., .18]	van der Post, *A View of all the Russias*, 315 says the Chinese believe the manroot or gingseng has indefinite power of rejuvenation.[11] EB "gingseng" says is shaped like mandrake

? 181.18	Swift and Vanessa met in the "sluttery"[12]
185.14	*altus prosator* begins hymn attributed to St Calumba—EB "Celt"
? 187.24	*brawd* = Welsh "brother"
? 190.33	[Robert] Graves says Antinous = "hostile mind"
194.11–12	Ir. *An-la'* = "the day" {I like this one}
200.12–13	{B. Tysdahl}[13] Nor. "Jeg elsker saaledes en smukke litten ung pige" = I love a pretty young girl
212.8–9	Sackville St 301—Teasy Ward a Dublin madam[14]
229.26	[i.e., .20] A beard splitter = a man given to wenching
?231.27	*esergi* = Ir. "ressurection"—EB "Celt"
234.21	*alauder* = Lat "lark"
241.27	*nahar* = Heb. "river"
254.18	Mermer = Summer[i]an god of sea, wind, storm
256.12 [i.e., .11]	Home Olga—Homo Logos—See Ellmann 714 [1982: 701 note]
?310.24	*lur* = prehistoric bronze horns found in Scandinavia, EB "Horns"
313.24	EB "Numismatics"—Sihtric made earliest Danish pennies in Ireland
323.26	Ukko = Finnic sky god
325.13	quotes I *Sam* IX, I[15]
331.20	Thwaits' soda water of Dublin is made of one of the wells ascribed to St. Patrick
332.36	*Dver* = Russ "door"
334.3	*milost* = Russ "grace" see Webster "Bogmik"
337.34	*Bettler* = Ger "beggar"—so there's the beggar with bowl
?346.2	Man in Macintosh?
??353.12	Reginald Fitz Urse = leader of murderers of Beckett[16] I would give a good deal to find the others
363.2–3	Hitchcock (who he?)
.34	? Bovary
?376.16	EB "Finn MacCool" says Finn[']s original name was Demni
378.22 [AG: .23]	*sor* = Heb. rock, also a title of Yaweh—153.23
379.4	O'Faolain, *Vive Moi*, says *Hound & Horn* known as *Bugle and Bitch*.[17] Does Bugle & Bitch come from something?
387.2	Afer, son of Hercules for whom Africa named
394.19 [i.e., .18]	*Erewhon Revisited* glances at story of Dogabert wearing his trousers backwards. FW has earlier ref[.] [274.29] Do you know story?

397.26–27	Spoonerism for Pachal Candle & Ir *casc*, Easter
?403.18 [i.e., .6]	Architectural saw (which I find so beautiful & fascinating I'd put it in a book were I a famous author) "The arch never sleeps." Hindus didn't like it on this account
?405.26	EB "grampus"—O. F. = *Graspois*
?407.20	Nelly Clifden, actress Edward VII carried on with at the Curragh
423.4	*tud* = Bret. "people"—EB "Celt"
430.29	Reason he smells so is because Shaun is stuffed like stuffing—see 456
452.24	*casc* = Ir Easter = Easter Duty
?456.23	XOANA = wooden statues of Apollo
468.33,36	*Judges* XX, i—Dan to Beersheba = limits of Palestine
?478.11	EB "Indo-European" *yava* = sanscrit "corn"
?491.17	*mareck* = Scotch Gaelic for "fou" v. drunk
498.19	*pani* = Hindu, "water"
499.10	*ser* = Welsh "stars"
501.19 [i.e., .17]	Ir *crain* = fig
?504.20	*corcur* = Ir "purple" / Corcoran
?510.4	In Babylonian myth all came into existence by the creative word, *Mummu* of Ea
534.18	Lane-Joynt, surgeon at Meath hospital, Dublin
.10	*babad* = Javanese "chronicle"—EB "Java"
541.24	EB "Torture"—*plumbatae* or leaden balls
553.21	?psychoponpos?
557.1	Esquara = Basque language
585.11	*paratonnere* or Fr. lightning-conductor
?598.33	[i.e., .32] *diurn* = day in Idiom Neubrat
.9	*Sé Dé* = 9th cent. hymn, ascribed Colman
602.1–3	EB "Celtic Languages"—famous grammarian's rule, *caol le caol agus leathan le leathan*—slender to slender, broad to broad. Has to do with placing consonants & vowels
606.13	Bishop's Rock, lighthouse in Scilly Islands
614.6	Heb *Shekinah* = "The Presence" {of God}
.8	Themes = *emeth*
619.33	Todd collaborated with Stokes in Ir archaeology[18]
620.21	Gorman,[19] 85: Arthur Symonds lived at 134 Lauderdale Mansions, Maida Vale. {Mean?}

So much for jotting. I have got a lot on Bucket-Tool a principal theme and a lot on use of "Ballad" in FW I, i which interests nobody but me.

Silliest book I ever read, *Alexander Pope* by Edith Sitwell p 140 (Penguin) describes a satire against Pope that reminds me (Maybe yes maybe no) of Mookse & Gripes.[20] A Pope was walking by the Thames & was recognized by his back by two gentlemen who whipped him & left. Then "good Mrs B. a good charitable woman, and near neighbor of Mr Pope's at Twickenham, chancing to come by, took him up in her apron, and carried him to the water-side, where she got a boat to convey him home."

Whether or not this applies, I wonder if obscure satires mayn't lie behind the slanging of the twins?

---

1. We place this letter here because of the reference to the 7 January 1965 issue of *The Listener*. Wilder returned this letter to Glasheen to help in the preparation of *Census III*.
2. In a letter to Frank Budgen, Joyce commented on the technique he employed on this page: ". . . the technique here is a reproduction of a schoolboy's (and schoolgirl's) old classbook complete with marginalia by the twins, who change sides at half time, footnotes by the girl (who doesn't), a Euclid diagram, funny drawings etc." (Joyce, *Letters I*, End of July 1939, 405–406).
3. Probably a reference to Brendan O Hehir's *A Gaelic Lexicon for 'Finnegans Wake' and Glossary for Joyce's Other Works* (Berkeley and Los Angeles: University of California Press, 1967). Glasheen added this information when she reviewed this letter in preparation for *Census III*.
4. The line is from Yeats's poem, "The Wild Old Wicked Man" (1938): "all those warty lads/That by their bodies lay." In a letter to Dorothy Wellesley, Yeats writes: "warts are considered by the Irish peasantry a sign of sexual power" (*Letters on Poetry from W. B. Yeats to Dorothy Wellesley*, London: Oxford University Press, 1964, 63).
5. Oliver St. John Gogarty's *Blight: The Tragedy of Dublin*, was first produced at the Abbey Theatre, Dublin, on 11 December 1917. Mr. Tumulty, Gogarty's *persona*, is a member of the Board of the Townsend Thanatorion.
6. Oliver St. John Gogarty's, *As I Was Walking Down Sackville Street* (New York: Reynal & Hitchcock, 1937). Gogarty is recounting a conversation in a pub about the economic and political situation in Ireland. Glasheen published a query about these lines in *A Wake Newslitter*, N.S. II, 4 (August 1965), 30, and asked "Is the earwigless state of the Park a fact? A cant Dublin phrase? What happened to the earwigs in Phoenix Park?"
7. Patrick Moore, "How old is the Earth?" in *The Listener and BBC Television Review*, LXXIII, No. 1867 (7 January 1965), 11–13.

8. In Atherton's edition of *A Portrait of the Artist as a Young Man* (London: Heinemann, 1964), he notes (249) that the phrase "A day of dappled seaborne clouds" (chapter IV) is quoted from Hugh Miller's *The Testimony of the Rocks* (Edinburgh, 1869), 237. In *The Books at the Wake* Atherton identifies references to two books by Hugh Miller (1802–1856): *The Old Red Sandstone* (1841) and *Footprints of the Creator* (1851). Glasheen finds a direct reference in these lines.

9. The references in this letter to "EB" are to the *Encyclopedia Britannica*, 11th edition.

10. Child prophet of the *camisards*, Protestant peasants of the Cévennes region of France who rebelled against injustices following the revocation of the Edict of Nantes (1685). They were so-named because of their white shirts.

11. Laurens van der Post, *A View of All the Russias* (New York: William Morrow & Co., 1964), 315.

12. Glasheen quotes from the *Wake*, but her meaning is not clear. Jonathan Swift met Esther Vanhomrigh (Vanessa), and her mother, the widow of a former Lord Mayor of Dublin, in London in the winter of 1707.

13. Bjorn Tysdahl was at the British Institute of the University of Oslo, Norway, working on Joyce and Ibsen. The copy he sent Glasheen of his *Joyce and Ibsen* (Oslo: Norwegian University, 1968) is in HWS. With Clive Hart he did a series of notes for *A Wake Newslitter*, "Norwegian Captions": N. S., I, 5 (October 1964), 6–9; I, 6 (December 1964), 11–13; II, 1 (February 1965), 7–9; II, 2 (April 1965), 13–15; II, 3 (June 1965), 28–30; II, 4 (August 1965), 29–30. The identifications deal with the *Wake*, 311–332 and 141, 186, 187.

14. Teasey Ward in Gogarty's *As I Was Going Down Sackville Street*.

15. Glasheen is in error. The reference should be to *Judges*, 6:12: "And the angel of the Lord appeared unto him, and said unto him, The Lord *is* with thee, thou mighty man of valour."

16. The English martyr, St. Thomas à Becket, who was murdered in 1170 for defending the rights of the Church against King Henry II.

17. Seán O' Faoláin (1900–1991), the Irish writer born John Francis Whelan (he adopted the ancient Gaelic form of his name). In his autobiography *Vive Moi!* (Boston: Little, Brown and Co., 1964), O'Faoláin writes this, without explanation, about the magazine *Hound and Horn* founded by Lincoln Kirstein, a fellow student at Harvard University when O'Faoláin studied there from 1926 to 1928. In his text, page 314, the dates for his own first publication, and for the founding of the *Hound and Horn* are incorrect. Joyce's essay "From a Banned Writer to a Banned Singer" was published in *Hound and Horn*, V, 4 (July–September 1932), [542]–546.

18. James Henthorn Todd (1805–1869) and Whitley Stokes (1830–1909) each published books on Irish archaeology and Celtic society.

19. Herbert Gorman (1893–1954), the American newspaper reporter and writer. His *James Joyce: His First Forty Years*, 1924, was the first biography of Joyce. The references here are to his *James Joyce* (New York: Farrar & Rinehart, 1939).

20. According to Sitwell, Pope thought that Lady Mary Wortley Montagu and Lord Hervey, whom he had satirized in *The Dunciad*, were joint authors of "a coarse and witless pamphlet, called 'A Pop upon Pope; or a True and Faithful

Account of a late horrid and barbarous whipping committed on the body of Sawney Pope, a Poet, as he was innocently walking in Ham Walks, near the River of Thames, meditating Verses for the Good of the Publick. Supposed to have been done by two evil-disposed Persons, out of Spite and Revenge for a harmless Lampoon which the said Poet had writ upon them'" (1728). (Harmondsworth, England: Penguin Books, 1948, 140–141; London: Faber & Faber, 1930, 168–169).

☐

To Adaline Glasheen, Farmington, Connecticut

[MS. ALS—HWS]

[?10] February 1965   Cannes—Tomorrow
                             American Exp. Co. NICE (A-M)

Dear Adaline =
    It was the last words of your letter that knocked me over.[1] Francis's knee-cap stuck. The most delicate part of the body—all that labyrinthine care that Nature went to in order to perfect the joint. (I once hurt mine—falling down East Rock as an undergraduate—got water-on-the-knee... was laid up for weeks.)
    Do give him all my sympathy.
    Give all our cordial greetings to Alison and Newton Osborne.[2] Isabel and I want to give them something pleasing and useful when I get back and can consult with you about it *sotto voce*. I remember how you kept weeping all day when Alice [i.e., Alison] went West to study—have you been dabbing your eyes again now that your chick and child has left the nest? I remember that your way to console yourself is resolutely to cook something. I might add that I pity people who don't have an FW to plunge into.
    [Jack] Dalton has just sent me a photostat of a page from a J. J. notebook challenging me to read the last line. I can't. He hints that it's something pertinent to me. Isabel—passing it on to me—read, "Hi there, Erasmus!" which it's not. People who have bad handwriting are not thereby particularly endowed to read the bad handwriting of others.
    Do go and teach at Buffalo.[3] I think 1966 is far too soon to write a book (a whole book!) on Narrative in FW.

I loved your finding those Ballad women fighting their several battles behind the "narrative" in Book One. When I finish my novel[4] I've decided to write one or two more "Seven Ages" playlets; and then go back to FW for three or four months. Lordy, probably I'll be 70 by then. Does one have any memory at 70? You sure need memory when you work on that opus.

Forgive the lack of pep in this letter. I drag a bad cold (caught in the air-conditioned hotel in the tropics at Curaçao) that like a golf ball in my throat—and oh, the constant Kleenex at my nose.

All devoted best to you all—

Ever
Thornt.

1. A reference to a lost letter.
2. Alison, the Glasheens's daughter, had married Newton Osborne, a medical student.
3. Thomas E. Connolly invited Glasheen to participate in the summer program in modern literature at the State University of New York at Buffalo which he directed. The program, which lasted thirteen years, involved scholars, poets, and novelists. Each year a distinguished Joycean was invited to work in Buffalo's extensive Joyce collection. Glasheen declined, and the invitation for a Joyce scholar was extended to James Atherton, who accepted.
4. Wilder's *The Eighth Day*.

□

To Isabel Wilder, Hamden, Connecticut
[MS. ALS—YCAL]

7 March 1965   Farmington, Connecticut

Dear Isabel,

Since I accepted joyfully your lovely invitation[1] I have sat and told my neuroses like rosary beads, cheap and depressing rosary beads, and decided I'd give you more annoyance than pleasure if I went to

New York with you. I am a very nervous traveller. I am liable to panic in crowds or places I can't get out of. I live with the damn things and can cope very fairly with them but not with all of them at once.

I am terribly sorry to cry off. We would have loved to come to dinner with you and hope you'll ask us another time. Indeed the whole scheme was so lovely I could weep with annoyance at my tom-foolery. Don't you, please, be angry.

You know there's a little *FW Newslitter* we all—even Thornton—contribute to. I know they would be thrilled if you reviewed the movie for them. They need new contributors and they need good prose. Please think of it.[2]

Again, all sorrow,

        Yours,
        Adaline

---

1. Isabel Wilder had invited Glasheen to accompany her to New York for a private screening of Mary Ellen Bute's film *Passages from 'Finnegans Wake'*. Bute, who was a classmate of Isabel's at the Yale School of Drama in 1925, came to know of Thornton's enthusiasm for Joyce at meetings of the James Joyce Society. Isabel may have attended a screening at the Museum of Modern Art on 16 February 1965, for members of the James Joyce Society of New York. Bute's film is based on a stage adaptation of the same name by Mary Manning (Cambridge: Harvard University Press, 1957). At the Cannes Film Festival in 1965, Bute's film won a prize for the best first feature by a director. So impressed was Wilder by Bute's film that he assigned her the film rights for his play *The Skin of Our Teeth*, a project that she never completed. See Kit Basquin, "Mary Ellen Bute's Film Adaptation of *Finnegans Wake*" in *James Joyce's 'Finnegans Wake': A Casebook*, ed. John Harty, III (New York: Garland Publishing Inc., 1991), 177–188.

2. Isabel did not write a review for the *Newslitter*. Instead, James Blish reviewed the film. See IW to AG, 20 March 1965, n. 3.

ISABEL WILDER:

To Adaline Glasheen, Farmington, Connecticut

[MS. ALS—HWS]

[9 March 1965] 50 Deepwood Drive
Tuesday morning Hamden, Connecticut

Dear Adaline:
    I'm truly bitterly disappointed not to have you along on the jaunt but I do understand. I often wonder HOW I ever get off when I truly like to be here every short minute there's left of life & so much to be done that I want to do & never do, even if here. I'll miss you greatly & report. I don't feel I know enough about FW to review a movie on the subject but I'll try. It's an amusing challenge & I'd like to surprise T. W. as well as J. J.!
    When spring is more settled you & Frank run down & we'll talk & talk, lunch early here—whichever suits—

                affe-
                Isabel

ISABEL WILDER:

To Adaline Glasheen, Farmington, Connecticut

[MS. TL—carbon—YCAL]

20 March 1965 [50 Deepwood Drive
                                          Hamden, Connecticut 06517]

Dear Adaline:
    Because of the St. Patrick's day Parade, crowds, etc. the time of the screening was put off until Thursday at 2.[1] A much more christian hour for one arriving from New Haven!

I can say honestly that for reasons I will soon name, I was glad you were not there. (This, of course, does not mean that I did not miss you as a person and companion.) The reason I say this is that the film was run in a small projection room with a very small screen. If I had not seen it on a large,—that is not the great wide screen of some theatres but a good sized screen such as small art theatres have,— I would have no comparison. However, having seen it, I can assure you the difference was immense and I would have been bitterly disappointed for you. The difference is so great because light and shade alone are affected so think how much an image is; and the relation of image to image. And it seemed to effect sound. The words and music were affected, also in relation to each other. The score is VERY good and exciting, in fact I found it remarkable and perfectly suited. But on the smal[l] screen it seemed to get in the way of the words and drown them out while at other times it was right. All very curious. I asked Miss Bute about this and she said odd things happened like this. She, knowing the film so well was not so conscious as I but she knew this happened and the problem arose at times and was interested that I had been so upset by it. I begged her never to show it under these circumstances. It destroyed a very special and important quality. It was still, of course, very good and challenging but not good enough. The two people there that afternoon who were "professionals" and could speak for or against it loudly on the air and in a certain part of the press, were Dwight McDonald and Otis Guernsey.[2] They each have wide audiences. Happily, they not having my knowledge of a large clear print and better adjustment of words, musical background and other sounds, were immensely impressed and what they said to Miss Bute, most enthusiastic.

It is to be shown next week at least once to members of certain categories of memberships in The Museum of Modern Art.

It has been officially invited to be shown at the Cannes Film Festival in May. Columbia University wants the big N. Y. opening for a Benefit in the autumn but they hope to get a "distributor" before then so the backers can have some advance money. They need it badly. It will have an opening in Dublin and London the same time as N. Y. There is so much humor in it for those who are at ease, as it were and not worrying about understanding the words they don't get. To others to think they know English, to *think* English is being spoken and then find it is not English as THEY know it, is baffling and to some annoying. They are trying my suggestion which I think is not a "compromise" but a necessity for an audience which is intelligent, open-mind[ed] and interested in a challenge—a brief introduction that takes a little over a minute, using a quote from J. J. and a few score words naming the family make-up, etc. How this goes at the March 30th screening in the good auditorium will be important. I know an English professor from Brooklyn College who is to be there and he is going to report to me.

I don't think I could possibly write a review,—not for the Newslitter.[3] That must be a true J J Scholar. I don't know enough. A layman's reaction would have no value whatsoever. I would be afraid of [Jack] Dalton! I must have a chance to tell my histoire Dalton. I've really got him buffaloed. I write him such polite, old-world courteous notes, making myself into an old-world dumbbell that he gets befuddled and walks on eggs sending his thanks for my thoughtfulness and that it was not necessary for me to go to the trouble of letting him know that Mr. Wilder was away. . . . But, you see HE is the one writing the unnecessary letter to thank ME! I'm sure he thinks I'm a fool but he takes care to reach me on my elegant frosty level. Very funny. Yet he gets VERY sincere doing it. I've made him aware that perhaps there is SOMETHING he doesn't KNOW, so he now takes no chances when I carry on treating him elaborately like a person of manners and importance.

I can't believe you have a married daughter. She was just a little girl and you didn't look old enough to have her even 15–16 when I saw you both. You and Frank wander down in a few weeks and have our rendez-vous just the same.

Best to you both.

1. Mary Ellen Bute's *Passages from 'Finnegans Wake'* (also titled *Finnegans Wake*) did not have a commercial release until October 1967. The film, completed in 1965 is a 92 minute black and white film.

2. Dwight MacDonald's 1965 *Esquire* review is reprinted in his *Dwight MacDonald On Movies* (1969; rpt., New York: Da Capo Press, 1981), 461–462. We have not located a review by Otis Guernsey, a well-known theatrical critic.

3. James Blish reviewed Bute's film for *A Wake Newslitter*, N.S., II, 6 (December 1965), 29–30. Blish's review echoes many of Isabel Wilder's reservations about the movie.

To Isabel Wilder, Hamden, Connecticut

[MS. TLS—YCAL]

23 March 1965 Farmington, Connecticut

Dear Isabel,

Yes please, do let's meet. We would love it dearly.

Please also, do still think of writing about the movie for the Newslitter. One must not—repeat not—be buffaloed by [Jack] Dalton. He is, as a lady who actually had him to dinner, said to me, "Somebody who shouldn't be let to be with people." She said this, not in anger or disgust, but as one who has come to a truly serious decision.

And yet Dalton is very good at FW.

Mercy yes, I have a married daughter and I'm going to have a grandchild come late fall. How will you like being a grandmother? people say, and I reply truly that I will like it fine because I like to hold babies and crumple their ears and this you cannot do to stranger babies. In the teeth of all this evidence, I still manage to think of myself as a fascinating woman of thirty. This is called having the best of two worlds.

I'm sure you're right about the necessity of a brief introduction to the FW movie. Who is going to write it? Who is going to give it? I wish the answer to both questions was—your brother, but I daresay he would not even if he were home.

Till we meet.

Yours,
Adaline

To Adaline Glasheen, Farmington, Connecticut

[MS. ALS—HWS]

29 April 1965   [Florida]
en route North

Dear Adaline

I loved your letter.[1]
Can't send anything 1/10th as vivid in reply.
But do attribute these stamps to my gratitude and appreciation.[2] I went to some pains to acquire them (in Miami.)
No news to report. Just the daily chore.
Returned from Europe on a slow Italia ship (Naples—Cannes—Canary Islands—etc—Panama—Santiago de Chile) and met a delightful Panamiania[3] lady. I wish I'd known your son-in-law's name[4]; she was eager to know it. Said she knew everybody there.
When I finally get to Connecticut I shall call you up (a) about what would please the young couple and (b) about all those dazzling new "break throughs" in FW. There MUST be some!
It was morn on the 17th of last month before I suddenly remembered that it was my birthday. I burst out laughing. It pleased me to see how little consideration I give to the passing of time. I found this in a paper recently: Secretary (entering room with breakfast tray): Happy birthday, Willie. Mr. Somerset Maugham (92 or 93) Oh, hell! Another birthday!
Someone called attention to the fact that the days of the week fall on the same numbers in 1965 as in 1897. So I learn for the first time that I was born on a Saturday—Easter Eve. Isn't the old English name for that Saturday "The Raking of Hell"?—i.e. when Our Lord gathered from the underworld the Righteous who had lived before His coming? It must be in FW. Somewhere.
I hope Francis's knee is all restored now and that he's begun to forget that miserable time.

                       All devoted best to you all—
                       Ever
                       Thornton

1. A reference to a lost letter.
2. At the top left and the top right of the page Wilder affixed a stamp from the Republic of Ireland.
3. Wilder's word.
4. Glasheen's son-in-law, Newton Osborne, was Panamanian.

☐

To Adaline Glasheen, Farmington, Connecticut

[MS. ALS—HWS]

[postmark: 12 May 1965]   50 Deepwood Drive
                                 Hamden, Connecticut 06517

Dear Adaline =
   Lately, I'm the victim of outside pressures.
   Had to go to Washington[1]
   Have to go now to New York. (Will see *Hello Dolly* for the first time. It had begun to look mean or ugly-spirited that I hadn't seen it.)[2]
   All this interruption when my own stuff was going on so well.
   Oh beata solitudo! O sola beatitudo!
   Many thanks for the enclosed.[3] Love that tobacconist's allusion—it doesn't clear up the passage—*au contraire*: why, oh, why—does he mix up those wares with the Gracchi?
   [Jack] Dalton's phone to you!!—he's nuts. He sees himself as an impish little boy and that's dangerous!
   I'm off to Atlantic City (Spas out of season are very good working places.[)]
   Will be in New Haven in mid-summer ("nobody in town") and will ask for a cup of tea in Farmington.
   So you're to be a grandmother—The (H)uman (C)hain (E)xtends.

            This is in haste.
            All best to you both
            Old Thornt

1. On Tuesday, 4 May, Wilder received the first National Book Committee medal for literature. The award was presented by the first lady, Lady Bird Johnson, at a ceremony in the East Room of the White House. See *New York Times*, 5 May 1965, 43.

2. Wilder was in Europe when the Jerry Herman musical *Hello Dolly!* opened in New York on 16 January 1964. Wilder saw the musical, suggested by his *The Matchmaker*, on 13 May and the next day he left for Atlantic City, New Jersey.

3. A reference to a lost letter with enclosures.

□

To Thornton and Isabel Wilder, Hamden, Connecticut

[MS. ALS—YCAL]

13 July 1965 [22 Carrington Road
  Farmington, Connecticut]

Dear Thornton and Isabel,

We had a simply heavenly time with you on Saturday.

I'm home for a couple of days and right wondery in the head after the excitement of a faculty apartment in Storrs, Conn. Alison was fine, scarcely needed me except as slavey, but there is something about me—a kind grandmotherly presence, do you think?—that caused a series of young married women with predictable problems to lay them—problems—before me for such footling solution as I could give. So I footled and had to cope with nothing more serious than two flat* tires on Alison's car.

Newton back safe & happy for his father took a violent turn for the better[.] The children are thrilled with your check, your book, your records[.]

If you will bear with me this vapid or active or real life will come to an end and I will return to rapt contemplation of FW[.]

 Yrs,
 Adaline

F[rancis] had a terrible time alone for the cats bullied him and he cooked unfetching messes that he was obliged to eat[.] Men without wives—another vapid subject—a small subject[.]

*I don't mean I changed the flat tires. I just wheedled & flattered strange men into doing so.

☐

To Isabel Wilder, Hamden, Connecticut

[MS. TL—YCAL]

17 July 1965 [22 Carrington Road
Farmington, Connecticut]

Dear Isabel,

I wish it was a week ago tonight. We had such a lovely time with you all. I wish it was happening all over again.

But this is not to dwell on past felicities but to ask you about those glasses that let you read a book which is flat on your stomach. I called two optical places in Hartford and found out they are called "Bed Specks," a name of singular unfelicity. At both places Bed Specks—doesn't that suggest to you a bed littered with crackers and cheese?—cost about fourteen dollars and you had said you knew of their being 6.95 or something like that. I desperately need the damn things, and I will pay 14 dollars, but of course I'd rather not. So could you tell me?

We mean to hold you, you know, to our promise to come to us in fall.

Yours,
Adaline

I read the [Frank] Budgen book right off and will get it right back to you so you can give it to the Croat. Does he have [Harry] Levin's book on Joyce?[1]

1. Frank Budgen's *James Joyce and the Making of 'Ulysses'* (1934; rpt. 1960) and Harry Levin's *James Joyce: A Critical Introduction* (1941; rpt. and augmented, 1960). The "Croat" has not been identified.

☐

To Adaline and Francis Glasheen, Farmington, Connecticut
[MS. ALS—HWS]

[17 July 1965]   50 Deepwood Drive
Saturday   Hamden, Connecticut 06517

Dear Adaline and Francis =
    It was a treat—as always—to see you.
    And I thought that Francis was in better spirits and "tone" than the last time at the Lawn Club.
                        x
    That volume FIVE Simenons in one!—follows.[1] Isabel—the book-wrapper—has been in Canada and just got home. Went to *Hello Dolly* in Toronto, and to the Ontario Shakespeare Festival.
                        x
    Very pleased to see J. A.'s [James Atherton] letter.[2] I always cringe when the USA fails to show one of its better faces to visiting foreigners—even in such matters as the weather.
    Too bad they've poured so much work on him. It'd be invaluable if he could have a summer just to sit before those notebooks. He has a different kind of discernment from the [Jack] Dalton.
                        x
    I can make nothing of the column of letters—except an increase of my old dread that J J has buried schemata so deep that it's folly for us to try and dig them up {unless the Buffalo books also contain greater aids than that.}
                        x
    All happy wishes to the young people.
                        x
[drawings of ribbons]
    Those are pink and blue ribbons.

                    Ever
                    (T)

[new page]
POST SCRIPTUM
July 22.
Your letter—the letter *to* you, with others—has lain on my desk all these days.
I forget to mail 'em.
Since then I've received a lovely letter from Alison.
And I've written a letter to them—the letter that should have accompanied the wedding present long ago.
H[orace]. Walpole, writing to Lady Ossory, says there's a lovely joke about being a (new) grandparent in the then newly printed letters of Madame de Sévigné.[3]
Well, it is a lovely joke, but it's very high-brow involving a latin phrase—the Emperor Nero—a heroic wife stabbing herself. . .etc, etc.
I'll tell it to you when I see you.
Anyway, it's about first learning that you are a grandmother.
Paete, non dolet [Paetus, it is not painful]

Best to you both
(TN)

1. Georges Simenon, *The Second Maigret Omnibus* (New York: Harcourt, Brace & World, 1964).
2. Atherton participated in the summer program in modern literature at the State University of New York at Buffalo directed by Thomas E. Connolly. Glasheen had forwarded a letter from Atherton and two typed pages of transcriptions Atherton had made of selected passages from Joyce's notebooks in the Buffalo collection: VI B 24, pp. 205–206 and VI B 46, pp. 17–20. The first notebook entry lists American notes to *Finnegans Wake* and were mostly used in the *Wake*, pages 531–554. The second entry concerns references to Mark Twain's *Huckleberry Finn*. On this page Wilder entered page and line references from the *Wake* to correspond to the notebook entry. The American notes were discussed in an article, "Some American Notes to *Finnegans Wake*" by Stephen B. Bird in *A Wake Newslitter*, N.S., III, 6 (December 1966), 119–124. Atherton commented on Bird's article and noted that it was he who "started this particular hare by directing Mr. Bird's attention to the New York City entry in the notebook, when he attended a seminar I conducted at Buffalo in 1965. Unfortunately I lost touch with Mr. Bird afterwards and was not able to tell him that I had found the source-book for these particular notes. It is not the very surprising one of the article on New York City in the 11th edition of the *Encyclopedia Britannica*" (*A Wake Newslittler*, N.S., IV, 5, October 1967, 102–103). Wilder returned the two pages with his letter of 10 September 1965.
3. *Horace Walpole's Correspondence with The Countess of Upper Ossory*, ed. W. S. Lewis, et. al. (New Haven: Yale University Press, 1965), Vol. 32: I, Thursday, 19 January 1775, 224–230. The reference is to a letter by Madame de Sévigné to

Philippe Moucleau, 27 January 1687, letter 952 in volume III, *Madame de Sévigné Correspondence* (Paris: NRF, Éditions Gallimard, 1978), 275–276. See TW to AG, 26 July 1965.

□

ISABEL WILDER:

To Adaline Glasheen, Farmington, Connecticut

[MS. TL—carbon—YCAL]

22 July 1965

50 Deepwood Drive
Hamden 17, Connecticut

Dear Adaline:

What a pleasure it was to have you and Frances here for a few hours. It did us both a great deal of good. It was such FUN, too!

As to the glasses;—I have picked up some information which explains the two prices I quoted. The place here where I get my glasses tells me this:

The $14.95 ones used to be $19.95 and this type are prisms.

There is a kind based on the same idea which are mirrors. They cost, he thought, $6.95. So that is what I heard of and thought they were the same, reduced in price years after launching the invention. He claims they are VERY different items and that it pays to get the better ones for they are less strain on the eyes. I would only have to take his word for it. You might ask someone else for His (her) opinion. Now I am going to fall down on the job. I don't know WHERE to get the mirror ones. I saw an ad on them several years ago and never heard of them again.

The [Frank] Budgen book arrived today. Thanks. I think the Croat wrote that the [Harry] Levin book was among the three he had been able to get in his brief stay in London. Thanks for the tip if he hasn't it. I'm having great difficulty getting the one you recommended. . . something Traveller.[1]

Hasn't it be[en] elegant to be a little cooler!

Best to you both,
Affectionately,

1. Probably Richard M. Kain's *Fabulous Voyager: James Joyce's 'Ulysses'* (Chicago: The University of Chicago Press, 1947). For Budgen and Levin, see AG to IW, 17 July 1965, n. 1.

☐

To Alison and Newton Osborne, Storrs, Connecticut

[MS. ALS—HWS]

22 July 1965   50 Deepwood Drive
                                       Hamden, Connecticut 06517

Dear Mrs. Osborne:
Dear Dr-to-be Osborne:
Dear Little Bienvenida or Bienvenido Osborne:
    It's been a great pleasure hearing all about yourselves and your interests from Francis and Adaline G., and when I heard that the Bacteriologist was also a great lover of music it gave me an idea for my long-delayed wedding present.
    (Two eminent scientists from among my friends have been *mélomanes* also:
    Almost every Friday night of my six half-years at the University of Chicago I used to play piano four-hands with Professor Ralph Lillie—co-founder of the Woods Hole Biological Laboratory;
    and I used to see a lot of Dr. Percival Bailey, the brain-surgeon—co-author with Dr. Harvey Cushing of *Tumors of the Brain and Spine*. After those long exhausting days of operating at the Billings Clinic he used to come home for a drink and music before dinner. But he could only listen to *one* composer: Beethoven. Fortunately, his wife is an accomplished pianist. I used to tell him that "Beethoven wouldn't like it"—he venerated Haydn, Mozart, and Bach. But no! Beethoven was his only spiritual nourishment.)
    So the present was first designed for records.
    Then the Glasheens came to town and I gave them some records for you, and hoped that the present might be for the baby.
    Anyway, it's heart felt and for anything that will give you pleasure.
    Forgive me for not having accompanied it immediately with a letter. At that time I was in and out of doctors' offices and my poor sister was

in and out of doctors' offices and all letter-writing was delayed until our little crises were past.

Anyway, it's still a wedding present and brings the wish that you may long be happy.

Some day I hope to renew my *felicitations* in your own home in Panama.

A world of cordial regards to you both,—to you all!

> Sincerely yours,
> Thornton Wilder

To Adaline Glasheen, Farmington, Connecticut

[MS. ALS—HWS]

26 July 1965

50 Deepwood Drive
Hamden, Connecticut 06517

Dear Adaline:
  I hear and obey.

x

Madame de Sévigné had a cousin who wrote to her in doleful consternation that he was about to become a grandfather. He looked upon himself as still a gay young cavalier.

She—who had several grandchildren—replied encuragingly: *Paete, non dolet.*[1]

x

Paetus, a member of Nero's court, received a command from the Emperor to kill himself. These commands were frequent and admitted of no evasion. Paetus didn't like it a bit. He wandered around Rome all day in a slow burn.

Returning home, he found his wife waiting for him on the doorstep. She plunged a dagger in her heart, saying, "Paetus, it doesn't hurt."

x

Coming on it without this laborious explanation it is very funny and very freighted.

x

I am, madam,
Your ladyship's obedient servant,

T. N. W.

1. See TW to AG, 17 July 1965, n. 3.

☐

To Thornton and Isabel Wilder, Hamden, Connecticut
[MS. ALS—YCAL]

30 July 1965   [22 Carrington Road
Farmington, Connecticut]

Dear Thornton and Isabel,

Just a tidying-up note before I plunge into my two weeks in Stoors.[1]

Richard Francis was born yesterday, healthy mother & baby. He's right cunning.

The Semeon [TW: SIMENON] came,[2] great thanks

The joke   "   "   " [3]

Did you know—I didn't—negro babies are born white and migrate in the first few days?

Richard's ears are darkening like a siamese's.

I should think that, given the semantic white = good, black = bad, ignorant and superstitious people must be impressed by the initially white & rosy child who darkens—oncoming of original sin, mark of Ham, what have you, and yet I've never come on this curious fact in any book by or about the negro, have you?

Father Noon writes that another Jesuit, Father Boyle is going to write a book about FW.[4]

      Yrs,
      Adaline

1. Adaline planned to stay with Alison and her husband Newton in Stoors, Connecticut, while Alison was recuperating from giving birth.
2. *The Second Maigret Omnibus*. See TW to AG, 17 July 1965, n. 1.
3. Wilder's letter of 26 July 1965.
4. Father William T. Noon, S.J., author of numerous articles on Joyce and *Joyce and Aquinas* (New Haven: Yale University Press, 1957). Father Robert J. Boyle, S. J., also the author of numerous articles on Joyce and *James Joyce's Pauline Vision: A Catholic Exposition* (Carbondale: Southern Illinois University Press, 1978).

To Thornton Wilder, Hamden, Connecticut

[MS. TLS—YCAL]

7 August 1965   [22 Carrington Road
                 Farmington, Connecticut]

Dear Thornton,

Alison turns out to be like one of those Russian peasant women who drop a child and finish the turnip harvest. She was in the hospital two and a half days and on the fourth day home went to a baseball game, a movie and dispensed with my services, in order to be queen of the hearth, reigning alone. Naturally I was mad as hell at the time but when I'd gotten some sleep, I saw I admired her spirit. We made up but I still went home.

So home late last Thursday and a lot of Joyce mail and a house to clean up since the Grahams and Jim Atherton are coming to dinner Wednesday and he is going to stay till Saturday. Then Friday turned up the young Dutch medical student, Thon Tellegen, who invited himself to dinner Wednesday, too. He is tall and willowy and liable, I daresay, to deep disillusion when elder Joyceans turn out to be mortal.

My most interesting letter was from Jim [Atherton] who had just made the compulsory trip to Cornell to view the Joyce to Nora letters which somewhat put him off Joyce and seemed to him deeply obscene. He went with Father Noon and with another S. J. Father Boyle who is going to write a book on FW. Jim sent me a copy of a letter from Nora, thanking her husband for a book she liked because it was by Masoch.[1] From what Jim told me, I assume that, as Bloom (a non-author) bought *Sweets of Sin* for Molly, so Joyce wrote pornography for Nora.

What the Jesuits make of it, I don't know, for Jim only quoted Father Boyle as saying that Jesuit education fitted a boy to face every problem presented by the twelfth century.

Did I say the baby—Richard—is v[ery]. handsome, sort of Latin-colored with black eyes and long silky black hair and a dimple in one cheek? He is also a rather haughty, fastidious and touchy baby and I do not suppose I am ever going to be particularly sensible about him.

Yrs,
Adaline

---

1. An unpublished letter in the Cornell Joyce Collection. Richard Ellmann writes about Joyce sending Nora a book by Leopold von Sacher-Masoch in August 1917 (1959: 430–431; 1982: 417).

ISABEL WILDER:

To Adaline Glasheen, Farmington, Connecticut

[MS. ALS—HWS]

13 August [19]65   c/o Charles H. Morgan
　　　　　　　　　　West Tisbury, Mass.

Dear Adaline
　　Congratulations. Wonderful to have the waiting over & everyone doing fine plus. You were a dear to send us (*us* for you so sweetly included me) bulletins so promptly. We *were* & *are* interested & care.
　　See what was in a Sunday—before-last N. Y. Times! Wish I could have got a pair for you.[1] Saw the ad late. Getting off was as usual, fierce. Goodness, easier to stay here. And since now I can't, darn it, drive myself so far, I'm dependent on finding someone to drive up the 220 mi[les] & get himself by bus & train back to N[ew]. H[aven]. I wasn't minding old age so much until real decline of health sets in & goes apace! T. comes Sun.—Have the niece here for 3 days now. Vacation comes in Heaven & I'd rather stay here until it's complete senility!

　　　　　　　　Affection to you & Francis—
　　　　　　　　Isabel

1. Glasses or "bed specks" discussed in AG to TW and IW, 13 July 1965 and IW to AG, 22 July 1965.

To Adaline Glasheen, Farmington, Connecticut

[MS. ALS—HWS]

10 September 1965

50 Deepwood Drive
Hamden, Connecticut 06517

Dear Adaline =

Forgive me keeping these enclosures so long.[1]

They were forwarded to me when I went on the 15th to visit Isabel on Martha's Vineyard. I didn't take my FW with me. Returned here today at 2:30 and only now 8:30 have been able to transcribe them.

I've penciled in the page references to most of the Huck Finn allusions. As you say, it doesn't seem to reveal much.

Gorgeous story about [Jack] Dalton knowing more English slang than Mr. Atherton.

I assume your Northwestern Press has sent you a copy of Mrs Christiani's book for review.[2]

I don't review, but I'd send them a blurb, if they asked for it—one can't send one unasked.

It's a useful book—but as you say of the Buffalo notebooks; it doesn't unlock any basic material. (I'm still hoping the Buffalo material does—at least *one* lead as important as your Morton Prince discovery.)[3]

I'm about to attack my last chapter[4]; will probably ship abroad for a short spell.[5]

I hope all's well with the young family.

Forgive my being so late in returning this material. I had a good time with it.

        Best to Francis,
        Toujours
        Thornton

1. See TW to AG, 17 July 1965, n. 2.
2. Glasheen reviewed Dounia Bunis Christiani's *Scandinavian Elements of 'Finnegans Wake'*, (Evanston: Northwestern University Press, 1965) in *Criticism: A Quarterly for Literature and the Arts*, IX, 1 (Winter 1967), 104–105.
3. Glasheen's 1954 article, "*Finnegans Wake* and the Girls from Boston, Mass."

4. Wilder's novel, *The Eighth Day*.
5. Wilder sailed on the SS *Independence* on 6 October 1965. He remained in Europe, traveling in Italy, France, and Switzerland for several months.

To Thornton Wilder, Hamden, Connecticut

[MS. TL—YCAL]

14 September 1965 [22 Carrington Road
Farmington, Connecticut]

Dear Thornton,

Happy last chapter. Happy abroad.

We're well. Children well and happy. Baby of solemn, unearthly beauty.

Thank you for suggesting I get the new Scandinavian FW book out of Northwestern. I wrote them. They have, by the way, started advertising my book again.

Did I tell you there was this young (23) Dutch medical student who wrote me very nice letters[1]—the one who was coming to New York to get inspiration for a play he and another Dutch were writing about Jimmy Walker. We know a girl who goes to NYU and is a siren. A real siren—men's mouths just drop open when they see her. She is also very intelligent and writes poetry for *The Realist*. She's tall, so I asked the Dutch—Thon Tellegen—if he was tall and he said, yes, and so I fixed them a date. Thon Tellegen turned out to be a child, six feet tall, and the girl thought him a perfect baby. Moreover, as (obviously I didn't know at the time) she was pregnant by the only one of her lovers who she really would like to marry. So, to her, Thon was a baby whose idea of romance was to call her "Monica" because he thought her real name too plain and unevocative. Anyway the child fell very badly for Monica and yearned and yearned and yearned and bored and bored both Monica and me—to whom he wrote yearning letters, trying to get me to place him in a favorable light. Monica is a very gentle girl but, in the end, she told him to get lost and refused his offer of marriage. Whereupon in a letter I wish I could show you (but it would not be honorable) Thon denounced me for having, as it were, gotten him a blind date with Circe.

In short, it was Henry James in reverse—European innocence meets American experience and limps off, licking its wounds. Also, in short, I have now learned why elderly ladies fix young men up with the sort of nice girl who ought to have been married but has not been.

The more I think about Jim Atherton, the less satisfied I am with our encounter. It was my opinion—which I didn't dare express—that while he was here he was like a man, holding his breath till he can get home and start swearing. I thought, well he just doesn't like us—there's no law says he has to. But the Grahams and Father Noon felt exactly the same way. And—this is quoting Father Noon from memory—he acted as if *his* opinions of FW were from Mt Sinai and we would, in all courtesy, not talk about anybody else's opinions.

Would your dear sister, Isabel, like to come see us this fall if we could make transportation easy? We'd love to have her, would you tell her?

I seem to know more news about Joyceans than about Joyce. I have been Joyce-engaged but in a nasty way. I mean I have been, [Jack] Dalton-like, tearing Nathan Halper's Joyce and TSE article[2] to pieces and jumping on his face with hob-nail boots. This is not a pleasing occupation for a lady, but he started it by saying he was going to attack me for being the symbol of self-indulgence and permissiveness in reading FW. Still, I admit it, this is a nasty occupation and a decadent one. I had always thought the most decadent thing I ever did was sit in Amsterdam and work a jig-saw puzzle of Edward VII and Alexandra on top of an elephant at a Burbar. But Now I have really touched bottom.

                Yrs
                Adaline

1. See AG to TW, 7 August 1965. There are no Thon Tellegen letters in HWS.
2. Halper's "Joyce and Eliot: A Tale of Shem and Shaun," *The Nation*, 200 (31 May 1965), 590–595. The article, in a slightly different form, was published as "Joyce and Eliot," in *A Wake Newslitter*, N.S. II, 3 (June 1965), 3–10; and 4 (August 1965), 17–23. Glasheen did not write for publication about Halper's article. There are no letters from Halper in HWS.

1966

To Thornton Wilder, Hamden, Connecticut
[MS. ALS—YCAL]

28 July 1966   [22 Carrington Road
 Farmington, Connecticut]

Dear Thornton,

Where are you? How are you?[1]

FW {do you remember FW?} stands as ever—reserved and irritating here and there. I have done a dull and worthy list of Dublin street names mentioned in FW. Did I tell you I found out who the Sullivani are?[2] I can't remember what I've told anybody.

We are a family blown about with as many ills as Job, F[rancis]. is just home from Hartford Hospital and shock-treatments, Alison's husband was accepted for medical school but can't get a grant. Alison also lost a second baby.[3]

I sit amid the general ruin and am no special comfort to anyone, I should say. But I am going to stop sitting next week and go to work oiling 18th century leather books for Mr. Wilmarth Lewis. This oiling seems to require a fine precision and a pair of surgeons hands. I was born ham-handed so I see myself not giving satisfaction and that right rapidly.

I guess I must know some FW news. Well, LSU Press has probably accepted Ruth von Phul's 698 page book.[4] Clive Hart is at Buffalo for the summer and reports that Jack Dalton is green—his face, you know, literally green. Father Noon has multiple sclerosis. {My, what a cheerful letter this is turning out to be!} I had better stop gossiping about Joyceans.

I hope all's well with you.

> Yours,
> Adaline

1. There is no extant correspondence since September 1965.
2. In *Census III* Glasheen identifies, 573.7, the Sullivani, as a gang of twelve mercenaries.
3. At the end of this paragraph, in a note meant for his sister Isabel, Wilder writes: "Oh! Oh! Does that mean the first wonder-baby died?"
4. The book was never published.

To Adaline Glasheen, Farmington, Connecticut

[MS. ALS—HWS]

August—the fifth, some say.   50 Deepwood Drive
1966.   Hamden, Connecticut 06517

Dear Adaline:
    Forgive my long silence.
    I always devour your letters with delighted appreciation, but now in my 70th year I'm sinking into sloth.
    Deeply concerned by what you tell me: Alison's loss. I wish I knew medical circles and could be of use toward a grant (I've often been successful in "cultural" hand-outs of far less importance) for her husband. Is he an American citizen now?
    Convey my friendship to Francis and my appreciation of his quality.
    When I got back I sat down and gave three days to F. W.— copying in data from that new book on it and many items from the

accumulated Newslitters, but the spell it had over me so long is broken. It's a book of power and fascination, but I can no longer "dig" in it.

Mrs Boldereff from Princeton sent me her book on Joyce-Blake with a flattering inscription.[1] All I can say is to swing my gavel like a judge and cry NOT PROVEN.

Lots of pressure is being put on me to contribute to the FESTSCHRIFT for Lefty Lewis.[2] But I'm not an "eighteenth century" man—I'm a dilettante in literary history and criticism. They blithely suggest that I write about 20 pages on "The Gothic Novel": I don't know anything about it. I respect scholarship too much. Could it be possible, dear Alison [i.e., Adaline] that because I acquired a brief sixpenny name in other fields that they want me included—even though I wrote tripe? Oh, no, it can't be.

My novel is finished,[3] but don't tell anybody. The typist is "wrapping it up." But I'm back at work on that series of one-acts and I'm just as inaccessible as ever—and so shall be to the end of my days.

Fritz Senn sent me two articles he had written for Swiss papers in connection with the monument for Joyce's grave.[4] He writes very well,— clear, well-ordered, free of the abstract-noun barnacles that adhere to professorial German. I hope he soon will get the academic or editorial jobs he so deserves.

Now, Adaline, don't get down-hearted.

You are a splendid vital intelligent inspiriting (and goodlooking) girl.

You have done a notable work and are forever ensconced in literary history.

Keep it up.

Write the flock faithfully—even when you don't feel like it.

You are what the Army used to call a *Communications Center*.

A ganglion.

Rally the Troops.

Start another book. Why not do the long delayed Place-Names in F. W. ("Geographical and Sociological References in F. W.") I'll lend you the scrappy notes I made toward it, to start your card file— superficial though they are.

You will prove most useful to those who now turn to you if—at the same time—you are fulfilling yourself also in that kind of work.

Courage—dear friend—high heart—

   Affectionately
   Thornton

1. Frances Motz Boldereff's *A Blakean Translation of Joyce's Circe* (Woodward, PA: Classic Non-Fiction Library, 1965).
2. Wilder did not contribute to the Festschrift for Wilmarth S. Lewis (known to his friends as Lefty) (1895–1979), published to commemorate the 250th anniversary of Horace Walpole's birth, *Horace Walpole: Writer, Politician, and Connoisseur*, ed. Warren Hunting Smith (New Haven and London: Yale University Press, 1967). Wilder met Lewis in 1912 when they were both students at the Thatcher School in Ojai, California. Lewis and Amos Wilder, Thornton's older brother, were also roommates at Oberlin College, and Wilder and Lewis renewed their friendship when he entered Yale College in 1917. Wilder served as a member of the advisory committee for several volumes in the Yale University Press edition of Lewis's *Horace Walpole Correspondence*, and his annotated copy of the edition, along with his correspondence with Lewis, is in The Lewis Walpole Library in Farmington, Connecticut. Lewis was one of the speakers at the memorial service for Wilder on Sunday, 18 January 1976, at Yale's Battell Chapel. His talk is reprinted in a pamphlet printed by Isabel Wilder, *Thornton Niven Wilder: 1897–1975* (n.d.), 11–13.
3. Wilder's *The Eighth Day*.
4. Senn wrote, "James Joyce: Eigenheiten im Werk des grossen Iren," in *Zolliker Bote* (Zollikon), 24 June 1966, 9–11 about the monument to Joyce by Milton Hebald which was dedicated on Bloomsday 1966 at Joyce's grave. Senn also sent Wilder "Joyce im Gespräch," from *Neue Zürcher Zeitung*, 15 March 1964, 59.

1967

To *Adaline Glasheen, Farmington, Connecticut*

[MS. APCS—HWS]

[Postcard: Dachs / Blaireau / Badger]

[? March 1967]   [Atlantic City, New Jersey]
a few days in Atlantic City—hard at work at *another*!¹

Dear Adaline:
   All of us children born in Wisconsin² (see over) are badgers. We have pretty markings but our noses are too long. ¶ Yes that "Stephen Crane" man is a former pupil of mine—nice and bright but ebullient.³ ¶ Your John Philips didn't meet me at a ball, because I've never in 70 years been to a ball.⁴ ¶ Delighted that you're in "health." You will be superb at Buffalo.⁵ ¶ Haven't see[n] movie Ulysses.⁶ Isabel found it incoherent—more illustrations to a book she never read. ¶ Yes, Ellen Mary Bute⁷ who did the FW movie has all production rights to *SKIN OF OUR [TEETH]* and is star-hunting. ¶ I devotedly want Francis to get well. ¶ Saw Fritz [Senn] in Zurich.⁸ He's better and is slowing [i.e., slowly] arriving at a "position"; but I don't think he'd be happy if he had everything.

          Affectionate greetings to all.
          Thornt'

---

1. Wilder's novel *The Eighth Day*, after a delay of almost a year from its promised date, was published on 29 March 1967, less than a month before Wilder's seventieth

birthday. It is not clear whether at this time Wilder had begun work on his next novel *Theophilus North* (1973) or was working on new plays for his one-act cycle plays. This is the first extant letter since TW to AG, 5 August 1966. On 27 October 1966, Wilder sailed on the *France*. He spent time traveling in France, Germany, Austria, Italy, and Switzerland. He returned from Genoa on the *Cristoforo Colombo* on Sunday, 19 March 1967.

2. Wilder was born in Madison, Wisconsin, on 17 April 1897.

3. Glasheen had met Robert Wooster Stallman (1911–1982), an authority on Stephen Crane. He was a student of Wilder's at the University of Chicago, and, in March 1935, he participated in Gertrude Stein's seminar at the university. Wilder provided Stallman, who owing to an illness was unable to work, with a monthly stipend paid anonymously through the university. His book *The Houses that James Built and Other Literary Studies* (East Lansing: Michigan State University Press, 1964) is dedicated to Wilder: "In token appreciation for his sponsorship of an apprentice poet and critic: 1934–1935." Stallman writes about his relationship with Wilder at the University of Chicago in "To Thornton Wilder: A Note in Gratitude," in *Four Quarters: Thornton Wilder Number*, La Salle College, Philadelphia, 16, 4 (May 1967), 28–29.

4. A reference to a lost letter.

5. Glasheen had accepted an invitation to teach in the summer program in modern literature at the State University of New York at Buffalo.

6. *Ulysses*, a film produced and directed by Joseph Strick which starred Barbara Jefford as Molly Bloom, Milo O'Shea as Leopold Bloom, and Maurice Roeves as Stephen Dedalus.

7. Mary Ellen Bute's *Passages from 'Finnegans Wake'*. See Isabel Wilder to AG, 20 March 1965.

8. Wilder saw the Senns several times in December 1966.

To Thornton Wilder, Atlantic City, New Jersey

[MS. TL—YCAL]

2 April 1967
22 Carrington Road
Farmington, Connecticut]

Dear Thornton,

I read *The Eighth Day* and it was—as book jackets say—engrossing. F[rancis]. is reading it now and is greatly taken with the idea of our being the eighth day.[1]

I have read your book only once and I'm not sure what I think of it. I like it, of course, but I haven't taken it in, made it out. In "Illinois to Chile" I was distracted by trying to make out a myth that governed the whole—I didn't succeed but then I had to read in an article that "The Cocktail Party" was based on *Alcestis*. Mr. Wellington Bristow[2]— Mercury and Accuser—oh he is a lovely character and a completely original character. Fine, fine. But is "I to C" a myth? Or is John Ashley just like one of those Greek murderers who had to go into exile and meet with gods? Was Eumaeus a murderer?

Mr Bristow is my second favorite character. My favorite—or at least the one that seems to me most interesting and beautifully done—is Breckenridge Lansing. Here, too, I was distracted by speculating—is he Ernest Hemingway? I decided yes he was, whether you knew it or not. Then I began to speculate—did you know he was? And I decided yes you did. Then I decided Lansing-Hemingway is, as it were, your Mulligan-Gogarty, but forgiven.

I don't think I'm within a mile of understanding your book. But I read two reviews of it (Time and today's Sunday NYTimes)[3] and they were cret [paper torn, Wilder adds: cretinous]

    Yrs
    Adaline

---

1. Wilder found the concept of humankind's "second week" in the writings of Pierre Teilhard de Chardin. In the novel, Dr. Gillies, responding to a question about what the new century will be like says: "Man is not an end but a beginning. We are at the beginning of the second week. We are children of the eighth day" (New York: Harper & Row, 1967), 16. The novel has a Prologue and six titled sections—"Illinois to Chile 1902–1905" is the second section. In the novel Wilder tells of two Mid-West families brought together through a murder charge. John Ashley has been accused of the murder of his friend and senior colleague Breckenridge Lansing. He is tried and condemned but saved by unknown rescuers on his way to execution. Wilder narrates what becomes of his wife and children to learn what might have contributed to this crime. In the "St. Kitts" chapter, it is revealed that George Lansing killed his father because of his cruelty to his wife and family.

2. John Ashley escapes from Coaltown, Illinois, to Manantiales, Chile, where he lives in a hotel managed by a Mrs. Wickersham. A frequent visitor to the hotel is "the famous Wellington Bristow, a businessman, owner of an import-export office in Santiago de Chile. He was an American citizen, he said, born in Rome of an English father and a Greek mother, but he had been heard to describe his origins differently" (183). He keeps a list of people who have committed crimes, his "rat

list." Mrs. Wickersham learns that John Ashley is on his list and arranges for his escape. After Ashley is declared drowned at sea, a disbelieving Bristow continues to search for him.

3. *Time*, an unsigned review, "Books: Everytown," 89 (31 March 1967), 96. Benjamin De Mott, "Old-Fashioned Innovator," *New York Times Book Review*, 2 (April 1967), 1, 51–52.

To Adaline Glasheen, Farmington, Connecticut

[MS. APCS—HWS]

[? April 1967]   Clamming at Atlantic City

Dear Adaline =
 Don't grope too hard. I don't go in for deep symbolic stuff. But I'll tell you one bit (not necessary for a reader, really): a woman is lucky if her life completes The Trajectory: Artemis—Aphrodite—Hera—Athene. Beata got stuck in Hera. Eustacia (and Lauradel) are Aphrodite but she's journeying through Hera to Athene.[1] Your friend Bristow is Hermes—finagler and Psychopompos—so is Roger. Your friend Breckenridge is shoddy—Ares, married to Aphrodite (he flunked out of West Point). Félicité[2] and all nuns are born Athene—even if they have lots of children.
 You were Artemis and Aphrodite (with occasional time-out for Hecate) and the author of the Census and the professor at Buffalo is entering into her happiest expression as Pallas Athene—friend of good men and patroness of mind and culture. ¶ Now reread the Lauradel-scene[3]: Black Venus—island and shells—and even she is pushing on to the next stage which is Athene.
 Oh, no—I never thought of Hemingway. He was an Apollo and ashamed of it. He wanted to be Ares—and fouled up his life.

       Thorny

1. Beata Ashley whose husband John is accused of murdering Eustacia Lansing's husband Breckenridge. Lauradel is a "singer and part owner of the 'Old Dixie

Ballroom, a Refined Dance Floor for Ladies and Gentlemen'" in Chicago. She forms an attachment with Roger Ashley, who, using the name Trent Frazier, has become a respected Chicago journalist.

2. A daughter of Eustacia and Breckenridge Lansing.

3. *The Eighth Day*, 253–259.

☐

To Thornton Wilder, Atlantic City, New Jersey

[MS. TL—YCAL]

7 April 1967   [22 Carrington Road
                                           Farmington, Connecticut]

Dear Thornton,

Tell me where to stay in Atlantic City off-season. The information will not, I assure you, bring F[rancis]. and me hot-foot into y[ou]r vicinity, but we are v[ery]. fond of deserted resorts. In exchange (maybe you already know it) may I mention an island off New Bedford called Cutty Hunk, populated (in Oct) by nothing but enthusiastic bass fishers who turned out to be v[ery]. relaxing company as they never talked about anything but the minutiae of bass fishing.

I'm sorry if you didn't meet John Philips (gawd he is not MY John Philips) at a ball, for (though utterly detestable) he is one whose career cannot but be followed with wrapt attention. The son of a New Jersey dentist he conned the Walpole factory[1] into hiring him, sight unseen— no 18th cent. articles published, no nothing, sheer gall. After a year in New Haven he was let go, came to teach at Mrs Riddle's school, Avon Old Farms. While there he attempted to abjure his Jewish faith and enter—well, he tried to become a Congregationalist, an Episcopalian, a Catholic and was turned down by all 3 faiths (so the Congregational minister told me—I admit it was very odd for a clergyman to tell [t]his at a dinner party, but strange things happen to people who know John Philips). The reason he wanted to become a Christian was that he was courting a girl named March Enders, who is the daughter of the president of the biggest Hartford bank, and the niece of Dr Enders who won part of a Nobel prize for measles vaccine. March was an enchanting girl who found herself tied down in a little rich social world and being urged to marry a college friend of her father's, when all she wanted was to go to McGill medical school. As I read March, she used John Philips (a desperately unwantable son-in-law by any standards) to threaten her parents so that they would let her go to McGill. In any case, after going with John for a year she did go off to medical school and I have not heard of her since.

While at Avon Old Farms John found a box of Henry James Letters, written to Mrs Riddle.[2] He proposed to edit them and publish them in the Atlantic—this was all agreed to by the magazine. But when he called on H. James descendant to ask permission, John's impossibleness infuriated the descendant so that he refused permission for publication. The letters are now on display at the Hillstead Museum—one of them is great.

All this bad luck would, you'd think, flatten any man, but John left America and went to teach at a Swiss school, La Rosay (sp?). There, he drifted quite out of my ken but not out of the ken of people who'd known him in New Haven. They kept meeting him in Florence where he lived (with some person of presumed rank, sometimes said to be male, sometimes female) in a most wonderful palace in Florence where he entertained people to tea, wearing sometimes a black velvet mask. Is this not pure Firbank or Corvo?[3]

Luck to y[ou]r new novel. I think-thought the character was E. Hemingway because of his passion for shooting, his "manliness," his wanting to shoot Spaniards, his lodge connections (G. Stein "you're 40 percent Rotarian"),[4] madness at end of life, unsuccess with Aphrodite.

No, I never have been Hecate, if by Hecate you mean a woman who believes in her irrational powers. This is a great lack in any woman.

                Yrs
                Adaline

1. Wilmarth S. Lewis's project of the correspondence of Horace Walpole.
2. See TW to AG, 6 January 1954, n. 1.
3. Two eccentric English novelists: Ronald Firbank (1886–1926) and Frederick William Rolfe (1860–1913) who wrote under the pen name Baron Corvo.

4. The remark by Gertrude Stein, in the voice of Alice B. Toklas, is, "They [Stein and Hemingway] sat and talked a long time. Finally I heard her say, Hemingway, after all you are ninety percent Rotarian. Can't you, he said, make it eighty percent. No, she said regretfully, I can't" (Gertrude Stein, *The Autobiography of Alice B. Toklas*, New York: Harcourt, Brace, & Co., 1933, 270).

☐

To Adaline Glasheen, Farmington, Connecticut

[MS. APCS—HWS]

29 April [1967] P. O. Box 862
 Edgartown Mass #02539

Dear Adaline =
 Your letter about the Roman painter[1] made me happy from one point of view—to see you as Central Inspiritrix of the FW worker. ¶ I don't think much of the treasure hunt—partly because Joyce detested Rome and everything about it—perhaps because it was the center of Christendom. ¶ When I was at the Academy[2] I often went to sit under Tasso's oak—one of the great VIEWS of the world. ¶ [Fritz] Senn has sent me instal[l]ment II of his Zürich review of J. J.'s letters.[3] Senn writes awfully well—in a really distinguished German. Isabel gave me the *Letters* for my birthday.[4] I found them desolating for egocentricity. ¶ I find Svevo[5] more and more interesting. ¶ I think with a glow of you at Buffalo. It'll be terrible to leave Francis but since it must be—go into it with your contagious handsome convincing self. ¶ Dear Francis—grin and bear it while her Ladyship's away. A world of cordial regard to you. ¶ Adaline, don't waste your precious time on me, but. . . .but. . . I love to hear from you.

 Sez your devoted
 old friend
 Thornton.

1. A reference to a lost letter.
2. After graduating from Yale College in 1920, Wilder spent 1920–1921 at the American Academy in Rome where he was involved in archeological studies. It

was this year in Rome that provided him with the background for his first novel, *The Cabala*.

3. Senn's review of volumes II and III of Richard Ellmann's *Letters of James Joyce* appeared in the *Neue Zürcher Zeitung*, no. 814, 26 February 1967, 61–63.

4. A three-volume boxed set of Joyce's letters was published by the Viking Press in 1966. The first volume, edited in 1957 by Stuart Gilbert, was reissued with corrections. The second and third volumes were edited by Richard Ellmann.

5. Italo Svevo (1861–1928), the pseudonym of the novelist Ettore Schmitz. Svevo, who had worked in a bank, wrote two novels that were almost totally forgotten: *Una vita* (*A Life*) and *Senilità* (*As a Man Grows Older*). He and Joyce met in Trieste, in January 1908, when Svevo took private English lessons to prepare for visits to his wife's family's paint factory in England. Svevo's essay on Joyce, "Scritti su Joyce," is in *Opera omnia*, vol. 3, *Racconti, saggi, pagine sparse*, ed. Bruno Maier (Milano: Dall'Oglio), 1966–1969, [706]–748.

□

To Thornton Wilder, Hamden, Connecticut

[MS. TL—PRIVATE COLLECTION]

2 May 1967   [22 Carrington Road
                                          Farmington, Connecticut]

Dear Thornton,

I have always got the time and the will to write you letters. Usually I just don't have the subject matter, and don't tell me that if I were Madame de Sevigny (sp?) I would always be able to find the subject matter—I deny it.

This summer at Buffalo ought, I fancy, to provide a fair field full of folk. William Empson is listed as being there, though I've heard he may have cancer and not be, poor man. A Pole Jan Kott (*Shakespeare our Contemporary*—I liked the essays on Lear and The Tempest, rest just adequate)—he is going to be there. And some Irishman, Austin Clark[e],[1] who was one of the founders of the Irish Literary society that Joyce wouldn't join. The rest are poets I never heard of.

So maybe I will have something to write letters about.

Yrs
Adaline

A friend of ours Warren Smith[2] (you've met him, he works for Mr Lewis) read *The Eighth Day* and thinks it the finest American novel since Willa Cather.

---

1. Austin Clarke (1896–1974), the Irish poet, playwright, and novelist.
2. Warren Hunting Smith worked on Wilmarth S. Lewis's Horace Walpole correspondence project and was co-editor of several volumes. It was to the library named in his honor at Hobart and William Smith Colleges, Geneva, New York, that Glasheen gave Wilder's letters and her Joyce research archive.

To Adaline Glasheen, Farmington, Connecticut

[MS. APCS—HWS]

[Postcard: Surf at South Beach on Martha's Vineyard Island]

5 May [1967] Martha's Vineyard

Dear Adaline =
   Yes, I read Jan Kott—some long needed insights from the Marxian wing, but too few. I worship Empson—I read *Versions of Pastoral*[1] three times a year. . . . I buy the *New Statesman*, all over Europe and NY, in the hope of finding his occasions—and book reviews. I hope he'll be at Buffalo. ¶ Get ready to be an admired and intimidating Blue Stocking. ¶ I love your letter; but my new glasses—for eye-strain—come back next Tuesday. ¶ All cordial best to Francis and to M'lady

Thornton

---

1. Empson's *Some Versions of Pastoral* (1935).

To Adaline Glasheen, Buffalo, New York

[MS. ALS—HWS]

11 July 1967   last days at Stockbridge Mass

Dear Adaline =
Your wonderful letter very welcome but I was horrified by the night drive you describe—45 minutes in the riot area![1] With the worst kind of neurotic—the ostentatious neurotic.

You don't say a word about classes or lectures or discussion groups.

But in spite of that lunatic's drive—which *I* shall never forget—it does sound as though you've had and shall continue to have some very good times. And among the good times will be hearing your own voice on the podium. Madame Frau Professora Glasheen, in person.

Since [Jack] Dalton has dropped FW, please cultivate and inspirit the next generation of FW workers.

Wouldn't it be Heaven, if a young woman or a young man got up and calmly revealed the thematic structure of "A. L. P." chapter? or the City-Builder proclamation?

They're all taking you out for a "beer,"—so, soon you'll be led out by Leslie Fiedler.[2]

There's no news in my life so I'll simply tell you what I've been reading:

Bleak House {neither a previous reading nor much critical reading on Dickens had led me to expect the sombre black power of the earlier portions. And Orwell says that he did not record the proletariat!!!}[3]

To the Finland Station {Best thing he ever did}[4]

Tolstoi's *The Cossacks* {the wonderful things you can pick off the racks of a rural drugstore these days.—What a wellspring of youth it is!}

Brown's *Life against Death*[5] {Have read "in" Freud for 40 years, but never understood the import of his "death instinct" until this week}

Two novels sent me by acquaintances—both first novels—with much Talent, but constantly undermining their own best qualities by an inexperienced and self-indulgent insertion of themselves into the development.

Have a great time.
Thanks for your fascinating letter.

     Devotedly
     Thornton

My best to Francis, when you write

1. A reference to a lost letter. In late June and early July there were almost daily riots in Buffalo, New York, by young African-Americans protesting the lack of summer jobs. There was a massive armed patrol by police of the East Side ghetto. Hundreds of young people were arrested, and the police used buckshot pellets to disperse the rioters.

2. The literary critic and author of, among other books, *Love and Death in the American Novel* (1960). Fiedler was teaching at SUNY Buffalo when Glasheen was there.

3. Orwell's "Charles Dickens," first published in his *Inside the Whale, a Book of Essays* (1940).

4. Edmund Wilson's *To the Finland Station: A Study in the Writing and Acting of History* (1940).

5. Norman O. Brown's *Life Against Death: The Psychoanalytical Meaning of History* (1959).

□

To Thornton Wilder, Hamden, Connecticut

[MS. TL—YCAL]

16 August 1967   [22 Carrington Road
                                  Farmington, Connecticut]

Dear Thornton,

I feel fairly foolish at having come away from Buffalo with no treasure trove of Joyceana.[1] The Muse (Clio I suppose) will remove her countenance.

I read 25 FW holograph workbooks. That is, I turned their pages and looked at the pages. I found Joyce's explanation of ALP = 111 in Hebrew numbers. I found $1 + 2 + 3 + 4 + 5 + 6 + 7 = 28$.[2] But these things have already been troved. With the best will in the world, I did not find anything to write a note about.[3]

On the other hand, I had a simply wonderful summer socially. I sister-souled like crazy, lent an avid and appreciative ear to Jack Dalton's textual finds[4] (while he was eating 18, yes I don't care if you don't believe me, 18 deserts),[5] to a young millionairess who was married only 7 hours to her 3rd husband, to a poet who has left his wife nine children and the Catholic Church for a barman, to a (she *said*) member of the jet-set a name dropper of truly fantastic proportions, to a novelist whose dead serious novel was taken by the critics as a farce, to a farcical novelist whose two books have been taken dead serious, to Robert Graves' ex-private secretary, to a Harvard boy with the theory that only a bourgeois can write a great novel. Impressions, indeed, came crowding too fast—autumn leaves in Val[l]ombrosa—too fast for one who has lived out of the world and is almost always surprised by the things she hears.

My Joyce lectures were decent, not glorious.[6] I had no student of first-rate abilities, but some of the auditors were very good indeed.

After Buffalo I visited the children in Ann Arbor.[7] They are very happy, esthetically pleasing (Alison has thinned down and grown-up—I sort of miss the puppy child she was) and cultivating their garden without knowing they should have suffered first.

Then I came home. F[rancis]. is neither better nor worse. I'm working—it isn't easy—to get him to a new set of doctors.

I am reading *Mansfield Park*, FW, and *Chronicles of the House of Borgia* by Baron Corvo. This last is a book worth mining. Over all it is possessed of a high silliness which is most taking.[8]

So now you know about my summer and my present condition. How was your summer? Did I tell you Alison has read *The Eighth Day* twice?

      Yours,
      Adaline

---

1. Glasheen had taught at the SUNY Buffalo Summer School in Modern Literature. See TW to AG, [?10] February 1965, n. 3.

2. All Hebrew letters have numeric value. "Both entries... are in [Buffalo Notebook] VI.B.15..."

    $A = 1$
    $L = 30 = 111 = \wedge$
    $P = 80$

(VI.B 15: 23; *JJA* 32: 253 [*The James Joyce Archive*, ed. Michael Groden, et al. New York and London: Garland Publishing, 1977–1979]) . . . 1 + 2 + 3 + 4 + 5 + 6 + 7 = 28 ([Buffalo Notebook] (VI.B 15:83; *JJA* 32: 283)." (Email received from Sam Slote, 1 September 1999.)

3. In the margin Wilder wrote: "for the magazine," meaning *A Wake Newslitter*.

4. Dalton had not "dropped FW" as Wilder thought in his letter of 11 July 1967. He was continuing his study of the *Finnegans Wake* notebooks in the Library of the State University of New York at Buffalo for which he was awarded a Guggenheim Fellowship in 1964–1965. See TW to AG, 24 October 1963, n. 2. For Dalton's work on the text of *Finnegans Wake* see his "Advertisement for the Restoration," in *Twelve and a Tilly: Essays on the Occasion of the 25th Anniversary of 'Finnegans Wake'*, ed. Jack P. Dalton and Clive Hart (Evanston: Northwestern University Press, 1965), [119]–137.

5. Wilder has underlined this parenthetical in red.

6. Glasheen's "Joyce lectures" have not been located.

7. Glasheen's daughter Alison and her husband, Newton Osborne.

8. Frederick [Rolfe] Baron Corvo, *Chronicles of the House of Borgia* (London: Grant Richards; New York: E. P. Dutton & Co., 1901). The book chronicles the house of Borgia from its rise in the twelfth century to its subsequent decline in the nineteenth. The book's main focus is the Borgia family from 1455 to 1572, when they, as Baron Corvo writes, "sprang to the pedestal of fame; leaping at a bound, from little bishoprics and cardinalates, to the terrible altitude of Peter's Throne; producing, in those years, two Popes, and a Saint and General of the Jesuits" (vii).

☐

To Adaline Glasheen, Farmington, Connecticut

[MS. ALS—HWS]

22 August [1967]   Hotel Algonquin
                                           59 West 44th Street
                                           New York, N. Y. 10036

Dear Adaline =
     Wonderfully relieved that you're back home safe and sound and delighted that you had a rip-roaring good time
     that'll teach you not to tremble with trepidation before future engagements.

x

Spending August in N. Y. To see my niece,—my invalid sister on Long Island—and to meet my English godson[1] arriving this morning on the *Queen Mary*—it got in at 8 and still no sign of him at 11:20. (He's going to get a doctorate in Economics at the University of Pennsylvania.)

x

The weather has been excruciating.

Air-conditioning is unable to mitigate it. But New York is fantastically buoyant, proud of itself, and at its best. Expo tourists throng here—photograph her endlessly, and I've seen no shadow of disappointment on their faces—I've been stopped for directions by a teacher for the blind from Ghana, by Brazilians (what appeared to be a Family of ten); this hotel is filled with French. . . .

Leaving for a week at the Hotel Taft New Haven Saturday (Eyes giving me trouble—doctor's exams.) Isabel's on Martha's Vineyard, exhausted by summer guests.

My best to you Francis.

Will you be able to apply yourself to some writing this autumn?

devotedly
Thorny

1. Julian Le Grand, son of his wartime English friends Roland and Eileen Le Grand.

□

To Adaline Glasheen, Farmington Connecticut

[?28 August 1967] [50 Deepwood Drive
 Hamden, Connecticut]

"THE NATION"

On the chance you missed this—The Farmington Library doesn't take "The Nation"[1]

Ever
(T. N.)

1. Wilder sent pages from the section "Books & The Arts" (*The Nation*, 28 August 1967) which included: a review by Kevin Sullivan of *A Short History of Irish*

Literature: A Backward Glance, by Frank O'Connor (149–150); "Listening to Frank O'Connor," a memoir by O'Connor's widow, Harriet O'Connor (150–151); "Events," a poem by Harvey Shapiro (150); "Swift Conviviality," a review by Vivian Mercier of the Swift Tercentenary Symposium held in Dublin (151–153); "Driving Through Minnesota During the Hanoi Bombings," a poem by Robert Bly (152); "Tall-Tale Americana," an article by Rolfe Humphries about the writings of Alfred Henry Lewis (153–154); page 155, which concludes the article was not included.

☐

To Adaline Glasheen, Farmington, Connecticut

[MS. APCS—HWS]

[Postcard: Gay Head cliffs on beautiful Martha's Vineyard Island]

23 October [1967]   Edgartown, Mass

Dear Adaline:
 Thanks.[1] Eyes much better. ¶ Terribly sorry you had bad luck with picking a shore place on Rhode Island. ¶ Rê Proust—yes, Albertine is dim and boring—but the other major characters are absolute creations. Why must you compare them with others? I suspect that you are an impatient reader; you refuse to submit to an author's scale and time plan. Besides it's that unfoldment of six or seven great ideas that is half the greatness of Proust, a seriousness beyond Trollope. ¶ Today's mail brought on brochures by [Fritz] Senn and Father Noon.[2]
 Good news that you feel like writing.

      Ever your old
      Thornton

Sailing for Germany in two weeks.

1. A reference to a lost letter.
2. The "brochures" or perhaps offprints have not been identified.

To Adaline Glasheen, Farmington, Connecticut
[MS. ALS—HWS]

31 October 1967
50 Deepwood Drive
Hamden, Connecticut 06517

Dear Adaline =

Yes,[1] I knew Prof. Robert Ernst Curtius—and his widow now in Bonn. Cannot see that the doubling of the *Lion and the Mouse* with the *Fox and the Grapes* is very much of a break-through. But I hope Breon Mitchell does see Curtius's copy: some very helpful notes might be there.[2]

A doubling of Lion and the Mouse with the Fox and the Grapes[3] merely makes me mad. So you can see how unhooked I've become toward that book that rivetted me for so many years.

I don't know much about places or seasons in Sicily. (I only spent one day there in 1920—en route to the Americ[an]. Academy at Rome = disembarked at Palermo—saw Norman remains and the wonder of Monreale.)

Everybody talks about Taormina. Pick your pension carefully. Do you want to look at Greek Temples (Agrigente) or just bask? I can't imagine you "idling"!

My ship sails one minute after midnight on Sunday.

Sat. night in N. Y. we're seeing Gertrude Stein's play "*In Circles*."[4] (It is published as *A Circular Play*. The first line is "Pappa dozes Mamma blows her noses.")

Recall me cordially to Alison and Francis.

devotedly
Thornton

See you in the spring

---

1. A reference to a lost letter or a telephone conversation.
2. Wilder twists the name; it should be Ernst Robert Curtius (1886–1956), a literary historian and critic who wrote on Joyce. In 1924, Joyce wanted him to supervise the German translation of *Ulysses* being prepared by Georg Goyert (published in 1927). His study *James Joyce und sein 'Ulysses'* was published in Zurich (Neue Schweizer

Rundschau) in 1929. A translation by Eugene Jolas, "Technique and Thematic Development of James Joyce," was published in *transition*, No. 16–17 (June 1929), 310–325. In September 1936, on his way from Copenhagen to Paris, Joyce visited Curtius in Bonn to encourage his support for *Finnegans Wake*. Joyce made sure that Curtius received a press copy of *Finnegans Wake* (letter to Georg Goyert, 12 August 1939, *Letters III*, 452), and it is that copy referred to in this letter. Curtius's letters to Wilder are in YCAL. There are no letters from Breon Mitchell to Wilder in YCAL or to Glasheen in HWS.

3. Fables by Aesop and La Fontaine.

4. Wilder saw *In Circles*, a musical by Al Carmines and directed by Lawrence Kornfeld, at the Judson Memorial Church, New York, on Saturday 4 November. The musical is based on Stein's play *A Circular Play: A Play In Circles*, written in May–June 1920 and first published in Stein's *Last Operas and Plays* (1949). The authoritative text of the play is in Ulla E. Dydo, *A Stein Reader* (Evanston, Illinois: Northwestern University Press, 1993), 326–342. The next evening Wilder sailed on the *Bremen*. He arrived in Cherbourg on 12 November. For the next three and a half months he traveled in France, Switzerland, Germany, Austria, and Italy. He returned to New York on the *Michelangelo* on 14 March 1968.

Adaline Glasheen at the Fifth International James Joyce Symposium, Paris, June 1975
Photograph by Fritz Senn

1968

To Thornton Wilder, Hamden, Connecticut
[MS. TL—YCAL]

4 June 1968 [22 Carrington Road
Farmington, Connecticut]

Dear Thornton,

Are you in America?[1] Are you on earth?

I wish I could write you—after all this while—a memorable letter but I likely can't. How are you? I'm as always. F[rancis]. had a way out operation which has, so it seems, pretty well restored him to life. If we are all creatures of our hormones, Freud is a pearl of absolutely no price and high literary coinage is debased to reportage. Alison had a second child, Sara, and I've not long been back from attending on that event. I fell in love with my grandchildren, which is a serious but not specially graceful emotion. Northwestern (maybe Faber) is going to bring out a Third Census in 1972–73.[2] I'm not going to try to cozen you back to FW now, for I am floundering about in the Salmon theme, which is neither very hard to make out (so I can't ask you any intelligent questions) nor very attaching.

My purpose in writing is to tell you—if you don't know already—that Fritz Senn is coming to Buffalo. He's going to speak to the J J Society on Bloomsday—June 17,[3] this year—and he is going to be on a symposium at Buffalo with Hugh Kenner and William Empson.[4]

If you were around, he would (I suppose, I haven't asked) love to see you. So, of course, would I.

       Yrs
       Adaline

1. This is the first extant letter since Wilder's letter of 31 October 1967 where he announced a trip to Europe. Wilder returned to the United States on 14 March 1968.
2. On 29 February 1968, Glasheen wrote John Putnam, a senior editor at Northwestern University Press, proposing a third edition of her *Census* to be published in "three or four years" or asking whether they would give her permission to find another publisher. Putnam's reply on 18 March 1968 suggested that her "new findings" might be put into a supplementary appendix which "could be added to the text as it now stands, or as a pamphlet to be issued with the existing book." He wrote that one thousand copies of the book remained, and that he anticipated at the current rate of sale it would take five years to deplete the stock. After an exchange of letters, it was agreed that a third *Census*, completely resetting *Census II* would be issued, but not in the immediate future. Glasheen wrote Putnam on 13 May 1968, "mercy not, I won't hurry about it. *Finnegans Wake* is not to be taken by storm. You muddle along for years with reference books and you wait for happy accidents and you have dreams—always respectable ones—and you pester people with simple-minded questions." Over the next few years Glasheen reviewed her correspondence and solicited corrections and new identifications. The manuscript of *Census III* was mailed to Northwestern on 28 September 1972. In late January or early February 1973, Ralph Carlson, director of the Press, solicited comments from J. Mitchell Morse, Hugh Kenner, and William York Tindall about a third census. Each responded enthusiastically to the proposal. Kenner's letter of 9 February 1973 echoes the comments of both Morse and Tindall. Kenner wrote: "It is exciting to know that Mrs. Glasheen's *Third Census of Finnegans Wake* is ready. The First Census established her as one of the very few workers in the field who needs to be taken very seriously; she deals in information, not in theory, and the kind of information moreover which it is essential to have if we are going to penetrate Joyce's local effects. The Second Census has been an indispensable tool for all students of the labyrinth. I am not surprised to hear of the length to which the Third Census has grown; there is simply more and more to be found out, and she has been diligently finding it. There are sure to be some disputed entries, but Mrs. Glasheen has the reputation of being 99% solid. I very much look forward to the new book." A contract for *Census III* was signed on 4 March 1973, and Joy Neuman, acting director of the Press, began the in-house editing. On 16 April 1974, Neuman wrote Glasheen that the "administration of Northwestern University has decided to discontinue the publishing operations of the Press." The Press, Neuman continued, was prepared to fulfill their contractual obligations, or they extended to Glasheen the option of withdrawing her manuscript and seeking another publisher. In a letter of 28 May 1974 to Lawrence Nobles, Dean of Administration, Glasheen agreed to leave the manuscript at Northwestern. But when news of the closing down of the Press spread, Glasheen was advised by friends to seek a publisher who would actively

promote her book. Through Hugh Kenner's efforts the book was accepted and published by California in March 1977. (The letters cited in this note are the originals or office copies in the University Archives, Northwestern University Library.)

3. Bloomsday, 16 June, was celebrated by the James Joyce Society at the Gotham Book Mart on Monday, 17 June. The speakers were Senn and Thomas Staley who spoke on "Five Years in the Joyce Industry."

4. Empson was to have participated in the summer program in modern literature at Buffalo in 1967, but he withdrew because of ill health. See AG to TW, 2 May 1967.

☐

To Adaline Glasheen, Farmington, Connecticut

[MS. ALS—HWS]

[? June 1968] Last days on Martha's Vineyard[1]
Friday

Dear Adaline =
    Delighted to hear from you.
    With the good news about Francis and your joy in your grandchildren.
    And the call on you for a Third CENSUS—I hope you still get some fun out of that, as well as all the hard work.
    Oh, yes, I've been in lively correspondence with Fritz Senn. Offered to put him up at the Mermaid Tavern (I mean: the Algonquin Hotel) but it turns out happily that he's being overwhelmed with hospitable attentions. He's full of trepidation about the speech he has to make at the Bloomsday meeting and the classes he must meet in Buffalo. . . .
    I have to go to N. Y. to my nephew's wedding on the 15th and I shall stay over to see him on the 18th. I'm a hermit and I don't go to group gatherings—even at the wedding I put my nose in the church and in the reception for a moment; but don't go to those dinners etc etc. (We all *love* the bride and are very happy for young "Tappie"—Amos Tappan Wilder.)
    As to Buffalo—oh, to be 21½ again and going to Empson's classes (and the bars he frequents.) He's my idol.

Many thanks for your letter—give my cordial best to Francis and to the young people.

> and lots of admiration
> and devotion to you
> Ever
> Thornton

1. Wilder remained on Martha's Vineyard until 12 June when he returned to Hamden, Connecticut, on Friday, 14 June he left for New York. Senn arrived from Dublin late in the afternoon of Monday, 17 June, and spoke that evening.

☐

To Thornton Wilder, Hamden, Connecticut

[MS. ALS—YCAL]

29 June 1968 [Buffalo, New York]

Dear Thornton,

My two weeks at Buffalo are nearly gone by—home tomorrow[.] I have done lots of Joyce work, found things—lots to be found—in the workbooks and I wish I had the money to go on panning for gold, but I am not sure I could stand the pace—too exciting altogether.

I met a poet whose parents belong to the Bakersville California branch of the same Hermetical society as Yeats did,[1] and he had to have his palm read every year. Every seven years the scry-lady said— truly sinister—"I find Daemon and Pythias in this hand or—as I prefer to call it—Demon and Python." Surely a novelist can use that remark[.]

I attended the same poet's reading and was passed an envelope on which Hugh Kenner had written: "Banality was the dominant note of his temperament, but it was a banality tempered by outbursts of platitude, repetition and simple blah."

Hugh is the only mind in attendance {W. Empson comes tomorrow}. He takes me out to lunch and addresses me as if I was a public meeting. He is a pretty brilliant addresser. He wants me to put in for a Guggenheim for doing my 3rd Census. If I do put in will you write me a recommendation?

Fritz [Senn] is, of course a very nice man. I have decided—grossly unfair—that I want him to treat me the way Disraeli treated Queen Victoria, but he does not.

I have also spent much time listening to a young woman who is involved in *two* love triangles and is breaking, she says, her heart. Do you think it possible to be tragic in two triangles? I don't think so, but she does try.

Love,
Adaline

1. In 1888 Yeats joined the Esoteric Section of Madame Blavatsky's Theosophical Society.

☐

To Thornton Wilder, Hamden, Connecticut

[MS. TL—YCAL]

29 July 1968 [22 Carrington Road
Farmington, Connecticut]

Dear Thornton,

Did you get the letter I wrote you? I thought to hear from you, and of course I wouldn't pester a real author to answer my letters—but you have had an operation and I picture you perhaps having a relapse and I want to be told you have not.[1]

Last week, you'll never think who we had for dinner and the night (uninvited but preeminently there) but Jack Dalton. He behaved—out of consideration for F[rancis]'s health and maybe a little out of the small liking he has for me—with an unholy quiet and correctness that made him absolutely dull, which—to do him justice—he is not usually.

Distress he showed about one thing. He had always told me how very fond he was of cats and how in his various apartments he always had cats. So, natch, I sought to divert him with our mother cat, and her two pure white kittens with blue eyes which are in the finest hour of kittenhood, and playing all about the yard. The mother cat is teaching them to hunt and every time I took JD out to see the dear little kittens they were eating mice or rabbits, and this distressed him very much. "Well, what do you think cats do?" I asked. "My cats ate out of cans," he said miserably. When he was about to drive off, along came a kitten with a dead bat. "I think you are in rat's alley where dead men lost their bones," he said and left without more adieu.

I had a letter from Fritz [Senn] who, I guess, is not any happier.

I am corresponding with a 22 yr English boy ("I would like to get married but my relations with young ladies is just like Glugg's."—sad)[2] who is in Paris working at some laboratory on "the acoustics of insects." Today I got a letter from someone living in Gravesend who is terribly grateful to my First Census who signs himself (him? her?) G. Beetle.[3]

Dear Thornton, I hope you're well.

            Love
            Adaline

---

1. Glasheen had probably heard from Isabel Wilder that Thornton underwent an operation on 2 July to correct a hernia problem. He remained in the hospital until 12 July.
2. In the play "The Mime of Mick, Nick, and the Maggies" (the *Wake*, 219–259), Glugg, "the bold bad bleak boy of the storybooks" (219.24), played by Shem, unsuccessfully tries to answer the three versions of a riddle put to him by Issy and the Maggies (multiple manifestations of Issy herself). The English boy is not identified.
3. The letter is not in HWS.

To Adaline Glasheen, Farmington, Connecticut

[MS. ALS—HWS]

8 August [1968]   50 Deepwood Drive
                                          Hamden, Connecticut 06517

Dear Adaline =
    Thanks.
    I'm fine, convalescent but languid.
    Loved your letter. Will answer more spiritedly later.
    Fritz Senn writes to you "not any happier?"
    Hell, to me he's mad about the U. S. A. and refers vaguely to hoping to live here permanently. "Just a dreamer."
    [Jack] Dalton wishes that cats weren't predatory carnivores. We could have forseen that = he wants the world to conform to his way or he'll smash it to pieces.

                     More anon
                     Best to all
                     Old T.

To Thornton Wilder, Hamden, Connecticut

[MS. TL—YCAL]

11 August 1968   [22 Carrington Road
                                      Farmington, Connecticut]

Dear Thornton

We are so glad you are getting well. How, commonly, do you divert yourself in convalescence? What do you read?

I should hate to think you really thought you needed to write me spirited letters. I've never known you to write any other kind. What I lack, for the moment, is matter—for the spirited letter, I mean. I have been painting walls and cleaning letter files and today being a heavenly day I walked five miles around a reservoir in the morning and gardened in the afternoon. I feel marvelous and euphoric as all get out, but stupid as a milkweed plant.

Next Wednesday Fritz [Senn] asked me to be part of a symposium at the Gotham Book Mart.[1] I shan't be. But the following week we're going to some sort of Joycean party the Grahams[2] are giving in Bronxville. Fritz will perhaps spend the night before or the night after the party with us. All uncertained by possible commitments he maybe has.

Did I tell you I drive now? That's another occupation that you can't make much of in letters.

You can, if you like, keep the enclosed. Jack [Dalton] sent me two offprints.[3] I do like the pictures.

Whatever it is you want I wish you.

Adaline

---

1. Not a regular meeting of the James Joyce Society.
2. Philip Lamar Graham, attorney, *Wake* enthusiast, and friend of the Glasheens.
3. In "Two New Fadographs of James Joyce," in the *James Joyce Quarterly*, V, 2 (Winter 1968), 168–170, Dalton published two photographs of Joyce by Ruth Asch of Berlin made in 1929, probably at the behest of Joyce's German publisher Rhein-Verlag. The offprint he sent Glasheen is in HWS.

To *Adaline Glasheen, Farmington, Connecticut*

[MS. APCS—HWS]

13 August [1968] [50 Deepwood Drive
 Hamden, Connecticut 06517]
 in his DEN

Dear Adaline
 What a hospitable angel you are—furnishing lodging for migrant Joyceans.
 Thank you for the off-prints.[1] I'll stick them in my Concordances. If ever you want them back for some new Joyce-Idolator (you find in Holland, for example) let me know. I've 'ad Joyce.
 You've been painting walls!
 And walking around the reservoir!
 Be ready for Fritz [Senn] to sound you out about how he can get a job in New York. As I see it he must return to a wife and three children in a country where he can live *with them* far more cheaply than here. Rabelais said "Destiny aids them [who] recognize her and drags those who resist."

 devotedly
 Thornton

---

1. One of the offprints was by Jack Dalton, the second is unknown. See AG to TW, 11 August 1968, n. 3.

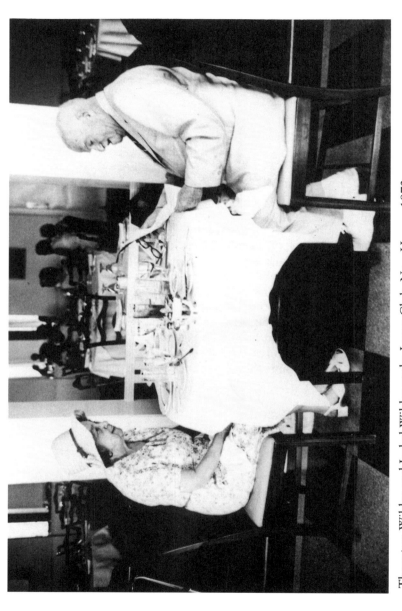

Thornton Wilder and Isabel Wilder at the Lawn Club, New Haven, 1972
Photographer unknown, Private collection

1970

To *Thornton Wilder, Hamden, Connecticut*

[MS. TL—YCAL]

20 May 1970[1] [22 Carrington Lane]
Farmington, Connecticut

Dear Thornton,

How goes it and I'm ever so sorry if mention of FW is too sick-making, BUT I thought you'd like to know I think I've found a lot of fairly involved and not-uncomplimentary references to Gertrude Stein in FW I vi #11 [148.33–168.12].[2]

I don't tell you about it because, if you are interested at all at all, it's best to see for yourself by rereading #11 along with the, say, first half of *Time and Western Man*—through the chapter on Joyce's mind anyway.[3]

I hope you're well. I am. We are. F[rancis]. splendid now after his operation. Pulled from the gaping jaws of modern psychiatry which gives me unkind pleasure. Alison is still married, two children, her husband's going to intern at the University of Michigan hospital. I'm just back from a visit.

I really DO hope you are well and writing.[4]

Yrs
Adaline

I think I've found Picasso in #11 too[5]

1. This is the first extant letter since 13 August 1968. Nothing is stated in the letters to explain this silence. In the intervening period Wilder and Glasheen did, however, speak on the telephone. Wilder had a number of health problems in this period which he discusses in subsequent letters.

2. See Glasheen's entry for Gertrude Stein (1874–1946) in *Census III*. Glasheen's research notes on *Wake* references to Stein and Alice Toklas (1877–1966) are in HWS.

3. In *Time and Western Man* (London, 1927), Wyndham Lewis discussed Stein in chapter XII, "'Time'-Children. Miss Gertrude Stein and Miss Anita Loos," and chapter XIII, "The Prose-Song of Gertrude Stein." The final chapter in the book, chapter XVI, is "An Analysis of the Mind of James Joyce."

4. Following the publication of *The Eighth Day* in 1967, Wilder returned to the two one-act play cycles hoping to polish drafts of additional plays, but eventually he abandoned the project. In December 1967 he began a memoir which fictionally recalled his boyhood days in China, where his father had been American Consul General in Hong Kong and later in Shanghai, and where, in 1911, Wilder attended the China Inland Mission School in Cheefoo. Intermittently until his death, Wilder worked on significant experiences in his life which he treated as a fictional memoir. The work, which he called "Zen," remains unpublished. In 1969 he began writing a novel, *Theophilus North*. As chapters were completed, they were sent to Robert Maynard Hutchins (1899–1977), the educator and lawyer, who had been a fellow student with Wilder at Oberlin College and at Yale University and President of the University of Chicago when Wilder taught there in the 1930s. Wilder dedicated the book to him. The outline of *Theophilus North* parallels incidents in Wilder's life; for example: North, like Wilder, taught at a boys' preparatory school (in the 1920s, Wilder taught at the Lawrenceville School in New Jersey). Feeling a need to change his life, North goes to Newport, Rhode Island, where he had served in the Coast Artillery during World War I (as Wilder had). In the last paragraph of the novel Wilder writes: "Imagination draws on memory. Memory and imagination combined can stage a Servants' Ball or even write a book, if that's what they want to do" (New York: Harper & Row, 1973).

5. In *Census III* Glasheen cites three references to Pablo Picasso (1881–1973): 157.13; 159.4; 166.20–.21. Glasheen's research notes on Picasso are in HWS.

To Adaline Glasheen, Farmington, Connecticut

[MS. ALS—HWS]

24 May 1970 [50 Deepwood Drive]
Hamden, Conn 06517

Dear Adaline=
 Many thanks for your letter. Oh what good news about Francis. Give him my felicitations and congratulations and also to Adaline who's having her additional jubilation over the mortification to psychiatry. I hope this beautiful springtime (though today is overcast) is adding new well-being to convalescence. *Praise the Lord on the shawm and on the seven stringed lyre.*
 The advance to the stage of internship for Alison's husband is also good news. The M. D.'s road is a long hard grind. I hope those babies are giving you as much pleasure as my four-and-a-half-weeks old great nephew right here in New Haven. (Two hours in labor; the mother strolled down the hospital corridor to take a shower four hours after the birth, and was elected committee chairman of the First Ward on the same day. Cccrazy!) My correspondence has been full of babies. Mia Farrow[1] writes storms of joy about her twin boys but the rest of her letter is asking suggestions about what roles she should play on the (British) TV and in a repertory company. She says that one of her little nippers is a little devil and I point out that the boy's father (director of the London Symphony Orchestra) can find additional employment for his *baton*.
 My eye-sight's in trouble, but I'll look up the Stein and Picasso references. I remember having glimpsed some. {If I remember correctly a *picasso* is a thorny plant.} I very much doubt your observation that J. J.'s reference to these persons could be "non-complimentary." Joyce's belly was filled with bile and envy and *resentment*. The greater the rival, the more violent his denigration: sneers at Goethe, sneers at Shakespeare. He'd have turned on Ibsen, but Ibsen once wrote him a letter.[2]
 It's also good news that Fritz Senn concedes that he feels a little better, more self-confident. I saw him and the whole family in Zurich in December.[3] He's planning to come over here for many months. Given our troubled times in academic circles. . . will Indiana and Columbus,

Ohio[4] be able to follow through with their promises? I hope so. I wish you knew his wife and *vice-versa*.

    Please recall me cordially, affectionately, to Alison.

    And to FRANCIS.

    Am delighted to hear of a new englarged CENSUS.[5] Your correspondence must be mountainous. And your filing cabinets!

    On June 11-15 I'm to meet with my 50th Class Reunion. Imagine that.

    In the meantime I'm going Wednesday to Stockbridge for a week's uninterrupted work (we've been tormented by a smutty-nuisance phone-caller—I judge a girl of about 15 years old—we can't take the receiver off, nor let the bell ring because we're expecting calls from our brother and sister and nephew and certain workmen on our cottage on Martha's Vineyard which was half-ruined through the negligence of our winter-caretaker—so we answer the phone and hear the cackle of this idiot foul-mouthed girl. What times we live in![)]

              Ever fondly
               Old Thornt.

---

1. The actress Mia Farrow, and her husband, the conductor-composer Andre Previn were neighbors on Martha's Vineyard, where Wilder had a summer house.

2. On 20 January 1900, Joyce read an essay, "Drama and Life" (*Critical Writings*, 38-46), before the Literary and Historical Society at University College, Dublin. The essay reveals the impact that Henrik Ibsen (1828-1906) had on Joyce's thinking about drama, and it closes with the curtain speech of Act I of Ibsen's *Pillars of Society*. Joyce's review of Ibsen's *When We Dead Awaken*, "Ibsen's New Drama," was published in the *Fortnightly Review* on 1 April 1900 (*Critical Writings*, 47-67). The article was read by Ibsen, and through his English translator William Archer (1856-1924), Ibsen expressed his gratitude to Joyce (Ibsen to Archer 16 April 1900, British Library, the text of the letter is in Ellmann, 1959: 76-77; 1982: 74). Archer wrote Joyce telling him of Ibsen's comments on 23 April; Joyce responded on 28 April (*Letters II*, 7; see also Joyce to Ibsen, March 1901, *Letters I*, 51-52). Joyce sent Archer some of his poems and his now lost "A Brilliant Career." Archer was supportive of Joyce's writing, but eventually their friendship cooled when Archer argued against Joyce's going to Paris to teach English. In 1915 and 1917 Joyce asked Archer for his assistance in having *Exiles* produced in London. Archer apparently did little to help Joyce.

3. As had become his habit, Wilder had spent several months in Europe in 1969-1970.

4. Senn had been invited to teach summer seminars on Joyce at the University of Indiana, Bloomington, and Ohio State University, Columbus.

5. Glasheen was working on *Census III*; see AG to TW, 4 June 1968, n. 2.

To Thornton Wilder, Hamden, Connecticut

[MS. TL—PRIVATE COLLECTION]

27 October 1970 [22 Carrington Road
 Farmington, Connecticut]

Dear Thornton

I heard you've lost the sight of one eye. I am terribly sorry. It's hell for you. What's to say? Except prayers and a long stream of swear-words. I wish it hadn't happened to you.

We're fine. F[rancis]. is super-fine. Children also fine. My son-in-law is interning in obstetrics at the university of Michigan. Alison has a bad back about which she is heroic (you never expect your own child to be heroic, do you?) and is taking 11 hours of work. If she passes the 11 hours, she'll be a junior and she talks vaguely of being a city planner, but her academic advisor is sensibly and I hope successfully pushing her into majoring in history.

Joyceans go on. Jim Atherton broke his back in two places, poor man, falling down his own stairs at 7 in the morning. He taught at Buffalo this summer and he and his wife, Nora, visited us for 3–4 days. I have tried but I can't describe Nora, save to say she is in her old-fashioned Lancashire way exotic, more exotic than a southseas islander and I hope you'll meet her one day. It is worth a good deal of effort. Fritz [Senn], you probably know, taught at Indiana in the summer and is at Ohio now. He went to Europe (it's not a secret or anything) with a megalithic 20 yr old Italian-American girl, built like a Henry Moore statue. But that didn't work out, for reasons I haven't heard. Clive Hart, now at the university of Dundee, is giving up indefinitely the Newslitter to Fritz. I daresay Clive won't take it up again. It will go out of existence perhaps I fear.

I have my Third [TW: {CENSUS}] in abeyance while I try to write a piece long overdue for a *Ulysses* anthology on "Calypso."[1] It is v[ery]. surprising how much there is to say about so quiet a section as "Calypso." I have a hang-up about the piece because if I carry it to its logical conclusions I'm going to have to say things about *Ulysses* that I myself think good things, but taken out of context will give aid and comfort to enemies. *Ulysses* scares me rather. It is at heart a very very cold book. FW (excuse me mentioning it) is lots warmer.

I'm sorry this is so dull a letter. I always wish I could be brilliant and amusing. I am slightly comforted in my dullness by a friend who [h]as gone to King's College Cambridge where he says everybody is very nice, but conversation at the high table, he says, does not coruscate. Everybody talks about either the faculty club or car pools.

Dear Thornton, I hope all will be well with you.

        Yrs
        Adaline[2]

1. Glasheen's essay on "Calypso" chapter of *Ulysses* was published in *James Joyce's 'Ulysses': Critical Essays*, edited by Clive Hart and David Hayman (Berkeley and Los Angeles: University of California Press, 1974), [51]–70. The book contains essays on each chapter of *Ulysses* by a different Joyce scholar.
2. Under Glasheen's signature, Wilder has written, "a remarkable girl."

1974

To Thornton Wilder, Hamden, Connecticut
[MS. TL—YCAL]

5 March 1974[1]   Carrington Lane
                                       Farmington, Connecticut

Dear Thornton

I just read *Theophilus North* and I loved it. It is a pleasant book and an elegant and it is a sort of game-playing book and it is a ruthless regal book that with the greatest courtesy makes no compromises anywhere. I felt proud to have known its author.

                Yrs
                A. Glasheen

---

1. This is the first extant letter since Glasheen's letter to Wilder of 27 October 1970. Neither Wilder nor Glasheen explains the gap in their correspondence. In the intervening years, Wilder's health deteriorated; his eyesight continued to fail, he had trouble with his hearing, he had a prostate operation, and had bouts with vertigo. He continued spending several months each year traveling in Europe. He returned from what would be his last trip to Europe on 22 February 1971. Thereafter, he would spend time in Edgartown, Massachusetts, Florida, Puerto Rico, or Mexico. Wilder finished his novel *Theophilus North* in April 1973, and it was published in September 1973.

To Adaline Glasheen, Farmington, Connecticut

[MS. ALS—HWS]

8 March 1974 50 Deepwood Drive
Hamden, Connecticut 06517

Dear Adaline =
What a blood-warming note from you.
For years I've been "mad" at J. J. and at the years I spent with him—but you can see what they gave me, just the same—nobody could see better than you what I owe him. So I've got over my resentment against him.
    I'm real old now, but I'm cheerful inside
and positively uplifted since receiving your beautiful letter
To you and to Francis and to your daughter

           affectionate greetings ever
           Thornton

Isabel joins me.

To Adaline and Francis Glasheen, Farmington, Connecticut

[MS. APCS—HWS]

30 May [1974] [50 Deepwood Drive]
Hamden, [Connecticut] 06517

Dear Friends—
    Delighted to have seen you.[1]
    Thanks for your radio guide. I found 88.5 but haven't yet been here at exactly noon—when Francis reads, I assume.[2] ¶ Yes, several of

Landor's Imaginary Conversations are of high quality and of astonishing diversity.[3]

¶ I didn't read enough of M. Baring to converse about him[4]. . . I kept thinking of the line from an old hymn: *Fleeting is the worldling's pleasure*.

¶ I wish I could think of a title for the Third Census.[5] I must leave Wednesday for Edgartown Mass 02539

devotedly
Thornton

1. The Glasheens visited Wilder and his sister for dinner in Hamden, Connecticut, on Wednesday, 22 May.
2. Francis Glasheen had a radio program on a Hartford station where he would read from works of literature. There are two cassette tapes in HWS: on the first he reads episode 12, "Cyclops," from *Ulysses* and "The Ondt and the Gracehoper" (414.16–419.10) and selections about "King Roderick O'Connor" from *Finnegans Wake*. On the second tape he reads "Characteristics of Yorkshiremen" from Book I, chapter 2 of Elizabeth Gaskell's *The Life of Charlotte Brontë* (1857) and excerpts from Lawrence Sterne's *Tristram Shandy* (1760–1767).
3. Walter Savage Landor (1775–1864), the English writer, wrote two sets of dialogues or conversations between characters from classical times to his own time. There are about 150 dialogues where Landor expresses his opinions on literary, social, and political issues. The first set of dialogues, *Imaginary Conversations*, was published 1824–1829; a second set, *Imaginary Conversations of Greeks and Romans*, was published in 1853. Among the dialogues are "Dante and Beatrice" and "Calvin and Melancthon."
4. Maurice Baring (1874–1945), the English novelist, journalist, and playwright.
5. Glasheen was working on *Census III*, which would be published in 1977.

To Adaline Glasheen, Farmington, Connecticut

[MS. APCS—HWS]

[postmark: 28 June 1974] Edgartown, Mass. 02539

Dear Adaline =
Sure! I believe that hundreds of thousands are reading *Ulysses* every day.
Harrah! Temple Press.[1]
Bartleby[2]—you're quite right close to S. Beckett (see below)[3]
Isabel left me here and is back in Hamden. But this town of narrow streets is crowded by tourists' cars and tourists' cars already. Daily I want to get my "Times" and my mail and my eatable but you have to go great distances to find a parking place[.]
Cudgeling my wits for suggestions for Francis's . . . lots of dialogue, if Adaline would only go in the air with him[.][4]

Best to all
Thornt'

---

1. When Northwestern University Press announced that it was suspending publications, Glasheen sought another publisher. J. Mitchell Morse, of Temple University, was influential in having Temple University Press offer to publish *Census III*. Eventually, through the efforts of Hugh Kenner, the book would be published by the University of California Press. See AG to TW, 4 June 1968, n. 2.

2. The main character in Herman Melville's allegorical tale, "Bartleby the Scrivener: A Story of Wall Street," first published anonymously in *Putnam's Magazine* in 1853.

3. There is no "below" on this postcard, and, therefore, no connection between Melville's story and Samuel Beckett (1906–1989), the Irish writer and one time secretary to Joyce.

4. See TW to AG and FG, 30 May 1974.

To Adaline Glasheen, Farmington, Connecticut

[MS. ALS—HWS]

Oct[ober] 4 or 5 1974   Post Office Box 862
                        Edgartown, Massachusetts 02539

Dear Adaline =
   Many thanks.[1]
   Yes, I'm much better.
   You can imagine my surprise at the T. L. S. (the Daily Times was kind[)] (two syllables, please) but nowhere near so well written. The Commercial Times (also London) had a very well written one by a woman. (They tell me that paper, like our Wall Street Journal has a reputation for superior reviews of books and plays. Can you explain that?[)] [2]
   I can understand them asking you for a review—you are the *doyenne* of Joyce studies, but if the books were as poor as you say, I have confidence in your judgment to refuse. They'll knock at your door again.[3]
   I got a letter from Fritz Senn at the U. of Hawaii today.[4] I glanced at it and then mislaid it. I wish him well.
   You speak of C. S. Lewis—Norman Pearson happened to arrive on this island yesterday with BRYHER (a darling) and happened to mention that he was a fellow-grad-student with him at Oxford years ago.[5]

   Have found Senn's letter. "I cannot hope that the round of visiting professorships will go on; I wish it did. . . ." He's having a wonderful time, but. . . "One doesn't alas, escape from one's problems." (nor ever forget to mention them.)

   Cheers to your book
   All cordial best to Francis. I hope he continues to find more and more real right material to read. I'm ashamed that I couldn't think of anything.
   Devoted best, dear Adaline

             Old Thornt'

   Isa sends her admiring best

1. Reference to a lost letter or to a telephone conversation.

2. References to favorable English reviews of *Theophilus North*: "Angelism in New England," in the *Times Literary Supplement* (London), 12 July 1974, 741; Paul Theroux's review, "A Sunny Sprawl" in *The Times* (London), 27 June 1974, 9. There was no newspaper "The Commericial Times" published in London. Wilder may mean *The Financial Times*, but we have been unable to locate a review. The novel was reviewed in the *Wall Street Journal* by Edmund Fuller, "Thornton Wilder's Cosmopolitan Tales," on 13 November 1973, 26.

3. On 7 August 1974 (HWS), John Gross, editor of the *Times Literary Supplement* (London), wrote Glasheen asking her to review *A Conceptual Guide to 'Finnegans Wake'* ed. Michael H. Begnal and Fritz Senn (University Park: Pennsylvania State University Press, 1974). Glasheen declined, but she expressed her willingness to review for the *TLS*. In a letter of 27 September 1974 (HWS), Gross wrote suggesting she review Arthur Power's *Conversations with James Joyce*, ed. Clive Hart (London: Millington, 1974). Glasheen's review appeared in the *TLS* of 9 January 1976, 4, under the title "Talk of the Town" (in the typescript at HWS, Glasheen titles the review "Man of the Old Black Church"). When Gross sent Power's book, he also sent Mark Shechner's *Joyce in Nighttown: A Psychoanalytic Inquiry into 'Ulysses'* (Berkeley: University of California Press, 1974) which Glasheen did not review.

4. Senn participated in the "James Joysymposium" organized by Margaret Solomon at the University of Hawaii from 26 to 30 August 1974. For a review of the symposium, see Philip W. Kenny, "James Joysymposium; Hawaii 1974," in *The James Joyce Quarterly*, XII, 3 (Spring 1975), 205–209. In the Fall semester he taught an undergraduate course "Kafka, Joyce, and Beckett" and a seminar on Joyce (email received, Fritz Senn, 1 October 1998). Senn's letter is not in HWS.

5. C[live]. S[tapkes]. Lewis, the pseudonym of the English writer Clive Hamilton (1898–1963). Norman Holmes Pearson (1909-1975), a professor of American Literature at Yale University, was a close friend of the English novelist, Annie Winifred Ellerman, known as Winifred Bryher (1894–1983).

To Adaline Glasheen, Farmington, Connecticut

[MS. ALS—HWS]

22 October 1974   50 Deepwood Drive
                                         Hamden, Connecticut 06517

Dear Adaline =
    Many thanks for sending me CALYPSO.[1]
    It seems to me an admirable exposition—brings together all those strands of reference.
    But you know me and Joyce. William James[2] used to warn his students from lingering long in the realm of the "abject truth." Joyce was certainly in relation with truth and all honor to him, but he also exhibited a delectation in the abject. We know many greater writers than he of whom that could not be said. How "unengaging" is the man we see in the letters and the biography. He was never "at home with himself," *dans sa peau*, and had little warmth to extend to others,—neither were Eliot and Thomas Mann (cold fishes) nor Pound (in his later years—when young he was wonderfully generous—indeed) nor, I suspect Yeats. Yet how one would like to have been in familiar relations with Chekhov or Turgenev or H. James or Freud (I was)[.][3]
    I assume you know Empson's paper on what happened after the close of *Ulysses*. I can give you it—Kenyon Review: Winter 1956. Just drop me a card (or phone); otherwise I'll keep it in my Empson-collection.[4]
    Next time I'm in Zürich I'll go to the Kronenburg Restaurant[5] where they have Joyce's table marked as a shrine. I know a number of waitresses there who are proud to have served him often (on Mrs Edith Rockefeller McCormick's money I assume). I'm going to ask them if he took Norah[6] there often. I'll bet I know the answer. I'd like to have known Norah.

                 Sez your old friend
                 Thornton

---

1. Glasheen sent Wilder a copy of her essay on episode four, "Calypso," which was published in *James Joyce's 'Ulysses': Critical Essays*, ed. Clive Hart and David

Hayman (Berkeley and Los Angeles: University of California Press, 1974), [51]–70.

2. The American philosopher and psychologist (1842–1910).

3. Wilder first met Freud when he visited him on 13 October 1935 in his home in Grinzing, a wine village (*Heurigen*), in the countryside north of Vienna. A second meeting took place on the evening of 25 October. Wilder writes of his first meeting with Freud in a letter to Gertrude Stein and Alice Toklas on 14 October 1935, see Burns and Dydo, Stein/Wilder Letters, 63–65. Wilder saw Freud again in London in June 1939. See Wilder to Stein and Toklas in Burns and Dydo, Stein/Wilder Letters, [24 June 1939], n. 9.

4. William Empson, "The Theme of *Ulysses*," in *The Kenyon Review*, XVIII, 1 (Winter 1956), [26]–52, is the text of a BBC Third Programme talk he delivered on Bloomsday, 1954.

5. Wilder is confusing incidents from two periods when Joyce lived in Zurich. During World War I, Joyce was often at the Pfauen Restaurant. In February 1918, Mrs. McCormick, who lived in Zurich, where she was an analysand of Carl Jung, deposited 12,000 Swiss francs in Joyce's name in a Zurich Bank. Beginning in March 1918 until October 1919, Joyce received an additional one thousand francs per month. Mrs. McCormick stopped her support of Joyce in part because of his refusal to be analyzed by Jung. The Kronenhalle restaurant, not the Kronenburg, was owned by Gustav Zumsteg and his wife. Joyce and Nora had eaten there on 9 January 1941, five days before his death on 13 January 1941. Fritz Senn recalls that Wilder took him there when they met in 1969 and that, "There were indeed two waitresses claiming they remembered Joyce (Schwester Emma and Schwester Klara, as they were called, as well as Frau Zumsteg)" (email received, 24 September 1998).

6. Wilder's spelling.

1975

To Thornton Wilder, Hamden, Connecticut

[MS. TL—YCAL]

17 March 1975   [22 Carrington Road
                                             Farmington, Connecticut]

Dear Thornton,

How are you? I heard vaguely that you and Isabel are back in New Haven. How went it with Florida?[1]

Do you remember giving me a copy of crazy Miss Boldereff's book about FW?[2]

We went to the Joyce birthday celebration at Wesleyan. Where there was a sort of beautiful young man gotten up like the young Bernard Shaw—Sean Golden.[3] He is professional Irish and writing (predictably) a dissertation on Joyce and Beckett at UConn.

According to Sean, UConn has the biggest Charles Olson (I haven't read any of his poetry) collection in the world and that Olson scholars and cultists are gathering collections of letters. They have discovered that Miss Boldereff was a longtime secret sweetheart and correspondent of Olson's. (Why are all good American stories by Henry James?) And, as of Joyce's birthday, nobody had been able to locate Miss Boldereff because she had perhaps moved, perhaps got married, perhaps changed her name. But a couple of scholars in spring vacation were going to search house by house in the Pennsylvania mountains where she used to live because she must have Olson letters and because maybe Olson wrote one or both of her crazy FW books.[4]

I thought it would entertain you to be told this story.

          Yrs
          Adaline

1. Wilder flew from New York to Fort Meyers, Florida, on 12 December 1974. He then settled in the Island Inn, on Sanibel Island, until early March 1975.

2. The copy of Frances Motz Boldereff's *Reading 'Finnegans Wake'* (1959) which Wilder gave to Glasheen is in HWS. Boldereff's other books are: *A Blakean Translation of Joyce's 'Circe'* (1965), *Hermes to his Son Thoth: Being Joyce's Use of Giordano Bruno in 'Finnegans Wake'* (1968), *Time as Joyce Tells It* ([1977] published under the pseudonym, Reighard Motz), *Verbi-Voco-Visual: The Presence of Bishop Berkeley in 'Finnegans Wake'* (1981, published under the pseudonym, Thomasine Rose), and *Let Me Be Los: Codebook for 'Finnegans Wake'* (1985, rpt., Barrytown NY: Station Hill Press, Inc, 1987, published under the pseudonym, Frances Phipps).

3. The celebration at Wesleyan University in Middletown, Connecticut, organized by Louis Mink, a professor of Philosophy and Joyce scholar, included a non-stop reading of *Ulysses*. Sean Valentine Golden, a doctoral candidate at the University of Connecticut at Storrs, participated in the reading. He completed his dissertation, "Bygmythster Finnegan: Etymology as Poetics in the work of James Joyce," in 1976 (*DAI*, 38/01, p. 278, July 1977). With Peter Fallon he edited *Soft Day: A Miscellany of Contemporary Irish Writing* (Notre Dame, Ind.: University of Notre Dame Press, 1980). Glasheen attended Golden's defense of his dissertation in the summer of 1976 (email received, Sean Golden, 11 April 1996).

4. For Charles Olson's relationship with Boldereff, see Tom Clark, *Charles Olson: The Allegory of a Poet's Life* (New York: W. W. Norton & Co., 1991). See also *Charles Olson and Frances Boldereff: A Modern Correspondence*, ed. Ralph Maud and Sharon Thesen. Hanover, NH: Wesleyan University Press/University Press at New England, 1999. Charles Olson (1910–1970) was teaching at the University of Connecticut at Storrs at the time of his death on 10 January 1970.

To Adaline Glasheen, Farmington, Connecticut

[MS. ALS—HWS]

15 November 1975   Hamden Conn 06517

Dear Adaline:

    We loved your letter.[1]

    Rejoiced that you got to see Paris[2]. . . . Oh, I wish it were twenty years ago and I could have been there at the same time. ¶ Oh, yes, I know about [Jacques] Lacan—my brother admires him as on the psychology of religion and I admire him as one appearing occasionally in the footnotes of Levi-Strauss's *l'Anthropologie structurale*.[3] ¶ Am I right in recalling that *escabeau* or *escumbeau* [escarbot] means a dung-beetle? Did Lacan call Joyce that!! I'm only pretending to be surprised.

    Sorry it [?word] so much of the time. Some traveler tells me that even the little simple lunch for one costs ten dollars.

    I've been flying in and out of the doors of hospitals on Martha's Vineyard and in Boston. I'm now very old and grungy; but—I'll tell you a secret—when THEY aren't around I'm cheerful and chipper and mad about walking on the ceiling.

    I think Isabel and I are going down to N. Y. soon[4] and I think I may take her to see *Travesties*[5]—though I shrink from plays that are written in over-labored wit. (and that goes for some early Shakespeare and all Giraudoux[6].) They say the widow of Carr (Harry Carr?) was helpful in building up the lampoon of her husband. ¶ Anyway, we're going to see two great movies *Distant Thunder* by the Hindu S[atyajit]. Ray[7] and Ingmar Bergman's *The Magic Flute*.[8] Isabel's coming up for about three days around Thanksgiving Day. A friend has got me a guest card at the Harvard Club—imagine that! Unrecognized—Ignored—invisible! Sheer Heaven.

    Convey my regards to all your family down to the latest grandchild—and LOTS of affection to Francis.

                  Devotedly
                  Thornton

P. S. You remember the pleasure that Loreley Lee had in Paris seeing "Coty's and Chanel's and all the other old French monuments"?[9]

1. A reference to a lost letter.

2. Glasheen attended the Fifth International James Joyce Symposium in Paris, 15–21 June 1975. She had planned to travel to the symposium with Mabel Worthington, but Worthington became ill after arriving in Dublin. Worthington had arranged for them to meet Joyce's daughter Lucia Joyce at St. Andrews Hospital in Northampton, England, after the conference. In the absence of Worthington, Glasheen decided to return to the United States after the conference to await the galleys of *Census III*. A photographic essay by Fritz Senn, one of the co-chairmen of the conference was published in *The James Joyce Quarterly*, XIII, 2 (Winter 1976), [133–142].

3. Wilder read *Anthropology structurale* by Claude Lévi-Strauss shortly after it was published in Paris in 1958. The book, a collection of seventeen papers by Lévi-Strauss, written between 1944 and 1957, was published as *Structural Anthropology*, translated by Claire Jacobson and Brooke Grundfest Schoepf (New York: Basic Books, 1963). A second volume, *Anthropologie structurale deux*, a collection of papers written both before and after the first volume, was published in Paris by Plon in 1973; the English translation, *Structural Anthropology, Volume 2*, translated by Monique Layton was published by Basic Books in 1976. The are no references in either the text or the notes to Jacques Lacan (1901–1980), the practitioner and theorist of psychoanalysis. Glasheen met Lacan at the Fifth International James Joyce Symposium in Paris. See note 2.

4. Wilder stayed in New York from 22 November to 6 December. Wilder died at his home in Hamden, Connecticut, in the afternoon of 7 December.

5. The Royal Shakespeare Company's production of Tom Stoppard's *Travesties* opened in New York at the Ethel Barrymore Theatre on 30 October 1975 (it had opened in London at the Aldwych Theatre on 10 June 1974). *Travesties* is set in Zurich in 1917 and is based on the life and times of Henry Carr. In the play Carr, as an old man, reviews his life and the people he met or could have met in Zurich in 1917–1918. Among them are James Joyce, who is writing *Ulysses*, Tristan Tzara, a founder of the Dadaist movement, and the revolutionary Vladimir Lenin and his wife, Nadezhda (Nadya) Krupskaya. Stoppard based his play on the amateur acting troup, The English Players, formed in Zurich by Joyce and the actor Claud Sykes in the spring of 1918. In "Henry Wilfred Carr, (1894–1962)," included with the printed play (New York: Grove Press, 1975, 11–13), Stoppard writes of how he was contacted by Carr's second wife, Noël, after the play had opened in London. She supplied him with biographical details of Carr's life not found in Richard Ellmann's biography of Joyce. Wilder saw the play on Saturday, 29 November, with his friends Garson Kanin and Ruth Gordon. Isabel Wilder had arrived in New York on 25 November and returned to Hamden on the 28th.

6. The French playwright and novelist Jean Giraudoux (1882–1944).

7. *Distant Thunder* (*Ashani Sanket*), directed by Ray from his own screenplay is based on the novel by Bibhuti Bhusan Bannerjul. The story, set against the war-induced famine of 1943 in which five million people died, concerns the awakening to the evils of the social system of Gangacharan, a young Brahmin teacher, physician, and priest and his wife Ananga.

8. Ingmar Bergman's version of Mozart's *The Magic Flute*.

9. In *Gentlemen Prefer Blondes* (1925) by Anita Loos, Lorelei Lee and her friend Dorothy visit Paris and stay at the Ritz Hotel. The novel is in the form of Lorelei's diary, and for 27 April she writes, "Because when Dorothy and I went on a walk, we only walked a few blocks but in only a few blocks we read all the famous historical names, like Coty and Cartier and I knew we were seeing something educational at last and our whole trip was not a failure" (Chapter four, "Paris Is Devine").

☐

To Thornton Wilder, Hamden, Connecticut

[MS. TLS / AL[1]—YCAL]

21 November 1975   [22 Carrington Road
                                                        Farmington, Connecticut]

Dear Thornton,

I just mailed you an offprint and a letter.[2] Then on the instant I received from Warren Smith, the enclosed.[3] I don't know—did Donald Gallup tell you?

While I was in Paris, DG said to WS in passing "Has Mrs Glasheen managed to sell her Wilder collection of Joyce manuscripts?"

"Who told you she had ~~one~~ a collection?" Warren asked.

"Why you did," said Donald.

Warren was horrified, denied it, took my husband out to lunch at Mory's and told him. My husband told me when I got back.

I wrote Warren and said I hadn't any collection. I had some books you had given me over the years with some of your Joyce notes in them. I had letters you had written me. I had no Joyce MSS of any kind, given by anybody.

I also told Warren I had never offered for sale any letter you wrote me or book you gave me. And it would never occur to me to do so. I said that rumors about somebody were always rampant and it wasn't for him (Warren Smith) or me (Adaline Glasheen) to deny since we were in this matter conscious of our ignorance. I did think of writing you to repeat the rumor and say I was sorry the rumor arose, but I am always afraid of being some artist's person from Porlock,[4] so I didn't.

Now Donald Gallup has remembered that it wasn't Warren who told him. But it still leaves me, I guess, lied about (an amateur—I must look up the Goldstone book) by Mister Goldstone in his goddam book which I will now have to read instead of reading a good book. And I suppose I could also write his publishers if he, Mr Goldstone, didn't answer my letter.

But of course you mightn't want me to write Mr Goldstone. And if you don't want me to write him, say so and I will stamp and bite my ribbons, and live with the opprobrium of being an amateur lady Joycean. (Me with my Census III on the pop of going to press.)

In other words, you tell me what to do and I'll do it. Occurs to me if you have an extra copy of Goldstone, you could send it to me, or, just copy out the part about me.

The oddest things happen to me. I bet I didn't tell you the TLS asked me to review James Stephens letters[5] and I did and they diametrically altered every opinion I expressed or castrated and rearranged so that phrases became banal—e.g. I said the Irish Revivers were "heirs of guilty colonials" which became "heirs of colonials." Very few people could write a review of J Stephens Letters that would get them politically censored [inserted: like Orwell & The New Statesman] and very few people have been falsely accused of having and planning to sell y[ou]r annotated FW. And accused of being an Amateur.

I must be a more remarkable person than I have ever thought.

        Yrs
        Adaline

Please send back enclosed & tell me what to do right off because I have to read proof on III very soon

1. The postscript to this letter, and several additions to the text are handwritten.

2. Much of this letter is a reference to Richard H. Goldstone's *Thornton Wilder: An Intimate Portrait* (New York: Saturday Review Press, 1975). Goldstone wrote: "He [Wilder] summarily deprived the Yale Library of his annotated text of James Joyce's *Finnegans Wake*, placing it in the hands of a woman friend, who despite long-standing lively amateur interest in Joyce expressed indifference to Wilder's speculations (recorded in the book's margins) and regarded the gift merely as a windfall which at the appropriate time she would sell to the highest bidder." In a letter, published in the *James Joyce Quarterly*, XIV, 1 (Fall 1976), 114, Glasheen quoted this passage and added: "Mr. Goldstone has told two or three people that I am the lady of long-standing lively amateur interest. I am not. I thought Joyceans might like to know where Thornton Wilder's copy of *Finnegans Wake* is now, so I wrote Isabel Wilder and asked her. She says: 'That Joyce copy I had in my hands a few days ago. It's been safely locked up in the Beinecke in our private locked files. I handed it over to Don [i.e., Donald Gallup]... It's been there for years.'" Goldstone met Wilder when they were both in the officer training school of the Army Air Corps in 1942. They met again after the war, and on 14 to 15 December 1956, Goldstone interviewed Wilder for the *Paris Review* (see *Writers at Work: 'The Paris Review' Interviews, First Series*, ed. Malcolm Cowley, New York: The Viking Press, 1958; rpt., 1977, Penguin Books, [99]–118). Initially, when Goldstone, a professor of English, suggested a study of Wilder's work, Wilder cooperated. But when Goldstone changed his focus to the more personal, Wilder disassociated himself from Goldstone. The book was published shortly before Wilder's death. Isabel Wilder always maintained that Wilder never read it. Through Earl H. "Bud" Rovit, his colleague at the City College of New York, Goldstone had learned of Glasheen's friendship with Wilder. He wrote Glasheen on 30 May 1974 (HWS) asking to meet with her and to compare his impressions of Wilder with hers. After speaking with Isabel Wilder, Glasheen declined to meet Goldstone. There is only this one letter from Goldstone in HWS.

3. Warren Hunting Smith's letter to Glasheen of 19 November 1975 (HWS), in which he reports that Donald Gallup, Curator of the American Literature Collection of the Beinecke Library, and Wilder's Literary Executor, recalled that it was Goldstone who told him "that you [Glasheen] were selling the Joyce MSS given by the Wilders... No wonder that the Wilders think Goldstone is a snake in the grass!"

4. A reference to the man who allegedly interrupted Samuel Taylor Coleridge while he was writing "Kubla Khan: Or, a Vision in a Dream."

5. On 11 November 1974 (HWS), John Gross, editor of the *Times Literary Supplement* (London), wrote Glasheen asking her to review *Letters of James Stephens*, ed. Richard J. Finneran (London and New York: Macmillan, 1974). She agreed, and on 26 November Gross wrote that he was sending the book. Glasheen wrote her review and sent it to Gross in the Spring of 1975. Glasheen responded to the proofs on 11 October 1975 (HWS): "May I repeat what I wrote you last spring— if you don't like the review, I will write another. How much space can I have." It would appear that Glasheen neglected to send this letter to Gross together in the envelope that contained an offprint of her "Calypso" article, and the proofs of her review of Arthur Power's *Conversations with James Joyce*. On 3 November 1975 (copy, HWS) she again wrote Gross thanking him for a copy of his *James Joyce*

(New York: Viking Press, 1970) which he had sent her, and to remind him that she had sent back the proofs of the Power review. Page proof of the *TLS* review of *Letters of James Stephens* is in HWS. The text of Glasheen's original review is in Appendix XI.

☐

To Adaline Glasheen, Farmington, Connecticut
[MS. AL—HWS]

25 November 1975[1]   Harvard Club
  27 West 44th Street
  [New York, New York]

Dear Adaline:
 Total confession.
 I never owned a Joyce MSS.
 If they're talking about Wilder's comments on books by and about Joyce, I had dozens—all worthless, alas—eight years—groping futile scribbling.

---

1. This letter was begun shortly after Wilder arrived in New York on 25 November and was found unfinished after he died on 7 December 1975. It was sent to Glasheen by Isabel Wilder.

Appendix I

On The Four Old Men in Finnegans Wake[1]

THORNTON WILDER

Just as the sleeping Mr. Earwicker identifies himself with his two sons—seeing in them his youthful energies, his unexploited powers, his good and bad propensities—but not reliving in them the experiences of his own youth,—so in the Four Old Men he anticipates his old age,—sometimes as wise and venerable, but mostly as impotent, prurient, senescent and finally all but destitute. The principle [i.e., principal] evocation arrives with the chapter devoted to them alone on pps 383–399, where they are in Mrs MacCawley's poor house (i.e. his own wife's—Mrs "Finn McCool's"), concerned over their food, Shackleton's bread and milk, butter and ham, scratching their bedsores, suffering indigestion from having eaten a bad crab, and in delirium counting and recounting the mother-of-pearl buttons on their nurse's glove. Here is fully established the songs they sing, "Auld Lang Syne," "Far from the Land," "Coming through the Rye" and "Glory be there are no more of us"[2]; and their obsessive concern with saying Grace.

However, through the night they are identified with (1) Geography of Ireland and the Points of the Compass. (2) The Four Masters of Ireland, historians. (3) The Four Evangelists, with the animals that tradition has associated with them. (4) The Four Waves of Ireland, etc.

Geographical: Matthew Gregory, North, Ulster; Marcus Lyons, South, Munster; (Dr) Luke (Metcalfe) Tarpey, East, Leinster; and John MacDougal, West, Connaught.[3] This last always arrives late in the tabulation (the distance he has to come? because the Gospel of John was the last written, and is so different from the others?) and is accompanied by a donkey. All of them occasionally take on the name Walker, also, probably from the Whiskey manufacturer and maybe in reference to the fact that two of the Four Masters are called Peregrine.

They are present at the drunken evening in H. C. E.'s bar in Chapter II 3[4] and when they go home from their [i.e., there] in the rain they are represented as living in parts of Dublin which likewise denote the four parts of the compass: number one lived at Bothersby North [372.36]. . . . . and number two digged up Poors Coort, Soother [373.1] {The Fore Courts}. . . . and number three he slept with Lilly Tekkles at the Eats [373.3] {with A. L. P.}. . . and the last with the sailalloyd donggie he was berthed on the Moherboher to the Washte [373.4–.5] . . {Boher = Irish Road, Moore Road?}

At one point they are identified with the four mythical cities of Ireland (p. 219[.11]). Findrias, Murias, Gorias, and Falias, from whence the Tuatha Da Danaan [381.6] came. Gorias was in the East; from it was brought the "sword of light" [TW insert: Lug's invincible spear]; from Murias, came the [TW insert: Dagda's] cauldron of plenty; Falias, Fal's stone which roared under a King; Find[r]ias, Nuada's unescapable sword.

On p. 270–271, judging by the marginal note, they are identified with family-tribes of the counties, respectively: the O'Brien, the O'Connor, the Mac Loughlin and the Mac Namara.

Mark Lyons arriving at the examination of the dead "Yawn" on p. 475[.25], comes "trailing the wavy line of his partition footsteps"— perhaps a reference to the fact that Munster was formerly divided into East and West Munster. The name Tarpey for Luke may be due to some Tarpeyan betrayal in the history of Leinster and its Pale.

As an example of Joyce's diabolic complication it may be pointed out that Mark Lyons lives at the Fore Courts—a well-known landmark in Dublin. {All four are referred to this place—as the Poor Courts, the Four Porkers, etc}. The sleeping H. C. E. confers on Marcus the title of Marquis, and gives him the name of Pawerschoof [386.18],—Poor + German Hof = Court = coalesced into a horse?—image, with the German word Schuft, rascal suggested. The title is spelled with an *e* to suggest the ocean; the two *u*'s are retained for some philological reason plus cloacal reason discussed on p. 120 and the result becomes Merquus of Pawerschoopf. The horse or goat image in the pawing hoof may be due to some astronomical reason still undeciphered.

As The Four Masters of Ireland: These famous [TW space] century historians were Michael O'Clery, Farfassa O'Mulconry, Peregrine (Cucoigriche) O'Clery and Peregrine O'Duigenan. Their first names are given in a different order (Per; Mich; Farf; Peregr.) on p. 398[.15]; and the murky notes on Irish and Earwickian history on pps 13–14 are ascribed to them under their name Mammon Lujius [13.20] (see Mamalujo, below) and with the phrase (p. 14) "Now after all that tarfatched and peragrine or dingnant or clere" [14.28]—where the order would be 2-3-4-1. The original Four Masters came from Donegal, Roscommon, Leitrim, and? [TW space], respectively.[5] On p. 395[.3-.4] "John" is represented as "hacking away at a parchment pied." The *O'Clery* in the confused reminiscences of p. 385, and 386, must be some memory of the chief of the Four Master[s].

Query: Does Ireland identify its Four Masters with its Four Waves? The names of the waves (absurdly) are given on p. 23[.26-.29]. The four winds perhaps are given on p. 228.

I doubt whether any further or particularized use is made of the Four Masters besides the fact that their authority and dignity contribute to the Four Old Men as Judges, Doctors, and "Shanators" [475.23, .24].

N. B. Three assistants to the Four Masters were Maurice O'Mulcorny, Conary O'Clery and Paul O'Calla. The middle one of these may be alluded to in the list beginning at the bottom of p. 397[.36].

The Four Evangelists

The first two letters of their names make up the frequent Mamalujo, which occurs once in a feminine form Mamalujah,[6] which is the Russian word for Mother Puddle. The four old men derive some names and attributes from the Evangelists: Matthew—man; [TW space] Mark, accompanied by a lion, hence Marcus Lyons {Marcus, to prevent too much identification with H. C. E. in his character of King Mark to Shem's Tristan}. Luke, the sacrificial ox or calf—hence Luke Metcalfe Tarpey; also like the evangelist, often called Doctor. John, the Eagle.

1. An unpublished journal entry of 23 February 1940.
2. A line in the song "One More Drink for the Four of Us."
3. [Wilder's footnote:] In addition: Luke Tarpey seems to have some Welsh in him, and John McDougal some Scotch ("the poor senitsman") p. 390[.20]—which may lead to an identification with the Three Fusileers, accosted in the Park, who likewise recur as Irish, Welsh and Scotch.
4. Wilder here means *Finnegans Wake*, Book II, section iii (309–382) which takes place in Earwicker's pub where the innkeeper and the customers spend the hour before closing time watching two plays and a musical program on a television set.
5. [Wilder's footnote:] Michael O'C[l]ery, Donegal, Ulster; Farf O'M, Roscommon, Connaught; Pereg O'Clery, Leitrim, Connaught.
6. This word, as such, is not in the *Wake*.

Appendix II

Memorandum: rê Frank Budgen's
"Joyce's Chapters of Going Forth By Day"[1]

THORNTON WILDER

Nothing is more difficult than such a preliminary article on F—n's W., outlining for the still innocent reader the plan of the book, some indications of its method, and giving the elements of the objective data,— Mr. Earwicker's situation, his family and his recent actions which during his dream are elevated to myth.

This article does it very well, but falls short in two respects: (1) its [i.e., it] gives no idea of the difficulty nor of the intrinsic justification for the style and (2) it gives no idea of the grandeur of the object proposed.

The subject of the novel is Original Sin. Out of remorse from crimes committed in thought or even in the subconscious, man is stirred to intelligence and creativity.

The motto of the book is St. Augustine's *O felix culpa* ("Oh, Phoenix culprit").

In sleeping, it seems to say, everyman nightly descends to the basfonds of his primitive atavistic nature and wrestles with the monstrous forbidden temptations of pure impulse: theft, murder, incest, homosexuality, and blasphemous pride. And every dawn he emerges, relatively triumphant, haunted by shame, but ready to face another day.

The justification of the polyglot puns is

(1) In those depths all the languages are one. Human speech is mere *stoff*.

(2) The pun is the *lapsus linguae* whereby the forbidden confessional matter eludes the censor.

(3) Only by superimposed meanings can be conveyed synchronously, Mr. Earwicker, the publican of Chapelizod; the myth-figure he is identifying himself with at the moment; and the poet-author's comment on the moment.

Mr. Budgen cites passages at length, in all their apparent incoherence, certainly inducing in the reader that resentful repudiation that was aroused in Desmond McCarthy and Harold Nicolson when the book first appeared,[2] and which should stand against them as a black mark for a long time to come. The amount of time which a periodical reviewer can give to a book is not one of the coefficients of its merit.

In each expository article like this one there should be one passage, however brief, analyzed in detail to show the skill, beauty and profundity of the effects that Joyce can obtain from his method.

E. G.: (your page 181)[3] {The work [i.e., word] *tusker* [245.1] on the preceding page has started in Earwicker's mind thoughts of the lighthouse on the Eastern coast, for Tusker Light is near the bay of Dublin.} *When otter leaps in outer parts* [245.5–.6] . . . {The ear hears: "When other lips and other hearts"—from *The Bohemian Girl* of the Dubliner Balfe.[4]} . . . . Then Yul remembers Mei [245.6]. (1) Then you'll remember me (2) Then Sir Henry Yule, the classic translator of Marco Polo, remembers the Chinese girl he left behind him, (3) and— as elsewhere in the book, where this is a recurrent expression—age remembers youth, and December remembers May. This starts an Oriental foliation: (The German for poppy is *Mohnblume*): her lighthouses, like moons, like flowers, like Chinese lanterns. . . . etc. At Arklow, like an arclight's gleam. Their sapphire rays allure sailors to those lights erected by the German engineering company of Siemann [i.e., Siemens].

Middle of page 182: Kerrse is Perrse, not only because the Irish may interchange K for P,[5] but because the whole book avails itself of Grimm's laws of phonetic changes, a philologist's riot. Just as the hero is Proteus, [Wilder at margin: Proteus is never mentioned save by anagram and phonetic change. H. C. E. is Mr. Porter, and Tolper and on page one [3.17] '—t oldparr.'] and like the unborn child, passes from fish, to bird, to vertebrate, so language developes[6] before our eyes, l's interchange with r's, and b's with m's. In the chapter on the letter dug up from the rubbish heap [10.25–13.3], Joyce half gives and half cryptically withholds the keys for deciphering this language.

x   x

p. 187

The pretty nurse[7] who attends the four old men is still Maggie Earwicker, Anna Livia Plurabelle. In this aspect they are H. C. E.'s prevision of his old age and decay. (The number four is throughout the symbol of seniority. A. L. P.'s "my mad feary father" on the last page of the novel [628.2] is a play on the German form of it, just as his terrifying trident is a last appearance of the fork that pursued her as a child.)

x x[8]

1. This manuscript, written on stationery from the Savoy Hotel in London, is part of the papers of Cyril Connolly (1903–1974) in the Harry Ransom Humanities Research Center at the University of Texas at Austin. At the top of the first page, Connolly wrote: "from Thornton Wilder to Cyril Connolly on Joyce. TW was in London in the war. Cyril Connolly." Wilder may have been asked to comment on Budgen's essay, "Joyce's Chapters of Going Forth By Day," which was published in *Horizon*, the journal edited by Connolly, in its September 1941 issue (172–191). The essay has been reprinted several times including in Budgen's, *James Joyce and the Making of 'Ulysses' and Other Writings*, with an introduction by Clive Hart (Oxford and New York: Oxford University Press, 1972; rpt., 1989, [323]–342). Wilder and John Dos Passos were the two American delegates to the Seventeenth International Congress of P. E. N. held in London from 10 to 13 September 1941.

2. Neither McCarthy nor Nicolson wrote a review of *Finnegans Wake* when it was first published. Wilder may have been told of remarks each made about the book.

3. Budgen quotes from the *Wake*, 244.22–245.9, the passage describing "the coming on of night and the animals in the Zoo going to rest."

4. Michael Balfe (1808–1870), Irish born composer; *The Bohemian Girl* (1843) is his best-known opera.

5. The point is made by Budgen when he writes about Joyce's invention of names.

6. Wilder uses the rare form of the verb.

7. Budgen is discussing Book II, section iv (383–399).

8. The manuscript ends here. Wilder normally used "x x" to indicate the end of one section of thought and the beginning of another, suggesting that this manuscript is unfinished or incomplete.

Appendix III

Finnegans Wake: *The Polyglot Everyman*[1]
Draft A

THORNTON WILDER

An increasing number of writers have been publishing papers on general aspects of Finnegans Wake,—its philosophical and religious implications or its implied treatment of the institutions of society or the family. Only a small number have been heard from who do the basic work of decyphering[2] line by line that unbroken succession of devilishly ingenious verbal constructions. This paper is intended to aid and stimulate this latter group of students,—not to map the jungle from the air, but to cut some paths through it.

I shall begin by naming and illustrating certain structural devices which James Joyce employed throughout the book. Apter names may be discovered later, for in several cases they are applied to devices which are not found elsewhere in literature; it is thought that it is well that a beginning be made, and I begin by calling attention to the grid, the sequence, the semé, and the foliation.

James Joyce's mind worked under a compulsion to present his thought and images in rigorous numerical and associational systems. It is well that it was, in view of the subject that he'd chosen. This is not the first cosmological novel, but it is the most ambitious; its subject is Man, his instincts, his intellect, and the institutions he has created from an effort to harmonize the two. This Man is presented to us through the person of one man, a very modest representative of his genus, a pub-keeper on the outskirts of Dublin. Joyce's problem has been to ensure that every detail concerning his individual be a reflection of the universal and this requirement has entailed a most extraordinary machinery of allusions, relationships, ever-shifting identifications, and symbols. The first device toward this requirement I call the *grid*, borrowing the word from the [space in manuscript[3]] of map-making,—a pattern of horizontal and vertical lines upon which any desired figuration may be superimposed. It differs from a *cadre* in that the grid-lines enter into the figure itself, as control, orientation, and significance. There are many grids beneath the complex text of *Finnegans Wake*; it is difficult to say which is more basic. The entire book is based upon—or accorded to—the Service of the Mass. It is also *hung upon* (the grid is now overhead) Vico's theories of the development of society. There is an astronomical grid [on] which no competent scholar has yet published his findings.[4] We do not yet know the date of this [space in manuscript] night, but we can be very certain that Joyce has indicated it in many ways and places. There are the hours and the watches of the night, both civil (Roman) and ecclesiastical. These grids are continually entering into the text, in complicated polylingual puns. Some student will some day show us in detail (the things which now we can only glimpse) the regularity with which the dreamer hears the horological bells on a ship at sea, the canonical hymns and prayers in the religious houses (I have counted the Trisagion, or rather the Tersanctus eight times). Moreover, I suspect that the *Purgatorio* of Dante subtends the book, which does not prevent a constant play of allusion to the other canticles. Most awe-inspiring of all, Joyce has surrounded the sleeper (who is everyone who has ever slept) with grids of the physical world, of matter and sound. Through long passages (intermitted from time to time for reasons we cannot yet determine, though everything in Joyce has such a reason) the atomic series is written into the text

[space in manuscript]

and for sound, Guido da Arezzo's scale.

[space in manuscript]

A second device and the easiest to recognize, is the Sequence. The best known of these is the rainbow, generally identified, but not always, with the hero's daughter Isabelle (Yseult), with girlhood, with hope, with Noah. With many languages at his disposal, Joyce has had little trouble with six of the colors, but his ingenuity has been hard pressed to run the changes on indigo. He has had to remind us that the word comes from the Greek for Indian and that the syllable *ind* should be sufficient:
As

[space in manuscript]

Joyce's passion for scheme and order and numerically determined elements has led to his making sequences the very bricks of Finnegans Wake, as grids are the foundations and struts and girders. Here are the Seven Deadly Sins and the Nine Worthies, the Five Sacred Wounds and the Twelve Paladins of France, the *processus prophetarum* and the wives of Henry VIII[.] The Ten Wonders of the Ancient World coalesce with the fine things that can, or could be found in Dublin (553:10–12). Man—after a night of humiliation—is justifying his existence by announcing all the benefits he has bestowed and the cities and monuments he has raised:

. . . . chopes pyramidous and mousselimes and the ["the" added by Wilder] beaconphires and colos[s]ets and pensilled {these are the hanging gardens of Babylon; Spanish: jardines pensiles} turisses for the busspleaches of the summiramies and esplanadas and statuesque and templeogues {this is the Temple of Zeus at Olympia: Ogue, the All-Father of early Celtic religion; Templogue is also a suburb of Dublin}

These were more difficult to identify on page 261 lines [space in manuscript]. It is at the beginning (the cosmological beginning) of the schoolboy's lessons. Ainsoph, the creator of all being in the Kabala, has called the feminine principle into existence by sheer longing and on her has engendered the world, the human race and its creations (261.7–13):

. . . when old is said in one and maker mates with made (O my!)[,] having conned the cones {the pyramids} and meditated the mured and pondered the pensils and ogled the olymp and delighted in her dianaphous and cacchinated behind his culosses, before a mosoleum. {He has substituted the walls—mured—of Babylon for the Pharos of Alexandria}

There are hundreds of these sequences throughout the book. Perhaps the most extraordinary use to which he has put the device is found on page [605] where seven sequences are in play at the same time. The page is written in the manner of an old Saint's legend: our hero's son, the revolting good little Kevin, is about to take his bath. The Saint whose name he bears made a dwelling for himself at the center of seven lakes in Glendalogh—we are in a heptarchy of sevens, with the nine orders of the angels thrown in for good measure: the orders of the church, the canonical watches, the gifts of the spirit, the sacraments. The colors of the spectrum must be there (gold [.10] . . . vert [.11] . . . rubric [.23] . . . cardinal [.25] . . . violet [606.4] . . .)[.] Though I cannot find orange or the other blues, knowing Joyce's thoroughness we can assume that they are there in Erse or Finnish or Japanese.[5] This passage is saved—as many are not—from blasphemy by the droll and winning charm of this infant in his "hanbathtub" [606.2]. (A word which reminds us of the Moslem sect of the Hanbalites, just as "amiddle" [605.12] is intended to recall the Amidists of Japanese Buddhism who hold that salvation is by faith in Amita. *Finnegans Wake* is

[space in manuscript]

There is another device which I call the Semé—a word used in the decorative arts and in heraldry and which has been in the English language for some time. It means a sprinkling or a strewing. A grid and a sequence are systems of a known number and of a recognized order. Joyce does not omit an element or alter their order without special intention. A semé, however, is a mere profusion. Woven into the Anna Livia Plurabelle chapters are the names of over five hundred rivers; into the section which Joyce published separately Haveth Childers Everywhere[6] are the names of hundreds of cities, monuments, and streets. Half buried in the text of the Fable of the Moo[k]se and the Gripes[7] are the names of a score of philosophers and the terms given to geological strata under France and the adjacent countries. These semé cannot include all the cities, philosophers, or geological epochs in history. There is a delightful semé on page [583] where we learn that our dear Isabelle's 28 companions (she is a leap year girl) are the heroines of operas and operettas—from Die Walküre to The Pirates of Penzance. (She is herself Isolde, and lives in Chapelizod, a village near Dublin, "Castle of Iseult.") There are some very [space in manuscript] semés. The coitus of our archetypical pair is conducted to the accompaniment of the names of at least 25 celebrated cricketers, giving place to the sequences of the satellites of Jupiter, Neptune, Saturn and Uranus. We may be certain that these curious associations of idea are in obedience to some demand of the overall grids which are not yet apparent to us.

One can easily distinguish a semé from a sequence, but a foliation often resembles a brief or light semé. If we were not dealing with Joyce we would say that a word or an image "sets off" a train of association[.]

Finnegans Wake is filled with the most astonishing semés. There are 114 Suras, or chapters, in the Koran, each with its identifying title. All of them are in Joyce's book,—sprinkled, sown throughout it—some in English, some in Arabic (Joyce's English and Arabic!). Tom Moore wrote Irish Melodies, each poem accompanied by an indication of the tune to which it is to be sung. All of them are in *Finnegans Wake*. We are indebted to Mr. [space in manuscript][8] of Wigan in North England for the discovery and analysis of these interpolations. Moore's "How dear to me the hour when daylight fades" is sung to the air "The Twisting of the Rope." On page 427 lines 17 and 19, we read ". . . . (how dire do we thee hours when thylike fades!). . . . with a twhisking of the robe. . ." We are beginning to think that we shall find *all* the Saints in the calendar, *sown* throughout the texts, *all* the writers who have been valued (we have recently uncovered from heavy disguise Kalidasa, Camoens, and Manzoni) as well as some delightful play with Marie Corelli, Rhoda Broughton and Ouida. Each of Shakespeare's plays is given not a passing allusion but a deep searching—not primarily because they are works of literature, but because they exhibit some aspect of the book's tireless preoccupation, the situation in which Man finds himself. The reader will have gathered how difficult it is to quote any single sentence from this book—so inextricably is it bound up with the unresting play of its varied patterns—but for lovers of "Measure for Measure" and Cymbeline there is a grandeur in the following lines (251.9, 10, 16, 17):

> "For all of these have been thisworlders, time liquescing into state, pitiless age grows angelhood {Angelo}. . . . . . The specks on his lapspan aare his foul deed thoug[t]hs, wishmarks of mad imogenation."

Allusions to many of Trollope's and Henry James's novels—including the less well known ("Miss MacKenzie," "The American Senator," "Guy Domville," "Julia Bride") have been found; they are probably all there.[9]

> Though the last nine pages of the book offer us a semé of the pantomimes that Margaret Earwicker (Anna Livia Plurabelle) had heard as a girl & a quasi-sequence of the places she passes on a walk from the Liffey to the Head of Howth, a sequence of the seven deadly sins and their absolution (the peccata that are erased in the *Purgatorio*[)], the sequence of her husband's achievements, the Seven Wonders of the Ancient World, the sequence of his achievements (the labors of Hercules), poor bumbling fellow though he is,—that in the blaze of Joyce's genius it is scarcely possible to distinguish one modality from another.[10]

One can generally distinguish a semé from a sequence, but a FOLIATION often resembles a brief or light SEMÉ. If we were not dealing with James Joyce we would say that a word or an image "sets off" a train of association; but that is not the way that Joyce's mind works; he is the master in the free association of the interior monologue of his characters, but he is the slave of the demands laid upon him by his imperative designs. The foliation is, in appearance, a divagation into[11] a language, a mythology, a nexus of allusions; but nothing in Joyce is arbitrary. All is under the governance of an overruling plan. For example, in line 35 of page 28 we find the word: "that samesake sibsubstitute of a hooky salmon": Now, the salmon plays a large role in this book. Finn McCool, the eponymous hero of Ireland, our Finn of Finnegans Wake, by tasting of a salmon's flesh—like Adam of the forbidden fruit—learned the distinction between good and evil. And the "samesake" of a salmon is a smolt. And the smolt reminds us of Tobias Smollett. Page 28, line 36: . . . rody ram . . . at random . . . {the next page:} . . . .humphing . . . . pickle . . . . clinkers [29.5–.8]. What are these side-glances at the English novelist doing here? And— as Mrs. Glasheen has shown us—in the same opening chapter—there is a foliation of association with the Brontë family,— Pages 7 and 8: ". . . . brontoichthyan . . . . Anny . . . Heather . . . belles' . . . villagettes . . . Patkinses . . . . Kathe . . . ." [7.20–8.8]. There is no system, no order. Is this merely a semé? For a reason which I shall propose later I suggest that the whole first chapter—the death and wake of Finnegan, the fall of Humpty-Dumpty, with the promise of resurrection—is the history of Everyman and the history of the English novel.

Foliation is everywhere and Joyce has been under the necessity of curbing his hyperactive mind from wandering down the avenues of digression and comment. (As Gertrude Stein said to Ernest Hemingway: "Hemingway, Hemingway, comment is not literature").[12] "Comment" is ultimately valuable to us only when it is built into a larger compassing field of ideas.

There is a very beautiful and despairfully complicated passage on pages 244 and 245: "how night falls on the zoological gardens in Phoenix Park, Dublin." At one moment Joyce is prompted to give us a foliation of Chinese associations. The animals are sleeping:

> "Hopopodorme. So-beast! No chare of beagles, frantling of peacocks . . ." [245.2–.3]

Joyce found this phrase in [Thomas] Urquhart's translation of Rabelais!

> "Lights, pageboy, lights! Brights will [i.e., we'll] be brights. With help of Hanoukan's lamp" [245.4–.5].

[at margin: SALOME]

The distorted spelling reminds us that we must remember the Jewish Feast of Lights and the flashlight of our little Shaun-John-Kevin;—

the unremitting interplay of the macrocosms and our humble family in Chapelizod, the microcosms.

"When otter leaps in outer parts then Yul remembers Mei" [245.5–.6].

The ear hears a song from [Michael] Balfe's The Bohemian Girl: "When other lips and other hearts"; the eye begins to see the animals playing about the lighthouses on the coast of Ireland; and the reader catches an allusion to one of the basic themes of the book: When the ageing man (Yule-Christmas-December) remembers May—the young girl in his life. Mei is Chinese for young girl and the blossom of the flowering tree; and Sir Henry Yule, the early explorer to China remembers the girl he left behind him. The word Mei starts an oriental foliation:

"Her hung maid mohns are bluming . . ." [245.6–.7]

The German for poppy is Mohnblume; the Chinese lanterns of the Hang dynasty that a girl has hung on the terrace are like the lighthouses of the Irish coast:

". . . .arcglow's seafire siemens lure and wextward warnerforth's hooker-crookers" [245.8–.9].

The light at Arklow, sapphire-blue, built by the German engineering firm of Siemen[s], an enticement to sailors, and at Wexford that deceptive beam—like Captain John Warneford Armstrong, the base informer, trying to shipwreck navigators in the straits of the Hook and the Crook[.]

There are innumerable foliations in Finnegans Wake: grandiose, tender, indecent, informative, or very funny, but they are all under the stern governance of a grid. The moment has come when Joyce *must* introduce the Orient, or one of the arts;—music, or the influence of one of the planets, Saturn-Wisdom-Old Age. Nothing is arbitrary or self-indulgent in Finnegans Wake. I shall presently submit other illustrations of the foliation.

Now I enter upon devices that Joyce has employed that, to my knowledge, have never been employed in literature before.

Another device I call the paroidia (Greek). I shall conclude this paper with an illustration of Joyce's basing a passage of his book on a page of *The Illiad*. Parody? In our time the word has come to imply an attempt to ridicule a predecessor. It is not in Joyce that we shall find any ridicule of Homer, to whom he had previously offered the most signal homage that Europe has extended for several centuries. The etymology of the word encourages us to return to its spelling after the Greek: "beside a song." Joyce has shown us in the Oxen of the Sun chapter in Ulysses that he possesses the last virtuosity in the imitation of other authors. There is little of that in Finnegans Wake, though the entire book is in large part an imitation of various speakers—mostly pedants, gossips, journalists, and vulgarians.

These then are the four principal devices as *method* (there are still other ones, less frequently employed, which I shall illustrate later); what devices does he call upon to [space in manuscript]. Those that I have described are the canvas and paint, what devices does he employ as draughtsman? Those are the conventions of tonality and counterpoint, what are the characteristics of the music he writes by their aid?

It is difficult to find a name that will characterize the most important of these. The principal personages in the book are Everyman, Everywoman, and so on; but such persons have never existed and Joyce would be [the] last man to attempt to describe such an abstract. There have been men, women and children, beyond all counting; and those in literature (good and bad literature) are as real to Joyce, for his purposes, as those in history. Man appears in this book *in* thousands of persons. The words *persona* and *personifications* are misleading; these are not masks, which imply concealment or a division of the person into a real and a temporarily or permanently assumed. Our hero is frequently Abraham or Lot or Napoleon—he is not presented to us as *playing* such roles. Nor is the word *avatar* suitable, bringing with it associations of the incarnation of divine beings. There is a report that Joyce first intended to call this volume "Proteus" and its subject is, indeed, proteiform man. {On pages 120 to 139 there are 389 characterizations of our hero, all insulting to the last degree, hurled at him by one of his sons who is also a portion of himself deriding himself.} As in much modern literature, the connections are rejected; our hero is not felt in a given situation to be "like" Noah or Jonathan Swift or even one of his sons: he *was* them and the situations in which they found themselves are permanently in being. Joyce has liquidated time; the generations of men traverse time like a great river; each man carries Everyman within himself and Everyman; the falls of Niagra present themselves to our eyes, *also*, as motionless column of water (the semé of rivers in the Anna Livia Plurabell chapter impresses this compellingly upon our attention). Let us call this device: [space in manuscript]

In Humphrey Earwicker's broadcast address of self-justification, declaring all the benefits he has conferred on human society:

> ". . . . in my bethels of Solyman's I accouched their rotundaties and I turnkeyed most insultantly over raped lutetias in the lock:" [542.27–.29]

I founded maternity hospitals (like the Rotunda Hospital in Dublin, of which my schoolday friend Dr. Bethel Solomon[s][13] was for a time president[)]; and I was [sic] set up prison-hospitals for delinquent women like Dublin's Hospital of St. Margaret of Cortona, popularly known as the "lock"; in fact, like some sultan in Turkey I ruled over the unfortunates tyrannically. Throughout this passage at least two grids are in operation: all the cities that Man has made. Solyman is an ancient name for Jerusalem; every city of refuge is a bethel; Lutetia is an old name for Paris. Another grid introduces all the masterpieces of literature: "I wrote the Rape of the Lock and the Rape of Lucrece."

> "I richmounded the rainelag in my bathtub of roundwood and conveyed it with cheers and cables . . . . through my longertubes of elm: out of fundness for the outozone I carried them amd curried them in my Putzemdown cars to my Kommeandine hotels:" [542.4– .9]

{Grid of cities: Richmond, Ranelagh, Bata Roundwood, Ulm, Punchestown, outside Dublin with its race tracks, the Condamare Avenue at Monte Carlo. We are constantly returned to Dublin, but Joyce has forged a style that can convey simultaneously the microcosm and the macrocosm. Did you notice that in Germany likewise the artisans were given pleasure resorts where they could eat and wash themselves?[}]

His wife likewise reappears under innumerable names.

> ["]Then a toss nare scared that lass, so aimai moe, that's agapo! Tell me, tell me, how cam she . . . through all her fellows, the neckar she was, the diveline? Casting her perils before our swains. . . ." [202.6– .9][14]

She's not only the river Liffey, but the Cam and the Neckar and Nare and the Aimini in Iran and the Anapo in Italy. And she's the heroine of a story in Joyce's *Dubliners*, Eveline; and she's the girl Byron loved in Athens, for neither Death (than-a-tos) nor Love ever frightened Anna Livia Plurabelle.

And who shall number the existences that the twin sons, Shaun-Kevin who lives through the Holy Week as protagonist! and Shem-James who reached a lowness never yet sunk to, especially when he wrote that book, that epical forged cheque on the universe, Finnegans Wake. And little Isabelle, sleeping so sweetly in her little April cot but whose image returns to us as girls ranging from Mallarmé's Salome to Dante[']s Beatrice[.]

Another device that Joyce employs to alert our attention to the fact that he is alluding to one of his characters is to write a phrase that exhibits the character's initials. When I read that a man, "with Hirish tutores

Cornish made easy" [126.24] I not only see a recommendation for language lessons and a ribald reference to Tristram's conquest of Iseult of Cornwall, but I see that we are talking about H. C. E.—Humphrey Chimpden Earwicker. His wife's A. L. P. is omnipresent. Most double v's and double w's allude to her. I think most words where two separated m's are emphasized allude to Mallarmé whose *Coup de Dés* and "Faunagain" play a large rôle.[15]

But the most striking device and one totally new, that Joyce extracts from these procedures is what he can accomplish by employing several of them *simultaneously*. This is a device well known to musicians— one has only to think of the superimposed *motifs* at the close of the Meistersinger Overture, or the triple-fugue of Bach where his themes for the members of the trinity are finally combined. In the graphic arts juxtaposition is more practicable than coalescence. Joyce's style delights in superimposing image upon image with effects that are often gloriously funny, often touching and impressive, and always illuminating. On page [234], Joyce amalgamates two persons whom no one would [have] ever thought of ever juxtaposing: Eamon de Valera and Melville's Billy Budd. Joyce hated de Valera (it was no recommendation that they were born on the same day—Joyce was very susceptible to such coincidental conjunctions). Rightly or wrongly, he charged his co-eval with encouraging bigotry in Ireland and robbing Catholicism of its potentialities for joy. Joyce's last two books are still barred from Dublin. Their author did not wish, however, openly to offend the statesman and the passages concerning him are more cyphered than most. When we find Spanish phrases, and the words basque and beret and the Bay of Biscay and Geneva councils and Eucharistic congresses in the text we are probably in the vicinity of "I mean" and "Edward." In this passage Billy Budd is robbed of the pathos that surrounds him in Melville's story; his much advertised beauty is reduced to sugariness and his stutter is recalled. Joyce insists that the women of Ireland lavished on the statesman a sickly adulation and halfway through the paragraph the double-image is swept up into the image of HCE's son Kevin-Shaun. Everyone who has ever lived, in life or in art, has his correspondence in the Earwicker household. Needless to say, I have oversimplified the content of the page: Buddha and his mother Maya cross the scene; there is a foliation from Don Quixote. The book's grid involving the Mass and the Nightwatches sends us a *Kyrie* and a litany and a Soul-netzer is opposed to a Leib-netz. {For those who are following those lines in the text, I shall recall that Billy Budd wore cotton breeches (here they are in the colors of de Valera's Free State[)] and that Melville called him a "cynosure" and spoke of his "game-cock spirit." The result is, as generally throughout the book, occasionally obscure,

often blasphemous, and very funny. It is a pleasure to add that the irruption of poor Billy Budd here was first detected by Mrs Glasheen of Farmington, Connecticut, the Egeria of Finnegans Wake studies.
[margin: crush the slander's head 102.27, i.e., .17]

A more winning example of the effects that Joyce can obtain from combining his procedures appears on page [270]. Anna Livia Plurabelle decides to go out and silence those malicious gossips that have been defaming her husband. She resolves, like Eve, to put her foot on the schlangder's head (Genesis [Chapter 3]; German; schlange, a serpent). But first the mother of us all dresses up in some very fine clothes, indeed,— page 207 line 31 to page 208 line 26.[16]

1. Wilder spoke before members of Yale University's Romance Language Club, German Club, and Slavic Club on 23 April 1959. The talk is mentioned and titled in his letter to Glasheen of [? April 1959]. We have labeled this Draft A, and the second, which appears to be a revision with additions, Draft B. Wilder left spaces in his manuscript where he intended to fill in a detail or develop an idea. We have indicated this by the phrase "space in manuscript." At the head of the first manuscript page Wilder wrote in a number of words with page and line references. Some items from the list refer to words from *Finnegans Wake*; some words are to be found in the *Wake* but not on the page Wilder includes. For example, Clarke Dual does not appear on page 294—the word Clarke is on page 558.20 and the word Dual on 105.20. For 58.19 it is not clear what word in the line Wilder means to cite. It is possible that some of the notations refer to reading Wilder was doing at the time. The words are:

    Haughty cacuminal
    55.29
    58.19
    Hepar = lien 166
    Clarke Dual 294
    Hohner Poetic 821 H 73
    Antad 817.32
    Crinoline = Antad 19
    Didascoles [?23]
    Frisette 30
    Cicero-
    chick pea 157
    Last rose of Summer 371[.15]

2. We have retained Wilder's spelling.

3. In Draft B Wilder writes "games and the art."

4. The next sentence is written in the margin but with no indication where it is to be inserted.

5. At the top of this manuscript page Wilder has written "ynisled—analive." These words do not appear in the *Wake*. On page 605 Joyce uses many words with a "y," replacing an "i," for example, "ysland of Yreland" [.4].

6. *Haveth Childers Everywhere*, a fragment of *Finnegans Wake*, III, iii (532.1–554.10), was published in June 1930 by Henry Babou and Jack Kahane in Paris and by the Fountain Press in New York.

7. *Finnegans Wake*, I, iv (152.15–159.18).

8. Wilder left a space here intending to write in the name of James Atherton, author of *The Books at the Wake* (1959).

9. The first two titles are by Anthony Trollope, and the last two are by Henry James.

10. This indented paragraph is written in the margin but with no indication of where it was to be inserted.

11. The manuscript page ends here. On the verso Wilder has written:

112	OR 7-2138
Suras	James Atherton Wigan Lancas
Moore's Melodies	Matthew J. C. Hodgart of Cambridge, England
	Don at Pembroke
Songs	Hodgart and Miss Mabel Worthington

12. In *The Autobiography of Alice B. Toklas* (1933) Stein writes: "Once when Hemingway wrote in one of his stories that Gertrude Stein always knew what was good in a Cézanne, she looked at him and said, Hemingway, remarks are not literature" (Chapter IV, "Gertrude Stein Before She Came to Paris").

13. For information on Dr. Solomons see Wilder to Glasheen, 7 December 1950.

14. In his manuscript Wilder put the first sentence of the quoted text as the last sentence. We have restored the order as it is in *Finnegans Wake*.

15. Poems by Stéphane Mallarmé (1842–1898). "Faunagain" is undoubtedly Mallarmé's poem "L'Après-midi d'un Faune"; "Malster Faunagon" is in the *Wake*, 337.28.

16. The manuscript ends here. On the verso of the final manuscript page are the following citations from the *Wake*:

The woods are fond always . . . As were we their babes in. And robins in crews so. [619.23–.24]
We'll not disturb their sleeping duties. [620.36–621.1]
I thought you were all glittering in the noblest of carriage. You're only a bumpkin. [627.21–.23]
My currant bread's full of sillymottocraft [623.19]
bigmaster 624[.11]
Laddies Lampern [621.5]

Appendix IV

Finnegans Wake: *The Polyglot Everyman*
Draft B

THORNTON WILDER

An increasing number of writers have been publishing papers on the general aspects of *Finnegans Wake*,—its philosophical or religious implications or its attitudes to the family or to the institutions of society. A smaller number have been heard from who are engaged in the basic work of decyphering that unbroken succession of verbal deformations,— its "sleep language" of *paronomasia*. This paper is intended to aid and stimulate this latter group; to suggest ways of clearing paths through the jungle rather than of mapping it from the air. I shall begin by naming and illustrating certain structural and stylistic devices which Joyce employed throughout the book. To be aware of their presence does not in itself, elucid a passage but it reduces the number of problems that confront a reader on a given page and releases it to concentrate upon others. First, I shall call attention to the *grid*, the sequence, the semé, and the foliation.

James Joyce's mind worked under a rigorous compulsion to present his thoughts and images in systems. It was well that it did in view of the subject that he had chosen. This is not the first cosmological novel but it is the most ambitious. His subject is Man, his instincts, the operation of his mind, the institutions he has created, and, above all, the documents he has made in an effort to give an account of himself. This Man he presents to us in the person of one man, a very modest representative of his kind, a pub-keeper on the outskirts of Dublin. Joyce's problem has been to ensure that every detail concerning his individual carries a relation to every man in every place and every age and this requirement has entailed a most extraordinary machinery of allusions, ever-shifting identifications, and symbols.

GRID

The first device he employs to satisfy this requirement I call the grid. The word is borrowed from games and from the art of map-making. It denotes a pattern of regularly drawn vertical and horizontal lines upon which a desired figuration may be drawn. It differs from a *cadre* in that the interior lines and not merely the boundaries enter into the figuration itself, as control, orientation, and significance. There are many grids beneath the text of *Finnegans Wake*. The entire book is based upon—or accorded to—the service of the Mass, and not only, as in one extended passage to the Good Friday Mass of the Presanctified in the Maronite Rite & The Lesson. Vico's theories of the successive stages in the development of society furnish another grid. There is an omnipresent astronomical grid which no competent scholar has yet studied. We suspect that the volume was dreamed on an All Souls' Halloween night, but we do not yet know the year though we can be certain that Joyce has indicated it in many ways and places. The watches of the night, civil and ecclesiastic, the bells on ships at sea constitute a grid. Just as Homer's Odyssey subtended *Ulysses*, so Dante's *Purgatorio* seems to be lending pattern to the novel, which does not prevent many an allusion to the other two canticles of Dante. Most awe-inspiring of all, Joyce has surrounded the sleeper—who is everyone who has ever slept—with a grid-system of the physical world, of matter and of sound. For long sections the atomic series ascends or descends the page in polyglot puns, and for sound, the syllables of Guido d'Arezzo's scale.

SEQUENCE

A second device, and the easiest to recognize, is the *sequence*. The best known of these is the rainbow or spectrum, generally identified, but not always, with girlhood, with the hero's daughter, with hope and with the story of Noah. With many languages at his disposal Joyce has little trouble with six of the colors, but for *indigo* he must remind that the word itself comes from the Greek for Indian and that the syllable *ind* should be sufficient. The spectrum can be tenderly delicate, as in the view of the daughter lying in her [margin: "GIRLS"] "april cot" on page 556 (". . boyblue . . . orange blossoming . . . greengageflavoured . . . primarose . . ."); or scurrilous on the bottom [margin: "PRIEST"] of page 432, where a priest is looking for his place in the Missal; or vituperative on page 339[.27–.29], where the twin sons have a vision of their father as the Tsar of all the Russias and, on another level, the [margin: "Tolstoi"] Russian authors are expressing their resentment at the preëminence of Tolstoi: "A bear raigning" (*Baron* for *Count*) in his heavenspawn consomation robes. ["]Rent, outraged, yewleaved, grained, ballooned, hindergored and voluant." Sequences are the very bricks of Finnegans Wake as grids are the struts and girders. Here are the seven deadly sins and the graces, the Nine Worthies, the Twelve Paladins of France [margin: "CHEOPS"] and the six wives of Henry VIII. The Seven Wonders of the Ancient World coalesce with the things that can, or could be found in Dublin. Man, after a night of humiliation, is enumerating all the benefits he has bestowed and the cities and monuments he has raised (page 553)[.10–.12]

> ". . . chop[e]s pyramidous and mousselimes and the ["the" added by Wilder] beaconphires and colos[s]ets and pensil[l]ed turisses {in Spanish the hanging gardens of Babylon are the jardines pensiles[}] . . . and esplanadas and statuesques and templeogues."] {This is the Temple of Zeus at Olympia; *Ogue* is an All-father in early Celtic religion, and Templogue is a suburb of Dublin}.

These appear again on page 261. This is the beginning of the schoolboys? lessons, their first cosmological lesson. Ainsoph, the creator of all being in the Kabal [space in manuscript], has called the feminine principle into existence by sheer longing and on her has engendered the world, the human race, and its creations:

> ". . . . when old is said in one and maker mates with made . . . having conned the cones {pyramids} and meditated the mured {Joyce has substituted the walls of Babylon for the Pharos at Alexandria} and pondered the pensils and ogled the olymp and delighted in her dianaphous and cacchinated behind his culosses, before a mosoleum."
> [261.7–.13]

Perhaps the most extraordinary display of this device is found on p 605 where seven sequences are in operation at the same time. The passage is written in the manner of an old celtic saint's legend. Our hero's son, the revoltingly good little Kevin is about to take his bath. The saint whose name he bears built a dwelling for himself at the center of the seven lakes of Glendalough. We are in a heptarchy of seven, with the nine orders of the angels thrown in for good measure: the orders of the Christian ministry, the canonical watches, the gifts of the spirit, the sacraments, the colors of the spectrum, the notes of the scale. In addition, we are told that little Kevin is in his "hanbathtub" which reminds us of the Moslem sect of the Hanbalites, just as "amiddle" recalls the Amidists of Japanese Buddhism who hold that salvation is by faith in Amida. Joyce is working on so vast a scale that the innumerable passages of extreme indecency and blasphemy demand an exercise of judgment other than that accorded to more narrowly circumscribed works.

SEME
A third device I call the *semé*. This word, from a French past participle, "strewn," has long been incorporated in the English language as a term in heraldry and decoration. It means the scattering on a background of a graphic image a field of fleur-de-lys or a sea of stars. A grid and a sequence are a system of a known number and of an established order; in using them Joyce does not omit an element or alter their order without a special intention. A semé, however, is mere profusion. Woven into the Anna Livia Plurabelle chapter are the names of over four hundred rivers; in the chapter which section which Joyce first published separately as Haveth Childer Everywhere are the names of hundreds of cities, monuments, and streets. Half buried in the Fable of the [Mookse and] Gripes are the names of many philosophers and (why?) some geological strata under France and the adjoining countries. There are many astonishing semés. The sexual congress of our archetypical pair is conducted to the accompaniment of the names of at least 25 celebrated cricketers, a device which gives place to the sequences of the satellites of Jupiter, Neptune, Saturn, and Uranus. There are 114 Suras or chapters in the Koran. We are indebted to Mr. James Atherton of Wigan, Lancashire for finding them sprinkled throughout the book, some in English, some in Arabic,— Joyce's English and Arabic. Joyce has not only woven into the text the first lines of all of Tom Moore's Irish Melodies, but has given with them the name of the air to which they are sung. (Moore directs that "How dear to me the hour when daylight fades" be sung to the air "The Twisking Twisting of the Rope"; so we read on page 427: " . . . . (how dire do we thee hours when thylike fades!) [.17] . . . . with a twhisking of the robe . . . ." [.19])

The entire book is a vast semé of references to authors and their works, but in the most autobiographical of the chapters, that devoted to Shem the Penman, the names of novelists, poets and critics attain a profusion and density equal to those of the rivers in the Anna Livia Plurabelle chapter. The list of objects littering the "mousefarm filth" [183.4] of Shem's lodging is funny enough, but read as allusions to literature they are even funnier. Some are easy to see (André Gide— "counterfeit franks," Oscar Wilde—"best intentions," [183.19] Wyndham Lewis— "lees of whine"? [183.22] and the allusion to the Marquis de Sade, which shall not be reprinted here), but Joyce has been writing an entire book of puns and wishes us to catch the mere flick of a syllable. There is a particularly beautiful semé in the closing pages of the book where Anna Livia Plurabelle takes leave of her husband and children to return to her father, the ocean, and be reborn again to cloud, rain, and river. Through and under her words we hear the names of the pantomimes she had delighted in as a child: "The woods are fond always. As were we their babes in. And robins in crews so . . . . . I won't take our laddy's lampern . . . . ". [619.23–24, 621.5]

One can generally distinguish a semé from a sequence, but a *foliation* often resembles a brief semé. If[1]

---

1. Wilder's manuscript ends here.

Appendix V

THORNTON WILDER

To Dounia Bunis Christiani, Scarsdale, New York

[MS. APCS—Photocopy—Northwestern University Library]

4 June 1963   P. O. Box 144.
                                                   Douglas, Ariz[ona]

Dear Miss Christiani:
    Perfectly delighted to receive your dissertation.[1] You have found an enormous amount of material for which readers will be deeply indebted to you. This is just a brief note; I shall send you a letter with tentative comments later.
    All FW students are greedy for more. Couldn't you do a paper on H. C. Andersen in FW?
    Let me also compliment you on your translation—the passages from "Solness"[2] are better than any translation I know. The theatre needs you!
    With thanks and many regards.

                     Sincerely yours
                     Thornton Wilder

1. Dounia Bunis Christiani (d. 1982) received her doctorate from Columbia University in New York where she worked with Professors William York Tindall and Elliott V. K. Doobie. It is not clear how Christiani came to write to Wilder. The two letters printed here were transcribed from photocopies Christiani made for her editor at Northwestern University Press, publisher of her *Scandinavian Elements of 'Finnegans Wake'* (1965). We have not located any other correspondence between Wilder and Christiani.

2. In her chapter, "H. C. Earwicker as Bygmester Ibsen" (46–56), Christiani translates passages from Henrik Ibsen's 1892 play *Bygmester Solness* (*The Master Builder*).

☐

To Dounia Bunis Christiani, Scarsdale, New York

[MS. ALS—Photocopy—Northwestern University Library]

6 June 1963 P. O. Box 144
[postmark: 10 June 1963] Douglas, Arizona.

Dear Miss Christiani:
 As I wrote you your thesis is a most valuable contribution to FW knowledge. Thank you many times for letting me see it. I have written Mrs Glasheen (Mrs Francis G., Farmington, Conn.) of all my pleasure in it.[1] I hope you will let her see it next. She is the "telephone central" of FW workers all over the world. In addition, she is level-headed and sensible, which cannot be said of the most of us! Her CENSUS TWO is just out; you will have richly swelled CENSUS THREE.
 I accompany this sheet with another of stray tentative comments on the Lexicon.[2] Please forgive my using "work paper"[3]—I always feel more at ease on it when there is a serious discussion going.

STRINDBERG. I agree with you that *The Dream Play* must play a considerable rôle; but, oh, I wish you could find a few more allusions of a concrete character. As [James] Atherton says: "Joyce always names his sources"—however indirectly and slyly. I don't know the title in Swedish,[4] but could it be hidden in:
420.33. . . . {wrongly} SPILLED. TRAUMconductor. Joyce has distorted *spelled* and *Drumcandra* to arrive at it.
 Incidentally, Strindberg's 3rd wife—29 years younger!—Harriet Bosse is
221.30 Bosse and stringbag.

HAMSUN[5] Joyce has a way of making a "foliation" of an author—
 generally concealing the most important clue: 28.35 {SALMON = SMOLT = SMOLLET}—29.1– 8. {Incidentally, that may be the

GROWING PLANT. . . 29.2 BAY TREE putting out branches, of The DREAM PLAY}; {the BRONTES, with their pen-names under BELL 7.22—8.6}

188.29–30   HANDSOME PAN:. . . . 27 pipes. . . . 29 buttonmuttonlegs. 30 syringe = SYRINX 188.27 VIKTORIA. . . . .36 HUNGER.

Do I imagine it? Are there other Hamsun titles hidden there? If so, why is it on a page subtended by the CONFITEOR. . . . "peccavi nimis cogitatione, verbo, et opere["]6 188.4. . . . . . 8 thought, would, and did. Cur. . . etc. Oh, why?!

KIERKEGAARD[7]   I think there's a third ENTEN-ELLER in FW 201.31 kirkeyaard. . . . . . 34 ayther nayther. {Maybe 8.26 nayther. . . nor}

I feel he plays a large part. Have you explored the title in Danish—"Diary of a Seducer" in ENTEN ELLER? And the Danish for *Fear and Trembling*? I seem to see him in the text on p. 467 aided by 19 Diarrhio. . . 24 churchyard. . . 36 serving = Severinus.

I forget REGINA'S last name.[8] Is she there? Explore Soubrignets and the mottoes in his books (as Joyce took Bruno's *hilaris. . . tristis*) and those *noms de plume* (Joyce uses 6 of Mangan's *noms de plume*.)

Incidentally: Terribly disappointed to read in your thesis that O[e]hlenschläger[9] is so mediocre a writer. Kierkegaard—whom I profoundly admire—frequently alludes to him.

IBSEN, a vast subject. Very grateful for what you have found. I am told that there is a book coming out in Germany about Ibsen in FW, detailing it play by play.[10] I seem to see him everywhere, esp. *When we Dead Awaken* (Irene sings 5 times "I am free!"; the last words "*pax vobiscum*").[11] Even the last pages of FW: Ellida rec'd the letter from her "man of the sea" from Archangel.[12]

I hope you aren't going to rest from your labors now. You have shown us how omnipresent Danish is, and things Danish. (Incidentally, I suspect that the many uses of COPENHAGEN include not only city, battle, and horse, but COBHA (COVA), wife of NOAH, and ancestress of the Irish (and of all of us!) through SHEM to *Nemedius*, and through JAPHETH to Parthalon.[)]

As I wrote you I think it would be wonderful if a Danish reader would pursue H. C. Andersen. Could you examine that Danish handyman of 141.8–26. He is JOE; but Joyce uses Robert Burns' song

"JOHN (HANS) ANDERSON, my JOE["], elsewhere in connections that might bring in H. C. A. See that whole complex on pp 412–414 Ender-Sanders-Shunders-von Andersen and 413.14 "sweet Standerson my ski." (Is that the princess with the pea under her 413.2?). Note 138.16 [i.e., .15]—I suspect those "CHArms" to be the initials pied: H. C. A. (Joyce is a devil!) Joyce makes such vast use of Lewis Carroll's "unwholesome" infatuation for young girls—does he play the same game with H. C. A.? # There he is again 221.6 as SAUNDERSON whom you are inclined to see as O[e]hlenshläger. Are there any obscurer works of HCA in there? Joyce loves to drag in the less known works. (I vaguely remember a novel called *To be or not to be*[13] which would lead us quite a chase, but is "Danish.")

Forgive all this vague conjecture. It's just to show you again how greedy I am for more.

I cannot say too often how grateful I am for your kindness in letting me see the thesis and grateful for all the material it brings.

      With many regards, Dr. Christiani
      Sincerely yours
      Thornton Wilder

The typescript[14] goes to you under separate cover with every safeguard the P. O. affords

GLOSSARY[15]

5.31	KIST-VAEN = CISTVAEN, boat shaped tomb (I don't know where I found this note)
18.13	Could this be translating into Danish Ibsen's Warrior's Home, Kjaemphga?[16]
20.28	Joyce could never get over hearing that Rebecca West (whose charge that he was "vulgar" he much resented) had "forty bonnets."
23.19	Norroena—*old dial*. Orkneys-Shetlands!
76.14 [i.e., 77.14]	Yes, in *Transition* Joyce published *wacht*.[17]
86.26	I didn't know PIKE Norw. girl. Notice, the fish PIKE is a LUCE 525.12 LUCIA JOYCE however, veiled, about the book. She is also a fleur de lys. . . lily. . . flag
87.25	NOAH = Benjamin Lee Guinness. The Guinnesses had an estate at CONG which they gave to the nation. See 87.10 Ham Shem and Japheth.

102.13	For your amusement: what A. L. P. has astride of her nose, like a clothespeg 208.22– 23 is a "barnacle"—sic . . . . .high spirited circus rider that she is. CIRCUS = menagerie = Mrs Noah.
123.16	ulykke. . . .!! Thanks!
126.	{your line 4 [i.e., .5]; my line 17} Ma'am, you don't pause to call our attention to HENDRIK?
133.36	KONGSEMNERNE = Ibsen's[18]
155.25	Delightful. . .thanks Lucia Joyce is also a LUCIOLE, firefly, glowworm throughout.
187.10	VITGAAF = Flemish: edition?
200.33	Yes, Joyce first printed: Oh, that!
236.9– 10	Mrs Glasheen reads D. Parelhoen = guinea-hen = Artemis.
244.7– 8	recently discovered: ONDSLOBU bog Latin, Great Britain; but your readings are fine
245.6	for your pleasure: MEI Chinese for young girl: Sir Henry Yule = traveller to China remember, the girl he left behind him.
306.3	could one add the Pope = Daddy of the Helvetia's Swiss guards will surprise us with the Papal Bull: Laudabilitur?
310.3	ALSO: Petersen Coil (protection against lightning—Joyce's dread). Joyce added Jomsborg, Selver later: the text first read "Synds, Bergen" (capitalized). I'm tempted to see Thor{e. . . peter. . e}sen, Ibsen's wife.[19]
414.34	Tingsom—etc. Many thanks! Joyce first printed singsomingenting. Perhaps a misprint, or an allusion to "La cigale agent chanté." But 416.27 was T—g. I suspect his house was also called Nixnix and nix because ⊙⊙ was the sign of an outhouse and you remember what was written over the door: 182.32
444.11	Thanks!!
452.8ff	For your amusement. Joyce told Miss Weaver that in this chapter Shaun was Hermes Trismegistus—i.e. IBIS-headed THOTH. So his sister is SISSIBIS and 452.10 thauthor .13 th'other. . . th'ether. The .12 phono is the Maronite cope PHAINO.—Oh, Lord, there's no end to it.
469.18	Will you accept a Spoonerism? J/ules V/erne—he's going round the world. . . 11 like Drake (quackquack . .9)
494.34	I'm glad to learn she's Cinderella. The spelling perhaps admits ASCOPART / ASKAPART conquered giant—Ballad of Sir Bevis of HAMPTON[20]
498.11	The Guinnesses Cong estate again. This among other things is the funeral of NOAH-GUINNESS. . . 497.27 Ma

	GENNIS... bott.. departure? There are his 498.13 gemini.. sons LORD IVEAGH and ARDILAUN... there is his lord mayor's chain 498.29 (he was the first *Lord* Mayor of Dublin). It looks to me that Bulg... Belg... etc is often Ben—Le—Guinness 498.36.
513.8	FLUT flood ORKAN hurricane. NOAH 513.23 is drunk on his liquor and is dancing. Singing Ta Ra Ra boom de ay. [.12] (TARARA = ARARAT!) CONG this astute (Guinness) was in LOUGH CORRIB (513.5 mARCus of CORRIG.[)] On the previous page: all those other great sea voyagers: Magellan... Columbus.. Vasco da Gama.. Cabot [.5, .7, .15, .18]
[Christiani: 525.12 Luce.]	
526.34	Yes, indeed. SCHIELEN. Yes indeed. One of the ugliest things in all literature is his LOUCHER-LUCIA and other jokes about the girl's squint.
536.1—ff	This is principally O. Wilde dying in the Rue des Beaux Arts (..10 Belle Arts =) with some Henry James (.17 Vereker "Lesson of the Master"); but do you see Ibsen getting in there? dying in Kristiana[21] capital of AKERSHUS country (... 13). Solness is identified with Towers of Babel...8 and steeples... 9.
538.32–33	CONG...Deucollion NOAH-GUINNESS
539.35	somewhere I found SKATHI, norse giantess, SKULD one of the norns.
550.14 [i.e., .15]	a big bakery-restaurant called that (Dampkok[k]en) in Oslo? It's in Hamsun's "Hunger"
561.8	SOVE is also sleep in Romany!
572.2–6	Is there any direct quotation from "SOLNESS" in this passage?
597.1	LAMFHADER—Lug of the long arms = i.e. of coincidences.
627.27 [i.e., 625.27]	Sw[edish]. still-silent. SAME = Lapp; sitta {city / to sit?[}] This was suggested to me by the Swedish Ambassador in Washington who is fascinated by the book![22]

I suspect that many of the knock-knock... and Castleknock... are Hilde Wangel at the door.[23] And 572.1–6 youngfries... backfrisking... who was that girl that Ibsen met in the Tyrol and served as model for Hilde. Is she here?

> Joyce read Ibsen in Danish! (Ellmann p. 707) [1982: 694].
> Well, that's the opposite of Unamuno[24] who learned Norwegian in order to read Ibsen but "was rewarded by being able to read Kierkegaard in Danish"!

1. See TW to AG, [? June 1963] and [? November 1963].

2. Part two of Christiani's book is a glossary of Scandinavian words (Danish and Dano-Norwegian) in *Finnegans Wake*. The first part of the book contains short essays on Joyce's use of Scandinavian materials and writers in the *Wake*. Christiani reviewed this letter when she revised her dissertation for publication, and, although she marked some of Wilder's notes with a check mark or "add," Wilder is not acknowledged in her Foreword.

3. The "work paper" for the letter and the Glossary is lined, three-hold loose leaf paper.

4. August Strindberg's *Ett drömspel* (*A Dream Play*) was written in 1902 and first produced in 1907.

5. Knut Hamsun (1859–1952), the Norwegian writer who won the 1920 Nobel Prize for literature. Among his novels are: *Pan* (1894), *Victoria* (1898), and *Hunger* (1890).

6. Part of the prayer, "I Confess": "I have sinned exceedingly in thought, word, and deed."

7. Søren Kierkegaard (1813–1855), the Danish religious philosopher. The first part of *Enten-Eller* (*Either/Or*) was published in Copenhagen in 1843 under the pseudonym Victor Eremita; *Forforenens dagbog* "The Diary of a Seducer" is contained in *Enten-Eller*. *Frygt og bæven* (*Fear and Trembling*), under the pseudonym, Johannes de Silentio, was published in Copenhagen also in 1843.

8. Kierkegaard broke his engagement to Regine Olsen in September–October 1841. In their "Historical Introduction" to *Either/Or* Howard V. Hong and Edna H. Hong write: "There was one reader, however, Regine Olsen, whom Kierkegaard wanted to discern him behind the pseudonyms, especially the writer behind the pseudonymous diary, as part of his plan to make it easier for her to part with him. 'When I left 'her,' I begged God for one thing, that I might succeed in writing and finishing *Either/Or* (this was also for her sake, because *The Seducer's Diary* was, in fact, intended to repel, or as it says in *Fear and Trembling*, 'When the baby is to be weaned, the mother blackens her breast.')" (*Either/Or: Part I*, edited and translated by Howard V. Hong and Edna H. Hong, Princeton University Press, 1987, xvi).

9. Adam Gottlob Oehlenschläger (1779–1850), the Danish poet and dramatist.

10. It is not clear what book Wilder means. He may have heard from Glasheen that a student in Oslo, Bjorn Tysdahl, was working on a doctoral dissertation on this subject later published as *Joyce and Ibsen: A Study in Literary Influence* (Oslo and New York: Norwegian Universities Press, 1968).

11. It is Maia Rubek, not Irene, who sings "I am free, I am free, I am free!/No longer the prison I'll see!/I am free as a bird, I am free!" after her husband, Professor Rubek, and Irene walk off into the mist and are then buried in an avalanche. The final words of the play, "Pax vobiscum!" are said by the Nun.

12. Ellida Wangel, the second wife of Dr. Wangel, a country doctor, in Ibsen's *The Lady from the Sea* (1888). Arkhangelsk, Archangel in English, is a port city in Russia named after a monastery dedicated to the Archangel Michael.

13. Hans Christian Andersen's novel *At være eller ikke være* (*To Be, or Not to Be?*) (1857).

14. Christiani's dissertation.

15. In this Glossary Wilder comments and offers suggestions on entries in Christiani's dissertation.

16. Ibsen's play, *Kjæmpehøjen* (1850) has been variously translated as *The Warrior's Barrow* or *The Burial Mound*.

17. The first printing of pages 75–103 of the *Wake* appeared in *transition*, 4 (July 1927), 46–65.

18. Ibsen's *The Pretenders* (1863).

19. Ibsen met his future wife, Suzannah Thoresen in 1856; they were married in 1858.

20. A medieval romance which exists in several versions including Scandinavian and Celtic.

21. K/Christiana, now Oslo.

22. Wilder met Gunnar Jarring, the Royal Swedish Ambassador to the United States, at Yale University in November 1960. See Jarring to Wilder, 15 December 1960 (YCAL).

23. Hilde Wangel, in Ibsen's *The Lady from the Sea* (1888), is Dr. Wangel's daughter from his first marriage.

24. Miguel de Unamuno (1864–1936), the Spanish philosopher and writer.

Appendix VI

A Puzzle[1]

THORNTON WILDER

Who were our hero's ancestors?
Finnegans Wake is largely about the successive invasions of Ireland—Norse, Norman, British (Cromwell's and the "Black and Tans")
The hero was Norse—Earwicker—Eyrvikr or Eyrawwyggla.
To begin first with the ancestry of his son SHEM. 169.13 ff[2] [169.1 ff].

169.16 [169.4] RAGNAR LODBROG. In her census Mrs Glasheen has found seven allusions; to these should be added 19.4; 343.31; 440.29. (Joyce gives Ragnar Bluebeard because, I think, he is superimposing the pre-Norman Jarl van Hoother, Earl of HOWTH—see HOFED BEN EDAR 30.23 [30.11] Head of, Hill of, Howth—these Earls are represented as Bluebeards.)

169.16 [169.4] Horrild Hairwire. Looks like Harald Fairhair (Haarfager) but we see another collocation on
      p. 444.5 (family) both harefoot and loadenbrogued.
Which gives us
RAGNAR and Harold Harefoot, King of the Anglo-Saxons, 1035–40

{One might say that Joyce intends to give a *general* impression of early raiders, but we tend to find that he is very precise within the general. Here, for instance, his spelling of RAGNAR is meant to remind us of Vico's mythical-semi-divine cycle: regin x rögn = the Gods.}

169.17 [169.5]   None of us know what to do with "Mr. Bbyrdwood de Trop Blogg." A friend of Joyce's father was a Mr. Beardwood.

{Before I leave this page—though it is not pertinent to the proposed puzzle—let me point out how closely packed the text is:
        169.23 [169.11] St. Patrick was called "Adzehead" by the Irish.
        169.24 [169.12] Hoel, duke of Burgundy.
        169.24 [169.12] Nuad, hero-semi-divinity of Ancient Ireland had a "silver arm"
        170.25 [i.e., 169.13] Parnell was called the "uncrowned King of Ireland." Etc.}

NOW TO EARWICKER'S ANCESTRY 30.13–ff. [30.1-ff]
There is the HAROLD again—three times 30.14 [30.2], 33 [30.21]; 31.8–9—but coalescing this time with HAROLD II defeated by William the Conqueror 31.14 at the Battle of Hastings 30.34 [30.23–.24]

What we *don't* see are all these
30.18 [30.6–.8]
    GLUES 97.20
    GRAVYS = (gravy duck 224.6 [i.e., 224.7]) 97.20
    NORTHEASTS
    ANKERS
    EARWICKERS of Sidlesham
    HUNDRED of MANHOOD
329.7 FF 375.3–4; 9

    Is it possible that this is Saga or Edda material?
    It may be Hebrew. For DUMLAT 30.22 [30.10] read TALMUD.

    We assume that this page (recurrent throughout the book) is a dream-development of a picture hanging on Mr. Earwicker's wall; entitled and based on the Ballad of Chevy Chase,—an innkeeper greeting Royalty which stops at his door while hunting. (It[s] last appearance is quite beautifully in his wife's farewell 622.24–33)
                      x x
    The christening of the Norse invader begins 325.30 {note St Clotilde who converted her husband Clovis, king of the Franks to Xity [i.e., Christianity]} and in the pages following his marriage to a daughter of Ireland. All terribly mixed up with other things. You'll see Woden's ravens Huggin and Munin on 327.36 combined with the ravens and doves that Noah sent from the ark.
                      x
    Lund's Tower is twice in the book: 137.9; 320.22 (and 372.23).
                      x

I'm sure you're right about SAM[a] and LAPP in 625.27; because I found somewhere (but now I've lost it) that Our Heroine is described as wearing a "lapsummer dress" [199.13].

x

We're continually find new beauties in that closing "fare well to the world."

She is Noah's wife and she is Eve. As Noah's wife,:

622.15 "Afartodays, afeartonights, and me as with you in thadark." So: 619.20–21 Folty and folty all the nights . . . .30 [i.e., .36] comfort {Noah in Hebrew}

She is many Eves, including Eva MacMurrough married by the Norman invader Strongbow 626.2

So: 619.28 makmerriers {Her head is singing "Old King Cole["] etc}

619.34 Yawhawaw = Jalaveh and Hebr. HAWWAH, Eve

And since it's the Christmas season, there are five Christmas carols or anthems near the top of p. 502; but I don't know why they're there.

LATER: Some Norse material:

539.35 my skat and skuld (SKATH and Norse SKULD) . . FLUKIE of the Ravens: seems to be WODEN. . . . . . .via LOKI?

---

1. This undated text (probably written between 1957 and 1963) is among Wilder's notes for *Finnegans Wake*. These notes appear at certain points to be lecture notes and at other points to be addressed to someone in particular as a letter.

2. In his early work with the *Wake*, Wilder counts up from the last line on pages that open chapters. We include the line numbering counting from the top line as line 1.

Appendix VII

Twins[1]

THORNTON WILDER

BOANERGES. A name given to James and John, the sons of Zebedee, because they wanted to call down "fire from heaven" to consume the Samaritans for not "receiving" the Lord Jesus. It is said in the Bible to signify "sons of thunder," but "sons of tumult" would probably be nearer its meaning (Luke 9,54; see Mark 3,17) (Brewer's Dict.)[2]

        22.32   Boanerges, Jarl von Hoother
        26.19   Mr. Tumulty
J. Rendel Harris[3]   *The Dioscuri in [the] Christian Legends,*[4]
                                                    Cambridge 1903
———   *The Cult of the Heavenly Twins,*   "   1906
———   *Boanerges*   "   1913

These books discuss the importance of TWINS in mythology. Twins are often treated as marvels and subject to taboos. They appear in mythology are [i.e., as] children of the sky or children of the Thunder-God (Kabiri); associated with fertility, rain-charms, healings and are patrons of marriage, sailors and horses. They are often to be detected in mythology by pairs of names, which closely resemble each other, or alliterate or rhyme etc. The chief twin deities in Greek mythology are [the] Dio[s]curi, Castor and Pollux[5]: others include Herakles and Iphikles, Idas and Lynceus, Amphion and Zethus.[6] Dioscurism is not confined to Greek mythology: cf. The Sanskrit Acvins[7]; Semitic Jabal, Jubal and Thubal. (N. B. triads of names of the same kind are sometimes found occasionally female pairs or triads).

Harris saw survivals of Dioscurism in early Christian mythology, especially in the saints. Twin saints include SS Acius and Aceolus,

Donatianus and Rogatianus, *Crispin* and Crispinian, Speusippus Mesippus & Elasippus, Protasius and Gervasius, Vitalis and Agricola, Florus and Laurus. Even St Michael seems to have started as a Dioscurus.

Twin-lore is found in the apocryphal books of the New Testament especially the 'Acts of St Thomas.' Judas Thomas is the twin of Christ, known as Didymus which means 'twin.' 'Thomas' also means 'twin' though it is mistranslated as 'abyss.' For 'Acts of ST T' see Brewer's Dict: T in India, patron saint of masons and architects, symbol a builder's square. A different apocryphal tradition calls him *James* Thomas; yet another speaks of Judas *Thaddeus*, the Lord's brother. There is also Addai, the brother of Jesus.

Rendel Harris was not at first widely accepted but was taken up by A. H. Krappe; see his standard work The Science of Folklore for summary.[8] Rendel appears in FW on p. . . .[9] (Rendel's are also a popular brand of contraceptives[)].

There are hundreds of these Dioscuric doublets or triads in FW, from p. 3[.25] Jhem or Shen. 7[.22] Bronto. . . Brunto (Thunder plus Giordano Bruno); long lists on p. 44 and 325 gosse and bosse [.16] &c. Hengist and Horsa [272.17], Heber and Heremon [14.35– .36] etc must be taken as in this category.

The most important of the TIM-TOM series is 258 even Garda Didymus and Garda Domas [.30–.31]. . . pray-your-prayers Timothy and Back-to-Bunk Tom [.35–.36].

431.32 dieobscure
456.30 THADDEUS
491.6 crispin

1. This may be the "leaf" referred to in TW to AG, [? October 1962–II]. The typed sheet has some additional notes in Wilder's hand. At several points in the text there are check marks which may have been made by Glasheen. We have changed Wilder's page and line references to *Finnegans Wake* from his 22/32 to the format used throughout this book: 22.32. Wilder's interest in twins was more than simply academic as he had a twin brother, Theophilus, who died at birth.

2. It is not known which edition of *Brewer's Dictionary of Phrase and Fable* Wilder is using. The Rev. Ebenezer Cobham Brewer's *Dictionary* was first published in 1870.

3. Throughout this note Wilder types "Rendell" in the name of J[ames]. Rendel Harris (1852–1941). We have silently corrected this error.

4. Published in London by the firm of C. J. Clay and Sons in 1903 and not Cambridge as Wilder has typed.

5. Wilder here follows Rendel in using the Roman names. In Greek mythology they are Kastor and Polydeuces.

6. Rendel's definition of twins goes beyond identical or fraternal twins. Herakles and Iphikles, for example, were half-brothers, Idas and Lynceus and Amphion and Zethus were brothers but not identified in mythology as twins.

7. Açvins or Celestial Horseman in the Rig-Veda.

8. Alexander Haggerty Krappe (1894–1947), *The Science of Folk-Lore* (London: Methuen, 1930).

9. Wilder does not indicate the page in the *Wake*, and Glasheen has no entry for J. Rendel Harris in any edition of the *Census*.

Appendix VIII

The Strange Cold Fowl in Finnegans Wake[1]

ADALINE GLASHEEN

A Grail Quest starts on the first page of *Finnegans Wake* when an "unquiring one" is sent "west in quest" of the ultimate truth about Everyman Earwicker, his "tumptytumtoes,"[3.33] which are said to stick up like pikes in the sign of Virgo (26.13). We glimpse the chalice not being drained (31) and the chalice being broken (44), but the quest soon peters out in blind upon blind and arid alley. Folk memory fails us, and the man-in-the-street, and the judge on the bench.

    Then we come to the section that Joyce called "The Hen" (104–124) and are promised the guidance of the woman who knew him well, his wife, Mrs. Anna Livia Earwicker. Earlier (11.12–.13) we have seen her "picking here, pecking there," gathering spoils from a darkling battlefield; later she takes those spoils out of her "culdee sacco" [210.1] and gives them to her children; but her great treasure is a letter from America which will clear her husband's name, rehabilitate that Everyman, whose inception, descent, and destination are "*temporarily* wrapped in obscenity" [150.31–.32].

    Anna Livia wants to write an impressive defense of Man, but she cannot so much as settle on a title, and finally hands over the battered letter to her son, Shem the Penman, and settles for a collaboration. Shem has not got the remotest idea what the letter is about, but he is the artist as a clever young man and cannot admit ignorance. Mock heroic, echoing "The Rape of the Lock" and "The Nun's Priest's Tale," he tells how his mother, a little hen, scratched on a dunghill and produced the wonderful letter; he subjects the letter to the scrutiny of paleontology, bibliography, conjectural biography, psychoanalysis, Marxism, and what not, making a merry rout of higher criticism, seemingly only to enrich the confusion of the Quest. One thing is plain, the letter is not much to make scholarly ado about; yet throughout the rest of the book, it is pursued for its own sake. Shem and Shaun, his twin, once fought over who stole a pig (or a *Hamlet*); from now on they fight over who owns the letter. In a later section of *Finnegans Wake* we learn why they both can claim it.

Now, however, here is the hen, Belinda Doran (a *poule*), scratching a letter (a *poulet*) and watched by a shivering boy (to all purposes, a *poulard*):

> About that original hen. Midwinter . . . was in the offing and Premver a promise of a pril when . . . an iceclad shiverer, merest of bantlings observed a cold fowl behaviourising strangely on that fatal midden or chip factory or comicalbottomed copsjute (dump for short) . . . (110.22–.26)

In a later passage "original hen" becomes "our regional's hin and the gander of Hayden" (482.16–.17), meaning that hen and boy have been the temptress Eve and whoever took a gander at her in the Garden of Eden. ("Hayden" mixes up Eden with B. R. Haydon's picture *The Curse of Adam*[2] and Haydn's *Creation*, which is based on *Genesis* and *Paradise Lost*.) The dump or dunghill is the body of Humpty-Dumpty Everyman, recumbent in the landscape after fall. It is also the dunghill that John Shakespeare kept on Henley Street; and it is William Shakespeare, whom Voltaire described as a dunghill, containing some pearls of genius.

Intent, shivering boy and strange fowl suggest Freud's Little Arpad[3] and his chicken. Later on, sure enough (478–482), they are tricked out with glosses from *Totem and Taboo*, but now we are quickly assured that the pair are, of all things, respectable. The cold (chaste) boy is "keepy little Kevin in the despondful surrounding of such sneezing cold" (110.32–.33). Kevin is Shaun, the good Earwicker twin, honest Kevin, frank Kevin. As the Irish St. Kevin he figures in *Finnegans Wake* as a type of religious male frigidity, and the word "keepy" ties him to the equally frigid saint of science, the child Elizabeth called her "young Lord Keeper," Francis Bacon.

As for the cold fowl, Belinda (usually Biddy or Bridget) Doran, she exemplifies all that led Thackeray to complain that since *Tom Jones*, no one has been allowed to create a man. Shem mocks at those who oppose her:

> . . . they are not justified, those gloompourers who grouse that letters have never been quite their old selves again since that weird weekday in bleak Janiveer (yet how palmy a date in a waste's oasis!) when to the shock of both, Biddy Doran looked at literature (112.23–27).

I had reasons, unconnected with my present subject, for thinking Biddy Doran might be America's own strange Delia Bacon, a Victorian lady who found Shakespeare low and replaced him with a chaste and unreal Francis Bacon; though there is no open mention of her in "The Hen," Joyce has a way of blazing his trails. He may camouflage them, he may let them take on protective coloring, but he blazes. It occurred to me that Delia was a lady who gave life and reason to hunting out Francis Bacon from "hides and hints and misses in prints" [20.11] in the texts of Shakespeare's plays. Joyce likes to imitate the activities of the people he writes about and he likes his readers to participate strenuously in his prose. If Delia was hiding and hinting, her disguise would not be impenetrable, for Baconians are simple-minded. I looked up "Delia" in Webster because Joyce is obsessed with the magic meaning of names. In *Finnegans Wake* he uses them as a Morality uses Good Deeds or Mr. Worldly Wiseman, plays endlessly with Stephen-Crown, Peter-Rock, Anne-Grace, Margaret-Maggy-Gretta-Pearl-Daisy-Onion, Tristram-Sad, Shandy-Mirth, Francis-Free, Susanna-Lily, Ezekiel Irons-May God Stengthen You, etc.

Delia, I found, is Artemis, born on Delos. I went on to mythology— *The Golden Bough*, Robert Graves, the 11th *Britannica*—and was surprised to find how specifically Joyce links, not just Biddy, but Anna Livia herself to the goddess Artemis. I had known, of course, that Anna Livia is light in the dark night of *Finnegans Wake*, at once "Their mivver, Mrs Moonan" (157.14–.15) and something like the Virgin Muse of the Elizabethan poets. I had known Artemis was moon and virgin huntress and white goddess, but I had not known she was originally a goddess of fertility rites, chastened by myth-makers, as the Irish Brigit was chastened into St. Bridget. At all times, Artemis was a sort of rag-bag goddess of life and death, with many titles and attributes. Here are some of those attributes which Joyce uses in *Finnegans Wake*. Note how they cluster around the hen, especially on pp. 110–113.

In various times and places, Artemis or Delia healed and destroyed; she was peaceful, she was fierce and orgiastic; she was "The Lady of Rivers", and of the moon as the source of all fertilizing water; she took her share of first fruits (12.19); she collected "spoils" of vegetables and animals (11.18–.19, 209.28); she was goddess of the chase and of all wild animals (112.16, 113.3); as wildlife goddess she was worshipped in totemist cults, which explains her link to *Totem and Taboo*; she was virgin (110.25); she was a mother, patron of generation, the rearing of all young animals and humans, and of the field (112.13–.18, 244.8–.11); she was a bear goddess (110.2–.5), a lion goddess (112.22); she was worshipped as a fir-tree (113.6), a nut-tree (113.3, 273 note 3, 623.31–.32), a date-palm (112.26); and finally Delia was worshipped on the Acropolis as a guinea-hen; Joyce says (482.18–.20) that Kevin was in the High Street, "shooing a Guiney gagag, Poulepinter, that found the dogumen number one . . ." and elsewhere (236.9–.10) she is praised as "A paaralone!

A paaralone!," i.e. a *parelhoen* which is Dutch for "guinea-hen." Before I leave the subject, I had better add that to the Elizabethans a guinea-hen was a whore.

Delia is then the hen. I was only mildly surprised to find her a goddess, for New England spinsters are an eerie lot, and Delia Salter Bacon was no common woman. She wrote Nathaniel Hawthorne, apologizing for sending him a "patched and scratched and ill-looking manuscript," and he told her, ". . . you have acquired some of the privileges of an inspired person and a prophetess."[4] She was, in fact, possessed.

My information about her comes from Vivian Hopkins, *Prodigal Puritan* (1959), from F. W. Wadsworth, *The Poacher from Stratford* (1958), and from Joyce's source-book, Theodore Bacon, *Delia Bacon* (1888). From these I learned that Delia Bacon (1811–1859) was a sort of Margaret Fuller or Verena Tarrant, going about New England and speaking of the past, by inspiration, to enthusiastic audiences who found her "the very muse of history." Delia was born on the frontier, bred in New England, jilted by a Yale divinity student. Thereafter, she came to London to pull down the vanity of the boor she called "The Old Player," "The Poacher from Stratford," "Lord Leicester's Groom," "Will the Jester," etc. (71–72). In his place she raised a secret clique of genteel illuminati, who wrote all the best Elizabethan books in order to reach into the future and foster Science and Social Welfare. The clique, headed by Bacon and Raleigh, sounds a good deal like the Institute for Advanced Study. More dashing, of course.

Delia was not the first to believe Shakespeare did not write his plays, and she was a "Groupist" rather than a strict Baconian; but Bacon was her special knight in shining armor, and in popular opinion Delia is the original Baconian. Joyce treats her as such, usually, and so will I.

Nathaniel Hawthorne created Delia Bacon, his essay "Recollections of a Gifted Woman" set her image.[5] He was in his consulship when Delia came to England in 1856, and, unlike Emerson, who dropped her at a word from Carlyle, Hawthorne never stopped feeling that she mattered and ought to be right. He gave Delia money, got a publisher for *The Philosophy of Shakespeare's Plays Unfolded* (1857), and wrote a preface for it.

For this, Hawthorne got small thanks from that "sensitive," "tumultuous," and "most noble" character, Delia Bacon. When his preface pussyfooted and did not show absolute belief in Francis Bacon, she used the preface, but cast him off "with passionate resentment." Delia was one with her faith:

> . . . I used to be somebody . . . now I am nothing but this work . . . I have lived for three years as much alone with God and the dead as if I had been a departed spirit . . . I will put on one of the dresses I used

to wear the last time I made my appearance in the world, and try to look as much like a survivor as the circumstances will permit.[6]

This was when Hawthorne was still in her good graces and coming to call. He expected Delia to be an old biddy, but she charmed him. She had been beautiful and still had much of youth about her, when, eyes shining, color coming and going, she bubbled about the "clew and key" she had hunted out of Lord Bacon's letters, a clew and key which unlocked not only Shakespeare's plays, but also the "treasures of the tomb" at Stratford, for it was there that the posthumous papers of the Bacon society were hidden. (This ploy was not old hat in 1857. Delia was an original hen.)

She did not go after the papers until she finished her book. Then she went to Stratford and, unappalled by Shakespeare's doggerel curse on grave-robbers (102.21–.23), she took a dark lantern and stole into the church in dead of night, prepared to rape the lock of the tomb (423.25). Delia left no account of this excursion, but Hawthorne says that when she came face to face with the tomb, ". . . a doubt stole into her mind . . . she was afraid to hazard the shock of uplifting the stone and finding nothing" ["Recollections," 111].

Failure of nerve did not unsettle Delia's faith. She believed, went mad believing, died mad, and is buried in New Haven, Connecticut.

Hawthorne got out of it a symbol he never put in a novel. Joyce, the world's foremost snapper-up of symbols, did put her in *Finnegans Wake*, where at first he is content to follow Hawthorne—Delia is attractive, not mad in any vulgar, obvious way. Hawthorne says:

> Miss Bacon imagined herself to have received (what is certainly the greatest boon ever assigned to mortals) a high mission . . . with adequate powers for its accomplishment . . . special interpositions of Providence were forwarding her . . . I was sensible of a ladylike feeling of propriety in Miss Bacon, and a New England orderliness in her character, and, in spite of her bewilderment, a sturdy common sense ["Recollections," 108–109].

Joyce—or Shem—says:

> . . . her socioscientific sense is sound as a bell, sir, her volucrine automutativeness right on normalcy: she knows, she just feels she was kind of born to lay and love eggs . . . she is ladylike in everything she does and plays the gentleman's part every time (112.11–.17).

Hawthorne and Joyce agree, Delia is inspired, common sensical, ladylike. What Joyce calls her "automutativeness" refers to her writing, "I am only an automaton obeying some former purpose, obeying rather the Power above . . ."[7] The phrase, "plays the gentleman's part" has cricket connotations, but also refers to the snobbishness of the Baconians and allied heretics, who are anxious as Shakespeare for their candidate to be gentry.

It is mostly Joyce's way to subject characters to charm or guilt by association: a quotation turns Gretta Conroy into Cathleen ni Houlihan; if we did not know Buck Mulligan to be Antinous, Aegisthus, Claudius, we would not hate him near so much. Delia Bacon's attractions are defined when Joyce associates her with the only kind of female he thought worth putting in a novel, femalely female, all heart, not a brain cell ticking—Chaucer's, Partlet (124.23–.24), Pope's Belinda, Sheridan's Lydia Languish, and his own Maggy or Gretta Conroy. Twenty years ago, he thought Gretta out and now uses her for "a symbol of something" [*Dubliners*, 211] as Yeats uses Red Hanrahan in "The Tower." Joyce says of the hen:

> The bird in the case was Belinda of the Dorans, a more than quinquegintarian . . . and what she was scratching at the hour of klokking twelve looked for all this zogzag world like a goodish-sized sheet of letterpaper originating by transhipt from Boston (Mass.) . . . Dear whom it proceeded to mention Maggy well & allathome's health well only the hate turned the mild on *the van* Houtens and the general's elections with a *lovely* face of some born gentleman with a beautiful present of wedding cakes for dear thankyou Chriesty and with grand funferall of poor Father Michael don't forget unto life's & Muggy well how are you Maggy & hopes soon to hear well & must now close it with fondest to the twoinns . . . from . . . affectionate largelooking tache of tch. The stain, and that a teastain . . . marked it off on the spout of the moment as a genuine relique of ancient Irish pleasant pottery of that lydialike languishing class known as a hurry-me-o'er-the-hazy. (111.5–.24)

The letter's confused inanity may be a judgment on Delia's intellect, on all female intellect, but it does not mimic her prose—Delia wrote beautiful fanatic sentences which do not get anywhere. Rather, it is the letter of an uneducated woman, such a letter, I imagine, as Nora Joyce wrote home to Galway or got from girl friends gone to America. Joyce certainly associated the name Maggy or Gretta with Nora: he calls her Gretta in "The Dead," and she eloped with him under the name of Miss Gretta Greene. It is equally certain that the letter aims to establish the fact that Maggy is well, but, on careful reading, it is impossible to decide whether it is written to Maggy, about Maggy or by Maggy.

In any case, it is a splendid production because peculiarly feminine in its mixture of optimism and whine: there has been a wedding but "hate" (ate and heat) turned the milk in the Van Houtens cocoa, and since cocoa is a drink of peace with Joyce, it seems that the milk of human kindness has soured; Father Michael is dead; tea, a substance denoting sex with Joyce (and Ibsen) stains the page, blotting out the signature. Biddy has been Pandora (14.20)—Greek *doron* or gift—and will be again (209–212). The letter is Pandora's box of ills, with hope tucked in the corner.

From here on out, a deal of words is lavished on the letter.[8] Shaun the Post, who sets out to deliver the letter just at twelve (403–404) is obsessed with its importance and, unlike Shem, takes it very seriously. Shaun believes he is commanded to deliver the letter by "a power coming over me that is put upon me from on high" (409.36–410.1). His vocation was perhaps suggested by another passage in "Recollections of a Gifted Woman." Hawthorne tells how Delia's book failed: reviewers glanced at it and "essayed to kick the volume deeper into the mud . . ." (113.6–.7, 370.2).

> . . . it has been the fate of this remarkable book never to have had more than a single reader . . . since my return to America, a young man of genius and enthusiasm has assured me that he has positively read the book from beginning to end, and is completely a convert to its doctrines . . . it belongs surely to this one individual who has done her so much justice as to know what she wrote, to place Miss Bacon in her due position before the public and posterity ["Recollections," 116].

The young man was William O'Connor, author of *The Good Gray Poet*. He did deliver Delia's doctrines in a novel, *Harrington: a Story of True Love* (1860) in which he says he would rather be insane with Delia than sane with Dr. Johnson (370.4, .12–.13; 447.6–.19). It is not a position Joyce could take. In "Scylla and Charybdis" (*Ulysses*, 213–214), Stephen Dedalus disowns belief in the Platonic dialogue and parlor game he has made of Shakespearean biography, and Joyce seems to have thought that this denial gives him the right to be contemptuous of Delia's "dishorned discipular manram," who lies down in public with "the human lioness" (112.22). O'Connor may even have suggested the lovely sentence (120.12–.14) about the "ideal reader suffering from an ideal insomnia" who nuzzles the letter "till his noddle sink or swim," a gibe which persistent readers of *Finnegans Wake*—masochists all—take to themselves. I think it is a gibe at O'Connor or Shaun the Post or any man who fancies the eternal feminine to lead on to anything but the eternal feminine.

For that is the mystery revealed, or, at any rate, the last solution advanced. Some have thought the letter a message from Above, some have thought it a valuable artifact, dug up from the past; but, dying, Anna Livia tells her husband proudly that she herself scratched out the letter for herself to find someday. She did it for love of him.

> Scratching it and patching at with . . . what scrips of nutsnolleges I pecked up me meself . . . But once done, dealt and delivered, tattat, you're on the map. Rased on traumscript from Maston, Boss. (623.31–.36)

It is common enough for girls to write letters to the self they will be in ten or twenty years, but this is a little different. When young, Anna Livia splits into discrete personalities like Prince's Christine Beauchamp of Boston, the Chriesty of the letter.[9] Later, as we shall see, she is healed and made whole, but, like Miss Beauchamp, she always expects to find a letter from some one of those personalities, a letter containing she knows not what. Thus, the letter is from a woman to herself.

Woman is never more ambiguous than here. Will her message *raise* the man or *raze* him? I think she aims to do both, as Hilda Wangel raises and razes Master-builder Solness. Joyce's women are all two or more faced. And how can she think so frail a production as her letter can raise or raze? The answer to this was given by Pope in "The Rape of the Lock":

> Some secret truths, from learned pride conceal'd,
> To maids alone and children are reveal'd.
> What tho' no credit doubting Wits may give?
> The fair and innocent shall still believe.

And by Joyce in "The Hen" (109.30–.33):

> Who in his heart doubts either that the facts of feminine clothiering are there all the time or that the feminine fiction, stranger than the facts, is there also at the same time . . .

The Philosophy of Shakespeare's Plays Unfolded is precisely a letter from a woman to herself, sorely neglecting "the enveloping facts" (109.14); it is a feminine clothing of the starved body of Shakespearean biography with a feminine and ladylike fiction. When Delia Bacon did not put intuition to the test of truth and open the tomb, she became a matchless example of woman's capacity for creating illusion and choosing to live with it, go crazy with it. She is a purer example than Amelia Sedley or Emma Bovary.

In playful, Chaucerian anti-feminism, Joyce teases Delia by associating her with those light-comedy charmers, Partlet, Belinda, Lydia Languish: the first believes in her husband's wisdom, the second lives with gnomes and salamanders and makes the world's fuss about the least of rapes, the third writes letters to herself and dotes on an imaginary ensign. Fair, innocent, gay believers all.

There is, however, nothing gay about that powerful illusionist, Gretta Conroy. She defines the dreadful side of the hen goddess, and in order to show why Joyce associates those cold chickens, Gretta and Biddy Doran, I must digress and speak of "The Dead," a good story, woefully misread by male critics, who have learned to attend to what a woman seems to be doing rather than to what she accomplishes.

"The Dead" is thought suitable for the young, and I have read introductions to it in a good many Freshman texts. From these, I gather that "The Dead" is read either as a story in which the pretensions of an obtuse husband (say Torvald Helmer) are punctured and he enters into a more sensitive relation with his lovely wife, or it is read as a particularly "beautiful" account of a man's lyric acceptance of death. Certainly Gabriel Conroy is obtuse and has chilled his wife with some years of mild sexual neglect; but I see nothing beautiful in her throwing cold water on him when, at last, she rouses his desire for her, nor do I think it likely to lead to good understanding or happy relations. No. *Dubliners* is a series of horrid warnings, meant to make Irish flesh creep, and "The Dead" is the horridest warning of all. It is a ghost story, like *The Turn of the Screw*, in which the dead bring the living over to their side.

"The Dead" is about Gabriel who does his poor best to keep out of the clutch of romantic Ireland—reviews for an English paper, vacations on the continent. One night he watches his wife listen to an old Irish song and is swept by desire for her. She thoughtfully raises from the past the memory of a "gentle boy." Mr. Ellmann says the boy was a beau of Nora Joyce's from Galway, named Michael Bodkin, called Michael Furey in "The Dead," and Father Michael in *Finnegans Wake*. Gretta tells her husband how Michael came out to see her on a cold night, ". . . the poor fellow at the end of the garden, shivering. . . ." Michael died soon after.

> —And what did he die of so young, Gretta? Consumption, was it?
> —I think he died for me, she answered.
> A vague terror seized Gabriel at this answer as if, in that hour when he had hoped to triumph, some impalpable and vindictive being was coming against him, gathering forces against him in its vague world. But he shook himself free of it with an effort of reason. . .
> —It was in the winter, she said . . . [*Dubliners*, 221–222]

As in *The Turn of the Screw* it is not clear whether Gretta's revenant has its own malignant life, or whether it is the woman's vindictive cold that comes against her husband. Which it is, matters little to Gabriel who is easily unmanned by the beauty of Gretta's plain preference for the male of her own making, and by the neat staginess of her reply, "I think he died for me."

It is stagey, right out of Yeats' play, *Cathleen ni Houlihan*. Cathleen is like Gretta, no longer beautiful, but she has a glamour when she comes singing of "yellow-haired Donough that was hanged in Galway." Enchanted, her next victim asks, "What was it that brought him to his death?" Cathleen (whom Joyce elsewhere describes as "the old sow that eats her farrow") [*Portrait*, 203] answers, "He died for love of me: many a man has died for love of me."[10] The victim then leaves his human bride to follow the phantom sow. The young Yeats may have thought it beautiful to die for Ireland, but Joyce did not think a man should die for Ireland, or for a woman, or for anything. "Damn death. Long live life!" [*Ulysses*, 591]. He really did believe it.

I cannot feel much sympathy for Gabriel—he crosses so meekly to the dead, goes soft, embraces the romantic possibilities of endless cold, merges for good and all with Gretta's zombie, Michael Furey. Having eaten Gabriel, Gretta goes right off to sleep, not, I fancy, uncomplacent. As Ireland and/or a woman, she has revenged her neglect, brought down another man by her charms, and, like Delia Bacon, she has imposed her illusion on another person. In the first story of *Dubliners* a chalice was broken: in the last story lance and chalice lie paralyzed by "wholehail, snaeffell, dreardrizzle or sleetshowers of blessing, where it froze in chalix . . ." (552.35–.36).

Partlet, Belinda, Lydia define the silliness of female illusion: Gretta-Maggy defines its menace and contagion. In "The Dead" and in "The Hen" the same elements are present—cold female or chalice, cold female's document from the past, shivering boy; and, as Gretta's story keeps Gabriel from possessing her, so the hen's letter is credited with "euchring the finding of the Ardagh chalice" (110.34–.35), which I assume to be the True Grail. The Ardagh chalice is the greatest art-work out of the Irish past, and with its introduction, simple sexual cold becomes what keeps the artist from the cup of inspiration. In *Finnegans Wake*, as in *Ulysses*, the true artist is Shakespeare and the false is the Baconian's version of Bacon. I must warn against interpreting this duality in any simple fashion.

I do not think the common reader has any notion of the extent and fervor of the Victorian's idolatry of Francis Bacon. Bacon's writing was, I think, dead for the Victorians, as for us, but they were staunch in innocent trust of Science, a messiah Science; and Bacon was touted to them as Science's John the Baptist. His definitive biographer, James Spedding,[11] drools over "the sacred vision" of Bacon's youth, which was to "prophesy and prepare the way for the coming of the Kingdom of Man." Prophets are stainless; therefore Spedding, Basil Montagu, Delia Bacon and a good many more Victorians, took hold of Francis Bacon, the incredibly intelligent homosexual, toady, traitor friend, corrupt judge, and fashioned for him a life and character which resemble nothing so much as those of our dear Queen. Stephen Dedalus has this lay, saintly figure in mind: "Good Bacon: gone musty. Shakespeare Bacon's wild oats" (*Ulysses*, 195).

Then there is the more modern and ambiguous Bacon of Strachey's *Elizabeth and Essex*, whose "miserable end" must color our vision of his life:

> "Although our persons live in the view of heaven, yet our spirits are included in the caves of our own complexions and customs, which

minister unto us infinite errors and vain opinions." So he wrote; and so, perhaps, at last, he actually realized—an old man, disgraced, shattered, alone, on Highgate hill, stuffing a dead fowl with snow.[12]

The Baconian's Good Bacon is certainly present in *Finnegans Wake*, but the reality behind him is not so much Strachey's Lear-like Bacon as Macaulay's Ben Franklin-like Bacon, a cold, prudent man of great power, a doer, a take-charge man. I may add that Macaulay's account of Bacon's death is close to the spirit of Bacon's last letters.

> The great apostle of experimental philosophy was destined to be its martyr. It had occurred to him that snow might be used with advantage for the purpose of preventing animal substances from putrefying. On a very cold day, early in the spring of the year 1626, he alighted from his coach near Highgate . . . He went into a cottage, bought a fowl, and with his own hands stuffed it with snow. While thus engaged he felt a sudden chill, and was soon . . . much indisposed . . . after an illness of about a week, he expired . . . His mind . . . retained its strength and liveliness to the end. He did not forget the fowl which had caused his death. In the last letter that he ever wrote, with fingers which . . . could not steadily hold the pen, he did not omit to mention that the experiment of the snow had succeeded 'excellently well.'[13]

Finnegans Wake has a circular construction. Everything has happened before, everything will happen. I do not, therefore, know whether the young Lord Keeper, at the Shakespearean dunghill, sneezes in recollection or anticipation of the day on which he and the hen meet in mutual refrigeration. I do know that Biddy Doran is the very hen that Francis Bacon with his own hands stuffed with snow. Joyce calls her "that *original* hen" [110.22, Glasheen's emphasis]. Science's apostle and martyr told us in his last gasp that the experiment did "excellently well." The hen "shows her beaconegg" (382.11) and proclaims she is well, well, well, not forgot or forgetting to "life's &"[111.15]—which is life's end and life's going on.

To deprive the natural of life and preserve it unnaturally is the business of religion, no less than science. By associating Kevin-Religion with Bacon-Science, Joyce denies their traditional opposition and shows them at one in determining to change nature utterly. The hen, immortal subject of this change, proclaims it as good. Joyce, if I understand him, does not think that it is bad or illusory to alter nature—physical or human—but not in the hen's way.

Joyce seizes on the death-by-cold of Bacon and his hen and fashions it into an emblem of the Waste Land's circle of vicious sexual cold. It is a Bosch-like emblem, surprising, gruesome, funny, economical, apt, memorable. Which sex is responsible for the circle is often debated, variously answered, but each feels the original outrage was the other's, each chills in revenge for earlier wrong. Joyce himself attempts no answer, just sets it down as a condition of fallen humanity that cold and death are passed incontinent from sex to sex in the wintry waste. To be sure, there are other countries, other seasons in which the Grail is achieved. The Boschian emblem is itself a reminder that man and hen have behind them a lurid past in which they were warm and alive and did murder.

The "murders" are related in two widely separate parts of *Finnegans Wake*. The man is murdered on pp. 203–204, the woman on pp. 604–606.

Both murders take off from the boy at the dunghill who grows up to be St. Kevin. St. Kevin lived an eremite, in strict chastity, on the shores of Glendalough; a loving woman importuned him, and to her he was such a "coolcold douche" (290.15–.16) that she drowned herself. The legend lies behind George Moore's novel, *The Lake*, and has been the subject of Irish poems, serious and comic. In his first recension, Joyce stands the legend on its head, for the second, he contrives a happy ending. These recensions concern respectively the First and Second Adams; they are *Paradise Lost* and *Paradise Regained*.

The hen's auspices declare that "the golden age must return with its vengeance" (112.18–.19). The grateful hen must, in the cycling of time, become ungrateful and avenge her chilling, but bloody slaughter does not suit the feathered little divinity. Luckily for her, Joyce believes that murder, or any important activity, is as truly accomplished by symbolic act or state-of-soul as by deed. Bloom, for example, kills Penelope's suitors with kindness. They are none the less dead. Biddy's revenge is bloodless, perfectly charming, fatal.

In another goddess phase, as an unchaste Lady of Rivers, she murders in the prettiest part of *Finnegans Wake*, "Anna Livia Plurabelle" (196–216). Here we find her, a sprightly wife and mother, living chaste and not liking it, with an impotent old husband. He is the Fisher King, if you take it pagan; if you take it Christian, he is Adam bounded and grousing. It is winter, they are out of food, Anna Livia prays for a knight to give them food. She also prays for freedom, but is bound (201.5–.20).

We learn this from two washwomen who have differing versions of past events. One has heard Anna Livia was the moon and raped by the sun (202.26–.32); but the dominant version is that when Anna Livia was younger, long before she had to leave Eden and work for a living in man-made Dublin, she went along as a river on a warm "venersderg in junojuly" and tempted Michael Arklow. (He is called Arklow for geographical reasons.) He was a chaste priest and eremite, living in "the dinkel dale of Luggelaw," i.e. by Loch Tay in Wicklow—another reason for associating tea and sex. Michael was not a cold man, but a hot, thirsty one. He could not help himself, he "plunged both of his newly anointed hands" into her lovely hair, he drank her cool water, and, warning her never to do it, he kissed her, fell, and "Simba the Slayer of his Oga is slewd" (203.17–.36).

Siva the Slayer is, in one aspect, a great ascetic, in another, the linga. Now he has himself been slain when tempted to what he thinks is wrong, to lewdness. In the Christian context, he is the First Adam, falling into sin and death, slain by a woman's charms. He becomes the old husband, met earlier in "Anna Livia," who is furious with his wife, sits about "drammen and drommen, usking queasy quizzers of his ruful continence," "holding doomsdag over hunselv," and reading the death-notices of his children in the news papers (198.34–.35, 199.4–.5). Concupiscence, as St. Augustine saw it, is the mode of operation of original sin. Not Adam merely, but his children drink death from the unhallowed chalice. A woman, as Mr. Deasy says, brought sin into the world. "It was the first woman, they said, souped him . . ." (58.28–.29).

In *From Ritual to Romance* (1920) Miss Weston tells us that the Church set its face against the Grail legend because its symbols, cup, lance, etc., are au fond symbols of generation and hint at the rites of a never-quite-extinguished fertility cult, which aimed, as Joyce says, "to foster wheat crops and ginger up tourist trade" [76.35], to bring material plenty to a land made barren by drought or cold. The rites of many fertility cults include a ceremonial marriage, and, as an example of such a marriage, Miss Weston cites the story of Rishyacringa in the *Mahabarata*, a story which she compares to the Percival versions of the Grail legend: a kingdom suffers drought and starvation because Rishyacringa keeps chaste, an eremite in the wilderness; a wanton girl sails down the river to his hermitage, tempts him to her ship, carries him off to marry the king's daughter (who in earlier versions is herself), and the rains of course come in abundance.

There is strong resemblance between the tempting of Rishyacringa and Joyce's story of the River Lady, tempting the chaste Michael Arklow to be "slewd," and it is made plain that what is death in the Christian context is life in the pagan. Anna Livia is the yet unchastened Artemis or Brigit. She is not slain, she exults in the miracle of happy coition, happy conception; healed of "secheressa" or barrenness, she rises two feet in her own estimation and has walked on stilts ever since (204.1–.3). As life, she has overcome death and all the season of snows and sins. She is simply delighted.

That is worst of all—that Anna Livia's fall was not into but out of guilt. When she slips the Devil's clutches and falls into dirty water, it only renews her virtue, ". . . and she laughed innocefree with her limbs aloft and a whole drove of maiden hawthorns blushing and looking askance upon her" (204.18–.20).

Nothing is odder than to find Nathaniel Hawthorne here, Actaeon-like peeping at the goddess, naked in her bath. It really is Nathaniel, for in the next paragraph the washwomen, scrubbing the dirty linen of the fall, find a pair of drawers with scarlet letters on them. *The Scarlet Letter* takes place in Boston, Mass. and parallels the successful temptations of Rishyacringa and the First Adam, and to such temptings Hawthorne brings moral consciousness. Gretta Conroy's complacent, "I think he died for me," the mention of Father Michael's funeral in the hen's letter—these are much the same thing as Hester's scarlet and gold pride of accomplishment.

Anna Livia has pretty well fooled the world with her charm and saintly domestic abasement (101–102, 198–200, etc.), but we have seen that she is like Gretta-Maggy, most inimical to man when most winsome; and her husband hates her (199.11–.17) as Dimmesdale, D. H. Lawrence says, hates Hester. To be sure, Joyce did not need Lawrence to counsel him about the marital maladjustments of Adam and Eve, housekeeping outside Eden. They are implicit in Milton, but Milton's Eve is no avenger, no triumpher, no getter of her own back sexually. Lawrence's Hester-Eve is just that, and Joyce follows him by joining Hester to his main theme of female vengeance. In *Finnegans Wake* Hester is identified with Swift's Esthers, and the Esthers are rather frightening; they are the German stars of blindness; they turn into Philomela and Procne (307.5–.7 and left margin, 359.31–360.17) and reap the Tereus who ravished them with cold, reap him as the mistletoe, wielding golden sickles of the moon priestess. Like the "slewding" of Adam, the reaping of Tereus is contained in a passage of notable lyric sweetness.

Lawrence called Hawthorne a blue-eyed darling of absolute duplicity because he knew disagreeable truths in his inmost soul and "was careful to send them out in disguise," as, for example, the sending out of Astarte-Hester as St. Mary Magdalene. Similarly, Joyce calls Hawthorne "maiden" and presents him as a double-dealer because he does absolutely look, however askance, at the goddess exulting in her dirty bath. And, having looked, he sends her out disguised as a mid-Victorian Muse, that ladylike spinster, gifted Delia Bacon. In other words, Hawthorne knew Shakespeare's Muse was no lady, but he preferred the imposter Muse, and with masterly equivocation, did not give her the flat, Johnsonian, "No, ma'am."

Stephen Dedalus does indeed give a downright no to his own odd disingenuous game of Shakespeare, but within that game he insists Shakespeare's Muse is no lady, she's his wife—Ann. In the "Scylla and Charybdis" section of *Ulysses* Stephen spins a tale of the Muse's seduction of "our virgitarian swan" (171.3–.4) which is yet another analogue to the tempting of Rishyacringa and the First Adam, and it has about it the atmosphere of a fertility rite:

> He was chosen, it seems to me. If others have their will Ann hath a way . . . She put the comether on him, sweet and twentysix. The greyeyed goddess who bends over the boy Adonis, stooping to conquer, as prologue to the swelling act, is a boldfaced Stratford wench who tumbles in a cornfield a lover younger than herself (*Ulysses*, 191).

Stephen, of course, drastically tampers with the sense of "Venus and Adonis," turns Shakespeare's Adonis into Frazer's, and the encounter into another "slewding" in which Shakespeare gets the wound of Ulysses and the Fisher King:

> Belief in himself has been untimely killed. He was overborne in a cornfield first . . . and he will never be a victor in his own eyes after nor play victoriously the game of laugh and lie down . . . The tusk of the boar has wounded him there where love lies ableeding (*Ulysses*, 196).

Having made Shakespeare into a slain fertility god, Stephen goes on to talk about how Shakespeare hated the woman for his overthrow and to compare that overthrow with Adam's:

> The note of banishment, banishment from the heart, banishment from home, sounds uninterruptedly . . . it was the original sin that darkened his understanding, weakened his will and left in him a strong inclination to evil. The words are those of my lords bishops of Maynooth: an original sin . . . It is between the lines of his last written words, it is petrified on his tombstone under which her four bones are not to be laid. Age has not withered it. Beauty and peace have not done it away. It is in infinite variety everywhere in the world he has created . . . (*Ulysses*, 212).

Robert Graves points out that the white goddess—the "sow-white sponse" of *Finnegans Wake* (451.20–.21) is neither beautiful nor kind—just the poet's absolute necessity. Ann is white, beautiful, not kind. She brings Shakespeare down, banishes him from the realm of natural creation, but he goes out quickened to become a "lord of language" (Wilde's phrase) in the realm of unnatural, male creation. Because he is slain Adonis, he makes a world where love lies pretty generally ableeding, but can awake; because he is fallen Adam, "father of all his race" (*Ulysses*, 208), it is a world where all men wear her gift—that strong inclination to evil, and where all women have the look of her and her daughters. She is then necessary to the ends of his art, as he to her cornfield ends.

The domestic man, the husband may sit and gloom, but the undomestic man, the Masterbuilder answers her triumph with his own pagan joy. In a splendid Song of Myself (532–554) the Masterbuilder boasts of civilizing his wild girl, of bringing order out of chaos, and building all the cities of the world. This is the story the washwomen touched on—the sun's rape of the moon, Apollo the Maker's rape of the source of all fertility, man's struggle with nature that he may build a world. He declares that he built for love of her, and when his long brag is done, and when, with all his worldly goods, he tries to warm her heart, she is inimical to him as ever, her blessing frozen in the chalice (552.35–.36).

Stephen Dedalus says that Ann Shakespeare warmed to Puritan preachers, not to her husband's plays. Henry Adams learned at Boston dinner parties that women think masculine creation nothing but an excuse for the neglect of themselves. Nowhere in *Finnegans Wake* does Anna Livia praise or even memorialize the builder. She is anxious to replace the figure of hard-working, unregenerate old Adam-Finnegan-Shakespeare with a "hand-picked husband" who may for convenience be called Bacon. Anyone who tries to describe man as he actually is seems to her a slanderer. Satan is traditionally the slanderer of man, and it is her unending concern to "crush the slander's head" (102.17).

Enmity between the woman and the snake has, of course, its Scriptural authority, but the woman's attitude is older than the Bible, and in "Anna Livia" it is the first pagan woman, Pandora, who visits on the slanderers all the ills that flesh is heir to (Joyce to Miss Weaver, 7 March 1924).[14] I suppose this is Joyce's way of saying that Mother Nature is as unkind as Father Civilization and that it matters little whether our First Parents are in or out of the Christian Framework. We get it in the neck.

How did the slander start? Who spied on the fall? Anna Livia does not know (202.26), nor the washwomen (204.21). We are told that the sycamores listened (203.21–.22) and the hawthorns looked (204.20). The sycamores are the four old men or elders, who spy out of impotent envy; the hawthorns are blue-eyed and maiden; they look away; and since the Scriptural sycamore is the fig-tree, it combines very neatly with the maiden hawthorn. They communicate their distress to an interested world, start a scandal about two figures of supposed and unreal virtue, "cheeckin and beggin" (205.18–.19). The scandal gets in the papers, the theatres, the streets, and the rabble execrates their father as hangman god (206.3–.4), the term Stephen applies to Shakespeare and the Creator, to "The playwright who wrote the folio of this world and wrote it badly . . ." (*Ulysses*, 213).

The goddess is angry and swears to get even with the scandalmongers (206.4–.5) who are those men-in-the-street who so gladly contributed to an earlier opinion poll (58–61). To lull the suspicion that she is Artemis in vengeful mood or Pandora, the Greek bearing gifts, she disguises herself. First, she purifies herself, then she decks herself, Ophelia-like, in fantastic weeds (207.1–.4) to suggest that she is mad Delia Bacon, then she further disguises herself as "the dearest little moma," [207.34] not as tall as your elbow (207–208). She presents herself disguised as mad and a figure of fun, which is how Hawthorne's gifted woman has always looked to the world. She quite fools her children who think her a frumpy Ophelia and warn her to beware of water:

> Everyone that saw her said the dowce little delia looked a bit queer. Lotsy trotsy, mind the poddle! Missus, be good and don't fol in the say! (208.29–.31).

The Poacher is there (209.14) to watch her bestow her gifts—her flowers—"For evil and ever" (210.6). So Delia Bacon has a gratifying mad scene. If a lady must run mad in defense of falsehood, let her do it as moon goddess, play-acting one of Francis Bacon's most interesting heroines.

Death, disease, cold—the children accept these gifts from their delusive mother's "crinoline envelope." Too late, they "run from her pison plague" (212.22–.24), scatter to the ends of the earth, but not to safety, for their representatives, the washwomen, are condemned to toil and bring forth in pain and cold (213–214) until the Annunciation brings promise of a new day. This is Pandora's last gift—"hopes soon to hear well," [111.16] as the letter puts it. Hope causes the washwomen to forgive, call their parents' sin a happy one (215.12–.23), but for them at least, hope is another deluding gift. They are pagans, no hope for them in the new dispensation. Their night falls and they turn to a tree and a stone.

In "Anna Livia" we see how a woman killed a man, how the hen, that perfect lady, mother, and whore does murder. As whore, Eve cannot be other than deadly and deeply attractive. To Milton her attraction is the ultimate infuriation, the way of God's that he does not try to justify: to Joyce woman's attraction and man's creativity are mutually dependent, and if they do not justify God's ways, they are themselves God-like. What infuriates Joyce is woman in a phase of ladylike cold fowl of the Waste Land because then she kills man's impulse to create.

The passing on of cold is by no means a female prerogative in Joyce's works. If Gretta Conroy and Molly Bloom strike out at their husbands, it is because the men have failed to give, sympathize, control. They are not bad men, not actively bad. Gabriel is weak and foolish; Bloom is weak and wise, a Lancelot who cannot, for his sins, attain the Grail, but knows what the Grail is and worships. For the weak, Joyce has sympathy, but only hatred and bitterness for the man who is active in passing on cold.

Within the Grail context of *Finnegans Wake* (there are other contexts) Joyce takes up a position of strait-laced heterosexuality and from it, judges men with a grim consistency, likely to bewilder his readers. Why is he so terribly angry with Lewis Carroll, say, or Hamlet, Wilde, Swift? They are men that the world has settled to treat with charity, if not adulation. For Joyce, however, Lewis Carroll is an old man who tampers with girl children, indeed he is at least once identified with Francis Bacon (57.18–.19) who was unkind to a very young wife named Alice; Hamlet reads the book of himself instead of the book of Ophelia and drives her mad and dead with his cold; Wilde goes bankrupt for a trashy boy and from the depths, solicits pity for himself, not Mrs. Wilde; Swift is Tereus to his Esthers.

I don't say these hard judgments are complete or fair, but they are interesting, consistent, and not nearly so excited as Joyce's judgment of those who make capital of their cold. The righteous man of snow, the Angelo—one whiff of him and Joyce is Tom Sawyer, faced with a slicked-up boy who reels off the Kings of Judah to an admiring, feminine Sunday-school. The only decent reaction to that boy is—throw mud! Joyce throws and throws, and like all good haters, goes on throwing too long.

His target is not Michael Arklow, the erring man of God, the young Adam-Adonis-Shakespeare of the far-away fall. Michael Arklow, the Father Michael of the letter, is scarcely more than a name in *Finnegans Wake*. He and Anna Livia loved once, he worked a miracle, she hopes he will come again and work more miracles, just as Bertha hopes at the end of *Exiles*; but Father Michael is always absent. Joyce is not unfriendly to him, and I agree with Mrs. von Phul that Father Michael combines the actual young lover, Michael Bodkin with another actual young lover, James Joyce. He is not a woman's illusion, not sexuality recollected in the cold, but every woman's first, live, warm true love; he is the "boy in innocence" [621.30], slain by her love, lost beyond recall. From this boy, a woman takes the image of man's goodness, her passionate conviction that the world defames him.

For the real lover, once alive, now dead, Joyce has no bitterness. He hates the cold revenant, the model of virtue, the Michael Furey that woman creates within herself and sends walking about the world. This is not Father Michael, but Mike or Mick, roughly identical with keepy Kevin and with Anna Livia's son, Shaun the Post, who is called "gracious one" (424.15) to mark his identity with Michael Furey. In *Finnegans Wake* the revenant does take on his own malignant life, distorts the letter, carries it too far, and has the quite pathetic experience of having his mother choose his brother before him (194).

The cold boy at the dunghill grows up to be a "mothersmothered model" [191.25] of male frigidity, who wishes but acts not, pure of body, sewer of mind, a cheap lithograph saint, whose sugar coats twisted desires, bitter as gall. Flattered by the twenty-nine Biddies, "the Lunar Sisters' Celibacy Club," [92.24–.25] sure of success in Heaven, he has no success in delivering the letter to his father, old Adam (420–421). True, the father's blessing goes to Shaun, for men pay lip-service to virtue, but when the letter is around, the old man isn't.

Balked in this endeavor, Shaun changes into Jaun the Boast, "the killingest ladykiller all by kindness" (430.32–.33), and delivers the letter (grown like himself out of all recognition) as a Lenten sermon to his Biddies, Daughters of February or winter. Its virtuous message—never intended for womens' ears—is "Keep cool your fresh chastity which is far better far" (440.31–.32). It is an Ice-water sermon, preached to girls, a companion piece to the Hell-fire sermon, preached to boys by Father Arnall in *Portrait of the Artist*, and it is architectural and frightening as the Hell-fire sermon, only much longer because Jaun is Trismegistus or Thoth, the god of words (Joyce to Miss Weaver, 14 August 1927),[15] longer, broadly comic, openly perverse—out of the Church Fathers by Freudian error.

Now staunchly patriarchal, Jaun no longer admits female authorship of the letter, but claims he has put into "words of style" [432.17] the advice of the priest, Father Mike, who had them "From above" (432.19). The sermon is then an elaboration of the only words Father Michael speaks in all *Finnegans Wake*, speaks as he falls to the charms of the River Lady:

> He cuddle not help himself, thurso that hot on him, he had to forget the monk in the man so, rubbing her up and smoothing her down, he baised his lippes in smiling mood, kiss akiss after kisokushk (as he warned her niver to, niver to, nevar) . . . (203.32–.36).

Jaun takes the words of Adam in his fall and makes out of them the vulgarest pragmatism—chastity, girls, will get you a wedding ring in this world and me in the next; and though he excites the Biddies sexually—is he not pure?—they meet his pragmatism with their own, prepared to cheer him should he leap to heaven or curse him should he fall to hell (469.33–.34). The group female is eternally loyal to success, and, as the event shows, highly subject to illusion.

The individual female is the 29th daughter of February, thus a leap-year girl, permitted her own choice of lovers. She is Jaun's sister, Issy (who is the young Anna Livia) and to her, he directs his most lubricous appeals for a spiritual union, drinking "the coupe that's chill," [462.6] the "pale of sparkling ice" [451.25]. Issy says yes, "Only be sure you don't catch your cold and pass it on to us," (458.11–.12) but she can hardly wait to get him out of town so Shem can "Coach me how to tumble . . . "(461.30–.31).

So that Issy may not happily burn, Jaun institutes matrimony and preaches a pre-nuptial sermon, in the guise of a toast, to Shem, at once tempting him to the act and disgusting him with it. Jaun, as a sort of randy super-ego, assures Shem, a faltering libido, that he, Jaun, will have "all ringside seats" [466.7] at the marriage bed in which Shem and Issy will:

> Be kithkinish. Be bloodysibby. Be irish. . . . Be offalia. Be hamlet. . . .
> Be Yorick and Lankystare. Be cool. Be mackinamucks of yourselves.
> Be finish. (465.31–.34)

Jaun's Othello-like imagination turns sexual passion into a treacherous, bloody, cold, and envious war or a dirty joke. Under the lash of his language, Shem recoils, begins "sprouting scruples," and shame, the Irish national emblem, leaks out of him, "greeping ghastly" (466.8, 467.10). Finally Jaun has found someone to whom he can deliver his cold message—young, virgin, would-be Adam. Shem had meant to preach the sermon himself, but Jaun, his "everdevoting fiend" usurps the role (408.18) and converts Shem who crosses meekly to Jaun's side, is united with him, becomes Death and the Devil's own (468.20–.21). The events of "Anna Livia" are reversed: Adam withstands the temptation of woman's charms but not the Devil's clever tongue; perhaps he is to be thought of as the fruitful season overcome by the cold.

Joyce wrote Miss Weaver (24 May 1924)[16] that in this part of *Finnegans Wake* Shaun-Jaun is:

> . . . a postman travelling backwards in the night through the events already narrated. It is written in the form of a *via crucis* of 14 stations . . .

Jaun's walk is not just backward through events narrated in "Anna Livia," but also backward along the Way of the Cross, probably even Bach-ward in a mock Passion. The Devil, we know, blasphemes holy things by switching day to night, front to back, clockwise to "widdershins" [470.36, 511.1], and Joyce adds lots of wizard touches to make plain that the usurping postman plays the part of witch-god, preaching Manichean disgust of sex to a coven of hens and to a young male, extremely susceptible to language. Many of these touches, Joyce could have found in Margaret Murray's *The Witch-cult in Western Europe* (1921) where the witch heresy is explained as a survival of pagan nature rites. Whatever his sources, Jaun is mourned by the Biddies not only as Christ, but also as Osiris (470).

Finnegans Wake poses an overall uncertainty—are the characters acting in a divine or a human Mystery play? Is the author God? Shakespeare? In this backward Passion, however, we are told that Jaun is "the most purely human being that ever was called man," (431.11); furthermore, we see him, on Shem's advice, repeatedly trying to leap to heaven and falling, not to hell, but to the earth (469–470). Of this necessary return, he makes a virtue, a magic, hermetic resurrection (470.1–.3), whereupon February's daughters set up a wail for him as a dying god. The gentlest of these lambs gives him a yellow badge, testifying to their belief in him and, I suppose, to the renunciation of their sins. It is also a backward version of the hen presenting her letter of belief to the cold boy, and the fact that it is presented to the combined figure of Shem-Shaun explains why both brothers claim the letter later on. This gift restores Jaun's faltering confidence; he stamps the badge on his brow and prepares once more to soar.

By his powers of resurrection, Jaun has become the Biddies' yesterday and tomorrow (470.14), and looking back at that yesterday, that Sodom and Gomorrah of the Waste Land, the girls change, like Mrs. Lot and Gretta Conroy, to pillars of salt (470.13–.17) and cry joyous peace. Only Issy, the individual woman, is miserable, for her lover has been stolen from her (14.7–.9).

Shem and Shaun, united in Jaun, accepts the token of female belief and gives a tremendous leap, meaning to embrace the "pillarbosom" [471.7] of the Issy that he loves—Muse, Moon, Eve. Instead of a salt, peaceful female, he finds himself among the vengeful stars, "between estellos and venoussas, bad luck to the lie" (471.7–.8). He topples, not to rise again, and, as a postman must, departs on foot and at a "high bouncing gait of going" (473.14).

Among the evil and ever gifts which Pandora-Delia visits on her children is "a sunless map of the month, including the sword and stamps, for Shemus O'Shaun the Post" (211.30–.31). Joyce explained the gift as a Free State postage stamp, on which is a map of Ireland, including the counties of Ulster which the Free State does not possess. It is then a false map and it is given to Shem–Shaun when they combine to carry the letter. Moving back through the events of "Anna Livia," the postman—Shem–Shaun, Adam–Satan—accepts the fatal gift from the deadly woman, disguised as gentlest of lambs. A sunless map of the month is a sunless map of the moon, an unilluminated map of Woman or the Muse, who, in effect, puts him to the sword and gives him a stamp to get him sent out of her company. It is the old enmity of Eve and the Devil, but there is more to it than that.

In *Portrait of the Artist*, young Stephen Dedalus assumes the role of Satan and plays it as a rebel angel, glorious if tarnished, Milton's dasher, written in what Shem calls "pale blake" (563.15). Shem plays a burlesque version of this role in "The Mime" (219–259) and would doubtless have played it again in Book III had not Shaun usurped the role and played it, equally Blakian, as creeping Jesus. No interpretation, however fetching, saves the role: Satan is never the creative father, always the aspiring son, himself sonless, sunless. Moralizing Satan–Shaun fails with Eve, Bohemian Satan–Stephen with the Muse. Why? Because they talk and do not act, they do not rise, as the fallen father does, to lay hands on her, they work no miracles, physical or spiritual; and, therefore, united in *Finnegans Wake*, they fall before her extreme displeasure. The "high bouncing gait" [473.14] of their going reminds us that they are false god, false poet, combined in that symbol of falsity, the Baconian's Francis Bacon, who was vanquished by a hen on Highgate Hill.

When false gods and poets go, real ones arrive. In the cycling of *Finnegans Wake*, the female will meet up with the First Adam—poet and masterbuilder—in the Garden. He lays hands, he works a miracle of physical fertility on her, and the Quest of the pagan Grail is accomplished. The Second Adam, with more power over her than the First, lies also in her future (604–606), where the Kevin legend is comically replayed and she dies to natural life.

This time we are not at Loch Tay, but Glendalough. The holy man is alone—Christ in the wilderness. He is a lover of water, "Saint Kevin, Hydrophilos" [606.4–.5], but does not drink of water in her natural and unregenerate state. He collects, instead, seven tubs full of water (seven for the split selves of the Maggies, the seven devils of Magdalene), pours them into a hole he has dug, "exorcised his holy sister water, perpetually chaste" [605.36–606.1] and then gets into his "handbathtub" and meditates on "the regeneration of all man by affusion of water. Yee." [606.7–.12]. He has not talked, he has acted, laid hands, worked a miracle of spiritual fertility. The Quest of the Christian Grail is accomplished, natural water is made into the Water of Life, the "usqueadbaugham" [24.14], which will raise "all man" or Tim Finnegan from his bier. For the female or Nature, it means chastity, servitude, imprisonment in a "hen fine coops" (606.17) or cup, which more secular ages will call the invention of "franklings" [606.20], i.e. Ben Frankling and Frankling Bacon, those practical men of science.

The hen has met her match, met the reality behind her illusion. Delia Bacon rejected Shakespeare and replaced him with a made-up cardboard model of virtue, called Francis Bacon, but behind the cardboard there was the real and formidable figure of the man who invented modern science, who subdued physical nature "excellently well." In the same way, the womanish spirit of humankind has invented a cardboard

Christ of whom no one need really be afraid, but behind it there stands a formidable reality, which kills what is natural and preserves it.

St. Kevin's invention of the bath tub is a parable of *Paradise Regained*, of Christ entering the womb of Mary, of His union with His Church. It is Cana in Galilee and the Last Supper, it is the healing of Magdalene, it is the sanctifying of the pagan goddess Brigit and making her St. Bridget, the Mary of the Gael. Comic the parable may be, and the world will warp and corrupt it, but nothing suggests that a miracle of power does not take place, or that Joyce thinks it a pity for the spirit to seize on humankind.

1. This essay first appeared in *Spectrum*, V (Spring 1961), 38–64. The journal was published three times a year by the Associated Students of the University of California, Santa Barbara. Hugh Kenner, who taught at the University, was on the Advisory Board of *Spectrum* and solicited the article from Glasheen. Glasheen's page and line citations to the *Wake* are given in parenthesis; where we have added references these are given in square brackets. We have silently corrected printing errors and errors in transcribing from quoted material. Glasheen used a printing of the 1935 Modern Library edition of *Ulysses*; in checking quotations we have done this against the Vintage edition of 1961—and it is those page references which are cited. Quotations from *A Portrait of the Artist as a Young Man* are to the Penguin Books, Viking Critical Library edition, edited by Chester G. Anderson, 1977. Quotations from "The Dead" are to the Penguin Books edition of *Dubliners*, with an Introduction and Notes by Terence Brown, 1993. This essay should be read together with Glasheen's letters to Wilder beginning 10 October 1960 and continuing into her early 1961 letters.

2. Benjamin Robert Haydon (1786–1846), the British historical painter and diarist.

3. See also in the *Wake* 234.19: "ripidarapidarpad."

4. Bacon to Hawthorne, 24 May [1856] in Theodore Bacon, *Delia Bacon: A Biographical Sketch* (Boston and New York: Houghton Mifflin, 1888), 182; Hawthorne to Bacon, 12 May 1856 in The Letters, 1853–1856, in The Centenary Edition of the Works of Nathaniel Hawthorne, V. 15, ed. Thomas Woodson, James A. Rubino, L. Neal Smith, and Norman Holmes Pearson (Columbus: Ohio State University Press, 1987) 489.

5. In *Our Old Home: A Series of English Sketches*, The Centenary Edition of the Works of Nathaniel Hawthorne, V. 5, Fredson Bowers, textual editor (Columbus: Ohio State University Press, 1970), 90–119.

6. Bacon to Hawthorne, 26 June 1856 in *Delia Bacon*, 190. See also Nathaniel Hawthorne, *The Letters, 1853–1856* , 512–513.

7. Delia Bacon to Mrs. Sophia Hawthorne, 29–30 August 1856 , in *Delia Bacon*, 241.

8. Glasheen's phrasing in this sentence is awkward; we have let it stand.

9. See Glasheen's "*Finnegans Wake* and the Girls from Boston, Mass," *The Hudson Review*, VII, 1 (Spring 1954), 89–96.

10. *Cathleen ni Houlihan* in W. B. Yeats, *Plays for an Irish Theatre* (London and Stratford-upon-Avon: A. H. Bullen, 1913), 187.

11. James Spedding, *The Letters and the Life of Francis Bacon*, 7v., London: Longman, Green, Longman & Roberts, 1861–1874.

12. Lytton Strachey, *Elizabeth and Essex: A Tragic History*, (New York: Harcourt, Brace & World, Inc., 1928), 47.

13. Lord Macaulay, *Critical and Historical Essays Contributed to the 'Edinburgh Review'*, ed. F. C. Montague, (London: Methuen, 1903), Vol. II, 194–195.

14. Joyce, *Letters I*, 212–213.

15. Joyce, *Letters I*, 257–258.

16. Joyce, *Letters I*, 214.

Appendix IX

Helen Joyce 1962

ADALINE GLASHEEN

March 1, 1962[1]

On the preceding Sunday Helen Joyce called to tell me she had had pneumonia and had been operated on for cancer (of the ovaries). She was to have treatments for 3 weeks at Hartford Hospital and wanted to stay over some nights with us. I said Of course, made up a bed.

But I did not hear from her till March 1, Thursday, when she called from Hartford. She was staying at the Statler Hilton with her brother, Al Kastner [i.e., Kastor]. They asked us to dinner and we drove in over icy roads, met them in the hotel lobby and went to dinner at the Hearthstone Restaurant. After that we sat with them for a little in the hotel rooms and were home by 10.

Helen had lost 20–30 pounds and looked very refined and beautiful, well made-up, gray hair up on her head, elegant black wool suit and persian lamb jacket. What is admirable about Helen is her spirit, her determined femininity. This was in ascendance and she was impressive in bravery, sweetness, lack of the whine with which less graceful women invest their ills. The last few times I had seen her before this she was antagonistic to me, said wounding things. None of this [was] now apparent, and I was able to feel affection for her as well as the admiration I always feel.

Her brother Al is a sweet, terribly nervous old Jew with that quality of wanting to desperately please which I find attractive in Jews. He has a missing hand, wore a coat with a fur collar. He is a retired cutlery-maker, passes out pocket knives to waiters—and to we [i.e., us]. I liked him very much. He is Helen's "good" brother, the one who bought her house in

Washington Depot [Connecticut] for her, in contrast to her brother Robert, who, by Helen's account, is the "bad" brother who had her shut up and robbed her of the James Joyce letters which, again according to Helen, were hers by right of her divorce settlement.

When we met Helen in the Statler lobby, she muttered, "Don't mention Mr Joyce to Al. He hates him, writes my son Stephen poison-pen letters about him." So I did not mention "Mr Joyce." Aside from this, I must say I saw no friction between brother and sister, but my husband (who is better about these things than I) says he saw they were heading for a quarrel.

Today—March 4 Sunday—we were out sliding in the field next door when Alison called to say Mr Kastner [i.e., Kastor] was on the telephone. He was calling from Mt. Kisko [i.e., Kisco] where he lives. He and Helen had a big fight—whether last night or the night before I'm not sure—which ended with his taking a taxi to the railroad station (presumably from Washington Depot to New Milford). He was half in concern about Helen and half in concern about what Helen was going to say about him to us—this, at least, is my opinion.

In the fight she had said she would tell things about him and have him locked up. She accused him of having combined with Robert to have her locked up years ago. She was furious with him because the Joyce letters (Robert took them when she went to the asylum and wouldn't give them to her; then 3–4 years ago gave them to her son Stephen who took them to France;) which Stephen returned to Al, who—instead of returning them to Helen—gave them back to Robert who has them locked up again. She also, Al said, [is] angry because he wrote a letter to Stephen Joyce's wife in France ("the poison-pen" letter I suppose) saying that Helen had always been a spoiled child, but that what ruined her life was her second marriage with a man so much younger than she was—Giorgio Joyce. Al said, "We all know Helen never loved Giorgio. It was the old man, James Joyce, she was in love with. I wrote what's true—James Joyce was a drunkard, a sponger, a bamboozler. He took people in. Whenever there was a fight, he always got behind Hemingway."

All this went with a very genuine concern for Helen, who, he says, has three months to two years to live—bar miracles. The Sloan-Kettering Institute is in touch with her doctor. I promised not to say he'd called and to let him know if I thought Helen needed him.

A. Glasheen,
Farmington, Conn.
March 4, 1962

1. Contrary to this date, other references in the text suggest it was written on 4 March 1962.

Appendix X

Helen Joyce 1963

ADALINE GLASHEEN

My husband and I met Helen Joyce in the summer of 1957. She lived in a rented house in Cornwall, Connecticut. Later she moved to another rented house in Washington Depot, still later her brother, Al Kastor, bought her another house in Washington Depot. She always painted the name "Joyce" in big straggly letters on her rural mailboxes. The houses were nice houses, nicely not lavishly furnished. Helen had a fancy for Victorian glass and china and lots of potted plants; her bedroom was filmy, flouncy—lots of mirrors and the dressingtable covered with good scents and paints. Another bedroom was always screened and given over to parakeets not in cages. Cats (alley) and dogs (Skye terriers from a kennel the former Consuela Vanderbilt kept) were ubiquitous. Helen took dearest care of her animals who were mostly named Baby; she talked to them, fed them *oeufs en gelee* and *pate de foie gras* and what's wonderful they weren't fat or sickly animals. Helen made them all gentle and not nervous with each other and with her guests, but for my taste the animals were too many and at one New Year's dinner a cat kittened in a cardboard box at my feet.

We were introduced to Helen at a teaparty and a couple of weeks later she had us to lunch with Kevin Sullivan who later wrote *Joyce Among the Jesuits*. Helen hoped Mr Sullivan would collaborate with her on a book about her memories of the man she called "Mr Joyce." She paid Mr Sullivan a two hundred dollar advance, she said, for the project, but he did not collaborate or return the money. Helen bore him no malice, for she had no high expectations of people. Whether she deserved it or not, people had been, were, would be unkind to her. She complained of them constantly but without real bitterness, and any slight gesture of kindness—especially if you were a man—restored you to her good grace. Later on, she asked me to spend a summer with her and collaborate and she offered me an advance. I refused and saw plainly why her brother, Robert Kastor, had to tie up her money and have it doled out, month by month. Helen was a con-man's dream.

I know she was glad I refused because my feeling for Joyce came to chill her. She felt, for instance, that Mr Joyce should not be explained, but *Finnegans Wake* read by her quite beautifully in her beautiful voice. "My reading aloud inspired Mr Joyce when he was writing 'Anna Livia Plurabelle.'"

From my point of view—admittedly narrow and rather boorish— Helen had nothing much to communicate about Joyce. She had one letter from him, written in green ink, a short matter-of-fact note that sounded exasperated. She had a photograph of Joyce, taken in Berlin, very stunning and inscribed to "my daughter-in-law, Helen, with affection." The letter Helen kept in a drawer with her petticoats, the photograph was crumpled in a big box of other photographs. I had never seen the picture reproduced and persuaded her to take it out and put it under glass, which she did and had a copy made of it which she gave me for Christmas, making me swear I would never use the picture while she was alive and might still write her memoirs. Thereafter the photograph of Joyce and another of Nora were always in her livingroom, along with a copy of the Augustus John sketch of Joyce.

Helen had the one letter (she'd lent it to Kevin Sullivan but got it back), the photograph and her memories which she was always beginning to commit to a tape recorder. She remembered parties she had gotten up for Mr Joyce: one table centered around a cake baked to look like *Finnegans Wake*; another around a mirror converted into the Liffey with a swan on it. She remembered just what she wore to the parties—and to every other party she ever went to all her life and what every other woman at every party had also had on. She showed me once a cherry-colored dress by Sch[i]aparelli, velvet with a train and said Mr Joyce liked it because he could see the color. She remembered, too, that when women talked together Mr Joyce sat and listened to them and put his hand over his mouth to hide his laughter.

She would have more, much more, to say about Mr Joyce in her memoirs. Maybe. But I don't think so. Often and often she uttered— beautifully uttered—the name, Mr Joyce and it was big magic. About the man whose name it was, she had felt a great deal and—what was really remarkable—she still felt a great deal. It is not usual, it is even great for a woman of sixty years to feel directly and strongly. But I don't think she could ever have put what she felt into words.

We were Jamesian—she who had known the artist and said "Mr Joyce" as if it were a talisman—I who liked to play at his puzzles.

Helen had some sort of breakdown when her marriage with Giorgio Joyce was ending. "I was sick. I did things. I behaved very badly and made them all hate me," she said. "It was Nora who turned Mr Joyce against me. She would have hated anyone who married Giorgio. Nora had an awfully nasty disposition. She was cruel to Lucia, always comparing her with a girl named Kitten who was just naturally attractive to men. And Nora'd keep saying to Lucia, 'Why can't you be attractive like Kitten?' Nora hated me and so did Maria Jolas because Mr Joyce was so fond of Giorgio and me. Maria did it all, you know. She was the one that pushed and pushed her poor husband—he was an awfully nice man—into knowing Mr Joyce and then she wanted to run everything, but I soon let her know. She was a great big woman and always pretended to be so jolly. She'd say something perfectly awful to you and then say, 'Why of course I was joking. Don't you have any sense of humor?'["]

Later (I don't have the time straight) Helen was committed to a series of expensive mad-houses for nine years. She talked of them without compulsion or complaint. "There's a way you can always get out of them," she said. "You agree with everything the doctor says. You say everything is lovely. The patients are lovely. The nurses are lovely. The food is lovely. The doctor is right about you. Yes, you felt just like that about your father. Yes. If you don't say it you don't get out. And you have to do handicrafts."

Helen was good with her hands and at one asylum had hooked a rather pretty rug. She'd also painted in oils and made a compelling picture of a building where the worst cases were housed, where she'd been herself. The building was black, black.

When Helen lived in Cornwall so did the Mark van Dorens, and they were—I guess—the local, social cream of cream. When they gave a party they hired Helen's daily maid to do for them. Once when we were sitting on Helen's terrace, Mark van Doren drove up, parked across the road and sat waiting for the maid to join him. "He doesn't come to the door for her," Helen said, "because they don't invite me to their parties. He knows perfectly well who I am because we meet at the grocery and he asks questions about Mr Joyce. But it's his wife, Dottie, she just looks past me. They don't like Jews in Cornwall."

Helen mentioned her Jewishness two other times. When she moved to Washington Depot, some other friends of ours, the Hazens, moved to Washington village, and Helen remarked that they wouldn't sell her a house in the village because she was a Jew. She said, too, "It wasn't just my being so much older than Giorgio. Nora hated me because I was a Jew. Somebody said to her I was the best-dressed woman in Paris with a

Byzantine profile and Nora just made that sign in the air that people make when they mean a Jewish nose."

We went to Helen's many times. We spent a couple of weekends, we went to lunch or dinner alone with her maybe ten times, to a dozen of her parties. She was, however, nervous about driving on strange roads—we lived about an hour away from her—so she only came to our house twice, driven by a young man who was a ghost-writer for Mayor Wagoner [i.e., Robert Wagner] and other New York ward heelers. Helen brought her dogs who were taught to wet in the fireplace. She also brought us lavish presents of food and insisted on being given some gold-band dessert plates that matched a set she had inherited from her father, also a blue-and-bronze lustre pitcher. She was mad about pitchers.

My lunches were poor feeds by Helen's high, classic French cuisine. When she entertained tables groaned with infinite variety, prepared by her with genius and patience and extravagance. Her female guests muttered in corners that they could cook too if they used unlimited butter and had a maid to clean up the kitchen afterwards, but they could not have. Helen herself ate and drank very moderately and without any great pleasure. A lifelong watching of weight—she tended to be blowsy—had, I think quite killed her pleasure in food. She was rather like someone with perfect pitch who does not care for music.

Like all really interesting women Helen was always an actress and sometimes an accomplished comedienne. Once, I remember we arrived for the weekend and she said she had just enough gas to get to the village and no money to buy more gas. We offered her money, we offered to drive her. She said, "No dear. You come with me, Adaline." While we drove to the village she told me, resignedly, how her brother Robert had tied up all the trust funds so she couldn't touch a penny. A New York lawyer paid her household bills and had to approve any large expenses like a new car or a trip to Paris. He also paid her an allowance and she had spent it on the rent of a gallery that was to exhibit her paintings. There was, she vaguely indicated, lots and lots and lots of Kastor family money and she supposed she'd chucked it around like dirt all her life, but it was her money, why shouldn't she? She led me to the grocery, the liquor store, the hardware store, the antique shoppe and at each she bought lavishly, though with long deliberation. Every store-keeper handed her her parcels and a wad of money and every time she got the money Helen put on a charming little skit of the gleeful and con[n]iving child, getting candy out of elders.

"What was that?" I said when we had bought gas and were driving home.

"Oh I've made arrangements." Helen was pleased that I had noticed her performance. "They pad the bills and the lawyer pays them. And they and I split the difference. Of course I have to buy a great deal from them if I'm going to get any cash at all. It just wouldn't do for Robert's lawyer to get the idea I can live simply."

Helen also arranged—or anyway managed to have—comic social occasions. Once we came to lunch, bringing a guest of ours, a very conservative colonel, retired from the US Cavalry. We arrived to find our hostess still upstairs and on the flagstones of her patio, a man and woman, middle aged, in excellent condition and naked. The man sprang up and roared smilingly, in accents of deepest Dion Boucicault: "Sure, yer blood-slatherin' Protestants and black Republicans!"

Our retired cavalry friend said distinctly, "You may think of me as Colonel Blimp." He did not speak again till we got home.

Then Helen appeared, togged out in a sort of parody of youthful ingenuity, in a sleeveless pink-flowered organdy dress and a pink ribbon bow in her well-blued gray hair. The naked pair, who were her houseguests, began to tell Helen how much they were enjoying themselves. "It's been like a second honeymoon," the lady unfortunately said.

Helen curled her lip and sneered. "About time you had your first!"

The naked went to clothe and, with a kind of transcendent cattiness, Helen bawled their history to us in a voice that could not but reach the guest-room which gave on the patio. The man's name was Patrick (Patrick Something Very Irish, I have forgotten what, but he was later to be on the front page of the *New York Times* for abetting the man who got into the New York Public Library and memorized Joyce's letters to [John] Quinn). Patrick, Helen ranted, was a professional Irish. He had lived with the lady for twenty years and did not marry her because if he did that would put a stop to the alimony that a rich Swede had to pay her. If they married, Patrick would have to go to work—excuse the expression. And they were very very good at getting themselves asked to stay in the country during the summer. They'd come to her two weeks before after visiting a nephew of Teddy Roosevelt. "And they needn't think," Helen finished in fishwife vituperation, "they're going to stay with me—not after today."

When the pair, now clothed, rejoined us, they behaved as if they had not heard Helen. Patrick helped her fix drinks, while explaining who the greatest living Irish poet was. (I forget who.) The lady told me about drawings she had done for something the Joyce Society had printed.

Now Helen had told me before hand that she was inviting us solely so she could invite (without its looking particular) her next door neighbor Dan Parker and his daughter. He was a sports writer for one of the New York papers and a widower, my dear. Of course, there's a daughter, but Helen thought she was almost ready for college and need not count as a hindrance. I'd said, good, I believed in getting all the men you could and I'd be glad to talk to the daughter while Helen concentrated on Dan Parker. He was obviously the object of the organdy dress and pink bow.

When I saw Mr Parker I knew it was no good. Helen had stacks of the real authentic glamour and I don't think she'd lost a bit of it. I'd seen men of sophistication and humor look at her at parties; I'd seen my husband look when she came down to breakfast without a speck of make-up on and her gray hair hanging down her back and wearing a gold cotton robe, made in Egypt. But Mr Parker was the soul of bourgeois America, almost as exaggerated a type of good-fellow as Helen was an exaggerated type of the fatal woman. She was right out of his class and scared him to death. The whole party scared him. The colonel was silent and forbidding. Patrick was declaiming "Crazy Jane Talks to the Bishop," standing on a plywood chair. His lady and I were listening. His lady was also telling me about her hepatitis. Dan Parker had brought Helen a present, a Gilbert and Sullivan song book and accepting it, Helen said that Mr Joyce had been very fond of Gilbert and Sullivan. This led to her usual successful gambit about being James Joyce's ex-daughter-in-law. Mr Parker might have been told she was kin to the Marquis de Sade. He said stiffly that he had heard a good deal about *Ulysses* when he was younger. He fled to my husband and they talked batting averages till lunch. The Parker girl—a watchful type—sat by the colonel and did not speak either. Lunch was composed of the sort of food Mr Parker wasn't used to eating and it awed him. After lunch he said he had to get back to New York to cover a fight. Patrick and his lady asked, could they drive to New York with him? So Mr Parker and his watchful daughter and the professional Irishman and the grass widow went off together.

"I thought it went pretty well," Helen said. "And I thought of the right thing to say. I asked him, 'Do second basemen get to bat?'"

"Oh Helen," I said, "you'll never get him."

"I don't need you to tell me that," she said. "But there was a time when there wasn't any man I couldn't get."

I believed her.

It was, then, almost always Helen who entertained us and she gave us far more, materially, than we ever gave her. Immaterially, she gave us the most, too. She was a lonely woman and we gave her company. My husband she enjoyed as she enjoyed all attractive men. I could appreciate her—though she often annoyed the hell out of me—for she was just about what I think a woman ought to be. But I could give her next to nothing. All women were her natural enemies—I liked her for that—but I was so unlike her that I got on her nerves.

"I certainly don't know how you got Frank," she said waspishly.

And again: "Blank (a woman artist) says you're beautiful. I never noticed it. Now if you'd get some decent clothes and some color in your face, you might. . . etc. etc."

That was the difference. I could see how Helen got her men. I noticed she was beautiful. I knew she was right to snap at my retiring clothes and pallor. Most sixty-year-old women who blue their hair and wear pink bows in it, and put their hand on men's arm, and coo—well they're absurd. Helen never was. I don't think she ever was quite a lady but she never was a eunuch.

Of the men in her past she did not talk much. Once, referring to *Finnegans Wake*, 50.1: ". . .the Fleshmans may they cease to bidivil uns," she said Joyce must have meant her first husband, Leon Fleischmann, who "certainly did bedevil Giorgio and me." A guest at one of her parties said that Peggy Gug[g]enheim had said Helen had slept with every attractive man in Paris. Helen laughed, gratified, and shook her head. She gave no impression of regretting Giorgio Joyce. No magic in his name. She said once that Giorgio had had a good voice and that if Mr Joyce had taken half the trouble with him that he took with John Sullivan—whose voice had gone to pot—Giorgio might have gotten somewhere. Now Giorgio was married to some Scandinavian and was in Switzerland, living off his father's royalties.

When we first met Helen, her son Stephen Joyce, was going to Harvard, taking some course to fit him to be some kind of diplomat or UN official in Europe. (So far as I know Stephen has not practiced any calling.) I think Stephen was not then married but he married a French girl in the next year or two. Stephen, Helen said, hated being the grandson of Mr Joyce, hated Mr Joyce's books, hated people who liked Mr Joyce's books. During the Christmas vacation, Stephen came to stay with his mother and she called me up, pleased, and asked us to lunch to meet him. "When I told Stephen I was going to ask a Joyce scholar to lunch, he ran in the bedroom and locked the door," Helen said, "but you and Frank just come and Stephen'll have to come out to eat and then you can meet him."

I accepted, but my husband said he and I would not lie in wait for the grandson of a great man. So I called Helen back and regretted. She and I thought our son and husband impossibly finicky.

J. F. Byrne (Cranly in *Portrait of the Artist*) also hated anybody who liked Joyce, or so his son told me when I met him at lunch at Helen's. He was a nice boy, wearing a dark-brown shirt and no tie. Young Byrne had never read Joyce but he and I both liked Science Fiction and talked about it, especially as it was the day the Russians launched the first satellite. We agreed that life would be very exciting now if it continued to exist at all.

Helen had a great grievance, a real bitterness. When she was married to Giorgio Joyce, James Joyce wrote them certain letters and gave Helen the ms of "Ecce Puer" because she was the mother of his grandson, Stephen, and certain other small gifts, among them a little gold notebook that had a special value to her—I forget why. When she and Giorgio were divorced, the letters, the ms, the gifts came to her under the legal settlement.

When Helen went mad and was taken to a hospital (I think but am not sure this was in Europe) her possessions were dispersed and Helen thought that various people helped themselves to her Joyce momentoes. She told me of seeing the gold notebook (or was it a plain notebook with a gold pencil attached) in the Joyce collection at Buffalo. I have confused a recollection of who she thought stole the ms of "Ecce Puer" and so will not set it down here. The letters were what mattered to her most. They were taken by her brother, Robert, and put in his safe. When she came out of the asylum she claimed the letters. Robert refused, saying they ought to belong to Stephen. (How she got or kept her one letter I once knew but have forgotten.)

Joyce felt strongly about sons and sons' sons, so I think he, too, would have wanted the letters to belong to Stephen. Moreover, Helen did not strike me—a sympathetic observer—as a responsible person—she might have lost the letters or given them to the first attractive Joyce scholar (male) who asked for them. I can see, therefore, how Robert Kastor might refuse to give the letters to her. But, they were legally hers, she was sick and lonely, and she wanted them. To me, the letters are poor, rather nervous-making letters, but Helen thought them magic and begged Robert for them again and again. He let Stuart Gilbert publish them, but he said no to Helen. Instead, when Stephen and his wife were sailing to Europe, Robert came to the boat and gave Stephen the letters.

Helen was sure her son would give her the letters. "I've told Stephen so often what they mean to me." Stephen wrote from Paris to say he would not give her the letters. Helen begged him by letter, cable, trans-Atlantic telephone. Helen was terribly hurt. She rehearsed the story again and again. She consulted a lawyer who told her the letters could probably be recovered if she sued Stephen for them in the French courts. It was then—if I followed Helen—that her brother, Al Kastor offered to buy Helen a house in Washington Depot on the understanding that there be no suit in France. Helen agreed and a nice, rather dull, house was hers.

The story of the letters, as I have told it here, was repeated by me to Al Kastor's son and daughter-in-law who I met at the warming of this bought house. The son was a medical student; he and his wife were serious, credible young people, very unlike Helen and Al who were—well—

baroque. "Yes," the young people said, "it's all true. Uncle Robert is a terrible villain. So is Stephen."

Helen decided Stephen would sell the letters because he so hated his grandfather, but when I saw her last she said, "You'll never guess. Stephen has given the letters back to Robert. They're in his safe."

We had seen little of Helen in 1962. My husband wasn't well. She wasn't well. In February, 1962 she called and asked if I'd put her up, here in Farmington because she had had an operation for cancer of the uterus and had to have cobalt treatments at Hartford Hospital; she didn't want to drive home over icy roads at night. I said yes, of course, but she called back within the hour to say she was going to stay at the Statler Hotel in Hartford, instead, because her brother, Al, had come and offered to pay the bill. As it turned out Helen ended up being driven to and from Hartford every day because she wanted to be with her animals at night.

Next night, after her first cobalt treatment, she asked us to dinner with them in Hartford. Helen was in a moment of perfect beauty. Before, as I've said, she tended to be blowsy and tried to dress casually, as is correct to dress in the folksy Connecticut hills, inhabited by New Yorkers. Now she was slender, frail, with shadowy great eyes and delicate make-up most artfully applied. Utterly refined physically. She wore a black Balenciaga suit and a sable coat and diamonds. She was sweet, brave, vague.

Before she came down to the lobby Al told us she was going to die—two months—a year—doctors are never sure. Helen seemed to know and not greatly to care. "Oh the cobalt treatment wasn't too bad," she said. "At least I could walk to it and I didn't look like a hag."

We had a fine steak dinner—wine—brandy—best of everything at a restaurant filled with men who had responsible jobs with insurance companies and their unflamboyant wives. They couldn't keep their eyes off Helen and we ate in a little pool of conspicuousness. Helen, looking detached and musing and rather like Garbo at the end of *Camille*, basked in being seen by all those neat eyes.

Two or three days later Al Kastor called to say that after we left them that night, Helen had quarrelled with him and ordered him out of her life. I gathered they had quarrelled about Mr Joyce. Al said hoarsely, "James Joyce was an alcoholic, a sponger and a son of a bitch. I told Helen so. She was in love with him, not with Giorgio."

We thought to see Helen again but did not. I called her every Sunday and she always said she was too tired, but her maid told me afterwards that she would see no one because she thought she did not look well. After six months or so, Helen gave up answering the telephone and a nurse said invariably that Mrs Joyce was just the same or sometimes a little better today.

On January 9, 1963 Helen's maid called to say Helen had died at one o'clock. Al called later to say Helen was to be cremated in New York. He had never seen her after that night we all went out to dinner. He hoped we would come to the funeral, but my husband was sick and I told Al we couldn't come.

Appendix XI

Another Painful Case[1]

ADALINE GLASHEEN

Richard J. Finneran (Editor):
Letters of James Stephens
481pp. Macmillan. £10.00

James Stephens (1882–1950) was born in Dublin of poor white Irish Presbyterians ("strictly conservative in doctrine and practice"); parents cast him off, protestant orphanage brought him up to be useful—Joyce told him his "knowledge of Irish life was non-Catholic and, so, non-existent"; Stephens did what he could for the Irish when the English were bullying them; he chose to stay in England and broadcast for the BBC when Hitler was bullying the English; else, Stephens lived in literary circles in Dublin, London, Paris; he went on the dread American lecture circuit and though he drank a lot did not die; he had a pretty ghastly American patron who kept him as a jester on a Kentucky estate; he had a wife, a son who died untimely; latterly, his health was bad, he blacked out, he died after an operation for stomach ulcers.

The foregoing smatter of facts is culled mostly from: Brigit Bramsbäck, *James Stephens: A Literary and Bibliographical Study* (1959), Hilary Pyle, *James Stephens* (1965); James Stephens's letters. Brigit Bramsbäck gives a sympathetic short account of Stephens's life and her bibliography is detailed and useful. Hilary Pyle's biography is colorless; the biographer loses interest. Mr Finneran's *Letters* contains only some letters; others are printed by Hilary Pyle. Mr Finneran is a ham-handed editor without good judgment; he does supply pictures, a good index, and a useful appendix which sensibly deals with the vexed question of the date of Stephens's birth: he and Joyce said they had the same birthday; Gogarty said O no they hadn't. Of Stephens's birth and boyhood, it may be said that "the unfacts, did we possess them, are too imprecisely few to warrant our certitude." Stephens may even have invented his name.

Most of Stephens's personal letters are mild and non-commit[t]al, of interest only to the literary historian. Stephens was a great and commanding talker and a busy journalist—into talk and journalism the best of his surface experience went. His political journalism is good, still readable, and *The Insurrection in Dublin* (1916) is better than good, has the kind of honesty we call Orwellian. Stephens was not a good reviewer of novels, but he had a fine poetic ear—see his broadcasts about Yeats (collected in *James, Seumas & Jacques*, edited by Lloyd Frankenberg, 1964) and see his review of Gogarty's *An Offering of Swans* (*Letters*, 304–307).

Stephens was a loyal, hard-working foot-soldier of the Irish Literary Revival. As is well-known, the Revival was the work of conscience-hagged members of the Protestant Ascendency who knew that their own kind—"The people of Burke and of Grattan"—had for 700 years kept Ireland as a Belgian Congo for the Roman Catholic native Irish. Fearing that their own kind would break into another genocide, it became necessary to prove that the native Irish were people. Standish O'Grady, Lady Gregory, Yeats, Synge, George Moore, George Russell, Douglas Hyde, James Stephens and other intelligen[t]sia forged a literary language that, "adapts the Irish mode {of language} to the English tongue" (*Letters*, 197). There was no Gaelic on most Revivers but they knew it was a grand language because they read it in the English of Douglas Hyde and Kuno Meyer.

I cannot like "the Irish mode," whether used by Synge or Yeats or Stephens. For me, it is a patois that stops narrative dead and rudely rouses disbelief. Kicking and screaming, I reread Stephens's dialect-ridden fictions: *The Crock of Gold* (1912), *The Demi-Gods* (1914), *Irish Fairy Tales* (1920), *Deirdre* (1923). These are of the grown-up fairytale sort.

But *The Charwoman's Daughter* (1912) went down like good maple syrup, for it is written in the pleasant English that Barrie used when not writing Scots. Mary Makebelieve is a Dublin Cinderella and from her Joyce took hints for that fair specimen of winsome Irish girlhood, Gerty MacDowell.

It was Joyce who trained me to respond with snobbery and derision to the Irish Literary Revival. Joyce had intimations of immortality, knew himself to be the divinely right forger of Irish modes in English—all others are base coiners. Royal, Joyce was also a sorehead and, because the Irish Literary Revival did not ask him to a party, he went away and wrote the "Scylla and Charybdis" chapter of *Ulysses* which leaves Revivers up against the wall, punchdrunk with overkill.

The Irish Literary Revival had its humours—George Moore pointed them out before Joyce did. But the Revival was not the clumsiest rite of expiation ever performed by guilty heirs of brutal colonials: it meant well, had a high level of literary competence, and it had Yeats. It also had that minor poet, James Stephens, a very conscientious, sad man, who even wrote about "the duty of the lyric poet" in his preface to *Collected Poems* (1926, 1954). Stephens could not abide the facts of this world and he saw no exit.

Irish Presbyterians he left and, though not a mystic, became a lukewarm Theosophist. This was no turnabout for, however different their life-styles, Calvin and Madame Blavatsky both taught us to sit still because nature and human nature are depraved and preordained. This is a teleology that fit James Stephens all too well: when he was a child he tried to grow tall and did not, remained much smaller than other males; his wife said he had a grudge against nature for making him so small. (See the group picture, taken at the *Tailteann* games in 1924 in *Letters* between pp. 200–201[.]) Stephens thought childhood hell and had no taste for playing Peter Pan; he was, therefore, condemned to a life in which he was physically menaced by the large and knew himself a menace to small things.

Stephens was always afraid and out of his fear came a few sharp, scarifying lyrics of which "In Waste Places"[2] (1914) is the type.

> As a naked man I go
> Through the desert, sore afraid;
> Holding high my head, although
> I'm as frightened as a maid.
>
> The lion crouches there! I saw
> In barren rocks his amber eye!
> He parts the cactus with his paw!
> He stares at me, as I go by!
>
> He would pad upon my trace
> If he thought I was afraid!
> If he knew my hardy face
> Veils the terrors of a maid.
>
> He rises in the night-time, and
> He stretches forth! He snuffs the air!
> He roars! He leaps along the sand!
> He creeps! He watches everywhere!
>
> His burning eyes, his eyes of bale
> Through the darkness I can see!
> He lashes fiercely with his tail!
> He makes again to spring at me!

I am the lion, and his lair!
I am the fear that frightens me!
I am the desert of despair!
And the night of agony!

Night or day, whate'er befall,
I must walk that desert land,
Until I dare my fear, and call
The lion out to lick my hand!

This is a fear that is not susceptible to purgation by pity and terror nor to such comfort as may be had with apples and liedowns in green pastures. The poem is, however the expression of a noble mind, noble because it accepts responsibility.

Stephens would have been horrified by Tolkien's obsessive hate of Blacks, but Stephens lusted after righteousness and homeland: he would have liked to be a good hobbit, one of a virtuous people, somebody like verse-writing Bilbo Baggins.

Instead, Stephens physically embodied the primordial child that common-sized adults carry inside them, the threatened and threatening twin of us all. St. Augustine and Freud wrote in frank fear of the endangered-dangerous child, but its finest expression is in the wonderful, intolerable first act of *Little Eyolf*.

Here the hopeless, crippled child stands at bay, facing parents who wear thinnest masks of respectability, intend that the child shall be dead or gelded. They have struck once at him, will strike again. The preternatural battered child knows no way out of the human condition, and so issues the murderous challenge of infant Oedipus: "When I grow big, then I shall have to be a soldier. You know that, don't you?"

Ibsen's child is lucky; he finds his way out of the human race before he is killed or has got to kill. Non-human creatures die sweet innocent deaths. Eyolf triumphantly identifies with the non-human, drowns himself with a pack of rats.

In a truly remarkable act of understanding and cruelty, Joyce crossed Paris with a gift for Stephens, a copy of *Little Eyolf*. (*Letters*, 390–391).

---

1. The background of this review is given in AG to TW, 21 November 1975. The text printed here follows Glasheen's typescript in HWS.

2. Glasheen quotes the revised version of the poem. See *Collected Poems of James Stephens* (New York: The Macmillan Co., 1941), 233–234.

Appendix XII

City[1]

ADALINE GLASHEEN

Finnegans Wake is a famous work and a formidable. It has not bred a reasoned criticism, but instead, fosters high intolerant emotion. One either rejects *Finnegans Wake* in a storm of passionate exhaustion; or one finds that *Finnegans Wake* radically alters esthetic consciousness and provides an infinite variety of unstaled enjoyment and play. There are pretenders to a middle ground, but they are just that—pretenders.

Finnegans Wake is so dense in its textures, so dedalian in its structures, so many in its details that one's sense of the possible is offended by the hard, unquestioned fact that one mortal man wrote *Finnegans Wake*, 1922–1939, a mere seventeen years. He was James Joyce who was Irish, half-blind, sometimes distracted and disguised. He made his immense, surprising work when domiciled in a succession of bourgeois flats in the 7th arrondisement. "Paris is like myself a haughty ruin or if you like a decayed reveller."

The decayed reveller had a strong natural taste for cities—cities, grand opera, and the historical discipline were, one may say, his preferred art forms; he exploits his preference in *Finnegans Wake* and in the books he wrote before *Finnegans Wake*—*Dubliners, A Portrait of the Artist as a Young Man, Ulysses.*

A city is a man-made whole which contains men and the marvelous, amusing things that men have made. (For Joyce, as for Robbe-Grillet, the *thing* is the "fatal Cleopatra.") A city offers men and things the greatest opportunity for collision, multiplication, derision, evolution, separation, reformation, death, birth, metamorphosis and being blown to atoms, smashed to smithereens. A city—no less than a battlefield—is a primal scene where the gross, improbable, operatic melodramas of history can best be staged and are lik[e]liest to draw an exacting audience of rabblement and historians. A city is a convenient containing system, a delimiting device which is valuable to the artist as a proscenium arch.

These metropolitan commonplaces are the birthright, the naif unspoken assumption of artists who live in civilized countries. But Joyce was of Ireland. His people were native Irish, were turbulent, rural, tribal; they built no cities, made no complex, shapely works of literature; or if they did make complex literary artifacts something happened to them—fire, famine, plague, pillage—and only fragments, obscure or of no great interest remain to tantalize us like the remarkably flat letter that the hen scratches up from the dung-heap and scholars try to explain. (*Finnegans Wake*, 104–125.)

Joyce's people were the miserable Roman Catholic natives of "the island of saints and sages" (a bitter appellation) who had the really infernal bad luck to be paralyzed in their rural, tribal culture; they were invaded and colonized by the furious Northmen (–1014) and then by the English (–1922) who behaved, Joyce truly said, like Belgians in the Congo. The colonials knew how to build cities, forge iron swords, write *Paradise Lost*. The Irish had not these arts and were forbidden them. Overtaken by darkness, brutalized, pauperized, enslaved, the native Irish became absurdly brave and ignorant. For their bravery, they were bashed about and decimated [i.e., decimated]; for their ignorance they were tricked and mocked as racially incapable of the arts of civilization.

After seven hundred years of being Belgians in the Congo, some not untalented colonials took to writing "folk" plays about their victims. The "folk" appeared as suppositious saga heroes with names out of the ancient Irish, or else as peasants of the present day whose behavior and speech, Joyce denounced as "unreal and fabricated." (Power, 33.)[2]

Having the insolence and clear sight of a youth of cruel genius, Joyce told the playwrights that they had given themselves to ["]the most belated race in Europe," and added that his belated race "which never advanced so far as a miracle play affords no literary model for the artist, and he must look abroad." ("Day of the Rabblement")[3]

This is not the stuff to feed the troops of cultivated colonials or disadvantaged races. Joyce, therefore, went abroad, and true to his hard words and catholic taste he found models in many foreign parts.

He was an industrious and ingenious worker at his craft, and in his first twenty years of exile on the continent, he tried his hand with more or less success at most literary forms. His early poems, *Chamber Music* and his play, *Exiles* are inferior to their models—the Elizabethan lyric and Ibsen of the middle period—but Joyce's prose fiction—*Dubliners*,

Portrait, Ulysses—are at once an intensely individual literature of the first rank, beautifully executed, original in themes, inventive in techniques, AND they are a suite of tricky, Irish variations on some of the best known, routinely admired masterpieces of western civilization. With his models—he chose as surely boldly as Racine or Shakespeare—Joyce took the most dangerous and alarming liberties.

For example, the *Divine Comedy* is the model for a very funny, anti-clerical, novella, "Grace"; in "Grace" a tea-salesman gets drunk and falls down a public toilet in Dublin, he is purged of sin by his friends—good useful Catholics—who reenact the Vatican Council of 1870 round his bed of pain, and at a Jesuit retreat for erring business men, he is, so to speak, washed in the blood of the lamb.

For another, and more complex example, take Stephen Dedalus in *Portrait of the Artist* and *Ulysses*, whose character is modelled on the appropriate young man in the *Orestia*, the *Ring*, *Hamlet*, *Paradise Lost* within a framework of Joyce's own biography and a meticulous retelling of the *Odyssey*.[4]

For the last example, take Joyce's pleasantest act of insolence and remodeling, that chapter of *Ulysses* in which he rudely steals the sacred cows of English prose style and butchers them. Plagiary and travesty. The cry goes up: One of the natives has learned to write!

The act is witty, ferocious political. Joyce's best work is permeated with savage and minute intelligence of the indignities of Irish history. He does not express anger directly in his art; he tries not to spill a drop of blood—too much blood had been spilled in Ireland. Instead he goes in for the kill of the amour propre.

But *Ulysses* is an act of subversion—it is still not possible to buy *Ulysses* in the Soviet Union—and when *Ulysses* was published in Paris, its danger was understood and countered by an angry alliance of strange bedfellows—"Puritans, English Imperialists, Irish Republicans, Catholics" (*Letters* I, 147). These allies called *Ulysses* legally "indecent" ("reeling with indecency," said the English authoress, Virginia Woolf) and they ca[u]sed the book to be burnt by Customs officers in countries where English is principally spoken. Not until four or five years ago could Joyce's belated, battered race legally possess themselves of *Ulysses*.

Ulysses is Joyce's supreme proof of competence as a maker, proof that an Irishman, one of the belated natives, can, against all odds forge the previously uncreated prose literature of his race, and "lift the level of Irish prose to that of the international masterpieces" (Power 94–95).[5] *Ulysses*—which contains many literary forms within it (—give examples—) also provides the future Irish artist with the schema, models of literary forms which Joyce had to look for abroad.

Ulysses moreover, is an encyclopedic collection of elegant technical demonstrations of precisely How to Do It—how to do small jobs and very large ones—how to find the *mot juste* or the dialect word—how to do something high-flown like "transpose the myth *sub specie temporis nostri*" (*Letters* I, 147)—how to do something as pedestrian as get a character from street to Dublin street. How to join Ireland on to European civilization. Truly, there is a touch of the pedagogue about old Joyce. Pedagogues are not liked, but demonstrations of specific literary competence are substantially necessary for any young artist, any belated race. For fifty years foreign young men and artists have feasted on the plentitude of good things—on subject, techniques, trials that Joyce intended for his Irish natives. The natives have gone without.

Knowledge of Dublin and Dublin's absurd black, history, this was what Joyce took abroad with him. It was a subject no artist had touched on. Joyce knew he feared that the city was in danger of a deadly plague of paralysis. In *Dubliners* and *Portrait* a beautiful, lean, descriptive prose, is used conventionally, to project a physical image that sharply compels attention, is distinct from other cities say, El Greco's Toledo or Vermeer's Delft, but like those cities this Dublin is motionless as a painted city on a painted ocean.

Easter 1916 changed all that, and it also changed Joyce's "technic" for describing Dublin. Dublin had been proved paralyzed or dead, but, in Turgenev's sense had been "on the eve" of revolution, civil war, and the city put to the torch, gelignite, the long-range gun. If Dublin were here today it might be gone tomorrow. That is another thing about cities—people like to blow them up.

What Joyce did while Dublin was burning down, was write *Ulysses* in which he built Dublin up again with words, and after a method and a plan (described Messrs Hart and Knuth, *A topographical guide to James Joyce's Ulysses*, Colchester, 1976) such as had not been tried in fiction before. Of this odd, difficult linguistic exercise, Joyce was careful to say that he did not *remember* Dublin—a journalist tries to remember a house exactly, a creative writer *refashions* the house into a significant emotional image. (Power, 95)

Past Recaptured[6]

1. There are two extant typescripts of this text. The earlier shows Glasheen reworking ideas and making adjustments to the text. The second typescript incorporates those changes and contains a few further additions. This transcription follows the second typescript. Glasheen, as she often did with typescripts of her work, marked the first "Keep." We have not determined the occasion for this talk. It seems likely, however, that it was written in 1975, after she had read Arthur Power's *Conversations with James Joyce*, which she had reviewed for the *Times Literary Supplement* (London). Some of the phrasing in this essay is also used in Glasheen's review of *The Letters of James Stephens*. See Appendix XI.

2. Arthur Power in *Conversations with James Joyce*, ed. Clive Hart (New York: Harper & Row, 1974), quotes Joyce on John Millington Synge's work, "I do not care for it. . . for I think that he wrote a kind of fabricated language as unreal as his characters were unreal" (33).

3. "The Day of the Rabblement" (1901) in *James Joyce: The Critical Writings*, ed. Ellsworth Mason and Richard Ellmann (New York: The Viking Press, 1964, 68–72). See p. 70.

4. At the margin Glasheen drew a line alongside the entire paragraph and wrote: "specific?"

5. Glasheen misquotes from Arthur Power's *Conversations with James Joyce* where Power quotes Joyce as saying, "I have tried to lift Irish prose to the level of the international masterpieces" (94).

6. In the first typescript Glasheen, after the Power's page citation, Glasheen wrote: "?Proust, *Past Recaptured*."

Appendix XIII

Historical and Literary Figures in Joyce's Work[1]

ADALINE GLASHEEN

This panel—Ruth von Phul, Philip Graham, Louis Berrone—has come together here to swell Joyce's wonderfully crowded canvas, add figures to his cast of thousands.

By increase and multiply of persons, our panelists imitate a technic of Joyce's, play his own game of ineluctably increasing pressure of historical and literary population from first work to last, from "Et Tu Healy" to *Finnegans Wake*. "Et Tu Healy"—the very title is multiplication of Tim Healy into Brutus—a mild multiplication, nothing like *Finnegans Wake* where there is not a word which can not, at need, name and rename one or ten people. I take this expression of unity and diversity in *Finnegans Wake* to be imitation of Adam-as-Everyman who carries all the physical seeds of the human race inside his physical self.

Dubliners attempts no such linguistic tour de force, but shows a bare-seeming language, uttered on a bare-seeming stage—bare is esthetically necessary in Dubliners because (as Mrs Walzl has shown)[2] *Dubliners* represents a half-deserted city in a plague year.

The bareness is only seeming, for "issues from hand of Joyce no simple (i.e. single) soul"; unseen germs and iden[ti]ties hang about the plainest men and wonan [i.e., women]—identities hang like guilty secrets in Ibsen or Sophocles or *The Interpretation of Dreams*. While these presences are latent, they give a smell of unease, of something taking up space, using up the free air. Joyce is a very scary writer—"He wants to make our flesh creep," Mr Best says. And Joyce makes flesh move like Poe and the pornographer and the ad man and the maker of music and poetry. We are never let to be mere readers, passive in an idle hammock.

In short, *Dubliners* scares me a whole lot and is meant to scare, but its manifestations do more, they take the place of psychological analysis. Epiphany—multi-layered and ingeniously varied—epiphany enables Joyce to reveal people like Corley or Maria who are too ignorant or pigheaded or befooled to analyze and reveal themselves. I don't suppose Mr Kernan in "Grace," knows he is Ned Thornton and Dante; I don't suppose Joe Donnelly in "Clay" knows he is Joyce's maternal uncle John Murray and the Marquis of Lorne. Nor—for all their learning do Stephen and Buck Mulligan know they are Telemachus and Antinous.

The accomplished reader of Joyce's works is—by intellectual conceit or failure of apprehension or Joyce's slight of hand—just as prone as Joyce's characters to fall into blindness and error. I work on *Finnegans Wake* and those who do put by the fear—surely it is a pretentious fear—of being in error. And I certainly count myself blind, because I had read "Araby" a thousand times, and it was only recently on the 1001th reading that I connected John Bunyan with the boy at the fair who sees he is all "driven and derided by vanity."

Few are clearsighted as that child, and Joyce points out repeatedly that to know one's self is not to save one's self. At the end of *Dubliners*, Gabriel Conroy strips himself of pride, knows he is vain and has been fooled. But he is so weakened by loss of self-illusion that in weakness of will, he lets in, welcomes in "the hosts of the dead." Just so the men of Ireland let in the stranger who emasculated Irish men, engrossed the attention of Irish women.

Knowing himself defeats Gabriel Conroy, and it is left to Stephen and Bloom—profoundly secular men—to fight their way through the hosts of the dead. "Down with death! Long live life!" is Stephen's defiance. The two men save themselves, win a battle—not the war.

It is laudable for clever, always maligned members of the Joyce industry to come and do us the honor of clearing away splotches of opacity and darkness—to add children.

---

1. Introduction to a panel discussion with this title held on Friday, 18 June 1976, as part of Bloomsday Buffalo: A James Joyce Colloquium, organized by Thomas E. Connolly and Carole Brown at the State University of New York at Buffalo, 16–18 June 1976. Among other participants in the colloquium were James Atherton, Leslie Fiedler, Leo Knuth, Fritz Senn, and Mary Reynolds.

2. Glasheen may be referring to an article by Florence L. Walzl, "Pattern of Paralysis in Joyce's *Dubliners*: A Study of the Original Framework," in *College English*, 22, 4 (January 1961), 221–228.

Appendix XIV

George Reavey to Thornton Wilder

26th Sept. 1953[1]   121 WEST 15th Street
                                       NEW YORK.

Dear Mr. Wilder,
    I should have replied to your letter before, but I went off to the country to get away from the heat wave here and then have been trying to settle down.
    I am looking forward very much to meeting you. In the meantime, I'll tell you a little more about what I've been trying to do with Finnegan's [*sic*] Wake. The *trouble* a'beckets[2] is as you know that one thing leads to another.
    I started a) to explore Joyce's use of Russian vocabulary and references to find out if there was a pattern about them—I think there is; and then, of course, I stumbled on b) the Vasily Buslayev reference which seems to involve a whole world of cross reference in itself; further, I got involved in tracing all the references to the Russian General and the Crimean War; and finally, Buslayev suggested also an investigation of words begging and containing the letter B–b.
    A sample analysis of B reveals that Joyce uses 21.6 average B words in both *I.i.* and *IV.* In I.2 the average is higher—27.5. I must do a few more samples if not the whole. The average appears to be higher—almost double of B words normally (? aint s*u*ch a th*i*ng really) in a page of prose and points to a pattern—one connected with Buslayev—Buckley—Buck(-ram) and (Beech-tree)—I haven't really worked it all out yet if it's at all possible. The frequent use of *But* and *butt* is also intriguing and *But* is the inversion of *TUB*(lin?) and the Tale of . . . [Reavey margin: butt-*end* . . . v wall]

I think I've spread myself too much lately.

I should do a piece on the Russian vocabulary first, I think, and then go on to the other problems.

The theme of the Fall (with stone, tree and female) suggests a pendulum rhythm. The Buck-ram men (giants, adventurers, imperialists) all seem riding for a fall and they are connected with rivers and seas, hills and stones (also *monuments*). But the stone can become a tree and the tree can become stone (release and death of energies). The cultural period involved appears to me to be mainly from the Fall of the Roman Empire to the Decline of British Imperialism! ????. The language very often is that of the Dark Ages—the mixed "racings" of Slavs, Teutons, Celts, Arabs and Latins—the cacophany of Europe in the making and then in dissolution (with some Aryan roots and Chinese (the shadow of the Book of Changes—perhaps ?—and Marco Polo's Cathay?—and the Mongol invasion of Russia?). Jerusalem keeps falling . . . . a) wailing wall fall b) 1187 about the time of the Norman invasion of Ireland (1169–71)—(Chronicle Nikon mentions Vaska Buslayev under year 1171!) [Reavey margin: (page 5) and in *1170* Thomas à Becket *fell*. !!!] c) 1916 I think——same year as Irish Easter Rebellion (connected with G. P. O (Post Office) and general Peirce O'Reilly::: Easter—Fall and rebirth. . . .[)]

But to return to the *bucklied* (*lied*-song) (page 11[.26]). 12th century Novgorod was of course largely a Viking town (the merchants not only sailed to the Caspian and had connection with the Hanseatic League etc, but also sailed to the Dnieper, Black sea and *Constantinople*. The Norsemen reached Byzantium and Jerusalem via both Eastern and Western routes, completing circle.

In Buslayev saga No I (*Vas. Bus. and the Novgorod Men*), old Buslay dies at age of 90, leaving widow and young son Vassily Buslayev(ich)—son of. When Vassenka is seven, he learns Grammar, Letters and Liturgy. . .

"And there was no other singer so good
In the whole of glorious Novgorod
As this same Vassily Buslayev!"

[Reavey margin: (cf p 254[.32] "he's the best berrathon sanger in all the aisles of Skaldignavia.")]

Then, later, "Vassily began to drink and get drunk" (Wass*aily*!) and he began fighting everyone in the town, got him *twenty-nine* followers, and held the town to ransom. . . . they submit. . . . .

In Buslayev saga No 2 (*V. B. Went A-Praying*), after all his successes and sins, V. B. decides to go to Jerusalem and wash himself in the Jordan. He goes by rivers via the Caspian. On the way back comes across a "Saracen Hill," a skull and a Stone. On Stone is written: don't jump over me etc. V. B., who is always reckless and cares not a damn for anything, jumps and breaks his head (Humpty Dumpty!) and is buried there by his 29 boon companions. Such the fall. "Jerusalemfaring." (p. 26[.4] . . "since he went Jerusalemfaring in Arssia M[a]nor") (p 176 [i.e., 175.2–.22] "Madsons leap his Bier. . . ").

The drinking V. B. did with his boon companions suggests a PUB & and [sic] Festive Board. Drinking also suggests the liquid (river-sea) element and the warlike and merchant men who travel and gossip about women and the ends of the earth and *horse racing*. Wassaily is not only feasting but also *sailing*. [Reavey brackets text from here to "steeplechase!!!!" and writes: just ideas!] The racing is connected with "generations" ("experiencing a jolting series of prearranged disappointments[,] down the long lane of *generations* . . . " p 107 [.33–.35]) and "events grand and national" (p 13[.31–.32]), in this case the Easter Rebellion, but in general steeplechasing (The Grand National) which *generally* produces *falls* (*aside*: Perhaps the "*General*" has to do with the *death* of the *particular*??????) like the General's coffin getting mixed up with Che[k]hov's funeral????). A strange coincidence has just occurred to me: *Anna* Karenina watching Vronsky fall in the army steeplechase!!!! Joyce of course reported some race too. I wonder if there was a horse called the "Russian General" running?????? Also (back to page 13[.31–.32]) "events grand and national . . . . bring *fassil*wise [Reavey margin: Wassily?] to *pass how*." Is *pass how* by any chance *Pascha* (Russian—Greek) for *Easter*?—(*Jerusalem*) Pascal lamb for the slaughter?

I'm afraid this is a bit rambling (rody ram lad at random—p 28 [.36]), just as Trist-*ram* or *wramawitch* [27.28] son of a ram?, and without all the systematic references BUT it's just as it came just now and the firstfine time so perhaps something may come of it, vine or vinegar, or we'll be fined by the wail of the wall whence tri*boos* answer [11.2]. [Reavey margin: Horn: buckler!]

And, of course or off horse, I'd be after liking to know whether you think there's any stone upturned in this rough riding thesis?

Very Best Wishes
Sincerely yours
George Reavey

---

1. With his letter to Glasheen of 25 October [1953], Wilder enclosed this typed letter with numerous corrections and additions by George Reavey. At the top, in red pencil, Wilder wrote "To AG. Confidential TW."

2. Possibly a reference to FW 5.3: "tombles a'buckets."

Bibliographies

General Bibliography

Atherton, James S. *The Books at the Wake: A Study of Literary Allusions in James Joyce's 'Finnegans Wake'*. New York: Viking Press, 1959; rpt., Carbondale and Edwardsville, Illinois: Southern Illinois University Press, 1974.

Bauerle, Ruth H., ed. *Picking Up Airs: Hearing the Music in Joyce's Text*. Urbana and Chicago: University of Illinois Press, 1993.

Beckett, Samuel, et al. *Our Exagmination Round His Factification for Incamination of Work in Progress*. Paris: Shakespeare and Co. (Sylvia Beach), 1929; rpt., with an Introduction by Beach, New York: New Directions, 1961, 1972.

Benstock, Shari and Bernard Benstock. *Who's He When He's at Home: A James Joyce Directory*. Urbana: University of Illinois Press, 1980.

Briggs, Austin. "Rebecca West vs. James Joyce, Samuel Beckett, and William Carlos Williams," in *Joyce in the Hibernian Metropolis*, ed. by Morris Beja and David Norris. Columbus, Ohio: Ohio State University Press, 83–102.

Burns, Edward and Ulla E. Dydo, ed., with William Rice. *The Letters of Gertrude Stein and Thornton Wilder*. New Haven: Yale University Press, 1997.

Byrne, John Francis. *Silent Years: An Autobiography with Memoirs of James Joyce and Our Ireland*. Foreword by Harvey Breit. New York: Farrar, Straus & Young, 1953.

Campbell, Joseph and Henry Morton Robinson. *A Skeleton Key to 'Finnegans Wake'*. New York: Harcourt, Brace & Co., 1944; rpt. New York: Viking Press, 1961.

Cheng, Vincent John. *Shakespeare and Joyce: A Study of 'Finnegans Wake'*. University Park and London: Pennsylvania State University Press, 1984.

Christiani, Dounia Bunis. *Scandinavian Elements of 'Finnegans Wake'*. Evanston, Ill.: Northwestern University Press, 1965.

Connolly, Thomas E. *The Personal Library of James Joyce: A Descriptive Bibliography*. Buffalo: University of Buffalo Studies [v. 22, no. 1], April 1955; rpt., 2nd ed., University Bookstore, University of Buffalo, 1957.

———. *James Joyce's Books, Portraits, Manuscripts, Notebooks, Typescripts, Page Proofs: Together With Critical Essays About Some of His Works*. Lewiston, NY: Edwin Mellen Press, 1997.

Corfe, Tom. *The Phoenix Park Murders: Conflict, Compromise and Tragedy in Ireland, 1879-1882*. London: Hodder & Stoughton, 1968.

Deming, Robert H. *A Bibliography of James Joyce Studies*. 2nd ed., revised, and enlarged. Boston: G. K. Hall, 1977.
Dunleavy, Janet Egleson, ed. *Re-Viewing Classics of Joyce Criticism*. Urbana and Chicago: University of Illinois Press, 1991.
Ellmann, Richard. *James Joyce*. New York: Oxford University Press, 1959; revised ed., 1982.
———. *Oscar Wilde*. New York: Alfred A. Knopf, 1988.
Feshbach, Sidney. "Deeply Indebted: On Thornton Wilder's Interest in James Joyce," in *James Joyce Quarterly*, 31, 4 (Summer 1994), 495–517.
Frazer, Sir James G. *The Golden Bough: A Study of Magic and Religion* (1890–1915). London: Macmillan, 1980.
Gheerbrant, Bernard. *James Joyce; sa vie, son oeuvre, son rayonnement*. [Exposition á Paris, Octobre–Novembre, 1949.] Paris: La Hune, 1949.
Gillespie, Michael Patrick. *Inverted Volumes Improperly Arranged: James Joyce and His Trieste Library*. Ann Arbor, Mich.: UMI Research Press, 1983.
———. With the assistance of Erik Bradford Stocker. *James Joyce's Trieste Library: A Catalogue of Materials at the Harry Ransom Humanities Research Center, the University of Texas at Austin*. Austin, Texas: The Center, 1986.
Gorman, Herbert. *James Joyce*. New York: Farrar & Rinehart, Inc., 1939.
Hart, Clive. *A Concordance to 'Finnegans Wake'*. Minneapolis: University of Minnesota Press, 1963; rpt., corrected ed., Mamaroneck, N. Y.: Paul P. Appel, 1974.
Hayman, David, ed. *A First-Draft Version of 'Finnegans Wake'*. Austin: University of Texas Press, 1963.
Hodgart, Matthew J. C. and Mabel P. Worthington. *Song in the Works of James Joyce*. New York: Columbia University Press (for Temple University Publications), 1959.
Hodgart, Matthew J. C. and Ruth Bauerle. *Joyce's Grand OPEROAR: Opera in 'Finnegans Wake'*. Urbana and Chicago: University of Illinois Press, 1997.
Hollander, Lee M. trans. *The Poetic Edda*. 2nd ed. Austin: University of Texas Press, 1962.
Joyce, James. *Dubliners*. With an Introduction and Notes by Terence Brown. New York: Penguin, 1993.
———. *The Critical Writings of James Joyce*. Ed. Ellsworth Mason and Richard Ellmann. New York: Viking Press, 1959.
———. *Finnegans Wake*. New York: Viking Compass Edition, 1958.
———. *The Letters of James Joyce*. Vol. I, ed. by Stuart Gilbert. New York: Viking Press, 1957; reissued with corrections 1966. Vols. II and III, ed. Richard Ellmann. New York: Viking Press, 1966.
———. *Scribbledehobble: The Ur-Workbook for 'Finnegans Wake'*. Edited, with Notes and an Introduction by Thomas E. Connolly. Evanston, Ill.: Northwestern University Press, 1961.
———. *Ulysses*. New York: Random House, 1961.
Kee, Robert. *The Laurel and the Ivy: The Story of Charles Stewart Parnell and Irish Nationalism*. London: Hamish Hamilton, 1993.
Kenner, Hugh. *Dublin's Joyce*. Bloomington: Indiana University Press, 1956; rpt., with a new preface, New York: Columbia University Press, 1987.
Klein, A. M. *A. M. Klein: Literary Essays and Reviews*, ed. Usher Caplan and M. W. Steinberg. Toronto: University of Toronto Press, 1987.

Levin, Harry. *James Joyce, A Critical Introduction*. New York: New Directions Publishing Corp., 1941; revised and augmented edition, 1960.

———. Ed., *The Portable James Joyce*. New York: Viking, 1947.

MacDonald, John. *Diary of the Parnell Commission*. London: T. Fisher Unwin, 1890.

McHugh, Roland. *Annotations to 'Finnegans Wake'*. Revised Edition. Baltimore: Johns Hopkins University Press, 1991.

Nashe, Thomas. *The Unfortunate Traveller and Other Works*. Edited with an Introduction by J. B. Steane. Harmondsworth: Penguin, 1972.

O Hehir, Brendan. *A Gaelic Lexicon for 'Finnegans Wake' and Glossary for Joyce's Other Works*. Berkeley and Los Angeles: University of California Press, 1967.

Newman, John Henry Cardinal. *Apologia Pro Vita Sua: Being a History of His Religious Opinions*. Edited with an Introduction and Notes by Martin J. Svaglic. Oxford: Clarendon, 1967.

Magalaner, Marvin, ed. *A James Joyce Miscellany, Second Series*. Carbondale: Southern Illinois University Press, 1959.

Pound, Ezra and Rudd Fleming. *Sophokles/Elektra*. Introduction by Carey Perloff. New York: New Directions Publishing Corp., 1990.

Schoenbaum, S[amuel]. *Shakespeare's Lives*. Revised Edition. Oxford: Clarendon, 1991.

Scott, Bonnie Kime. *Joyce and Feminism*. Bloomington: Indiana University Press, 1984.

———. "A Consensus on Glasheen's *Census*," in *Re-viewing Classics of Joyce Criticism*, ed. Janet Egleson Dunleavy. Urbana and Chicago: University of Illinois Press, 1991, [46]–59.

Senn, Fritz. "Some Zurich Allusions in *Finnegans Wake*," *The Analyst*, XIX, December 1960.

Slocum, John J. and Herbert Cahoon. *A Bibliography of James Joyce, 1882-1941*. New Haven: Yale University Press, 1953.

Swift, Jonathan. *Swift: Satires and Personal Writings*, ed. and with an Introduction and Notes by William Alfred Eddy. London: Oxford University Press, 1937; rpt. 1973.

Spielberg, Peter. *James Joyce's Manuscripts & Letters at the University of Buffalo. A Catalogue*. Compiled and with an Introduction by Peter Spielberg. Buffalo: University of Buffalo, 1962.

Wallace, Emily Mitchell. *A Bibliography of William Carlos Williams*. Middletown, CT: Wesleyan University Press, 1968.

West, Rebecca. "The Strange Necessity," in *The Strange Necessity: Essays by Rebecca West*. Garden City, New York: Doubleday, Doran & Co., Inc., 1928, 1–213. The English volume by Jonathan Cape, *The Strange Necessity: Essays and Reviews by Rebecca West*, was published in July 1928. Prior to the volume's American publication on 9 November 1928, the first forty-four pages were published as "The Strange Case of James Joyce" in *The Bookman* (New York), 69 (September 1928), 9–23.

Wilder, Thornton. *American Characteristics and Other Essays*. Ed. Donald Gallup with a Foreword by Isabel Wilder. New York: Harper & Row, 1979.

———. *The Artist in Modern Society: Essays and Statements Collected by UNESCO*. Final Report of UNESCO International Conference of Artists, Venice 1952. Paris: UNESCO, July 1954, 121–124.

———. *The Collected Short Plays of Thornton Wilder*, Volume 1. Ed. Donald Gallup and A. Tappan Wilder, with additional material by F. J. O'Neil. New York: Theatre Communications Group, 1997.

———. "Five Thousand Letters to Alexander Woollcott," ed. Donald Gallup, in *Harvard Library Bulletin*, XXXII, 4 (Fall 1984), 401–407.

———. *The Journals of Thornton Wilder, 1939–1961, with two scenes of an uncompleted play 'The Emporium.'* Selected and Edited by Donald Gallup with a Foreword by Isabel Wilder. New Haven: Yale University Press, 1985.

———. Remarks on Sidney Kingsley in *Proceedings of the American Academy of Arts and Letters*, 2d series, no. 2 [1952], 20–21.

Williams, William Carlos. "A Point for American Criticism," in *Our Exagmination Round His Factification For Incamination of Work in Progress*. Paris: Shakespeare and Company (Sylvia Beach), 1929; rpt., with an Introduction by Beach, New York: New Directions, 1961, 1972. Williams's essay first appeared in *transition*, No. 15 (February 1929), 157–166.

Wilson, Edmund. *The Triple Thinkers & The Wound and the Bow* (combined volume). Foreword by Frank Kermode. Boston: Northeastern University Press, 1984.

Bibliography of the Published Works of Thornton Wilder on James Joyce

"James Joyce: 1882-1941," in *Poetry* (Chicago), LVII, 6(March 1941), 370–374. Reprinted in Wilder's *American Characteristics*, 167–171.

"Joyce and the Modern Novel," in *A James Joyce Miscellany*, ed. Marvin Magalaner. New York: The James Joyce Society, 1947-1957, 1957, 11-19. Adapted by Wilder from a tape recording of his talk before the James Joyce Society in New York on 2 February 1954. Reprinted in Wilder's *American Characteristics*, 172–180.

"Giordano Bruno's Last Meal in *Finnegans Wake*," in *A Wake Newslitter*, No. 6, October 1962, [1]–7. Reprinted with emendations in *Hudson Review*, XVI, 1 (Spring 1963), [74]–79. Reprinted in Wilder's *American Characteristics*, 278–285.

Bibliography of the Unpublished Works of Thornton Wilder on James Joyce included in this volume

1940
"On the Four Old Men in *Finnegans Wake*," journal entry, 23 February 1940 (YCAL).

1941
"Memorandum: rê Frank Budgen's 'Joyce's Chapters of Going Forth By Day,'" (Harry Ransom Humanities Research Center, University of Texas at Austin).

1959
"*Finnegans Wake*: The Polyglot Everyman," Draft A (YCAL).
"*Finnegans Wake*: The Polyglot Everyman," Draft B (YCAL).

1962
"Twins" (HWS).

UNDATED
"A Puzzle" (YCAL).

Bibliography of the Published Works of Adaline Glasheen on James Joyce

BOOKS

A Census of Finnegans Wake: An Index of the Characters and Their Roles. Evanston, Illinois: Northwestern University Press, 1956. Northwestern University Studies; Humanities Series Number Thirty-Two. London: Faber & Faber, 1957.

A Second Census of Finnegans Wake: An Index of the Characters and Their Roles. Revised and Expanded from the First *Census.* Evanston, Illinois: Northwestern University Press, 1963.

Third Census of Finnegans Wake: An Index of the Characters and Their Roles. Revised and Expanded from the Second *Census.* Berkeley: University of California Press, 1977.

ARTICLES—REVIEWS—LETTERS

1952
"Paracelsus," in *Notes and Queries*, 30 August 1952, 393. Response by Harold Williams, *Notes and Queries*, 11 October 1952, 459.

1954
"*Finnegans Wake* and the Girls from Boston, Mass.," in *The Hudson Review*, VII, 1 (Spring 1954), [89]–96. Reprinted in *Critical Essays on James Joyce's Finnegans Wake*, ed. Patrick A. McCarthy. New York: G. K. Hall, 1992, 169–175.

1956
Response to "The End of the 'Oxen of the Sun': An Analysis of the Boosing Scene in James Joyce's *Ulysses*" by Daniel Weiss (*The Analyst*, IX, December 1955, [1]–16) in *The Analyst*, X (March 1956), 11.

1957
"Another Face for Proteus," in *The James Joyce Review*, I, 2 (16 June 1957), 3–8.
Review, *James Joyce Epiphanies*, ed. O. A. Silverman. Buffalo: Lockwood Memorial Library, University of Buffalo, 1956, in *The James Joyce Review*, I, 3 (15 September 1957), 44–46.

1958
Corrections and Emendations to "From a Banned Writer to a Banned Singer, by James Joyce" in *The Analyst*, XV ([?September], 1958), 2, 4, 7.

1959

"Joyce and the Three Ages of Charles Stewart Parnell," in *A James Joyce Miscellany*, Second Series, ed. Marvin Magalaner. Carbondale, Illinois: Southern Illinois University Press, 1959, 151–178.

"Out of My Census," in *The Analyst*, XVII ([April 1959]), [i]–73.

1961

"The Strange Cold Fowl in *Finnegan's* [sic] *Wake*," in *Spectrum* (University of California, Santa Barbara), V, 1 (Spring 1961), [38]–64.

1963

"*Finnegans Wake* and The Secret Languages of Ireland," in *A Wake Newslitter*, No. 10 (February 1963), [1]–3. Reprinted in *A Wake Digest*, ed. Clive Hart and Fritz Senn. Sydney, Australia: Sydney University Press for Australian Humanities Research Council, 1968, 48–51.

"Solution to the Geometry Problem," *A Wake Newslitter*, No. 14 (June 1963), 3–4.

Notes in *A Wake Newslitter*, No. 15 (August 1963): (*a*) [Dilmun], 2-3. Reprinted with title "Dilmun" in *A Wake Digest*, ed. Clive Hart and Fritz Senn. Sydney, Australia: Sydney University Press, 1968, 71–72. (*b*) "Anna Livia's Delta," 3–4. (*c*) Untitled, "In the part of *Scribbledehobble* . . .," 4.

Review, *A Concordance to "Finnegans Wake"* by Clive Hart (Minneapolis: University of Minnesota Press, 1963), in *James Joyce Quarterly*, I, 1(Fall 1963), 36–37.

"Instances Perhaps of the Tetragrammation in 'Finnegans Wake,'" in *A Wake Newslitter*, No. 16 (September 1963), 5–6. Reprinted in *A Wake Digest*, ed. Clive Hart and Fritz Senn. Sydney, Australia: Sydney University Press, 1968, 73–74.

Notes in *A Wake Newslitter*, No. 18 (December 1963): (*a*) "On First Looking into the 11th Britannica, 'ALGEBRA: HISTORY,'" 3–4. (*b*) "avtokinatown," 4–5. (*c*) "Adam and Eve's," 5.

1964

"Semper As Oxhousehumper," in *A Wake Newslitter*, N.S., I, 1 (February 1964), 7–11.

Note, "hadding," in *A Wake Newslitter*, N.S. I, 1 (February 1964), 11.

Notes, Comments, Queries in *A Wake Newslitter*, N.S., I, 2 (April 1964), 12–13.

Notes and Comments in *A Wake Newslitter*, N.S., I, 3 (June 1964), 7–9.

Notes in *A Wake Newslitter*, N.S., I, 4 (August 1964): (*a*) "Two Shakespeare Quotations in FW," 5. (*b*) [Untitled], "Saint Patrick wrote . . . " 5. (*c*) [Untitled], "From Gogarty . . . " 6. (*d*) [Untitled], "our sovereign beingstalk . . . " 6. (*e*) [Untitled], Laurence Stallings . . . " 6.

Note, "Arms Without Appeal," in *A Wake Newslittler*, N.S., I, 5 (October 1964), 9.

"Part of What the Thunder Said in *Finnegans Wake*," in *The Analyst*, XXIII (November 1964), [1]–29. Three unnumbered pages of "Cletters" follow page 1; they are followed by page 2.

"Some References to Thoth," in *A Wake Newslitter*, N.S. I, 6 (December 1964), 6–8.

1965

[*Finnegans Wake*] "The Opening Paragraphs," in *A Wake Newslitter*, N.S., II, 2 (April 1965), 3–8; II, 3 (June 1965), 21–25; II, 4 (August 1965), 24–27; II, 6 (December 1965), 17–22; concluded in III, 1(February 1966), 6–14.

[Untitled], "(37) *As I was Going Down Sackville Street*" in *A Wake Newslitter*, N.S., II, 4 (August 1965), 30.

1966

Notes and Queries in *A Wake Newslitter*, III, 1(February 1966): (*a*) "A Few Welsh Words," 44. (*b*) "Hebrew," 44. (*c*) [Untitled], "The 11th E. B. . . ." 44. (*d*) "The Norwegian Captain," 44. (*e*) "Catherinettes," 45. (*f*) "The Witch," 45. (*g*) "Isolde," 45. (*h*) "Home Olga," 45. (*i*) [Untitled], "(42) During the Easter Rebellion," 46.

"A Garner of Littles," in *A Wake Newslitter*, N.S., III, 3 (June 1966), 63–65.

Note, "*New Statesman*, July 1, 1966," in *A Wake Newslitter*, N.S., III, 5 (October 1966), 117.

1967

"Joyce and Yeats," in *A Wake Newslitter*, N.S., IV, 1 (February 1967), 30.

Notes in *A Wake Newslitter*, N.S., IV, 3 (June 1967). (*a*) "Molly and FW," 56–57. (*b*) "Aesopian Language," 57.

"A Further Garner of Littles," in *A Wake Newslitter*, N.S., IV, 4 (August 1967), 77–78.

"Dublin Firms," in *A Wake Newslitter*, N.S., IV, 4 (August 1967), 78.

"Flesh and Blood Games," review of *Irish Folk Ways* by E. Estyn Evans (New York, 1957) in *A Wake Newslitter*, N.S., IV, 5 (October 1967), 99–100.

"A Riddle Not Answered," in *A Wake Newslitter*, N.S., IV, 5 (October 1967), 100–101.

[Untitled], "(44) Can anyone explain . . ." in *A Wake Newslitter*, N.S., IV, 5 (October 1967), 110.

Review, *Scandinavian Elements of 'Finnegans Wake'*, by Dounia Bunis Christiani (Evanston: Northwestern University Press, 1965) in *Criticism: A Quarterly for Literature and the Arts*, IX, 1 (Winter 1967), 104–105.

1968

"Notes Towards A Supreme Understanding of the Use of 'Finnegan's Wake' in *Finnegans Wake*," in *A Wake Newslitter*, N.S., V, 1 (February 1968), 4–[15].

Review, *Giacomo Joyce*, by James Joyce, with introduction and notes by Richard Ellmann (New York: The Viking Press, 1968) in *A Wake Newslitter*, N.S., V, 3 (June 1968), 35–47.

Notes in *A Wake Newslitter*, N.S., V, 5 (October 1968). (*a*) "Piping Pebworth," 75–76. (*b*) "Relittles," 76.

1969

Notes in *A Wake Newslitter*, N.S., VI, 1 (February 1969). (*a*) "Myself Corrected," 13–14. (*b*) "Rhymes," 14.

Review, *A Reader's Guide to Finnegans Wake*, by William York Tindall (New York: Farrar, Straus and Giroux, 1969) in *James Joyce Quarterly*, VII, 1 (Fall 1969), 70.

"Clay" in *James Joyce's "Dubliners": Critical Essays*, ed. Clive Hart. London: Faber & Faber, 1969, 100–106.

"Letters and FW," in *A Wake Newslitter*, N.S., VI, 2 (April 1969), 25–26.
Review, *James Joyce's "Ulysses"*, by Clive Hart (Sydney, Australia: Sydney University Press, 1968), and *Allusions in Ulysses: An Annotated List*, by Weldon Thornton (Chapel Hill: University of North Carolina Press, 1968), in *A Wake Newslitter*, N.S., VI, 2 (April 1969), 29–30.
Notes in *A Wake Newslitter*, VI, 5 (October 1969). (*a*) "Drisheens with Tansy Sauce," 76–77. (*b*) "Census Revisions," 77–78.

1970
Review, *Eternal Geomater: The Sexual Universe of Finnegans Wake* by Margaret C. Solomon (Carbondale and Edwardsville: Southern Illinois University Press, 1969) in *A Wake Newslitter*, VII, 3 (June 1970), 46–47.
"Another Note on *Ulysses*," in *James Joyce Quarterly*, VII, 4 (Summer 1970), 379.
"The Authoress of Paradise Lost," in *A Wake Newslitter*, N.S., VII, 6 (December 1970), 83-88.

1971
[Untitled], "In *Mont-Saint-Michel* . . .," in *James Joyce Quarterly*, VIII, 2 (Winter 1971), 185.
"Rough Notes on Joyce and Wyndham Lewis," in *A Wake Newslitter*, N. S., VIII, 5 (October 1971), 67–75.

1973
Notes in *A Wake Newslitter*, N.S., X, 1 (February 1973). (*a*) "Beaumont and Fletcher," 24. (*b*) "G. A. A.," 24–25. (*c*) "Schoppinhour," 25. (*d*) "Jon Jacobsen (424.27)," 25.
Notes in *A Wake Newslitter*, N.S., X, 5 (October 1973). (*a*) "The Yeats Letters and FW," 76. (*b*) "Laurens County," 77–78. (*c*) "!," 80. (*d*) "My Cubarola Glide (618.22)," 80. (*e*) "Riverrun," 80.
Notes and Queries in *A Wake Newslitter*, N.S., X, 6 (December 1973). (*a*) "Fay Arthur," 5. (*b*) "Phoenix Park," 95. (*c*) "Jonah in Dolphin's Barn," 96. (*d*) "Watches," 97. (*e*) Three Queries, 97.

1974
"Calypso," in *James Joyce's "Ulysses": Critical Essays*, ed. Clive Hart and David Hayman. Berkeley: University of California Press, 1974, [51]–70.
"Everyman and Noman," in *A Wake Newslitter*, N.S., XI, 6 (December 1974), 110.

1975
Two Queries in *A Wake Newslitter*, N.S., XII, 4 (August 1975), 73.
Notes in *A Wake Newslitter*, N.S., XII, 5 (October 1975). (*a*) "The Ould Plaid Shawl," 88. (*b*) "Cocke Lorell's Bote," 91. (*c*) "Misery of Boots," 92. (*d*) "Adam and Eve," 93.(*e*) "Dallan's Amra," 93–94. (*f*) "Hoang Ho," 94. (*g*) "Erigena," 94. (*h*) "Bennu," 95. (*i*) "Soft Youthful Bright Matchless," 95. (*j*) "Laura Bell," 95. (*k*) "The Battle of Brunanburgh," 96. (*l*) Two Queries, 97.

1976
Review, *Conversations with James Joyce* by Arthur Power, ed. Clive Hart (London: Millington, 1974) in *Times Literary Supplement*, 9 January 1976, 24.

Notes in *A Wake Newslitter*, N.S., XIII, 1 (February 1976). (*a*) "Everyman," 16. (*b*) "Butthead," 16.
Notes in *A Wake Newslitter*, N.S., XIII, 3 (June 1976). (*a*) "Les Vignes Sauvage," 55. (*b*) "Songs," 55. (*c*) "Aimee," 55. (*d*) "Thacka," 56.
"Beginning of All Thisorder," in *A Wake Newslitter*, N.S., XIII, 4 (August 1976), 59–62.
Notes in *A Wake Newslitter*, N.S., XIII, 5 (October 1976). (*a*) "Sylvia Beach," 95. (*b*) "Lieber Aleph," 99.
Letter to the Editor, *James Joyce Quarterly*, XIV, 1 (Fall 1976), 114.

1977
Notes and Queries in *A Wake Newslitter*, N.S., XIV, 1 (February 1977). (*a*) "Dolmens," 16. (*b*) "Unfacts," 16. (*c*) "Synecdoche," 17. (*d*) "Barbette," 17. (*e*) "Thornton Wilder," 17. (*f*) "Ulysses Glossary," 17. (*g*) "Queries," 18.
"A Deserted Vintner Dreams of Being a Beached Ark," in *A Wake Newslitter*, N.S., XIV, 3 (June 1977), 46–48.
Note, "Kate," in *A Wake Newslitter*, N.S., XIV, 4 (August 1977), 67.
"Queries About Mulligan as Heretic Mocker and Rhetorician," in *A Wake Newslitter*, N.S., XIV, 5 (October 1977), 71–76.
Note, "Albumblatt," in *A Wake Newslitter*, N.S., XIV, 6 (December 1977), 97.

1979
Review, *Id-Grids and Ego-Graphs: A Confabulation with Finnegans Wake*, by Jacob Drachler (Brooklyn, NY: Gridgraffiti Press, 1978), in *Times Literary Supplement*, 23 November 1979, 22.

1982–1986
"Notes on a Possible Structure of *FW*," in *A Wake Newslitter*, Occasional Paper, No. 1, August 1982, 1–4.
"Gleanings from a Reviewer of *Ulysses*," in *A Wake Newslitter*, Occasional Paper, No. 3, July 1983, 6.
"Addition/Correction to *Third Census*," in *A "Finnegans Wake" Circular*, I, 2 (Winter 1985), 42.
"A Kingdom Through a Fault," in *A "Finnegans Wake" Circular*, II, 2 (Winter 1986), 32.

Bibliography of the Unpublished Works of Adaline Glasheen on James Joyce included in this volume

(MS. HWS)

[Helen Joyce:] 4 March 1962
[Helen Joyce: January 1963]
"Another Painful Case," review, *Letters of James Stephens*, ed. Richard J. Finneran.
"City"
"Historical and Literary Figures in Joyce's Work"

Name Index

Abraham (*Old Testament*), 263
Aeschylus, 418
Aesop, 431n, 555n
Aguilar, Padre (Johnny MacDougal;
    see also "*Finnegans Wake*:
    Four Old Men"), 11, 254, 459
Alcott, Bronson, 31, 32n
Alcott, Louisa May, 390
Analyst, The, 121n, 143, 143n,
    144n, 159, 160n, 407
Andersen, Hans Christian, 384,
    385n, 386, 432, 471
Anderson, Margaret, 155n, 223,
    224n
Aquinas, Saint Thomas, 17, 166,
    342
Archer, William, 570n
Ardrey, Helen Johnson (Mrs.
    Robert), 163, 164n
Ardrey, Robert, 164n
Aristophanes, 396
Aristotle, 187–188
Arklow Lighthouse, 3, 42
Armstrong, John Warneford, 55
Armstrong, Robert, 253n
Asch, Ruth, 564n
Atherton, James S., 53n, 54, 57n,
    58, 59n, 67–69, 69n, 70n, 71,
    80n, 82, 84n, 87, 91n, 96,
    96n, 100, 105, 105n, 106,
    107, 107n, 108, 110, 111,
    111n, 112, 113, 113n, 114n,
    115n, 153, 154n, 156, 182,
    184, 184n, 186, 200, 202n,
    245, 317, 331, 332n, 337,
    354n, 413, 421, 506, 510n,
    512n, 522, 523n, 529, 531,
    533, 571
Atherton, Nora, 571
Aubrey, John, 279, 284n
Austen, Jane, 195
    Mansfield Park, 550

Bach, Johann Sebastian, 250, 251n,
    525
Bacon, Delia Salter, 261, 262n, 287,
    290–292, 295–297, 297n, 301,
    315, 319n
Bacon, Sir Francis, 109, 229, 261,
    262n, 266, 274–275, 276n,
    277, 278–284, 286n, 287–289,
    291–292, 294n, 297, 299–301,
    314, 315
Balfe, Michael, 42, 381n, 428n
Balzac, Honoré de, 105, 195, 196,
    426
Bankhead, Tallulah, 118n, 151
Baring, Maurice, 575, 575n
Barrie, James M., 303
Barrymore, John, 476
Bateson, F. W., 90n, 105, 112, 113n
Baudelaire, Charles, 174
Bauerle, Ruth, 264n, 273n, 329n,
    336n, 431n, 457n, 480n

Baxter, W. G., 55
Beach, Sylvia (Shakespeare and Company), 13n, 30n, 58, 59n, 500, 500n
Beauvoir, Simone de, 253, 256n
Becket, St. Thomas à, 507, 510n
Beckett, Samuel, 14n, 161, 162n, 576, 576n
Beethoven, Ludwig van, 525
Behan, Brendan, 260, 260n
Behan, Maurice, 55
Bellini, Vincenzo, 381n, 489, 490n
Belvedere College, 5n, 166, 167n
Benedict, Julius, 264n, 327, 328, 329n
Bennett, Charles, 8n, 47, 48n, 90n
Bergman, Ingmar, 583, 584n
Berlioz, Hector, 420
Bernhardt, Sarah, 56, 57n, 461
Besier, Rudolph, 57n
Best, Richard Irvine, 281, 285n
Bird, Stephen B., 523n
Bizet, Georges, 381n
Blake, William, 145, 506, 537
Blavatsky, Helena Petrovna, 174, 490, 561n
Boldereff, Frances Motz, 239, 241n, 366, 367n, 448, 537, 581, 582n
Boleyn, Anne, 181, 221, 427
Bonheim, Helmut, 335, 336n
Book of the Dead, The (Egyptian) (Frank Budge), 130, 131n, 210, 211n, 421, 423, 424, 428n
Booth, John Wilkes, 263, 264, 270
Ború (Bóroime), Brian, 343n
Boswell, James, 453
Boucicault, Dion, 80n, 321, 321n–322n, 328, 329n, 336, 450n
Bowen, Elizabeth, 155, 155n
Bowen, Zack, 408n
Boyle, Robert J., S. J., 528, 528n, 529

Brahe, Tycho, 447
Brandes, Georg M., 281, 285n, 315, 317, 337
Brewer, Ebenezer Cobham, 215, 216n, 229–230, 230n
Brinnin, John Malcolm, 159, 161n
Bromage, Mary C., 487, 494
Brooke, Tucker, 282, 285n, 315, 319n
Brooks, Cleanth, 4n, 91n, 153
Brontë Family, 173, 175n, 243, 383
Brown, Norman O., 548
Browning, Elizabeth Barrett, 398
Bruno, Giordano, 204–205, 205n, 375, 440
Bryher, Winifred (Annie Winifred Ellerman), 577, 578n
Budge, Frank (see "*Book of the Dead, The* (Egyptian)")
Budgen, Frank, 94, 95n, 385n, 490, 491n, 509n, 521, 522n, 524
Bunche, Ralph, 75, 75n
Burke, Thomas Henry, 8n
Burns, Robert, 29, 31, 462
Bute, Mary Ellen, 513n, 515, 516n, 539, 540n
Butler, Samuel (*Erewhon Revisited*), 507
Byrne, John Francis, 5n–6n, 170, 171n
Byron, George Noel Gordon, Lord, 190, 234–235, 344, 403, 404n

Cabot, John, 404
Cahoon, Herbert J., 4n, 52n, 92n, 155n
Caine, Sir Thomas Henry Hall, 228, 230n
Callanan, Jeremiah Joseph, 25, 26n
Cambrensis, Giraldus, 346, 347n, 356
Cambronne, Comte Pierre Jacques Étienne, 265, 267n
Camões, Luz Vaz de, 181, 182n
Campbell, Joseph, 59n, 84n, 152n, 246n, 388n

Campbell, Mrs. Patrick, 11
Caractacus, 350, 350n
Carey, James, 451, 457n
Carr, Henry, 583, 584n
Carroll, Lewis, 51, 217, 253, 255, 257, 291, 333, 334, 334n, 386, 387n, 397, 474
  Alice in Wonderland, 68, 160, 475
  Through the Looking Glass, 97
Carlyle, Thomas, 262n, 278n
Cary, Joyce, 89, 91n, 92
Castlereagh, Lord, 55
Cass, Andrew, 489, 491n
Cathleen ni Houlihan, 446, 450n
Cather, Willa, 547
Cavendish, Lord Frederick, 8n
Cenci Family, 392, 394n
Census of "Finnegans Wake", A
  (Adaline Glasheen)
  Precursor, mimeographed list, 7, 8n
  Wilder's idea for a census, 51
  Wilder's ideas for publishing, 106
  Yale UP, 117, 118n
  Wilder to Northwestern UP, 120, 121n
  Richard Ellmann and the *Census*, 121n
  Census published, 131, 132n
  Faber and Faber, 143, 143n–144n, 149, 152n, 170, 171n
  Census II, 149, 253n, 363–364, 365, 430n
  TLS review of, 157, 158n
  Census III, 409, 557, 558n–559n
Centlivre, Susannah, 215, 215n, 216
Cervantes, Miguel de (*Don Quixote*), 5n, 126, 127n, 152, 292, 370n
Chambers, Sir Edmund K., 280, 284n, 315, 319n
Chaplin, Charles, 396, 453, 457n, 472
Chardin, Pierre Teilhard de, 541n

Chaucer, Geoffrey, 27n
  "Wife of Bath's Tale, The", 76
Chekhov, Anton, 111, 111n, 418, 579
Christiani, Dounia Bunis, 431, 431n, 432, 434n, 461, 470, 471, 471n, 531, 531n
Chudleigh, Elizabeth, 453, 458n
Churchill, Winston, 11
Claudius, Emperor, 10
Cleland, John, 332n, 337
Clemens, Samuel L. (see also "Twain, Mark"), 20
Clift, Montgomery, 111n
Clodd, Edward, 224, 225n, 237
Clongowes Wood College, 166, 167n
Cloran, Peter, 88, 93
Coach With Six Insides, The (Jean Erdman), 388, 388n
Coleman, Elliot, 443n
Coleridge, Samuel Taylor ("The Rime of the Ancient Mariner"), 45, 587n
Colum, Mary, 53n, 155n, 389
Colum, Padraic, 50, 54, 154n, 155n, 280, 285n
Columbus, Christopher, 404
Congreve, William, 443n
Connolly, Thomas E., 512n, 522n
Copernicus, Nikolaus, 495
Coppée, François, 453, 457n
Coquelin, Benoit Constant, 56, 57n
Corneille, Pierre, 463n
Corvo, Baron (Frederick William Rolfe), 544, 544n, 550, 551n
Cowley, Malcolm, 8n, 32n
Coxey, Jacob S., 456, 458n
Crabtree, Lotta, 11
Crane, Stephen, 539, 540n
Criterion, The, 222
Cromwell, Oliver, 88, 271, 365, 421, 504
Curtius, Robert Ernst, 554, 554n, 555n

Dakin, Janet Wilder, 301n
Dalton, Jack, 405, 407n, 419n, 439,
    442n, 443n, 466, 467n, 469,
    492n, 493, 511, 516, 517, 519,
    522, 531, 533, 536, 548, 549,
    551n, 561, 562, 563, 564,
    564n, 565n
Dannebrog, Order of, 49, 49n
Dante Alighieri, 131n, 178, 181,
    196, 197, 226, 229, 245, 269,
    273n, 275, 339, 371, 386,
    411, 425, 445, 459, 460,
    463, 476
D'Arc Jeanne, 20
d'Arezzo, Guido, 20, 23n, 100,
    258–259, 260n
Davitt, Michael, 8n
Davenport, Arnold, 106, 107n, 108
Debussy, Claude, 242, 244n, 381n
Defoe, Daniel, 135, 462
Descartes, René, 140, 143
De Sica, Vittorio, 52n
Deslys, Gaby, 177–178, 188, 334
de Staël, Germaine, 194, 194n
De Valera, Eamon, 10, 12, 141–142,
    145, 149, 151–152, 152n,
    343n, 377, 446, 447, 449n,
    450n, 482, 487, 489, 494
De Vere, Aubrey Thomas, 180, 182n
Deucalion and Pyrrha, 40
Dial, The, 222
Dickens, Charles, 191n, 324n, 412,
    431n, 488n, 548
Dickinson, Emily, 5n, 30, 32n
Disraeli, Benjamin, 183, 561
Dobson, Henry Austin, 180, 182n
Dodgson, Charles Lutwidge (see
    "Carroll, Lewis")
Donizetti, Gaetano, 381n, 390n, 427
Donnelley, Ignatius, 109, 109n, 261,
    162n
Dostoyevsky, Fyodor Mikhailovich,
    199
Douglas, Lord Alfred, 173, 422
Dowden, Edward, 315, 319n

Drake, Sir Francis, 304, 403, 452,
    464
Drayton, Michael, 337, 338n
Dumas, Alexandre (Dumas fils), 133,
    463n
Dumas, Alexandre (Dumas père),
    321, 321n
Dunbar, William, 25, 27n, 157,
    158n
Durrell, Lawrence, 256
Duval, Claude, 10

Early, Jubal, 266, 268n
Eccles, John, 335, 336n
Edel, Leon, 4n, 155n, 175n
Edwards, Hilton, 57n, 137
Egoist, The, 222, 274n
Eisenstein, Sergei Mikhailovich,
    419n
Einstein, Albert, 89
Eliot, George, 181
Eliot, T. S., 38n, 126n, 153, 169n,
    192, 226–227, 231, 238, 238n,
    263, 264, 267n, 272, 273n,
    275, 276n, 327, 328, 329n,
    356, 476, 579
Elizabeth I, Queen, 292
Ellis, Havelock, 140
Ellmann, Richard, 36n, 119, 120n,
    121n, 126n, 143n–144n, 154n,
    170, 171, 172n, 184–185,
    186n, 240, 242, 300, 302n,
    312, 313n, 331, 332n, 338,
    363, 382n, 397, 411, 414,
    416, 429, 436, 438n, 440,
    478, 490, 495, 507, 529n,
    546n, 570n, 584n
Emerson, Ralph Waldo, 30, 262n,
    350
Empson, William, 546, 547, 547n,
    557, 559, 559n, 561, 579,
    580n
d'Eon, Charles, 394, 396
Epstein, Edmund, 164, 167n
Erdman, Jean, 388n

NAME INDEX

Faber and Faber, 157, 170, 171n, 222, 223n, 227, 476, 480n, 557
Fang, Achilles, 5n, 22, 23n, 44n
Farquhar, George, 443n
Farrow, Mia, 569, 570n
Faulkner, William, 6n, 24, 177, 179n
Fawkes, Guy, 305, 416
Fenollosa, Ernest, 223, 224n
Feuchtwanger, Lionel, 57n
Fiedler, Leslie, 548, 549n
Finnegans Wake (James Joyce)
    ALP (Anna Livia Plurabelle), 16, 28, 34, 35, 37, 41, 45, 49, 52, 54–55, 62, 71, 73, 79, 81–82, 83, 85, 88, 119, 122, 123n, 128, 130, 145, 154, 159, 162, 165, 168, 192, 195, 205, 213, 217, 220, 224n, 229, 235, 243, 250, 281, 282, 284, 287, 291–292, 301, 304, 307, 314, 318, 325, 326, 330, 332, 333, 335, 336, 348, 351, 365, 367, 370, 371, 384, 388n, 417, 428, 441, 472, 481, 497, 505, 548, 549
    Anna Livia Plurabelle (booklet, 1930), 476
    "Ballad of Finnegan's Wake, The", 500n
    Buckley and the Russian General, 46, 47n–48n, 81, 199, 248, 317, 318, 365, 448
    Burrus & Caseous, 308, 317–318, 337, 338n
    cad (with pipe), 17, 116
    Chapelizod, 36, 40, 351, 486, 488n, 490
    Earwicker, Margaret, 16, 117, 428
    Finn MacCool, 13n, 190, 432, 439, 451, 452, 464, 477, 507
    Four Judges, 12
    Four Old Men: Matthew Gregory, Mark Lyons, Luke Tarpey, Johnny MacDougal, also Mamalujo, 4, 15, 18, 19, 20, 21–22, 23n, 24, 26, 28, 31, 45, 47, 49, 55, 68, 79, 80n, 87, 88, 97, 178, 247–250, 250n, 283, 330, 335, 397, 399, 402, 406, 457n, 459, 460, 464, 483, 492
    Haveth Childers Everywhere (booklet, 1931), 195, 476
    HCE (Humphrey Chimpden Earwicker, Hircus Civis Eblanensis, Finn, Tim Finnegan), 17, 19, 20, 21, 26n, 35, 42, 43, 50, 54, 82, 88, 117, 145, 173, 192, 229, 234–235, 236n, 250, 259, 265–266, 271, 281, 287, 293, 299, 301, 314–318, 338, 347n, 348, 351, 365, 369, 399, 417, 432, 451, 462, 488n, 500n, 504, 519
    Issy (Isa, Isabel, Isolde), 10, 54, 63, 65n, 68–69, 81, 88, 89, 94, 98, 104, 174, 211, 235, 237, 315, 317, 335, 357, 365, 381n, 402, 441, 505, 562n
    Kate Strong, 17, 21, 50, 53n, 55, 281, 287–288, 315, 446, 461
    Liffey, 31, 40, 81, 122, 137, 200n, 243, 282, 364, 369, 486, 490
    Mime of Mick, Nick and the Maggies, The, 23n, 46, 48n, 81, 317, 376, 504
    Mookse and the Gripes, The, 20, 230n, 322, 323n
    Nocturne, 39, 44n

Norwegian Captain, 17, 31, 81, 317, 365
Ondt and the Gracehoper, The, 20, 175n, 307, 479
Prankquean, 17, 31, 176n, 345, 347n, 357
Shaun (Jaun, Kevin, Chuff, Yawn, Butt, John), 42, 46, 47, 50, 68, 73, 81–82, 88, 94, 97–98, 141, 142, 145, 152, 159, 160n, 176n, 187, 192, 205n, 221, 229, 234, 247–248, 261, 265, 275, 277, 279, 283, 291, 299, 301, 302, 307, 323, 327, 330, 335, 338n, 344, 357, 365, 392, 403, 424, 490, 504, 505
Shem (Glugg, Jerry, Taff), 36, 41, 56, 82, 88, 94, 97–98, 145, 152, 167, 176n, 178, 192, 195, 201, 205n, 214, 221, 229, 235, 253, 261, 263, 264, 265, 266, 275, 277, 279, 280, 281, 288, 299, 323, 338n, 340, 344, 349, 357, 365, 367, 371, 392, 403, 455, 460, 473, 479, 481, 504, 505, 562n
Tales of Shem and Shaun (booklet, 1932), 165
Thunder words, 347n
Tim Finnegan, 13n
Twin boys (Butt and Taff), 11, 68, 156, 183, 247, 404, 503, 505, 509
Finneran, Richard J., 587n
Firbank, Ronald, 544, 544n
Fitts, Dudley, 153
Fitzpatrick, Samuel A. Ossory, 312, 313n
Flaubert, Gustave, 254
Fleischmann, David, 406
Fleischmann, Mrs. David, 406–407, 465

Fleischmann, Martha, 380, 382n, 384, 393, 495n
Fleming, Polly (Mary Duke Wight, Mrs. Rudd Fleming), 37–38, 38n–39n
Fleming, Rudd, 38n–39n
Flemming, Elizabeth, 12
Fletcher, Elizabeth, 12
Flotow, Friedrich von, 395n, 450n
Ford, Ford Madox, 438n, 458n
Ford, John, 386, 387n
Forster, E. M., 76
Foster, Stephen, 273n, 450n
Frazer, Sir James G., 94, 95n, 224, 225n, 228–229, 230n, 302n, 506
Freud, Sigmund, 14n, 24, 26, 28, 29n, 100, 251n, 389, 548, 557, 579, 580n
Fuller, Margaret, 276, 278n

Gallup, Donald C., 238, 238n, 585–586, 587n
Galsworthy, John, 122, 123n
Gama, Vasco da, 377, 404, 445, 489
Gaskell, Elizabeth, 575n
Gate Theatre, Dublin, 5n, 57n
Gauguin, Paul, 429
gCopaleen, Myles na (see "O'Brien, Flann")
Genet, Jean, 384, 436
Gide, André, 188, 190, 201, 202
Gilbert and Sullivan, 422
Gilbert, Stuart, 112, 332n, 546n
Gilvarry, Jim, 4n
Giraudoux, Jean, 583, 584n
Gladstone, William Ewart, 56, 159–160, 160n, 161n, 274, 278
Glasheen, Adaline
  Writings
    "Another Face for Proteus", 90n, 91n, 96n, 103n, 105n, 107n, 109, 112, 113n
    "Calypso", 571, 572n, 579, 579n, 587n

NAME INDEX

Census of "Finnegans Wake", A
  (see "*Census of 'Finnegans Wake', A*")
"Dilmun", 444n
"*Finnegans Wake* and the Girls From Boston", 65n, 70n, 72, 73n, 79, 80n, 104, 108, 121n, 499n, 531n
"*Finnegans Wake* and the Secret Languages of Ireland", 362n
"Instances Perhaps of the Tetragrammation in *Finnegans Wake*", 466n
"Joyce and the Three Ages of Charles Stewart Parnell", 129n, 186n, 230n
"Laurens County", 52n
"Opening Paragraphs, The" [i.e., *Finnegans Wake*], 354n
"Out of My Census", 144n, 186n, 193n, 202n, 210n, 214n, 302n
"Part of What the Thunder Said in *Finnegans Wake*", 347n, 408n, 419n, 473n
"Rough Notes on Joyce and Wyndham Lewis", 146n
"Strange Cold Fowl in *Finnegans Wake*, The", 262n
TLS Reviews, 577, 578n, 587n
Glasheen, Alison (daughter; see also "Osborne, Newton"), 76, 77n, 80, 93, 108, 202, 220, 240, 243, 245, 310, 329, 362, 363, 407, 409, 430, 445, 451, 459, 464, 465, 469, 491, 493, 511, 512n, 520, 523, 525, 528, 528n, 535, 536, 550, 551n, 554
Glasheen, Francis J.(husband), 77n, 80, 83, 92, 93, 95n, 111n, 114, 118n, 119–120, 122, 123n, 126, 128, 165–166, 179n, 181, 183, 199, 204, 206, 207, 208, 212, 240, 243, 245, 252, 259, 260, 310, 329, 345, 408, 409, 445, 451, 466, 469, 493, 511, 514, 516, 518, 521, 522, 524, 525, 530, 531, 535, 536, 539, 540, 543, 545, 547, 548, 550, 552, 554, 557, 559, 560, 562, 567, 569, 570, 571, 574, 575n, 576, 577, 583
Glinka, Mikhail, 183, 184n
Godolphin, Sidney (Earl of Godolphin), 370, 370n, 458n
Goethe, Johann Wolfgang von, 105, 141, 142, 153, 180, 206, 378, 394, 395n, 416, 569
Gogarty, Oliver St. John, 81, 109, 110n, 504, 506, 509n, 510n, 541
Gogol, Nikolai Vasilevich, 199
Golden, Sean, 581, 582n
Goldmark, Karl, 441, 444n
Goldsmith, Oliver, 214n, 457n
Goldstone, Richard H., 586, 587n
Goldwater, Barry, 496
Gonne, Iseult, 221, 222n
Gonne, Maude, 29, 212–213, 217, 219n, 220, 222n, 223
Gordon, Ruth, 57n, 116n, 118n, 127, 128n, 169n, 197, 584n
Gorky, Maxim, 56, 199, 411, 426, 442, 444n, 481
Gorman, Herbert, 508, 510n
Gough, Sir Hugh, 10, 50, 53n
Gounod, Charles, 244n, 377, 378, 381n
Goya, Francisco de G. y Lucientes, 156
Graham, Philip Lamar, 305, 306, 306n, 309n, 394n, 402n, 418n, 467, 467n, 529, 533, 564, 564n
Grant, Ulysses S., 266, 267, 281, 395n
Graves, Robert, 226, 227n, 301, 302n, 318, 484, 485n, 507, 550

Gray, Sir John, 12
Greene, Letitia Tutt, 297, 298n
Greene, Robert, 283, 286n
Greene, Thomas, 298n
Greenwood, Sir George, 291, 294n
Gregory, Lady Augusta (née Isabella Augusta Persee), 450n, 487n, 488n
Griffin, Gerald, 327, 328, 329n
Grimm's Law, 56
Grolier Club, 4n
Grose, Captain Francis, 394n, 395, 399, 401n, 402n, 410
Gross, John, 578n, 587n
Guggenheim Fellowship (Glasheen's application), 128, 129n, 134, 135n, 179, 179n
Guinness, Alec, 489, 491n
Guinness Family, 348, 349n, 352, 354, 357, 358n, 429, 430, 436, 454, 458n
Gunning, Infanta, 346
Gunning, Mary and Elizabeth, 347n, 454, 458n
Guthrie, Tyrone, 116n

Hahn-Hahn, Baroness Ida, 330, 332n
Halévy, Frommental, 56, 378, 382n
Hall, Elizabeth, 316, 319n, 335
Hall, John, 302n, 319n, 335
Hall, Susanna Shakespeare, 300, 316, 317, 319n, 335
Hallam, Arthur Henry, 275, 276n
Halley, Edmund, 56, 478
Halper, Nathan, 4n, 47n, 413, 419n, 533, 533n
Hammer, Sir Thomas, 280, 282, 285n
Hamsun, Knut, 430
Hanley, Miles L., 29n, 121
Hardy, Thomas, 108
Harefoot, Harold, 344
Harmensen, James, 11
Harris, Frank, 317, 320n

Hart, Clive, 171, 172n, 185, 228, 308, 330, 338, 367n, 375, 407n, 418n, 423, 428n, 441, 442, 442n, 443n, 464, 498, 510n, 535, 571, 572n, 578n
Harte, Bret, 228, 230n
Hathaway, Anne (see "Shakespeare, Anne Hathaway")
Hawthorne, Nathaniel, 5n, 105, 240, 262n, 291, 295, 297n, 301
Haydn, Joseph, 525
Hayes, Richard J., 52n–53n
Hayman, David, 174, 176n, 451, 453, 455, 457n, 461, 463n, 458n, 460, 476, 478, 480n, 487, 488n, 489, 572n
Healy, Timothy Michael, 482, 483, 484n, 486, 487
Heap, Jane, 224n
Hecht, Ben, 52n
Hello Dolly! (see "Herman, Jerry")
Heltzel, Virgil B., 121n
Hemingway, Ernest, 170, 221, 541, 542, 544, 545n
Henry II, King, 149
Henry VIII, King, 221
Herman, Jerry (composer, *Hello Dolly!*), 484n, 519, 520n, 522
Herzogenberg, Elisabeth "Lisl" von, 412, 419n
Higginson, Fred, 154, 155n, 156, 158n, 215
Hodgart, Matthew John Caldwell, 67–68, 69n, 70n, 71n, 72–73, 73n, 76, 77n, 80n, 81–82, 85, 87–89, 91n, 96, 96n, 100, 105n, 106, 107–108, 112, 113n, 114n, 115n, 219n, 264n, 269, 273n, 277, 278n, 304, 306n, 328, 329n, 331, 336n, 393, 399, 408n, 450n, 465n, 480n
Hogg, James, 68, 70, 74
Hollander, Lee M., 434n, 457n
Holmes, Oliver Wendell, 456

NAME INDEX

Homer, 178, 292, 314, 371, 459
   Odyssey, The, 345
      Ulysses/Odysseus, 316
Hone, Joseph Maunsel, 411, 419n, 440, 490, 491n
Horace (Quintus Horatius Flaccus), 89, 415
Horniman, Annie E. F., 145, 146n
Howth Head (Earl of Howth), 22, 207n, 241, 266, 321, 340, 353, 364, 366, 369, 448, 451, 475
Hudson Review, The, 410, 419n
Hutchins, Patricia, 39n, 163
Hutchins, Robert Maynard, 457n, 468n
Hyde, Douglas, 230n, 231

Ibsen, Henrik, 54, 57n, 102, 133, 145, 182, 235, 325, 417, 459, 510n, 519, 570n
   Peer Gynt, 18

Jackson, General Thomas "Stonewall", 267n
James, Henry, 73, 85, 85n–86n, 90, 91n, 92, 93n, 164, 171, 184, 188, 195, 324, 326n, 337, 386, 533, 544, 579, 581
James Joyce Society of New York, 4n, 36n, 50, 53n, 84n, 85, 86n, 101n, 109n, 133, 134n, 154n, 155n, 162n, 164, 175n, 246n, 405, 407, 513n, 557, 559n, 564n
James, William, 90, 91n, 579
Jarrell, Mackie L., 234, 236, 236n
Jarring, Gunnar, 306n
Jenkins, William D., 499, 499n
Johnson, Hester (Esther, Swift's Stella), 234, 236n, 370, 371n
Johnson, Lady Bird, 520n
Johnson, Lionel, 180, 182n
Johnson, Samuel, 86, 137, 295
Johnston, Denis, 485, 487, 487n, 488n, 491n

Jolas, Eugene, 44n, 167n, 555n
Jolas, Maria, 155n, 165, 167n
Jonson, Ben, 285, 307–308, 337, 338n
Joyce, George (Giorgio), (son), 57, 132, 132n, 141, 145, 167n, 389, 390, 390n, 407n, 423
Joyce, Helen (Helen Kastor Fleischman), (daughter-in-law), 164–167, 167n, 168, 170, 171n, 193, 300, 405–407, 407n, 465
Joyce, James
   Chamber Music, 100, 101n, 108, 110n
   Dubliners, 92, 189n, 275, 419n
      "Araby", 92, 93
      "Grace", 29n
      "Dead, The", 171, 172n, 184, 228, 300
      "Sisters, The", 276n
   Exiles, 381n, 570n
   Finnegans Wake (see "*Finnegans Wake*")
   Giacomo Joyce, 381n
   Pomes Penyeach, 13n, 59n, 223n
   Portrait of the Artist as a Young Man, A, 88, 106n, 171n, 205n, 214, 388, 388n
      Stephen Dedalus, 171n, 214, 222n, 277, 280–283, 292–293, 299, 315, 316, 317, 318, 473n
   Stephen Hero, 171n
   Ulysses, 12, 14n, 28, 29, 29n, 30n, 39n, 45, 56, 59n, 63n, 81, 87, 89, 96, 109, 110n, 118n, 119, 120n, 121, 126n, 153, 155, 171, 174, 192, 205n, 221, 222n, 224n, 276n, 278, 278n, 280–282, 284, 285n, 289, 292, 299, 314, 331, 338, 352, 371, 373, 382n, 398, 402n, 473n, 554n, 571–572, 572n, 575n, 576, 579, 582n, 584n

"Aeolus" (7), 371, 372
Bloom, Leopold, 171, 275, 276n, 287, 292, 299, 315, 316, 338, 382n, 473n, 529
Bloom, Molly, 45, 117, 118n, 145, 170, 171n, 284, 299, 381n, 529
"Calypso" (4), 45, 371, 372, 579, 579n, 587n
"Circe" (15), 372, 373, 473n
Clifford, Martha, 382n
"Cyclops" (12), 45, 372, 575n
Dedalus, Stephen (see "Joyce, James: *Portrait of the Artist as a Young Man, A*: Dedalus, Stephen")
"Eumaeus" (16), 372, 373
"Hades" (6), 371, 372
"Ithaca" (17), 372, 373
"Lotus-Eaters" (5), 371, 372
"Lestroygonians" (8), 371, 372
MacDowell, Gerty, 382n
"Nausicaa" (13), 372
"Nestor" (2), 371, 372
"Oxen of the Sun" (14), 62, 62n, 372
"Penelope" (18), 372, 373
"Proteus" (3), 371, 372, 373
"Scylla and Charibdis" (9), 87, 277, 279–284, 285n, 287–290, 292–293, 314, 318, 319n, 335, 371, 372
"Sirens" (11), 371, 372
"Telemechaus" (1), 371, 372
"Wandering Rocks, The" (10), 371, 372
Joyce, John Stanislaus (father), 287, 486
Joyce, Lucia (daughter), 132, 132n, 166, 365, 383, 385, 385n, 386, 389, 390, 392, 396, 397, 451, 472, 473, 584n
Joyce, Mary Jane ("May") Murray (mother), 287
Joyce, Nora Barnacle (wife), 57, 109, 110n, 132n, 165–166, 197, 242, 494, 495n, 529, 529n, 579, 580n
Joyce, Stanislaus (brother), 57, 126n, 145, 185, 377
Joyce, Stephen James (grandson), 167n, 406, 407n
Jung, Carl Gustav, 26, 81, 82n, 100, 201, 453, 458n, 480n
Juvenal, 181, 182n

Kafka, Franz, 58, 59n, 251n
Kain, Richard M., 4n, 487n, 525n
Kalidasa, 180, 181
Kanin, Garson, 168, 169n, 584n
Kant, Immanuel, 177, 187
Kastor, Al, 405–406
Kastor, Mrs. Al, 406
Kastor, Robert, 167n
Kaye, Julian B., 155n
Keating, Geoffrey, 365, 367, 367n, 368n
Kelleher, John, 4n, 9, 13n, 16n, 32n, 36, 36n, 129, 129n, 149, 152n, 159, 160n, 330, 332n, 335
Kennedy, Jacqueline, 473n
Kennedy, John Fitzgerald, 473n
Kennedy, Walter, 157, 158n
Kenner, Hugh, 4n, 81, 87, 89, 90n–91n, 93, 95n, 129, 129n, 134, 153, 154n, 171, 557, 558n, 559n, 560, 561, 576n
Kerr, Alfred, 155n
Kettle, Andrew, 8n
Kierkegaard, Søren, 36, 59n, 153, 261, 280
King, Sir Abraham Bradley, 354, 354n, 357, 358n
Kingsley, Sidney, 52n
Kipling, Rudyard, 221, 267, 268n
Kirwan, William Burke, 207

NAME INDEX

Klein, A[braham]. M[oses]., 62n–63n, 82n, 86n, 100, 119, 120n, 129, 129n, 155, 352, 423, 428n
Kopper, Edward E., 407n
Kott, Jan, 546, 547

Lacan, Jacques, 583, 584n
La Fontaine, Jean de, 216n, 322, 431n, 480n, 555n
Laforgue, Jules, 38n–39n
Landor, Walter Savage, 575, 575n
Lane, Sir Hugh, 302n
Lane, John, 300, 302n
Lang, Andrew, 291, 294n
Langtry, Lillie (Lilly), 159, 160n
Laughlin, James, 4n
Le Fanu, Joseph Sheridan (*The House by the Churchyard*), 8n, 10, 36n, 141, 155, 155n, 158n, 420n, 478, 480n
Le Fevre, Raoul, 174, 176n
Lee, General Robert E., 267n
Lee, Sidney, 315, 317, 319n, 337
Lee, Vernon (pseud. Violet Paget), 91n
Lenin, Vladimir, 584n
Léon, Paul, 30n, 183
Lever, Charles, 145, 146n
Lévi-Strauss, Claude, 583, 584n
Levin, Harry, 9, 13n, 15, 18, 29, 31, 32n, 34, 36n, 154n, 200n, 332n, 393, 395n, 521, 522n, 524
Lewis, C.S., 577, 578n
Lewis, Sinclair, 221
Lewis, Wilmarth S., 535, 537, 538n, 544n, 547, 547n
Lewis, Wyndham (*Time and Western Man*), 81, 89, 140, 141, 145, 146n, 173, 175n, 202, 272, 274n, 286n, 412, 419n, 568n
Lichtenberg, Georg Christoph, 289, 290n

Liddell, Alice Pleasance, 332, 334, 334n, 387n, 474
Lincoln, Abraham, 263, 270–271, 273n, 276, 278
Lind, Jenny, 386
Listener, The, 506, 509n
Liszt, Franz, 420
Little Review, The, 222, 224n
Litz, A. Walton, 228, 331
Lloyd, Constance (Mrs. Oscar Wilde), 173, 175n, 182
Loechrich, Rolf, 107n
Longford, Lady, 5n
Longstreet, James, 267n
Loos, Anita, 272, 568n, 585n
Lortzing, Albert, 183, 184n
Lover, Samuel, 157, 158n
Lowell, Robert, 153
Lucian, 459
Lucy, Sir Thomas, 302n
Luhan, Mabel Dodge, 6n
Lyly, John, 312, 313n
Lyte, Henry Francis, 262, 264n, 323, 324n

Maeterlinck, Maurice, 438n, 442, 444n
Macaulay, Thomas Babington, 68, 70n, 71, 297, 298n, 301
MacBride, Major John, 217, 219n, 221
MacCarthy, Denis Florence, 418, 420n
MacDonald, John, 8n
MacDowell Colony, 58, 59n, 61–62, 75, 79, 80n, 84n, 123n, 132n, 164n, 252n
MacDowell, Edward, 59n
MacDowell, Marian Nevins, 59n
MacLeish, Archibald, 300, 302n, 474n
MacLiammóir, Micheál, 57n
Magalaner, Marvin, 154, 155n, 186
Magellan, Ferdinand, 452
Mallarmé, Stéphane, 174, 176n, 187, 195–196, 304

Mangan, James Clarence, 190, 269, 273n, 323, 324n, 397, 401n, 481, 482
Mann, Thomas, 195, 579
Manners, John Hartley, 431n
Marin, John, 110, 111n
Marivaux, Pierre, 195
Marlowe, Christopher, 292, 312
Martial (Marcus Valerius Martialis), 415
Martyn, Edward, 231, 231n
Marx Brothers, 306, 309n
Mascagni, Pietro, 382n
Massenet, Jules, 381n
Matthew, Father Theobald, 12, 187
Matthew, Thomas ("Bugge Bible"), 112, 113n
Maugham, W. Somerset, 225, 518
McCormack, John, 335, 336, 336n, 398, 480n, 484n
McCormack, Lily, 335, 336n
McCormick, Edith Rockefeller, 56, 57n, 579, 580n
McCullers, Carson, 61
McHugh, Roger, 443n
McPherson, Aimee Semple, 72, 73n, 475, 480n
Melville, Herman, 4n, 5n, 19, 30, 105, 192, 412, 576n
   Moby-Dick, 180
   Billy Budd, 270, 273n
Mercanton, Jacques, 439, 443n
Meres, Francis, 282, 285n
Mérimée, Prosper, 204, 205n
Merritt, Malcolm, 86n, 155n
Meyerbeer, Giacomo, 56, 198n, 244n, 377, 381n, 382n
Michelangelo Buonarroti, 156
Miller, Hugh, 506, 510n
Milton, John, 189
Mink, Louis, 582n
Misra, B. P., 498, 498n, 499n
Mistral, Frédéric, 449, 450n
Mitchell, Breon, 554, 555n

Modjeska, Helena, 461, 463n
Moe, Henry Allen, 129, 129n, 466
Monnier, Adrienne, 59n, 223, 223n
Montaigne, Michel Eyquem de, 292
Moore, Clement Clarke, 264n
Moore, George, 145, 146n, 411, 419n, 440
Moore, Henry, 571
Moore, Thomas (songs not listed separately), 25, 27n, 42, 44n, 76, 78, 135, 226, 263, 264n, 268–269, 272n–273n, 318, 321, 324n, 380, 473n, 480n
   Irish Melodies, 72, 74, 76, 264n, 268–269, 272n–273n, 321
Morgan, Frederick, 72, 73n, 419n
Morse, J. Mitchell, 170, 171n, 238, 330, 332n, 558n, 576n
Moseley, Humphrey, 308, 309n
Mozart, Wolfgang Amadeus, 178, 234, 236, 261, 262n, 381n, 525, 584n
Murphy, Father John, 360, 361n
Murphy, Father Michael, 361n

Napoleon Bonaparte, 95, 137, 267n, 279, 282, 284n, 339n, 346, 396
Nardi, Marcia, 163, 164n
Nash (or Nashe), Thomas, 25, 27n
Nelson, Admiral Horatio, 12, 257
Newman, John Henry, Cardinal, 25, 27n, 68, 70n, 88
Newton, Sir Isaac, 24, 89, 204, 205n, 234, 447
Nightingale, Florence, 385, 386
Niven, Charlotte Tappan Lewis (Wilder's aunt), 196, 198, 200n, 499n
Noon, Father William T. S.J., 184, 185, 186n, 328, 329, 330n, 528, 528n, 529, 533, 536, 553
Normand, Mabel, 453, 457n
Northwestern University Press, 557, 558n, 576n

NAME INDEX

Nyanza (Lakes) Albert and Victoria, 156, 158n

O'Brien, Flann (Brian O'Nolan, Brian Nolan, Myles na gCopaleen), 448, 450n, 491n
O'Casey, Sean, 235
O'Connell, Daniel, 63, 44–45
O'Connor, Frank, 553n
O'Connor, William D., 296, 298n
O'Connor, Ulick, 123n
O'Donovan Rossa, Jeremiah (Diarmuid), 360, 361n, 469, 469n, 479
O'Donovan Rossa, Margaret (Margaret O'Donovan Rossa Cole), 469, 469n, 471n, 479
O'Faoláin, Seán (John Francis Whelan), 507, 510n
Offenbach, Jacques, 382n
O'Flaherty, Gerard, 123n
O'Flanagan, Jane, 142
Oglethorpe, James Edward, 10
O Hehir, Brendan, 36n, 504, 509n
O'Leary, John, 175, 176n
Olson, Charles, 581, 582, 582n
O'Malley, Ernie (Earnâan), 347n
O'Malley Grace, 340, 342n, 347n, 353, 448, 468, 475, 487
O'Neill, Eugene, 169n, 198, 200n
O'Nolan, Brian (see "O'Brien, Flann")
Orwell, George, 548, 586
Osborne, Newton, 511, 512n, 519n, 520, 525, 528n, 535, 551n
Osborne, Robert Francis, 527, 529
Osborne, Sara, 557
O'Shea, Katharine (Kitty, Mrs. Charles Stewart Parnell), 160, 161n, 163, 163n, 175, 212, 275, 281, 285n, 339
O'Toole, St. Lawrence, 94, 149, 150, 340
Ovid (Publius Ovidius Naso), 386, 411, 415

Paddy, The Next Best Thing (John Hartley Manners), 429
Paleologue, Maurice, 440, 443n
Palestrina, Giovanni Pierluigi da, 9, 13n, 34
Paget, Violet (see "Lee, Vernon")
Palmer, Mrs. Bandmann, 280, 285n
Paracelsus, Philippus Aureolus, 218, 219n, 220
Parnell, Charles Stewart, 7, 8n–9n, 128, 135n, 139, 159–160, 160n, 161n, 163, 163n, 186, 275, 286n, 316, 323, 339, 341, 367n, 436
Pascal, Blaise, 134, 136n, 137
Pascal, Jacqueline-Euphemia, 134, 136n, 137
Pater, Walter, 19, 286
Patmore, Coventry, 162, 162n
Patti, Adelina, 368, 368n
Paul, Elliot, 44n, 167n
"Pearl, The", 24
Pearson, Norman Holmes, 577, 578n
Pereira, Irene Rice, 84n
Petrarch, 463
Philips, John, 543, 544
Phoenix Park, 8n, 34, 36, 39, 41, 50, 53n, 116, 286n, 369, 457n, 506, 509n
Phul, Ruth von, 212, 214n, 215, 228, 230, 266, 331, 332n, 451, 457n, 535
Picasso, Pablo, 567, 568n, 569
Pigott, Richard, 7, 138, 283, 286n, 323
Pilgrim's Progress (John Bunyan), 24, 45
Pilkington, Laetitia Van Lewin, 209, 235, 236n
Plato, 89, 188, 193, 193n, 196, 416–417
Poe, Edgar Allan, 5n, 8n–9n, 19, 270, 273n, 275, 301, 304, 322, 337, 389

Pomfret, John, 293
Ponikowski, Alexander, 30n
Pope, Alexander, 298n, 509, 510n
Pope, Major General John, 266, 267n
Pope Pius XI (Ambrogio Damiano Achille Ratti), 16n, 57
Popper Amalia, 377, 381n, 384, 495, 495n
Porter, Jane, 425, 429n
Pound, Dorothy (Mrs. Ezra), 38n
Pound, Ezra, 23n, 38n–39n, 56, 144n, 146n, 171, 177, 201, 212, 218, 219n, 223, 224n, 226–227, 231, 235, 240, 259, 304, 412, 436, 438n, 579
Power, Arthur, 578n, 587n–588n
Previn, Andre, 570n
Prince, Morton, 65n, 68–69, 70, 72, 73, 74, 104–105, 531
Pritchett, V. S., 125, 126n
Proust, Marcel, 137, 144n, 190, 195, 326, 407, 553
Puccini, Giacomo, 244n, 368n, 381n, 382n
Purcell, Henry, 321, 483
Pushkin, Alexander, 199

Quiney, Judith Shakespeare, 319n, 337, 338n
Quiney, Thomas, 319n, 338n
Quinn, John, 155n, 438n

Rabelais, François, 42, 151, 245, 246, 396, 459, 565
Rachel (Elisabeth Rachel Felix), 459, 463n
Ragnar Ladbrok, 341, 344, 490
Raleigh, Sir Walter, 262n
Ray, Satyajit, 583, 584n
Reavey, George, 47n, 83, 84n
Richard III, King, 28
Richardson, Samuel, 227n

Riddle, Theodate Pope, 85, 85n–86n, 90, 543, 544
Rimbaud, Arthur, 189, 240, 242
Ring, Blanche, 430, 431n
Robinson, Henry Morton, 59n, 84n, 152n, 246, 246n, 321
Roda Roda, Alexander, 217, 219n, 220
Rose, H. J., 436, 437, 438n, 454
Rossini, Gioacchino, 244n, 294n, 382n, 483, 484n
Rostand, Edmond, 57n
Rountree, Benjamin S., 52, 53n, 54, 55, 57n, 64, 64n
Russell, George (AE), 146n, 318

St. Augustine, 89, 185, 186n
St. Patrick, 94
Sacher-Masoch, Leopold von, 529, 529n
Sackville-West, Victoria, 207, 209, 210n, 270, 396, 398, 402n, 437
Sade, Donatien Alphonse François, Marquis de, 178, 201, 253–255, 256n, 256–257, 259, 268, 380
Saint-Saëns, Camille, 381n, 420
Saintsbury, George, 88
Sand, George, 142
Saroyan, William, 169n
Sartre, Jean Paul, 436
Sarraute, Nathalie, 467, 468n
Savage, Richard, 263, 264n, 274, 276n, 280, 414
Sawyer, Jonathan, 61, 339, 358n
Sawyer, Peter, 10, 50, 52n, 61, 145, 339, 342, 343, 357, 358n
Schiaparelli, Elsa, 165, 167n
Schiller, Johann Christoph Friedrich von, 270, 274n, 461
Schlauch, Margaret, 23n
Schrank, Franz von Paula, 455, 458n
Scott, Sir Walter, 46, 47n, 390n
Sechseläuten, 33, 34n–35n, 414

NAME INDEX

Senn, Fritz, 172n, 190, 191n, 204, 205n, 206, 206n, 207, 207n, 210, 224, 231, 245, 246n, 253, 270, 273n, 313n, 319, 320n, 326, 328, 331, 332n, 338, 339, 345, 356, 363, 364, 366, 367n, 373n, 374, 375, 380, 407, 407n, 409, 410, 419n, 435, 438n, 439, 442n, 464, 465, 465n, 476, 479, 480n, 491, 492n, 496, 499n, 537, 538n, 539, 540n, 545, 546n, 553, 557, 559, 559n, 560n, 561, 562, 563, 565, 569, 570n, 571, 580n, 584n

Sévigné, Madame de (née Marie de Rabutin-Chantal), 523, 523n, 526, 546

Sewanee Review, 482, 485n

Shackleton, Sir Ernest Harvey, 403, 404n

Shakespeare, Anne Hathaway (wife), 281–284, 287–288, 297, 298n, 299, 314, 315, 317, 319n

Shakespeare, Gilbert (brother), 307, 309n

Shakespeare, Hamnet (son), 315, 319n

Shakespeare, John (father), 279, 281, 284n, 286n, 287, 308

Shakespeare, Mary (mother), 287

Shakespeare, William, 4n, 67, 73, 85, 87, 109, 129, 130, 141, 160, 178, 229, 230n, 261, 262n, 266, 272, 275, 276n, 276–277, 278n, 278–284, 284n–286n, 286–290, 291–293, 294n, 295, 297, 298n, 299–301, 302n, 302–303, 307–308, 309n, 313–319, 319n– 320n, 321, 335, 337, 338, 338n, 377, 400, 442, 443n, 459, 463n, 569, 583

All's Well That Ends Well, 308
Antony and Cleopatra, 277
  Charmian, 293, 318
  Cleopatra, 76, 140, 283, 293, 318, 323
  Mark Antony, 283
As You Like It, 293, 323, 325
Comedy of Errors, The, 283
Coriolanus, 290n, 309n
Cymbeline, 150, 417
  Imogen, 56
Hamlet, 275, 278–284, 285n, 286, 288–289, 290n, 301, 308, 318, 377
  Hamlet, 277, 278–284, 284n–285n, 289, 293, 315, 378
  King Hamlet, 279, 290n
  Ophelia, 282, 286, 301, 378
1 Henry IV, 338
  Falstaff, 338, 365
  Robin Ostler, 67, 69n
2 Henry IV, 284n
Henry V, 284n
Julius Caesar, 272, 283, 284n, 308, 309n
  Mark Antony, 284n
  Julius Caesar, 272, 284n
King Henry VIII, 338, 339n
King Lear, 277, 288, 301n, 321n, 546
  Cordelia, 318, 319, 320, 335
  King Lear, 318, 320, 360
Love's Labour's Lost, 277, 283, 292
Macbeth, 275, 280, 284n, 290n, 318
Measure for Measure, 392
  Angelo, 130
Merchant of Venice, The, 283, 286, 309n
Midsummer Night's Dream, A, 229, 230n, 231, 280, 282, 283, 303, 318

Othello, 291–292, 335
    Iago, 133
Pericles, Prince of Tyre, 272, 320n
    Marina, 272, 282, 316, 317, 320n, 335
Romeo and Juliet, 54, 57n, 280, 377
    Juliet, 282
    Mercutio, 57n
    Romeo, 282, 481
    Tybalt, 54, 57n
Tempest, The, 214n, 303, 308, 320n, 546
    Miranda, 316, 317, 335
Timon of Athens, 190, 192
Troilus and Cressida, 329n, 442, 443n, 444n
Twelfth Night, 327, 329n, 496
Winter's Tale, The, 320n, 327
    Perdita, 282, 316, 317, 320n, 335
Shaw, George Bernard, 7, 10, 13n, 57n, 158n, 184, 235, 271–272, 273n, 318, 412, 581
Sheehy, Judge Eugene, 397, 401n
Shelley, Edward, 418, 420n, 422
Shelley, Percy Bysshe, 42, 394n, 415, 418, 422
Sheridan, John Desmond, 401n, 481
Sheridan, Richard Brinsley, 298n, 324n, 463n
Sheridan, Thomas, 222n, 463n
Sherwood, Robert, 147, 147n
Sidney, Sir Philip, 70n, 413
Simenon, George, 61, 62n, 522, 523n, 527
Simmons, Colonel William, 394, 395n
Sitric (Sitrec), 341, 343n, 346
Sitwell, Edith, 509, 510n
Skeat, Walter W., 282, 285n
Slataper, Scipio, 102, 102n
Slocum, John J., 4n, 52n–53n, 89, 92n, 154n

Smith, Warren Hunting, 8n, 547, 547n, 585–586, 587n
Smollett, Tobias, 134, 139n, 243
Smyth, Dame Ethel, 412, 419n
Solomon, Margaret, 578n
Solomons, Dr. Bethel, 3, 5n
Spenser, Sir Edmund, 262n, 292, 449
Sprigge, Elizabeth, 161, 162n
Staley, Thomas, 559n
Stallman, Robert Wooster, 540n
Stanihurst (or Stanyhurst), Richard, 50, 53n
Staples, Hugh B., 159, 160n
Stein, Gertrude, 28, 51, 59n, 117, 118n, 161, 162n, 201, 348, 540n, 544, 545n, 554, 555n, 567, 568n, 569, 580n
Stelloff, Frances, 4n, 119, 155n
Stendhal (Henri Beyle), 5n, 13n, 204, 205n, 234
Stephens, James, 361n, 586, 587n, 588n
Sterne, Laurence, 261, 414, 575n
Stevenson, Robert Louis, 221, 268n, 413
Strauss, Richard, 304
Strindberg, August, 432
Strong, L. A. G., 69n
Stoppard, Tom, 584n
Sudermann, Hermann, 414, 419n
Sullivan, John, 242, 244n, 377, 378, 379, 380, 381n, 398, 489
Sullivan, Kevin, 164–167, 167n, 170, 171n, 552n
Sullivan, Philip B., 382n
Sullivan, Timothy Daniel, 382n
Svevo, Italo (Ettore Schmitz), 545, 546n
Sweeney, James Johnson, 155n
Swift, Jonathan, 25, 27n, 28, 88, 92, 93, 186, 204, 205n, 209, 219n, 222n, 234–235, 236n, 261, 316, 323, 349, 358n, 370, 370n, 371n, 386, 391, 392, 394n, 414, 458n, 477, 507, 510n

NAME INDEX

Swinburne, Algernon Charles, 145, 146n
Synge, John Millington, 18, 142, 230n, 475, 480n

Talma, Louise, 123n, 126, 132n, 256n, 359n
Tellegen, Thon, 529, 532, 533, 533n
Temple, Sir William, 93, 235, 236n
Tennyson, Alfred Lord, 276n, 328
Thackeray, William Makepeace, 416, 420n
"Thistle and the Rose, The", 24
Thomas, Ambroise, 377, 378
Thomas, Dylan, 491n
Thomson, William, 294n
Thompson, John Hinsdale, 159, 160n
Thoreau, Henry David, 5n, 19, 30, 73, 74n
Thurber, James, 260n
Tillyard, E. M. W., 275, 276n, 280
Tindall, William York, 4n, 100, 108, 109, 109n, 155n, 430, 432, 488n, 558n
Toklas, Alice, 162n, 169n, 544n, 568n, 580n
Tolstoy, Leo, 5n, 38, 195, 196, 199, 201, 422, 426, 548
Tonnerre, Earl of, 398
Totévy, Georges Markow, 155n
Toulouse-Lautrec, Henri de, 76, 77n
Train, John, 15, 16n, 18
transition, 167n, 222, 391n, 437, 438n, 485, 500, 555n
Transatlantic Review, The, 455, 458n
Travers, Mary, 414, 419n
Trinity College Dublin, 5n
Trollope, Anthony, 26, 28, 67, 105, 106n, 441, 442, 443n, 476, 480n, 553
Troxell, Gilbert McCoy, 321, 322n
Turgenev, Ivan, 195, 579
Twain, Mark (all references to *Huckleberry Finn*), 20, 180, 183, 523n

Tysdahl, Bjorn, 507, 510n
Tzara, Tristan, 584n

Ulysses (film, dir. Joseph Strick), 539, 540n
UNESCO, 63, 63n, 64n, 71n
University College Dublin, 5n

Vanhomrigh, Esther, 236n, 358n
Vega, Lope de, 9, 13n, 34, 51, 53n, 61, 63n, 71, 78, 126, 127, 127n, 168
Vercingetorix, 350, 350n
Verdi, Giuseppe, 135, 136n, 140, 205, 243, 244n, 276n, 294n, 381n, 395n, 411, 421
Verlaine, Paul, 174, 240, 242
Verne, Jules, 303
Victoria, Queen, 45
Vico, Giovanni Battista, 20, 21, 23n, 31, 45–47, 47n, 185, 196, 316, 346
Vining, Edward Payson, 280, 283, 285n
Virgil (Publius Virgilius Maro), 415, 454

Wadding, Luke, 11
Wadsworth, Frank W., 291, 294n
Wagner, Richard, 105n, 133, 244n, 381n, 390n, 414
Wake Newslitter, A, 172n, 332n, 366, 367n, 374, 375, 375n, 380, 403, 407n, 410, 418n, 419n, 442n, 443n, 444, 457n, 464, 465, 465n, 466n, 471, 479, 480n, 492n, 493, 496, 498n, 499n, 509n, 510n, 513, 513n, 516, 516n, 517, 537, 551n, 571
Waller, Lewis, 272
Waln, Nora, 177, 179n
Walpole, Horace, 180, 346, 347n, 453, 458n, 523, 538n, 543, 544n, 547

Walsh, Ernest, 419n
Walton, Isaak, 342
Weaver, Harriet Shaw, 4n, 91n, 92, 92n, 93, 99n, 112, 185, 228, 233n, 274n, 299, 397
Weber, Carl Maria von, 382n
Welles, Orson, 54, 57n
Wellington, Arthur Wellesley, 1st Duke of, 45, 53n, 70n, 95, 279, 282, 283, 284n, 346, 347n, 352
Welty, Eudora, 95, 95n
Wesendonk, Mathilde, 389, 390n
West, Mae, 197
West, Rebecca, 12, 13n–14n, 134
Weston, Jessie Laidlay, 264–266, 267n, 272, 273n, 293
Wharton, Edith, 195
White, Blanco, 88
White, T. H., 469, 469n, 471n
Whitman, Walt, 5n, 259, 270, 273n, 296
Whittington, Richard (Dick), 357, 358n
Wiggin, Lawrence, 84n, 101n, 102n, 114n
Wilde, Oscar, 15, 45, 47n, 146, 175n, 188, 201, 275, 276n, 280, 282, 304, 322, 328, 331, 365, 373, 399, 413, 418, 419n, 422, 476
Wilde, Sir William, 414, 419n
Wilder, Amos Niven (brother), 130n, 179n, 200n, 419n, 473n, 538n
Wilder, Amos Tappan (nephew), 200n, 559
Wilder, Charlotte (sister), 75n, 83n, 429
Wilder, Isabel (sister), 5n, 69n, 126, 163, 196, 202, 203, 205n, 207, 212, 215, 225, 243, 309, 342, 362, 388, 393, 468, 470, 484n, 491, 493, 511, 512, 513n, 514, 516n, 517, 520, 521, 522, 524, 527, 530, 531, 533, 536n, 538n, 539, 545, 552, 562n, 574, 576, 577, 578n, 581, 583, 584n, 587n, 588n
Wilder, Katherine Kerlin (sister-in-law), 200n
Wilder, Thornton
Writings
Alcestiad, The (play, also titled *A Life in the Sun*), 116n, 118n, 119, 120n, 123n, 148n, 162n, 169n, 491n
Alcestiad, The: An Opera in Three Acts, 123n, 127n, 132n, 256n, 359n, 364n
"Beauty of the World: The Europeans and the American", 127n
Bernice, 169n
Cabala, The, 546n
Childhood, 251n, 362n
"Culture In A Democracy", 169n
Eighth Day, The, 127n, 404n, 468n, 484n, 496n, 499n, 512n, 532n, 538n, 539n, 540, 543n, 547, 550, 568n
"Emporium, The", 59n
"Exploration and Explanation", 77n
Happy Journey to Trenton and Camden, The, 169n
Heaven's My Destination, 119, 120n
Ides of March, The, 5n, 19, 96, 96n, 112, 161n
"Illinois, 1905", 71n
Infancy, 362n
"Ira", 251n
"Lope, Pinedo, Some Child Actors, and a Lion", 13n
Matchmaker, The, 116n, 123n, 163, 164n, 246n, 484n, 520n
"Martians, The", 116n
Merchant of Yonkers, The, 116n

"New Aids Towards Dating the Early Plays of Lope de Vega", 13n, 53n
Norton Lectures, 5n, 9, 16n, 17, 36n, 44n, 52n
Our Town, 238n, 493
Plays for Bleecker Street, 362, 362n
"Seven Ages of Man, The," "The Seven Deadly Sins" (cycle plays), 148n, 203n
Skin of Our Teeth, The, 59n, 77n, 112, 118n, 246n, 513n, 539
Someone from Assisi, 362n
Theophilus North, 540n, 568n, 573, 573n, 578n
Wreck on the Five-Twenty-Five, The, 169n
"Zen", 568n
Writings on Joyce
"*Finnegans Wake*: The Polyglot Everyman", 207, 207n
"Giordano Bruno's Last Meal in *Finnegans Wake*", 191n, 205n, 231n, 373n, 374n, 375, 376n, 382n, 407n, 419n
"Joyce and the Modern Novel", 86n, 101n, 154n, 158n, 160n
William III, King, 12
Williams, Tennessee, 169n
Williams, William Carlos, 14n, 164n
Wills, William Gorman, 339n
Wilson, Edmund, 26n, 31, 32n, 34, 62, 63n, 64, 64n, 392, 394n, 549n

Wilson, Woodrow, 336
Windle, Catharine F. Ashmead, 291–292, 294n
Wolff, Max J., 282, 285n
Woolf, Leonard, 398
Woolf, Virginia, 18, 207, 208, 210n, 211–212, 214n, 273n, 396, 398, 402n, 437
Woollcott, Alexander, 52n, 57n
Wordsworth, William, 160, 161n, 222n, 288
Worth, Irene, 489
Worthington, Mabel, 73n, 219n, 264n, 269, 273n, 278n, 304, 328, 393, 399, 407, 408n, 450n, 480n, 584n
Wycherley, William, 324n

Yaddo (writer's colony), 61
Yeats, Bertha Georgie (George) Hyde-Lees (Mrs. William Butler Yeats), 216, 218, 219n, 220, 222n
Yeats, J. B., 155n
Yeats, William Butler, 10, 13n, 36, 36n, 56, 145, 146n, 175, 180, 182n, 184, 186n, 189, 211–214, 214n, 216–218, 219n, 221, 222n, 223, 229, 230n, 231, 275, 285n, 411, 439, 440, 450n, 456, 458n, 475, 477, 480n, 504, 509n, 560, 561n, 579
Young, Brigham, 448
Yule, Sir Henry, 22, 42

Zola, Émile, 195

Finnegans Wake
Page/Line Index

Finnegans Wake page and line references are in bold followed by page references to this text.

Book I, i (**3–29**) 48n, 205n, 290, 500, 509
Book I, ii (**30–47**) 47n, 48n, 276, 278, 278n, 292
Book I, iii (**48–74**) 276, 278, 278n, 308
Book I, iv (**75–103**) 9n, 159, 276, 278, 278n, 288, 308, 323n, 363
Book I, v (**104–125**) 307
Book I, vi (**126–168**) 293, 443, 567
Book I, vii (**169–195**) 196n, 373n
Book I, viii (**196–216**) 79, 83, 85, 119, 123n, 155n, 162, 168, 205n, 224n, 243, 325, 335
Book II, i (**219–259**) 48n
Book II, ii, (**260–308**) 489, 503, 505
Book II, iii (**309–382**) 47n, 315
Book II, iv (**383–399**) 80n, 335
Book III (**403–590**) 94
Book III, i (**403–428**) 97–99
Book III, ii (**429–473**) 98–99, 424
Book III, iii (**474–554**) 160n
Book IV (**593–628**) 21, 94, 109, 499n

3 277, 347n
3.1–.14 339
3.4 233
3.5 232
3.7–.8 390
3.8 232
3.9 232, 353, 357
3.9–.10 366
3.11 28, 232
3.12 28, 232, 391

3.13 233
3.14 232, 278n
3.20 233
3.23 346
4.1 313
4.3–.4 174
4.8 453
4.15 431, 434n
4.18ff 366
4.24 366

4.30 366
4.31 340, 366
4.34 340
4.36 313, 340
5.3 340
5.5 279
5.5–.6 47n
5.18 312
5.22 190
5.27 372

5.30 378
5.31 378
5.35 378
5.36 11, 476
6.7 192
6.27 348
6.35 207
7.4 338, 348
7.9 475
7.13 338
7.15 348, 475
7.20–8.8 175n, 385n
7.20–10.24 385n, 401n
7.27 312
8–10 281
8.2–.3 383
8.3 384
8.4 383
8.9–11.28 346
8.14 383
8.15 349, 383
8.20–10.18 384
8.23 427
8.24 399
8.28 384
8.31 386
8.33 386
8.34 386
8.36 384
9 228, 346
9.2 383
9.4 350
9.5 350
9.5–9.26 384
9.6 346, 384
9.7 350, 383
9.10 399
9.13 3, 350
9.13–.14 346
9.14 384
9.17 384
9.20 384
9.21 384
9.26 383
9.27 267n, 350

9.31–.32 346
9.32 350
9.33 384
9.34 350, 384
9.35 95, 384
9.36 446
10.1ff 350
10.6 497
10.14 18
10.14–.19 95
10.15 18
10.18 497
10.19 350
10.21 349
10.35 346
10.36 176
11.3 431
11.11 353
11.13 431, 441
11.15 441
11.17 353
11.27 442
11.31 357
11.33 353
11.34 357
11.34–.35 441
11.35 353, 357, 441
11.36 441
12.11–.12 399
12.14 399
12.23 140, 144
12.26 312
12.31 346
13 94
13–14 163, 247
13.4–14.27 250n
13.9 11, 18, 462
13.10 462
13.13 11, 18, 462
13.14 462
13.22 248
13.24–.25 247
13.28 247
13.36 228
14.6 247, 248

14.13 370
14.20 432
14.36 440
15.9 440
15.11 399
15.16 440
16–17 95
16.1 95
16.11 311
16.15 183
16.36 346
17.2 240
17.2–.6 242
17.9 341
17.14 192
17.23 269
17.24 269
19.4 344
19.12–.19 293
19.15 293
19.15–.16 346
19.16 318
19.22 416
19.27 361
19.28 361
19.29 361
20.3 318
20.19–23.15 347n
20.27 14n
20.34–.35 55
21–23 176n
21.12 475
21.13 475
21.15 475
21.18–.19 473
21.25 475
21.30 17
21.36 340, 475
22.2 475
22.5–.6 473
22.12 340, 475
22.19 340, 475
22.36 490
23 11, 347n
23.6 472

FINNEGANS WAKE PAGE/LINE INDEX

23.20 46
24.6 446
24.18 15
24.20 11, 476
24.21 476
25.4 29n
25.5 477
25.9–.10 15
25.26 137
26.1 208, 490
26.2–.3 192
26.9 424
26.10 263
26.13 209
26.14 263
26.18 424
26.19 263
26.20–.24 424
27.1 17, 55
27.6 290
27.8–.9 192
27.11–.21 391
27.14 254
27.23 10
27.25 10
27.31 55
28.1 17, 192
28.5 10, 54
28.8 415
28.20 418
28.27 192
28.33 192
28.35 134
29.2 416
29.7 386
29.27 192
29.27–.28 192
29.35 192
30.2 344
30.6–.7 344
30.6–.8 334
30.11 135
30.35 192
31 274, 278, 289
31.6 346

31.11 274
31.11–.12 265
31.13–.14 266
31.14 274
31.16 159
31.17–.19 11
31.25 274
31.26 192
31.29 11
32.3 192
32–33 317
32.4–.5 506
32.7 311
32.9 270
32.23 192
32.29 270
33.1 346
33.8 270
33.24 270
33.29 270
33.34 127
34.1 192
34.8 136
34.15 291, 346
34.17 425
34.19–.23 333
34.23 192
34.32 333
34.33 333
35.2 417
35.14 278
35.15 36
35.15–.16 17
35.22 475
35.23 33
35.30 127
35.32 475
36.4 275
36.20 192
36.35 307
37.8 41
37.13 36
37.14 192, 275
38.10 224
38.14 411

39.4–.5 192
39.11 54
39.16–.17 278
39.17 275
39.29 279
40.1 440
40.3 262
40.11 192
40.13 275
40.14 275
40.15–.17 88
40.16 88, 92, 93
40.16–.17 397
40.23 373
40.23–.24 279
40.34 10
41.1 279
41.2 192, 490
41.3 389
41.3–.4 397
41.4 88
41.9 192, 487
41.12–.13 151
41.13 275
41.13–.14 279
41.16 189-190
41.17 192
41.18 279
41.28 400
42.2 127
42.4 192
42.11 279
42.20 146
43–44 265
43.2 279
43.5 279
43.7 459
43.10 50
43.23 413
43.31 265
43.32 138, 400
43.35 265
44 265, 347n
44-45 88
44–47ff 224, 265

44.3 265
44.9 265
44.10–.14 265, 292
44.11 275
44.13 279
44.16 157
44.19 265
44.19–.20 267n
44.19–.21 265
44.24–47.32 367n
48.3 317, 413
48.7 413
48.18 413
49–50 275
49.2 389
49.3 397
49.7–.8 88
49.14 389
49.24 393
49.26 413, 455
49.27 393
49.28 211n, 212
50.1 279, 406
50.9–.10 441
50.15 18, 55
50.17 400
51.7 446
51.8 446
51.12 446
51.12–.13 138
51.13 446
51.20 446
51.27 341
51.29 341
51.35 416
52 310
52.3 275
52.4–.5 279
52.16–.17 506
52.29–.30 12, 13
53.1–.3 279
53.1 88
53.15 88
53.36 279
54.5 89

54.22–.27 279
55 495
55.1 279
55.3–.4 437
55.10 279
55.16–.18 495
55.22 275
55.24 279
55.25–.26 495
55.27 275
55.28 275
55.31 279
55.33 495
55.34 495
56.1 495
56.14 462
56.16 279
56.22 279
56.27 279
56.28–.30 89
57 15
57.4 279
57.6 279
57.7–10 506
57.11 333
57.12 333
57.15 279
57.22 89
57.23–.29 333
57.28 333
58 33
58.6 383
58.8 393
58.18 383
58.24 33
58.30 383
59 137
59.1 413
59.2 373
59.2–.14 373
59.4 275
59.5 275
59.6–.7 18
59.8 373
59.11 373

59.12–.13 373
59.14 89, 373
59.20 275, 279
59.21 275
59.24 430
59.26 275
59.31 275, 279
59.33–.34 418
60.8 279
60.10 279
60.26 189, 279
60.31 150
61.1 150
61.14 341
61.19 342
61.24 342
62–64 280
62.5–.6 279
62.8 279
62.9–.10 275
62.11 275
62.13 275
62.15 279
62.17 280
62.19 280
62.25 283
62.26 280
62.34 11, 280
63.2 280
63.4 275, 280
63.10 280
63.15 280
63.16 280
63.19ff 280
63.20 275, 280
63.22 275
63.29 275, 399
63.30 280
63.31 280
63.33–.34 275
63.34 280
63.35 55, 280
63.36 280, 311
64.1 275, 280
64.3 275

64.4–.5 448
64.6 275
64.7 275
64.7–.8 280
64.9 275
64.9–.10 280
64.13 415
64.18 280
64.23 506
65 227
65.1 227
65.2 227, 280
65.5 494
65.7 227
65.11 280
65.12 227
65.14 280
65.17 275, 494
65.19 227
65.20 227
65.23 227
65.28 227
65.32 227, 476
65.32–.33 153
66.10 275, 280
66.13 259
66.14 259
66.18 275, 280
66.20 404
66.21 275, 280
66.22 275, 280
66.25 280, 482
66.26 482
66.29 275
67.15 280
67.18 275
67.20 275
67.23 280, 283
67.24 280, 283
67.33 212, 437
67.33–.36 209
68.9 437
68.20 258
68.27 275
68.32 280

68.33 417
68.34 417
69-70 354
69.3 280
69.6 432
69.7–.9 280
69.8 10
69.9 353, 354
69.10–.11 354
69.22 280
69.26 280
69.32 11
70.12 354
70.22 354
70.25 354
71–72 280
71.8 142
71.9 383
71.11 392
71.24 490
72.4 217
72.11 142, 144
72.15 280, 357
72.18 413
72.19 413
72.26 413
72.34–.35 280
73 41
73.1 440
73.16 280
73.21 281
73.32–.33 506
73.35 271
73.36 271
74.1 271
74.2 271
74.3 271
74.4 271
74.4–.5 209, 271
74.6 271
74.6–.7 271
74.9 437, 506
75–103 438n
75.1 506
75.15 281

75.20 56
75.21 281
76.5 281
76.10 281
76.21–.23 452
76.27–.28 342
76.31 56
76.33 281
77.7 415
77.13 20, 432
78 45
78.3 281
78.7 281
78.8 281
78.13 281
78.14 281
78.17 217
78.24 281
78.28 266
78.29 266
78.36 266
79.1 281
79.8–.9 281
79.18 281, 372
79.20–.21 281
79.22 281
79.23–.24 281
79.27 50, 281
79.30 281
79.31 399
79.33 281, 446
79.35 281
80 10
80.1–.2 341
80.1ff 281
80.8 281, 415
80.9 340, 415
80.13 282
80.14–.19 281
80.15 282
80.20 282
80.28–.29 10
81.2–.3 282
81.3 353
81.5 282, 462

81.9 217
81.10 282
81.11 282
81.16 282
81.17 282
81.23 282
81.28 282
81.30 282
81.34–.35 282
82.4 151
82.5 282, 399
82.9 282
82.11 282
82.12 282
82.13 151
82.14 282
82.15 495
82.17 151
82.19–.21 495
82.29 282
82.31–.32 282
83.3 282
83.5 282
83.7–.8 437
83.15 266, 437
83.21 266
83.23 282
83.28 282
83.29 282
84.2 266, 341, 437
84.4 283
84.6 266
84.7 266
84.11 437
84.15 437
84.17 495
84.20 495
84.23 341
84.34 283
84.36 151, 283
85.6ff 266
85.8 266, 283
85.10 283
85.14 266, 283
85.17 266

85.18 266, 283
85.23 89
85.27 415
85.28–.29 283
85.33 366
85.36 415
86 288
86.2 366
86.13 142, 283
86.14 283, 366
86.15 283
86.17 366
86.21–.22 283
86.27 283
87.1–.2 72
87.8 441
87.9 283
87.10 283, 328
87.20 283
87.22 283
87.25 312
87.26 275
88.6 492
88.15 283
88.24 454
88.30 24
88.31–.32 454
88.33 283
89.3–.4 283
89.4 352
89.13 352
89.15 352
89.18–.19 266
89.34 283
89.36 283
90 437n
90.31–.32 472
91.1 275
91.6 283
91.6–.7 318
91.7 283
91.13 141
91.22 269
91.24 269
91.30 432

92.4 283
92.6 142
92.6–.7 340
92.14 283
92.15 283
92.16 415
92.20 283
92.26 494
92.27 492
93 364
93.1 283
93.8 283
93.18 283
93.18–.19 283
93.22 410
93.27–.28 25
93.28–.29 25
93.30 379
93.34 192
93.35 145
94 15
94–95 283
94.3 283
94.29–.31 460
94.34 349
95 25, 45
96.2 283
96.4 283
96.10 399
96.33 25, 283
97.17 432
97.21ff 283
97.22 283
97.33 436
97.34 283
98.2 266
98.5 266, 283
98.21 449
98.29 459
98.30 459
99.10 415
99.15 433
99.16 176
99.19 283
99.22 266

99.29–.30 283
99.32–.34 459
100.2 455
100.6 284
100.25 432
100.28 284
101.3 284
101.9–.10 284
101.15 331
101.22 284
101.24 284
102.10 427
102.11 333
102.12 333, 428
102.12–.13 428
102.13 428
102.18 311
102.21–.22 284
102.27 284
103 284
103.5 284
103.8 411
103.10–.11 411
104ff 220
104.6–.7 221
104.10 221, 266, 352
104.11 352
104.18 270, 286
104.20 286
104.24 221
104.30–.31 72
105.1 286
105.3 221
105.8 221
105.10 436
105.11 448
105.14 221
105.18 286
105.19 19
105.22 286, 448
105.26 221
105.28–.29 180
105.34 286
105.35 221
106.2 286

106.9 221
106.11–.12 286
106.12 380
106.13 383
106.17 221
106.17–18 287
106.23 221
106.24 333
106.28 221, 352
106.28–.29 447
106.30 287, 352
106.33 353
107.8 150
107.15 287
107.18 235
107.22 235
107.34 432
108.1 287
108.21 266
108.26 367, 404
108.27 367, 506
109.1 287
110–113 287
110.7 187
110.13–.14 287
110.16 296
110.17 187, 287
110.18 287
110.23 287
110.30 287
110.35 328
111 88, 296
111–112 287, 295
111.5 287
111.6 221
111.8 296
111.11 287
111.13 288
111.16 288
111.20 221, 229
111.26 288
111.28 288
111.30 288
111.32 20
112.1 288

112.3–.4 267
112.5 288
112.7 452, 457n
112.8 506
112.11–.12 296
112.13–.14 296
112.16 296
112.21–.22 296
112.26 448, 475
112.26–.27 296, 301
112.27 296
112.28 475
112.29 475
112.30 221, 229
112.33 506
112.35 56, 296, 478
113 347n
113.16 333
113.35 333
113.36 506
114.2 430
114.16–.17 288
114.18–.19 288, 430
114.23 288
114.29 259, 413
114.30 259, 288
114.31 225
114.34–.36 288
114.35 288
115.14–.16 225
116.2 506
116.19 494
116.21–.22 288
116.25 288
116.36 221, 229, 288
117 221, 229
117.2 221, 229, 267
117.3 221, 229
117.4–.7 288
117.16 221
117.24 190
117.29–.30 174
118.1–.2 288
118.3–.4 288
118.13 56, 288

118.16 246, 288
118.19 288
118.20 221, 288
118.22 288
118.23 288
118.25 288
118.26 288
118.28 288, 313
118.32 288
119 88
119.5 288
119.7 288
119.9 221, 288
119.10 288
120.2 473
120.3–.4 499
120.5 288
120.7–.8 288
120.9 288
120.11 288
120.13–.14 296
120.15 288
120.27 288
120.35–.36 288
121.1 10, 288
121.2–.8 289
121.11–.12 289
121.20 289
121.27 289
121.31 289
121.31–.32 289
122.7 289
122.9ff 289
122.10 289
122.11–.12 289
122.12–.13 289
122.16 289
122.19 221, 289
122.23 289
122.31 289
122.33–.34 289
123.15 221
123.16 452
123.17 452
123.19 289

123.24 221
123.26 452
123.32 289, 452
124.1 221
124.2 289
124.3–.5 33
124.4–.5 26
124.6–.7 289
124.9 221
124.11 221
124.13 289
124.23–.24 289
124.27 289
124.29 432, 477
124.31 289-290
124.32 289
124.36 188
125.11–.12 290
125.21–.22 290
126 439
126–139 175
126.10 442
126.12 416, 451
126.13 31
126.17 333, 448
126.17–.18 448
126.18 448
127.1 308
127.36 389
128.20 142
128.–.29 259
128.32 137
129.16 178
129.23 414, 497
130.2 242
130.5 432
130.24 456
130.27 470
130.29 470
130.30 470
130.34 470
130.35 434, 470
131.8 436
131.13 436
131.14 436

131.18 436
131.33+ 223
131.33–.34 436
131.34 436
131.35 56, 240
132.8 461
132.10 461
132.27 11
132.32–.33 451
132.35 56
133.2 311
133.10 449
133.11 449
133.16–.17 448
133.19 56, 448
133.19–.20 378
133.20 243
133.21 17, 449, 461
133.23 427
133.25 416, 449
133.27 313n
133.28 449
134.4–.5 437, 454
134.4–.15 436
135.12 136
135.13 138, 399
135.17 138
136.16 476
136.20 269
136.21 269, 380
136.32 348
137.7 432
137.22–.23 45
137.23–.25 356
137.24 442
138.8 442
138.12 242
138.32–.33 180
139.6 390, 411
140 20
140.1 11, 453
140.30 133, 478
141 55, 510n
141.8–.26 55
141.9 55

141.14 55
141.29 356
141.32 415
142 55
142.31 339, 449
143 261
143.1–.2 431n
143.3 378
143.5 378
143.5–.6 506
143.7 378
143.8–.9 454
143.10 378
143.11 378
143.13 453
143.15 378
143.15–.16 261
143.19 378
143.20 261
143.22 261
143.24 378
143.26 378
144.5 479
144.6 441
144.8 477
144.10 328
144.14 211, 211n
144.17 211, 211n
144.29–.30 209
146.13 17, 361
146.17 506
146.17–.18 361
146.34 56
147.17 415
147.21 506
147.33 211
148.21 312
148.24 312
148.33–168.12 567
149.8 415
149.10 141
149.17 461
149.19 461
150.4 476
150.7 145

150.12 145
150.27 476
151 272
151.8 238
151.9 150
151.11 272
151.14 238
151.17 272
151.17–.21 272
151.18 238, 272
151.20 238, 272
151.21 238, 272
151.22 238, 272
151.23 238, 272
151.24 17, 272
151.30 272
152.4 145
152.15–159.18 230n
152.21 324
152.24 324
152.27 324
153.23 507
153.30 141
154.2 322
154.23 18, 20, 432
155 239
156.22 506
156.23 400
156.27 190
157.4 506
157.13 568n
157.17 476
157.34 11
158.7 56
158.15 304
158.16 304
158.25 304
158.26 304
158.32 304
158.33 304
159.4 568n
159.5–.6 304
159.8 304, 322
159.12 304, 322
159.14 153, 304, 322

159.15 304, 322
159.16 304
159.18 304, 322
159.34 141, 144
160.18 141
160.26ff 492
160.27–.28 47
161ff 271
161–.167 318
161–168 *passim* 338n
161.15 324
161.22 324
161.27–.32 271
161.28 272
161.30 272, 297
161.32 324
161.36 324
162 272, 506
162.1 272
162.8 272
162.9 272
162.11 272
162.12 272
162.14 272
162.16 272
162.27 417
162.27–.28 150
162.28 417
162.32 454
162.34 324
162.35 324
163.1 272
163.10 400
163.25 440
164 337
164.20 325
164.20–.21 308, 337
164.23 325
164.26 308, 325
164.27 325
165 505
165.2 17
165.15 145
165.22 140
165.24–.25 140

165.28 506
166.7 412
166.11 411
166.15 478
166.16 145, 412
166.20–.21 568n
166.24–.26 412
166.28 412
167.10 150
167.16 506
167.26–.27 141
168.5–.6 56
169.4 56, 344, 357
169.5 56
169.18 506
169.22 418
170.3 356, 358
171.16 473
171.25–.28 473
172.5 141, 279
172.5–.10 279
172.7 279
173.2 178
173.15 432
173.20 178
173.28 312
174.19 372
175.5 478
175.19–.20 333
175.28 265
175.31 372
175.33 372
175.35 356, 358
175.36 229
176.8 441
176.13 414, 425
176.28 373
176.34 372
176.36 372
177.4 479, 481
177.10 372
177.14 372
177.19 479
177.21 479, 481
177.22 29

177.27 479
178.22 412
178.27 237
178.30 237
178.31 237
178.32 237
179.17 372
179.31 324
179.33 324, 454
179.33–.34 324
180.5 393
180.6 393
180.11 393
180.15 393
181.2 150
181.18 507
181.25 426
181.26 195, 426
182.12 417
182.15–.16 373
183.11 201
183.12 201
183.14 201
183.17 201
183.18 201
183.19 201
183.20 201
183.22 201
183.23 201
183.24 201
183.25 201
183.27 201
183.28 201
183.29 201
183.30 201
183.30–.31 201
183.32 201
183.32–.33 201
183.33 201
183.35 201, 372
184 178
184–185 254
184.13 254
184.14 333, 334
184.15 268

184.16 268, 380
184.17 334
184.19–.20 235
184.20 178, 208
184.21 220, 254
184.23–.25 209
184.24 220
184.25 178
184.27 177, 334
184.27–.28 178
184.28 380
184.29 178, 253
184.30 178, 190, 253
184.32 254
184.33 178
184.34 187, 220
184.35 11, 254, 460
184.36 190, 254
185.14 326, 507
185.24 326
185.24–.25 312
185.25 254, 326, 441
185.29 312
185.31 326
185.33 326
186 510n
186–187 89
186.1 195, 312
186.4 196
186.7 92
186.8 196
186.23 180
186.25 196, 441
186.28 196
186.33 195
187 510n
187–193 308
187.7 180
187.11 93
187.11–.12 441
187.24 507
188 430
188.12 328
189 229
189.6 195

189.11 195
189.12 195
189.13 195
189.14 195
189.16 195
189.18 195, 432
189.19 195
189.25 477
189.28 195
189.29 195
189.31 56
190.8 195
190.33 507
191 238
191.9 227
191.9–.33 263
191.10 226
191.11 264
191.12 226
191.13 226, 328
191.18 263
191.21 227
191.23 227
191.24 227
191.26 226, 263, 328
191.30 227
191.34 428
192.3 209
192.4 209
192.5 209
192.11–.25 181
192.14 209
192.26 328
192.29 209
192.35 370, 411
192.36 370
193 505
193.1–.3 220
193.11 370
193.15 370
193.29 505
194.2 479
194.5 479
194.11–.12 507
194.17 478

194.22 481
195 505
195,5 505
196 229
196–216 391n
196.9 128
196.11 43
196.24 43
197.3 349
197.6 426
197.13–.14 494
197.14 452
197.28 349
197.31 372
197.36–198.1 24
198.17 424
198.30 399
198.31 290
199.1 448
199.2 426
199.29–.30 399
200.12–.13 507
200.25 326
200.27 426
200.33 190, 326
200.35 326
202 15, 16
202.8 307
202.8–.10 300
202.20–.21 426
203.9–.10 335
203.21–.22 335
203.26 57, 116
203.29–.30 209
203.31 211n
204.6 29
204.8 331
204.13 331
204.23 211n
205 287
205.13 413
205.21 427
205.28 340
205.31 357
205.33 340

205.34 340
205.35 178
206.14 372
206.31 426
207 239
207.16 325
207.19 326
207.24 325
207.24–.25 426
207.27 326
207.28 326
207.34 325
208ff 177
208.2 177
208.9 428
208.15 326, 449
208.18 417
208.18–.19 177
208.19 177, 326, 417
208.20 417
208.22 417
208.22–.23 428
208.23 413
208.25 177, 417
208.25–.30 417
208.29 261, 277, 287
208.29–.31 301
208.30–.31 325
209–212 301
209.14 261
209.34 34
210.7 89
210.8–.9 154, 413, 442
210.9 413
210.10 389
210.12 389
210.13–.14 390
210.14 400
210.15 425
210.20 425
210.28 400
210.29 427
210.30 12
210.33 427
210.33–.34 15

211.1 45, 426
211.2 10
211.9 254
211.10–.11 462
211.11 427
211.12 397
211.13 50
211.15 383
211.18 10. 459
211.22 426
211.24 45
211.25 10, 45
211.27 180
211.28 10, 342, 390
211.33 10
211.35 157
212.8–.9 507
213 13
213.4 427
213.5–.6 470
213.14 32
213.18–.19 33
213.30 427
213.32–.34 254
213.34 426
213.35 154
213.34–.35 13, 254
214.2 205
214.5 205
214.11 43
214.27–.28 418
215.33 490, 491n
219–259 23n, 562n
219.9 438n
219.21 438n
219.24 562n
220.19 150
221.6 432
221.30 432
221.33 411
221.34 341, 411
221.35 399
222.2 17
222.28 266
223 15

223.22 413
223.27–.33 89
223.19–.24 176n
223.28 45
224.32 400
226 229
226.24 454
226.34 258
226.35 258
227.14 417
227.16–.17 258
227.22 462
227.29–.30 258
227.35 384
228.10 456
228.14 177
228.15–.16 411
228.18 479
228.21 17
228.27 181
228.32–.33 399
228.33 15
228.36 432
229.13 372
229.20 507
229.21 462
229.26 462
230.9 188
230.12 389
231.12 418
231.27 507
231.30 150
232.36 145
233.16 400
233.30 460
233.35 446
234.1–.5 152
234.3 446
234.6ff 487
234.8 446
234.9 152
234.10 152
234.12 152, 446
234.15 478
234.16 487

234.20 152, 446
234.21 507
234.30 400
235 10
235.6 178
235.28 427
235.30 404
236.13 478
236.23 414
236.24–.25 414, 429
236.25 414
238.3 460
238.8–.9 455
239.18 312
239.19–.21 312
240.3 461
240.8 17
240.12 440
240.13 354
240.27 56
241.5 440
241.7 454
241.15 89
241.27 507
241.31 315
242 454
242.2 418
242.5 454
242.11 454
242.12 454
242.20 454
242.27 454
242.30 454
243.4 12
243.12 477
243.23 476
244 3, 4, 35, 39, 44n
244–245 23n, 44
244.4 44
244.13 22, 39, 40
244.14 40
244.14–.15 35, 40
244.15 40
244.16 40
244.16–.17 40

244.17 40
244.17–.18 40
244.18–.19 40
244.19 40
244.20 35, 40-50
244.21 41
244.22 434
244.23 35, 41
244.25 32
244.25–.26 41
244.26 41
244.28 41
244.29 41
244.30 35, 41, 432
244.31 35, 41
244.31–.32 41
244.32 41
244.33 41
244.34 41
244.34–.35 41
244.35 41-42, 137
244.36 42
245.1 42, 137
245.1–.2 42
245.3 42
245.4 42
245.5 42
245.5–.6 42
245.6 3, 42
245.7 42
245.8 3, 42, 55
245.10 263
245.33 55
245.34 55
248.2 386
248.3 474
248.8 386, 474
248.10 55, 386, 474
248.13 386
248.15–.16 456
248.17 386
248.18 386
248.20 386
249 229
251 130

251.11 399
251.17 56
252.6 23n
252.15 133, 417
252.16 417
252.26 23n
253.24 392
253.31 11
253.35 448
254 368
254.2 11
254.10 138
254.18 507
255.14 446
255.15 427
255.16 177
255.26 427
256.11 507
256.27 449
256.28 449
256.29 449
256.36 328
257 347n
257.5 150
257.7 449
257.8 151
257.11 188
258–259 46
258.5 112
258.13 46
260–261 504
260–308 341, 503
260 503. 504
260.4 212
260.8 212
260.12–.13 258
260 left margin 212,
   447, 504
260 note 1 503, 504
260 note 2 504
260 note 3 504
261.8 212
261.9 212
261.13 462
261.19 504

261.21 212
261.23 400
261.25 424, 436
262 193, 212
262.1–.2 417
262.2 193
262.16 342
262 note 1 358
262 note 3 55
262 note 6 342
262 note 7 112, 399
263.1 342
263.1–.3 354
263.2 342
263.18 212
263.21 354
263.22 212
263.23 354
263.30 354
263 note 1 354
263 note 2 400
264 486
264–265 487n
264.4 342
264.5 436
264.5–.6 455
264.6 417
264.7 417
264.24 242
264.30 212
264 note 1 400
264 note 3 212
266.19 213
266.21–22 217
266.27 242
266 note 2 213
267.1 213
267.3 460
267.12 472
267.13 258
267.14 258
267.15 258
267.16 258
267.17 258
267.18 454

267.19 432
267.22 454
267.24 454
267.24–.25 213
267 note 4 472
267 note 5 454
267 left margin 454
268.2 33
268.10 394
268.18 394
268 left margin 175, 213
269.17 323
269.18 323
269.24 463
269.25 463
269.28 213
269 left margin 229
269 note 2 140
270.19 489
270.20 333
270.20–.22 317
270.25 454, 477
270.26 477
271.1ff 488
271.3–.4 489
271.4 489
271.6 489
271.10 489
271.12 489
271.16–.17 489
271.18–.19 213
271.29 504
271 left margin 489
271 note 5 489
272.2 213
272.4 213
272.9 214, 446
272.14 446
272.20 446
272.25 414
272.25–.27 429
272.26 414
272.27 414
273.11 446

273.23 446
273.26 446
274.2 370
274.29 507
274.31 213
275.13 399
275 left margin 213
276.25 333
276 note 3 43
276 note 5 333
276 note 7 333
277.1–.3 43
277.2 43, 44
277.6 213
277.9 213
277.14 358
277.18 358
277.19 213
277 note 2 43
277 note 3 414
278.5 303
278.6 303
278.8 304
278.12 304
278.13 303
278 left margin 438
278 note 1 303
278 note 2 303
279.3 238
279.7–.8 416
279.14 398
279.15 398
279.16 398
279.18 398
279.21 398
279.32 398
279 right margin 238
279 note 1 18, 180, 190, 211, 211n, 229, 398, 428
279 note 1 line 10 442
279 note 1 line 18 442
279 note 1 line 19 442
279 note 1 line 28 442
280.1 215

280.6 213
280.34 213
281.14 415
281.17 261
281.21 133
281.23 213
281.27 153
281 left margin 261
281 right margin 212
281 note 1 151
281 note 2 425
281 note 3 109, 261
282 16, 261
282.4 261
282.5 454
282.8 453
282.25 432
283.4 400
283.7 460
283.8 460
283.17 177
283.19 226
283.23 213
283.24 460
283.26ff 180
283 note 1 12, 442
284.28–285.2 190
284 note 1 213
285.2 190
285.2–.3 216
285.3 213
285.4 213
285.15 213
285.27 417
285.28–.29 416
285 note 5 213
285 note 6 191
286 16
286.3 193
286.3–.24 416
286.4 416
286.5 213
286.6 416
286.13–.15 416
286.14 416

286.15 416
286.17 213
286.24 150
286.27 312
287.1 151, 446
287.4 151, 446
287.7 453
287.10 475
287.13 453
287.18 213
287.27 151
287.31 151, 446
287 note 1 475
287 note 3 151
287 note 4 446
288.1 151
288.1–.10 446
288.5 151, 213, 446
288.8 151, 213, 446
288.10 417
288.17 432
288.19–.21 235
288 note 2 213
288 note 4 55
288 note 7 151
289–292 226
289.2 432
289.8 10
289.9 56
289.15 226
289.25 263
289 note 3 213
290.1 339
290.2 226
290.2–.3 235
290.3 431n
290.17 412
290.20 412
290.21 412
290.24 339
290.25 339
290.26 339
290.28 476
290 note 1 339
290 note 7 229, 412

291 339
291.8 226
291.14 176, 180, 226
291.19 141
291.24 340
291.26 339
291.28 394
291 note 1 339
291 note 3 180, 226
291 note 4 414
291 note 6 238
291 note 8 394
292.1 269
292.1–.2 226, 273n
292.2–.3 226
292.3 269
293 503, 504, 505
293.3 213
293.11 213
293.18 344
293.21 344
293.27 353
293 right margin 504
293 note 2 353
294.2 495
294.8 140
294.12 188
294.23–.24 23n
294.27 213
294.29 141
294 note 1 495
295.1 141
295.10–.12 213
295.17 397
295.19 397
295.20 397
295.23–.24 213
295.33 397
296.9 333
296.21 213, 333
296.24 333
296.26 333
297.6 188
297.10 372
297.11 213

297.12 213
297.29 194
297.31 194, 215
298.3 213
298.16 213
298.24 187
298.28 213
298.32 213
298 left margin 187
299 88
299.13–.14 462
299.14–.15 218
299.22 11
299 note 2 462
300.3 416
300.9 416
300.12 218, 398
300.16 217, 218, 398
300.17 218, 398
300.18 398
300.20–.27 213
300.28 455
300.29 398
300.30 218
300 left margin 218
300 right margin 398
300 note 3 416
300 note 4 398
301.3 442
301.6 416
301.29 353
301 note 1 398
301 note 3 398
302.31–.32 213
303.5 215, 216
303.7–.8 213
303.16 218
303.17 141, 188, 216
303.19 216
303 left margin 213
304.8 392
304.25 212
304.27–.28 140
304.31 140
304 left margin 213

304 note 4 269
305.3 235
305.5 235
305.6 432
305.7 235
305.8 235
305.14 140
305.15 235
305.16 235
305.19 140
305.20 239
305.23–.24 235
305.33 235
305 right margin 174
305 note 1 235
305 note 3 492, 506
306–307 214
306.1 218
306.4 213
306.8 446
306 left margin 187
306 note 1 446
307.1 180, 353, 354, 416
307.3–.4 453
307.7 354
307.13 482
307.21 441
307.22–.23 353, 357
307.25 436
307 left margin 357
308 505
308 note 1 (and drawing) 505
308 note 2 (and drawing) 505
310.16 312
310.19 456
310.24 456, 507
310.27 448
310.31 452
310.32 433, 453
310.33 453
311–332 510n
311.12 344

311.15 344
311.27 399
312 307
312.19 353
312.20 353
312.22 353
313.15 341
313.24 341, 507
314 347n
314.33 333
315.25–.26 237, 462
315.28 432
315.30–.31 415
315.32–.33 411
316 452, 457n
316.1 25
316.2 269, 273n
316.5 191, 269
316.7 269
316.15–.16 415
316.19 412
316.21 412
316.21–.22 273n
316.27 452
316.27–.28 452
316.29 452
316.30 452
316.35 273n
317.2 415
317.9 433
317.18 178
317.28 433
317.36 487
318.2 174
318.10 383
318.12 479
318.14 383
318.32 240
318.33 433
318.34–.35 25
319 368
319.5 189
319.18 55
319.25 384
319.27 433

320.3 497
320.14 497
321.14–.15 430
322.6 434
322.35 400
323.4 487, 494
323.26 507
324.8 373
324.26 441
324.28 180, 487
325.13 507
325.14 436
325.32 150
326.2 353
326.3 353, 425
326.7 433
326.19 182
326.22 433
326.26 461
326.30 268
327 33
327.16 138
327.23–.24 33
327.28 138, 141
327.33 462
328.14 356
328.25 404
328.28–.29 229
329.2 404
330.5 187
331.15–.16 433
331.17 446
331.18 446
331.19 446
331.20 507
331.24 446
331.26 433
331.27 446, 456
331.31 446
332 15, 347n
332.1 25
332.2–.3 346
332.7–.8 426
332.18 433
332.22 344

332.25 448
332.36 507
333 497
333.1–.5 461
333.13 18
333.14 468
333.25 12
333.28 468
333.29–.30 178
333.30 433
333.31 446
333.31–.32 360
333.32 360
333.35 468
333.36 468
334.3 497, 507
334.5 446
334.17 133n, 400, 461
334.18 461
334.24 190
334.26 328
334.36 173, 183
335.2 461
335.24 461
335.32–.33 291
337.1 399
337.2 400
337.19 433
337.26 386
337.26–.27 386
337.27 440
337.30 414, 425
337.34 507
337.36 145
338.5–.6 199
338.6 199
338.13–.14 142
338.14 199
338.18 341
338.19 199, 422
338.23 199
338.26 269
338.28 341
338.29 269
338.30–.31 316

338.32 269
338.36 269
339–346 422
339.1 199
339.3 433
339.14 142
339.15 199
339.21 199
339.23 199
339.28–.29 190
339.29 199, 259
339.35 150
340.1 199
340.2 199, 422
340.16 199
340.22 142, 199
340.25 142
340.29 142
340.31 57n, 150
341.2 199
341.4 188
341.7 199
341.9 199
341.16 399
341.17 183
341.36ff 482
342.2 199
342.3 55
342.11 10, 482
342.13 482
342.22–.23 185
342.36–343 452
343.1 379
343.2 452
343.3 199, 452
343.4 379
343.6 379
343.8 379
343.15–.16 187
343.17 189
343.18 418
343.22–.23 418
343.30 180
343.31 490
344.2 199

344.3 433
344.8 404
344.10 404
344.12 142
344.17 142, 237
344.23 237
344.30 237
344.36 142
345.2–.3 365
345.4 190
345.22 188
346.2 507
346.4–.5 151
346.7 414
346.9 188
346.9–.10 199
346.11 414
346.13 199
346.26 183
346.27 415
347.14 328
347.19 199, 447, 456
347.26 151, 447
347.27 188
347.29 456
347.31 185
348.5 199
348.7 199
348.14 190
348.23 413
348.26 328
348.26–.27 25
348.27 199
348.35 417
349.2 199, 415
349.6 438n
349.10 328
349.19 185
349.20 185, 475
349.22 440
349.24 399, 475
349.29ff 199
350.5 441
350.16 173, 182
350.21 199

351 188
351.1 348
351.5 348
351.16 188
351.17 425
351.23 177
351.26 348
352.1–.2 199
352.3–.4 199
352.7 235
352.13 174
352.14 173
352.21–.22 456
353.7 174
353.8 174
353.10 199
353.12 507
353.14 341
353.28 199
353.35–354.1 272
354.10 199
354.14 188
354.24 404
356.14 25
357.2 190
357.4 174
357.7 199
357.18 174
357.30 420
357.31 173
358.1 199
358.3 140, 420
358.9 140
358.14 452
358.15 140
358.19 271
358.20 271
358.22 151, 271
358.23 271, 447
358.23–.24 151
358.27 447
358.28 271, 452
358.29 271, 452
358.30 271
358.32 447

359.1 259
359.4 142
359.10 360
359.12 271
359.15 271
359.16 354, 360
359.17 354, 360
359.18 353, 354
359.19 354
359.22 271, 353, 354
359.23 414
359.24 388
359.24–.25 382n
359.26 271
359.27 271
359.28 234
359.28–.29 234
359.31–360.16 385
359.32 333, 385
359.34 385
359.35 385
359.35–.36 386
359.35–360.2ff 235
360.2 386
360.3–.4 386
360.4 474
360.13 386
360.14–.15 235
360.23 433
360.28 400
361.10 418, 460
361.18 452
361.21 397
361.22 452, 474
362.5 10
362.22 269
363.2–.3 507
363.20 316, 372
363.22–.24 316
363.32 372
363.34 507
363.36 372
364.14ff 235
364.30–.31 361
364.34 452

364.35 361
365.6 142
365.12 456
365.16 185, 456
366.29–30 415
367 15
367.8 20, 394
367.11 394
367.13 394
367.25 394
367.28 28
368 15
368.29 55, 57n
368.30ff 492
369.18 180
369.25–.26 442
369.27 296
369.30 425
370.2 296
370.4 296
370.10 296
370.13 296
370.17 476
370.28 185
371.15–.16 393
371.36 357
372 15
372.1 357
372.2 357, 436
372.3 357
372.6 342, 357
372.7 357, 436
372.9–.10 174
372.9–.11 358n
372.17 357
372.23 357
373.1 11
373.4 182, 476
373.5 22, 476
373.8 211n
373.29 344
373.30 180
374.2 140
374.16 447
374.18–.19 447

FINNEGANS WAKE PAGE/LINE INDEX 723

374.34–.35 447
375.12 486
375.27 240
375.28 137
376.8–.9 341
376.16 507
376.31 341
376.32 456
377.14 401
377.24 418
377.35–.36 33
378.15–.17 28
378.15–.18 31
378.16 29
378.20 235
378.20–.21 25
378.22 507
378.23 507
378.24 177, 223
378.26 177, 235
379.4 507
379.17 177
379.23 14n
379.30 33
379.34 312
380.1–.2 411, 461
380.4–.5 411
381.14 263
382.21 367, 440
382.27 367
383 16, 33
383–399 458n
383.9 367
383.19 403
383.20 433
384.28 242
385.8 399
385.12 397
385.17 209
385.21 403
385.25 399
385.32 403
385.35 403
385.36 403
386.15 397

386.18 11
386.22 403
386.24 403, 440
386.31 403
386.35 403
387.2 507
387.5 403
387.6 403
387.9 433
387.10–.11 403
387.14 403
387.15 403
387.17 269, 323
387.18 269, 323
387.20 403
387.21 323
387.26 403
387.28 400
388.1 403
388.3 403
388.4 389
388.6 440
388.11 403
388.17 403
388.19 403
388.23 403
388.26 356
388.28 15
388.31 356
388.35 399
389.15 357
389.20 397
389.31 397
390.8 403
390.13 483
390.20 397
390.35 479
391.21 308
391.23 17
391.32 401
392.12 397
392.19 403
392.33 494
392.24 403
392.25 403

392.33 403
393.1 494
393.8 404
393.10 187
393.11 348
393.15 348
393.22–.23 402
393.26 404
394.7 404
394.18 507
394.25 403
394.30–395.2 187
394.35–.36 15
395.2 187
395.9 403
395.15 397
395.22 403
395.25 397
395.29 397
395.34 397
396.19 404
396.25–.26 456
396.36–397.1 402
397.2 358
397.3 358
397.11 358
397.17 413, 494
397.26–.27 508
397.27 403
398–399 20, 21, 45
398.12 403
398.15–.16 403
398.18 403
398.22 269
398.23–.24 269
399 317
399.9–.10 22, 24
399.14 24
399.22 24
399.25 21
399.28 476
403 33, 97
403.6 191, 508
403.8 190, 350
403.13 229

403.16–.17 229
403.17 191
403.18 229
403.32 456
403.33 456
403.34 456
404 336
404–407 234
404.4–405.7 229
404.15 189, 291
404.26–.27 235
404.29 235
404.30 235
405.4–.6 43, 45
405.26 508
405.33 229, 279
406.2 279
406.3 229
406.5 279
406.9 234, 333
406.10 229
406.11–.12 333
406.12 234
406.15 229
406.20 475
406.25 475
406.31 188
406.33 142
407.4 185, 229
407.4–.5 189
407.19 235
407.20 508
407.27 258
407.35 229
408.6 201, 229
408.11 481
408.23 414, 425
408.27 404
408.30 188
409.7 188
409.10 188
409.12 481
409.12–.13 189
409.13 481
409.14–.15 481

409.17–.18 94, 97
409.27 97
409.31 188
409.34 94
409.36 140
410.3 137
410.33 328, 333
410.34 333
411.26 333
411.27–.28 316
411.28 317
412.2 490
412.18 55
412.30 188
412.30–413.26 394n
412.31 229
412.33 140
413 25
413.1 140
413.5 182, 188
413.32 312
413.34 312
413.35 312, 494
413.36 312
414 229, 347n
414.4 358n
414.13 201
414.16–419.10 307,
  480n, 575n
414.19–.20 472
414.30 417
414.32–.33 141
415.2 307
415.8 416
415.9 420, 421
415.10 420
415.11 194, 410, 420
415.13 420
415.14 240
415.15 240
415.18 240
415.19–.20 240
415.24 421
415.25 140
415.26 421

415.29 140
415.31 421
415.32 421
415.33 421
415.36 183, 210, 358,
  421
416.1 210, 421, 424
416.6 357
416.7 357
416.13 177
416.30 178
416.36 453
417.11 453
417.12 416
417.16 187
417.17–.18 386
417.17–.19 178
417.29 386
417.30 386
417.32 187
419.17–.18 237
419.28 240
419.29 394n
420–421 25
420.20 448
420.31–421.1 477
420.35 18
422.13 151
422.26 201
422.28 151
422.29 151
422.30 151
422.33 383
423.4 508
423.6 327
423.10–.11 201
423.11–.12 327
423.13 327
423.17 327
423.22–.23 428
423.23–.24 327
423.26 327
423.28–.29 327
423.30 327
423.32 327

423.33 327
423.35 327
424 97, 347n
424–425 181
424.10 421, 426
424.20 433
424.20–.22 472
425.13 229
425.16 404
425.22 404
425.28 433
426.8 94
426.13 380
426.15 333
426.16 333
426.17 229, 333
426.25 133, 479
426.29–.30 399
426.30 97
427.17–.19 273n
427.17–.23 269
427.19 229
427.20 269, 273n
427.23 269
427.34 97
428.7 494
428.8 333
428.13–.14 477
428.18 360
428.21 333, 369
428.22 456
429 483
429–430 98
429–473 340
429.2 424, 483
430–432 98
430.2 327, 341
430.7–.25 482
430.10 185, 483
430.17–.18 98
430.20 392, 483
430.25 483
430.26 98
430.29 508
430.30 483

430.33 341
430.35 341
430.36 341
431 327
431–455 98
431.21–457.24 394n
431.23 341
431.30 341
431.34 229
431.35 238
431.36 341
432 98
432.21 133, 178, 461
432.22 461
432.24 185
432.25 483
432.26 357
432.28 258
432.30 258, 341
433 185
433.1 258, 392
433.2 258
433.4 258
433.5 150
433.10 357, 392, 448
433.10–.11 393
433.11 325
433.12 483
433.14 483
433.16 393
433.19 325
433.24 392
433.27–.28 357
433.32 392
433.35 325
434 242
434.5–.6 392
434.7 217, 255
434.24 483
434.27 17
434.29 242, 413
434.31–.32 369
434.32 412
435 242, 483
435.24 242

435.29 242
436.6 483
436.7 483
436.21 483
436.26 400
437.6 181
438.14 483
438.26 312
439.3 325
439.15–.17 399
439.17 54-55, 399
439.17–.18 18
439.36 325
440.10 15
440.14–.15 15
440.17 187
440.20 483
440.27 483
440.29 344, 490
441.11–.12 56
442.5 209
442.9 209
442.11 342
442.12 209
442.33 483
442.35 426
443.7 397
443.10 424
443.18 396, 453
443.21 396, 433, 453
443.25 397, 482
443.26 481
443.27 453
443.28 397, 482
443.30 397, 433, 453
443.31 453
443.33 453
443.34 397, 426, 481, 482
443.35 426, 481
443.36 397, 482
444.5 344
444.11 433
444.24 414
444.28 429

444.31 483
444.32 209
444.35 209, 254
444.36 209
444.36ff 252
445 483
445.1 254
445.2 472
445.4 472
445.5 254
445.7 254
445.8 254
445.11 254
445.14 255
445.17 254
445.18 254
446.1 354
446.6 354
446.8 483
446.14 269
446.15 269
446.28 483
446.30–.31 360
446.34 328
446.36 328, 440
447.9 138
447.12 17
447.13 183
447.14 17
449.3–.4 234
449.10 138, 342, 483
449.16 342
449.30 415
450.5 137
450.12 483
450.14 327
450.15 327
450.17 327
451.3 217
451.9 482, 483
451.23 188
452.8 424, 483
452.9 418
452.10 483
452.13 483

452.20–.21 429
452.24 508
452.28 483
452.36 177
453 184
453.13 490
453.16 490
453.18 483
453.19 490
453.32–.33 183
453.36 483
454 10
454.4 484
454.9 327
454.13–.14 201
454.15 201
454.16 393, 483
454.20 483
454.24 327
454.27 327
454.32 393
454.35 190, 428
455.1 428
455.2 428
455.5 448
455.6 180
455.11 484
455.23 392
455.28 428
455.32 229
455.33–.34 98
455.36 357
456.8 378
456.10 378
456.14 378
456.22 243, 378
456.23 481, 508
456.24 484
456.25 243, 378
456.26 378, 484
456.27 243, 378
456.28 484
456.29 484
456.30 378
456.31 225, 378

456.32 378
456.36 378
457–461 98
457.4 197
457.5 197
457.6 197
457.7 197
457.8 197
457.9 197
457.10 197
457.10–.11 197
457.11 10, 197, 482, 484
457.11–.12 197
457.12 484
457.12–.13 197
457.14 197
457.15 197
457.16 197
457.17 197
457.18 197
457.19 197, 325
457.20 197
457.21 198, 425
457.22 198, 425
457.25 357
457.27 325
457.28 325
457.29 186, 356
457.31 425
457.32 370
458 92
458.6 15, 57
458.14 89
458.16 325
458.18 325
458.21 325
458.23 325
458.25 188, 325
458.27 325
458.33 411
458.36 484
459.4 400
459.24–.25 188
459.33 482, 484

460.11 312
460.12 325
460.17 484
460.21 484
460.25 484
460.26 325
461 484
462.5 400, 484
462.7–.8 89
462.18 141
462.22 398, 484
462.26 135
462.32 135
463.4 413
463.5 98
463.14 135
463.15 304
463.21 304
463.31 304
463.35–.36 304
464.3 98
464.5 328
464.24 328
464.36–465.7 73
465 484
465.2–.3 323
465.4 323
465.12 321
465.16 321, 378
465.21 135, 378, 411, 421
465.22 378
465.24 378
465.27 378
465.29 15
465.32 378
465.35 137, 378
466.1 416
466.6 217
466.9 218
466.17 229
466.19 216, 217, 223, 447
466.19–.20 447
466.20 447

466.21 223, 413
466.25 11
467 98
467.14 418n
467.31 252
467.32 141, 251
467.33 251
467.35 251
467.36 251
467.36–468.1 251
468 98
468.23 303
468.24 303
468.26 400
468.27 268
468.29 303
468.30 303
468.33 303, 508
468.36 316, 508
469 98
469.2 303
469.4 303
469.7 303, 484
469.9 303, 452
469.10–.11 452
469.11 303
469.12–.13 303
469.14 137
469.18 303
469.21 41
469.23 303
469.24 303
469.25 303
469.29 484
469.32 303
469.34 217
469.35 303
470–471 93
470.2 425, 484
470.7 140. 478
470.8 478
470.9 440
470.20 188
470.21 303
470.26 484

470.29 484
471 94, 98
471.7 482, 484
471.17 482, 484
471.24 303
472.1 337
472.6–.7 393
472.15 15
472.22 484
472.34 484
473 98, 484
473.3 356
473.8 445, 447
473.9 312, 393
473.10 312
473.25 447
474–476 330
474.1 50
474.16 328
475.9–.10 477
476 15
476.1 356
477.29 268
477.33 268
478.8 43
478.11 508
478.13 217, 219n
478.23 424
479.9 452
479.32 452
479.32–.33 424
479.35 434
480.4 427
480.18 424
480.21 259, 449
480.23 153
480.25–.26 452
480.26 452
480.30 449
481.20 416
481.21 497
481.33 56
481.35 392
482.1 217
482.3 255

482.4 56, 255
482.7 434
482.15 255
482.33–.34 216
483.5–.6 216
483.14–.15 215, 216
483.19–.20 447
484.15 263
484.16 187
484.19 263
484.32 348
485.13 491n
485.19 348
485.21 348
485.35 210
485.36 210
486 88
486.1 208, 210
486.8 452
486.13 452
486.14 210
488 239
488.19 210
488.20 210
488.36 268
489.1 268
489.2 268
489.4 479
490.23 348
490.30 348
490.31–.32 431n
490.33 318
491.11 353
491.17 508
491.26 353
491.29 353
492 24
492.2 418
493.3 323
493.12 180
493.18–.19 318, 323
493.34 210
494 24
494.11 438
494.12 415

494.15 343
494.17 343
494.20–.21 436
494.21 460
494.23 343
494.24 436
494.25 436, 210
494.26 343, 478
494.34 434, 455
494.35 15, 210
495.6 210
495.15 243
495.16 243
495.24 183
496.20 255
496.30–.31 348
497–499 348
497.33 460
498.13–.14 348
498.19 497, 508
498.27 201
498.30 201
499.1 201
499.2 201
499.4 210
499.10 508
499.21 452
499.28 270
499.30 270
499.35 270
500.1 270, 271, 452
500.3 271
500.4 271
500.6 271
500.11 270
500.12 270, 452
500.13 270
500.14 270,
500.15 270, 271
500.19 270
501.17 508
501.26 365, 367
502.12 216
502.25 291, 294
502.25–.26 294n

502.29 308
503.12 94
504.2 441
504.20ff 482
504.20 508
504.22 417
505.1 190, 192, 237
505.20 357
505.21 357
505.27 429
506.25 349
507.15 151
507.33 349
508.22 240, 460
508.28 29, 240
508.29 334
508.30 334
508.32 334
508.34 334
510.4 508
511.10 402
512 404
512.4 45, 235
512.7 235, 404
512.10 235, 377
512.12 378
512.13 378
512.15 377, 404
512.16 377
512.17 377
512.18 377, 404
512.22 45
512.28 494
512.31 235
513.20 438
513.25 434
514 15
514.11 311
514.19 270
514.23 270
514.24 209, 270, 398
514.24–.25 270
515.9 422
516.12 360
516.12–.14 215

FINNEGANS WAKE PAGE/LINE INDEX

516.15 360
516.18 360
516.19 432, 434
516.24 441
516.27 360
517.10 269
517.15 269
518.9 494
519.7 14n
519.11ff 259
519.16 259
520.24 434
521.1 190
522.30–.31 453, 477
522.33 477
523ff–523.8 366
523.22 447
523.24 447
523.25 447
524.17 190
525.12 390
525.14 390
526.25 141
526.27 141
526.29 140
526.30 483
527.1 141
527.2 141
527.18 417
527.27 455
527.28 140
527.29 230
527.35 140
528 201
528.18 33
528.20 188
528.23 417
528.24 141, 185
528.26 33
528.31 367
528.32 269
528.33 269
529.20 266
529.25 360
529.30 399, 477

529.34 399
530.2 378
530.2–.3 478
530.3 378
530.14 472
530.16 378
530.21 428
531–554 523n
531.5–.6 413, 442
531.10 177
532.6 71
532.18 413
533 20
533.21–.22 11
534 16
534.8 399
534.10 145, 508
534.18 508
534.21–.22 18
534.25 476
534.31 18
534.36 399
535.6 441
536 15
536.9 33
536.11 33, 146
536.32 177
536.32–.33 12
537.9 180
537.12 404
537.30 414
538.1–.2 137
538.6–.7 414
539–554 4
539.3 177
540.22 145
540.26 462
540.27 462
540.28 462
540.29 462
540.30 223
540.33 462
540.35 462
541.5 353
541.6 494

541.23 415
541.24 508
542.2 478
542.14 472
542.18 5n
542.21 234
542.23 12
542.27–.28 5n
542.28–.29 3
542.29 5n
542.30 353
542.33 102
542.35 138
543–545 57n
543.2 12
543.14 441
543.18 12
543.19 462
544.1 497
545.4 57n
545.32 12, 353
546.5 342
546.6 342
546.9 342
546.14 353
546.18 342
546.21 262, 323
546.23 262, 323
547.8 342
547.14ff 342
547.24 186
547.36 416
548.19 454
548.22 177
548.26 12, 313
548.30 342
548.31 342
548.35 183
549.1 49
549.2 12
549.3 17
549.13 442
549.13–.16 356, 442
549.15 356
549.18 42

549.24 342
549.25 342
549.34 348
550.2 177
551.4 18
552.1 440
552.5 353
552.9 353
552.11–.13 133n
552.26 12
552.27 448
552.28 440
552.29 12
552.29–.30 428
552.30 353
552.31–.34 449
553.7 439
553.8 353
553.10 462
553.13–.14 12
553.14 43
553.21 508
553.24 63
553.35 136, 441
554 33
554.6 312
555 33
555.10 447
555.18–.19 447
555.23 440
556.1–.22 325
556.3–.18 191
556.9–.10 325
556.15–.17 325
556.17 323
556.17–.22 323
556.20 325
556.30 472
557.1 508
558.8 323
558.10 323
558.11 323
558.17 400
558.19 323
559.11–.12 462

560.8 348
560.9 348
560.14 40
560.16 348
560.22–.35 43
561.5 348
561.16 235
561.21 235
561.24 235
562.29 188
563.26 400
563.26–.27 455
563.27 186
563.31 180
565.5 434
565.8–.9 89
565.10 180
565.19 89, 92
566.36 186, 455
567.3 328
567.4 455
567.9 455
567.15 455
567.25 136, 402
567.27 335, 411, 421
567.29 397
568 10
568.2–.3 177
568.13 269
568.15 269
568.16 354
568.23 354
568.32 183
568.34 354
569 10
569.7 328
569.21 304
569.23 354
569.25 304
569.28 137, 183
569.29 150, 177
569.33 461
570.19 357
570.34 423
570.35 423

570.36 423
571.7 427
572.21 311
573 15
573.26 11, 18
573.32 466
574.36 416
575.6–.7 427
575.9 438
576.6 427
576.27 401, 416
576.36 177
577.1 452
577.4 415
577.16 431n
577.17 190
579.23–.24 361
580.4 342
581.10 456
581.12 456
582.29–.30 240
582.35 360
583 130
583.3–.4 137
583.9 312, 472
583.10 189, 417
583.17 321, 420
583.19 420
584.31 475
585.1 394
585.11 394, 508
586.6–.7 217
586.12 217, 263
586.13 217
586.14 217
586.15 263, 414
586.23 263, 414
588.27 348
588.33 142, 144
589.16 142
589.25 348
590.5 182
590.7 259
590.10 430
590.17 430

593.1 33
593.24 424
593.36 424
594 10
594.7 411
594.10 442
594.11 442
594.35 456
595.24 418
595.28 447
595.31–.32 450n
596.2 361
596.7 361
596.12 361
596.14 420
597.26 250
597.27 251
597.31 434
597.33 476
598.9 508
598.32 508
599.18 220
600.1 462
600.12 263
600.13 263
600.15 263
601.21 328
602.1–.3 508
602.22 474
602.26–.27 474
602.27 474
603.1 474
603.29 418
604.15 418
604.23 392
605.4 186
606.13 508
606.15 263
607.12 271
607.17 425
607.25 432
608.29–.30 137
609.20 448
610.8 393
610.10 393

611.20 89
611.28 335
611.34–.35 449
611.36 150
612.3 393
612.5 393
612.29 312
613 10
613.15 448
613.30 456
614.6 508
614.8 508
614.28 222
614.29 222
614.30 188
614.31 222
614.32 222
614.33 222
614.34–.35 188
614.36 222
615.1 223
615.2 223
615.3 223
615.4 223
615.5–.6 222
615.9 188
615.16–.17 314
616.1 182
616.32 177
617.31 269, 432
618.6–.7 137
618.12 136
619 185, 369
619.20 348
619.23 241
619.25 340
619.28 241, 340
619.33 508
619.34 340
619.36 340, 348
620.1 379
620.3 371
620.5 223
620.7 379
620.11 241

620.15 367
620.18 82
620.21 508
620.26 305
620.30 441
620.31 441
620.33 371
620.34 368
620.35 371
621.6 371
621.6–.7 400
621.11 379
621.13 236
621.14 372
621.15 371, 441
621.21 236
621.22 236
621.24–.25 379
621.25 371
621.26 371
621.30 236
621.34 236
621.35 305
621.36 236, 379
622.1 348
622.3 241
622.6 477
622.9–.10 372, 379
622.15 348, 367
622.18 340
622.23 379
622.23–.24 242
622.24 379, 425
622.25 379
622.28 379
622.30 379
622.31 379
622.32 371
622.33 379
622.35 241
623.1 379
623.12 379
623.16 379
623.21–.22 21
623.23 176, 241

623.24 371
623.31 241
623.35 304, 452
623.36–624.1 304, 452
624 54
624.12 305
624.16 133, 241
624.17–.18 54
624.18 10, 241
624.19 241
624.19–.20 379
624.21 241
624.26 241, 371
624.27 241
625.3–.4 379
625.15 241
625.22 241
625.35 379

626 319
626.1 369
626.2 340, 379
626.4 368, 369
626.5 320
626.6 241, 328, 368
626.7 369
626.19 371
626.33 321, 369
626.34 369
626.34–.35 321
627 54, 319
627–628 320
627.1 321
627.3 369
627.9 369
627.11 369
627.17–.18 361

627.26–628.3 319
627.28–.29 15
627.29 82
627.32 369
628.2–.3 360
628.3 369
628.4 361
628.6–.7 321
628.8 425
628.9 166
628.10 319, 320
628.11 320
628.12 369
628.13 320, 434
628.14 321
628.15 320, 328
628.15–.16 370